CAMBRIDGE
EDUCATIONAL SERVICES®

AMERICA'S PREMIERE TESTING READINESS PROGRAM

The Big Book of Skills

Comprehensive Coverage for College, Career, and the Common Core

S T U D E N T   T E X T

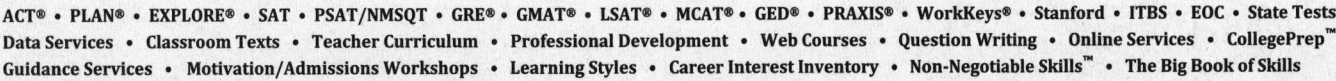

ACT® • PLAN® • EXPLORE® • SAT • PSAT/NMSQT • GRE® • GMAT® • LSAT® • MCAT® • GED® • PRAXIS® • WorkKeys® • Stanford • ITBS • EOC • State Tests
Data Services • Classroom Texts • Teacher Curriculum • Professional Development • Web Courses • Question Writing • Online Services • CollegePrep™
Guidance Services • Motivation/Admissions Workshops • Learning Styles • Career Interest Inventory • Non-Negotiable Skills™ • The Big Book of Skills

Our Mission: Progress Through Partnership

Cambridge Educational Services partners with educators who share the significant mission of educational advancement for all students. By partnering together, we can best achieve our common goals: to build skills, raise test scores, enhance curriculum, and support instruction. A leading innovator in education for twenty years, Cambridge is the nation's premiere provider of school-based test preparation and supplemental curriculum services.

Cambridge Publishing, Inc.
www.CambridgeEd.com

Certified Chain of Custody
Product Line Contains At Least
20% Certified Forest Content
www.sfiprogram.org
SFI-00756

TABLE OF CONTENTS

How to Use This Book..v

VERBAL SKILLS REVIEW

Grammar and Mechanics Skills Review   3

Course Concept Outline...3
Parts of Speech...7
Common Grammatical Errors 11
Analyzing Sentence Structure 29
Problems of Logical Expression 43
Idioms and Clarity of Expression 51
Punctuation 65

Diagramming Sentences Skills Review   81

Course Concept Outline...81
Subjects and Verbs 85
Modal Auxiliary Verbs 91
Conjunctions 97
Articles, Attributive Adjectives, and Direct Objects 101
Adverbs 107
Subjective Complements: Predicate Nominatives and Predicate Adjectives..........................113
Appositives 119
Prepositional Phrases 123
Indirect Objects and Objective Complements 129
Infinitives 135
Gerunds 145
Participles 151
Adverb Clauses 157
Adjective Clauses 167
Noun Clauses 173
Glossary of Grammatical Terms and Diagramming Symbols...179

English/Writing Mastery Test   191

English/Writing Mastery Test 193

Vocabulary Skills Review   205

Course Concept Outline...205
Building Vocabulary with Sentence Completions 207
Building Vocabulary Through Context..227

Reading Skills Review   287

Course Concept Outline...287
Honing Your Reading Skills...289

Reading Mastery Test   319

Reading Mastery Test 321

Writing Skills Review   333

Course Concept Outline 333
Planning an Essay 335
Composition 337
Revision and Scoring 343

MATH SKILLS REVIEW

Math Skills Review   349

Course Concept Outline 349
Numbers 355
Fractions 371
Decimals 385
Percents 397
Statistical Measures 409
Ratios and Proportions 419
Exponents and Radicals 429
Algebraic Operations 443
Algebraic Equations and Inequalities 461
Geometry 479
Coordinate Geometry 505
Story Problems 523

Math Mastery Test   549

Math Mastery Test 551

APPENDIX A: ANSWERS AND EXPLANATIONS

Grammar and Mechanics Skills Review 561
Diagramming Sentences Skills Review 569
English/Writing Mastery Test 589
Vocabulary Skills Review 591
Reading Skills Review 595
Reading Mastery Test 599
Writing Skills Review 601
Math Skills Review 605
Math Mastery Test 611

APPENDIX B: PROGRESS REPORTS

Progress Reports 615

Error Correction and Suggestion Form 631

HOW TO USE THIS BOOK

This text contains skills review lessons and items that will enable you to do three things: (1) review material that you may have forgotten; (2) learn material that you may never have learned; and (3) master the skills required to answer the more difficult multiple-choice items on the real test.

This book is divided into six chapters:

- Grammar and Mechanics

- Diagramming Sentences

- Vocabulary

- Reading

- Writing

- Math

Each chapter contains concept lessons and corresponding review exercises. For example, the lessons in the Math Skills Review cover the following topics: numbers, fractions, decimals, percents, statistical measures, ratios and proportions, exponents and radicals, algebraic operations, algebraic equations and inequalities, geometry, coordinate geometry, and story problems. The other chapters cover a similar range of topics that are appropriate to each subject.

The exercises in this book do not necessarily contain problems that mimic the items on the real test. The problems are designed to help you learn concepts—not necessarily to help you learn about how the concepts appear on the actual exam. This book also includes three Mastery Tests:

- English/Writing Mastery Test

- Reading Mastery Test

- Math Mastery Test

These tests will help you evaluate your progress after you complete the skills review material for each subject. After you have mastered the skills, you will be able to take full advantage of the concepts and test-taking strategies that are developed in Cambridge's Victory program.

Verbal
Skills Review

Grammar and Mechanics
Skills Review

Course Concept Outline

I. Parts of Speech (p. 7)

   A. Nouns (p. 7)

   B. Pronouns (p. 7)

   C. Verbs (p. 7)

   D. Modifiers (p. 7)

   E. Conjunctions (p. 8)

   F. Prepositions (p. 8)

   Exercise 1—**Parts of Speech** (Items #1–20, pp. 9–10)

II. Common Grammatical Errors (p. 11)

   A. Subject-Verb Agreement (p. 11)

      1. Material Inserted Between Subject and Verb (p. 11)
      2. Inverted Sentence Structure (p. 12)
      3. Use of Compound Subjects (p. 12)

   B. Pronoun Usage (p. 13)

      1. Pronouns Must Have Antecedents (p. 13)
      2. Antecedents Must Be Clear (p. 14)
      3. Pronoun-Antecedent Agreement (p. 15)
      4. Pronouns Must Have Proper Case (p. 15)

C. Adjectives versus Adverbs (p. 18)

1. Adjectives Modify Nouns; Adverbs Modify Verbs, Adjectives, and Other Adverbs (p. 18)
2. Linking Verbs (p. 19)
3. Watch for Adjectives Posing as Adverbs (p. 20)
4. Adjective Forms (p. 20)

D. Double Negatives (p. 23)

E. Nouns and Noun Clauses (p. 23)

Exercise 2—**Common Grammatical Errors** (Items #1–66, pp. 25–28)

III. Analyzing Sentence Structure (p. 29)

A. Sentence Fragments (p. 29)

B. Run-On Sentences (p. 30)

C. Faulty Parallelism (p. 31)

D. Incomplete Split Constructions (p. 32)

E. Verb Forms (p. 33)

1. Principal Parts of Verbs (p. 33)
2. Present, Past, and Future Tense (p. 34)
3. The Perfect Tenses (p. 36)
4. The Subjunctive Mood (p. 36)

Exercise 3—**Analyzing Sentence Structure** (Items #1–57, pp. 37–42)

IV. Problems of Logical Expression (p. 43)

A. Faulty or Illogical Comparisons (p. 43)

B. Unintended Meanings (p. 43)

C. Conciseness (p. 44)

1. Avoid Awkward Sentences (p. 44)
2. Avoid Passive Verbs (p. 44)
3. Avoid Needlessly Wordy Sentences (p. 45)

D. Misplaced Modifiers (p. 45)

Exercise 4—**Problems of Logical Expression** (Items #1–27, pp. 47–50)

V. Idioms and Clarity of Expression (p. 51)

A. Diction (p. 51)

1. Wrong Word Choice (p. 51)
2. Wrong Preposition (p. 53)
3. Gerund versus Infinitive (p. 54)

B. Ambiguity in Scope (p. 54)

C. Informal Usage (p. 55)

Exercise 5—**Idioms and Clarity of Expression** (Items #1–143, pp. 56–63)

VI. Punctuation (p. 65)

A. Commas (p. 65)

B. Semicolons (p. 69)

C. Colons (p. 70)

D. Periods (p. 71)

E. Exclamation and Question Marks (p. 71)

F. Dashes (p. 72)

G. Hyphens (p. 73)

H. Quotation Marks (p. 73)

I. Apostrophes (p. 75)

Exercise 6—**Punctuation** (Items #1–55, pp. 77–79)

PARTS OF SPEECH

Nouns

A *noun* is a word that refers to any one of the following items: persons, animals, plants, objects, times, places, and ideas.

Examples:

Persons:	Bob, woman, niece, student, doctor, men, brothers, teachers
Animals:	dog, mouse, cow, cats, elephants, birds
Plants:	grass, tree, bushes, oaks
Objects:	glove, car, building, sidewalk, desks, buses
Times:	hour, 8 o'clock, Thanksgiving, Mondays, weekends
Places:	home, office, city, Puerto Rico, Poland, Africa
Ideas:	democracy, love, youth, sisterhood, dreams

Pronouns

A *pronoun* is a word that can substitute for a noun.

Examples:

Hernandez hit a home run. He waved to the crowd.
The woman went into the store. She bought a book.
My sisters live in St. Louis. They are coming to visit.
The bull escaped from the pasture. The farmer caught him.
The plant seems dry. Julie should water it.

Verbs

A *verb* is a word that expresses activity, change, feeling, or existence.

Examples:

The dog is running down the street.
The weather became cold.
Carl worries that he might not pass the test.
The letter was several days late.

Modifiers

A *modifier* describes a word or makes the meaning of a word more specific. There are two types of modifiers. *Adjectives* modify nouns and pronouns.

Examples:

The <u>blue</u> car ran into the <u>red</u> car.
The <u>tall</u> woman was carrying an <u>expensive</u> umbrella.

Adverbs modify verbs, adjectives, and other adverbs.

Examples:

The farmer <u>patiently</u> waited for the cows.
My house was <u>badly</u> damaged after a large branch fell on the roof in the last thunderstorm.
With a full-time job and raising a child alone, Julie felt like she was <u>almost</u> always busy.

Conjunctions

A ***conjunction*** connects (1) words, (2) phrases, or (3) clauses.

Examples:

1. John <u>and</u> Mary are organizing a walk-a-thon.
   The book is on the table <u>or</u> the counter.
   Alex speaks <u>both</u> English <u>and</u> Spanish.
   Tina can play <u>either</u> offense <u>or</u> defense.
   The cookies contain raisins, currants, <u>and</u> nuts.
   All students must take physics, chemistry, <u>or</u> biology.

2. The tomatoes are packed into jars <u>and</u> shipped to a warehouse.
   Students must enter through the main gate on Elm Street <u>or</u> the side door on Broadway.
   Skimming the trees <u>and</u> banking sharply over the shoreline, the pontoon plane made a safe landing.
   Either the newly appointed dean <u>or</u> the assistant principal will make the presentation.

3. After the storm, the clouds dissipated, <u>and</u> the sun dried the field.
   The book was returned to the library last week, <u>or</u> it is still in the lounge.
   The ant worked hard <u>while</u> the grasshopper played.
   <u>Though</u> Victoria is only 13 years old, she is already a senior.

Prepositions

A ***preposition*** establishes a relationship between an object (usually a noun phrase) and some other part of the sentence, often expressing a location in time or place.

Examples:

Patty sat <u>on</u> the chair.
Cliff gave the apples <u>to</u> Tom.
Geneva is the owner <u>of</u> the diner.
The mop is <u>in</u> the closet <u>beside</u> the broom.

Parts of Speech
Exercise 1

DIRECTIONS: In items #1–20, identify each underlined word's part of speech. Use the following key:

N = Noun
V = Verb
Pro = Pronoun
M = Modifier
C = Conjunction
Prep = Preposition

Answers are on page 561.

1. The <u>taxi</u> wove in and out of <u>traffic</u> as <u>it</u> <u>hurried</u> to the <u>airport</u>.

taxi ___   traffic ___   it ___

hurried ___   airport ___

2. The <u>movers</u> <u>unloaded</u> the sofa <u>and</u> put <u>it</u> <u>in</u> the living room.

movers ___   unloaded ___   and ___

it ___   in ___

3. The <u>dark</u> <u>clouds</u> completely <u>blocked</u> <u>our</u> view of the mountains <u>and</u> the lake.

dark ___   clouds ___   blocked ___

our ___   and ___

4. After <u>dinner</u>, we <u>cleared</u> the dishes from the <u>table</u>, put them in the kitchen sink, <u>and</u> <u>sat</u> down to watch the game.

dinner ___   cleared ___   table ___

and ___   sat ___

5. One <u>room</u> in the library <u>was filled</u> <u>with</u> books written by <u>authors</u> of <u>Polish</u> ancestry.

room ___   was filled ___   with ___

authors ___   Polish ___

6. Some of the <u>first</u> television <u>shows</u> <u>were</u> adaptations of <u>earlier</u> radio versions of the same <u>programs</u>.

first ___   shows ___   were ___

earlier ___   programs ___

7. When the <u>waiter</u> <u>arrived</u>, <u>Victor</u> <u>ordered</u> pie with ice cream, chocolate syrup, <u>and</u> a cherry.

waiter ___   arrived ___   Victor ___

ordered ___   and ___

8. The building <u>inspector</u> <u>finally</u> <u>approved</u> the plans <u>and</u> <u>allowed</u> the construction to continue.

inspector ___   finally ___   approved ___

and ___   allowed ___

9. The superintendent <u>notified</u> the tenants <u>in</u> the building that the <u>water</u> <u>would be</u> off for two <u>hours</u>.

notified ___   in ___   water ___

would be ___   hours ___

10. Just as the <u>band</u> <u>finished</u> the number, the <u>crowd</u> <u>burst</u> into <u>loud</u> applause.

band ___   finished ___   crowd ___

burst ___   loud ___

11. Carlos <u>called</u> Iris to tell <u>her</u> that he <u>would be</u> late for <u>their</u> <u>date</u>.

called ___   her ___   would be ___

their ___   date ___

12. The <u>cat</u> <u>slept</u> on the windowsill in the <u>warmth</u> <u>of</u> the afternoon <u>sun</u>.

cat ___   slept ___   warmth ___

of ___   sun ___

13. As the <u>train</u> <u>pulled</u> into each station, the conductor <u>called</u> out the <u>name</u> of that station <u>and</u> the name of the next station.

train ___   pulled ___   called ___

name ___   and ___

14. By the time <u>we</u> got to Woodstock, the <u>children</u> <u>were</u> sound asleep <u>in</u> the <u>rear</u> of the car.

we ___   children ___   were ___

in ___   rear ___

15. Before <u>they</u> <u>leave</u> the camp, the guides <u>teach</u> the <u>hikers</u> how to identify poison ivy <u>and</u> warn them to avoid it.

they ___   leave ___   teach ___

hikers ___   and ___

16. Chuck <u>covered</u> the <u>steaming</u> hot pancakes with plenty of <u>melted</u> butter and sweet, <u>sticky</u> <u>syrup</u>.

covered ___   steaming ___   melted ___

sticky ___   syrup ___

17. Last <u>weekend</u>, we <u>made</u> a <u>special</u> trip to the mountains to see the <u>brilliant</u> colors of the <u>beautiful</u> fall leaves.

weekend ___   made ___   special ___

brilliant ___   beautiful ___

18. After that <u>eventful</u> afternoon, Art <u>wrote</u> to Cathy several times, <u>but</u> <u>his</u> letters all came back <u>unopened</u>.

eventful ___   wrote ___   but ___

his ___   unopened ___

19. Through the morning mist, we could just <u>barely</u> <u>make out</u> the headlights of the <u>bus</u> <u>as</u> <u>it</u> turned off the highway.

barely ___   make out ___   bus ___

as ___   it ___

20. Our host <u>offered</u> <u>us</u> a choice of coffee <u>or</u> tea and served some little cakes, which <u>were</u> <u>delicious</u>.

offered ___   us ___   or ___

were ___   delicious ___

COMMON GRAMMATICAL ERRORS

NOTE: Throughout this Grammar and Mechanics Skills Review, ✓ = correct, and ✗ = wrong.

Subject-Verb Agreement

One common grammatical error is lack of agreement between subject and verb. The simplest subject-verb disagreements are usually obvious, as in the following examples:

Examples:

The books <u>is</u> on the shelf. ✗
The books <u>are</u> on the shelf. ✓

My dog <u>eat</u> twice a day and <u>sleep</u> inside. ✗
My dog <u>eats</u> twice a day and <u>sleeps</u> inside. ✓

In order to test your ability to spot such errors, test-writers may use one of the three following distractions:

WHAT OBSCURES SUBJECT-VERB AGREEMENT?

1. Material Inserted Between Subject and Verb

2. Inverted Sentence Structure

3. Use of Compound Subjects

Material Inserted Between Subject and Verb

Examples:

Star <u>performers</u> in the movies or on television usually <u>earns</u> substantial income from royalties. ✗

One school of thought maintains that the federal <u>deficit</u>, not exorbitant corporate profits or excessively high wages, <u>cause</u> most of the inflation we are now experiencing. ✗

A recent survey shows that a <u>household</u> in which both the wife and the husband are pursuing careers <u>stand</u> a better chance of surviving intact than one in which only the husband works. ✗

In each of these three sentences, the subject and verb do not agree: "performers . . . earns," "deficit . . . cause," and "household . . . stand." However, the errors may not be immediately evident because of the intervening material. In the first sentence, the subject is separated from the verb by prepositional phrases. In the second sentence, the subject and the verb are separated by a parenthetical expression. In the third sentence, a clause intervenes between the subject and the verb.

The plausibility of the incorrect verb choice, and therefore the chance that the error will go unnoticed, is strengthened when there is a word or phrase near the verb that might be mistaken for the subject: "television . . . earns," "profits and wages . . . cause," and "careers . . . stand." If the first word of each of these pairs had been the subject, then there would have been no failure of agreement.

Inverted Sentence Structure

A second common problem of subject-verb agreement is ***inverted sentence structure***. In an inverted sentence, the verb precedes the subject. You should pay careful attention to the agreement between subject and verb, no matter how those elements are ordered.

Examples:

Although the first amendment to the Constitution does guarantee freedom of speech, the Supreme Court has long recognized that there <u>has</u> to be some restrictions on the exercise of this right. ✖

Jennifer must have been doubly pleased that day, for seated in the gallery to watch her receive the award <u>was</u> her brother, her parents, and her husband. ✖

In both of these sentences, the subjects and verbs do not agree. The relationships are obscured by the order in which the elements appear in the sentence—the verbs come before the subjects. These sentences should read:

Although the first amendment to the Constitution does guarantee freedom of speech, the Supreme Court has long recognized that there <u>have</u> to be some restrictions on the exercise of this right. ✓

Jennifer must have been doubly pleased that day, for seated in the gallery to watch her receive the award <u>were</u> her brother, her parents, and her husband. ✓

WATCH FOR INVERTED SENTENCE STRUCTURES

Regardless of the order of the sentence—subject-verb or verb-subject—the verb must always agree with its subject. If a sentence has a complex structure, it often helps to look at each element in isolation.

Use of Compound Subjects

Finally, be alert for ***compound subjects***. Usually, when the subject of a sentence consists of two or more elements joined by the conjunction "and," the subject is considered plural and requires a plural verb. Consider the following example:

Example:

Of the seven candidates, only John, Bill, and Jim <u>was</u> past office holders. ✖

The subject, "John, Bill, and Jim," is compound (joined by "and") and requires the plural verb "were"—even though the individual nouns are singular.

WATCH FOR COMPOUND SUBJECTS

Compound subjects, typically two or more subjects joined by "and," are plural and need a plural verb.

GRAMMAR AND MECHANICS SKILLS REVIEW • 13

Be careful not to confuse the compound subject with the disjunctive subject. When elements of the subject are joined by "or," the verb must agree with the element nearest to it. Replacing "and" with "or" changes our previous example:

> **Example:**
>
> Of the seven candidates, John, Bill, or Jim <u>is</u> likely to win. ✓

The elements are joined by "or," so the verb must agree with "Jim," which is the element closest to the verb. Therefore, the singular "is," as in "Jim is," is correct.

Additionally, watch out for subjects that are designed to look like plural but which are actually singular. Typically, these subjects are disguised using pronouns.

> **Example:**
>
> Neither one of those fools even <u>know</u> how to change a light bulb. ✗

The subject is not "those fools"; instead, it is the singular subject "Neither one." Thus, the singular verb "knows" is required.

<table>
<tr><td colspan="2">WATCH FOR DISJUNCTIVE AND SINGULAR SUBJECTS </td></tr>
<tr><td>1.</td><td>If the elements of the subject are joined by "or," the subject is disjunctive. The verb must agree with the closest element of the subject.</td></tr>
<tr><td>2.</td><td>Be alert for singular subjects that appear to be plural (typically pronouns).</td></tr>
</table>

Pronoun Usage

The rules for **pronoun usage** are summarized as follows:

<table>
<tr><td colspan="2">PRONOUN USAGE RULES </td></tr>
<tr><td>1.</td><td>A pronoun must have an antecedent (referent) to which it refers.</td></tr>
<tr><td>2.</td><td>The pronoun must refer clearly to the antecedent.</td></tr>
<tr><td>3.</td><td>The pronoun and antecedent must agree.</td></tr>
<tr><td>4.</td><td>The pronoun must have the proper case.</td></tr>
</table>

Pronouns Must Have Antecedents

A **pronoun** is used as a substitute for a noun. The noun that it replaces is called the **antecedent** (referent). With the exception of certain idioms such as "It is raining," a pronoun that does not have an antecedent is used incorrectly.

Examples:

Although Glen is president of the student body, he has not yet passed his English exam, and because of <u>it</u>, he will not graduate with the rest of his class. ✘

The damage done by Senator Smith's opposition to the policy of equal employment is undeniable, but <u>that</u> is exactly what he attempted to do in his speech on Thursday. ✘

In the first example, what is the antecedent of "it"? It is not "he has not yet passed his English exam," because that is a complete thought, or clause, not just a noun. "It" is not a pronoun substitute for that entire thought. Rather, "it" refers to Glen's "failure" to pass the exam, thereby providing "it" with the required antecedent. However, "failure" does not appear in noun form in the sentence. In other words, "it" wants to refer to a noun, but there is no noun to function as its point of reference. The sentence must be rewritten: "because of that fact, he will not graduate . . . ."

In the second example, "that" functions as a relative pronoun—it relates something in the first clause to the second clause. However, to what does "that" refer? Test possibilities by substituting them for "that" in the second clause. The sentence should make sense when you replace the pronoun with its antecedent. Is the antecedent "damage"?

but <u>damage</u> is exactly what he attempted to do . . . . ✘

Perhaps, then, the antecedent is "opposition" or "undeniable":

but <u>opposition</u> is exactly what he attempted to do . . . . ✘
but <u>undeniable</u> is exactly what he attempted to do . . . . ✘

There are no other candidates for the antecedent, so we must conclude that the use of "that" is incorrect. Most likely, what the writer intended to say was that the Senator attempted to deny the damage:

The damage done by Senator Smith's opposition to the policy of equal employment is undeniable, but he attempted to deny that damage in his speech on Thursday. ✓

PRONOUNS MUST HAVE ANTECEDENTS

Except for a few idiomatic expressions ("It" is getting late, "It" will be sunny today), every pronoun must have an antecedent. An antecedent must be a noun, not a thought or phrase. Identify a pronoun's antecedent and then check that it is correct by substituting it for the pronoun in the sentence.

Antecedents Must Be Clear

The antecedent of a pronoun must be made clear from the structure of the sentence. Consider these examples:

Examples:

Edward's father died before <u>he</u> reached his twentieth birthday, so <u>he</u> never finished his education. ✘

In 1980, the University Council voted to rescind Provision 3, <u>which</u> made it easier for some students to graduate. ✘

In the first example, it is not clear whether the father died before he reached the age of 20 or before Edward reached the age of 20. Furthermore, it is not clear whose education remained unfinished. Similarly, in the second example, the antecedent of "which" is not clear. "Which" may refer to Provision 3 or it may refer to the University Council's vote to rescind Provision 3.

> ## WATCH FOR UNCLEAR ANTECEDENTS
>
> The antecedent of a pronoun must be clearly identified by the structure of the sentence.

Example:

The letter is on the desk <u>that</u> we received yesterday. ✘
The letter <u>that</u> we received yesterday is on the desk. ✓

Finally, the impersonal use of "it," "they," and "you" tends to produce vague, wordy sentences.

Examples:

In the manual, <u>it</u> says to make three copies. ✘
The manual says to make three copies. ✓

<u>They</u> predict we are in for a cold, wet winter. ✘
The almanac predicts a cold, wet winter. ✓

Pronoun-Antecedent Agreement

The pronoun must agree with its antecedent. Consider the following example:

Example:

Historically, the college dean was also a professor, but today <u>they</u> are usually administrators. ✘

In the example, "they" must refer to "dean," but "dean" is singular and "they" is plural. The sentence can be corrected in one of two ways: by changing the first clause to the plural or by changing the second clause to the singular.

Historically, college deans were also professors, but today they are usually administrators. ✓
Historically, the college dean was also a professor, but today the dean is usually an administrator. ✓

> ## WATCH FOR PRONOUN-ANTECEDENT AGREEMENT
>
> If the antecedent is singular, the pronoun must be singular; if the antecedent is plural, the pronoun must be plural.

Finally, it is incorrect to use different forms of the same pronoun to refer to an antecedent. This error results in the sentence having different antecedents and therefore a ***shifting subject***.

Pronouns Must Have Proper Case

A pronoun must agree with its antecedent in case, number, and person. The pronoun's function in a sentence determines which case should be used. You should be familiar with the following three categories of pronoun case: nominative (or subjective), objective, and possessive.

TYPES OF PRONOUN CASE

1. Nominative (subjective) case pronouns are used as subjects of sentences.

2. Objective case pronouns are used as objects: direct objects, indirect objects, and objects of prepositions.

3. Possessive case pronouns are used to show possession. Use a possessive pronoun preceding a gerund. A gerund is the "-ing" form of a verb that is used as a noun.

The following examples illustrate correct usage of pronoun case:

Examples:

Nominative:
I thought he would like the gift we bought. ✓

Objective:
The choice for the part is between Bob and me. ✓ (The object pronoun me follows the preposition between.)

Possessive:
Do you mind my using your computer? ✓ (The possessive pronoun my precedes the gerund using.)

EXAMPLES OF PRONOUN CASE

		1st Person	2nd Person	3rd Person
Nominative Case	Singular:	I	you	he, she, it
	Plural:	we	you	they
Objective Case	Singular:	me	you	him, her, it
	Plural:	us	you	them
Possessive Case	Singular:	my	your	his, her, its
	Plural:	our	your	their

The following are additional examples of the **nominative**, or subjective, pronoun case:

Examples:

John and him were chosen. ✗
John and he were chosen. ✓ (He is the subject of the verb; we certainly would not say that him was chosen.)

It was her who was chosen. ✗
It was she who was chosen. ✓

Us student-workers decided to organize into a union. ✗
We student-workers decided to organize into a union. ✓

He is as witty as her. ✗
He is as witty as she. ✓

The following are additional examples of the *objective* pronoun case:

Examples:

They accused Tom and <u>he</u> of stealing. ✗
They accused Tom and <u>him</u> of stealing. ✓ (<u>Him</u> is the object of the verb <u>accused</u>; they accused <u>him</u>, not <u>he</u>.)

The tickets were given to Bill and <u>I</u>. ✗
The tickets were given to Bill and <u>me</u>. ✓ (<u>Me</u> is the object of <u>to</u>; the tickets were given to <u>me</u>, not to <u>I</u>.)

Finally, personal pronouns that express ownership never require an apostrophe. Also, a pronoun that precedes a gerund ("-ing" verb form used as a noun) is usually the possessive case.

Examples:

This book is <u>your's</u>, not <u>her's</u>. ✗
This book is <u>yours</u>, not <u>hers</u>. ✓

He rejoiced at <u>him</u> going to the party. ✗
He rejoiced at <u>his</u> going to the party. ✓

Some pronouns are either singular or plural, while others can be both. The structure and intended meaning of the sentence indicate whether the pronoun is singular or plural.

SINGULAR AND/OR PLURAL PRONOUNS

Singular:	anybody, another, everybody, everything, somebody, something, nobody, one, anyone, everyone, someone, no one, each, every, neither, either, much
Plural:	both, few, many, most, several
Singular and Plural:	all, any, half, more, none, some

Technically, pronouns are divided into seven formal categories:

FORMAL CATEGORIES OF PRONOUNS	
Personal:	I, we, my, mine, our, ours, me, us, you, your, yours, he, she, it, they, his, hers, its, their, theirs, him, her, them
Demonstrative:	this, these, that, those
Indefinite:	all, any, anything, both, each, either, one, everyone, everybody, everything, few, many, more, neither, none, somebody, someone, something
Relative:	(subjective) who, which, that; (objective) whom, which, that; (possessive) whose
Interrogative:	what, which, who, whom, whose
Reflexive/Intensive:	myself, ourselves, yourself, yourselves, himself, herself, itself, themselves
Reciprocal:	each other, one another

Adjectives versus Adverbs

Adjectives Modify Nouns; Adverbs Modify Verbs, Adjectives, and Other Adverbs

Adjectives are used to modify nouns, while **adverbs** are used to modify verbs, adjectives, or other adverbs.

Example:

No matter how <u>quick</u> he played, Rich never beat Julie when playing the card game "Speed." ✘

In the above example, "quick" is intended to modify the speed with which Rich played cards. However, "quick" is an adjective and therefore cannot be used to modify a verb. By adding "-ly" to the end of "quick," we can transform it into an adverb and the sentence reads: "No matter how quickly he played . . . ."

The following examples further illustrate the proper use of adjectives and adverbs:

Examples:

Adjectives:
Mr. Jackson is a <u>good</u> teacher. ✔
He is a <u>bad</u> driver. ✔
There has been a <u>considerable</u> change in the weather. ✔
My sister is a <u>superb</u> dancer. ✔
The teacher gave a <u>quick</u> explanation of the problem. ✔
This is a <u>slow</u> exercise. ✔

Adverbs:
Mr. Jackson teaches <u>well</u>. ✔
He drives <u>badly</u>. ✔
The weather has changed <u>considerably</u>. ✔
My sister dances <u>superbly</u>. ✔
The teacher explained the problem <u>quickly</u>. ✔
This exercise must be done <u>slowly</u>. ✔

The following examples underscore that adjectives, not adverbs, must be used to modify nouns:

Examples:

He said that the medicine tasted <u>terribly</u>. ✗
He said that the medicine tasted <u>terrible</u>. ✓

The dog remained <u>faithfully</u> to its master until the end. ✗
The dog remained <u>faithful</u> to its master until the end. ✓

I felt <u>badly</u> about forgetting the appointment. ✗
I felt <u>bad</u> about forgetting the appointment. ✓

In each of the above, the emphasized word modifies the subject of the sentence and not the verb. The following examples underscore that adverbs, not adjectives, must be used to modify verbs and adjectives:

Examples:

He can do the job <u>easier</u> than you can. ✗
He can do the job more <u>easily</u> than you can. ✓

The problem seemed <u>exceeding</u> complex to me. ✗
The problem seemed <u>exceedingly</u> complex to me. ✓

It rained <u>steady</u> all day yesterday. ✗
It rained <u>steadily</u> all day yesterday. ✓

The professor presented an <u>obvious</u> important point in class. ✗
The professor presented an <u>obviously</u> important point in class. ✓

We all agreed that the new film was <u>real</u> funny. ✗
We all agreed that the new film was <u>really</u> funny. ✓

The students found the physics examination <u>extreme</u> difficult. ✗
The students found the physics examination <u>extremely</u> difficult. ✓

If you speak <u>firm</u>, he will listen to you. ✗
If you speak <u>firmly</u>, he will listen to you. ✓

He made <u>considerable</u> more progress than I did. ✗
He made <u>considerably</u> more progress than I did. ✓

Linking Verbs

Linking verbs are followed by adjectives, not adverbs. The following is a list of common linking verbs:

COMMON LINKING VERBS				
be	become	appear	look	seem
remain	feel	smell	sound	taste

Note that some of the verbs listed as linking verbs may sometimes function as verbs of action. The following examples illustrate this point:

Examples:

Adjectives:
I feel <u>tired</u>. ✓
He looked <u>angry</u>. ✓
The pie tastes <u>delicious</u>. ✓

Adverbs:
I felt my way <u>slowly</u> in the darkness. ✓
He looked about the room <u>angrily</u>. ✓
She tasted the pie <u>cautiously</u>. ✓

Watch for Adjectives Posing as Adverbs

WATCH FOR ADJECTIVE-ADVERB SWITCHING

Be alert for adjectives posing in place of adverbs and vice versa. Adjectives can usually be transformed into adverbs by adding "-ly." However, verbs must be modified by adverbs, not simply by an adjective posing as an adverb.

Examples:

1. The girl looks <u>intelligently</u>. ✗
   The girl looks <u>intelligent</u>. ✓

2. That perfume smells <u>sweetly</u>, doesn't it? ✗
   That perfume smells <u>sweet</u>, doesn't it? ✓

3. The physician appeared <u>nervously</u> when he talked to the patient. ✗
   The physician appeared <u>nervous</u> when he talked to the patient. ✓

4. This bed seems very <u>comfortably</u>. ✗
   This bed seems very <u>comfortable</u>. ✓

5. Several people arrived too <u>lately</u> to be admitted to the performance. ✗
   Several people arrived too <u>late</u> to be admitted to the performance. ✓

   ➤ In the incorrect sentence, "lately" is not an adverb for "late." Instead, "lately" means "as of late."

6. The horse ran <u>fastly</u> enough to win the race. ✗
   The horse ran <u>fast</u> enough to win the race. ✓

   ➤ In the incorrect sentence, "fastly" is not a word.

7. The architect worked <u>hardly</u> to finish his drawings by the next day. ✗
   The architect worked <u>hard</u> to finish his drawings by the next day. ✓

   ➤ In the incorrect sentence, "hardly" is not an adverb for "hard." Instead, "hardly" means "barely."

Adjective Forms

Adjectives have three forms: the simple, the comparative, and the superlative. The simple form is used to attribute a characteristic to a noun by modifying it.

Examples:

The <u>blue</u> book is on the shelf.
The book is on the <u>top</u> shelf.

When two things are compared, the comparative form of the adjective should be used. The comparative is formed in one of two ways:

RULES FOR COMPARISONS BETWEEN TWO OBJECTS
1. Two objects can be compared by adding "-er" to the adjective. *or* 2. Two objects can be compared by placing "more" before the adjective.

Examples:

She is <u>more busier</u> than her sister. ✗
She is <u>busier</u> than her sister. ✓
She is <u>more busy</u> than her sister. ✓

Jeremy is <u>more wiser</u> than we know. ✗
Jeremy is <u>wiser</u> than we know. ✓
Jeremy is <u>more wise</u> than we know. ✓

If three or more things are being compared, the superlative form of the adjective is used. The superlative is formed in one of two ways:

RULES FOR COMPARISONS AMONG THREE OR MORE OBJECTS
1. Three or more objects can be compared by adding "-est" to the adjective. *or* 2. Three or more objects can be compared by placing "most" before the adjective.

Examples:

Mary is the <u>shorter</u> of all of her friends. ✗
Mary is the <u>shortest</u> of all of her friends. ✓

Of all the books, this one is the <u>more</u> difficult. ✗
Of all the books, this one is the <u>most</u> difficult. ✓

This is the <u>most sharpest</u> knife I have. ✗
This is the <u>sharpest</u> knife I have. ✓

Some comparative and superlative modifiers require changing the words themselves. A few of these irregular comparisons are given below. Whenever you are in doubt about the comparative forms of any adjective or adverb, consult your dictionary.

MODIFIERS THAT DO CHANGE

Positive	Comparative	Superlative
good	better	best
well	better	best
bad (evil, ill)	worse	worst
badly	worse	worst
far	farther, further	farthest, furthest
late	later, latter	latest, last
little	less, lesser	least
many, much	more	most

Some adjectives and adverbs express qualities that go beyond comparison. These adjectives and adverbs describe the highest degree of a given quality and, as a result, they cannot be improved. Some of these words are listed below.

MODIFIERS THAT DO NOT CHANGE

complete	horizontally	perfectly	square	unique
correct	immortally	preferable	squarely	uniquely
dead	infinitely	round	supreme	universally
exact	perfect	secondly	totally	

When the comparative form is used in an expression like "This thing is better than any other in the group," remember that "this thing" must be set off from the other members of the group by a word such as "other" or "else."

Example:

Our house is cooler than any house on our block. ✘

Since "our house" belongs to the group of houses on "our block," "our house" must be set off from the other houses by "other" or "else." To correct the above sentence, we could write:

Our house is cooler than any <u>other</u> house on our block. ✔

Example:

He has a better record than any salesman in our group. ✘

Again, since "he" belongs to the group of salesmen, "he" must be set off from the other salesmen by "other" or "else." So, the sentence should read:

He has a better record than any <u>other</u> salesman in our group. ✔

Finally, be aware of incomplete comparisons, which can be both illogical and confusing.

Examples:

The plays of Shakespeare are as good as Marlowe. ✘
The plays of Shakespeare are as good as <u>those</u> of Marlowe. ✔

His skill in tennis is far better than other athletes his age. ✘
His skill in tennis is far better than <u>that</u> of other athletes his age. ✓

His poetry is as exciting, if not more exciting than, the poetry of his instructor. ✘
His poetry is as exciting <u>as</u>, if not more exciting than, the poetry of his instructor. ✓

AVOID INCOMPLETE COMPARISONS

Double-check that the basis of any comparison is explicitly clear. This may include adding words such as "that" or "as" to ensure that the intended comparison is made.

Double Negatives

It is true that we all hear and sometimes say *double negatives* in daily conversation. However, double negatives are NOT acceptable in standard written English.

Example:

I <u>hadn't hardly</u> begun to understand Spanish when I had to move again. ✘

The phrase "hadn't hardly" is a double negative. The sentence should read: "I had hardly begun to understand . . . ."

WATCH FOR DOUBLE NEGATIVES

Watch for double negatives ("not barely," "hardly nothing")—they are always incorrect.

Nouns and Noun Clauses

Nouns are names of people, places, things, or ideas; they are used to indicate the subject of a sentence. Like pronouns, nouns have a case.

TYPES OF NOUN CASE

1. Nominative (subjective) case is used when the noun is the subject of the sentence.

2. Objective case is used when the noun is an indirect or direct object or is the object of a preposition.

3. Possessive case is used when nouns are intended to show possession.

English nouns do not change form between the nominative case and the objective case; however, because pronouns stand in for nouns and have distinct nominative and objective forms, it can be determined that nouns have cases as well.

Sometimes the place of the noun in a sentence is filled by a *noun clause* instead of a single noun. A noun clause is a dependent clause.

Example:

That Judy was chosen for the promotion is not surprising. ✓

The failure to properly introduce a noun clause is an error of sentence structure. "That" by itself is not the noun, nor is "Judy was chosen for the promotion" a noun. However, the two combined create a noun clause and function as the noun.

RULE FOR INTRODUCING NOUN CLAUSES
A noun clause is a group of words that functions as the subject (or another noun usage) of a sentence. "That" is often the best word to use to introduce noun clauses.

Examples:

The reason the saxophone is popular is because its timbre can approximate that of the human voice. ✗
The reason the saxophone is popular is that its timbre can approximate that of the human voice. ✓

Why American car manufacturers did not reduce car sizes earlier than they did is a mystery to most market experts. ✗
That American car manufacturers did not reduce car sizes earlier than they did is a mystery to most market experts. ✓

The above examples make the error of introducing noun clauses with "because" and "why." In both sentences, a noun clause is required; "that" should be used in both cases.

WATCH FOR "BECAUSE" AND "WHY" AS NOUN CLAUSE INTRODUCTIONS
Noun clauses must be introduced by "that," not "because" or "why."

Additionally, DO NOT use "where" for "that" in object clauses.

Example:

I saw in the bulletin where Mrs. Wagner's retirement was announced. ✗
I saw in the bulletin that Mrs. Wagner's retirement was announced. ✓

However, if the subject of the sentence actually is about where something is, then use "where."

Examples:

Where he went is not known now. ✓

Where the wedding had initially been scheduled is not where it ended up being held. ✓

All I want to know is where we are supposed to go for homeroom attendance. ✓

Common Grammatical Errors
Exercise 2

DIRECTIONS: For items #1–25, circle the letter of the underlined part of the sentence containing the grammatical error. Answers are on page 561.

1. The professor deals <u>harsh</u> with students <u>who</u>
   A   B
   <u>are not prepared</u>, and <u>he is</u> even <u>more severe</u>
   B   C   D
   with those who plagiarize.

2. A recent study <u>indicates</u> that the average
   F
   person <u>ignores</u> most commercial advertising
   G
   and <u>does not buy</u> products <u>because of them</u>.
   H   J

3. <u>Despite the fact</u> that New York City is <u>one of</u>
   A   B
   <u>the most</u> densely populated areas in the world,
   B
   <u>there are</u> many parks where one can sit on a
   C
   bench under the trees and <u>you can</u> read a
   D
   book.

4. Charles Dickens <u>wrote</u> about the <u>horrifying</u>
   F   G
   conditions in the English boarding <u>schools that</u>
   H
   he learned about on one <u>of his</u> trips to Yorkshire.
   J

5. André Breton <u>initiated</u> the Surrealist
   A
   movement <u>with the publication</u> of a manifesto,
   B
   <u>and it</u> incorporated the theories of Freud
   C
   <u>as well as</u> his own.
   D

6. The review of the concert <u>published</u> in the
   F
   morning's paper mentioned that the soloist <u>is a</u>
   G
   very promising talent and <u>that</u> the orchestra
   H
   <u>played capable</u>.
   J

7. During <u>the war</u>, there were many people in the
   A
   Polish countryside <u>that</u> sheltered <u>those</u> who
   B   C
   <u>had escaped</u> from concentration camps.
   D

8. The dean <u>lectured</u> <u>to we students</u> <u>on the</u>
   F   G   H
   <u>privilege and</u> responsibility <u>of attending</u> the
   H   J
   university.

9. <u>You taking the initiative</u> <u>in the negotiations</u> <u>will</u>
   A   B   C
   <u>profit</u> the company <u>to a great degree</u>.
   C   D

10. The members of the club <u>insisted that</u> <u>I be</u> the
    F   G
    representative of the organization at the
    <u>conference which</u> was something <u>I had hoped</u>
    H   J
    to avoid.

11. <u>No one</u> knows for sure <u>whether there was</u> a real
    A   B
    <u>person about which</u> Shakespeare <u>wrote</u> his
    C   D
    sonnets.

12. Although the director of the zoo takes great
      F   G

pains to re-create the natural habitats of the
       H

animals, few of the exhibits is completely
                      J

accurate in every detail.

13. Climatic differences between the north and

south of some countries helps to account for
        A   B   C

the differences in temperament of the
      C

inhabitants of the two regions.
            D

14. The month of August was particularly cold;
                       F

hardly no daily temperatures were recorded
      G   H

above 80 degrees, and only one was recorded
                  J

above 90 degrees.

15. The diaries of Stendhal, which make
                    A

entertaining reading, also provides a great
      A   B

wealth of information about musical taste and
                  C

performance practice in the last century.
                D

16. Given the evidence of the existence of a
      F

complicated system of communication used by
                    G

whales, it is necessary to acknowledge its
      G   H   J

intelligence.

17. Him being at the rally does not necessarily mean
      A   B

that the congressman agrees with the
  C   D

president's entire platform.

18. Although there is no perfect form of

government, representative democracy, as it is
                          F

practiced in America, is a system that is
      F   G

working well and more than satisfactory.
      H   J

19. George hired a caterer, who he later
           A   B C D

recommended, after tasting her specialty—
      D

spring rolls.

20. After driving past Trinity Church, the bus
                F

stopped at the recent constructed Exposition
                G

Tower, the tallest building in the city, to allow
            H   J

the passengers to take the special elevators to
         J

the observation tower.

21. The student senate passed the resolution
                A

banning smoking in the cafeteria with scarcely
              B   C

any dissenting votes which angered many
  C   D

members of the faculty.

22. Most employers assume that one's professional
               F

personality and work habits are formed as a
                  G   H

result of your early work experience.
  H   J

23. Only a small number of taxi drivers fail to insure
          A   B

their vehicles, but usually these are the ones
                       C

who need it most.
      D

24. <u>Angered</u> by the double standard society
    F

<u>imposed on</u> women, Edna St. Vincent Millay
    G

<u>wrote candid about</u> <u>her</u> opinions and her
      H   J

personal life.

25. Unless <u>they hire players</u> <u>who</u> <u>are</u> better hitters,
          A   B   C

the fans <u>will gradually lose</u> interest in the team
              D

despite the fine efforts of the pitching staff.

DIRECTIONS: For items #26–41, first identify each answer choice as an adjective or an adverb by writing ADJ (adjective) or ADV (adverb) on the line that follows each choice. Then, circle the adjective or adverb that best fills the blank in the item stem. Answers are on page 562.

---

26. Kathy does her homework ---------.

slow _____   slowly _____

27. We understand each other ---------.

really well _____   real good _____

28. Students should be --------- to their professors at all times.

polite _____   politely _____

29. Paula has adjusted to her new school. She is doing ---------.

good _____   well _____

30. I think the cake is done. It smells ---------.

good _____   well _____

31. Your room is a --------- mess. Clean it up at once!

terrible _____   terribly _____

32. When I found out that the accident was my fault, I felt ---------.

awfully _____   awful _____

33. The movie we saw last night wasn't --------- exciting.

terrible _____   terribly _____

34. Doing a job --------- right away saves time in the long run.

well _____   good _____

35. Cats have a developed sense of smell. They can smell ---------.

well _____   good _____

36. "Mrs. Chang, your son works --------- in class. You can be proud of him."

hard _____   hardly _____

37. In order to deliver the package on time, the messenger biked ---------.

fast _____   quick _____

38. The college I will be attending in September is ---------.

nearly _____   near _____

39. After contracting the disease, Marc's symptoms appeared ---------.

slow _____   slowly _____

40. Doctors need to remain --------- even during an epidemic.

healthy _____   healthily _____

41. Leo's stomach felt --------- after the terrific Thanksgiving feast.

heavy _____   heavily _____

DIRECTIONS: In sentences #42–66, circle the correct verb choice. Answers are on page 562.

42. Each year, many people who did not graduate from high school (receive, receives) GED diplomas.

43. The books on the top shelf (was, were) all written by Emily Brontë.

44. The stores in the downtown sector's newly renovated mall (offer, offers) brand name fashions at reduced prices.

45. Only a few dust-covered bottles of the vintage wine (remain, remains) in the cellar.

46. Each tourist who visits the caverns (is, are) given a guidebook.

47. Underneath the leaf covering (was, were) several different species of insects.

48. The young boys, who had never before been in trouble with the law, (was, were) worried about what their parents would say.

49. Several barrels containing a highly toxic liquid (has, have) been discovered at the abandoned factory.

50. The sponsors of the arts and crafts fair (hope, hopes) that it will attract several thousand visitors.

51. Dawn, Harriet, and Gloria, who have formed their own singing group, (is, are) auditioning for jobs.

52. According to insiders, the mayor, whose administration has been rocked by several crises, (worry, worries) that more layoffs are inevitable.

53. There (has, have) been several acts of vandalism in the cemetery in recent months.

54. Rock musicians who perform in front of large speakers often (loses, lose) part of their hearing.

55. The leaves from the branches of the tree that hang over the fence (falls, fall) into the neighbor's yard.

56. The computer and the printer, which are sitting on James' desk, (has, have) never been used.

57. Theresa, wearing her hip-length waders, (was, were) fishing in the middle of the stream.

58. The film critic for the *New York Times* (write, writes) that the film is very funny and entertaining.

59. Several of the ingredients that are used in the dish (has, have) to be prepared in advance.

60. The computer that controls the temperature of the living quarters of the ship (was, were) malfunctioning.

61. There (has, have) been some support for a proposal to build a new courthouse in the center of town.

62. Bill and Jean (is, are) going to the game tomorrow.

63. There (was, were) several students absent last week.

64. I hope that no one has left (his or her, their) homework at home.

65. Each of the sisters celebrated (her, their) birthday at the Plaza.

66. The music of Verdi's operas (is, are) filled with dramatic sweep.

ANALYZING SENTENCE STRUCTURE

When analyzing the structure of a sentence, ask yourself the following five questions:

CHECKLIST FOR ANALYZING SENTENCE STRUCTURE
1. Is the word group a complete sentence?
2. Is the sentence a run-on sentence?
3. Are the elements of the sentence parallel?
4. Are there any incomplete split constructions?
5. Do the verb tenses correctly reflect the sequence of events?

Sentence Fragments

A *sentence fragment* is a group of words that begins with a capital letter and ends with a period. A fragment looks like a sentence but really isn't because it lacks a main verb. Therefore, a fragment is a word grouping but not a complete thought.

Examples:

1. The regulation permitting camping in the state forest but not within 100 feet of a lake or stream. ✗
   The regulation permits camping in the state forest but not within 100 feet of a lake or a stream. ✓

   ➤ In the incorrect sentence, "permitting" is not a main verb.

2. Flights leaving the west coast and the Midwest were delayed. Because of severe thunderstorms in the east. ✗
   Flights leaving the west coast and the Midwest were delayed because of severe thunderstorms in the east. ✓

   ➤ In the incorrect sentence, "because" introduces a dependent, not an independent, clause. In the corrected sentence, the fragment is joined as a dependent clause to a proper independent clause.

3. While the carpenter finished framing the door, and the locksmith installed the hardware. ✗
   The carpenter finished framing the door, and the locksmith installed the hardware. ✓

   ➤ In the incorrect sentence, "while" makes the word group a dependent clause. In the corrected sentence, eliminating the "while" lets the word group stand as two independent clauses, each with its own main verb.

If you are editing your own work and find that you have written a sentence fragment, you have a lot of flexibility in how you eliminate the error. However, on a multiple-choice test, your options are limited. Typically, you have three choices for fixing a sentence fragment:

METHODS FOR FIXING SENTENCE FRAGMENTS
1. Change a verb form so that it becomes a main verb.
2. Combine the fragment with a true independent clause (sentence).
3. Convert a dependent clause into an independent clause.

Run-On Sentences

Be aware of sentences that carelessly run main clauses together without appropriate punctuation or connectors. **Run-on sentences** can be corrected in one of three ways: end-stop punctuation, a semicolon, or a connector.

The most common way to correct a run-on sentence is to divide the sentence using end-stop punctuation (a period, an exclamation mark, or a question mark).

Examples:

The lecture was dull you almost fell asleep. ✘
The lecture was dull. You almost fell asleep. ✓

Was the lecture dull you almost fell asleep. ✘
Was the lecture dull? You almost fell asleep. ✓

The lecture was incredibly dull you almost fell asleep. ✘
The lecture was incredibly dull! You almost fell asleep. ✓

The comma is not an end-mark. DO NOT use a comma by itself to separate two sentences.

Example:

Close the window, there is a draft in the room. ✘
Close the window. There is a draft in the room. ✓

Sometimes, two sentences are very closely related in meaning, and full end-stop punctuation may seem too strong. A semicolon can then be used to divide the two sentences.

Example:

It was a beautiful day there was not a cloud in the sky. ✘
It was a beautiful day; there was not a cloud in the sky. ✓

A third way to correct the run-on is to use a connector (conjunction) such as "and," "but," "for," "or," and "nor" if the two sentences are equally important. A comma is then placed before the connector.

Example:

I like to ski, my friend prefers to sit by the fire. ✘
I like to ski, but my friend prefers to sit by the fire. ✓

Particular problem words that may cause run-ons are "however," "therefore," "consequently," and "moreover." These words are not sentence connectors, and when they follow a complete thought, either a period or a semicolon should precede them.

Example:

Many asteroids are far away therefore they appear dim and are difficult to see. ✗
Many asteroids are far away. Therefore, they appear dim and are difficult to see. ✓
Many asteroids are far away; therefore, they appear dim and are difficult to see. ✓

Faulty Parallelism

Faulty parallelism is a common grammatical error. Whenever elements of a sentence perform similar or equal functions, they should have the same form. Consider the following faulty sentences; they are missing necessary words:

Examples:

At most colleges, the dominant attitude among students is that gaining admission to professional graduate school is more important than <u>to obtain</u> a well-rounded education. ✗

To demand that additional seasonings be placed on the table is <u>insulting</u> the chef's judgment on the proper balance of ingredients. ✗

The review was critical of the film, citing the poor photography, the weak plot, and the dialogue <u>was stilted</u>. ✗

In the first example, "gaining admission" and "to obtain" must both have the same form. Either both must be in the gerund form or both must be in the infinitive form. For example: "gaining admission . . . is more important than obtaining . . . ."

In the second example, the subject ("to demand") and the predicate complement ("insulting") must both have the same form: "To demand . . . is to insult . . . ."

In the last example, the last element of the list of film criticisms is not of the same form as the other two elements. The sentence should read: ". . . citing the poor photography, the weak plot, and the stilted dialogue."

CHECK THAT ALL ELEMENTS OF A SENTENCE ARE PARALLEL
Check that all elements of a sentence are parallel—including verb forms, noun forms, and word pairs such as "this . . . that," "either . . . or," and "neither . . . nor."

Examples:

He spends his time playing cards, swimming, going to the theater, and at school. ✗
He spends his time playing cards, swimming, going to the theater, and <u>going to</u> school. ✓

He manages his business affairs with knowledge, ease, and confidently. ✗
He manages his business affairs with knowledge, ease, and <u>confidence</u>. ✓

He was required by the instructor to go to the library, to take out several books on the Vietnam War, and that he should report to the class on what he had learned. ✗
He was required by the instructor to go to the library, to take out several books on the Vietnam War, and <u>to report</u> to the class on what he had learned. ✓

I am studying the sources of educational theory and how educational theory has evolved. ✘
I am studying the sources and <u>the evolution</u> of educational theory. ✓

He was not only sympathetic but also knew when to be considerate. ✘
He was not only sympathetic but also <u>considerate</u>. ✓

Not only did he enjoy the movie but also the play. ✘
<u>He enjoyed</u> not only the movie but also the play. ✓

I was concerned about the price of the car and if it was comfortable. ✘
I was concerned about the price and <u>the comfort</u> of the car. ✓

Neither does he speak Spanish nor Helen. ✘
Neither he nor Helen <u>speaks</u> Spanish. ✓

Incomplete Split Constructions

Split constructions refer to phrases in which a thought, interrupted by intervening material, is completed later in the sentence.

Example:

The officials were not only aware of, but actually encouraged, the misreporting of scores. ✓

This sentence contains a perfectly acceptable split construction. Ordinarily, the object of a preposition closely follows the preposition: "aware of the misreporting." Here, the object of the preposition is separated from the preposition by the phrase "but actually encouraged." This is unobjectionable as long as the thought is properly completed. There is a danger, however, that the intervening material will throw something off in the sentence.

CHECK THAT SPLIT CONSTRUCTIONS ARE COMPLETED

A split construction is a sentence structure in which two otherwise separate ideas are joined together by a later element. Be alert for split constructions and check that any interrupted thought is correctly completed.

Consider the following faulty sentences; they are incomplete split constructions:

Examples:

Her colleagues always speak of Professor Collins as a person who has and always will be sensitive to the needs of younger students. ✘

Judging from the pricing policies of many large corporations, maintaining a stable share of the market is as important, if not more important than, making a large profit. ✘

In the first sentence, the error is in the verb. The auxiliary verb "has" needs the verb "been," but "been" does not appear in the sentence. The sentence could be corrected by completing the construction: "... has been and ... always will be ...." In the second sentence, the error is an incomplete comparison. The sentence should read: "... as important as, if not more important than ...."

> ### RULE FOR CHECKING FOR SPLIT CONSTRUCTIONS
>
> The intervening material makes it difficult to spot errors of split construction. Therefore, when checking for split constructions, read the sentence without the intervening material—it should make sense, be grammatically correct, and be a complete sentence.

Examples:

George Washington <u>always has</u> and always will be <u>regarded</u> as the father of this country. ✗
George Washington <u>always has been</u> and always will be <u>regarded</u> as the father of this country. ✓

The smaller stone is just <u>as valuable</u>, and perhaps even more valuable than, <u>the larger stone</u>. ✗
The smaller stone is just <u>as valuable as</u>, and perhaps even more valuable than, <u>the larger stone</u>. ✓

Most television crime shows <u>are aimed</u> and appeal to <u>adults</u> over the age of 30. ✗
Most television crime shows <u>are aimed at</u> and appeal to <u>adults</u> over the age of 30. ✓

Verb Forms

Principal Parts of Verbs

The **principal parts** of verbs are the infinitive or present tense, the past tense, and the past participle. Most verbs are called regular verbs because the past tense and the past participle are formed by adding "-d" or "-ed" to the infinitive or present tense form:

Examples:

Present Tense:
borrow, dare, guard, miss, staple

Past Tense:
borrowed, dared, guarded, missed, stapled

Past Participle:
borrowed, dared, guarded, missed, stapled

Some verbs, however, do not follow the usual rule. They are called irregular verbs.

PRINCIPAL PARTS OF COMMON IRREGULAR VERBS

Present	Past	Past Participle
arise	arose	arisen
be	was, were	been
bear	bore	borne
become	became	become
begin	began	begun
bid	bade	bid, bidden
blow	blew	blown
break	broke	broken
bring	brought	brought
build	built	built
buy	bought	bought
catch	caught	caught
choose	chose	chosen
cling	clung	clung
come	came	come
cut	cut	cut
do	did	done
draw	drew	drawn
drink	drank	drunk
drive	drove	driven
eat	ate	eaten
fall	fell	fallen
feed	fed	fed
feel	felt	felt
fight	fought	fought
find	found	found
flee	fled	fled
fling	flung	flung
fly	flew	flown
forget	forgot	forgotten
forgive	forgave	forgiven
freeze	froze	frozen
get	got	gotten
give	gave	given
go	went	gone
grow	grew	grown
hang (a person)	hanged	hanged
hang (an object)	hung	hung
hear	heard	heard
hide	hid	hidden
hold	held	held
hurt	hurt	hurt
keep	kept	kept
know	knew	known
lay	laid	laid

Present	Past	Past Participle
lead	led	led
leave	left	left
lend	lent	lent
lie	lay	lain
light	lit, lighted	lit, lighted
lose	lost	lost
make	made	made
meet	met	met
read	read	read
ride	rode	ridden
ring	rang	rung
rise	rose	risen
run	ran	run
see	saw	seen
send	sent	sent
sew	sewed	sewn
shake	shook	shaken
sit	sat	sat
shoot	shot	shot
shrink	shrank, shrunk	shrunk, shrunken
slay	slew	slain
sleep	slept	slept
slide	slid	slid
speak	spoke	spoken
spend	spent	spent
spin	spun	spun
spring	sprang, sprung	sprung
stand	stood	stood
steal	stole	stolen
sting	stung	stung
swear	swore	sworn
swing	swung	swung
swim	swam	swum
take	took	taken
teach	taught	taught
tear	tore	torn
tell	told	told
think	thought	thought
throw	threw	thrown
wake	waked, woke	waked, woken
wear	wore	worn
weave	weaved, wove	woven
win	won	won
wring	wrung	wrung
write	wrote	written

Present, Past, and Future Tense

The tense of a verb indicates whether the action or condition described by the verb belongs to the present, to the past, or to the future.

Examples:

Present Tense:
deliver, learn, open, respond

Past Tense:
delivered, learned, opened, responded

Future Tense:
will deliver, will learn, will open, will respond

A problem of logical expression is poor choice of verb tense. The **verb tenses** in a correctly written sentence accurately reflect the **sequence** and/or **logic** of events described. The following examples contain verb tense errors:

Examples:

As soon as Linda finished writing her dissertation, she <u>will take</u> a well-earned vacation in Paris. ✘

A recent study shows that many mothers re-enter the labor force after their children <u>left</u> home. ✘

The first sentence is incorrect because the initial verb phrase ("As soon as Linda finished") describes an action that was entirely completed in the past; however, the subsequent verb phrase ("she will take") makes it sound as if that first action had not been completed and was instead on-going. Depending on whether Linda has already completed the dissertation, the sentence could be corrected in one of two ways:

As soon as Linda <u>finishes</u> writing her dissertation, she will take a well-earned vacation in Paris. ✓
As soon as Linda finished writing her dissertation, she <u>took</u> a well-earned vacation in Paris. ✓

The first corrected version states that neither event has yet occurred and that the writing will precede the vacation. The second corrected version states that both events are completed and that the writing preceded the vacation.

In the second sentence above, the verb "left" is incorrect because the verb "re-enter" describes a present, on-going action. The sentence can be corrected by making it clear that "children leaving home" is also a present, on-going phenomenon:

A recent study shows that many mothers re-enter the labor force after their children <u>leave</u> home. ✓
A recent study shows that many mothers re-enter the labor force after their children <u>have left</u> home. ✓

Either sentence is acceptable since both make it clear that leaving home is not a completed past action but an ongoing phenomenon.

WATCH FOR SHIFTING VERB TENSES
Make sure that verb tenses properly reflect the sequence, as well as the duration, of any action described in the sentence.

Examples:

Charles came to town last week and <u>goes</u> to a resort where he <u>rests</u> for three days. ✘
Charles came to town last week and <u>went</u> to a resort where he <u>rested</u> for three days. ✓

Joan came home last week and <u>goes</u> to her summer cottage where she <u>spends</u> the last weekend of her vacation. ✗

Joan came home last week and <u>went</u> to her summer cottage where she <u>spent</u> the last weekend of her vacation. ✓

The Perfect Tenses

Use the ***present perfect*** for an action begun in the past and extended to the present.

Example:

I am glad you are here at last; <u>I have waited</u> an hour for you to arrive. ✓

In this case, "I waited" would be incorrect. The action "have waited" (present perfect) began in the past and extended to the present.

Use the ***past perfect*** for an action begun and completed in the past before some other past action.

Example:

The foreman asked what <u>had happened</u> to my eye. ✓

In this case, "happened" would be incorrect. The action "asked" and the action "had happened" (past perfect) are used because one action (regarding the speaker's eye) is "more past" than the other action (the foreman's asking).

Use the ***future perfect*** for an action begun at any time and completed in the future. When there are two future actions, the action completed first is expressed in the future perfect tense.

Example:

When I reach Chicago tonight, my uncle <u>will have left</u> for Los Angeles. ✓

The action "will have left" is going to take place before the action "reach," although both actions will occur in the future.

The Subjunctive Mood

The ***subjunctive*** is used to express a wish, a command, a supposition, or a condition that is contrary to fact. The subjunctive is very important in other languages, but only a few remnants survive in English. The most important forms of the subjunctive are the use of "were" in place of "was" and the use of "be" in place of "am" in clauses requiring the subjunctive.

Example:

I wish that I <u>were</u> on a tropical island lying on the beach. ✓

In this sentence, "were" is used rather than "was" in order express the subjunctive (contrary to fact) idea that the speaker is not lying on the beach of a tropical island.

Example:

The teacher required that all reports <u>be</u> typed. ✓

In this example "be" is used rather than "are" because the teachers wishes or commands that the reports be typed.

Analyzing Sentence Structure
Exercise 3

DIRECTIONS: For items #1–28, choose the verb form that completes the sentence correctly. Answers are on page 563.

1. A gentleman is ------- to see you.

   A. comes
   B. came
   C. come
   D. coming
   E. will come

2. Bill was ------- to telephone you last night.

   F. to suppose
   G. supposed
   H. suppose
   J. supposing
   K. will suppose

3. My friend has ------- to get impatient.

   A. to begin
   B. began
   C. begin
   D. beginning
   E. begun

4. He has ------- a serious cold.

   F. catched
   G. caught
   H. catch
   J. catching
   K. will catch

5. He could ------- before large groups if he were asked.

   A. sing
   B. sang
   C. sung
   D. singed
   E. singing

6. She has ------- before large groups several times.

   F. sing
   G. sang
   H. sung
   J. singed
   K. singing

7. They have already ------- to the theater.

   A. go
   B. goes
   C. going
   D. gone
   E. will go

8. He has ------- me excellent advice.

   F. give
   G. gave
   H. gived
   J. giving
   K. given

9. He is ------- to his parents.

   A. to devote
   B. devote
   C. devoted
   D. devoting
   E. will devote

10. The engineer has designed and ------- his own home.

   F. to build
   G. builds
   H. building
   J. built
   K. had built

11. He ------- as he ran onto the stage following the clown and the magician.

    A. to laugh
    B. laughing
    C. laughed
    D. laughs
    E. had laughed

12. She ------- the high-jump so well at trials that she is going to the Olympics this summer.

    F. had jumped
    G. to jump
    H. jumping
    J. jumps
    K. jumped

13. It ------- that she continued to blame me even after she knew it wasn't my fault.

    A. hurt
    B. hurts
    C. has hurt
    D. hurting
    E. will hurt

14. The man ------- the murder occur if he had really been on that street corner when he said he was.

    F. see
    G. sees
    H. would have saw
    J. seen
    K. would have seen

15. The child ------- everywhere now that she is able to stand up by herself.

    A. to walk
    B. walks
    C. walked
    D. walking
    E. had walked

16. Tomorrow morning, Sam ------- his sister.

    F. was calling
    G. called
    H. calling
    J. has called
    K. will call

17. After she had completed her investigation, the state trooper ------- her report.

    A. was writing
    B. wrote
    C. has written
    D. writes
    E. will write

18. When I was growing up, we ------- every summer at my grandmother's home in the country.

    F. spend
    G. will spend
    H. have spent
    J. were spending
    K. spent

19. Whenever we get a craving for a late-night snack, we ------- a pizza.

    A. order
    B. ordered
    C. had ordered
    D. have ordered
    E. were ordering

20. For years now, John ------- his milk at the corner grocery.

    F. buys
    G. will buy
    H. has bought
    J. is buying
    K. bought

21. We were just leaving when the telephone -------.

    A. rang
    B. will ring
    C. was ringing
    D. has rung
    E. had rung

22. We arrived at the house by noon, but the wedding ------- over.

    F. is
    G. will be
    H. had been
    J. has been
    K. was

23. We ------- to drive to the game, but the car stalled.

    A. plan
    B. will plan
    C. had planned
    D. are planning
    E. have planned

24. The roofers were putting the last shingles on the house while the plumber ------- the water lines.

    F. is testing
    G. was testing
    H. tests
    J. will test
    K. had tested

25. A large flock of Canadian Geese ------- over the meadow and landed in the pond.

    A. will fly
    B. were flying
    C. fly
    D. flew
    E. are flying

26. Hui worked very hard to complete her course-work before the baby ------- due.

    F. is
    G. are
    H. was
    J. will be
    K. were

27. We ------- to drive from Wisconsin to Washington in two days, but we were late.

    A. want
    B. are wanting
    C. were wanted
    D. wants
    E. had wanted

28. Earl and I ------- to eat lunch together outside if it doesn't rain.

    F. will hope
    G. had hoped
    H. hope
    J. did hope
    K. hoped

DIRECTIONS: For items #29–52, circle the letter of the underlined part of the sentence containing the error. Answers are on page 563.

---

29. The owner of the collection <u>requested that</u>
                                            A

    the museum <u>require</u> <u>all people with a camera</u>
                    B   C

    <u>to leave</u> them at the door.
      D

30. The young comic <u>found</u> that capturing the
                         F

    audience's attention was easy, <u>but to maintain</u>
                                  G

    <u>their</u> interest <u>was</u> difficult.
     H   J

31. The whale had been <u>laying</u> on the beach for over
A

two hours before the rescue teams <u>were able to</u>
B

<u>begin</u> <u>moving</u> it <u>back into</u> the water.
B   C   D

32. The praying mantis <u>is welcomed by</u>
F

homeowners for <u>its</u> ability <u>to control</u>
G   H

destructive garden pests, <u>unlike the</u>
J

<u>cockroach, which serves no useful function.</u>
J

33. The <u>newly</u> <u>purchased</u> picture was <u>hanged</u> on the
A   B   C

back wall <u>nearest</u> the bay window.
D

34. The <u>opening scene</u> of the film was a <u>grainy,</u>
F   G

<u>black-and-white</u> shot of an empty town square
G

<u>in which</u> an outlaw was <u>hung.</u>
H   J

35. <u>We spent</u> an exhausting day <u>shopping we</u>
A   B

<u>could hardly</u> wait <u>to get</u> home.
C   D

36. The fact that she is bright, articulate, and <u>has</u>
F

<u>charisma</u> <u>will serve</u> her well in her campaign for
F   G

governor, <u>particularly</u> since her opponent <u>has</u>
H   J

<u>none</u> of those qualities.
J

37. Puritans such as William Bradford <u>displaying</u>
A

the courage and piety <u>needed to survive</u> in the
B

New World, a world <u>both</u> promising and
C

threatening, <u>which</u> offered unique challenges
D

to their faith.

38. The woman to <u>whom</u> I take my clothes <u>for</u>
F   G

<u>tailoring</u> has <u>sewed</u> the hem on this skirt
G   H

<u>perfectly.</u>
J

39. Unfortunately, <u>before</u> cures are found for
A

diseases such as cancer, many lives <u>would</u>
B

<u>have been</u> lost and millions of dollars in
B

medical services <u>spent to</u> treat symptoms
C

<u>rather than to</u> provide a cure.
D

40. The <u>house on</u> the corner was <u>completely</u> <u>empty,</u>
F   G   H

<u>no one</u> <u>came</u> to the door.
H   J

41. For many people, it is difficult <u>to accept</u>
A

compliments graciously and <u>even more</u>
B

<u>difficult</u> <u>taking</u> criticism <u>graciously.</u>
B   C   D

42. <u>Due</u> to the <u>extremely warm</u> weather this winter,
F   G

the water has not <u>froze</u> on the pond <u>sufficiently.</u>
H   J

43. The French poet Artaud <u>believed</u> <u>that, following</u>
A   B   C

the climax of a drama, the audience <u>experienced</u>
D

a violent catharsis and is thereby "reborn."

44. <u>Where</u> had <u>everyone</u> <u>gone</u> <u>all</u> the lights were <u>off</u>.
　　F　　　　G　　　H　　　　　　　　J

45. <u>Rather</u> than <u>declaring</u> bankruptcy, he <u>applied</u> for
　　　A　　　　B　　　　　　　　　　　C
a loan, and the bank <u>loaned</u> him the money.
　　　　　　　　　　　D

46. <u>Wagering</u> on the Kentucky Derby favorite <u>is</u> a
　　　F　　　　　　　　　　　　　　　　　　　G
bad <u>betting</u> proposition, for in the last fifteen
　　　H
years, the horse that has been the crowd favorite
at post time of the Kentucky Derby <u>loses</u> the
　　　　　　　　　　　　　　　　　　J
race.

47. We entered the cave <u>very</u> <u>slowly almost</u> afraid of
　　　　　　　　　　　　A　　　　B
what we <u>might find</u> <u>there</u>.
　　　　　C　　　　D

48. After he <u>had learned</u> <u>of</u> her suicide, he <u>drunk</u> all
　　　　　F　　　　　G　　　　　　　H
of the poison <u>from the vial</u>.
　　　　　　　　J

49. <u>During the years</u> she spent <u>searching for a cure</u>
　　　A　　　　　　　　　　　B
for the disease, Dr. Thompson interviewed
hundreds of patients, ran thousands of tests, and
<u>cross-checking</u> <u>millions of bits of data</u>.
　　C　　　　　D

50. <u>After struggling with the problem</u> for most of the
　　　　　　　　F
afternoon, he finally <u>flinged</u> the papers <u>on</u> the
　　　　　　　　　　　G　　　　　　H
desk and <u>ran out of the room</u>.
　　　　　J

51. <u>Suddenly,</u> I felt that something <u>was going to</u>
　　　A　　　　　　　　　　　　　B
<u>happen my</u> heart began to <u>beat furiously</u>.
　　C　　　　　　　　　D

52. <u>Early in his career</u>, the pianist entertained
　　　F
thoughts <u>of becoming</u> a composer; but after
　　　　　G
receiving bad reviews for his own work, <u>he</u> <u>had</u>
　　　　　　　　　　　　　　　　　H　　J
<u>given up</u>.
　　J

DIRECTIONS: For items #53–57, analyze the given sentence for sentence fragment errors. If an error exists, choose the answer choice that best corrects the error. If the sentence is correct as written, choose (A). Answers are on page 563.

53. <u>During the time that I was in the hospital. I</u>
<u>read</u> every one of the Sherlock Holmes stories.

A. NO CHANGE
B. During the time that I was in the hospital, reading
C. During the time that I was in the hospital, I read
D. During the time of being in the hospital. I read
E. Being in the hospital during the time reading

54. A city ordinance <u>prohibiting the construction</u> <u>of any structure that is</u> taller than the statue of Minerva, the Roman goddess of wisdom, on the dome of City Hall.

F. NO CHANGE
G. which prohibits the construction of any structure that is
H. that prohibits the construction of any structure that is
J. prohibits the construction of any structure that is
K. prohibiting the construction of any structure being

55. Because the low-lying land was very <u>marshy and the construction of a complex system of drainage ditches was</u> necessary before construction could begin.

    A. NO CHANGE
    B. marshy and the construction of a complex system of drainage ditches being
    C. marshy with the construction of a complex system of drainage ditches
    D. marshy, the construction of a complex system of drainage ditches being
    E. marshy, the construction of a complex system of drainage ditches was

56. The loud noise from the overly sensitive alarm on the car <u>parked in front of the building making</u> it difficult for the audience to understand the speaker.

    F. NO CHANGE
    G. that was parked in front of the building making
    H. which parked in front of the building making
    J. parked in front of the building made
    K. parked in front of the building to make

57. <u>Calling Wyoming the "Equality State," and</u> women were permitted to vote in the territory as early as 1869.

    A. NO CHANGE
    B. Called Wyoming the "Equality State," and
    C. Calling Wyoming the "Equality State, because
    D. Wyoming is called the "Equality State," because
    E. The "Equality State" being the name of Wyoming,

PROBLEMS OF LOGICAL EXPRESSION

Faulty or Illogical Comparisons

One problem of logical expression is faulty or illogical comparisons. A faulty comparison is the attempt to compare two things that cannot logically be compared. Consider the following faulty examples:

Examples:

Today, life expectancies of both men and women are much higher compared to the turn of the century when living conditions were much harsher. ✗

The average salary of a professional basketball player is higher than the top-level management of most corporations. ✗

A comparison can only be made between like or similar items. Yet, in the first sentence, we see an attempt to compare "life expectancies" with "the turn of the century"—two dissimilar concepts. The sentence can be corrected simply by adding "life expectancies at" before "the turn of the century." Now we have life expectancies compared to life expectancies, and that is a logical comparison.

The same error occurs in the second sentence. An attempt is made to compare "average salary" to "management." The error can be corrected in the same way as in the first example. In short, we can simply add "the average salary of" before "the top-level management."

WATCH FOR ILLOGICAL COMPARISONS	
Be alert for sentences that attempt to make an illogical comparison between two dissimilar concepts.	

Unintended Meanings

Another problem of logical expression relates to whether a sentence says what it intends to say. Sometimes, a sentence intends to say one thing but actually says another.

Examples:

A childless charwoman's daughter, Dr. Roberts was a self-made woman. ✗

If the present interest rates fall, the dollar will lose some of its value on the foreign exchange. ✗

At first, both sentences may sound plausible. However, a closer reading shows that each contains an error of logical expression.

The first example asserts that Dr. Roberts was the daughter of a childless charwoman. However, this is not possible; if Dr. Roberts' mother had been childless, there would be no Dr. Roberts. Of course, the sentence intends to say that Dr. Roberts was both childless as well as the daughter of a charwoman ("Childless and a charwoman's daughter, Dr. Roberts was a self-made woman.").

The second example contains a more subtle error. It asserts that "present interest rates" might change. However, that is logically impossible. By definition, a "present rate" cannot change. If the rate changes, the result is a new interest rate; the result is not a changed "present rate." The sentence is corrected simply by deleting the word "present."

There are countless ways in which sentences can include unintended meanings. So, when you review a sentence, always remember to ask yourself if the ideas or actions being described are logically accurate and/or possible.

> ## VERIFY THAT EACH SENTENCE HAS ITS INTEDED MEANING
>
> Use logic to verify that each sentence has its intended meaning.

Conciseness

There are many kinds of conciseness errors. Several examples are below.

Avoid Awkward Sentences

A sentence may be grammatically and logically correct but still be awkward.

Examples:

The giant condor is able to spread its wings up to 25 feet. ✘
The giant condor has a wingspan of up to 25 feet. ✓

Although most students would benefit from further study of the sciences, doing so is frightening to most of them in that science courses are more difficult than liberal arts courses. ✘
Although most students would benefit from further study of the sciences, most of them are afraid to take science courses because they are more difficult than liberal arts courses. ✓

Given that the Incas lacked the wheel, the buildings at Machu Picchu are more astonishing than any Greek temples that are comparable as an achievement. ✘
Given that the Incas lacked the wheel, the buildings at Machu Picchu are more astonishing than any comparable Greek temple. ✓

In each example above, the second sentence is better because it is more concise.

Avoid Passive Verbs

Another common error involves passive verbs. The examples below show how active verbs (instead of passive verbs) produce sentences that are more clear and concise.

Examples:

One-fourth of the market <u>was captured</u> by the new computer firm. ✘
The new computer firm <u>captured</u> one-fourth of the market. ✓

The winning lottery ticket <u>was sold</u> by the gas station attendant. ✘
The gas station attendant <u>sold</u> the winning lottery ticket. ✓

The lesson <u>was finished</u> by the teacher, so she let us leave class early. ✘
The teacher <u>finished</u> the lesson, so she let us leave class early. ✓

AVOID PASSIVE VERBS

A passive verb combines a form of the verb "to be" or "to have" with an active verb (e.g., "The ball <u>was thrown</u>."). Avoid passive verbs. Active verbs are stronger and more direct.

Avoid Needlessly Wordy Sentences

Sometimes, a sentence will be incorrect because it is needlessly wordy.

Examples:

The protracted discussion over what route to take continued for a long time. ✘
The discussion over what route to take continued for a long time. ✓

An aim of the proposal is chiefly to ensure and guarantee the academic freedom of students. ✘
An aim of the proposal is to guarantee the academic freedom of students. ✓

In the first example, "protracted" is unnecessary because it means "to continue for a long time." In the second example, "chiefly" is unnecessary because an "aim" is a chief concern. Likewise, "ensure" is unnecessary because it has the same meaning as "guarantee."

Misplaced Modifiers

Another error of logical expression involves misplaced modifiers. A modifier should be as close as possible to what it modifies. If a modifier is too distant from what it is supposed to modify, it can modify the wrong part of the sentence.

Examples:

Stuffed with herb dressing, trussed neatly, and baked to a golden hue, Aunt Fannie served her famous holiday turkey. ✘

The doctor said gently to the patient that there was nothing wrong with a smile. ✘

At the party, Fred served cold lemonade to his thirsty guests in paper cups. ✘

In the first example, the introductory modifier immediately precedes Aunt Fannie. As a result, it sounds like she was stuffed, trussed, and baked. To correct the sentence, simply relocate the introductory modifier: "Aunt Fannie served her famous holiday turkey stuffed with herb dressing, trussed neatly, and baked to a golden hue."

In the second example, there is ambiguity because "with a smile" is improperly placed. As a result, the doctor's meaning is unclear: he either means there is nothing wrong with smiling; or, more likely, the doctor smiled as he informed the patient that nothing was wrong. To correct the sentence, simply relocate the modifier: "With a smile, the doctor said gently to the patient that there was nothing wrong."

Finally, in the third example, there is ambiguity because "in paper cups" is improperly placed. As a result, the sentence implies that the guests themselves are in paper cups. To correct the sentence, simply relocate the modifier: "At the party, Fred served cold lemonade in paper cups to his thirsty guests."

WATCH FOR MISPLACED MODIFIERS	

Watch for sentences with ambiguous or incorrect modification. A modifier should be as close as possible to what it's supposed to modify.

Examples:

I bought a piano from an old lady with intricate carvings. ✗
I bought a piano with intricate carvings from an old lady. ✓

I read about the destruction of Rome in my history class. ✗
In my history class, I read about the destruction of Rome. ✓

The word "only" can also cause confusion depending on how it's placed in a sentence.

Examples:

<u>Only</u> he kissed her. ✓
He <u>only</u> kissed her. ✓
He kissed <u>only</u> her. ✓

All of these sentences are logically possible. However, each sentence has a different meaning simply because the word "only" is placed differently in each one.

Finally, participle phrases can create confusion if they're improperly placed.

Examples:

Answering the doorbell, the cake remained in the oven. ✗
Answering the doorbell, we forgot to take the cake from the oven. ✓

Falling on the roof, we heard the sound of the rain. ✗
We heard the sound of the rain falling on the roof. ✓

As with previous examples, we can correct the sentences by moving the modifier (i.e., the participle phrase) as close as possible to what it's supposed to modify.

Problems of Logical Expression
Exercise 4

(1) When I was a child, my grandmother's kitchen was the scene of feverish activity during the early fall. (2) One morning, she would go to the farmers' market and return with baskets of fruits and vegetables. (3) Then, she would spend the rest of the day preparing the fruits and vegetables for the wide-mouthed canning jars that will be preserved through the winter. (4) Until the late fall, the pantry shelves were lined with rows of jars containing pickled peaches, creamed corn, and many varieties of jams and jellies.

(5) Today, we are able to buy fresh fruits and vegetables at the local grocery store even during the winter. (6) Indeed, years ago, home-canning was a practical solution to one of nature's dilemmas. (7) On the one hand, the harvest produced more fruits and vegetables than could be consumed immediately, so without some way to preserve the produce, it would spoil. (8) On the other hand, during the winter months, fresh produce was not available, so it was important to have preserved foods available.

(9) There is nothing any more mysterious about home-canning than any food preparation. (10) Special canning jars are packed with prepared food, fitted with self-sealing lids, which are submerged in boiling water. (11) The sustained high heat kills dangerous organisms causing the food to spoil. (12) As it gradually cools, a vacuum pulls the lid down against the mouth of the jar to make an airtight seal. (13) Unless the seal is broken, no organisms can enter the jar to cause spoilage.

(14) Although we no longer depend on home-canning, home-canning can be fun. (15) Spread on hot toast on a cold winter morning, a homemade jam just tastes better than a store. (16) You also will enjoy giving jars of homemade preserves to friends and relatives that are both unusual and personal as gifts. (17) All you need to do to get started is to find a book at the local library or bookstore and follow the directions about home-canning.

1. Sentence (2): <u>One</u> morning, she would go to the farmers' market and return with baskets of fruits and vegetables.

    A. NO CHANGE
    B. Some
    C. Each
    D. Once
    E. This

2. Sentence (3): Then, she would spend the rest of the day preparing the fruits and vegetables for the wide-mouthed canning jars that <u>will be preserved</u> through the winter.

    F. NO CHANGE
    G. preserve them
    H. preserved them
    J. were preserved
    K. would be preserved

3. Sentence (4): <u>Until</u> the late fall, the pantry shelves were lined with rows of jars containing pickled peaches, creamed corn, and many varieties of jams and jellies.

    A. NO CHANGE
    B. Since
    C. By
    D. Up to
    E. Then

4. Sentence (6): <u>Indeed,</u> years ago, home-canning was a practical solution to one of nature's dilemmas.

    F. NO CHANGE
    G. Indeed
    H. Furthermore,
    J. Moreover,
    K. However,

5. Sentence (7): On the one hand, the harvest produced more fruits and vegetables than could be consumed immediately, <u>so</u> without some way to preserve the produce, it would spoil.

   A. NO CHANGE
   B. meanwhile
   C. anyway
   D. instead
   E. otherwise

6. Sentence (8): <u>On the other hand</u>, during the winter months, fresh produce was not available, so it was important to have preserved foods available.

   F. NO CHANGE
   G. In fact
   H. Really
   J. Still
   K. Yet

7. Sentence (9): There is nothing any more mysterious about home-canning <u>than any</u> food preparation.

   A. NO CHANGE
   B. than any other
   C. as any
   D. as any other
   E. than

8. Sentence (10): Special canning jars are packed with prepared food, fitted with self-sealing lids, <u>which are submerged</u> in boiling water.

   F. NO CHANGE
   G. that are submerged
   H. submerging
   J. submerged
   K. and submerged

9. Sentence (11): The sustained high heat kills dangerous organisms <u>causing</u> the food to spoil.

   A. NO CHANGE
   B. that caused
   C. that could cause
   D. to cause
   E. which caused

10. Sentence (12): <u>As it gradually cools,</u> a vacuum pulls the lid down against the mouth of the jar to make an airtight seal.

   F. NO CHANGE
   G. As they gradually cool,
   H. Gradually cooling,
   J. Gradually cooled,
   K. As the jars gradually cool,

11. Sentence (13): Unless the seal is broken, no organisms <u>can enter</u> the jar to cause spoilage.

   A. NO CHANGE
   B. are entering
   C. entered
   D. have entered
   E. had entered

12. Sentence (14): Although we <u>no longer</u> depend on home-canning, home-canning can be fun.

   F. NO CHANGE
   G. usually
   H. never
   J. constantly
   K. perhaps

13. Sentence (15): Spread on hot toast on a cold winter morning, a homemade jam just tastes better than <u>a store</u>.

   A. NO CHANGE
   B. a store's
   C. the store
   D. some store
   E. any store

14. Sentence (16): You also will enjoy giving jars of homemade preserves to friends and relatives <u>that are both unusual and personal as gifts</u>.

   F. NO CHANGE
   G. as gifts that are both unusual and personal
   H. being gifts both unusual and personal
   J. which are gifts that are both unusual and personal
   K. that are gifts which are both unusual and personal

15. Sentence (17): All you need to do to get started is to find <u>a book at the local library or bookstore and follow the directions about home-canning</u>.

    A. NO CHANGE
    B. a home-canning book at the local library or bookstore with directions
    C. a book about home-canning at the local library or bookstore and follow the directions
    D. a book with directions about home-canning at the local library or bookstore and follow them
    E. a local library or bookstore with a home-canning book and follow the directions

---

DIRECTIONS: For items #16–27, circle the letter of the underlined part of the sentence that contains an error. Answers are on page 563.

---

16. <u>Written in almost total isolation from the world,</u>
                                  F

Emily Dickinson <u>spoke of</u> love <u>and</u> death in <u>her</u>
                  G   H   J

poems.

17. <u>Being highly qualified for the position,</u> the bank
                    A

president <u>will conduct</u> a final interview with the
               B

new candidate tomorrow, <u>after which</u> <u>he will</u>
                     C   D

<u>make</u> her a job offer.
   D

18. <u>In broken English,</u> the police officer patiently
         F

listened to the tourist ask for directions to Radio

City Music Hall, <u>after which</u> she <u>motioned</u> the
              G   H

tourist and his family into the squad car and

drove <u>them</u> to their destination.
     J

19. <u>Following the recent crash of the stock market,</u>
                  A

Peter <u>bought</u> a book on portfolio management <u>in</u>
      B   C

<u>order to learn</u> methods to protect his
    C

investments <u>from a well-known investment</u>
                  D

banker.

20. <u>Recent</u> research indicates that people <u>who</u> lived
    F   G

agrarian lifestyles in the Middle Ages had <u>much</u>
                          H

<u>more</u> leisure time <u>than people</u> today.
   H   J

21. <u>Since</u> we have a <u>broader</u> technological base,
    A   B

American scientists believe that our space

program <u>will ultimately prove</u> superior <u>to Russia.</u>
           C   D

22. Although a person may always represent
<u>himself</u> in a judicial proceeding, licensed
   F

lawyers <u>only</u> may represent <u>others</u> in <u>such</u>
        G   H   J

proceedings for a fee.

23. <u>Unlike the pale and delicately built ballerinas of</u>
                  A

<u>romantic ballet,</u> Judith Jamison's movement
    B

<u>seems more African than</u> European-American,
        C

and her physical appearance <u>reinforces</u> the
                      D

contrast.

24. Market experts <u>predict</u> that in ten years, when
          F

the harmful effects of caffeine become <u>more</u>
                      G

<u>generally known,</u> the number of tons of
    G

decaffeinated coffee <u>consumed by</u> Americans
              H

each year will exceed <u>coffee containing caffeine.</u>
                J

25. Illiteracy, <u>a widespread problem in the United</u>
                        A

<u>States,</u> <u>undermines</u> productivity because many
  A   B

mistakes <u>are</u> made by workers who do not know
              C

how to read <u>on the job</u>.
                    D

26. As sailors <u>are often assigned</u> to ships <u>that</u>
                      F   G

<u>remain</u> at sea for months at a time, men in the
  G

Navy <u>spend</u> more time away from home <u>than</u>
          H   J

<u>any branch of the service</u>.
          J

27. <u>Like A. J. Ayer</u>, much of Gilbert Ryle's
        A

philosophical argumentation <u>relies</u> on analysis
                              B

of the way <u>people</u> <u>ordinarily</u> use language.
              C   D

IDIOMS AND CLARITY OF EXPRESSION

Standard English contains numerous idioms and two-word verbs that are perfectly acceptable to use. Here are a few examples:

about time, about to	have in mind	sleep on it
bank on	keep an eye on	up against
fly off the handle	move on, move up	work out

A non-idiomatic expression is not acceptable standard written English for any of the following reasons:

CHECKLIST FOR IDIOMATIC EXPRESSION ERRORS

1. Diction
   a) Wrong Word Choice
   b) Wrong Preposition
   c) Gerund versus Infinitive
 	
2. Ambiguity in Scope
 	
3. Informal Usage

Diction

The first category of idiomatic expression errors involves *diction*, i.e., word choice.

Wrong Word Choice

Sometimes, a word can be used incorrectly and lead to a construction that is non-idiomatic or not acceptable standard written English.

Example:

The techniques of empirical observation in the social sciences are different <u>than</u> those in the physical sciences. ✘

The above example is wrong because "different than" is a non-idiomatic expression. The correct idiomatic expression is "different from": "The techniques of empirical observation in the social sciences are different <u>from</u> those in the physical sciences."

Sometimes, words whose meanings are very similar can be used incorrectly and lead to a construction that is non-idiomatic or not acceptable standard written English.

Examples:

John expressed his intention to make the trip, but <u>if</u> he will actually go is doubtful. ✗
John expressed his intention to make the trip, but <u>whether</u> he will actually go is doubtful. ✓

Herbert divided the cake <u>among</u> Mary and Sally. ✗
Herbert divided the cake <u>between</u> Mary and Sally. ✓

Herbert divided the cake <u>between</u> Mary, Sally, and himself. ✗
Herbert divided the cake <u>among</u> Mary, Sally, and himself. ✓

The <u>amount</u> of students in the class declined as the semester progressed. ✗
The <u>number</u> of students in the class declined as the semester progressed. ✓

There are <u>less</u> students in Professor Smith's class than there are in Professor Jones' class. ✗
There are <u>fewer</u> students in Professor Smith's class than there are in Professor Jones' class. ✓

Finally, some sentences are incorrect because they include words that fail to convey the author's intended meaning. An author sometimes makes this mistake because the wrong word and the correct word are actually quite similar.

CONFUSING WORD GROUPS

accept—*to receive,* or *to agree to something*
except—*to exclude* or *excluding*
access—*availability,* or *to get at*
excess—*state of surpassing specified limits* (noun), or *more than usual* (adjective)
adapt—*to adjust or change*
adept—*skillful*
adopt—*to take as one's own*
advantage—*a superior position*
benefit—*a favor conferred or earned*
build—*to erect, construct* (verb), or *the physical makeup of a person* (noun)
built—*the past tense of build*
adverse—*unfavorable*
averse—*having a feeling of repugnance or dislike*
advice—*counsel, opinion* (noun)
advise—*to offer advice* (verb)
affect—*to influence* (verb)
effect—*to cause or bring about* (verb), or *a result* (noun)
all ready—*everybody or everything ready*
already—*previously*
all together—*everybody or everything together*
altogether—*completely*
allude—*to make a reference to*
elude—*to escape from*
allusion—*an indirect reference*
illusion—*an erroneous concept or perception*
alongside of—*side by side with*
alongside—*parallel to the side*
among—*a term used with more than two persons or things*
between—*a term used with two persons or things*

ante—*a prefix meaning before*
anti—*a prefix meaning against*
capital—*place of government,* or *wealth*
capitol—*building that houses legislatures*
click—*a brief, sharp sound*
clique—*an exclusive group of people or set*
cloth—*fabric or material*
clothe—*to put on clothes, to dress*
coarse—*vulgar,* or *harsh*
course—*a path,* or *a plan of study*
complement—*a completing part*
compliment—*an expression of praise or admiration*
conscience—*the ability to recognize the difference between right and wrong*
conscious—*aware*
desert (DEZZ-ert)—*an arid area*
desert (di-ZERT)—*abandon,* or *a reward or punishment*
disburse—*to pay out*
disperse—*to scatter, distribute widely*
discomfit—*to upset*
discomfort—*lack of ease*
dual—*double*
duel—*a contest between two persons or groups.*
emigrate—*to leave a country*
immigrate—*to enter a country*
eminent—*of high rank, prominent, outstanding*
imminent—*about to occur, impending*
epitaph—*an inscription on a tombstone or monument*
epithet—*a term used to describe or characterize the nature of a person or thing*

CONFUSING WORD GROUPS

expend—*to use up*
expand—*to spread out*
faze—*to worry or disturb*
phase—*an aspect*
formally—*in a formal way.*
formerly—*at an earlier time*
fort (fort)—*a fortified place*
forte (FOR-tay)—*a strong point*
forte (FOR-tay)—*a musical term that means loudly*
idle—*unemployed or unoccupied*
idol—*image or object of worship*
in—indicates *inclusion or location,* or *motion within limits*
into—*motion toward one place from another*
incidence—*to the extent or frequency of an occurrence*
incidents—*occurrences, events*
it's—the contraction of *it is,* or the contraction of *it has*
its—possessive pronoun meaning *belonging to it*
knew—the past tense of *know*
new—*of recent origin*
know—*to have knowledge or understanding*
no—a negative used to express *denial or refusal*
later—*after a certain time*
latter—*the second of two*
lay—*to put*
lie—*to recline*
lightening—*making less heavy*
lightning—*electric discharge in the atmosphere,* or *moving with great speed*
loose—*not fastened or restrained,* or *not tight-fitting*
lose—*to mislay, to be unable to keep,* or *to be defeated*
moral—*good or ethical* (adjective), or *a lesson to be drawn* (noun)
morale—*spirit*
passed—the past tense of *to pass*
past—*just preceding or an earlier time,* or *in a direction going close to and then beyond*

personal—used to describe *an individual's character, conduct, or private affairs*
personnel—*an organized body of individuals*
precede—*to come before*
proceed—*to go ahead*
principal—*chief or main* (adjective), *a leader,* or *a sum of money* (noun)
principle—*a fundamental truth or belief*
prophecy—*prediction* (noun, rhymes with *sea*)
prophesy—*to predict* (verb, rhymes with *sigh*)
raise—*to lift, to erect*
raze—*to tear down*
rise—*to increase in value,* or *to get up or move from a lower to a higher position*
seem—*to appear*
seen—the past participle of *see*
set—*to place something down* (mainly)
sit—*to seat oneself* (mainly)
stationary—*standing still*
stationery—*writing material*
suppose—*to assume or guess*
supposed—past tense and past participle of *suppose*
supposed—*ought to or should* (followed by *to*)
than—used to express *comparison*
then—used to express *time,* or *a result or consequence*
use—*to employ or put into service*
used—past tense and the past participle of *to use*
used—*in the habit of or accustomed to,* (followed by *to*)
used—an adjective meaning *not new*
weather—*atmospheric conditions*
whether—*introduces a choice* (*whether* should not be preceded by *of* or *as to*)
your—a possessive showing *ownership*
you're—the contraction of *you are*

Wrong Preposition

In standard written English, only certain prepositions can be used with certain verbs. As a result of daily conversation and writing in standard written English, you should know which prepositions and verbs can be used together.

Example:

I asked him repeatedly if he was from <u>about</u> here, but he never answered me. ✘

The phrase "was from about here" is incorrect. From daily conversation, you should recognize the correct phrase: "he was from *around* here."

Gerund versus Infinitive

The *gerund* is the "-ing" form of a verb, and it is used as a noun.

Examples:

My doctor recommends <u>bicycling</u> as an alternative form of exercise. ✓
The company discontinued <u>testing</u> on animals. ✓

The *infinitive* is the "to" form of a verb. It is used as a noun.

Examples:

Our new physics professor prefers <u>to teach</u> by example. ✓
The restaurant requires men <u>to wear</u> a coat and tie. ✓

In some circumstances, you can use either the gerund or the infinitive.

Examples:

<u>Adding</u> an extra room to the house is the next project. ✓
<u>To add</u> an extra room to the house is the next project. ✓

However, in some circumstances, the gerund and the infinitive are NOT interchangeable. The difference is not a matter of grammar because both the infinitive and the gerund are used as nouns. Instead, the difference is a matter of what fluent English speakers would regard as idiomatic (acceptable).

Examples:

Tania says that <u>to open</u> the window will keep the room cool. ✘ (The infinitive is not idiomatic.)
Tania says that <u>opening</u> the window will keep the room cool ✓ (The gerund is idiomatic.)

She intends <u>calling</u> her mother on Sunday. ✘ (The gerund is not idiomatic.)
She intends <u>to call</u> her mother on Sunday. ✓ (The infinitive is idiomatic.)

WATCH FOR GERUND-INFINITIVE SWITCHING

Sometimes an infinitive can replace a gerund (or vice versa) and the result is non-standard written English.

Ambiguity in Scope

Watch for *ambiguity in scope*. This occurs when there is not a clear division between two ideas; as a result, two ideas that should be separate seem to merge.

Examples:

After the arrest, the accused was charged with resisting arrest and criminal fraud. ✘

The recent changes in the tax law will primarily affect workers who wait tables in restaurants, operate concessions in public places, and drive taxis. ✘

In the first example, the scope of "resisting" is not clear. As a result, the sentence could be interpreted to mean that the accused was charged with resisting criminal fraud. To correct the sentence, simply insert "with" before "criminal fraud": "... charged with resisting arrest and with criminal fraud." The intended scope of "resisting" is now made clear, and the clear division between the two separate ideas is established.

In the second example, the scope of "workers" is not clear. In short, the sentence uses "and" to join together the three types of workers described: "... workers who wait tables in restaurants, operate concessions in public places, *and* drive taxis." As a result of this word choice, the sentence could be interpreted to mean that the changed tax law will affect only those workers who do all three jobs. Clearly, this is not the intent of the sentence. To correct the sentence, simply change "and" to "or," or give the job descriptions in a series of parallel constructions: "... workers who wait tables in restaurants, workers who operate concessions in public places, and workers who drive taxis." If either of these corrections is made, the intended scope of "workers" is made clear.

WATCH FOR AMBIGUITY IN SCOPE

Watch for sentences that run two or more ideas together. Correct the error by adding words that make it clear the two ideas are distinct.

Informal Usage

Some expressions heard in daily conversation are regarded as *informal* or *low-level usage* and are unacceptable in standard written English. You will need to recognize the difference between standard and non-standard written English.

Example:

She <u>sure</u> is pretty! ✘
She <u>certainly</u> is pretty! ✓

Idioms and Clarity of Expression
Exercise 5

DIRECTIONS: In sentences #1–99, circle the correct word choice. Answers are on page 563.

1. He is the (principal, principle) backer of the play.

2. I hope your company will (accept, except) our offer.

3. We hope to have good (weather, whether) when we are on vacation.

4. Put the rabbit back (in, into) the hat.

5. The attorney will (advice, advise) you of your rights.

6. She is far taller (than, then) I imagined.

7. Are they (all ready, already) to go?

8. She answered the letter on shocking pink (stationary, stationery).

9. What is the (affect, effect) you are trying to achieve?

10. I want to (set, sit) next to my grandfather.

11. He's going to (lay, lie) down for a nap.

12. I'm (all together, altogether) tired of his excuses.

13. He saluted when the flag (passed, past) by.

14. I'd like another portion of (desert, dessert).

15. Try not to (loose, lose) your good reputation.

16. How much will the final examination (effect, affect) my grade?

17. What is it (you're, your) trying to suggest?

18. She's not (use, used) to such cold weather.

19. The cost of the coat will (raise, rise) again.

20. You are (suppose, supposed) to be home at six o'clock.

21. Her cat ran straight for (its, it's) bowl of food.

22. Are you (conscience, conscious) of what you are doing?

23. It will (seen, seem) that we are afraid.

24. His essays are filled with literary (allusions, illusions).

25. This wine will be a good (complement, compliment) to the meal.

26. It's (later, latter) than you think!

27. My cousin has a swimmer's (build, built).

28. I never (knew, new) him before today.

29. She asked her a (personal, personnel) question.

30. The golf (coarse, course) was very crowded.

31. The costume was made from old (cloth, clothe) napkins.

32. The ball carrier was trying to (allude, elude) the tacklers.

33. There are (know, no) more exhibitions planned.

34. I will wait for you in the (anteroom, antiroom).

35. Her (moral, morale) is very low.

36. Begin the sentence with a (capital, capitol) letter.

37. The fact that he nearly had an accident did not even (faze, phase) him.

38. He earns royalties in (access, excess) of a million dollars a year.

39. Now, may we (precede, proceed) with the debate?

40. Her (fort, forte) is writing lyrics for musical comedy.

41. They wondered how they were going to (disburse, disperse) the huge crowd.

42. Everyone was dressed (formally, formerly) for the dinner party.

43. I am not (adverse, averse) to continuing the discussion at another time.

44. Can something be done to diminish the (incidence, incidents) of influenza in that area?

45. "Seeing the film in class will serve a (dual, duel) purpose," he explained.

46. I'm not sure I want to (expand, expend) so much energy on that project.

47. Imagine my (discomfit, discomfort) when she showed up at the party too!

48. He was a famous matinee (idle, idol) many years ago.

49. When did they (emigrate, immigrate) from New York to Paris?

50. I think she is part of a (click, clique) of snobs and creeps.

51. She paid little attention to the fortune-teller's (prophecy, prophesy).

52. The lights went out when the (lightning, lightening) hit the house.

53. I'll provide you (what ever, whatever) assistance you require.

54. We are in (eminent, imminent) danger of losing our reservations.

55. Will she be able to (adapt, adopt) to our way of performing the operation?

56. As we went through the old cemetery, we were fascinated by some of the (epitaphs, epithets).

57. He shared the riches (between, among) Laura, Millie, and Ernestine.

58. The housing law was rewritten for his (advantage, benefit).

59. (Alot, A lot) of the time, he falls asleep at nine o'clock.

60. It was difficult to keep track of the (amount, number) of people who visited him last week.

61. I see him in the park (almost, most) every day.

62. Are you certain that he is (alright, all right) now?

63. She is just beginning to (aggravate, annoy) her mother.

64. He is the school's oldest living (alumni, alumnus).

65. He spotted the riverbank and then guided the canoe up (alongside, alongside of).

66. (Being as, Since) it is Wednesday, we are going to a Broadway matinee.

67. He is (anxious, eager) to be finished with the dental treatment.

68. Where do you want to (meet, meet at)?

69. My aunt just went inside to rest (awhile, a while).

70. It was (about, around) noon when we met for lunch.

71. I brought a (couple, couple of) books for you; both are historical novels.

72. Between (you and I, you and me), I think that her hat is very unbecoming.

73. The (continual, continuous) ticking of the clock was very disconcerting.

74. She (cannot seem, seems unable) to get up early enough to eat breakfast with him.

75. I (assume, expect) that you really earned your salary today.

76. I'm (disinterested, uninterested) in seeing that movie.

77. You must be (every bit as, just as) sleepy as I am.

78. I doubt (that, whether) it will snow today.

79. Sam, Joe, Lou, and Artie have worked with (each other, one another) before.

80. She asked him (if, whether) he wanted to have lunch with her or with her sister.

81. All (humans, human beings) need to take a certain amount of water into their bodies every week.

82. We hope to (conclude, finalize) the deal this month.

83. We were upset when she (flaunted, flouted) her mother's orders.

84. His girlfriend only eats (healthful, healthy) foods.

85. He said such terrible things about her that she is suing him for (libel, slander).

86. I would like to see you in (regard, regards) to the apartment you plan to rent.

87. She is always late for work, (irregardless, regardless) of how early she wakes up in the morning.

88. He'll (loan, lend) you a hand carrying the groceries.

89. The media (are, is) doing the job poorly.

90. The art director was taken (off, off of) the most profitable gallery show.

91. I hope that she will (quit, stop) sending us the job applications.

92. The reason the baby is crying is (because, that) she is hungry.

93. Does he (manage, run) the department efficiently?

94. Anyone who wants to have (his or her, their) conference with me today is invited to meet in my office at ten o'clock.

95. She scored more points than (any, any other) player on the team.

96. His room is very neat (but, while) hers is very messy.

97. He will (try and, try to) be more pleasant to his sister.

98. I shall give it to (whoever, whomever) arrives first.

99. This time, we will not wait (for, on) you for more than ten minutes.

DIRECTIONS: In sentences #100–114, determine whether the gerund choice, (A); the infinitive choice, (B); or BOTH the gerund and the infinitive, (C), is the correct answer to fill in the blank. Answers are on page 565.

100. After the break, the teacher continued -------.

   A.   lecturing
   B.   to lecture
   C.   BOTH

101. He forgot ------- me at the party last year, so he introduced himself again.

   A.   meeting
   B.   to meet
   C.   BOTH

102. Please remember ------- five minutes early on the day of the test.

   A.   arriving
   B.   to arrive
   C.   BOTH

103. He hesitated ------- for the assignment.

   A.   volunteering
   B.   to volunteer
   C.   BOTH

104. After her speech, the lecturer proceeded ------- questions.

   A.   taking
   B.   to take
   C.   BOTH

105. The politician continued ------- soft money contributions during his campaign.

   A.   accepting
   B.   to accept
   C.   BOTH

106. "I will not tolerate -------," the professor said.

   A.   talking
   B.   to talk
   C.   BOTH

107. Taking sixteen credit hours, the student has neglected ------- some of her essays.

   A.   writing
   B.   to write
   C.   BOTH

108. She has not even begun ------- for the exam even though it is tomorrow.

   A.   preparing
   B.   to prepare
   C.   BOTH

109. The applicant tried ------- for an extension of the deadline, but his request was turned down.

   A.   asking
   B.   to ask
   C.   BOTH

110. The class has been warned not -------.

   A.   cheating
   B.   to cheat
   C.   BOTH

111. The senior anticipates ------- next month.

    A. graduating
    B. to graduate
    C. BOTH

112. Knowing that the deadline is tomorrow has forced me ------- on the project.

    A. concentrating
    B. to concentrate
    C. BOTH

113. Cats cannot stand ------- the sound of a vacuum cleaner.

    A. hearing
    B. to hear
    C. BOTH

114. I do not want to spend any more time ------- these equations.

    A. solving
    B. to solve
    C. BOTH

> **DIRECTIONS**: For items #115–129, circle the letter of the underlined part of the sentence containing the error and write the correct word or phrase. Answers are on page 565.

115. Economists <u>have established</u> that there is a
                  A

<u>relation</u>—albeit an indirect one—between the
  B

<u>amount</u> of oil imported into this country and the
  C

<u>number</u> of traffic accidents.
  D

Correct Word/Phrase: _____

116. Ironically, today Elizabeth I and <u>her</u> rival for the
                           F

English throne, Mary Stuart, <u>whom</u> Elizabeth
                        G

<u>had</u> executed, <u>lay</u> side by side in Westminster
 H   J

Abbey.

Correct Word/Phrase: _____

117. Although the script is interesting and well

written, it is not clear <u>whether</u> it can be <u>adopted</u>
                  A   B

for television since the original story contains

scenes that <u>could not be broadcast</u> <u>over</u> the
             C   D

public airwaves.

Correct Word/Phrase: _____

118. If he <u>had known</u> how difficult law school would
        F

be, he <u>would of chosen</u> a different profession or
        G

perhaps even <u>have followed</u> the <u>tradition</u> of
           H   J

going into the family business.

Correct Word/Phrase: _____

119. When shopping malls and business complexes

<u>get built</u>, quite often the needs of the
 A

handicapped <u>are</u> not considered; as a result, it
        B

later becomes necessary to make <u>costly</u>
               C

modifications to structures to make them

<u>accessible</u> to persons of impaired mobility.
 D

Correct Word/Phrase: _____

120. Researchers <u>have found</u> that children
                     F

<u>experience</u> twice as much deep sleep <u>than</u>
  G   H

adults, <u>a fact which may</u> teach us something
         J

about the connection between age and

learning ability.

Correct Word/Phrase: _____

121. <u>Despite</u> the ample evidence that smoking <u>is</u>
   A   B

<u>hazardous</u> to one's health, <u>many</u> people seem to
   B   C

find the warnings neither frightening <u>or</u>
                                           D

convincing.

Correct Word/Phrase: _____

122. No matter how <u>many</u> encores the audience
                       F

demands, Helen Walker <u>is always willing</u> to sing
                                 G

<u>yet</u> another song <u>which pleases</u> the audience.
 H   J

Correct Word/Phrase: _____

123. In light of <u>recent</u> translations of stone carvings
            A

<u>depicting</u> scenes of carnage, scholars are now
  B

questioning <u>as to whether</u> the Incas were <u>really</u>
            C   D

a peace-loving civilization.

Correct Word/Phrase: _____

124. In galleries containing works of both Gauguin

and Cézanne, you will find an equal <u>number</u> of
                                       F

admirers <u>in front of</u> the works of <u>each</u>, but most
            G   H

art critics agree that Gauguin is not of the same

artistic stature <u>with</u> Cézanne.
              J

Correct Word/Phrase: _____

125. The board of education <u>will never be</u> <u>fully</u>
                           A   B

<u>responsive</u> to the needs of Hispanic children in
  C

the school system so long <u>that</u> the mayor refuses
                         D

to appoint a Hispanic educator to the board.

Correct Word/Phrase: _____

126. The judge <u>sentenced</u> the president of the
              F

corporation to ten years in prison for <u>embezzling</u>
                                             G

corporate funds but <u>gave</u> his partner in crime
                       H

<u>less of a sentence</u>.
 J

Correct Word/Phrase: _____

127. Scientists <u>have recently discovered</u> that mussels
                      A

<u>secrete</u> a powerful adhesive that allows them
  B

<u>attaching</u> themselves to rocks, concrete pilings,
  C

and <u>other</u> stone or masonry structures.
     D

Correct Word/Phrase: _____

128. Wall paintings found recently in the caves of

Brazil are <u>convincing</u> evidence that cave art
               F

<u>developed</u> in the Americas at an earlier time <u>as</u> <u>it</u>
   G   H J

did on other continents.

Correct Word/Phrase: _____

129. The <u>drop</u> in oil prices and the slump in the
        A

computer industry <u>account for</u> the recent <u>raise</u>
                   B   C

in unemployment in Texas and the <u>associated</u>
                                                D

decline in the value of real estate in the region.

Correct Word/Phrase: _____

> **DIRECTIONS:** In items #130–143, correct or omit the underlined preposition as necessary. If the preposition is correct as written, select NO CHANGE. Answers are on page 565.

130. Where are you going <u>to</u>?

  F. NO CHANGE
  G. from
  H. in
  J. OMIT the underlined portion.

131. He has not yet taken advantage <u>off</u> the sale.

  A. NO CHANGE
  B. of
  C. from
  D. OMIT the underlined portion.

132. The teacher broke the news <u>to</u> the student.

  F. NO CHANGE
  G. too
  H. two
  J. OMIT the underlined portion.

133. Due to decreased sales, the workers were laid <u>off</u> by the company.

  A. NO CHANGE
  B. of
  C. down
  D. OMIT the underlined portion.

134. The manager promised to look <u>in to</u> the customer's complaint.

  F. NO CHANGE
  G. into
  H. unto
  J. OMIT the underlined portion.

135. The lawyer voiced his objection <u>on</u> the recount of the votes.

  A. NO CHANGE
  B. to
  C. about
  D. OMIT the underlined portion.

136. The office will open sometime <u>in</u> a half hour.

  F. NO CHANGE
  G. within
  H. inside
  J. OMIT the underlined portion.

137. There are many students waiting <u>on</u> the instructor during her office hours.

  A. NO CHANGE
  B. for
  C. to
  D. OMIT the underlined portion.

138. Please save energy by turning <u>of</u> the lights before you leave the house.

  F. NO CHANGE
  G. off
  H. in
  J. OMIT the underlined portion.

139. The dancers swung <u>in</u> motion when the music started.

    A. NO CHANGE
    B. in to
    C. into
    D. OMIT the underlined portion.

140. I work at the bank <u>in</u> the corner of Main and Packard.

    F. NO CHANGE
    G. on
    H. around
    J. OMIT the underlined portion.

141. He took it <u>up on</u> himself to schedule the meeting.

    A. NO CHANGE
    B. on
    C. upon
    D. OMIT the underlined portion.

142. Ralph had difficulty getting to sleep <u>till</u> very late.

    F. NO CHANGE
    G. up to
    H. until
    J. OMIT the underlined portion.

143. This class is different <u>than</u> the other.

    A. NO CHANGE
    B. of
    C. from
    D. OMIT the underlined portion.

PUNCTUATION

It is important to be familiar with the principal rules governing **punctuation**. This section is not intended to give a definitive set of punctuation rules; instead, it provides a basic overview of correct usage.

Commas

USE A COMMA BEFORE COORDINATING CONJUNCTIONS

Coordinating conjunctions ("and," "but," "nor," "or," "for," "yet," "so") join two independent clauses. Use a comma before coordinating conjunctions unless the two clauses are very short.

Examples:

The boy wanted to borrow a book from the library, <u>but</u> the librarian would not allow him to take it until he had paid his fines. ✓

Joe has been diligent about completing his work, <u>but</u> he has had many problems concerning his punctuality. ✓

I sincerely hope that these exercises prove to be of assistance to you, <u>and</u> I believe that they will help you to make a better showing on your examinations. ✓

Generally, a comma is not used before a subordinate clause that ends a sentence. However, in some circumstances a comma can be used to emphasize the point of the subordinate clause.

Examples:

I cannot possibly find the time to study for the test, unless I rearrange my piano lessons and only work on the weekends. ✓

My mother always scolded my brother and me for being loud and obnoxious, even though the silence worried her more. ✓

If there is no subject following the conjunction, a comma cannot be used since this would create a sentence fragment. If there is a subject following the conjunction, the comma can be omitted if the two clauses are very short.

Examples:

She went to the cafe <u>and</u> bought a cup of coffee. ✓

Roy washed the dishes <u>and</u> Helen dried them. ✓

I saw him <u>and</u> I spoke to him. ✓

A restrictive phrase or clause is vital to the meaning of a sentence. DO NOT set off restrictive phrases or clauses with commas.

Example:

A sailboat, without sails, is useless. ✘
A sailboat without sails is useless. ✓

USE COMMAS FOR CLARITY

1. Use a comma if the sentence might be subject to different interpretations without it.

2. Use a comma if a pause would make the sentence clearer and easier to read.

The following examples show how commas can change the meaning of a sentence:

Examples:

The banks that closed yesterday are in serious financial trouble. (Some banks closed yesterday, and those banks are in trouble.)
The banks, which closed yesterday, are in serious financial trouble. (All banks closed yesterday, and all banks are in trouble.)

My cat Leo fell down the laundry chute. (The implication is that I have more than one cat.)
My cat, Leo, fell down the laundry chute. (Here, "Leo" is an appositive. Presumably, he is the only cat.)

Inside the people were dancing. ✘
Inside, the people were dancing. ✓

After all crime must be punished. ✘
After all, crime must be punished. ✓

If you read the last two examples aloud, you will hear how a natural pause suggests where a comma should be inserted. This practice of listening for a pause is not infallible. However, it is the best practice when all other rules governing use of the comma seem to fail.

USE COMMAS TO SEPARATE COORDINATE ADJECTIVES, WORDS IN A SERIES, AND NOUNS IN DIRECT ADDRESS

1. Use a comma between coordinate adjectives. Coordinate adjectives are adjectives of equal importance that precede a noun. If the word "and" can be added between two adjectives without changing the sense of the sentence, you are dealing with coordinate adjectives and should separate them with commas.

2. Use commas to separate the words in a series when three or more elements are present. In such a series, use a comma before "and" or "or." If the series ends in "etc.," use a comma before "etc." DO NOT use a comma after "etc." in a series, even if the sentence continues.

3. Use commas to set off nouns in direct address. The name of the person addressed should be separated from the rest of the sentence by commas.

Examples:

The jolly, fat, ruddy man stood at the top of the stairs. ✓
He is a wise, charming man. ✓
She is a slow, careful reader. ✓

Coats, umbrellas, and boots should be placed in the closet at the end of the hall. ✓
Pencils, scissors, paper clips, etc. belong in your top desk drawer. ✓

Bob, please close the door. ✓
I think, José, that you are the one who was chosen. ✓

USE A COMMA TO SEPARATE QUOTATIONS AND INTRODUCTORY PHRASES	

1. Use a comma to separate a direct quotation from the speaker.

2. Use a comma after an introductory phrase of two or more words.

3. Use a comma after an introductory phrase whenever the comma would aid clarity.

4. Use a comma after introductory gerunds, participles, and infinitives regardless of their length.

However, if a subordinate clause follows the main clause, it is not necessary to set it off with a comma.

Examples:

She said, "I must leave work on time today." ✓
"Tomorrow I begin my summer job," he told us. ✓

As a child, she was a tomboy. ✓
She was a tomboy as a child. ✓

To Dan, Phil was a friend as well as a brother. ✓
Phil was a friend as well as a brother to Dan. ✓

In 1998, hundreds of people lost their lives in an earthquake. ✓
Hundreds of people lost their lives in an earthquake in 1998. ✓

When you come home, please ring the bell before opening the door. ✓
Please ring the bell before opening the door when you come home. ✓

Because the prisoner had a history of attempted jailbreaks, he was put under heavy guard. ✓
The prisoner was put under heavy guard because he had a history of attempted jailbreaks. ✓

Finally, commas must be used to set off certain phrases and elements that interrupt the natural flow of a sentence.

USE PAIRS OF COMMAS TO SET OFF APPOSITIVE, PARENTHETICAL, AND NONRESTRICTIVE ELEMENTS

1. An appositive phrase follows a noun or pronoun and has the same meaning as that noun or pronoun. For example, "Mrs. Walker, a teacher, walked up the steps."

2. Parenthetical expressions are words that interrupt the flow of the sentence without changing the meaning of the sentence. Examples include "however," "though," "for instance," "by the way," "to tell the truth," "believe me," "it appears to me," "I am sure," and "as a matter of fact."

3. A nonrestrictive element introduces material that is not essential to the sentence and, if removed, will not change the meaning of the original sentence. For example, "The blanket, which was red, lay on the grass."

Examples:

Mr. Dias, <u>our lawyer</u>, gave us some great advice. ✓
Bob, <u>an industrious and hard-working student</u>, will run for class treasurer. ✓

This book, <u>I believe</u>, is the best of its kind. ✓
Julie and her three dogs, <u>I am sure</u>, will not easily find an apartment to rent. ✓

Sam, <u>who is a very well behaved dog</u>, never strays from the front yard. ✓
Millie, <u>who is a fine student</u>, has a perfect attendance record. ✓

Read a sentence aloud to determine if commas should be used to set off a parenthetical expression. If you pause before and after the parenthetical expression, use commas to set it off. In general, if material can be omitted without changing the meaning of the main clause, the material is nonrestrictive and should be set off by commas.

USE COMMAS TO SEPARATE DATES, ADDRESSES, AND SPECIFIC LOCATIONS

Use commas to separate the different parts of a date and address. Be sure to include a comma after the last item, too.

Examples:

The train will arrive on Friday, February 13, 2003, if it is on schedule. ✓

My new address is: 2040 Winnebago Ave., Apt. #2, Madison, WI. ✓

My daughter traveled from Cambridge, Massachusetts, to Albany, New York, in three hours. ✓

The above rules summarize the most important uses of commas. If you follow these rules, you will not make a serious mistake involving commas.

WHEN SHOULD COMMAS NOT BE USED?

1. DO NOT use a comma to separate a subject from its verb.

2. DO NOT use commas to set off a restrictive or necessary clause or phrase. For example, do not write "The dog, that was barking, bothered me."

3. DO NOT use a comma in place of a conjunction.

Semicolons

USE A SEMICOLON TO SEPARATE A SERIES OF NUMBERS OR A SERIES OF PHRASES THAT CONTAIN COMMAS

1. Use a semicolon to avoid confusion with numbers.

2. Use a semicolon to separate a series of phrases or clauses, each of which contains commas.

Examples:

Add the following prices: $.25; $7.50; and $12.89. ✓

The old gentleman's heirs were Margaret Whitlock, his half-sister; James Bagley, the butler; William Frame, companion to his late cousin, Robert Bone; and his favorite charity, the Salvation Army. ✓

USE A SEMICOLON TO SEPARATE TWO INDEPENDENT CLAUSES

A semicolon may be used to separate two independent clauses when they have a close relationship and are NOT connected with a coordinating conjunction.

Example:

The setting sun caused the fields to take on a special glow; all was bathed in a pale light. ✓

A *semicolon* is often used between two or more independent clauses that are connected by conjunctive adverbs. Examples of conjunctive adverbs include "consequently," "therefore," "also," "furthermore," "for example," "however," "nevertheless," "still," "yet," "moreover," and "otherwise." (**NOTE:** A comma must follow the adverb.)

USE SEMICOLONS ONLY WITH INDEPENDENT CLAUSES

Use a semicolon only if each clause can function as an independent sentence.

Examples:

He waited at the station for well over an hour. However, no one appeared. ✓
He waited at the station for well over an hour; however, no one appeared. ✓

Anne is working at the front desk on Monday. Ernie will take over on Tuesday. ✓
Anne is working at the front desk on Monday; Ernie will take over on Tuesday. ✓

She waited for her check to arrive in the mail for two weeks. However, the check never appeared. ✓
She waited for her check to arrive in the mail for two weeks; however, the check never appeared. ✓

DO NOT use a semicolon between an independent clause and a phrase or subordinate clause.

Example:

She worked extra hours every night; yet, was not able to finish the project on time. ✗
She worked extra hours every night yet was not able to finish the project on time. ✓

To summarize, there are three different ways to separate two independent clauses: (1) use a comma followed by a conjunction; (2) use a semicolon; or (3) use a period.

Example:

Autumn had come, and the trees were almost bare. ✓
Autumn had come; the trees were almost bare. ✓
Autumn had come. The trees were almost bare. ✓

If you are uncertain about using a semicolon to connect independent clauses, write two sentences instead.

Colons

The *colon* is always used in the following situations:

RULES FOR SITUATIONS REQUIRING A COLON
1. A colon should be placed after the salutation in a business letter.
2. A colon should be used to separate hours from minutes.
3. A colon should be used to precede a list of three or more items or a long quotation.
4. A colon should be used to introduce a question.

Examples:

Dear Board Member: ✓

The eclipse occurred at 10:36 a.m. ✓

There are three branches of government: executive, judicial, and legislative. ✓

My question is this: Are you willing to punch a time clock? ✓

DO NOT use a colon directly after a verb.

Examples:

We played: volleyball, badminton, football, and tag. ✗
We played volleyball, badminton, football, and tag. ✓

We purchased: apples, pears, bananas, and grapes. ✗
We purchased apples, pears, bananas, and grapes. ✓

DO NOT USE COLONS TO CALL ATTENTION TO ELABORATION OR EXPLANATIONS IF ALREADY SIGNALED	
A colon may be used to call attention to elaboration or explanation. However, DO NOT use colons after expressions such as "like," "for example," "such as," and "that is." In fact, colons are intended to replace these terms.	

Be careful not to use a colon to introduce or call attention to material that is already signaled by some other element of the sentence.

Example:

We did many different things on our vacation, such as: hiking, camping, biking, canoeing, and kayaking. ✗
We did many different things on our vacation, such as hiking, camping, biking, canoeing, and kayaking. ✓
We did many different things on our vacation: hiking, camping, biking, canoeing, and kayaking. ✓

Periods

RULES FOR SITUATIONS REQUIRING A PERIOD	
1. Use a period at the end of a sentence that makes a statement, gives a command, or makes a polite request in the form of a question that does not require an answer. 2. Use a period after an abbreviation and after the initial in a person's name.	

Examples:

He is my best friend. ✓

There are thirty days in September. ✓

Would you please hold the script so that I may see if I have memorized my lines. ✓

Gen. Robert E. Lee led the Confederate forces. ✓

NOTE: DO NOT use a period in postal service name abbreviations such as AZ (Arizona) or MI (Michigan).

Exclamation and Question Marks

RULES FOR SITUATIONS REQUIRING AN EXCLAMATION MARK	
Use exclamation marks after commands or expressions that show strong emotion. Only use exclamation marks to express strong emotion or to imply urgency.	

Examples:

Wonderful! You won the lottery! ✓

Oh no! I won't go! ✓

> ## RULES FOR SITUATIONS REQUIRING A QUESTION MARK
>
> Use a question mark after a request for information. A question mark is used after a direct question. A period is used after an indirect question.

NOTE: A question must end with a *question mark* even if the question does not encompass the entire sentence.

Examples:

At what time does the last bus leave? ✓

"Daddy, are we there yet?" the child asked. ✓

Did you take the examination on Friday? ✓

The instructor wanted to know if you took the examination on Friday. ✓

Dashes

The material following the *dash* usually directs the reader's attention to the content that precedes it. Unless this material ends a sentence, dashes, like parentheses, must be used in pairs.

> ## RULES FOR SITUATIONS REQUIRING A DASH
>
> 1. Use a pair of dashes to set off an explanatory group of words. If the group of words appears at the end of a sentence, it can be preceded by a single dash.
>
> 2. Use a dash before a word or group of words that indicates a summation or reversal of what preceded it.
>
> 3. Use a dash to mark a sudden break in thought that leaves a sentence unfinished.

Examples:

The tools of his trade—probe, mirror, and cotton swabs—were neatly arranged on the dentist's tray. ✓

Patience, sensitivity, understanding, and empathy—these are the marks of a friend. ✓

He was not pleased with—in fact, he was completely hostile toward—the takeover. ✓

Dashes can be used like commas to set off parenthetical remarks. The difference is a matter of emphasis. Dashes mark a more dramatic shift or interruption of thought. DO NOT mix dashes and commas.

Hyphens

RULES FOR SITUATIONS REQUIRING A HYPHEN
1. Use a hyphen when creating a compound modifier that will precede a noun. A compound modifier is an adjective or adverb phrase that consists of two or more words (e.g., "a <u>walk-in</u> closet").
2. Use a hyphen when creating adjective or adverb phrases that involve numbers (e.g., "a <u>three-course</u> meal").
3. DO NOT use a hyphen if the compound modifier includes an adverb ending in "-ly" (e.g., "a <u>highly praised</u> singer").

The following examples illustrate when it is correct to use a hyphen and when it is correct to NOT use a hyphen:

Examples:

There was a sit-in demonstration at the office. ✓

We will sit in the auditorium. ✓

I purchased a four-cylinder car. ✓

I purchased a car with four cylinders. ✓

His perfectly formed vase earned him praise from the teacher. ✓

His well-formed vase earned him praise from the teacher.

Quotation Marks

WHEN TO USE QUOTATION MARKS
1. Use quotation marks to enclose the actual words of a speaker or writer.
2. Use quotation marks to emphasize words used in a special or unusual sense.
3. Use quotation marks to set off titles of short themes or parts of a larger work.

Examples:

Jane said, "There will be many people at the party." ✓

He kept using the phrase "you know" throughout his conversation. ✓

"Within You, Without You" is my favorite song on the *Sgt. Pepper's Lonely Hearts Club Band* album by The Beatles. ✓

WHEN NOT TO USE QUOTATION MARKS

1. DO NOT use quotation marks for indirect quotations.

2. DO NOT use quotation marks to justify a poor choice of words.

Examples:

He said that "he would be happy to attend the meeting." ✗
He said that he would be happy to attend the meeting. ✓

I gave her research summary article a low score because I didn't think she "got it right." ✗
I gave her research summary article a low score because I didn't think she understood the methods or results. ✓

PUNCTUATION RULES FOR SITUATIONS WITH QUOTATIONS

1. Always place periods and commas inside quotation marks.

2. Place a question mark inside quotation marks if it is part of a quotation. For example, "Do you like ice cream?" Place a question mark outside quotation marks if the entire sentence is a question that involves the quotation. For example:

   Do you think he was serious when he said "I don't like you"?

3. Place an exclamation mark inside quotation marks if it is part of a quotation. For example, "I'm rich!" Place an exclamation mark outside quotation marks if the entire sentence is an exclamation that involves the quotation. For example:

   I can't believe he said "I don't care"!

4. Always place colons and semicolons outside quotation marks.

Examples:

The principal said, "Cars parked in the fire lane will be ticketed." ✓

The first chapter of *The Andromeda Strain* is entitled "The Country of Lost Borders." ✓

My favorite poem is "My Last Duchess," a dramatic monologue written by Robert Browning. ✓

Three stories in Kurt Vonnegut's *Welcome to the Monkey House* are "Harrison Bergeron," "Next Door," and "EPICAC." ✓

Mother asked earlier tonight, "Did you take out the garbage?" ✓

Do you want to go to the movies and see "Jurassic Park"? ✓

The sentry shouted, "Drop your gun!" ✓

Save us from our "friends"! ✓

My favorite poem is "My Last Duchess"; this poem is a dramatic monologue written by Robert Browning. ✓

He was quoted as supporting the investigation in *The Washington Post*: "I don't know of any proof of misappropriation of funds; however, I support a full investigation into any possible wrongdoing by government officials." ✓

Apostrophes

The apostrophe is used for possession and contraction.

USE APOSTROPHES TO INDICATE POSSESSION

Use apostrophes to create the possessive case of nouns. However, DO NOT use apostrophes with possessive pronouns (e.g., "yours," "hers," "ours," "its," "theirs," and "whose").

Examples:

lady's = belonging to the lady ✓

ladies' = belonging to the ladies ✓

To determine if an apostrophe has been used properly, read the apostrophe as "of the."

Example:

childrens' = of the childrens ✗
children's = of the children ✓

This rule applies at all times, even with compound nouns separated by hyphens and with entities made up of two or more names.

Examples:

Brown and Sons' delivery truck = the delivery truck of Brown and Sons ✓

Lansdale, Jackson, and Smith's law firm = the law firm belonging to Lansdale, Jackson, and Smith ✓

If a singular or plural noun doesn't end in "s," simply add "'s" to create the possessive form (e.g., "Smith's farm"). If a singular or plural noun does end in "s," either add "'s" or simply add an apostrophe to create the possessive form (e.g., "James's farm" or "James' farm").

USE APOSTROPHES FOR CONTRACTIONS

Use an apostrophe when creating a contraction; insert the apostrophe in place of the omitted letter(s).

Examples:

haven't = have not ✓

o'clock = of the clock ✓

class of '85 = class of 1985 ✓

Be careful with "its" and "it's." "It's" is the contraction of "it is." "Its" is the third-person possessive pronoun. Also, DO NOT confuse "they're" ("they are"), "their" (possessive), and "there" (preposition).

Examples:

The cat knows when <u>it's</u> time for <u>its</u> bath. ✓

They're happy to be done with <u>their</u> work. ✓

Punctuation
Exercise 6

DIRECTIONS: Punctuate sentences #1–55 with commas, semicolons, periods, exclamation marks, question marks, dashes, hyphens, quotation marks, and apostrophes as necessary. Answers are on page 566.

1. He was not aware that you had lost your passport

2. Did you report the loss to the proper authorities

3. I suppose you had to fill out many forms

4. What a nuisance

5. I hate doing so much paperwork

6. Did you ever discover where the wallet was

7. I imagine you wondered how it was misplaced

8. Good for you

9. At least you now have your passport

10. What will you do if it happens again

11. I dont know if they are coming though I sent them an invitation weeks ago

12. Neurology is the science that deals with the anatomy physiology and pathology of the nervous system

13. Nursery lore like everything human has been subject to many changes over long periods of time

14. Bob read Joyces *Ulysses* to the class everyone seemed to enjoy the reading

15. In order to provide more living space we converted an attached garage into a den

16. Because he is such an industrious student he has many friends

17. I dont recall who wrote *A Midsummer Nights Dream*

18. In the writing class students learned about coordinating conjunctions and but so or yet for and nor

19. Those who do not complain are never pitied is a familiar quotation by Jane Austen

20. Howard and his ex wife are on amicable terms

21. Her last words were Call me on Sunday and she jumped on the train

22. He is an out of work carpenter

23. This is what is called a pregnant chad

24. Come early on Monday the teacher said to take the exit exam

25. The dog mans best friend is a companion to many

26. The winner of the horse race is to the best of my knowledge Silver

27. Every time I see him the dentist asks me how often I floss

28. The off duty officer witnessed the crime

29. *Anna Karenina* is my favorite movie

30. Red white and blue are the colors of the American flag

31. Stop using stuff in your essays its too informal

32. She was a self made millionaire

33. The Smiths who are the best neighbors anyone could ask for have moved out

34. My eighteen year old daughter will graduate this spring

35. Dracula lived in Transylvania

36. The students were told to put away their books

37. Begun while Dickens was still at work on *The Pickwick Papers Oliver Twist* was published in 1837 and is now one of the authors most widely read works

38. Given the great difficulties of making soundings in very deep water it is not surprising that few such soundings were made until the middle of this century

39. Did you finishing writing your thesis prospectus on time

40. The root of modern Dutch was once supposed to be Old Frisian but the general view now is that the characteristic forms of Dutch are at least as old as those of Old Frisian

41. Moose once scarce because of indiscriminate hunting are protected by law and the number of moose is once again increasing

42. He ordered a set of books several records and a film almost a month ago

43. Perhaps the most interesting section of New Orleans is the French Quarter which extends from North Rampart Street to the Mississippi River

44. Writing for a skeptical and rationalizing age Shaftesbury was primarily concerned with showing that goodness and beauty are not determined by revelation authority opinion or fashion

45. We tried our best to purchase the books but we were completely unsuccessful even though we went to every bookstore in town

46. A great deal of information regarding the nutritional requirements of farm animals has been accumulated over countless generations by trial and error however most recent advances have come as the result of systematic studies at schools of animal husbandry

47. *Omoo* Melvilles sequel to *Typee* appeared in 1847 and went through five printings in that year alone

48. Go to Florence for the best gelato in all of Italy said the old man to the young tourist

49. Although the first school for African Americans was a public school established in Virginia in 1620 most educational opportunities for African Americans before the Civil War were provided by private agencies

50. As the climate of Europe changed the population became too dense for the supply of food obtained by hunting and other means of securing food such as the domestication of animals were necessary

51. In Faulkners poetic realism the grotesque is somber violent and often inexplicable in Caldwells writing it is lightened by a ballad like humorous sophisticated detachment

52. The valley of the Loire a northern tributary of the Loire at Angers abounds in rock villages they occur in many other places in France Spain and northern Italy

53. The telephone rang several times as a result his sleep was interrupted

54. He has forty three thousand dollars to spend however once that is gone he will be penniless

55. Before an examination do the following review your work get a good nights sleep eat a balanced breakfast and arrive on time to take the test

Diagramming Sentences
Skills Review

Course Concept Outline

I.   Subjects and Verbs (p. 85)

   A. Subjects (p. 85)

   B. Verbs (p. 86)

   C. Diagramming Subjects and Verbs (p. 88)

   Exercise 1—**Subjects and Verbs** (Items #1–5, p. 90)

II. Modal Auxiliary Verbs (p. 91)

   A. Indicative (p. 91)

   B. Subjunctive (p. 92)

   C. Diagramming Modal Auxiliary Verbs (p. 93)

   Exercise 2—**Modal Auxiliary Verbs** (Items #1–5, p. 95)

III. Conjunctions (p. 97)

   A. Coordinating Conjunctions (p. 97)

   B. Subordinating Conjunctions (p. 97)

   C. Correlative Conjunctions (p. 97)

   D. Diagramming Conjunctions (p. 98)

   Exercise 3—**Conjunctions** (Items #1–5, p. 100)

IV. Articles, Attributive Adjectives, and Direct Objects (p. 101)

A. Articles (p. 101)

B. Adjectives (p. 101)

C. Attributive Adjectives (p. 101)

D. Direct Objects (p. 102)

E. Diagramming Articles, Attributive Adjectives, and Direct Objects (p. 103)

Exercise 4—**Articles, Attributive Adjectives, and Direct Objects** (Items #1–5, p. 106)

V. Adverbs (p. 107)

A. Adverbs that End in "-ly" (p. 107)

B. Adverbs that Do Not End in "-ly" (p. 107)

C. Adjectives that Also Function as Adverbs (p. 108)

D. Diagramming Adverbs (p. 108)

Exercise 5—**Adverbs** (Items #1–5, p. 111)

VI. Subjective Complements: Predicate Nominatives and Predicate Adjectives (p. 113)

A. Predicate Nominatives (p. 113)

B. Predicate Adjectives (p. 114)

C. Diagramming Subjective Complements (p. 114)

Exercise 6—**Subjective Complements: Predicate Nominatives and Predicate Adjectives** (Items #1–5, p. 117)

VII. Appositives (p. 119)

A. Restrictive and Nonrestrictive Appositives (p. 119)

B. Intensifying Pronouns (p. 120)

C. Diagramming Appositives (p. 120)

D. *Exercise 7*—**Appositives** (Items #1–5, p. 122)

VIII. Prepositional Phrases (p. 123)

A. Prepositions (p. 123)

B. Adverbial Prepositional Phrases (p. 124)

C. Adjectival Prepositional Phrases (p. 124)

D. Diagramming Prepositional Phrases (p. 125)

Exercise 8—**Prepositional Phrases** (Items #1–5, p. 127)

IX. Indirect Objects and Objective Complements (p. 129)

A. Indirect Objects (p. 129)

B. Objective Complements (p. 129)

C. Diagramming Indirect Objects and Objective Complements (p. 131)

Exercise 9—**Indirect Objects and Objective Complements** (Items #1-5, p. 133)

X. Infinitives (p. 135)

A. Transitive Infinitives (p. 135)

B. Complementary Infinitives (p. 136)

C. Diagramming Infinitives (p. 138)

Exercise 10—**Infinitives** (Items #1-10, pp. 142-143)

XI. Gerunds (p. 145)

A. Modifiers and Tense (p. 145)

B. Diagramming Gerunds (p. 146)

Exercise 11—**Gerunds** (Items #1-5, p. 149)

XII. Participles (p. 151)

A. Nominative Absolutes (p. 152)

B. Dangling Participles (p. 152)

C. Diagramming Participles (p. 153)

Exercise 12—**Participles** (Items #1-5, p. 156)

XIII. Adverb Clauses (p. 157)

A. Subordinating Conjunctions (p. 157)

B. Relative Adverbs (p. 157)

C. Equal and Unequal Comparisons (p. 158)

D. Diagramming Adverb Clauses (p. 160)

E. Diagramming Equal and Unequal Comparisons (p. 162)

Exercise 13—**Adverb Clauses** (Items #1-10; pp. 164-165)

XIV. Adjective Clauses (p. 167)

A. Relative Clauses (p. 167)

B. Adjective Clauses Introduced by Relative Adverbs (p. 168)

C. Diagramming Adjective Clauses (p. 168)

Exercise 14—**Adjective Clauses** (Items #1-5, p. 171)

XV. Noun Clauses (p. 173)

    A. Noun Clauses Introduced by the Expletive "That" (p. 173)

    B. Noun Clauses Introduced by the Expletives "Whether" and "If" (p. 173)

    C. Noun Clauses Introduced by Interrogative Words (p. 174)

    D. Diagramming Noun Clauses (p. 174)

    Exercise 15—**Noun Clauses** (Items #1–5, p. 177)

XVI. Glossary of Grammatical Terms and Diagramming Symbols (p. 179)

SUBJECTS AND VERBS

Subjects

Subjects are difficult to define simply. Here is one incomplete definition: the subject of a sentence is the noun, pronoun, phrase, or clause about which the sentence says or asks something.

Examples:

1. Susan finished her report and handed it in.

   ➤ The sentence says something about Susan. It tells the reader what Susan did. "Susan" is the subject of the sentence.

2. Is patience a virtue?

   ➤ The sentence asks the reader something about patience. "Patience" is the subject of the sentence.

So far so good; nevertheless, this definition has its weaknesses. Let's examine a few more sentences.

Examples:

1. Carla's blatant impatience caused everyone in the restaurant to laugh.

   ➤ The sentence tells the reader something about Carla and something about her impatience. Is "Carla's" or "impatience" the subject? "Carla's" is a possessive, so it cannot be a subject.

2. It is raining.

   ➤ "It" is the subject. But does the sentence really tell something about "it"?

3. You know that mighty Casey struck out.

   ➤ Is the subject of the sentence "you" or "Casey"? "You know" is the main clause (which always contains the subject of the sentence, in this case "you"), and the rest of the sentence is a dependent clause (which never contains the subject of the sentence, but like all clauses has a subject, in this case "Casey").

As you can see, we need a better definition. So, here is a more helpful one: the subject of a sentence is the word with which the verb agrees. This definition is more helpful than you may at first realize. Consider the following:

Examples:

1. On the lake they see a sailboat.

   ➤ What is the subject of the sentence—"lake," "they," or "sailboat"? It can only be "they" because "see" does not agree with either of the other words.

2. Across from the library there will be state-of-the-art tennis courts.

➤ If a verb is in the future tense, you may want to change it mentally to the present tense before looking for agreement. In this case, the change would be from "will be" to "are." You can see that the verb agrees with "tennis courts," not with "library."

In standard prose, the subject of a sentence usually comes before the verb. There are two main exceptions:

SITUATIONS IN WHICH THE VERB COMES BEFORE THE SUBJECT
1. When "there" or "here" is used to announce the delayed appearance of the subject (e.g., "Next week there will be a birthday party at school.")
2. With questions (e.g., "Have you seen the toys in the attic?")

An ***expletive*** is a word that has a syntactic function but really doesn't contribute to the meaning of a sentence. In the sentence, "There are two books on the table," "there" doesn't add anything to the meaning of the sentence, as you can prove by dropping it: "Two books are on the table." "There" does, however, fill the usual place of the subject and announce to the reader or listener that the order of words in the sentence may be different from what is expected. So, "there" announces that the verb will precede the subject.

Verbs

Let's consider the tenses (present, past, future, present perfect, past perfect, and future perfect), voices (active and passive), and forms (simple, progressive, and emphatic) of two ***verbs***: "play" and "sell."

ACTIVE VOICE OF THE VERB "PLAY"
1. *Simple Present:* plays, play
2. *Simple Past:* played
3. *Simple Future:* will play, shall play
4. *Simple Present Perfect:* has played, have played
5. *Simple Past Perfect:* had played
6. *Simple Future Perfect:* will have played, shall have played
7. *Present Progressive:* am playing, is playing, are playing
8. *Past Progressive:* was playing, were playing
9. *Future Progressive:* will be playing, shall be playing
10. *Present Perfect Progressive:* has been playing, have been playing
11. *Past Perfect Progressive:* had been playing
12. *Future Perfect Progressive:* will have been playing, shall have been playing
13. *Present Emphatic:* does play, do play
14. *Past Emphatic:* did play

PASSIVE VOICE OF THE VERB "PLAY"

1. *Simple Present:* am played, is played, are played
2. *Simple Past:* was played, were played
3. *Simple Future:* will be played, shall be played
4. *Simple Present Perfect:* has been played, have been played
5. *Simple Past Perfect:* had been played
6. *Simple Future Perfect:* will have been played, shall have been played
7. *Present Progressive:* am being played, is being played, are being played
8. *Past Progressive:* was being played, were being played

ACTIVE VOICE OF THE VERB "SELL"

1. *Simple Present:* sells, sell
2. *Simple Past:* sold
3. *Simple Future:* will sell, shall sell
4. *Simple Present Perfect:* has sold, have sold
5. *Simple Past Perfect:* had sold
6. *Simple Future Perfect:* will have sold, shall have sold
7. *Present Progressive:* am selling, is selling, are selling
8. *Past Progressive:* was selling, were selling
9. *Future Progressive:* will be selling, shall be selling
10. *Present Perfect Progressive:* has been selling, have been selling
11. *Past Perfect Progressive:* had been selling
12. *Future Perfect Progressive:* will have been selling, shall have been selling
13. *Present Emphatic:* does sell, do sell
14. *Past Emphatic:* did sell

PASSIVE VOICE OF THE VERB "SELL"

1. *Simple Present:* am sold, is sold, are sold
2. *Simple Past:* was sold, were sold
3. *Simple Future:* will be sold, shall be sold
4. *Simple Present Perfect:* has been sold, have been sold
5. *Simple Past Perfect:* had been sold
6. *Simple Future Perfect:* will have been sold, shall have been sold
7. *Present Progressive:* am being sold, is being sold, are being sold
8. *Past Progressive:* was being sold, were being sold

The *imperative* mood includes the verb forms used to command someone to do something.

Examples:

1. Go!

2. Run!

3. Sit!

4. Speak!

In each case, the imperative has the same form as the present infinitive (e.g., "to go," "to run," "to sit," "to speak") but without the particle "to." This is even true of the infinitive "to be," whose imperative form is "be" (as in "Be good!" or "Be quiet!"). Imperatives do not have to be followed by an exclamation mark, but they often are.

Diagramming Subjects and Verbs

Every diagram of a sentence has at least two lines. First, there is a horizontal base line, which is used for subjects, main verbs, direct objects, predicate nominatives, predicate adjectives, and objective complements. Second, there is a vertical line that passes through the base line and divides the subject of the sentence from the predicate of the sentence (the predicate is the main verb and its objects or complements).

All finite verbs (verbs that can serve as main verbs) are diagrammed in the space provided for the verb. This space starts immediately to the right of the line that divides the subject from the predicate. This is true for all finite verbs regardless of tense (present, past, future, present perfect, past perfect, and future perfect), voice (active and passive), mood (indicative, imperative, and subjunctive), and form (simple, progressive, and emphatic). This does not apply, however, to so-called "verbals," which cannot serve as main verbs in a sentence (infinitives, gerunds, and participles).

NOTE: As you work through the Diagramming Sentences Skills Review, you may want to check the Glossary of Grammatical Terms and Diagramming Symbols at the end of the Diagramming Sentence Skills Review (pp. 179–190) for the meanings of words and expressions that you do not understand.

In diagramming, the subject is always placed on the far left of the horizontal base line. As mentioned above, the vertical line passing through the base line serves to separate the subject from the verb. The examples that follow are very simple sentences that include only a subject and verb; these diagrams will help you to understand the basics of diagramming sentences.

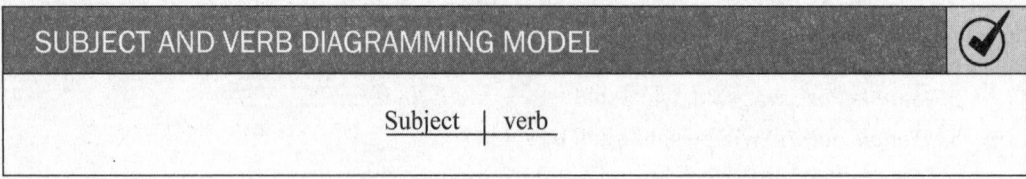

Examples:

1. Children play.

   Children | play

   The noun "children" is the subject of the sentence. The verb "play" is in the present tense.

2. They were selling.

| They | were selling |

The personal pronoun "they" is the subject of the sentence. The past progressive "were selling" is the verb. The nominative (subject) forms of the personal pronouns are "I," "you," "he," "she," "it," "we," "you," and "they."

3. It had been played.

| It | had been played |

The subject of the sentence is the personal pronoun "it." The verb "had been played" is in the past-perfect tense, passive voice.

4. Sandwiches are being sold.

| Sandwiches | are being sold. |

The subject of the sentence is the plural noun "sandwiches." The verb "are being sold" is a progressive form in the present tense, passive voice.

Subjects and Verbs
Exercise 1

DIRECTIONS: Create a diagram for each of the following sentences. Answers are on page569.

1. Ducks quack.

2. Mosquitoes are buzzing.

3. People have been talking.

4. They will be captured.

5. Money had been collected.

MODAL AUXILIARY VERBS

Authorities differ as to which verbs should be called *modal auxiliary verbs*. In this lesson, the list of modal auxiliary verbs will include "can," "could," "may," "might," "must," "should," and "would." It is impossible to discuss modal verbs without referring to the indicative and the subjunctive moods, so let's be sure we have a clear understanding of those terms.

Indicative

The *indicative* mood is used for pointing out, describing, or asking. Most verb forms are indicative. Here are some sentences whose verbs are in the indicative mood.

Examples:

1. It is snowing.

2. That has been my house for the last ten years.

3. When does the movie begin?

4. I had a headache.

5. Will you be my friend?

Three modal forms, "can," "may," and "must," are always indicative.

Examples:

1. Ronald <u>can</u> run fast.

   ➤ This sentence says simply that Ronald has the ability to run fast.

2. The children <u>may</u> go with us.

   ➤ This sentence says either that the children have permission to accompany us or that it is possible they will go with us.

3. Stella <u>must</u> stay home this evening.

   ➤ This sentence tells of a particular obligation incumbent upon Stella.

In the first of these examples, if we talk about Ronald's ability to run fast in the past, we would say, "When he was young, Ronald could run fast." However, if we want to talk about the characters in the other sentences in the past, we must use altogether different verbs. For the second sentence, we would say, "The children were permitted to go with us. And for the third sentence, we would say, "Stella had to stay home that evening."

Subjunctive

The modal auxiliary verb "could" is used not only in the past indicative but also in the present *subjunctive*.

Examples:

1. If Ronald had not injured his foot, he <u>could</u> run fast.

   ➤ In this sentence, "could" does not refer to an actual ability. Instead, it refers to an ability Ronald would have if he hadn't hurt himself. This sentence rules out Ronald's ability to run fast here and now.

2. If Ronald wanted to do so, he <u>could</u> run fast.

   ➤ This sentence has two possible meanings. The first meaning is that it's impossible for Ronald to run fast because he doesn't want to do so. The second meaning is that it's improbable Ronald can run fast because it's improbable he wants to do so. If you make a small change and use the indicative in this sentence, its meaning becomes less ambiguous: "Ronald can run fast if he wants to do so."

"Might" is the present subjunctive form of "may." Note the difference between the following sentences:

Examples:

1. If she is here, she <u>may</u> be able to help us.

   ➤ In this sentence, her ability to help is possible (because it is possible that she is here).

2. If she were here, she <u>might</u> be able to help us.

   ➤ In this sentence, her ability to help is purely speculative (because she is not here).

"Would" is used in unreal (contrary-to-fact) conditional sentences.

Example:

If I had time, I <u>would</u> help you.

Contrast the above example with a sentence containing a real condition.

Example:

If I have time, I <u>will</u> help you.

"Would" is also used to express habitual action in the past (e.g., "Back then, people would often sit on their front porch and talk with passing neighbors.").

"Should" is seldom used these days as a future-tense indicator.

Example:

Next year I <u>should</u> like to visit my cousin in New York.

Instead, it is more widely used to express obligation and expectation.

Examples:

1. I really <u>should</u> do my homework.

2. You <u>should</u> be able to find our house.

"Must" has no past tense and no subjunctive form. If we want to use the verb "must" in the past or as a subjunctive, we have to choose another verb.

Examples:

1. They had to leave early. (past)

2. If he had to work harder, he would. (subjunctive)

All seven modals can be used with basic present-perfect forms (present-perfect infinitives without "to").

Examples:

1. He <u>cannot</u> have finished so soon.

2. She <u>could</u> have pouted, but she didn't.

3. If she were there, she <u>may</u> have been able to help them.

4. If she had been there, she <u>might</u> have been able to help them.

5. If I had had time, I <u>would</u> have helped you.

    ➤ This is an unreal conditional sentence in past time.

6. I really <u>should</u> have done my homework.

7. They <u>must</u> have left.

    ➤ This sentence is not the same as "They had to leave."

Notice that in the third and fourth examples, the use of "may" and "might," respectively, helps to distinguish between real and unreal situations.

Finally, with regard to the subjunctive mood, many grammarians claim that it is almost dead in English. They say it is used only in an occasional expression such as "If I were you." For example, if you were asked the verb tense of "gave" and "lived," you would likely say that both are past tense verbs. You would be half right. These verbs are past indicative forms, but they are also present subjunctive forms: "If we gave him five dollars [right now], he would be able to eat"; "If you lived closer [right now], we could get together more often."

Diagramming Modal Auxiliary Verbs

A modal auxiliary verb and the verb it modulates are considered a single verb phrase. In a sentence diagram, this verb phrase is placed in the normal position of the verb (i.e., right after the vertical line that follows the subject):

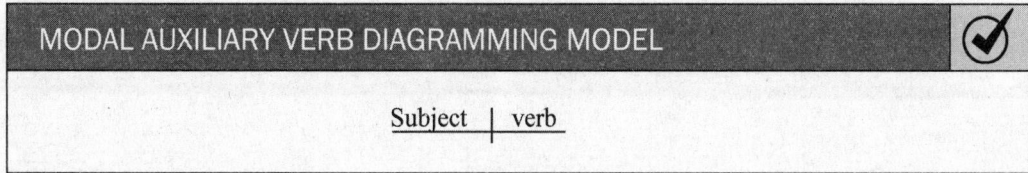

MODAL AUXILIARY VERB DIAGRAMMING MODEL

Subject | verb

Examples:

1. This must leak.

   This | must leak

   The demonstrative pronoun "this" is the subject of the sentence. The complete verb consists of the modal auxiliary verb "must" and the present infinitive of the intransitive verb "leak." Intransitive verbs have no passive voice.

2. They should have hurried.

   They | should have hurried

   The subject of the sentence is the personal pronoun "they." The complete verb consists of the modal auxiliary verb "should" and the basic present perfect form of "hurry."

3. Homes may have been destroyed.

   Homes | may have been destroyed

   The subject of the sentence is "homes." The verb phrase "may have been destroyed" consists of the modal auxiliary verb "may" and the basic present perfect passive form of "destroy."

Every sentence has a subject and a predicate. The predicate is everything in the sentence that is not the subject, modifiers of the subject, or independent elements. Up to this point, you have only been asked to diagram sentences that have unmodified subjects and predicates that consist only of a verb or verb phrase. As you proceed through this skills review, you will be asked to diagram increasingly complex sentences. Regardless of how complex the sentences become, though, remember that every diagram must include a horizontal base line and a vertical line passing through that base line.

Modal Auxiliary Verbs
Exercise 2

DIRECTIONS: Create a diagram for each of the following sentences. Answers are on page 569.

1. You may stay.

2. They should be scolded.

3. She must have been delayed.

4. That could have been done.

5. They might be coming.

CONJUNCTIONS

Coordinating Conjunctions

Coordinating conjunctions connect words, phrases, and clauses of equal importance. Almost always, they connect words, phrases, and clauses of the same kind (i.e., nouns with nouns, verbs with verbs, etc.). Coordinating conjunctions include "and," "but," "or," "nor," "for," "so," and "yet."

Examples:

1. Hansel and Gretel marked the trail through the forest. (***compound subject***)

2. The children laughed and played. (***compound verb***)

3. The stepmother commanded, "Hansel and Gretel, wait here until your father and I return." (***compound vocative***)

4. In which song is America called "the land of the free and the home of the brave"? (***compound predicate nominative***)

5. They have a mountain of money but a thimbleful of time. (***compound direct object***)

6. Would you call a tadpole a fish or a reptile? (***compound objective complement***)

7. The project manager was excited but too exhausted to think straight. (***compound predicate adjective***)

8. The students were urged to express their ideas clearly and concisely. (***compound adverb***)

9. Ours is a government by and for the people. (***compound preposition***)

10. She yearned to go to Colorado and ski all winter. (***compound infinitive phrase***)

11. She went shopping but he stayed home. (***compound sentence***)

Subordinating Conjunctions

Subordinating conjunctions are conjunctions that introduce dependent clauses. Subordinating conjunctions include "because," "since," "although," and "if."

Example:

If you take Brenda, and Josh rides with Amelie, I'll see to it that Johanna and Natalie find a way. (***compound adverb clause***)

Correlative Conjunctions

Correlative conjunctions are paired conjunctions that link balanced words, phrases, and clauses. Correlative conjunctions include "both . . . and," "either . . . or," "just as . . . so," "neither . . . nor," and "whether . . . or."

Examples:

1. She likes to ride the roller coaster with <u>either her parents or her grandparents</u>. (***compound object of a preposition***)

2. The meet director gave <u>both the winner and the runner-up</u> a large trophy. (***compound indirect object***)

3. He could live <u>neither with her nor without her</u>. (***compound prepositional phrase***)

Diagramming Conjunctions

When diagramming a compound subject, place the individual subjects on parallel horizontal lines and put the coordinating conjunction on a broken vertical line between the two horizontal lines. In the diagramming model below, the "c.c." stands for "coordinating conjunction":

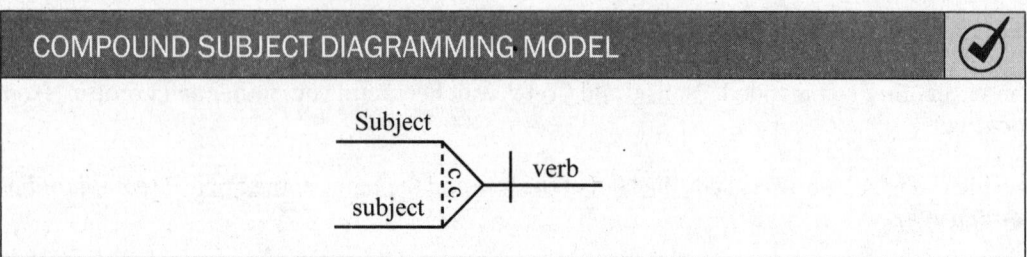

Example:

Jack and Jill are falling.

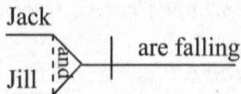

"Jack and Jill" is a compound subject. "And" is a coordinating conjunction.

Do the same with compound verbs.

To diagram a compound sentence, diagram the first main clause above the second, and put the coordinating conjunction on a broken-line step-down between the verbs of the two diagrams:

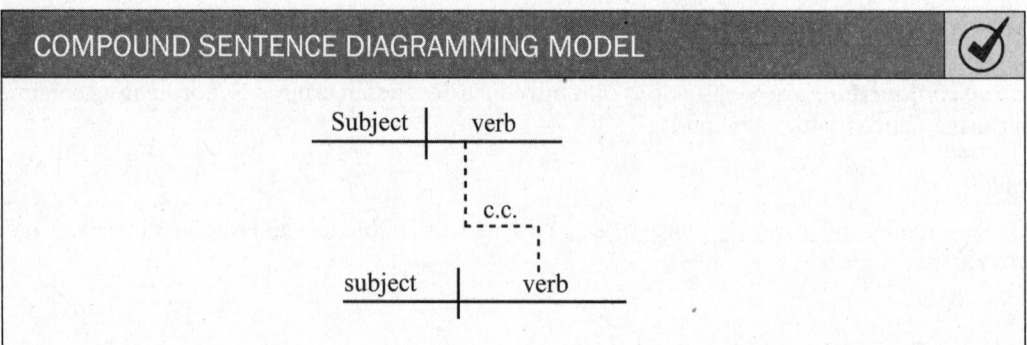

Example:

We are working but you are playing.

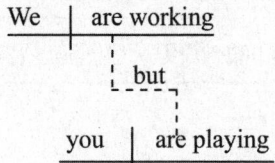

"We are working" is an independent clause (i.e., it can stand alone as a complete sentence), and the same can be said of "you are playing." These two clauses are joined in this compound sentence by the coordinating conjunction "but."

Conjunctions
Exercise 3

DIRECTIONS: Create a diagram for each of the following sentences. Answers are on page 570.

1. Buses come and go.

2. Deer were running and jumping.

3. Children run, jump, and play.

4. Doctors and nurses are scurrying.

5. Bombs fell and people died.

ARTICLES, ATTRIBUTIVE ADJECTIVES, AND DIRECT OBJECTS

Articles

Although not all languages have *articles*, English has three: "the" (definite article), "a" (indefinite article), and "an" (indefinite article).

Adjectives

Adjectives modify nouns; in other words, they describe or limit nouns in some way. If we call something "a house," we don't differentiate it from any other house. If we call a house "a beautiful house," we restrict the house to that subset of houses that are beautiful. If we call the house "a beautiful white house," we further restrict or modify it by the addition of the adjective "white"; in other words, we restrict the house to that subset of houses that are both beautiful and white.

Attributive Adjectives

Attributive adjectives usually appear right before nouns or pronouns, either following an article ("a <u>beautiful</u> house," "the <u>beautiful</u> house") or not preceded by an article ("<u>beautiful</u> houses"). Sometimes, a noun is modified by two or more attributive adjectives.

Examples:

1. We entered the <u>beautiful</u> <u>white</u> house.

2. A <u>tall</u>, <u>dark</u>, and <u>handsome</u> stranger approached us in the living room.

Attributive adjectives are distinguished from predicate adjectives, which come after linking verbs.

Example:

The house is <u>white</u>.

Occasionally, though, an attributive adjective follows its noun.

Examples:

1. There will be time <u>enough</u> to finish the gardening.

2. The boys were waiting for something <u>else</u> to happen.

Direct Objects

Direct objects receive the action of a verb directly; however, not all verbs take direct objects. Verbs that do are called transitive verbs; verbs that do not are called intransitive verbs. The following are examples of intransitive verbs: all forms of the verbs "be," "become," "seem," "come," aspire," and "squirm."

Here is a way to identify direct objects: as you read a sentence, ask "whom?" or "what?" immediately after a non-linking verb. The answer, if you get one, is a direct object.

Examples:

1. That is a tree.

   ➢ If you ask "what?" right after "is," you get the answer "tree"; however, "tree" is a predicate nominative since it follows the linking verb "is."

2. They saw a tree.

   ➢ If you ask "what?" right after "saw," the answer is "tree." "Saw" is not a linking verb, so "tree" is a direct object.

3. In college she studied economics.

   ➢ Is there a direct object in this sentence? To find out, ask "what?" right after "studied" (i.e., "In college she studied what?" ⇒ "In college she studied economics"). "Studied" is not a linking verb, so "economics" is a direct object.

4. In college she sometimes studied until two in the morning.

   ➢ Is there a direct object in this sentence? If you ask "She sometimes studied whom?" or "She sometimes studied what?" you see that the answer is not present in the sentence; therefore, the sentence has no direct object. Not every non-linking verb will have a direct object.

5. They like Amy but dislike her friend.

   ➢ Are there direct objects in this sentence? To find out, ask "whom?" right after the verb "like" (i.e., "They like whom?" ⇒ "They like Amy"). Similarly, ask "whom?" right after the verb "dislike" (i.e., "They dislike whom?" ⇒ "They dislike her friend"). Neither "like" nor "dislike" is a linking verb, so both "Amy" and "her friend" are direct objects (the noun that serves as the direct object is "friend"; "her friend" is referred to as the complete direct object).

6. He has been an accountant for nine years.

   ➢ If you ask "what?" right after the verb "has been," the answer is "accountant"; however, "accountant" is a predicate nominative since it follows the linking verb "has been," a form of "be."

7. They hiked out into the country and enjoyed the sights.

   ➢ There are two verbs in this sentence: "hiked" and "enjoyed." Does either have a direct object? If you ask "They hiked what?" or "They hiked whom?", you see that the answer is not present in the sentence. In contrast, if you ask "They enjoyed what?", the answer to the question is "sights"; so, "sights" is a direct object.

8. We planted flowers and vegetables in our garden.

➤ If you ask "what?" after the verb "planted," the answer is "flowers and vegetables." "Planted" is not a linking verb, so "flowers and vegetables" is a direct object.

9. She can read and write French, but she does not speak the language well.

➤ There are three verbs in this sentence: "read," "write," and "speak." Do they all have direct objects? If you ask, "She can read and write what?" you see that the answer is present in the sentence (i.e., "She can read and write French"). Similarly, if you ask, "She does not speak what?" you see that the answer is "language." None of the verbs are linking verbs, so "French" and "language" are direct objects.

Diagramming Articles, Attributive Adjectives, and Direct Objects

An article is diagrammed on a slanted line below the noun it modifies. The top of the slanted line touches the horizontal line underneath the noun:

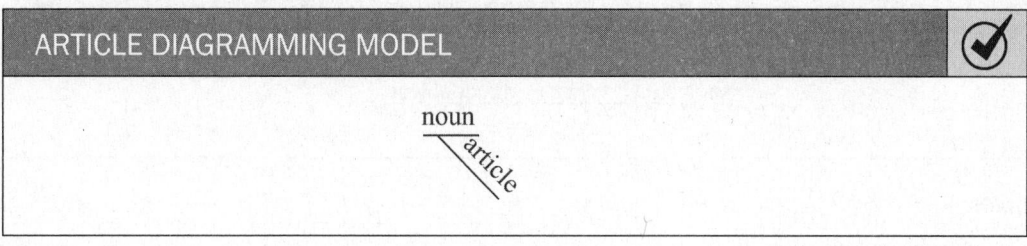

Example:

The flowers are blooming.

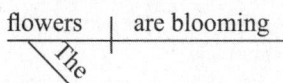

An attributive adjective is diagrammed on a slanted line below the noun it modifies. It is placed to the right of an article:

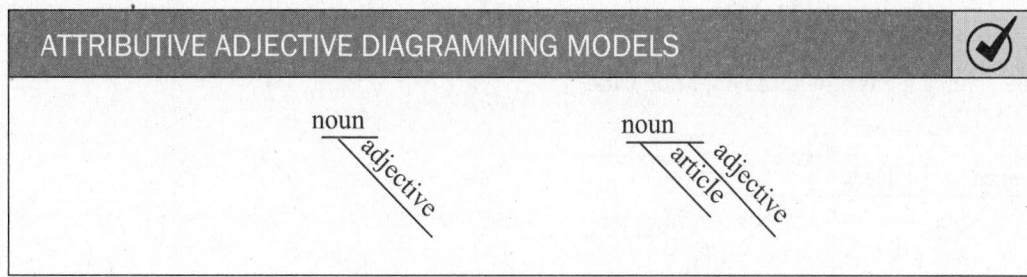

Examples:

1. Wonderful things are happening.

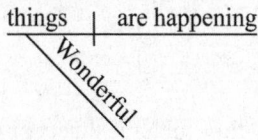

2. A full moon shone.

A direct object is diagrammed after its verb. A vertical line touching the base line from above separates the verb from the direct object:

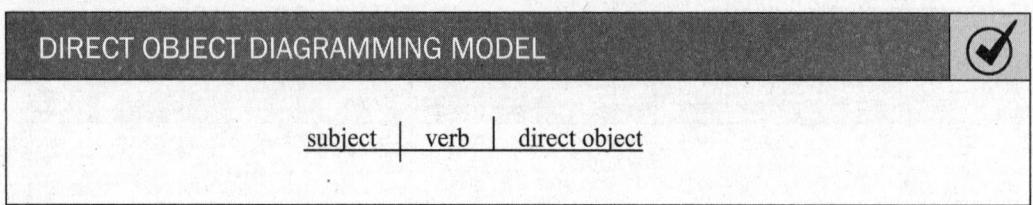

DIRECT OBJECT DIAGRAMMING MODEL

subject | verb | direct object

Examples:

1. Most people saw the comet.

2. They have a cat and a small dog.

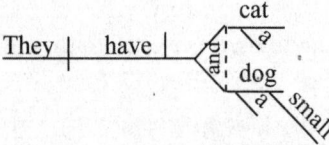

3. The agency feeds unwanted dogs and cats.

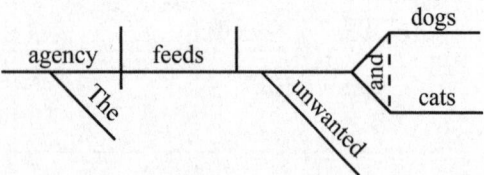

"Unwanted" modifies both "dogs" and "cats." Therefore, it must be placed on a segment of the direct object line that pertains to both direct objects.

4. They splurged and bought a house.

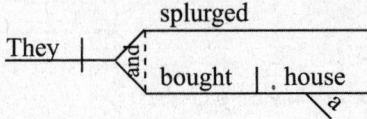

5. She mowed and watered the lawn.

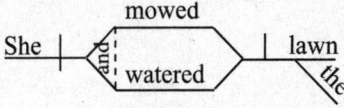

Both verbs have the same direct object.

Articles, Attributive Adjectives, and Direct Objects
Exercise 4

DIRECTIONS: Create a diagram for each of the following sentences. Answers are on page 570.

1. We must consider a different plan.

2. Either the county or the city must assume primary responsibility.

3. The new store sells athletic clothing and equipment.

4. Employers appreciate honest and diligent employees.

5. She buys and restores old furniture.

ADVERBS

In general, **adverbs** modify verbs, adjectives, and other adverbs. Less frequently, they are also used to modify prepositions, prepositional phrases, conjunctions, clauses, and sentences. There are transitional adverbs, which function both as conjunctions and as adverbs, and there are independent adverbs, which modify nothing at all. So, how does one recognize an adverb?

Adverbs that End in "-ly"

The list of **adverbs that end in "-ly"** extends into the thousands. Here are just a few: "thoroughly," "pleasantly," "helpfully," "dearly," "horribly," and "astutely." However, some words that end in "-ly" aren't adverbs at all but are adjectives (e.g., "manly," "costly," and "portly"), as illustrated in the first three of the following examples:

Examples:

1. She speaks <u>friendly</u> to everyone. ✘
   She is a <u>friendly</u> person. ✓

2. He smiles <u>manly</u>. ✘
   They admire his <u>manly</u> qualities. ✓

3. She listens to her patients <u>motherly</u>. ✘
   She shows a <u>motherly</u> concern for her patients. ✓

4. The assistant principal spoke softly, patiently, and supportively to the troubled student.

   ➤ The adverbs "softly," "patiently," and "supportively" modify the verb "spoke." They tell how the assistant principal spoke.

5. Honestly, I don't care.

   ➤ "Honestly" is an independent adverb; it does not modify any word in the sentence.

Adverbs that Do Not End in "-ly"

And then there are **adverbs that do not end in "-ly,"** e.g., "also," "too," "quite," "very," "here," and "there."

Examples:

1. The motives of the exceedingly gracious hostess were quite political.

   ➤ The adverb "exceedingly" modifies the attributive adjective "gracious." The adverb "quite" modifies the predicate adjective "political."

2. Ray answered the question quite hastily and altogether incorrectly.

   ➤ The adverb "quite" modifies the adverb "hastily." The adverb "altogether" modifies the adverb "incorrectly."

Adjectives that Also Function as Adverbs

What's more, there are quite a few *adjectives that also function as adverbs*, e.g., "fast," "high," "low," "long," "right," "left," "late," and "early."

Examples:

1. Only racecar drivers need <u>fast</u> cars. ✓ (adjective)
   He drives too <u>fast</u>. ✓ (adverb)

2. It was a <u>long</u> wait. ✓ (adjective)
   They had to wait <u>long</u>. ✓ (adverb)

3. She made a <u>right</u> turn. ✓ (adjective)
   She turned <u>right</u>. ✓ (adverb)

4. The <u>early</u> bird gets the worm. ✓ (adjective)
   That bird arrives <u>early</u>. ✓ (adverb)

Diagramming Adverbs

Every adverb is diagrammed on a slanted line. If the adverb modifies a verb or a predicate adjective (predicate adjectives are introduced in the next lesson), the slanted line is extended down from the horizontal line under the verb or predicate adjective:

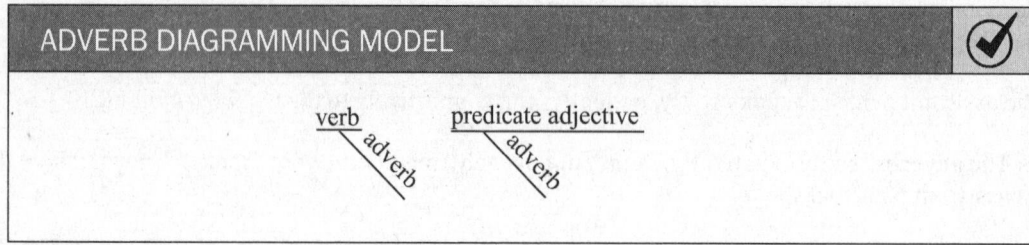

ADVERB DIAGRAMMING MODEL

Example:

The neighbor talks incessantly.

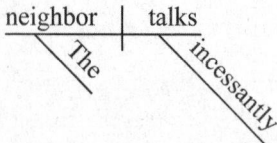

If the adverb modifies an attributive adjective or another adverb, the slanted line underneath the adverb is placed on the left of and parallel to the slanted line of the attributive adjective or of the adverb and is hooked at the top onto this line:

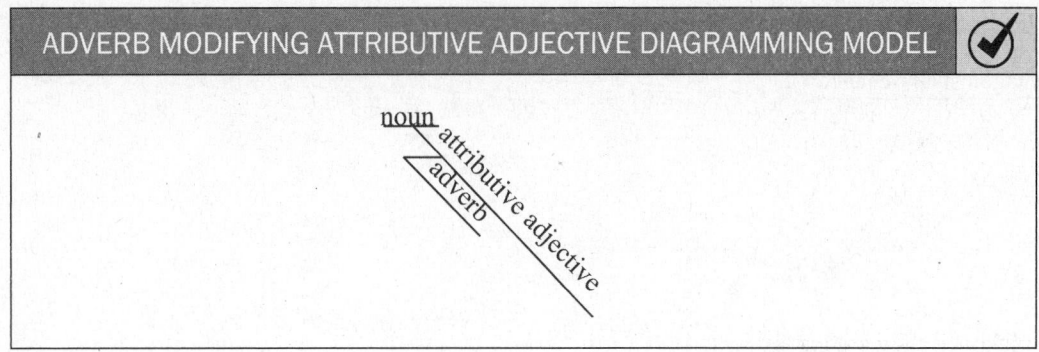

Example:

The thoroughly bored students were fidgeting.

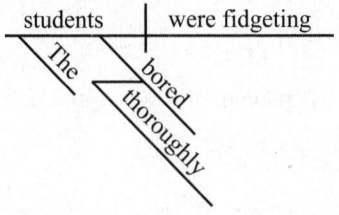

If two adverbs or a compound adverb modify a verb, two slanted lines are extended down from the horizontal line underneath the verb:

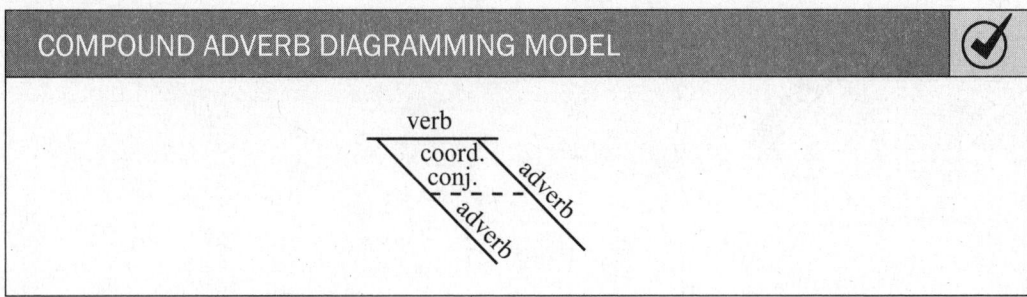

Examples:

1. We awoke very early.

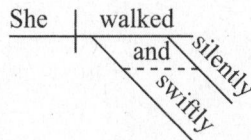

2. She walked swiftly and silently.

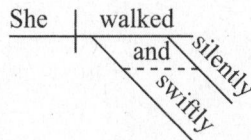

3. The strikingly but superficially beautiful antagonist entered.

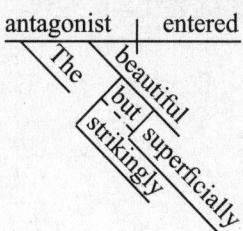

4. Quickly he showered and dressed.

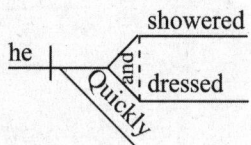

Some adverbs are independent words, modifying nothing at all. Such an adverb is placed on a horizontal line above and separate from the rest of the sentence, as in the following example:

Example:

Not surprisingly, the fatuous man loves a diffident woman.

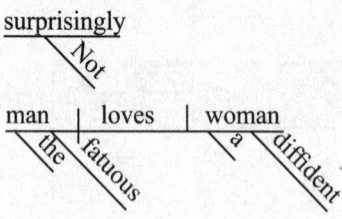

Adverbs
Exercise 5

DIRECTIONS: Create a diagram for each of the following sentences. Answers are on page 571.

1. Angrily and inexorably the storm devastated the coastal regions.

2. Not all Americans favor bigger and more expensive cars.

3. I did the assignment fast and inattentively.

4. She wrote an exceedingly but unexpectedly beautiful poem.

5. This subdivision has about fifty residences.

SUBJECTIVE COMPLEMENTS: PREDICATE NOMINATIVES AND PREDICATE ADJECTIVES

Subjective complements are nouns or adjectives (or the equivalent of either) that complete linking verbs. Such nouns and equivalent expressions are called *predicate nominatives*; such adjectives and equivalent expressions are called *predicate adjectives*. Subjective complements can also follow certain intransitive verbs as well as passive-voice forms of factitive verbs (i.e., verbs that make someone or something someone or something else, such as "make," "choose," "appoint," or "designate").

Predicate Nominatives

Examples:

1. The woman in the blue dress is my sister.

   ➤ The predicate nominative is the noun "sister," which follows a form of the verb "be."

2. It is I.

   ➤ The predicate nominative is the personal pronoun "I."

3. Have you ever been a lifeguard?

   ➤ The predicate nominative is "lifeguard." The verb "have been" is a present-perfect form of the verb "be."

4. This could be an important clue.

   ➤ As you would probably expect, modal forms of the verb "be" (such as "may be," "should be," "could have been," and "must have been") can take subjective complements.

5. She was elected president.

   ➤ "President," a predicate nominative, follows a passive-voice form of the factitive verb "elect." Predicate nominatives can also be preceded by the expletive "as" (e.g., "He was chosen as leader of the small delegation."). (An expletive is a word with a function but with little or no meaning.)

Predicate Adjectives

Examples:

1. I had been sick for a week.

   ➤ "Sick" is a predicate adjective. "Had been" is a past-perfect form of the verb "be."

2. She felt sad.

   ➤ "Sad" is a predicate adjective. In addition to "feel," the verbs "seem," "become," "look," "remain," "taste," and other similar verbs can be followed by predicate adjectives. You can test them with the adjective "good" (e.g., "it seems good," "he is becoming good," "you look good," "we want to remain good," or "the water tastes good").

3. Blackberries grow wild along the south edge of the woods.

   ➤ "Wild" is a predicate adjective. In this sentence, the verb "grow" is intransitive; in other words, it has a meaning in this sentence ("to thrive" or "to become larger") that does not take a direct object. In other contexts, "grow" can function as a transitive verb meaning "to cause to grow" (e.g., "She is growing green beans and tomatoes").

4. They left angry but arrived happy.

   ➤ "Angry" and "happy" are predicate adjectives; each follows an intransitive verb. "Arrive" is always intransitive. "Leave" can be either intransitive or transitive depending on the context. For example, it is transitive in the sentence "Most customers and employees have already left the building."

5. Tom was made livid by the derogatory remark about his daughter.

   ➤ The predicate adjective "livid" follows a passive form of the factitive verb "make."

Diagramming Subjective Complements

In a sentence diagram, a backslash is used to separate verbs from subjective complements (predicate nominatives and predicate adjectives):

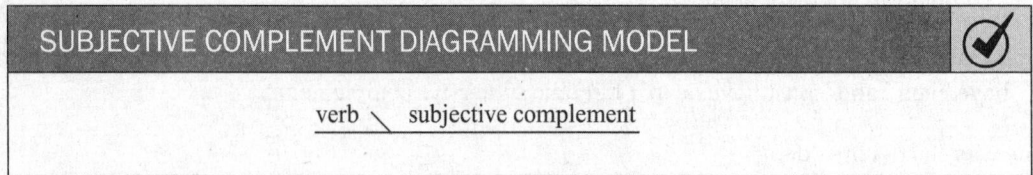

SUBJECTIVE COMPLEMENT DIAGRAMMING MODEL

verb \ subjective complement

Examples:

1. One uncle is an attorney.

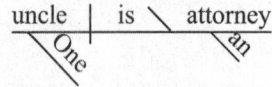

2. The best student became a philosophy professor.

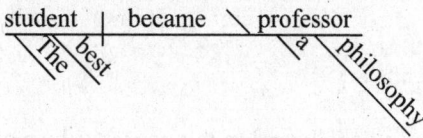

"Became" is a linking verb. "Philosophy" is a noun used as an adjective.

3. Two seniors were made co-captains.

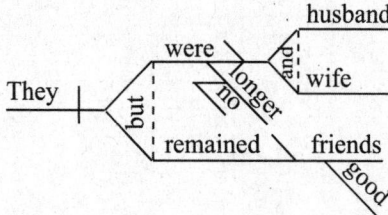

"Were made" is a passive form of a factitive verb.

4. They were no longer husband and wife but remained good friends.

This sentence has a compound predicate and a compound predicate nominative.

5. The stranger was tall, dark, and handsome.

Note the tripartite predicate adjective.

6. He feels good, but he doesn't look good.

7. I am getting sick.

When "get" means "become," as it does in this sentence, it is a linking verb.

8. Here the corn grows tall.

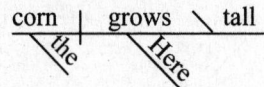

The intransitive verb "grows" is followed in this sentence by a predicate adjective, "tall."

9. She is just playing stupid.

She | is playing \ stupid
just

When "play" means "pretend to be," it can be followed by a subjective complement.

Subjective Complements: Predicate Nominatives and Predicate Adjectives
Exercise 6

DIRECTIONS: Create a diagram for each of the following sentences. Answers are on page 572.

1. Our waiter was both efficient and courteous.

2. She was feeling happy, but he was feeling sad.

3. He is a truly remarkable scholar but a lousy poet.

4. He became angry and silent and left the room.

5. She has been, is, and will be a very effective mayor.

APPOSITIVES

Appositives are words, phrases, or clauses that identify or explain other words in the same sentence. Appositives are said to be in apposition with the words they identify or explain. Most appositives are nouns in apposition with preceding nouns; however, they can also be pronouns, verbs, adjectives, adverbs, prepositions, phrases, or clauses. Occasionally, they can also precede the word or words with which they are in apposition. Appositives are set off with parentheses or commas.

Examples:

1. We planned to travel (fly) to Seattle.

   ➤ This sentence contains a verb in apposition with a verb.

2. These flowers are for my best friend, you.

   ➤ This sentence contains a personal pronoun in apposition with a noun.

3. She regrets the disappearance of many feral (wild) animals.

   ➤ This sentence contains an adjective in apposition with an adjective.

4. He removed the books clandestinely (secretly).

   ➤ This sentence contains an adverb in apposition with an adverb.

5. We live on (beside) a river.

   ➤ This sentence contains a preposition in apposition with a preposition.

6. The office workers were told to be less officious (to mind their own business).

   ➤ This sentence contains an infinitive phrase in apposition with an infinitive phrase.

7. On Friday evenings we go out to eat (the only excitement of the week), and then we work all weekend.

   ➤ This sentence contains a noun phrase in apposition with a clause.

In English, when a proper name is in apposition with a possessive noun, only the proper name has a possessive ending.

Example:

I borrowed my friend Melvin's car.

Restrictive and Nonrestrictive Appositives

There is an important distinction between *restrictive and nonrestrictive appositives*: the former are necessary for identification, and the latter are unnecessary for identification.

> **RESTRICTIVE VERSUS NONRESTRICTIVE APPOSITIVES**
>
> Restrictive: "My cousin Alan broke his arm." (noun in apposition with a noun)
>
> Nonrestrictive: "My father, a skiing instructor, broke his arm." (noun in apposition with a noun)

Intensifying Pronouns

Certain pronouns are both reflexive and intensifying. As **_intensifying pronouns_**, they are appositives: "myself," "yourself," "himself," "herself," "itself," "ourselves," "yourselves," and "themselves."

Examples:

1. The author herself will be there to sign copies of her new book.

   ➢ This sentence contains an intensifying pronoun ("herself") in apposition with a noun ("the author").

2. They themselves will be there.

   ➢ This sentence contains an intensifying pronoun ("themselves") in apposition with a pronoun ("they").

Diagramming Appositives

Appositives are placed in parentheses immediately after the word or words with which they are in apposition:

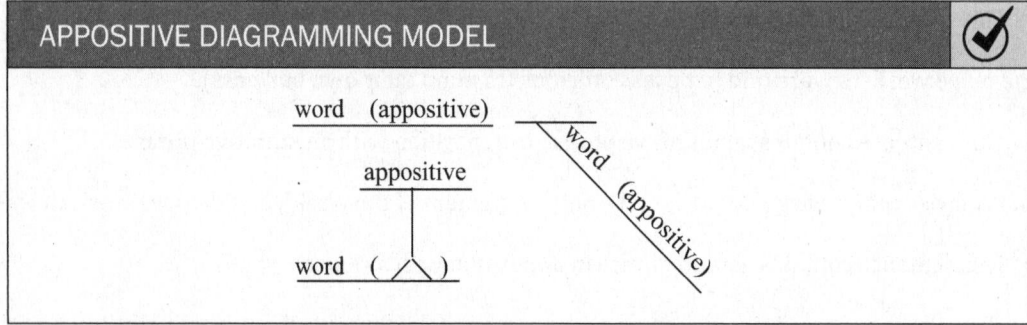

APPOSITIVE DIAGRAMMING MODEL

You can disregard the appositive on a pedestal for now. It is a topic for later consideration.

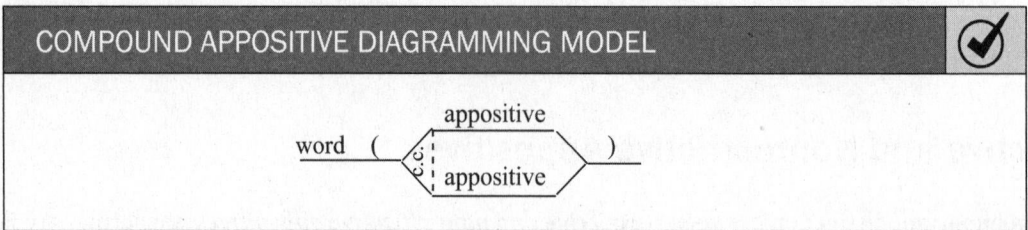

COMPOUND APPOSITIVE DIAGRAMMING MODEL

Examples:

1. Everyone likes my friend Jacob.

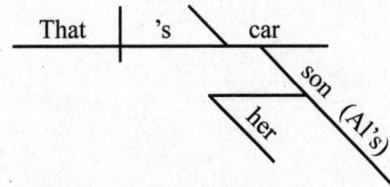

"Jacob" is in apposition with the direct object "friend."

2. That's her son Al's car.

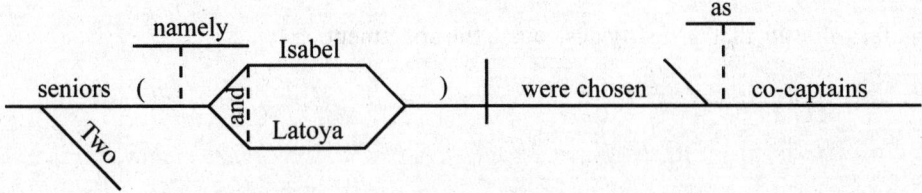

The sentence has two possessives: the pronoun "her" and the noun "Al's." If the appositive "Al's" is omitted, one says "her son's car." Notice, too, the "'s" in the verb position. When diagramming sentences, contractions that combine the subject and a form of the verb (e.g., "that's," "they're," etc.) are separated as shown.

3. Two seniors, namely Isabel and Latoya, were chosen as co-captains.

The sentence has two expletives: "namely," which introduces the compound appositive "Isabel and Latoya," and "as," which introduces the predicate nominative "co-captains."

Appositives
Exercise 7

DIRECTIONS: Create a diagram for each of the following sentences. Answers are on page 573.

1. Her cousins Jack and Jill climbed a hill.

2. J. J., a four-year band member, was chosen as the most outstanding musician.

3. The renters altered, that is, nearly destroyed, the apartment.

4. They have strength, speed, and mental toughness—the right qualities.

5. Have you met my friend Marcy?

PREPOSITIONAL PHRASES

Prepositions

Prepositions are particles (small, uninflected words) that show relationships between their objects and other words. You can name many prepositions by thinking of any place a mouse can go: "in," "into," "around," "up," "down," "over," "under," and "through." Many prepositions, however, have nothing to do with place: "with," "without," "for," "besides," "since," "of," and "except."

When used in a sentence, a preposition must have an object. If a particular word does not have an object, it is not a preposition. It may look exactly like a preposition (i.e., it may be spelled the same), but without an object it functions as an adverb, a conjunction, or as part of a phrasal verb.

Examples:

1. Jack Horner was sitting <u>in</u> a corner.

   ➤ The preposition "in" has the object "corner."

   They just walked <u>in</u>.

   ➤ Here, "in" is an adverb. Adverbs do not have objects.

2. Poor Jethro had to stay <u>after</u> school.

   ➤ The preposition "after" has the object "school."

   He stayed for an hour <u>after</u> the other students had left.

   ➤ Here, "after" is a subordinating conjunction, introducing an entire clause ("the other students had left").

3. The dog chased the cat <u>around</u> the house.

   ➤ The object of the preposition "around" is "house."

   The flu is going <u>around</u>.

   ➤ Here, "around" is an adverb.

4. There is no one here <u>but</u> us.

   ➤ The object of the preposition "but" is the pronoun "us."

   She went to school <u>but</u> her brother stayed home.

   ➤ Here, "but" is a coordinating conjunction.

For now, only nouns and pronouns will be used as objects of prepositions; later, however, you will see how gerunds and gerund phrases, infinitives and infinitive phrases, as well as noun clauses can be objects of prepositions. It is even possible for prepositional phrases to be used as objects of prepositions.

Some prepositions consist of more than one word. Examples of these phrasal prepositions are "out of," "along with," "as for," and "by means of."

Adverbs, too, can modify prepositions and prepositional phrases.

Examples:

1. The fireworks display will begin right after the game.

   ➢ The adverb "right" modifies the preposition "after."

2. The food arrived just in time for the party.

   ➢ The adverb "just" modifies the prepositional phrase "in time."

Adverbial Prepositional Phrases

Most prepositional phrases are adverbial or adjectival. *Adverbial prepositional phrases* modify verbs, adjectives, and adverbs.

Examples:

1. Carolyn and Barbara strolled through the park.

   ➢ The prepositional phrase "through the park" modifies the verb "strolled." It tells where Carolyn and Barbara strolled.

2. Transparent in the middle, the glass is increasingly opaque as it approaches the frame.

   ➢ The prepositional phrase "in the middle" modifies the adjective "transparent."

3. Everyone moved closer to the storyteller.

   ➢ The prepositional phrase "to the storyteller" modifies the adverb "closer."

Adjectival Prepositional Phrases

Adjectival prepositional phrases modify nouns and pronouns.

Examples:

1. All eyes were focused on the woman on the tightrope.

   ➢ The prepositional phrase "on the tightrope" modifies the noun "woman."

2. Someone in the corner stood up.

   ➢ The prepositional phrase "in the corner" modifies the pronoun "someone."

3. As far as anyone knew, he was in good health.

   ➢ The prepositional phrase "in good health" functions as a predicate adjective, modifying the pronoun "he."

Diagramming Prepositional Phrases

To diagram a prepositional phrase, place the preposition on a diagonal line connected to the horizontal or diagonal line of the word or words modified. From a point near the bottom of this diagonal line, draw a horizontal line to the right, and put the object of the preposition on this line. Any modifiers of the object are diagrammed in the expected manner:

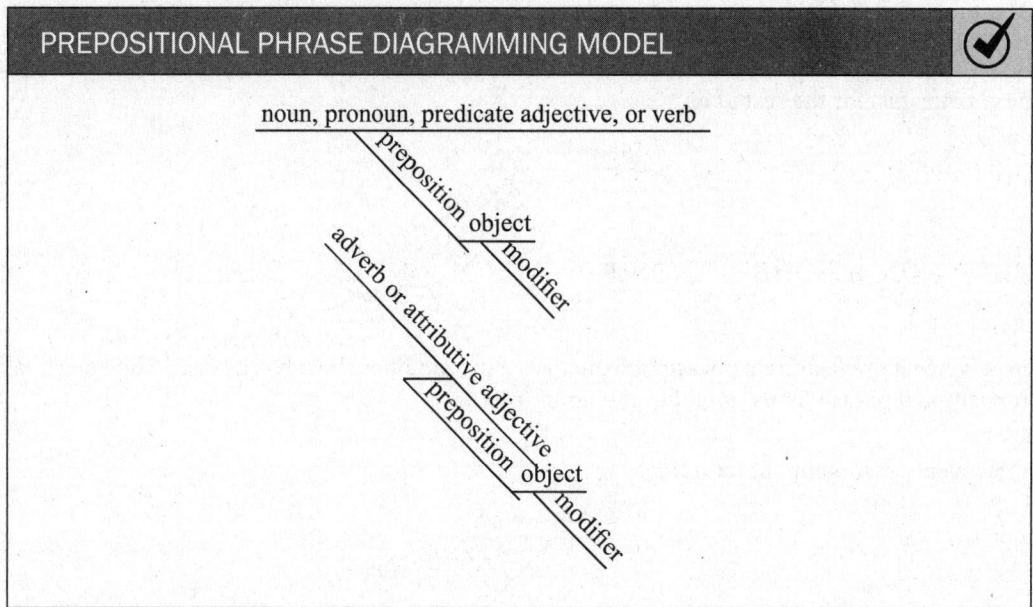

PREPOSITIONAL PHRASE DIAGRAMMING MODEL

Examples:

1. A porter carried our baggage to the car.

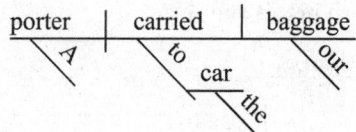

The prepositional phrase "to the car" is adverbial; it modifies the verb "carried."

2. Late for her doctor's appointment, Susan was driving dangerously.

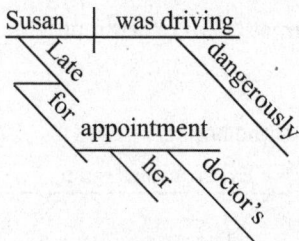

The adverbial prepositional phrase "for her doctor's appointment" modifies the attributive adjective "late."

3. He is of sound mind and body.

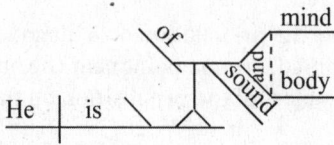

"Of sound mind and body," a prepositional phrase with a compound object, serves in this sentence as a predicate adjective, modifying the pronoun "he."

4. She eats too fast for the rest of us.

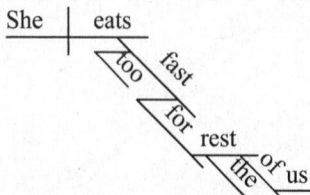

The adverbial prepositional phrase "for the rest of us" modifies the adverb "fast." The adjectival prepositional phrase "of us" modifies the noun "rest."

5. In the evening we went out for a ride.

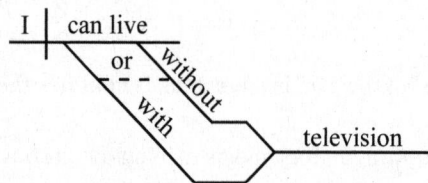

"In the evening" and "for a ride" are prepositional phrases modifying the verb "went." "Out," which looks like a preposition, is an adverb in this sentence.

6. I can live with or without television.

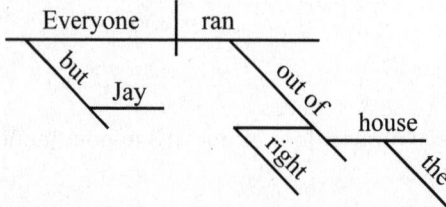

The adverbial prepositional phrase "with or without television" features two prepositions and a single prepositional object.

7. Everyone but Jay ran right out of the house.

Everyone | ran

but Jay

out of house

right the

In this sentence, "but" is a preposition. "Out of" is a phrasal preposition. The adverb "right" modifies the prepositional phrase "out of the house."

Prepositional Phrases
Exercise 8

DIRECTIONS: Create a diagram for each of the following sentences. Answers are on page 574.

1. Early in the week, friends of ours are coming for dinner.

2. They approach every new challenge with enthusiasm and determination.

3. We can go through the narrow tunnel or over the narrow bridge.

4. The principal is taking a group of teachers out for lunch.

5. She acted in accordance with the express wishes of her clients.

INDIRECT OBJECTS AND OBJECTIVE COMPLEMENTS

Indirect Objects

Indirect objects tell to whom or for whom direct objects are given, said, or shown. In the sentence "He showed them the picture," the direct object is "picture." The indirect object (i.e., the people to whom the picture was shown) is "them." An indirect object is not preceded by a preposition. "He showed them the picture" means the same thing as "He showed the picture to them." However, in the latter sentence, "them" is not an indirect object; instead, it is the object of the preposition "to."

Examples:

1. Fred gave his sister a present.

    ➤ "Present" is a direct object. The indirect object is "sister."

2. Will you lend me a dollar?

    ➤ "Dollar" is a direct object. The indirect object is "me."

3. She is telling her students a story.

    ➤ "Story" is a direct object. The indirect object is "students."

Remember: Not every sentence that has a direct object has an indirect object as well. Indirect objects are found only in sentences that have verbs of giving, telling, or showing, such as "offer," "hand," "teach," "lend," "promise," "bring," and "get." Even verbs like "sing" and "find" can take indirect objects if they imply a kind of giving or offering, as in "Will you sing us a song?" and "Find me a pretty flower!" In the previous sentences, the indirect objects are "us" and "me." "Do" doesn't seem to be a verb of giving, but it is in a sentence like "Please do me a favor."

Objective Complements

Objective complements are nouns or adjectives (or the equivalent of nouns or adjectives, like pronouns or participles) that complete verbs with respect to direct objects. The verb in a sentence with an objective complement is often factitive: "elect," "appoint," "choose," "render," "name," "call," "entitle," "color," "dye," and "make."

Examples:

1. They called their mascot Herbie.

    ➤ The noun "Herbie" is an objective complement; the verb "called" is factitive.

2. The summer job will make him strong.

   ➤ The adjective "strong" is an objective complement; the verb "make" is factitive.

3. The shock of standing in front of the class has rendered the poor boy speechless.

   ➤ The adjective "speechless" is an objective complement; the verb "rendered" is factitive.

4. The parents named their daughter Aphrodite.

   ➤ The noun "Aphrodite" is an objective complement; the verb "named" is factitive.

5. One of my classmates dyed his hair purple.

   ➤ The adjective "purple" is an objective complement; the verb "dyed" is factitive.

Like predicate nominatives, some objective complements are introduced by the expletive "as."

Example:

The European travelers chose a bilingual woman as their spokesperson.

Objective complements appear only in active sentences. To change a sentence with an objective complement into its corresponding passive sentence, one takes the direct object of the sentence and makes it the subject. The passive factitive verb acts as a linking verb, and the objective complement of the original sentence becomes a subjective complement (either a predicate nominative or a predicate adjective). To see how this works, let's change the five example sentences above into their corresponding passive forms.

Examples:

1. Their mascot was called Herbie.

   ➤ "Herbie" is a predicate nominative.

2. He will be made strong by the summer job.

   ➤ "Strong" is a predicate adjective.

3. The poor boy has been rendered speechless by the shock of standing in front of the class.

   ➤ "Speechless" is a predicate adjective.

4. The daughter of the parents was named Aphrodite.

   ➤ "Aphrodite" is a predicate nominative.

5. The hair of one of my classmates was dyed purple.

   ➤ "Purple" is a predicate adjective.

The above rules hold when the objective complement is a noun, a pronoun, or an adjective. We will see in the next lesson that it does not apply when the objective complement is an infinitive.

Diagramming Indirect Objects and Objective Complements

An indirect object is diagrammed like an object of a preposition, on a horizontal line that extends to the right from a point near the bottom of a diagonal line whose top touches the base line under the verb. Leave the diagonal line empty:

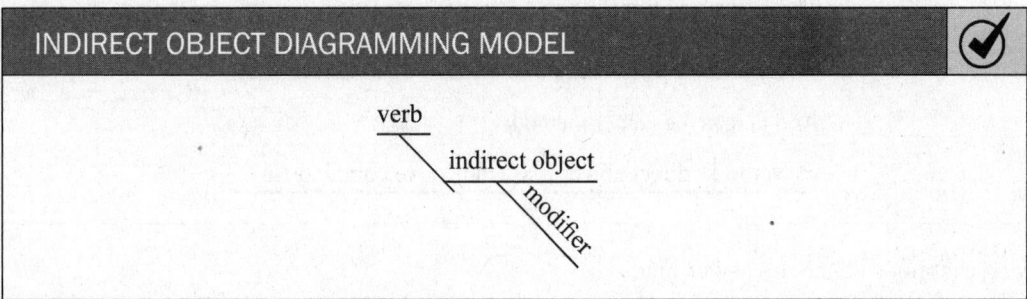

INDIRECT OBJECT DIAGRAMMING MODEL

verb

indirect object

modifier

Examples:

1. Show Jenny the letter from Theresa.

The noun "Jenny," which indicates the person to whom something is to be shown, is an indirect object. The "*x*" represents the unexpressed subject "you." The prepositional phrase "from Theresa" is adjectival.

2. She gave him her phone number.

The personal pronoun "him" is an indirect object. "Phone" is a noun used as an adjective.

3. I told William and Sarah the news.

"William and Sarah" is a compound indirect object.

4. Play me my favorite melody.

In this context, playing is a kind of giving; thus the verb "play" can have an indirect object.

There are two acceptable ways of diagramming objective complements. The one has tradition on its side, while the other is more appealing to most people today:

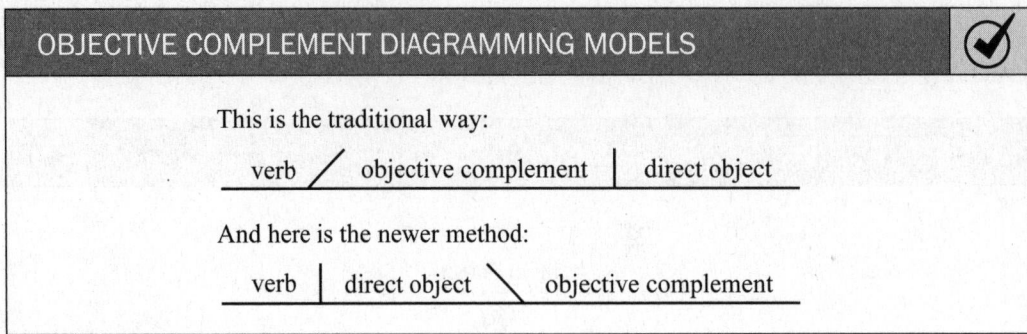

The following examples utilize the newer method:

Examples:

1. The class elected him treasurer.

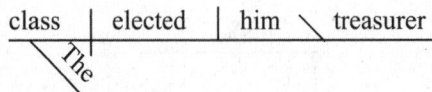

The noun "treasurer" is an objective complement.

2. I chose you as my friend and confidante.

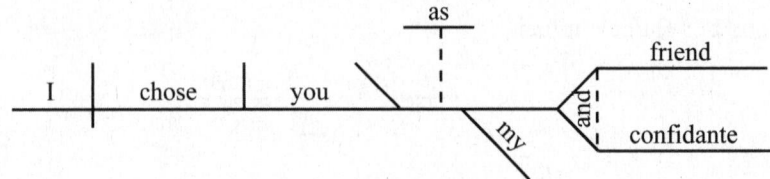

"Friend and confidante" is a compound objective complement. "As" is an expletive.

Indirect Objects and Objective Complements
Exercise 9

DIRECTIONS: Create a diagram for each of the following sentences. Answers are on page 575.

1. John gave Judy an engagement ring.

2. The governor gave each distinguished student and his or her mentor a monetary award.

3. The rescue team found the campers alive and declared them extremely fortunate.

4. Jamie told Shanika, her next-door neighbor, the news about their friend Pam.

5. Humpty-Dumpty was found in pieces, and neither the king's horses nor the king's men could make him whole again.

INFINITIVES

Transitive Infinitives

The basic form of a verb—the form that is usually preceded by the particle "to"—is called an infinitive. All **infinitives** have tense, and **transitive infinitives** have voice as well as progressivity; however, they do not have person and number.

INFINITIVES OF THE TRANSITIVE VERB "FIND"
1. *Present Active:* to find
2. *Present Passive:* to be found
3. *Present Perfect Active:* to have found
4. *Present Perfect Passive:* to have been found
5. *Progressivity:* to be finding, to have been finding

An infinitive with its modifiers and objects is called an infinitive phrase. Like simple infinitives, infinitive phrases can be used as adverbs, adjectives, or nouns.

Examples:

1. They are playing <u>to win</u>. (as an **adverb**)

2. We drove fifty miles <u>to see the performance</u>. (as an **adverb**)

3. You have nothing <u>to do</u>. (as an **adjective**)

4. I am looking for something <u>to read on vacation</u>. (as an **adjective**)

5. Who doesn't want <u>to succeed</u>? (as a **noun**)

6. The children are learning <u>to write correctly</u>. (as a **noun**)

When used as nouns, infinitives and infinitive phrases can be subjects, direct objects, predicate nominatives, appositives, objects of prepositions, and objective complements.

Examples:

1. <u>To die</u> is our common destiny. (as a **subject**)

2. <u>To fly</u> is fun for a while. (as a **subject**)

3. <u>To stand up for the rights of the underprivileged</u> is admirable. (as a **subject**)

4. <u>To drive a car properly</u> requires practice and a respect for the rights of others. (as a **subject**)

5. Do you want <u>to rest</u>? (as a ***direct object***)

6. Children like <u>to run and play</u>. (as a ***direct object***)

7. She tried <u>to read a good book</u>. (as a ***direct object***)

8. Would you prefer <u>to go to a movie today or to eat out tomorrow</u>? (as a ***direct object***)

9. Their goal will be <u>to survive</u>. (as a ***predicate nominative***)

10. Her job was <u>to hire the best people available</u>. (as a ***predicate nominative***)

11. To strive is <u>to succeed</u>. (as a ***predicate nominative***)

12. It was not my idea <u>to leave early</u>. (as an ***appositive***)

13. Sometimes it is necessary <u>to stand and fight</u>. (as an ***appositive***)

14. Nothing remained except <u>to fold our tents and go home</u>. (as the ***object of the preposition "except"***)

15. The waiter did everything but <u>pay the bill</u>. (a "*to*-less" infinitive as the ***object of the preposition "but"***)

16. Do you really have nothing to do except <u>disturb others</u>? (a "*to*-less" infinitive as the ***object of the preposition "except"***)

17. She made them <u>stay after school</u>. (a "*to*-less" infinitive as an ***objective complement***)

18. He heard someone <u>come in the back door</u>. (a "*to*-less" infinitive as an ***objective complement***)

19. We watched the red sun <u>sink below the horizon</u>. (a "*to*-less" infinitive as an ***objective complement***)

In these cases where the infinitive is used as an objective complement, the infinitive is quite often "*to*-less."

One might consider the phrase "to be honest" as an objective complement in the sentence "I believe him to be honest." However, a better analysis of this sentence might be to consider the phrase "him to be honest" as an objective-case subject with a verb in the infinitive form. The sentence can be restated as "I believe <u>that he is honest</u>" (i.e., with the indirect statement underlined.

Complementary Infinitives

The modal auxiliary verbs "may," "might," "can," "could," "should," and "must" are so closely tied to their complements (the verbs that complete them) that the two (modal auxiliary and complement) are considered single verb forms ("may arrive," "can help," "should wait," "must have seen," etc.) and are so diagrammed. Other verbs achieve this same closeness with their complements ("ought to hurry," "am going to meet," "used to watch," etc.). In such constructions, the infinitives that complement the introductory words are usually preceded by the particle "to" and are called ***complementary infinitives***.

Examples:

1. Students <u>have to stay</u> in their homerooms until the bell rings.

2. Students <u>ought to stay</u> in their homerooms until the bell rings.

3. Students <u>are to stay</u> in their homerooms until the bell rings.

4. Students <u>are going to stay</u> in their homerooms until the bell rings.

5. Students <u>used to stay</u> in their homerooms until the bell rang.

Do not confuse complementary infinitives with direct objects. In general, sentences that contain transitive verbs (i.e., verbs that take direct objects) are able to be restated in the passive voice. Even though "have" and "used" can take direct objects, they can't do so in the above sentences because their meanings there do not allow them to be used passively. If you try to express these sentences in the passive voice, you get nonsense.

Example:

To stay in homerooms until the bell rings is had by students. (Nonsense, right?)

Above, you were introduced to infinitives and infinitive phrases used as predicate nominatives; now, you will meet infinitives and infinitive phrases used as predicate adjectives. The infinitives may be preceded by forms of the verb "to be," but they can also follow other linking verbs (e.g., "seem," "appear," and certain passive verbs).

Examples:

1. He seemed <u>to have all his ducks in a row</u>. (as a ***predicate adjective***)

2. One contestant appears <u>to lack self-confidence</u>. (as a ***predicate adjective***)

3. The Royal Library of Alexandria is thought <u>to have contained more than 500,000 books</u>. (as a ***predicate adjective***)

4. This is said <u>to be the best Vietnamese restaurant in town</u>. (as a ***predicate adjective***)

In a peculiar construction, the particle "for" is used as an expletive to introduce an infinitive phrase used as a subject, a direct object, a predicate nominative, or an appositive. Such infinitive phrases have subjects.

Examples:

1. For us to deny our common humanity would be harmful to society. (subject of infinitive: "us")

2. The old man does not like for others to do his work for him. (subject of infinitive: "others")

3. The plan was for him to read the script first. (subject of infinitive: "him")

4. It is essential to the success of the company for all employees to contribute their time and talents. (subject of infinitive: "employees")

An infinitive phrase can also be used as the object of the preposition "for."

Examples:

1. The salespeople were itching for the last customers to leave the store. (subject of infinitive: "customers")

2. The boss bought a second car for the staff to use. (subject of infinitive: "staff")

Finally, infinitives and infinitive phrases can also be used as independent expressions.

Examples:

1. To tell the truth, I've never caught a really big fish in my life.

2. Kay made a good impression, to say the least.

Diagramming Infinitives

Most infinitives are preceded by the particle "to"; however, some are "*to*-less":

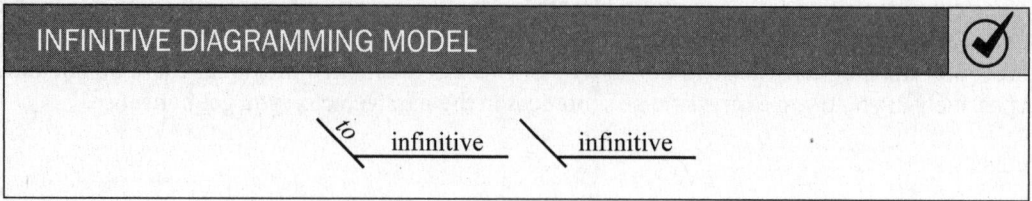

Examples:

1. To own her own car has long been her desire.

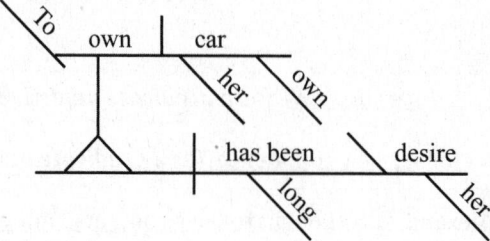

The infinitive phrase "to own her own car" is the subject of the sentence.

2. He hates to wash dishes and take out the garbage.

This sentence features a compound infinitive phrase used as a direct object.

3. To love is to live fully.

The subject of the sentence is the infinitive "to love"; the infinitive phrase "to live fully" is a predicate nominative.

4. We have nothing to do, we are ready to go, and we can't wait to leave.

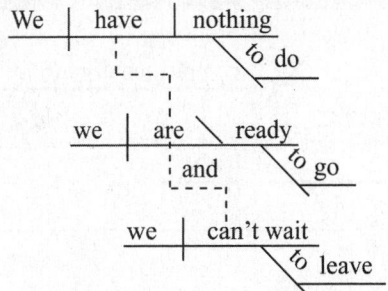

"To do" is an adjectival infinitive; it modifies the noun "nothing." "To go" is an adverbial infinitive; it modifies the adjective "ready." "To leave" is an adverbial infinitive; it modifies the verb "can't wait."

5. The weather forced him to head south.

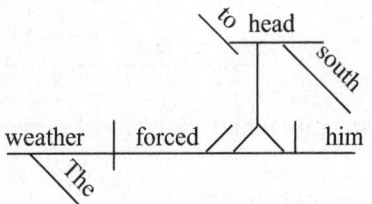

The infinitive phrase "to head south" is an objective complement. Don't forget the other way of diagramming objective complements, as follows:

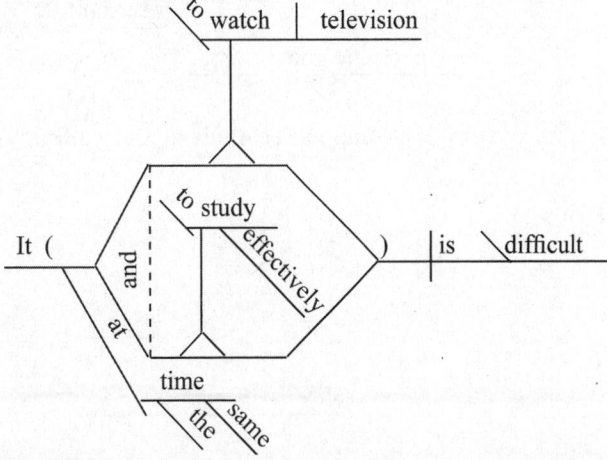

6. It is difficult to watch television and to study effectively at the same time.

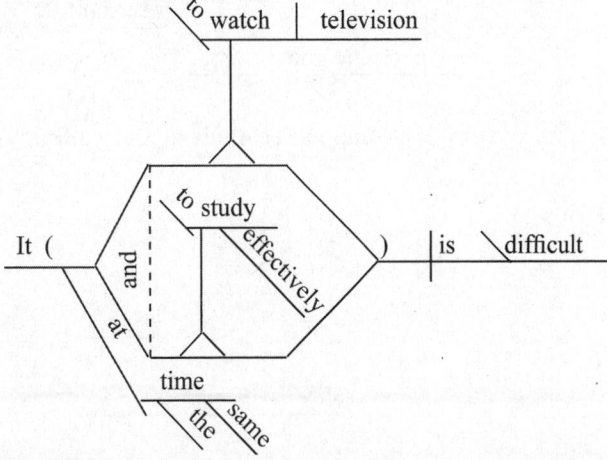

The compound infinitive phrase "to watch television and to study effectively at the same time" is in apposition with the subject of the sentence, "it."

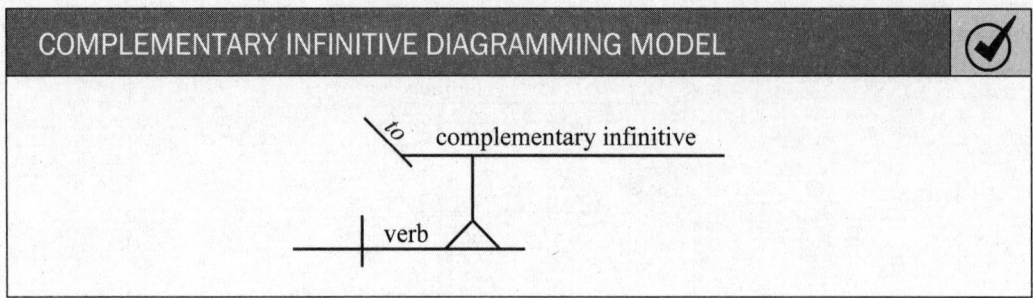

COMPLEMENTARY INFINITIVE DIAGRAMMING MODEL

Examples:

1. The wedding is to be held in an azalea garden.

The complementary infinitive "to be held" is in the present tense, passive voice.

2. You ought to have been there.

"To have been" is a complementary infinitive. It is in the present perfect tense.

3. We are going to go to the game and scream.

"To go to the game and scream" is a compound complementary infinitive phrase.

4. She is about to speak.

"About to" is a phrasal particle.

5. A small dinosaur appears to have been partially digested by the large dinosaur.

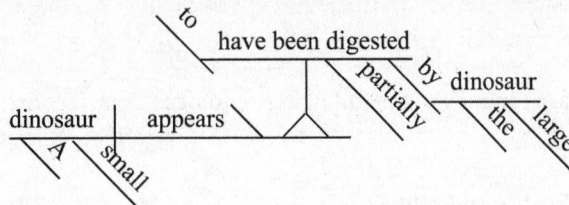

The infinitive phrase introduced by the present perfect passive infinitive "to have been digested" functions as a predicate adjective after the linking verb "appears."

6. It is said to be a good idea to rise early.

The passive verb "is said" functions as a linking verb. The infinitive phrase "to rise early" is in apposition with the subject, "it."

7. To be sure, the second computer is for the children to use.

"To be sure" is an independent infinitive phrase; therefore, its diagram is completely separate from the rest of the diagram. "For the children to use" is a prepositional phrase that functions as a predicate adjective. "Children" is the subject of the infinitive "to use."

Infinitives
Exercise 10

DIRECTIONS: Create a diagram for each of the following sentences. Answers are on page 576.

1. Their plan was to fly to Seattle and rent a car.

2. That is easy to promise but hard to do.

3. She spoke too softly to be understood.

4. He walks three miles every day to stay cardiovascularly healthy.

5. Domestic responsibilities compelled them to stay at home.

6. The students are to go immediately to their desks.

7. For them to become angry is not helpful to our cause.

8. To have to be told three times to behave is a sign of immaturity.

9. She said for the children to be ready to leave in ten minutes.

10. They are thought to have been kidnapped by insurgents.

GERUNDS

The "-ing" form of a verb that is functioning as a noun or in a noun phrase is known as a *gerund* (be careful not to confuse the gerund form of a verb with its participle form, which will be discussed on p. 151). Gerunds are verbal nouns; in other words, they are both nouns and verbs. When a gerund is functioning as a noun, it can function as other nouns function. This means that a gerund could be the subject of a sentence, the direct object, a predicative nominative, or any other form of a noun.

When a gerund is functioning as a verb, the gerund is usually part of a larger group of words that includes complements, objects, and modifiers and that is known collectively as a *gerund phrase*. As a verb in a gerund phrase, a gerund can have several different functions. If the gerund is derived from a linking verb, it can be followed by a predicate nominative or a predicate adjective. For example, in the sentence "The child being stubborn did not get the candy he demanded in the grocery store," "being" is a gerund that links "the child," the subject, with "stubborn," a predicate adjective. Furthermore, a transitive gerund can take a direct object. In the sentence "Raising children is a difficult task," "children" is the direct object of the gerund "raising." Finally, if the gerund is a verb of saying, giving, or showing, it can take an indirect object. In the sentence "Johnny was not happy about awarding Jason the prize," "the prize" is the direct object and "Jason" the indirect object of the gerund "awarding." And the whole gerund phrase is the object of the preposition "about."

Modifiers and Tense

Since gerunds can be nouns and verbs, they can also be modified like nouns and verbs. As a noun, a gerund can be modified by adjectives and by words functioning as adjectives (i.e., nouns, prepositional phrases, etc.). In the example "Mountain biking is Bernie's favorite sport," the adjective "mountain" modifies the gerund "biking." As a verb, a gerund can be modified by adverbs and by words functioning as adverbs (i.e., adverbial objectives, prepositional phrases, etc.). In the sentence "Driving the car slowly is one of my father's worst traits," the adverb "slowly" modifies the gerund "driving" in the gerund phrase "driving the car."

Like infinitives, gerunds have tense and (in the case of transitive gerunds) voice; however, gerunds do not have person or number. If a verb is intransitive, it has only two gerund forms. For example, the intransitive verb "be" has only two gerund forms: present ("being") and present-perfect ("having been"). These two gerunds could be used in a sentence like "Being in love is better than having been in love." If a verb is transitive, it has two active forms and two corresponding passive forms. For example, the transitive verb "to see" has not only a present active gerund ("seeing") and a present perfect active gerund ("having seen") but also a present passive gerund ("being seen") as well as a present perfect passive gerund ("having been seen").

Examples:

1. <u>Waiting</u> is not fun. (as a *subject*)

2. <u>Walking for at least thirty minutes daily</u> is healthy. (as a *subject*)

3. <u>Eating out</u> can get boring. (as a *subject*)

4. Her hobby is <u>running</u>. (as a *predicate nominative*)

5. Giving free food to friends is regarded by the manager as <u>stealing</u>. (as a *predicate nominative*)

6. Learning to walk is <u>putting one foot in front of the other</u>. (as a *predicate nominative*)

7. These are a few of my grandchildren's favorite things: <u>coloring, listening to stories, and watching videos</u>. (as an ***appositive***)

8. It was a pleasure <u>getting to know you</u>. (as an ***appositive***)

9. This is the life for me, just <u>lying on the sand and soaking up the sun</u>. (as an ***appositive***)

10. She doesn't like <u>hitting</u>. (as a ***direct object***)

11. Do you enjoy their <u>ranting and raving</u>? (as a ***direct object***)

12. Have you tried <u>starting at the beginning</u>? (as a ***direct object***)

13. In the wintertime you can lower your heating bill by <u>lowering the temperature in your house</u>. (as the ***object of a preposition***)

14. Sunday afternoons are reserved for <u>doing fun things with their children</u>. (as the ***object of a preposition***)

15. Since his heart surgery, he has given much thought to <u>eating and drinking healthfully</u>. (as the ***object of a preposition***)

16. Do you call that <u>dancing</u>? (as an ***objective complement***)

17. The judge condemned their door-to-door sales as <u>taking advantage of the elderly</u>. (as an ***objective complement***)

18. Anyone in his right mind would consider that strategy <u>manipulating the books</u>. (as an ***objective complement***)

19. Anything worth <u>doing</u> is worth <u>doing right</u>. (as an ***adverbial objective***)

Diagramming Gerunds

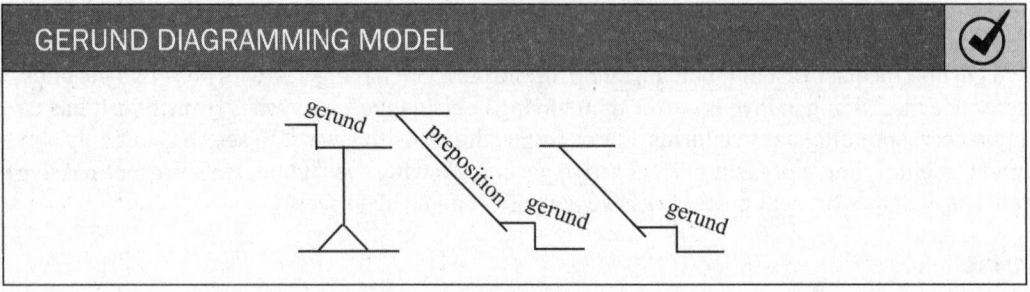

Examples:

1. Diagramming is a symbolic way of showing grammatical relationships between the words of a sentence.

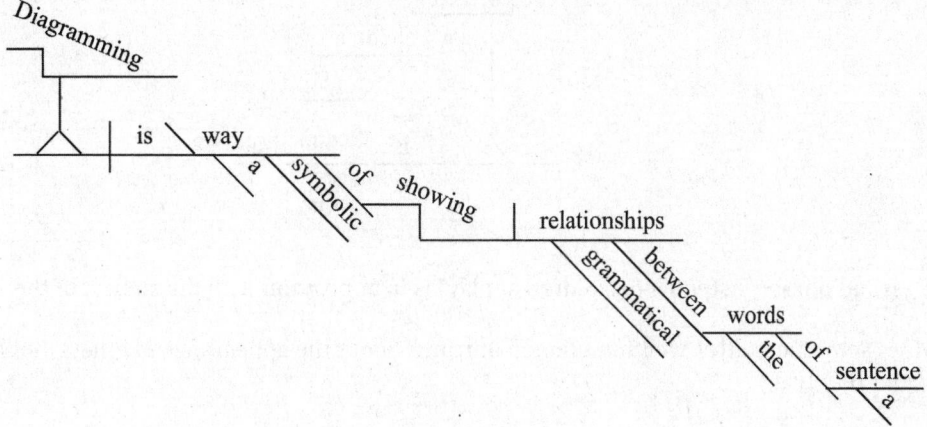

In this sentence, the gerund "diagramming" is the subject. Another gerund, "showing," introduces a gerund phrase that serves as the object of the preposition "of."

2. His basketball strong points are rebounding and blocking shots.

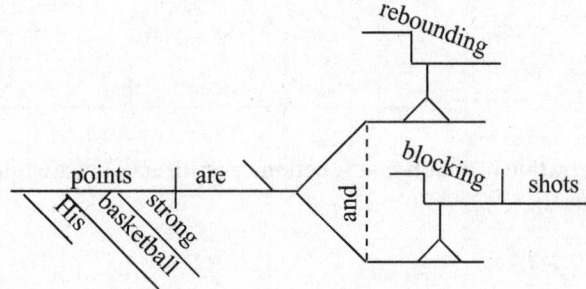

The compound predicate nominative comprises a gerund and a gerund phrase. Because gerunds are not only nouns but also verbs, some of them take direct objects.

3. Everyone in the family teases him about his snoring during our favorite TV programs.

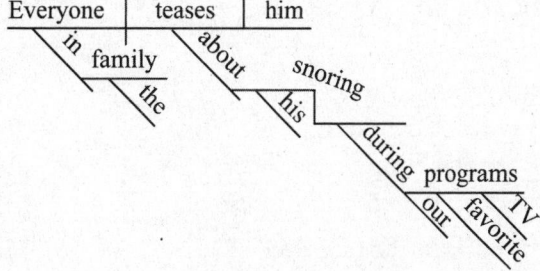

Adjective modifiers of gerunds (i.e., "his") hang from the upper horizontal line of the gerund step-down, whereas adverbial modifiers (i.e., the prepositional phrase "during our favorite TV programs") hang from the lower line.

4. It is usually delightful listening to children at play.

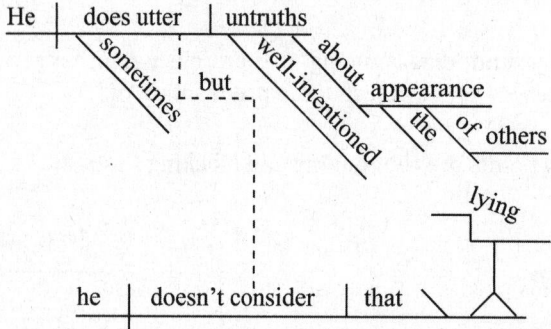

The gerund phrase "listening to children at play" is in apposition with the subject of the sentence, "it."

5. He does sometimes utter well-intentioned untruths about the appearance of others, but he doesn't consider that lying.

"That" is a demonstrative pronoun that functions as a direct object while the gerund "lying" is an objective complement.

Gerunds
Exercise 11

DIRECTIONS: Create a diagram for each of the following sentences. Answers are on page 579.

1. Ms. Shelby, a teacher at our school, calls her friendship with Mr. Moss, a teacher at a rival school, "fraternizing with the enemy."

2. Something worth quoting is worth quoting accurately.

3. The landlord increased his profit by raising the rent and reducing the amenities.

4. The men are playing golf and the women are going shopping.

5. The joylessness in Mudville is the result of Casey's not having hit a home run.

PARTICIPLES

Participles are verbal adjectives; in other words, they are both verbs and adjectives. Like infinitives and gerunds, participles have tense and voice but no person and number. There are five participial forms of most transitive verbs:

PARTICIPIAL FORMS OF THE VERB "CARRY"
1. *Present Active:* carrying
2. *Present Passive:* being carried
3. *Present Perfect Active:* having carried
4. *Present Perfect Passive:* having been carried
5. *Simple Past:* carried

Participles can function both as attributive adjectives and as predicate adjectives. They can also serve as objective complements. They have an essential role in nominative absolutes, and they have an independent use.

Participles and participial phrases can modify subjects, predicate nominatives, direct objects, indirect objects, objects of prepositions, appositives, objective complements, and adverbial objectives.

Examples:

1. <u>Lost</u>, the puppy wandered from house to house in search of food. (as an ***attributive adjective***)

   ➤ A past participle modifies a subject.

2. <u>Having run all the way from Marathon to Athens</u>, the messenger died. (as an ***attributive adjective***)

   ➤ A participial phrase introduced by a present-perfect participle modifies a subject.

3. <u>Having been shot</u>, he was rushed to a nearly hospital. (as an ***attributive adjective***)

   ➤ A present-perfect passive participle modifies a subject.

4. The first thing they saw was a uniformed man <u>riding a white horse</u>. (as an ***attributive adjective***)

   ➤ A participial phrase introduced by a present active participle modifies a predicate nominative.

5. Do you know the person <u>being arrested</u>? (as an ***attributive adjective***)

   ➤ A present passive participle modifies a direct object.

6. They gave the girl <u>sleeping in the corner</u> an award for honesty. (as an ***attributive adjective***)

   ➤ A participial phrase introduced by a present participle modifies an indirect object.

7. The children found all the eggs except the one <u>hidden in an old flower pot</u>. (as an ***attributive adjective***)

   ➤ A participial phrase introduced by a past participle modifies an object of a preposition.

8. Mary's life was saved by her sister, the woman <u>standing next to her</u>. (as an ***attributive adjective***)

   ➤ A participial phrase introduced by a present participle modifies an appositive.

9. Thomas Heywood considered Mistress Frankford a woman <u>killed with kindness</u> and so titled his play. (as an ***attributive adjective***)

   ➤ A participial phrase introduced by a past participle modifies an objective complement.

10. The finished product did not seem to be worth the time and effort <u>invested in it</u>. (as an ***attributive adjective***)

    ➤ A participial phrase introduced by a past participle modifies a compound adverbial objective.

11. The children came <u>running</u>. (as a ***predicate adjective***)

    ➤ The intransitive verb "came" functions as a linking verb in this sentence.

12. You were seen <u>lying on a park bench across from the train station</u>. (as a ***predicate adjective***)

    ➤ The passive verb "were seen" acts as a linking verb.

13. They feel themselves <u>being drawn through a tunnel</u>. (as an ***objective complement***)

14. Each morning, the neighbors heard him <u>whistling the same tune</u>. (as an ***objective complement***)

Nominative Absolutes

Nominative absolutes are grammatically independent expressions consisting of nouns or pronouns modified by participles.

Examples:

1. <u>Their funds exhausted</u>, they knew one of them had to find a job fast.

2. <u>Victory having been accomplished at a terrible price</u>, the homecoming was bittersweet at best.

Dangling Participles

A ***dangling participle*** is a participle that does not modify the intended word or phrase or simply does not modify anything at all. While careful speakers and writers of English avoid dangling participles like the plague, they typically allow themselves to dangle the present participle "speaking."

Example:

<u>Speaking of food</u>, it's time to head home and light the grill.

➤ The participle "speaking" is used independently with nothing to modify; one can argue that it functions here as a preposition.

Diagramming Participles

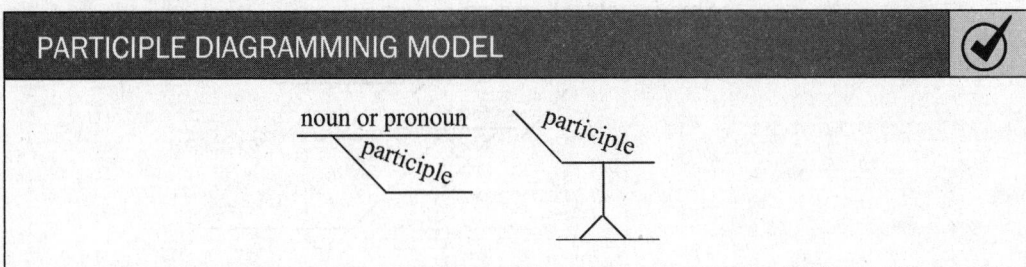

PARTICIPLE DIAGRAMMING MODEL

Examples:

1. Letting the guests wait, she kept talking on the phone.

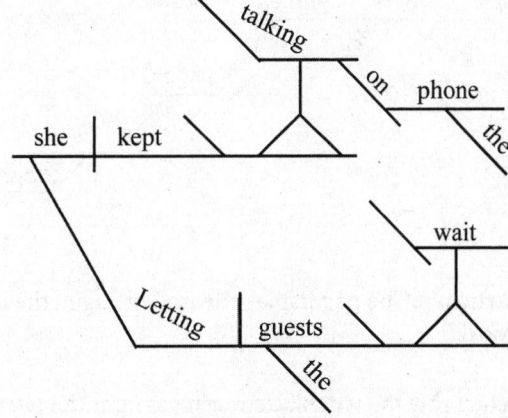

"Letting" and "talking" are present participles. The former serves as an attributive adjective, the latter as a predicate adjective after the verb "kept," which in this sentence is a linking verb. The "*to*-less" infinitive "wait" is an objective complement.

2. Speaking of superfluity, you will find at least forty boxes stacked in the closet.

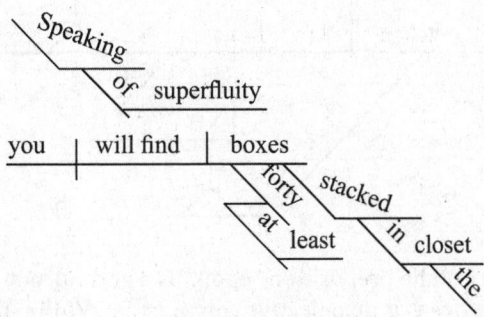

"Speaking of superfluity" is a dangling participle. "Stacked" is a past participle. The participial phrase "stacked in the closet" modifies "boxes," a direct object.

3. She told the person being interviewed the reason for her unusual questions.

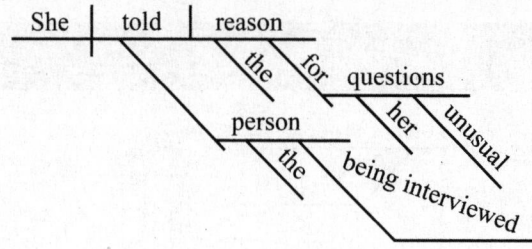

The present passive participle "being interviewed" modifies the indirect object, "person."

4. Her eyes turned toward two people sitting in the corner.

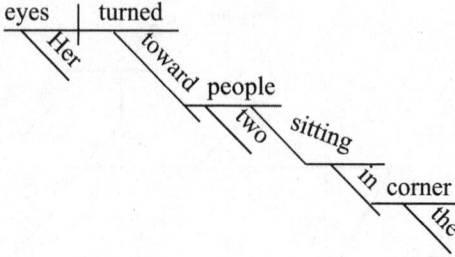

"Sitting" is a present participle. The participial phrase "sitting in the corner" modifies "people," the object of the preposition "toward."

5. Upon awakening, Gretchen saw the witch attempting to light the oven.

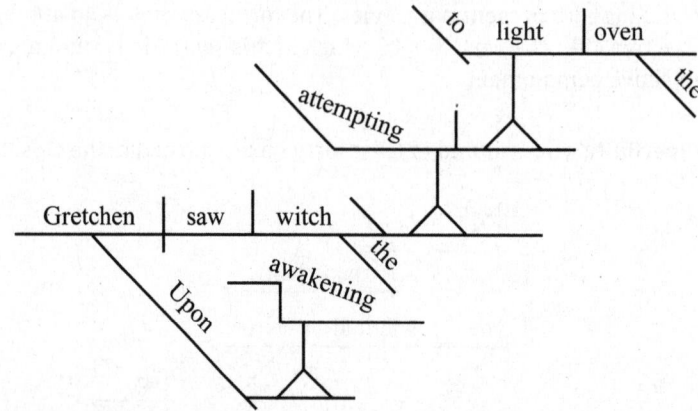

"Awakening," the object of the preposition "upon," is a gerund, not a participle. The participial phrase "attempting to light the oven" is an objective complement. Within this phrase, the infinitive phrase "to light the oven" functions as the direct object of the present active participle "attempting."

6. With her chores finished, she went outside to play.

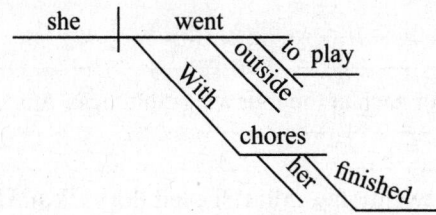

"With her chores" is a prepositional phrase modifying the verb. "Finished" is a past participle modifying "chores."

Participles
Exercise 12

DIRECTIONS: Create a diagram for each of the following sentences. Answers are on page 581.

1. Still running smoothly after twenty-five miles, she left the park and headed for the finish line.

2. Chewing, spitting, and occasionally talking, the three old-timers watched the people and the trains go by.

3. Having reached the end of her twelve-hour shift, the exhausted nurse heaved a sigh of relief.

4. The bridge having collapsed, some interstate commuters were forced to drive much farther each day.

5. Speaking of rascals, Oscar just knocked at the door.

ADVERB CLAUSES

A clause is a group of words that has a subject and a predicate (i.e., the verb, its objects, and the modifiers of the verb and of its objects). An independent, or main, clause is a clause that can stand alone as a complete sentence. Every sentence must have at least one main clause. A dependent, or subordinate, clause cannot stand alone as a complete sentence but is dependent upon another clause.

Up until now, we have been considering (and diagramming) only independent clauses. There are three types of dependent clauses: adverb clauses, adjective clauses, and noun clauses. In this lesson, you will be introduced to *adverb clauses*.

Subordinating Conjunctions

Some adverb clauses are introduced by subordinating conjunctions (e.g., "because," "since," "although," and "if").

Examples:

1. Stacy stayed home on Derby day because it was raining.

2. Since none of us has a basketball, we can't play basketball.

   ➢ For "since" to be a subordinating conjunction, it must be causal (i.e., it must mean "because").

3. Although she had just bought a new dress, she decided to wear an old one.

4. I would have left earlier if I hadn't had to clean my room.

   ➢ "If" is a subordinating conjunction only when it is conditional.

Relative Adverbs

Other adverb clauses are introduced by *relative adverbs* (e.g., "when," "where," "after," "before," "while," "since," and "as"). Relative adverbs are adverbs because they modify the kinds of words that adverbs modify. They are called relative adverbs because, in part, they function as prepositions with relative-pronoun objects. This will become clear as you examine the following examples:

Examples:

1. We can do our homework when we return.

   ➢ The relative adverb "when" can be expressed as "at the time at which." This expression comprises two prepositional phrases: "at the time" and "at which," the former modifying the verb "do" and the latter modifying the verb "return." "Which" in "at which" is a relative pronoun. Relative pronouns and relative clauses are discussed in the next lesson.

2. Dorothy wanted to go where her friends were going.

   ➢ The relative adverb "where" is the equivalent of "to the place to which."

3. When we retire, we can go hiking whenever the weather is accommodating.

> Both "when" and "whenever" are relative adverbs. The latter is the equivalent to "at any time at which." "When" and "where" can also be interrogative adverbs and, as such, introduce direct and indirect questions (the latter being noun clauses, which is the topic of the lesson on p. 173).

4. Make hay while the sun shines.

> "While," a relative adverb, can be restated as "during the time at which."

5. After he had worked in the garden for an hour, he sat down and fell asleep.

> The relative adverb "after" can be restated as "after the time at which." Notice that "after" in the expression "after the time at which" is not a relative adverb but a preposition.

6. He hasn't stopped talking since he got here.

> The relative adverb "since" is temporal, not causal. It is the equivalent of "since the time at which." The latter "since" is a preposition.

Equal and Unequal Comparisons

There are two types of comparison: equal and unequal. Both are expressed by using relative adverbs and (often elliptical) subordinate clauses. **Equal comparisons** require the positive (or basic) form of an adjective or adverb preceded by "as" or "so" (ordinary adverbs) and followed by "as" (a relative adverb). **Unequal comparisons** require the comparative form of an adjective or adverb followed by the relative adverb "than."

Adjectives and adverbs have three gradations:

POSITIVE, COMPARATIVE, AND SUPERLATIVE ADJECTIVES AND ADVERBS

1. *Adjectives:* tall, taller, tallest; good, better, best; beautiful, more beautiful, most beautiful

2. *Adverbs:* soon, sooner, soonest; well, better, best; awkwardly, more awkwardly, most awkwardly

The sentence "You are as tall as she" expresses an equal comparison (i.e., the two people being compared are equal in height). Every comparison contains a subordinate clause, which is usually expressed elliptically. For example, "You are as tall as she" in its expanded form is "You are as tall as she is tall." The first "as" of the correlatives "as . . . as" is a regular adverb; it modifies the adjective "tall" (the first one). The second "as" is a relative adverb and modifies the second (or unexpressed) "tall." To see why the second "as" is not an ordinary adverb but a relative adverb, consider this equivalent restatement: "You are tall in the degree in which she is tall." The first "as" is rendered by "in the degree," the second by "in which." Since this "which" is a relative pronoun, the second "as" is called a relative adverb.

Examples:

1. Jessica can run as fast as her brother.
   Expanded sentence: Jessica can run as fast as her brother can run fast.
   Equivalent sentence: Jessica can run fast in the degree in which her brother can run fast. ("Fast" is an adverb in this sentence.)

2. The Smiths are not so wealthy as the Joneses.
   Expanded sentence: The Smiths are not so wealthy as the Joneses are wealthy.
   Equivalent sentence: The Smiths are not wealthy in the degree in which the Joneses are wealthy.

3. They are as honest as they are kind. (This sentence is not elliptical.)
   Equivalent sentence: They are honest in the degree in which they are kind.

The sentence "You are taller than she" expresses an unequal comparison (i.e., the two people being compared are unequal in height). The expanded form of this elliptical sentence is "You are taller than she is tall." This is equivalent to "You are tall beyond the degree in which she is tall." In this restatement, "taller" is rendered as "tall beyond the degree," and "than" is expressed as "in which," a prepositional phrase containing a relative pronoun; thus, "than" is called a relative adverb.

Examples:

1. Her work is more difficult than his.
   Expanded sentence: Her work is more difficult than his is difficult.
   Equivalent sentence: Her work is difficult beyond the degree in which his is difficult.

2. Jack was hurt worse than Jill.
   Expanded sentence: Jack was hurt worse than Jill was hurt badly.
   Equivalent sentence: Jack was hurt badly beyond the degree in which Jill was hurt badly.

3. I would rather write a report than read one.
   Expanded sentence: I would rather write a report than I would gladly read one.
   Equivalent sentence: I would write a report gladly beyond the degree in which I would gladly read one.

You have been introduced to the correlatives "as . . . as" and "so . . . as" and have noted that they are used with the positive degree of adjectives and adverbs (in so-called equal comparisons). Another correlative expression, "the . . . the," is used with the comparative degree. In the sentence "The bigger they are, the harder they fall," which can be rephrased as "They fall harder in the degree in which they are bigger," "the" in "the bigger" is a relative adverb, while "the" in "the harder" is a regular adverb.

In the sentence "We were so tired that we fell asleep right away," "so . . . that" is a correlative expression expressing result. It is not to be confused with "so that", which expresses purpose (e.g., "She turned off the TV so that she could study better."); "so that" is a phrasal subordinating conjunction. In the case of "so . . . that," "so" is a regular adverb and "that" is a relative adverb. The sentence "We were so tired that we fell asleep right away" can be restated as "We were tired to the degree at which we fell asleep right away."

Diagramming Adverb Clauses

Adverb clauses are introduced by subordinating conjunctions and relative adverbs:

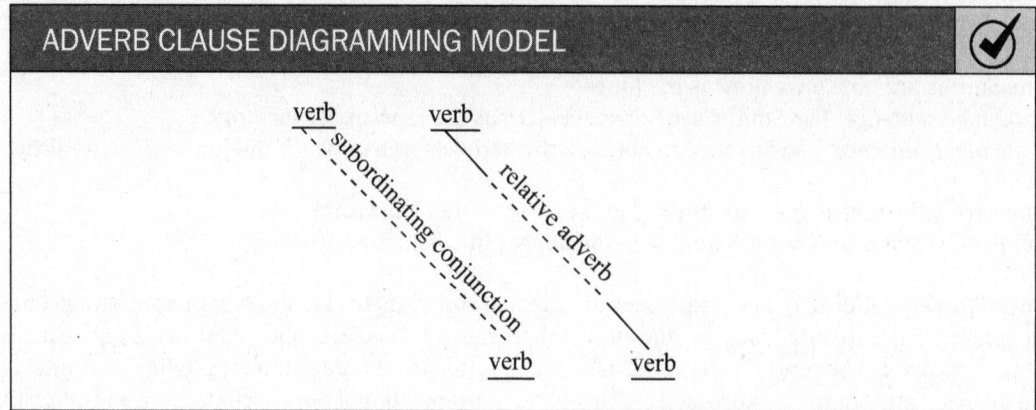

ADVERB CLAUSE DIAGRAMMING MODEL

Examples:

1. They want to climb Mt. Everest because it is the world's highest mountain.

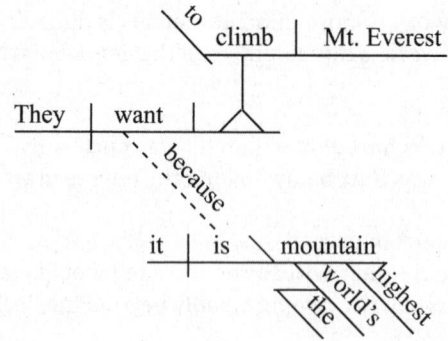

The subordinating conjunction "because" introduces a dependent clause. The infinitive phrase "to climb Mt. Everest" is a direct object. "Mountain" is a predicate nominative. "The" modifies "world's," not "mountain." (For example, in the phrase "my teacher's grade book," "my" modifies "teacher's," so it must follow that "the" would also modify "teacher's" if the phrase were changed to "the teacher's grade book.")

2. Although school had been dismissed early, we got home late.

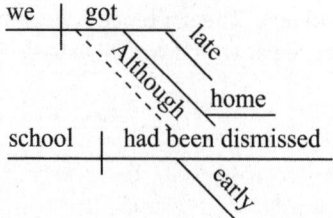

In sentence diagrams, dependent clauses are placed below independent clauses regardless of word order. "Home" is diagrammed as an adverbial objective here. It can also be construed and diagrammed as a simple adverb.

3. He finished planting the tree just when the rain began.

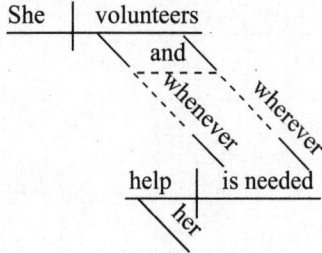

The solid lines at both ends of the broken line show that "when" modifies both "finished" and "began." The relative adverb "when" is modified by the adverb "just." The gerund phrase "planting a tree" functions as a direct object.

4. She volunteers whenever and wherever her help is needed.

The dependent clause is introduced by the compound relative adverb "whenever and wherever."

5. Although the store is closed on weekends, we will arrange to deliver on Saturdays if the customer agrees to pay a delivery charge.

This sentence has two subordinate clauses, each introduced by a subordinating conjunction. "Closed" is not a participle in this sentence but a simple adjective.

Diagramming Equal and Unequal Comparisons

ATTRIBUTIVE ADJECTIVE DIAGRAMMING MODELS

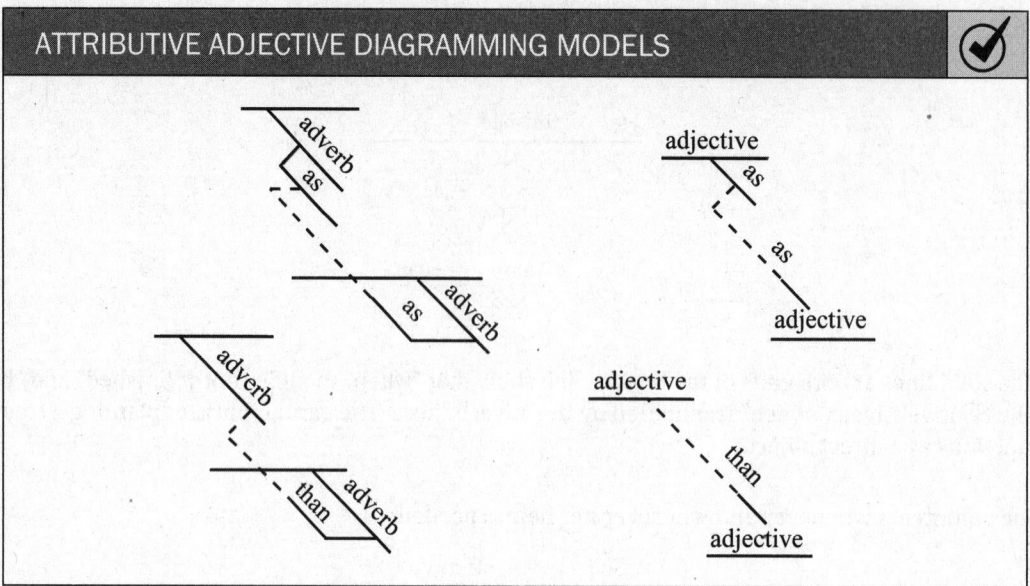

Examples:

1. This store is as large as that one.

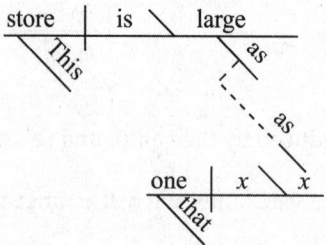

The sentence expresses an equal comparison. Like most comparative sentences, it is elliptical. The expanded sentence is "This store is as large as that one is large." The instances of "*x*" in the diagram represent the words "is" and "large." The sentence can be restated as "This store is large in the degree in which that store is large." The first adverb is a regular adverb; it modifies the first "large." The second "as" is a relative adverb. In the rephrased sentence, it is expressed by "in which," a prepositional phrase containing a relative pronoun.

2. My dog is friendlier than my cat.

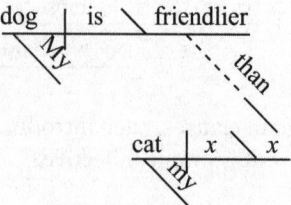

This sentence, which expresses an unequal comparison, is elliptical. The expanded sentence is "My dog is friendlier than my cat is friendly"; hence, the instances of "*x*" in the diagram represent the words "is" and "friendly." An equivalent sentence is "My dog is friendly beyond the degree in which my cat is friendly." "Than" is a relative adverb.

3. The tan chair is softer and more comfortable than the green one.

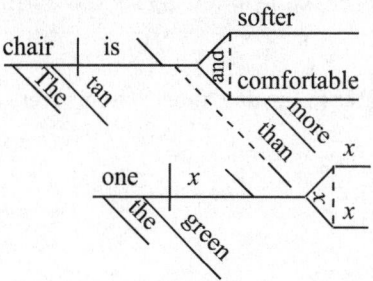

An equivalent sentence would be "The tan chair is soft and comfortable beyond the degree in which the green one is soft and comfortable." "Than" is a relative adverb.

4. The more time we have, the more time we seem to waste.

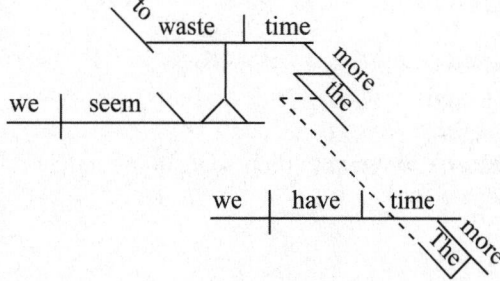

This sentence can be rephrased as "We seem to waste more time in the degree in which we have more time." "The" in "the more time we have" is a relative adverb, and "the" in "the more time we seem to waste" is a regular adverb.

5. I was so hungry that I ate ten pancakes.

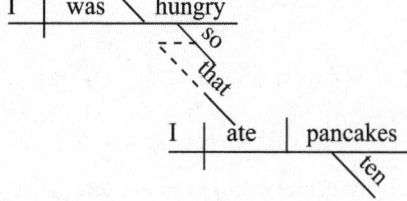

This sentence is equivalent to "I was hungry to the degree at which I ate ten pancakes." "So" is a regular adverb, and "that" is a relative adverb.

Adverb Clauses
Exercise 13

DIRECTIONS: Create a diagram for each of the following sentences. Answers are on page 582.

1. Although snow was expected later in the day, most schools were open.

2. She knows a lot about the world because she travels a lot.

3. When they entered the theater, they went to their seats immediately.

4. She arrived after the party had begun but before the food had been served.

5. Whenever she crossed the old bridge, she thought of a night many years ago.

6. The more it rains, the faster the grass grows.

7. It was so late that no more trick-or-treaters were expected.

8. After the guests arrive, but before the food is brought out, let's remind them of the reason for the party.

9. He is kinder and more generous than his sister.

10. When our family does a jigsaw puzzle, the children always put in more pieces than the parents.

ADJECTIVE CLAUSES

Adjective clauses are clauses that modify nouns or any words that substitute for nouns. There are two kinds of adjective clauses: those introduced by relative pronouns and those introduced by relative adverbs.

Relative Clauses

Adjective clauses introduced by relative pronouns (e.g., "who," "whom," "whose," "which," and "that," among other words) are called ***relative clauses***. Every relative pronoun has an antecedent (i.e., a preceding word or words to which the relative pronoun refers). A relative pronoun agrees with its antecedent in number and gender but not in case. It takes its case from its use in its own clause. A good understanding of this idea allows one to choose confidently between "who" and "whom."

Examples:

1. That is the man whom (or that) we saw at the game.

   ➢ The relative pronoun "whom" (or "that") is the direct object in its clause. "Man," the antecedent, is a predicate nominative. Careful speakers and writers do not use "who" in the objective case.

2. Do you know the person who (or that) wrote this book?

   ➢ The relative pronoun "who" (or "that") is the subject of its clause. Its antecedent, "person," is a direct object. One never uses "whom" in the nominative case.

3. They are the neighbors whose cat was stolen.

   ➢ "Neighbors," a predicate nominative, is the antecedent of "whose," a relative pronoun in the possessive case.

4. Distracted, Joe nearly pulled out in front of a fast-moving truck, which made him look twice at the next intersection.

   ➢ The antecedent of the relative pronoun "which" is not "truck" but the entire clause "he nearly pulled out in front of a fast-moving truck." In other words, it wasn't the truck itself but instead his experience of nearly pulling out in front of the truck that made him look twice at the next intersection. "Which" is the subject of the relative clause.

Sometimes, when the relative pronoun "whom" or "that" is a direct object or the object of a preposition, we omit it. Of the previous examples, only the first can be expressed without an expressed relative pronoun: "That is the man we saw at the game." Another example would be "Those are the tools I work with every day." In this sentence, the relative pronoun "that," the object of the preposition "with," is unexpressed.

The indefinite relative pronouns "whoever," "whomever," "whichever," and "whatever" (along with those with an inserted "so," such as "whosoever") ordinarily do not have expressed antecedents.

Examples:

1. "I'll give a bonus point to whoever can tell me what page we're on," said the frustrated French teacher.

   ➤ Many people, even many educated people, would say "whomever" here, thinking (incorrectly) that the indefinite relative pronoun is the object of the preposition "to." It isn't. The unexpressed antecedent "anyone" is the object of the preposition; "whoever" is the subject of the relative clause.

2. They plan to give the money to whomever they find in the shelter.

   ➤ This time "whomever" is correct because it is the direct object in its own clause. The object of the preposition "to" is the unexpressed antecedent "anyone."

The word "what" can mean "that which." When it does, it is considered a relative pronoun.

Example:

They did what the lieutenant ordered.

➤ In this sentence, an unexpressed "that," the direct object of the verb "did," is the antecedent of "what," a relative pronoun. "What" is the direct object of the verb "ordered."

Relative pronouns also agree with their antecedents in person. Notice the subject-verb agreement in the following:

Example:

You, who <u>are</u> my child, love me, and I, who <u>am</u> your father, love you.

Adjective Clauses Introduced by Relative Adverbs

Examples:

1. That is the reason why I was late.

   ➤ Since "why" is equivalent here to the prepositional phrase "for which," it is called a relative adverb. Notice that this sentence can be expressed without an expressed "why" (i.e., "That is the reason I was late.").

2. From here you can see the hospital where our children were born.

   ➤ "Where," a relative adverb, is equivalent to "in which."

3. Clayton remembers a time when candy bars cost five cents.

   ➤ The relative adverb "when" is equivalent to "at which."

Diagramming Adjective Clauses

In diagramming, one draws a broken line between a relative pronoun and its antecedent. Like all other dependent clauses, a relative clause is diagrammed below its main clause:

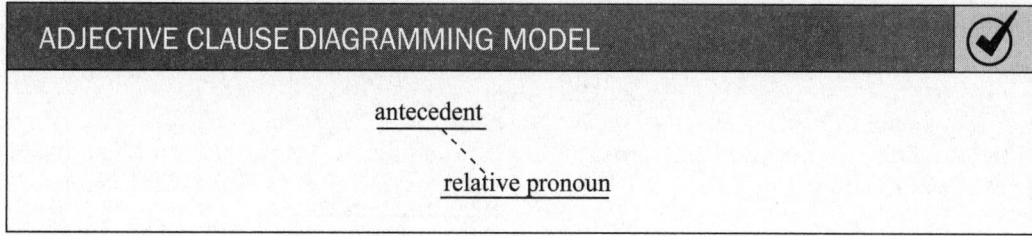

Examples:

1. I have to see the shipment that came in today.

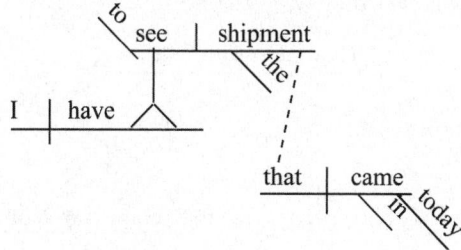

The relative pronoun "that" is the subject of its clause. Its antecedent, "shipment," is a direct object. "To see" is a complementary infinitive.

2. I know the person whose ring was stolen.

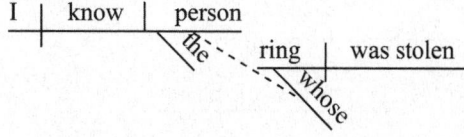

"Person," a direct object in its clause, is the antecedent of the possessive relative pronoun "whose."

3. That's the book that I've been waiting for.

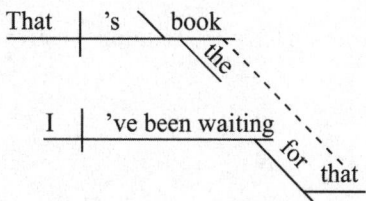

"That," the object of the preposition "for," is a relative pronoun. Its antecedent is "book," a predicate nominative. The second "that" could be omitted (i.e., "That's the book I've been waiting for."). In diagramming this sentence, one would represent the missing relative pronoun with an "*x*":

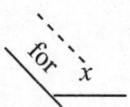

4. Tell whoever asks.

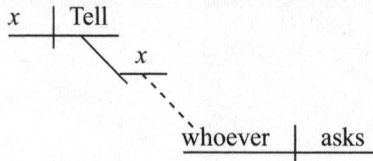

The first "*x*" stands for the unexpressed subject, "you." The second "*x*" stands for "anyone," the unexpressed antecedent of the indefinite relative pronoun "whoever."

5. They read into the text whatever they want to find.

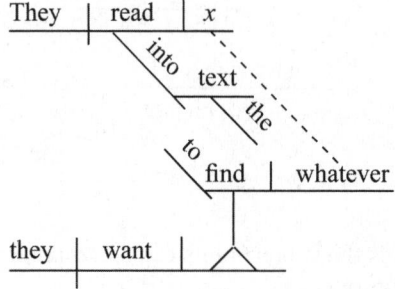

The indefinite relative pronoun "whatever" is equivalent to "anything that." The antecedent is represented in the diagram by an "*x*."

6. I know a place where we can have the reunion.

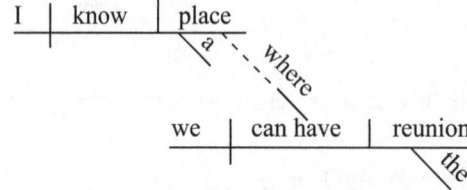

The adjective clause "where we can have the reunion" is introduced by the relative adverb "where" (the equivalent of "at which").

Adjective Clauses
Exercise 14

DIRECTIONS: Create a diagram for each of the following sentences. Answers are on page 585.

1. Choose carefully the person in whom you place your full trust.

2. The guy whose car is parked illegally may soon be looking for a ride.

3. The accident happened on the day they arrived in Miami.

4. The other prizes will be given to whoever answers correctly.

5. I have already told you the reason I can't be there.

NOUN CLAUSES

Noun clauses are clauses that function as nouns. Noun clauses are used as subjects, predicate nominatives, direct objects, objects of prepositions, adverbial objectives, and appositives. They may be introduced by the expletives "that," "whether," and "if" (in the sense of "whether"); by the interrogative pronouns "who," "whom," "whose," "which," and "what"; by the interrogative adjectives "which" and "what"; and by the interrogative adverbs "how," "when," "where," and "why." Some noun clauses have no special introductory word or words.

Noun Clauses Introduced by the Expletive "That"

Examples:

1. He knew that he had forgotten something.

   ➤ The noun clause "that he had forgotten something" functions as a direct object. The same sentence can be expressed without "that": "He knew he had forgotten something."

2. That they scored so few points is a source of great embarrassment to the team, which prides itself on its potent offense.

   ➤ The noun clause "that they scored so few points" is the subject of the sentence.

3. Why doesn't it bother the teacher that most of her students are talking?

   ➤ The noun clause "that most of her students are talking" serves as an appositive. It is in apposition with the subject "it."

4. The answer is that she encourages group work at certain times of the day.

   ➤ The noun clause "that she encourages group work at certain times of the day" is a predicate nominative.

5. I'm sorry that we can't wait that long.

   ➤ The noun clause "that we can't wait that long" functions as an adverbial objective. It modifies the predicate adjective "sorry." The same sentence can be expressed with an understood "that": "I'm sorry we can't wait that long."

Noun Clauses Introduced by the Expletives "Whether" and "If"

Examples:

1. Whether we succeed or not often depends on how much effort we are willing to expend.

   ➤ "Whether we succeed or not" is the subject of the sentence. "Whether or not" is a phrasal expletive.

2. Can you tell me if the Kramers live on this street?

    ➤ "If the Kramers live on this street" is a direct object. "If" can sometimes be used as an introductory expletive instead of "whether."

3. The big question was whether it was going to rain.

    ➤ The noun clause "whether it was going to rain" functions as a predicate nominative. "Whether" is an expletive.

4. The two brothers disagree about whether the pope is infallible.

    ➤ "Whether the pope is infallible," a noun clause, is used here as the object of the preposition "about."

Noun Clauses Introduced by Interrogative Words

Noun clauses can be introduced by interrogative pronouns, interrogative adjectives, and interrogative adverbs.

Examples:

1. Who was required to attend the meeting had never been clarified.

    ➤ The noun clause "who was required to attend the meeting" acts as the subject of the sentence. "Who" is an interrogative pronoun.

2. They asked what they could do to help and what tools were available.

    ➤ The noun clauses form a compound direct object. The first "what" is an interrogative pronoun, and the second "what" is an interrogative adjective.

3. We are puzzled about why we have to stay.

    ➤ The noun clause "why we have to stay" is the object of the preposition "about." "Why" is an interrogative adverb.

4. It is amazing how long she can remain under water.

    ➤ The noun clause "how long she can remain under water" is an appositive. It is in apposition with the subject of the sentence, "it." "How" is an interrogative adverb.

Diagramming Noun Clauses

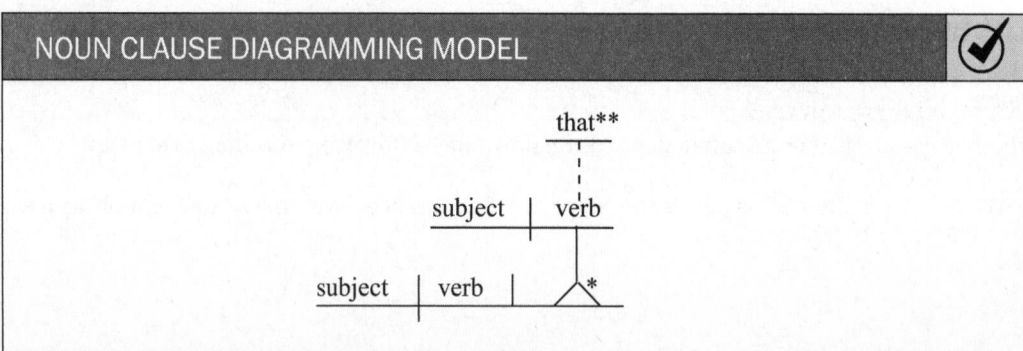

*This particular noun clause is a direct object; however, noun clauses can also function as subjects, predicate nominatives, objects of prepositions, appositives, and adverbial objectives.

**If the expletive "that" is unexpressed, an "*x*" represents it in a diagram. Other words that can introduce noun clauses are the expletives "whether" and "if" as well as interrogative pronouns, adjectives, and adverbs.

Examples:

1. The trouble is that she doesn't do her homework.

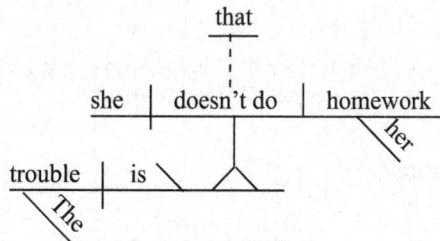

The noun clause "that she doesn't do her homework" functions as a predicate nominative. "That" is an expletive.

2. She wondered whether he was sorry he had hurt her.

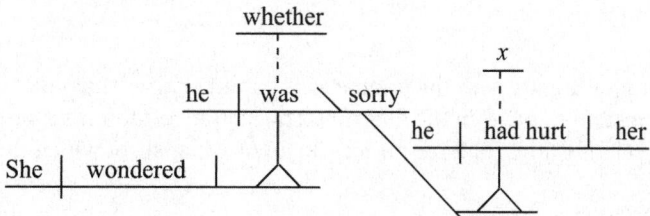

This sentence features a noun clause within a noun clause. The larger noun clause, "whether he was sorry he had hurt her," functions as a direct object. The smaller noun clause, "he had hurt her," is an adverbial objective. The expletive "that" is unexpressed. It is represented in the diagram by an "*x*."

3. Robert is always uncertain about which pages he should study.

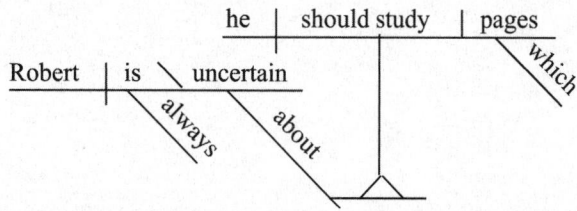

The noun clause "which pages he should study" is the object of the preposition "about." "Which" is an interrogative adjective.

4. It has never been disclosed why they did what they did.

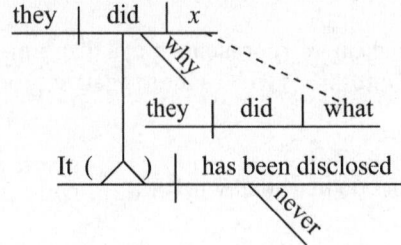

The noun clause "why they did what they did" is in apposition with the subject of the sentence, "it." The relative pronoun "what" is the equivalent of "that which."

5. You are not as big as you think.

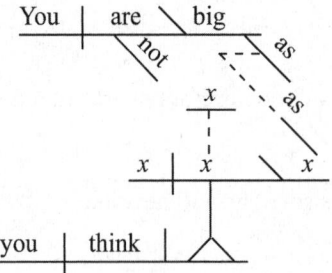

This elliptical sentence ends with the unexpressed noun clause "that you are big." These four words are represented by instances of "*x*" in the diagram. The sentence contains a so-called equal comparison. The second "as" is a relative adverb; it introduces an adverb clause, of which the unexpressed noun clause is a part.

Noun Clauses
Exercise 15

DIRECTIONS: Create a diagram for each of the following sentences. Answers are on page 587.

1. An unintended result of the experiment was that many birds died.

2. It is a widespread belief that poinsettias are poisonous.

3. The professor attempted to find out who damaged his car.

4. The station manager claimed to be uncertain as to why the station had lost so many listeners.

5. How many angels could fit on the head of a pin was a question that some medieval theologians are said to have found intriguing.

GLOSSARY OF GRAMMATICAL TERMS AND DIAGRAMMING SYMBOLS

Absolute phrase – a phrase that has a logical, but not a grammatical, connection to the rest of the sentence (see "nominative absolute").

Active voice – a characteristic of transitive verbs that indicates the relationship of the verb to the subject as doer or performer. A transitive verb is in the active voice when the subject of the sentence is the agent (i.e., when the subject is doing something).

Adjective – a word that modifies (qualifies, describes, limits) a noun, pronoun, or equivalent expression. Attributive adjectives and predicate adjectives are differentiated according to their position relative to the modified nouns and pronouns.

Adjective clause – a clause that functions as an adjective by modifying (qualifying, describing, limiting) a noun, pronoun, or equivalent expression. There are two types of adjective clauses: 1) relative clauses and 2) clauses linked to nouns in other clauses by means of a relative adverb.

Adverb – a word that modifies verbs, adjectives, other adverbs, prepositions, prepositional phrases, conjunctions, clauses, and sentences.

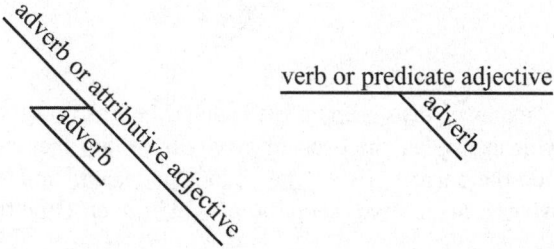

Adverbial objective – a noun or pronoun used as an adverb (indirect objects are included among adverbial objectives).

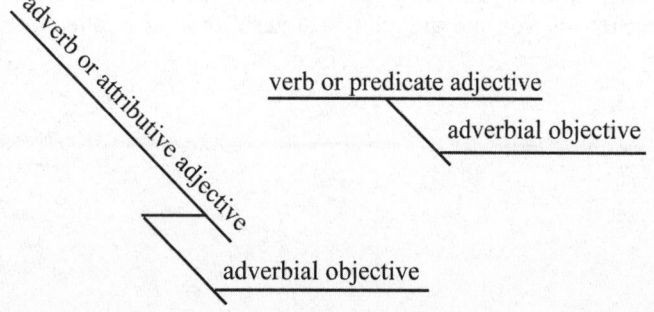

Antecedent – a word, phrase, or clause to which a pronoun refers (for which a pronoun stands).

Appositive – a word or group of words whose purpose is to identify or explain another word or group of words in the same sentence. The appositive usually follows the word(s) with which it is in apposition. Appositives can be restrictive or nonrestrictive. An example of a restrictive appositive is the word "John" in "his brother John." In this first example, there is more than one brother (e.g., "His brother John, his brother Sam, and his brother Will are all tall"); so, no comma is used between "brother" and "John." An example of a nonrestrictive appositive is the word "John" in "his brother, John" (e.g., "His brother, John, is a good man."). In this second example, John is the only brother, so a comma separates "brother" and "John."

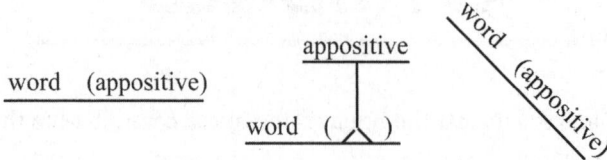

Article – definite ("the") and indefinite ("a," "an").

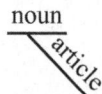

Attributive adjective – an adjective that either precedes the noun or pronoun it modifies (e.g., "a pleasant evening," "a certain someone") or comes immediately after it (e.g., "there will be time enough for that tomorrow" or "let's do something different").

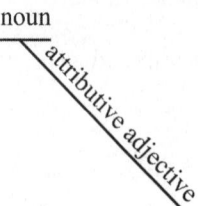

Auxiliary verb – a helping verb. Auxiliary verbs help to form such things as tense, voice, emphasis, and mood. They are underlined in the following examples: the present progressive "am seeing," "are seeing," and "is seeing"; the emphatic "do see" and "did see"; the perfect tenses "has seen," "had seen," and "will have seen"; the future "will see" and "shall see"; the passive "is seen," "was seen," and "will be seen"; and the modal forms "must see," "can see," and "may see."

Clause – a group of words with a subject and predicate.

Comparative degree – forms of adjectives and adverbs with the suffix "-(e)r" or with a preceding "more" (e.g., "larger," "more beautiful," "faster," and "more abundantly"). "Worse" is also an adjective of comparative degree. Comparisons using the comparative degree and the relative adverb "than" are called unequal comparisons.

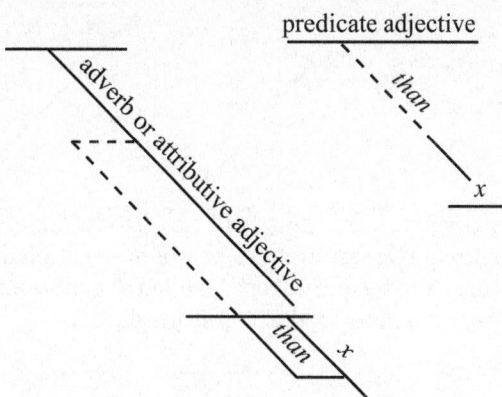

Complement – a term that includes subjective complement (predicate nominative and predicate adjective), direct object, indirect object, objective complement, and retained object.

Complementary infinitive – an infinitive used to complete certain verbs. The complementary infinitives are underlined in the following examples: "They ought <u>to study</u>," "She used <u>to collect</u> stamps," "I have <u>to prepare</u> a speech," "He is going <u>to announce</u> the winners," and "You are <u>to travel</u> to London."

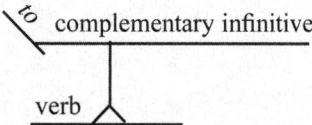

Complex sentence – a sentence containing at least one dependent (subordinate) clause.

Compound sentence – a sentence containing at least two independent (main) clauses.

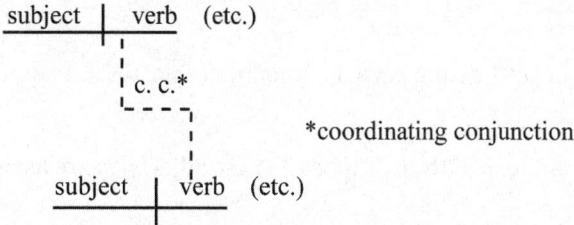

Compound-complex sentence – a sentence containing two or more independent (main) clauses and at least one dependent (subordinate) clause.

Conjunction – a word that connects words, phrases, and clauses. There are three kinds of conjunctions: coordinating conjunctions, subordinating conjunctions, and correlative conjunctions.

Conjunctive adverb – a word that connects (like a conjunction) and modifies (like an adverb). There are two kinds of conjunctive adverbs: transitional adverbs (e.g., "however," "moreover," "therefore," etc.) and relative adverbs (e.g., "when," "while," "where," etc.).

Coordinating conjunction – a word that connects words, phrases, and clauses of equal importance. The principal coordinating conjunctions are "and," "or," "but," and "nor." (See "compound sentence.")

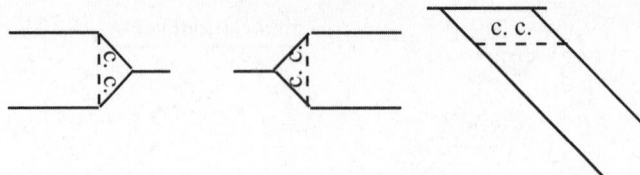

Correlative adverbs – the adverb pairs "as . . . as," "so . . . as," "so . . . that," "then . . . when," "there . . . where," and "the . . . the." Each of these adverb pairs can be restated as a pair of prepositional phrases, with the second of the two containing a relative pronoun (thus, the second adverb is called a relative adverb) and the first containing the antecedent (e.g., "as . . . as" can be restated as "in the degree in which").

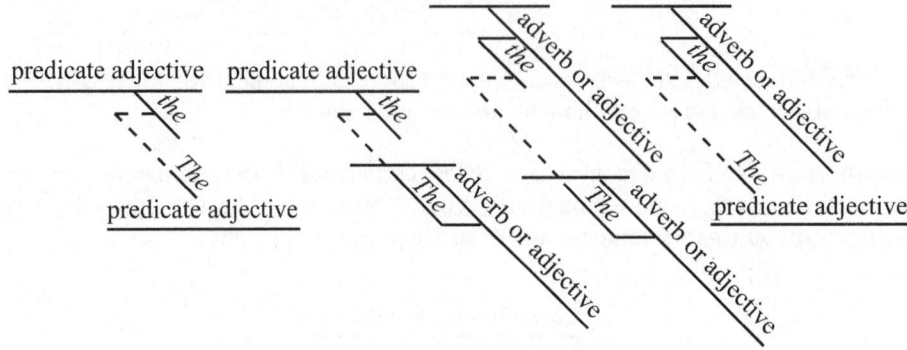

Correlative conjunctions – two-part conjunctions, such as "both . . . and," "either . . . or," and "neither . . . nor."

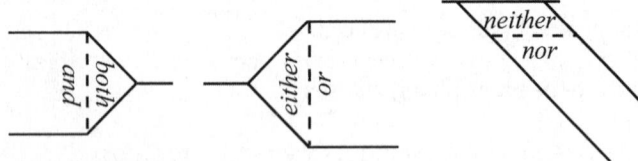

Definite article – English has only one definite article: "the." It designates the noun it modifies as specific or as previously mentioned.

Demonstrative adjective – "this," "that," "these," "those." These adjectives are used to point out someone or something.

Demonstrative pronoun – "this," "that," "these," "those." Like all pronouns, they are used as noun substitutes.

Dependent clause – also called a subordinate clause. A dependent clause functions as an adverb, an adjective, or a noun; it is dependent upon, or subordinate to, an independent (main) clause.

Direct address – a noun or phrase indicating the person(s) spoken to; sometimes called a vocative.

$$\frac{\text{vocative}}{\text{subject} \mid \text{verb}}$$

Direct object – a noun, pronoun, or equivalent expression that names the direct recipient of the action of a transitive verb. Not all sentences have direct objects. You can identify a direct object by asking "Whom?" or "What?" immediately after a non-linking verb.

Elliptical clause – a clause with an unexpressed, but understood, word or words. In diagrams, the variable *x* represents an unexpressed word or words.

Equal comparison – a comparison using the positive degree of the adjective or adverb and the correlatives "as ... as" or "so ... as."

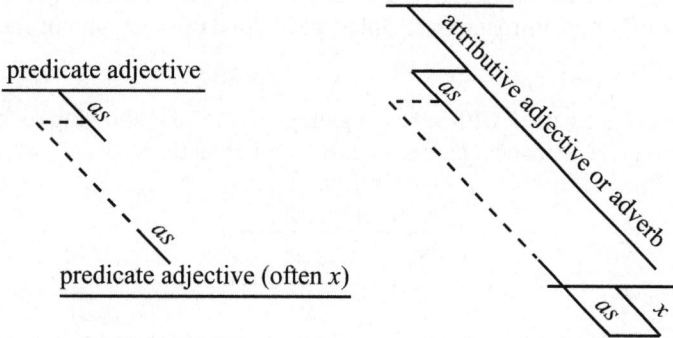

Expletive – a word with a function but with little or no meaning. For example, in the following sentences, "there," "that," and "whether" are expletives: "<u>There</u> is a cat on the roof." "Did you hear <u>that</u> the game has been canceled?" "I don't know <u>whether</u> she will be able to attend."

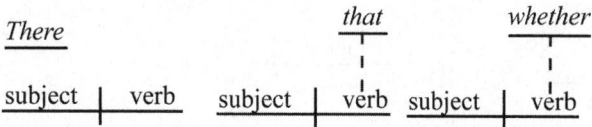

Factitive verb – a verb (such as "choose," "elect," "make," or "name") that is used to make someone or something someone or something else.

Finite verb – a verb that has person and number. Participles, gerunds, and infinitives are non-finite verbs.

Future tense – a tense that is formed by combining the auxiliary verbs "shall" and "will" with the present infinitive (without "to").

Future-perfect tense – a tense that is formed by combining the auxiliary verbs "shall" and "will" with the present-perfect infinitive (without "to").

Gerund – a verbal noun; a word ending in "-ing" that is both verb and noun.

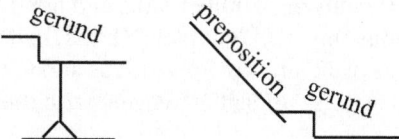

Imperative sentence – a sentence that expresses a command or a request. The subject, "you," is usually unexpressed.

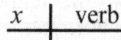

Indefinite article – English has only two forms of the indefinite article: "a" and "an."

Indefinite pronoun – a word like "each," "every," "enough," "much," "any," "either," and "some."

Indefinite relative pronoun – "whoever," "whomever," "whosever," "whichever," and "whatever," as well as "whosoever," "whomsoever," "whosesoever," "whichsoever," "whatsoever," and "what." Indefinite relative pronouns refer to unexpressed indefinite antecedents, such as "anyone" or "anything."

Independent expression – a word or group of words with no grammatical connection to the rest of the sentence. Independent expressions include vocatives, interjections, and nominative absolutes. Not only nouns, but also adverbs, infinitives, infinitive phrases, participles, participial phrases, and prepositional phrases can be used independently.

Indirect object – a noun or pronoun used with verbs of giving, saying, and showing to indicate to whom or for whom the direct object is intended. Indirect objects are adverbial objectives.

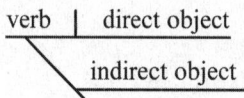

Indirect question – a question expressed as part of a sentence without the use of a question mark. The following sentences contain indirect questions: "He asked <u>why we were late</u>." "She wondered <u>if she had to go to school</u>." "The teacher wants to know <u>who said that</u>."

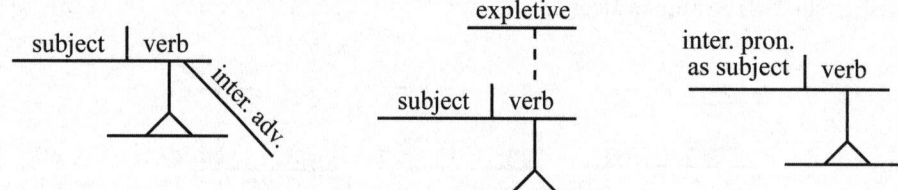

Infinitive – the basic form of any verb (usually preceded by the word "to"). Infinitives have tense and voice (present active, "to call"; present passive, "to be called"; present-perfect active, "to have called"; and present-perfect passive, "to have been called") as well as progressivity ("to be calling," "to have been calling"). Infinitives can function as adverbs ("they are running <u>to win</u>"), as adjectives ("you have nothing <u>to do</u>"), and as nouns ("we all want <u>to succeed</u>").

Infinitive phrase – an infinitive with its modifiers and objects. Like simple infinitives, infinitive phrases can be used as adverbs, adjectives, or nouns.

Intensive pronouns – pronouns that intensify or identify nouns and other pronouns. In form, they are indistinguishable from reflexive pronouns: "myself," "yourself," "himself," "herself," "itself," "ourselves," "yourselves," and "themselves." Intensive pronouns are appositives and are so diagrammed. Examples: "she <u>herself</u> made the dress" (or "she made the dress <u>herself</u>"), "we met with the manager <u>herself</u> to discuss the problem."

noun or pronoun   (intensive pronoun)

Interjection – a word or group of words with no grammatical connection to the rest of the sentence, used to express feeling or emotion (e.g., "wow," "holy Toledo," "for crying out loud," "hurrah").

interjection

subject | verb

Interrogative adjectives – adjectives used in direct and indirect questions: "which," "what."

Interrogative pronouns – pronouns used to ask direct and indirect questions: "who," "whom," "whose," "which," "what."

Intransitive verb – a verb that does not need a direct object. Some intransitive verbs are "go," "sleep," "grin," and "travel." Many intransitive verbs can also be transitive; for example, a tent can "sleep three people," a boss can "grin his approval," and one can "travel the world."

Linking verb – a verb that requires a predicate nominative or a predicate adjective for completion. The most common linking verb is "be," including the participles and gerunds "being" and "having been" as well as the finite forms "is," "am," "are," "was," "were," etc. Some other verbs that can be linking verbs are "seem," "become," "feel," "look," "remain," and "taste." Factitive verbs (e.g., "make," "call," "elect," etc.) can function in the passive voice as linking verbs: "He <u>was made</u> rich," "She <u>is called</u> Kathy," and "You <u>will be elected</u> president." Some scholars put the verb "be" in a category of its own and do not include it among the linking verbs.

Modal auxiliary – a verb used with a main verb to add a note of necessity, possibility, permissibility, or the like: "can," "could," "may," "might," "must," "should," "would."

Nominative absolute – a noun or noun substitute (also called a substantive noun) modified by a participle or a participial phrase and having no grammatical connection to the rest of the sentence. The participle "being" is sometimes unexpressed (e.g., "His money [being] safely in the bank, he relaxed at last").

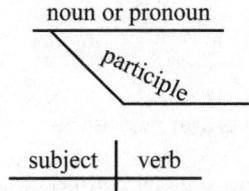

Noun – the name of anything (e.g., "Mr. Smith," "John," "woman," "principal," "student," "Atlanta," "country," "kindness," "hatred," "dawn," "darkness," "sound," "loudness," "lion," "lemur," "book," "computer," "alertness," "curiosity," "weight," "water," "wish," and thousands of others).

Noun clause – a clause that functions as a noun.

Noun phrase – a noun and its modifiers (including articles, adjectives, prepositional phrases, relative clauses, and infinitives).

Nouns as adjectives – a noun placed before another noun such that the former modifies the latter (e.g., "<u>wastepaper</u> basket," "<u>K-Mart</u> special," "<u>holiday</u> blues," "<u>cabin</u> fever").

Number – singular or plural. Nouns and pronouns have number (they are singular or plural), and so do verbs. The number of the subject of a sentence must agree with the number of the verb. If one says, "They eats later," one makes an agreement error involving number.

Objective complement – a noun, adjective, or equivalent expression (prepositional phrase, infinitive, infinitive phrase, participle, participial phrase, gerund, or gerund phrase) that completes the action of the verb and in some way either repeats (i.e., is identical with) or describes the direct object. Consider these sentences:

"They named their baby daughter <u>Estelle</u>."
"That makes me <u>angry</u>."
"We found the book <u>difficult</u>."
"I saw them <u>leaving</u>."
"The weather forced him <u>to stay at home</u>."
"She asked him <u>to help with the groceries</u>."

Most authorities agree that the first four sentences contain objective complements; however, there is significant disagreement concerning the last two. In this skills review, all underlined words above are considered objective complements. One way to recognize an objective complement, when it is a substantive, is this: if a verb seems to have two direct objects, and the first of the two is not an indirect object, then the second is an objective complement.

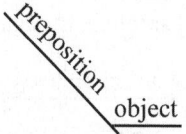

Object of a preposition – a noun or other substantive that follows a preposition and completes it. Without an object, a particle cannot be a preposition.

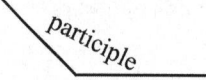

Participial phrase – a participle with its objects and modifiers

Participle – a verbal adjective. Transitive verbs have five different kinds of participles: present active ("giving," "speaking"), present passive ("being given," "being spoken"), present-perfect active ("having given," "having spoken"), present-perfect passive ("having been given," "having been spoken"), and past ("given," "spoken").

Particle – a subordinate word that is uninflected (i.e., does not change its form to reflect changes in tense, number, or the like). In English, nouns, pronouns, verbs, adjectives, and adverbs are inflected; prepositions, conjunctions, interjections, articles, and expletives are not.

Passive voice – a characteristic of transitive verbs that indicates the relationship of the verb to the subject as receiver of the action. A transitive verb is said to be in the passive voice when the subject of the sentence is acted upon (i.e., when something is done to the subject). (See "active voice.")

Past participle – a verb form used with various tenses of the verb "have" to form the perfect tenses (e.g., "driven," "called," "gone," and "seen").

Past tense – This tense is subdivided into three groups: (1) simple past (e.g., "saw," "gave," "hunted," "was (were) seen," "was (were) given," and "was (were) hunted"; (2) past progressive (e.g., "was (were) seeing," "was (were) giving," "was (were) hunting," "was (were) being seen," "was (were) being given," and "was (were) being hunted"; (3) emphatic past (e.g., "did see," "did give," and "did hunt."

Past-perfect tense – the tense in which verbs use "had" as an auxiliary verb (e.g., "had worked," "had been reading," "had been planted").

Person – an expression used to distinguish among the speaker (or writer), the person spoken (or written) to, and the person spoken (or written) about. There is first person ("I," "we"), second person ("you"), and third person ("he," "she," "it," "they"). The person of the subject must agree with the person of the verb. If one says, "I likes him," one makes an error in subject-verb agreement.

Personal pronouns – pronouns that denote person (first, second, third) and, in some instances, number (singular, plural), gender (masculine, feminine, neuter), and case (nominative, objective, possessive). There are nominative forms (e.g., "I," "you," "he," "she," "it," "we," and "they"), objective forms (e.g., "me," "you," "him," "her," "it," "us," and "them"), and possessive forms (e.g., "my," "mine," "your," "yours," "his," "her," "hers," "its," "our," "ours," "their," and "theirs").

Phrasal prepositions – prepositions that consist of more than one word (e.g., "out of," "because of," "instead of," "along with," "as for," "by means of," "in addition to," "in spite of," etc.).

Phrasal verb – a verb-particle combination with an idiomatic meaning such that the meaning cannot be known from the separate meanings of the verb and the particle (e.g., "she looked up the word" or "he carried out the command"). Notice that one cannot say "the word up which she looked" or "the command out which he carried," which shows that "up" and "out" are not prepositions here.

Phrase – a group of words in a sentence that forms a unit but that does not have a subject or a predicate.

Possessive – the inflected forms of nouns (e.g., "Mary's," "the workers'," "the men's") and pronouns (e.g., "my," "mine," "your," "yours," "his," "her," "hers," "its," "our," "ours," "their," "theirs") used to show possession or the idea of belonging to.

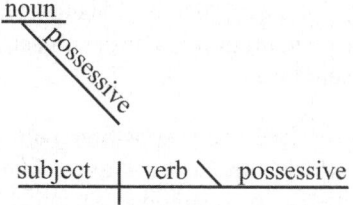

Predicate – the verb together with its modifiers and complements.

Predicate adjective – an adjective or equivalent expression that follows a linking verb and refers to the subject.

subject | linking verb \ predicate adjective

Predicate nominative – a substantive that follows a linking verb and refers to the subject.

subject | linking verb \ predicate nominative

Preposition – a particle that requires an object (noun, pronoun, or the equivalent) for completion. Prepositions usually precede their objects.

Prepositional phrase – a preposition with its object (including article and adjectives, if any). Prepositional phrases function as adverbs and as adjectives. (See "object of a preposition.")

Present participle – a verb form ending in "-ing" that can function (1) both as a verb and as an adjective (e.g., "a woman wearing a blue skirt," "lovers holding hands"); (2) as a verb only (e.g., "the deer were running through the woods," "we are planning a party"); (3) as an adjective only (e.g., "a sinking ship," "the loving mother").

Present-perfect tense – the tense in which verbs use "has" or "have" as an auxiliary verb (e.g., "has (have) held," "has (have) woven," "has (have) been holding," "has (have) been weaving," "has (have) been held," "has (have) been woven").

Present tense – This tense is subdivided into three groups: (1) simple present (e.g., "see," "give," "hunt," "am (are, is) seen," "am (are, is) given," and "am (are, is) hunted"); (2) present progressive (e.g., "am (are, is) seeing," "am (are, is) giving," "am (are, is) hunting," "am (are, is) being seen," "am (are, is) being given," and "am (are, is) being hunted"); (3) emphatic present (e.g., "do (does) see," "do (does) give," and "do (does) hunt").

Progressive verb forms – verb forms in various tenses used to show action going on or a state continuing. These forms occur in all six tenses of finite verbs (e.g., "is showing," "was showing," "will be showing," "has been showing," "had been showing," "will have been showing") and in the present and past tenses of the passive voice (e.g., "is being shown," "was being shown"). Infinitives have progressive forms in the present and present-perfect tenses (e.g., "to be showing," "to have been showing").

Pronoun – a word that takes the place of a noun. There are various kinds of pronouns: personal pronouns (e.g. "I," "you," "he," "she," "it," etc.); relative pronouns (e.g., "who," "whom," "whose," "which," "that," etc.); interrogative pronouns (e.g., "who," "whom," "whose," "which," "what"); demonstrative pronouns (e.g., "this," "that," "these," "those"); reflexive and intensive pronouns (e.g., "myself," "yourself," "himself," "herself," etc.); indefinite pronouns (e.g., "someone," "anyone," etc.); and reciprocal pronouns (e.g., "each other," "one another").

Reflexive pronoun – "myself," "yourself," "himself," "herself," "itself," "ourselves," "yourselves," "themselves." A reflexive pronoun can be used as a predicate nominative, a direct object, an indirect object, or an object of a preposition to refer to the subject of the sentence.

Relative adverb – an adverb that can be restated as a prepositional phrase containing a relative pronoun, or as two prepositional phrases, the second of which contains a relative pronoun. For example, "where" in the expression "the hotel where we are staying" can be restated as "in which"; similarly, "when" in the sentence "We can go when the light turns green" can be restated as "at the time at which." (See "correlative adverbs.")

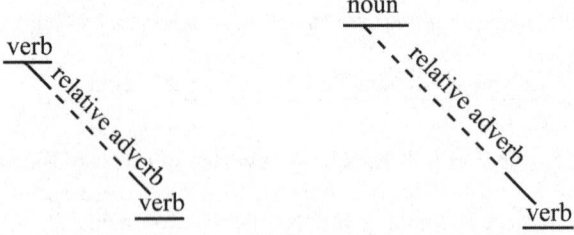

Relative clause – an adjective clause introduced by a relative pronoun. (See "relative pronoun.")

Relative pronoun – a pronoun that introduces a dependent clause and has an antecedent (a previously mentioned noun, pronoun, or the equivalent to which it refers) within the same sentence. The principal relative pronouns are "who," "whom," "whose," "which," and "that." Additional relative pronouns include the indefinite forms "what," "whoever," "whomever," "whosever," "whichever," "whatever," "whosoever," "whomsoever," "whosesoever," "whichsoever," and "whatsoever"; these have an unexpressed antecedent. "As" can be a relative pronoun (e.g., "He liked the same songs as his parents had liked when they were young.").

```
antecedent
        ⟍
         ⟍
         relative pronoun
```

Retained object – a direct object that continues to function as a direct object when the indirect object of a sentence in the active voice becomes the subject of a corresponding sentence in the passive voice. The retained object is underlined in the following example: "Someone gave the youngster a new baseball glove" (active). "The youngster was given a new baseball glove" (passive).

Sentence – an independent clause that begins with a capital letter and ends with a period, a question mark, or an exclamation point. (See "clause.")

Sentence modifier – a word, phrase, or clause that modifies an entire sentence or a major portion thereof, like a clause or an entire predicate.

Subject – a noun, pronoun, or equivalent word, phrase, or clause about which the sentence says something.

```
subject | verb
```

Subjective complement – a noun, adjective, or the equivalent of either, that completes a linking verb. Such substantives are called "predicate nominatives"; such adjectives and equivalent expressions are called "predicate adjectives."

Subjunctive mood – the modification of verbs used for contrary-to-fact conditions (e.g., "if she were here," "if I had a million dollars"), unreal wishes (e.g., "I wish I were an astronaut," "he wishes he could fly"), and indirect commands and suggestions (e.g., "she insists that he go along"), etc. (e.g., "Be it ever so difficult").

Subordinate clause – See "dependent clause."

Substantive – a noun or a noun substitute (such as a pronoun, adjective, phrase, or clause).

Tenses – present, past, future, present perfect, past perfect, future perfect. Tense has a lot to do with time but is not synonymous with it.

Transitional adverb – an adverb used to join clauses. Examples are "consequently," "furthermore," "however," "moreover," "nevertheless," "therefore," etc.

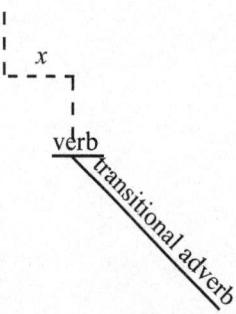

Transitive verb – a verb that needs a direct object for completion. (See "intransitive verb.")

Unequal comparison – (See "comparative degree," "equal comparison.")

Verb – a word expressing action or state. Most verbs end in "-s" in the third person singular of the simple present tense. An "-ing" ending is used to express verbs as participles and gerunds. The simple past of most verbs differs in form from the present tense, as does the past participle.

Verbals – non-finite verb forms: gerunds, participles, and infinitives.

Vocative – See "direct address."

Voice – a term that refers to the relation of the verb to the subject as doer of the action of the verb or as recipient of the action. A transitive verb is said to be either in the active voice (when the subject of the sentence is acting) or in the passive voice (when the subject is acted upon).

English/Writing
Mastery Test

ENGLISH/WRITING MASTERY TEST

54 Items

DIRECTIONS: In the following passages, certain words and phrases are underlined and numbered. In the right-hand column, alternatives for the underlined part are listed. Choose the one that best expresses the idea, makes the statement consistent with standard written English, or is most consistent with the style and tone of the entire passage. Choose "NO CHANGE" if you think the original version is best. Some items do not correspond to underlined parts but ask about a section of the passage or the passage as a whole. These items are identified by a number in a box.

For many of the items, you must read one or more sentences beyond the item to determine the answer. Be sure that you have read far enough ahead each time you choose an alternative. Once you have chosen the best alternative, fill in the corresponding oval on your answer sheet. Answers are on page 589.

Passage I

The History of Air Traffic Control

In the earliest days of aviation, there weren't very many aircraft <u>flying up there</u> in the skies.
1
So, at first, the rules for flying were brief and basic. For example, pilots were told not to begin their takeoff until other aircraft were <u>out</u> the way.
2

As traffic increased, however, airport operators

realized that such general rules were not <u>collision</u>
3
<u>preventing enough</u>. They began to use a form of air
3
traffic control based on visual signals. The early controllers stood on the field and waved flags to tell pilots what to do. <u>The very earliest person to pilot a</u>
4
<u>powered aircraft was Orville Wright.</u>
4

1. A. NO CHANGE
   B. flying up
   C. up flying
   D. OMIT

2. F. NO CHANGE
   G. out of
   H. of
   J. outside

3. A. NO CHANGE
   B. enough to prevent collisions
   C. preventing collisions enough
   D. to prevent enough collisions

4. The writer is considering deleting this sentence from the essay. Should the writer delete it?

   F. No, because the first flight in a powered aircraft was an event of historical significance.
   G. No, because some readers may not know that Orville Wright made the first flight in a powered aircraft.
   H. Yes, because the writer does not mention any other pilot by name anywhere else in the essay.
   J. Yes, because the information does not help the reader understand the system of visual signals.

In 1930, the first radio-equipped control tower was built in the United States. Within a few years, about 20 radio control towers were <u>operating, almost</u>
5
all airline aircraft were equipped with radio-telephone communication. Further increases in flights created a need for air traffic control not just in and around airports but also out along the airways. The major airlines <u>serving Chicago, Cleveland,</u> and
6
Newark opened the Airway Traffic Control Center at Newark. The early en route controllers tracked planes using maps and blackboards and little boat-shaped weights that came to be called "shrimp boats" by the controllers. 7 These early air traffic controllers had no direct radio link with aircraft but used telephones to stay in touch with airline dispatchers, airway radio operators, and airport traffic controllers. These individuals fed information to the en route controllers and also relayed their instructions to pilots.

The air traffic control system was originally private and under the direction of the airlines, but in 1941, Congress appropriated funds for the Civil Aeronautics Administration to construct and operate air traffic control towers. In response to wartime needs, the CAA greatly expanded its en route air traffic control system. After World War II, air traffic control became a permanent federal responsibility. 8

5. A. NO CHANGE
B. operating, and almost
C. operating almost
D. operational, almost

6. F. NO CHANGE
G. serving Chicago Cleveland
H. serving Chicago Cleveland,
J. serving, Chicago, Cleveland,

7. The writer is considering deleting the following phrase:

and little boat-shaped weights that came to be called "shrimp boats" by the controllers

Should the writer delete the phrase?

A. No, because the information is essential to the reader's understanding of the operation of the tracking system.
B. No, because the information provides an interesting detail about the operation of the early tracking system.
C. Yes, because the writer goes on to explain that the weights were replaced by a radar-based system.
D. Yes, because many readers may be confused by the reference to "boats" in a passage about airplanes.

8. The writer is thinking of adding the following sentence to the fourth paragraph after the second sentence.

During the war, women constituted well over 40 percent of the controller workforce.

Should the writer add the sentence?

F. Yes, because the sentence shows that women were an important part of the air controller workforce.
G. Yes, because the sentence presents a positive image of women in positions with important responsibilities.
H. No, because the makeup of the workforce is not relevant to shifting responsibility to the federal government.
J. No, because the writer does not discuss the number of men in various positions at any point in the essay.

The postwar years saw the beginning of a <u>totally</u>
₉
<u>rad</u> development in air traffic control: the
₉
introduction of radar. Originally developed by the British for military <u>defense, this</u> new technology
₁₀
allowed controllers to see the position of aircraft tracked on video displays.

In the 1960s, new rules required planes to carry a radar beacon called a transponder that identified the aircraft and helped to improve radar performance. Pilots were also required to fly on instruments regardless of the weather and to remain in contact with controllers. The Federal Aviation Administration also standardized the settings for the new all-weather instruments, created navigation checkpoints, and established a Central Flow Control Facility. In 1994, the FAA opened a new Air Traffic Control System Command Center with advanced equipment. 11

Today, air traffic control monitors the movements of all aircraft. In flight, an aircraft follows en route air traffic control instructions. When it approaches an airport for <u>landing, the</u>
₁₂
aircraft enters the terminal control area where it is monitored by controllers using radar and who constantly tell pilots how to navigate within the area. Finally, the controllers tell the pilots how to reach their final location where the passengers will disembark. 13

9. A. NO CHANGE
B. rad
C. dramatic
D. totally dramatic

10. F. NO CHANGE
G. defense, and this
H. defense this
J. defense. This

11. The writer wishes to add the following sentence to paragraph six:

Together, all of these changes contributed greatly to the safety of the skies.

The most logical place for the additional sentence is:

A. after the first sentence.
B. after the second sentence.
C. after the third sentence.
D. after the fourth sentence.

12. F. NO CHANGE
G. landing the
H. landing, and the
J. landing. The

13. The writer wishes to add the following sentence to the final paragraph:

Controllers also monitor the aircraft all the way to the ground and tell the pilots how to maneuver on the ground to avoid collisions on the airfield.

The most logical place for the sentence is:

A. after the first sentence.
B. after the second sentence.
C. after the third sentence.
D. after the fourth sentence.

14. The writer is considering adding a subtitle to the title "A History of Air Traffic Control" that would summarize the main theme of the essay. Which of the following statements would best accomplish that purpose?

F. The Development of Radar
G. A Study in Government Inaction
H. From Flags to Electronics
J. The Dangers of Uncontrolled Air Space

Passage II

The Building of the Capitol

On September 18, 1793, George Washington laid the cornerstone for the foundation of the U.S. Capitol. <u>A celebration marked the event big time.</u>
15
President Washington and a company of volunteer artillery from Alexandria crossed the Potomac River and joined <u>to</u> Masonic Lodge members from
16
Virginia, Maryland, and the Federal City, later named Washington, D.C. They marched to the beating of drums and the cheering of spectators with the colors flying to the Capitol site about a mile and a half away. Following the laying of the <u>cornerstone ceremony, the</u> festivities included a
17
barbecue that continued until after dark.

The Capitol is the home of the U.S. Congress, which consists of the House of Representatives and the Senate. The competition for its design was won by Dr. William Thornton, a gifted amateur architect who had studied medicine. <u>Dr. Thornton, however,</u>
18
<u>rarely practiced medicine as a doctor.</u> Thornton
18
placed a shallow domed rotunda <u>centrally in the</u>
19
<u>middle</u> between the Senate (north) and House
19
(south) wings.

Construction proceeded slowly with a series of architects <u>who followed one after another</u>. James
20
Hoban<u>, the architect of the White House,</u> completed
21
the Senate wing in 1800. His successor, Benjamin Henry Latrobe, completed the House wing in 1803.

15. A. NO CHANGE
B. A celebration marked the event, big time.
C. A big celebration marked the event.
D. Marking the event big time was a celebration.

16. F. NO CHANGE
G. up
H. onto
J. with

17. A. NO CHANGE
B. cornerstone ceremony. The
C. cornerstone, ceremony the
D. cornerstone. The ceremony

18. F. NO CHANGE
G. Dr. Thornton, a doctor, rarely practiced medicine, however.
H. As a doctor, Dr. Thornton rarely practiced medicine, however.
J. OMIT

19. A. NO CHANGE
B. centrally in the middle in
C. in the middle centrally
D. centrally

20. F. NO CHANGE
G. after another
H. one another
J. OMIT

21. The writer is thinking of deleting the underlined phrase. If the phrase is deleted, what information will be lost from the paragraph?

A. James Hoban designed another famous building.
B. The Capitol was designed by a series of architects.
C. British forces nearly destroyed the Capitol in 1814.
D. The Capitol was completed according to plan in 1826.

Then, in 1814, British troops set fire to the Capitol as well as the White House and other District buildings during the War of 1812. Fortunately, a rainstorm prevented the fire from <u>completely</u>
                                                    22
<u>destructing</u> the Capitol. Charles Bulfinch, the
   22
brilliant Boston architect <u>who succeeded Latrobe in</u>
                                               23
<u>1818,</u> completed the building in 1826 with only
   23
slight modifications of Latrobe's interior plan.

By 1850, the number of states in the union had more than <u>doubled, as had</u> the number of members of
                                          24
Congress. Instead of 30 senators, there were <u>now 62,</u>
                                                              25
<u>the</u> House had grown from 69 representatives to 233.
 25
With Congress expanding so rapidly, it was obvious that the building was too small.

In 1850, President Millard Fillmore selected architect Thomas U. Walter to construct large northern and southern wings containing new legislative chambers. <u>Fillmore had the first bathtub</u>
                                                               26
<u>installed in the White House.</u> As work progressed,
   26
Walter also designed a new cast-iron dome <u>to better suit the larger building.</u> By 1868
                                          27
it was completed, and the grounds were subsequently enlarged.

22. F. NO CHANGE
  G. completely destroying
  H. destructing completely
  J. the complete destruction of

23. The writer is considering deleting the phrase:

who succeeded Latrobe in 1818

If the writer deletes this phrase, what information will be lost from the paragraph?

  A. The name of the architect who finally completed the building of the Capitol
  B. The date that construction of the Capitol was finally completed
  C. The fact that no architect worked on the Capitol between Latrobe and Bullfinch
  D. The fact that the Capitol was completed substantially according to Latrobe's plan

24. F. NO CHANGE
  G. doubled. As had
  H. doubled. So too
  J. double, as

25 A. NO CHANGE
  B. now 62 the
  C. now 62, and the
  D. now 62 with the

26. F. NO CHANGE
  G. (Fillmore had the first bathtub installed in the White House.)
  H. He was the one who installed the first bathtub in the White House.
  J. OMIT

27. The writer is considering deleting the phrase:

to better suit the larger building

If the writer deletes this phrase, what information will be lost from the paragraph?

  A. The reason for designing a new dome
  B. The reason for enlarging the building
  C. The name of the designing architect
  D. The completion date of the renovation

The nation and its government, however, continued to grow; and in 1897 the Library of Congress moved out of the Capitol into its own building, making space for new committee rooms. In the twentieth century, separate buildings were constructed to provide offices and committee rooms for the House and Senate. The Supreme Court moved into its own building in 1935. [28]

28. The writer is considering adding the following sentence to the essay:

Today's Capitol complex includes the Capitol, six major House and Senate buildings, three Library of Congress buildings, the Supreme Court Building, the U.S. Botanic Garden, and other facilities.

What would be the most appropriate place for the new sentence?

F.   The first sentence of the essay
G.   The last sentence of paragraph two
H.   The last sentence of paragraph four
J.   The last sentence of paragraph six

29. Suppose the writer's assignment had been to write a short essay about the way that laws are made by the Congress. Would this essay successfully fulfill that assignment?

A.   No, because the essay is mainly about the design and building of the Capitol.
B.   No, because the essay is mainly about the lives of the architects who designed the Capitol.
C.   Yes, because the essay mentions that the Congress has both a Senate and a House of Representatives.
D.   Yes, because the essay describes how the number of members of Congress has increased.

Passage III

African-American Troops During the Civil War

When the Civil War began, Jacob Dodson, a free black man living in Washington, D.C., wrote to Secretary of War Simon Cameron and informed him that he knew of "300 reliable colored free citizens" who wanted to enlist and defend the city. Cameron replied that "this department has no intention at present to call into the service of the government any colored soldiers." It didn't matter that black men, slave and free, had served in colonial militias and had fought on both sides of the Revolutionary War. [30]

On March 31, 1862, Union troops commanded by General David Hunter took control of the islands off the coasts of <u>Georgia, and South</u> Carolina.
31
<u>Fort Sumter in Charleston Harbor in South Carolina,</u>
32
<u>where the war began, was not even finished when</u>
32
<u>the first shots were fired.</u> Local whites who owned
32
the rich cotton and rice <u>plantations, and they fled</u> to
33
the Confederate-controlled mainland. Most of their slaves remained on the <u>islands, and they</u> soon were
34
joined by black escapees from the mainland. Hunter needed more soldiers to control the region's many tidal rivers and islands against guerrilla <u>resistance,</u>
35
<u>so reasoned</u> that the African Americans who lived in
35
the area and were familiar with local conditions would be <u>an awesome</u> solution.
36

30. If the writer were to substitute paraphrases for the quotations in paragraph one, the paragraph would primarily lose:

   F. wording that adds detail to the historical context of the essay.
   G. evidence that black soldiers fought effectively in the Civil War.
   H. details about the battles that included black Civil War soldiers.
   J. descriptions of heroic acts by African-American soldiers.

31. A. NO CHANGE
   B. Georgia and South
   C. Georgia and, South
   D. Georgia and South,

32. F. NO CHANGE
   G. Fort Sumter, South Carolina, in Charleston Harbor was where the first shots of the war were fired and was not even finished.
   H. Not even finished at the time the first shots were fired, Fort Sumter in Charleston, South Carolina Harbor was where the war began.
   J. OMIT

33. A. NO CHANGE
   B. plantations and they fled
   C. plantations, they fled
   D. plantations fled

34. F. NO CHANGE
   G. islands, they
   H. islands and they,
   J. islands and, they

35. A. NO CHANGE
   B. resistance, the reason
   C. resistance, and he reasoned
   D. resistance, reasoning

36. F. NO CHANGE
   G. a dynamite
   H. a cool
   J. an excellent

Hunter, <u>a staunch abolitionist</u>, recruited black
                    37
men capable of bearing arms as Union soldiers. He
was planning to form the first all-black regiment of
the Civil War, but when President Abraham Lincoln
heard about the plan, it came to an end. Though
Lincoln <u>opposed slavery he</u> was afraid of moving
              38
more quickly than public opinion in the embattled
North would allow. In an angry letter, the president
ordered Hunter to disband the regiment.

Yet in August 1862, two weeks after Hunter
had dismantled his regiment, the War Department
allowed General Rufus Saxton to raise the Union
Army's first official black regiment, the First South
Carolina Volunteers. This and other black regiments
organized in the coastal regions successfully
defended and held the coastal islands for the
duration of the war.

By the fall of 1864, some 140 black regiments
had been raised in many northern states and in
southern territories captured by the Union. About
180,000 African Americans served during the Civil
War, including more than 75,000 northern black
volunteers. Although the black regiments were
segregated from their white counterparts, they
fought the same battles. Black troops performed
bravely and successfully even though they coped
with both the Confederate enemy and the suspicion
of some of their Union military colleagues.

Despite these handicaps, the United States
Colored Troops participated <u>for</u> 449 military
                                    39
engagements, 39 of them major battles. More than a
dozen USCT soldiers were given <u>the award of</u> the
                                          40
Congressional Medal of Honor for bravery.

37. The main purpose of the underlined phrase is
to:

A. explain why so many African-Americans
   wished to enlist.
B. cast light on Hunter's motivation for
   organizing black troops.
C. question Hunter's ability to lead African-
   American troops.
D. show the strategic importance of Hunter's
   position.

38. F. NO CHANGE
     G. opposed, slavery he
     H. opposed slavery, he
     J. OMIT

39. A. NO CHANGE
     B. by
     C. with
     D. in

40. F. NO CHANGE
     G. the awarding of
     H. and awarded
     J. OMIT

41. The writer is thinking of adding the following
sentence to the essay:

*It was not until 1865, the year the war ended,
that Congress passed a law providing equal pay
for black soldiers.*

This sentence would be most logically placed
after the last sentence of the:

A. third paragraph.
B. fourth paragraph.
C. fifth paragraph
D. sixth paragraph.

42. If a student were researching a term paper and
wanted to find this essay, what would be the
mostly likely place to look for it?

F. An army manual on military strategy
G. A book on important Civil War battles
H. A history of African-Americans in the
   military
J. A compilation of narratives of enslaved
   African-Americans

43. If the writer had been asked to write an essay on the causes of the Civil War, would this essay fulfill that assignment?

A. No, because an essay on the cause of the war would not discuss the early stages of the war.

B. No, because the essay focuses upon the role of African-American soldiers during the war.

C. Yes, because the essay discusses slavery, one of the most important issues debated before the Civil War.

D. Yes, because the essay explains that Lincoln was constrained by public opinion in the North.

Passage IV

Protesting for the Vote

On Monday, March 3, 1913, there was a big parade down Pennsylvania Avenue in Washington, D.C., to protest in favor of the cause of suffrage for women. The parade was led by a lawyer in front, Inez Milholland. She wore a white cape and rode a white horse. Stretched out behind her was a long line including nine bands, four mounted brigades, three heralds, about twenty-four floats, and more than 5,000 marchers.

Women from countries that had already enfranchised women occupied the place of honor in the first section. Then came the "Pioneers" who had been struggling for so many decades to secure women's right to vote. The next sections celebrated working women, who were grouped by occupation. There were nurses in uniform, women farmers in work clothes, homemakers in aprons, women doctors and pharmacists in lab coats, and college women in academic gowns. The state delegations followed. People had come from around the country to march in protest against the existing political organization of society which excluded women. 46

Everything went well for the first few blocks, but then the crowd of spectators, mostly men in town for Wilson's inauguration the next day, pushed into the street making it almost impossible for the marchers to pass. Women were jeered, tripped, grabbed, and shoved. The men made crude remarks and were totally uncool. The police seemed to enjoy the jokes and laughter, and some even participated. The men in the procession heard shouts of "Henpecked" and "Where are your skirts?" The spectators seemed to think the heckling was great fun.

To the women, however, the harassment was very serious. Helen Keller was so exhausted and unnerved by the experience that she was unable to give her speech scheduled for later at Continental Hall. In 1962, they made a movie about Helen Keller's life called "The Miracle Worker."

44. F. NO CHANGE
G. in the front
H. out in front
J. OMIT

45. A. NO CHANGE
B. with
C. over
D. against

46. If the writer wanted to add the sentence below to paragraph two:

Finally, there was the separate section for male supporters of women's suffrage.

The most appropriate place for the sentence would be immediately after:

F. sentence 2.
G. sentence 3.
H. sentence 5.
J. sentence 6.

47. A. NO CHANGE
B. and were being totally uncool
C. and acted totally uncool
D. OMIT

48. F. NO CHANGE
G. until
H. by
J. since

49. The writer is considering deleting the underlined sentence. The writer:

A. should not delete the sentence because the movie establishes that Helen Keller was a famous person.
B. should not delete the sentence if the protest of March 13, 1913, was also included in a scene in the movie.
C. should delete the sentence because Helen Keller was prevented from actually making the speech.
D. should delete the sentence because a movie made nearly 50 years later is irrelevant to the events of March 13, 1913.

Two ambulances came and went constantly for six hours. The emergency vehicles were always impeded and at times actually prevented from getting through the crowd. One hundred marchers had to be <u>hurriedly</u> rushed to the local emergency
50
hospital.

Despite the enormous difficulties, most of the marchers in the parade completed the route. When the procession reached the Treasury Building, one hundred women and children presented a tableau written especially for the event to show the ideals towards which both men and women have been struggling through the ages. The pageant began with "The Star-Spangled Banner." The impressive figure of Columbia dressed in red, white, and blue emerged from behind the huge columns at the top of the Treasury Building steps. Charity came next. Liberty followed with the band playing a triumphal march, and a dove of peace was released. In the final tableau, Columbia, surrounded by Justice, Charity, Liberty, Peace, and Hope, all in flowing robes and colorful scarves with trumpets sounding, stood to watch the oncoming procession. *The New York Times* described the pageant as "one of the most impressively beautiful spectacles ever staged in this country."

During all of this, president-elect Wilson and the presidential party arrived <u>to</u> the railway station
51
a few blocks away. A member of Wilson's staff asked "Where are all the people?" And a policeman said, "Watching the big show."

50. F. NO CHANGE
G. in a hurry
H. hurrily
J. OMIT

51. A. NO CHANGE
B. at
C. for
D. with

52. The author is considering adding the following sentence to the essay:

Before the afternoon was over, Secretary of War Henry L. Stimson, responding for a request from the chief of police, authorized the use of a troop of cavalry from nearby Fort Myer to help control the crowd.

The sentence would most logically be added to Paragraph:

F. 1.
G. 2.
H. 3.
J. 4.

53. If the writer had been asked to write a piece about an important event in the movement for women's suffrage, would this essay be acceptable?

A. Yes, because the event was attended by thousands of people and received national press coverage.
B. Yes, because the event coincided with the scheduled inauguration of President-elect Wilson.
C. No, because the event triggered a violent counter-demonstration by those who opposed suffrage.
D. No, because the parade ended at the Treasury Building rather than some more important location.

54. Which of the following statements most effectively summarizes the essay as a whole?

F. Women from many different walks of life wanted the vote and participated in the suffrage movement.

G. The March 3, 1913, parade for women's suffrage was a dramatic event that publicized the cause of women's suffrage.

H. The women who protested on behalf of women's suffrage often used parades and entertainment to rally support.

J. Most men in the United States during the early 1900s were opposed to granting women the right to vote.

Vocabulary Skills Review

Course Concept Outline

I. Building Vocabulary with Sentence Completions (p. 207)

   A. Sentence Completion Difficulty Factors (p. 208)

      1. Vocabulary (p. 208)
      2. Complexity (p. 209)

   B. Sentence Completion Strategies (p. 210)

      1. Anticipation (p. 210)
      2. Analysis (p. 211)
      3. Substitution (p. 212)

   Exercise 1—**Anticipating Sentence Completions** (Items #1–20, pp. 213–215)

   Exercise 2—**Analyzing Sentence Completions** (Items #1–20, pp. 216–218)

   Exercise 3—**Substituting Sentence Completions** (Items #1–17, pp. 219–220)

   Exercise 4—**Building Vocabulary with Sentence Completions** (Items #1–40, pp. 221–226)

II. Building Vocabulary Through Context (p. 227)

   Exercise 5—**Building Vocabulary Through Context** (Items #1–10, pp. 228–229)

   Exercise 6—**Vocabulary Builder: Prose Fiction Passages** (Items #1–45, pp. 230–238)

   Exercise 7—**Vocabulary Builder: Social Science Passages** (Items #1–90, pp. 239–255)

   Exercise 8—**Vocabulary Builder: Humanities Passages** (Items #1–75, pp. 256–269)

   Exercise 9—**Vocabulary Builder: Natural Science Passages** (Items #1–90, pp. 270–286)

BUILDING VOCABULARY WITH SENTENCE COMPLETIONS

This Vocabulary Skills Review can be used either in preparation for a specific exam or as a general tool for building vocabulary and reading skills. Whether your objective is to perform well on an exam or to improve your vocabulary and reading skills, you will find the exercises in this review useful.

A good way to build your vocabulary and reading skills is with *sentence completion* items. These items will help to improve your knowledge of sentence structures, transitions, logic, and vocabulary. Sentence completions are also called *completions* or *fill-in-the-blanks.*

Studies have shown that people don't need to hear every word that is said in order to understand the point of what was said. If you think about it, these findings make sense. For example, you could be talking to someone on a cell phone in an area with poor reception and hear: "On your way back to the house, please pick up a medium ------- with mushrooms on it but no anchovies." The most important word in the sentence is missing, but you understand that you're supposed to pick up a pizza. Of course, most sentence completions are not so simple. Consider the following examples of sentence completions:

Examples:

1. To compensate for the funds that will no longer be available due to a decline in the value of the endowment's portfolio, the university will need to find an ------- sum from another source.

    A. anticipated
    B. equivalent
    C. unofficial
    D. unstated
    E. inconsequential

    (B) is the correct answer choice. Since funds will no longer be available from the present source, it will be necessary to replace those funds: to do so, the university will need to find an equivalent sum from another source.

2. Although the mobster's efforts to appear mentally unstable and therefore unable to stand trial were ------- and even -------, the defense lawyers, through clever strategies, were able to postpone the criminal proceedings for several years.

    A. unrelenting .. predictable
    B. contrived .. convincing
    C. unpersuasive .. ludicrous
    D. predictable .. amusing
    E. ill-advised .. heroic

(C) is the correct answer choice. The "were ------- and even -------" tells you that the second substitution word makes a more extreme statement than the first. Also, the conjunction "although" at the beginning of the sentence tells you that the substitutions describe an effort that seemed unlikely to work, but that in fact resulted in partial success for the lawyers.

Sentence Completion Difficulty Factors

There are two difficulty factors involved in every sentence completion item. The first factor is vocabulary. The second factor is complexity or sentence structure.

Vocabulary

Vocabulary can determine if a sentence completion item is easy or difficult. Compare the two sets of answer choices that follow each of the item stems in the following examples:

Examples:

1. After working together for several years, members of the crew had developed specialized terms for the tools they used, a(n) ------- only they could understand.

A.	procedure	vs.	A. procedure
B.	custom		B. custom
C.	jargon		C. argot
D.	appetite		D. appetite
E.	rhythm		E. rhythm

   (C) is the correct answer in both sets of answer choices. A specialized vocabulary is called "jargon" or, less commonly, "argot." Although (C) is the answer in both cases, the difficulty level is not the same for the two sets of answer choices. The second set of answer choices is more difficult because "argot" is a less familiar word. So, the difficulty of a sentence completion item can depend upon the vocabulary in the answer choices.

2. Awed by the credentials of the reviewing committee, the doctoral candidate set forth the central thesis of the paper tentatively and answered questions with -------.

A.	confidence	vs.	A. aplomb
B.	delight		B. relish
C.	uncertainty		C. diffidence
D.	recklessness		D. abandon
E.	directness		E. imperviousness

   (C) is the correct answer in both sets of answer choices. The candidate was awed and set forth the argument tentatively (i.e., not confidently). We can logically assume that the candidate would answer questions in a similar manner, so "uncertainty" is the best word to complete the sentence. Similarly, "diffidence" would also be the best answer here since it means "reserve, shyness, or modesty." Again, although (C) is the answer in both cases, the difficulty level is not the same for the two sets of answer choices. Note too that all of the answer choices in the second column are expressed in less familiar vocabulary. As you can see, an entire set of answer choices that consists of more difficult vocabulary words makes for an even more difficult item.

Complexity

Sentence structure can also determine if a sentence completion item is easy or difficult. In short, more difficult items will involve more difficult sentence structures. Compare the following two item stems:

Example:

Every society has a concept of justice, but what counts as a just or an unjust act is -------.

vs.

The concept of justice is universal, found in every society from the most primitive to the most advanced; but the actions to which these terms attach are -------.

A. variable
B. laudable
C. foreseeable
D. crucial
E. implicit

(A) is the correct answer choice in both cases. In either sentence, the "but" sets up a contrast between an idea in the first part of the sentence and an idea in the second part of the sentence. The important idea in the first part is universality, so the important idea in the second part must be the opposite (i.e., uniqueness or variability).

Of course, the most difficult sentence completion items will include unfamiliar vocabulary as well as a complex sentence structure. Consider the following example, which is presented with two different sentence structures and sets of answer choices:

Example:

Although the Best in Show was awarded to a dog owned by a relative of the judge, the decision was entirely -------.   vs.   Although the Best in Show was awarded to a dog owned by a relative of the judge, it cannot be argued that the decision was -------.

A. wrong
B. happy
C. biased
D. pleasant
E. justified

A. warranted
B. inconclusive
C. acceptable
D. appropriate
E. unjustified

(E) is the correct answer choice for both items. The conjunction "although" sets up a contrast between the two parts of the sentence. The first part of the sentence explains that the prize was awarded to a relative of the judge, which might suggest unfairness. However, "although" signals that the opposite is true; in other words, the judging was fair. So, (E) is the correct answer choice in both cases. It is more difficult to arrive at the correct answer in the second column, though, for the reasons mentioned above. Specifically, the vocabulary in the second column is less familiar. Also, the sentence structure in the second column is more complicated. As you'll see, sentence structures can be more complicated for several reasons, including the presence of extra clauses, parenthetical notes, or "negative" sentence constructions (i.e., "it cannot be argued that the decision was unjustified" instead of "the decision was entirely justified").

Sentence Completion Strategies

Anticipation

The first step when solving a sentence completion item is to read the sentence for meaning. Read the sentence at normal speed, as though someone were speaking to you. Then, identify one or two words that could complete the sentence successfully. If you're lucky, one of your words will appear in the list of answer choices. If that does not happen, look for the answer choice that is most similar to what you anticipated and that completes the sentence successfully.

Examples:

1. After his novel was rejected by six publishers,
    John became embittered and -------, so much so
    that his friends feared for his sanity.

    A. gentle
    B. wary
    C. morose
    D. pacified
    E. prudent

    The question stem establishes that John was embittered, which is a negative state of emotion. So, you want to select the answer choice that also describes a negative emotional state. You might have anticipated words such as "disappointed," "angry," "depressed," or "sullen" to complete the sentence. These words do not appear in the list of answer choices, but "morose" is a negative emotional state consistent with feeling embittered. So, (C) is the correct answer choice.

2. Given the rapidly changing nature of today's
    technological society, schools can no longer hope
    to teach eternal principles, for by tomorrow,
    today's knowledge is -------.

    A. enriched
    B. reproduced
    C. adequate
    D. precarious
    E. obsolete

    The question stem sets up a contrast between "eternal principles" and knowledge that is not eternal. You might have anticipated words such as "temporary," "outdated," or "transient" to complete the sentence. These words do not appear in the list of answer choices, but "obsolete" has a similar meaning. So, (E) is the best answer choice.

3. Retiring by nature and ------- even in private,
    Eleanor hardly ever spoke in public.

    A. confident
    B. taciturn
    C. preoccupied
    D. untamed
    E. courageous

The question stem tells you that Eleanor was unwilling to speak. So, the sentence could be completed with words such as "quiet" or "silent." Those words do not appear in the list of answer choices, but "taciturn" has a similar meaning. So, (B) is the correct answer choice.

Analysis

When reading a sentence completion item, pay attention to verbal signals. Verbal signals will tell you how the parts of a sentence fit together. For example, they can tell you:

- if one part of a sentence clarifies or adds detail to another;

- if a later element contradicts an earlier element; and

- if one idea is qualified or overruled by another.

Examples:

1. It is a rare individual who bothers to examine his or her fundamental ethical beliefs; indeed, the effort required ------- most people from even starting.

   A. cautions
   B. discourages
   C. sustains
   D. recalls
   E. withdraws

   In this item, "indeed" is an important verbal signal. It indicates that the second part of the sentence supports or underscores the first part. So, if the first part states that few people bother to examine their beliefs, the second part goes one step further and says that the effort required "discourages" most people from doing so. Therefore, the correct answer is (B).

2. Although ------- in her criticism of the minutest details, she often ------- the larger picture; so her input was incomplete.

   A. understated . . conspired
   B. sparing . . omitted
   C. exhaustive . . overlooked
   D. creative . . presented
   E. meticulous . . emphasized

   In this item, "although" is an important verbal signal. It indicates that the second part of the sentence will contrast with the first part. As a result, the two substitutions must be opposites or express dissimilar ideas. One would not expect someone described as "exhaustive" to have "overlooked" any detail, so (C) is the correct answer.

Finally, the following table has two columns. The first column is a list of signal words that are frequently used in sentence completion items. The second column explains the function of each signal word (i.e., it summarizes the logical relationship that is suggested or established by the signal word) and should be helpful when reviewing answer choices for sentence completion items.

SIGNAL WORD	WHAT TO LOOK FOR IN SENTENCE COMPLETIONS
therefore, thus, consequently, so, as a result	a further conclusion, the effect of a cause, an expected outcome
if, since, because	a premise of a logical argument, a cause leading to an effect, a condition or conditions leading to an outcome
and, additionally, further, moreover, similarly, likewise	further extension of a thought, a parallel or similar idea, added emphasis
although, though, while, but, rather, however, despite, unlike, yet, not	contrasting ideas, an exception, a reversal of thinking
indeed, in fact	an example, an idea for added emphasis
(:) *colon*	enumeration, clarification, further detail

This list of signal words is not exhaustive, but it highlights the type of verbal clue that can be very important in sentence completion items.

Substitution

In the end, some items still might seem too difficult to solve. The sentence structure might be too complex; the vocabulary might be too unfamiliar; or, even after evaluating verbal signals, the logic of the sentence might not make sense to you. If this happens, try substituting or plugging the answer choices into the sentence. You might find that, in the end, this simple step will help you to locate the correct answer choice.

Anticipating Sentence Completions
Exercise 1

DIRECTIONS: For items #1–10, read each sentence through for meaning. Then, in the space provided, write a few possible words that you anticipate could be used to complete the sentence. Answers are on page 591.

1. Stress is the reaction an individual feels when he believes the demands of a situation ------- his ability to meet them.

_____

_____

_____

2. The ------- of his career, capturing the coveted "Most Valuable Player" award, came at a time of deep personal sadness.

_____

_____

_____

3. Martin's opponent is a(n) ------- speaker who is unable to elicit a reaction from a crowd on even the most emotional of issues.

_____

_____

_____

4. The cold weather caused ------- damage to the Florida citrus crop, prompting growers to warn that the reduced yield is likely to result in much higher prices.

_____

_____

5. The report is so ------- that it covers all of the main points in detail and at least touches on everything that is even remotely connected with its topic.

_____

_____

_____

6. The Constitution sets up a system of checks and balances among the executive, the legislative, and the judicial branches to ensure that no one branch can establish ------- control over the government.

_____

_____

_____

7. The females of many common species of birds have dull coloring that ------- them when they are sitting on a nest in a tree or other foliage.

_____

_____

_____

8. She was one of the most ------- criminals of the 1930s, her name a household word and her face in every post office.

_____

_____

_____

9. Although he had not been physically injured by the explosion, the violence of the shock left him temporarily -------.

_____

_____

_____

10. Good teachers know that study habits learned at a young age stay with a student for life, so they try to find ways to ------- enthusiasm for studies.

_____

_____

_____

DIRECTIONS: For items #11–20, read each sentence through for meaning. Then, in the space provided, enter your anticipated completion. Finally, match your anticipated completion to one of the answer choices for that item. Answers are on page 591.

11. Even those who vigorously disagreed with the goals of the plan ------- admitted that it had been well designed.

_____

A.   erroneously
B.   valiantly
C.   successfully
D.   defiantly
E.   grudgingly

12. So-called road rage is just one example of a more general ------- that includes disrespect for rules, traditions, and institutions.

_____

A.   incivility
B.   caution
C.   curiosity
D.   passion
E.   apprehension

13. Random noises have been shown to ------- sleep cycles, causing fatigue and irritability in test subjects.

_____

A.   reinforce
B.   disrupt
C.   solidify
D.   undermine
E.   fracture

14. Increasingly, state legislatures have enacted laws that use a standardized exam as the sole ------- by which the success or failure of a school system is to be judged.

_____

A.   prediction
B.   guarantee
C.   actuality
D.   criterion
E.   aspiration

15. A fine public servant with an otherwise untarnished reputation has become the latest ------- in a war being waged by unscrupulous journalists against those who espouse principles they reject.

_____

A.   happenstance
B.   victory
C.   casualty
D.   detriment
E.   fiasco

16. The new bookstore, with its coffee bar and classical music, hopes that its literature selections will appeal to a ------- clientele.

A. sophisticated
B. conventional
C. provocative
D. restrictive
E. passive

17. The corporation's spokesperson ------- the report as junk science and accused the researchers of pursuing a political agenda.

A. highlighted
B. denounced
C. withdrew
D. fomented
E. inscribed

18. By the terms of the extremely ------- curriculum, all students at the academy were required to take two years of Latin, two years of algebra, and two years of fine arts.

A. industrious
B. fractured
C. provocative
D. valiant
E. regimented

19. The polite veneer that John exhibits in public ------- a violent temper that frequently erupts in private, especially when his authority is challenged.

A. condemns
B. belies
C. validates
D. queries
E. presages

20. Long hours of ------- rehearsal ensured that the orchestra performed the difficult piece flawlessly.

A. arduous
B. spontaneous
C. influential
D. jubilant
E. temporary

Analyzing Sentence Completions
Exercise 2

DIRECTIONS: For items #1–10, analyze each sentence by underlining a few words or phrases that provide clues for the completion of the sentences. Then, write down a few possible words that you anticipate could be used to complete the sentence. Answers are on page 591.

1. The survivors had been drifting for days in the lifeboat, and in their weakness, they appeared to be ------- rather than living beings.

2. The guillotine was introduced during the French Revolution as a(n) -------, an alternative to other less humane means of execution.

3. Because of the ------- nature of the chemical, it cannot be used near an open flame.

4. The Mayor's proposal for a new subway line, although a(n) -------, is not a final solution to the city's transportation needs.

5. In a pluralistic society, policies are the result of compromise, so political leaders must be ------- and must accommodate the views of others.

6. The committee report vigorously expounded the bill's strengths but also acknowledged its -------.

7. Because there is always the danger of a power failure and disruption of elevator service, high-rise buildings, while suitable for younger persons, are not recommended for -------.

8. For a child to be happy, his day must be very structured; when his routine is -------, he becomes nervous and irritable.

   _____

   _____

   _____

9. The current spirit of ------- among different religions has led to a number of meetings that their leaders hope will lead to better understanding.

   _____

   _____

   _____

10. Our modern industrialized societies have been responsible for the greatest destruction of nature and life; indeed, it seems that more civilization results in greater -------.

    _____

    _____

    _____

DIRECTIONS: For items #11–20, answer each sentence completion using verbal signals to analyze the logical structure of the sentence. Circle the letter of your answer choice. Answers are on page 592.

11. When Ghana achieved independence from colonial domination in 1957, the first country in sub-Saharan Africa to do so, it ------- economic and political advantages unrivaled elsewhere in tropical Africa.

    A. demanded
    B. enjoyed
    C. proclaimed
    D. denounced
    E. incited

12. *Fraktur*, a genre of folk art that has its roots in the Rhine Valley, is ------- to the Pennsylvania Dutch region, though Russian-German Mennonites produced similar but ------- ornamental drawings.

    A. endemic .. characteristic
    B. inherent .. distinct
    C. native .. unusual
    D. reduced .. inconsequential
    E. unique .. unrelated

13. The Free Trade Zone law was enacted in order to ------- legal issues left open by the Supreme Court case of *California v. Bond*.

    A. resolve
    B. undermine
    C. redress
    D. present
    E. nullify

14. Scholars often speak of an early and a late Heidegger, but a more careful reading reveals only a(n) ------- shift rather than a radical ------- in his thought.

    A. evolutionary .. bent
    B. discernible .. consistency
    C. inevitable .. temper
    D. unpredictable .. change
    E. gradual .. discontinuity

15. Van Gogh was virtually ------- at the time of his death: his agent, brother Theo, had sold only one of his paintings.

    A. unknown
    B. famous
    C. wealthy
    D. victorious
    E. adored

16. Legalized gambling seems to offer unlimited governmental revenue without the need to raise taxes; however, experience shows that casino gambling is not the financial ------- claimed by its proponents.

    A. panacea
    B. calamity
    C. incentive
    D. predicament
    E. validation

17. Low on supplies and badly in need of fresh troops, General Burgoyne's ------- and even ------- decision to push ahead resulted in disaster at Saratoga.

    A. reflective . . conscientious
    B. valorous . . cowardly
    C. rash . . foolhardy
    D. ill-advised . . calculated
    E. victorious . . generous

18. Although the Ford Edsel of the 1950s is commonly thought of as a "lemon," the car was actually -------; it was the victim of marketing, not -------, failures.

    A. attractive . . sales
    B. well-made . . engineering
    C. high-priced . . design
    D. desirable . . advertising
    E. well-known . . manufacturing

19. No reasonable trade-off between unemployment and inflation can be achieved by either monetary or fiscal policy alone; rather, both must be regarded as ------- tools for managing the economy.

    A. complementary
    B. intelligible
    C. unnecessary
    D. delicate
    E. unlimited

20. Professional schools assemble a(n) ------- student body not for the sake of enriching extracurricular life, but for the variety of personal and academic backgrounds that enhance the learning experience.

    A. homogeneous
    B. knowledgeable
    C. elite
    D. unexceptional
    E. diverse

Substituting Sentence Completions
Exercise 3

DIRECTIONS: For items #1–12, select an appropriate completion for the corresponding blank in the following paragraph. Answers are on page 592.

Today, the Surgeon General announced the findings of a new **(1)**------- that concludes that smoking represents a serious **(2)**------- to non-smokers as well as to **(3)**-------. According to the Surgeon General, disease risk due to **(4)**------- of tobacco smoke is not limited to the **(5)**------- who is smoking, but can also extend to those who **(6)**------- tobacco smoke in the same room. Simple **(7)**------- of smokers and non-smokers within the same airspace may reduce, but does not **(8)**-------, exposure of non-smokers to environmental smoke. A spokesperson for the tobacco industry **(9)**------- the report, saying the available **(10)**------- does not support the conclusion that environmental tobacco smoke is a hazard to non-smokers. On the other hand, the Coalition for Smoking on Health, an anti-smoking organization, **(11)**------- the report and called for **(12)**------- government action to ensure a smoke-free environment for all non-smokers.

1. (A) movie
(B) election
(C) report
(D) advertisement
(E) scholarship

2. (A) consciousness
(B) hazard
(C) remedy
(D) possibility
(E) adaptation

3. (A) cigarettes
(B) fumes
(C) alcoholics
(D) non-smokers
(E) smokers

4. (A) observation
(B) criticism
(C) improvement
(D) inhalation
(E) incorporation

5. (A) individual
(B) corporation
(C) doctor
(D) campaign
(E) reporter

6. (A) create
(B) breathe
(C) enjoy
(D) ban
(E) exhibit

7. (A) encouragement
(B) prohibition
(C) separation
(D) intermingling
(E) cooperation

8. (A) imagine
(B) increase
(C) prepare
(D) intimidate
(E) eliminate

9. (A) purchased
(B) prepared
(C) understood
(D) criticized
(E) underscored

10. (A) alibi
(B) publicity
(C) evidence
(D) reaction
(E) conversation

11. (A) praised
(B) rejected
(C) prolonged
(D) denied
(E) criticized

12. (A) minimal
(B) immediate
(C) reactionary
(D) uncontrolled
(E) eliminating

DIRECTIONS: For items #13–17, answer each sentence completion using substitution. Circle the letter of your answer choice. Answers are on page 592.

13. The Senator frequently ------- other members of the chamber with unwarranted attacks on their personal lives.

    A. provokes
    B. analyzes
    C. enhances
    D. deprives
    E. elevates

14. Clyde's ------- occasionally astonished even his closest friends who knew full well that his had been a(n) ------- childhood.

    A. sophistication . . extended
    B. naiveté . . sheltered
    C. wit . . precocious
    D. knowledge . . difficult
    E. wisdom . . uneducated

15. Research into sleep suggests that there are several ------- states between sleeping and waking and that it is difficult to determine where one ends and another begins.

    A. serious
    B. permissive
    C. predetermined
    D. unalterable
    E. intermediate

16. The playwright took a story so sublime that it has offered the ultimate challenge to composers, choreographers, and writers for centuries and, with a wanton heavy-handedness, gave the audience a hackneyed version that descended into -------.

    A. confusion
    B. bathos
    C. inattention
    D. significance
    E. indecision

17. Sensing his position was all but lost, the speaker launched into -------, hoping to save the day by rhetoric rather than reason.

    A. rationalization
    B. recapitulation
    C. dramatization
    D. exactitude
    E. peroration

Building Vocabulary with Sentence Completions
Exercise 4

DIRECTIONS: Each of the following sentences has one or two blanks. Choose the word or phrase for each blank that best fits the meaning of the sentence in its entirety. Circle the letter of your answer choice. Answers are on page 592.

1. While the fame of musical geniuses like Mozart and Beethoven endures for centuries, the idols of pop music quickly fade into -------.

   A. obscurity
   B. disbelief
   C. permanence
   D. poverty
   E. notoriety

2. In order to prevent an increase in the number of unemployed people, the economy must expand to ------- new jobs to offset those lost to factories in other countries.

   A. extinguish
   B. create
   C. prolong
   D. conceal
   E. avoid

3. In order to protect her privacy, the former employee spoke to reporters about the safety violations only after they guaranteed her -------.

   A. compensation
   B. publicity
   C. representation
   D. anonymity
   E. loyalty

4. In the State of Nature, described by Thomas Hobbes in *Leviathan* as a state of war, one against all others, no individual has sufficient physical strength to be assured of personal security, so all rely on -------.

   A. animosity
   B. premeditation
   C. principles
   D. prowess
   E. allies

5. Members of the Research and Development Council had been warned that the prototype was extremely -------, but were pleasantly surprised to see a model with many ------- usually incorporated only much later in the design process.

   A. crude .. refinements
   B. flexible .. advances
   C. rudimentary .. deficiencies
   D. unreliable .. trappings
   E. casual .. advantages

6. Although the developmental sequence of the reproductive cycle in insects is similar for many species, the timing can ------- greatly in regard to the beginning and duration of each stage.

   A. endure
   B. accelerate
   C. vary
   D. proceed
   E. coincide

7. The "framers' original intent" theory of Constitutional interpretation, though now ------- within academic circles, still has considerable practical effect because it is ------- by many sitting judges.

   A. propounded .. accepted
   B. disseminated .. rejected
   C. corroborated .. critiqued
   D. dismissed .. espoused
   E. encapsulated .. emphasized

8. Proponents of a flat tax hope to substitute a single federal revenue-raising measure for the ------- of convoluted and even self-contradictory provisions of the present tax code.

   A. tapestry
   B. concordance
   C. cacophony
   D. duplicity
   E. welter

9. An examination of the psychological forces that shape the personality of the title character of *The Magus* naturally invites closer study of its form, as story content and form are carefully ------- by Fowles in the novel.

   A. delineated
   B. anticipated
   C. integrated
   D. determined
   E. reserved

10. The broadcast of the story has seriously compromised the credibility of the entire news department: the key piece of information, though not ------- on the one particular point, is expected to support a vast ------- of implications for which no other proof is offered.

    A. fabricated .. contradiction
    B. unconvincing .. superstructure
    C. persuasive .. convocation
    D. inextricable .. skein
    E. conclusive .. facsimile

11. By and large, Wittgenstein's treatment of language in *The Philosophical Investigations* will be ------- to the lay person, but the more ------- points will be grasped only by specialists in the philosophy of language.

    A. granted .. general
    B. accessible .. esoteric
    C. concrete .. ingenious
    D. alien .. technical
    E. attractive .. abstract

12. For many years, the cost of faculty salaries and benefits rose faster than tuition and contributions to endowments so that some ------- were in danger of becoming -------.

    A. colleges .. expensive
    B. universities .. insolvent
    C. students .. dropouts
    D. unions .. superfluous
    E. teachers .. replaceable

13. In an effort to render as accurately as possible ------- lighting conditions, French Impressionist Claude Monet worked on several paintings at once, frantically changing canvases as ------- alterations in illumination created almost imperceptible new visual effects.

    A. essential .. unimportant
    B. transitory .. subtle
    C. momentary .. evident
    D. prototypical .. minute
    E. classical .. improbable

14. During the 1980s, fortunes were made on a seemingly daily basis by ------- traders who ------- conventional wisdom on investing in the stock market.

    A. maverick .. flouted
    B. rogue .. applied
    C. impoverished .. acknowledged
    D. devious .. promulgated
    E. renegade .. propounded

15. A fire in the People's Republic of China destroyed the factory responsible for producing most of the world's RAM memory components; the ensuing shortage was so ------- that computer users came to believe that the high prices were the result of ------- by suppliers.

    A. prolonged .. coddling
    B. insignificant .. touting
    C. ineffectual .. directing
    D. severe .. gouging
    E. unpredictable .. misleading

16. The idea that a single individual can alter the course of history is not mere speculation; in fact, well-documented instances are not even -------.

A. established
B. confirmable
C. conceivable
D. actualized
E. exceptional

17. Some proponents of an author's lending royalty plan argue that borrowing a book from a library is a form of ------- since the reader enjoys the intellectual property without ------- the author.

A. theft . . acknowledging
B. piracy . . protecting
C. contract . . paying
D. servitude . . releasing
E. larceny . . compensating

18. Though it seemed that director Robert Altman had firmly established his artistic reputation with the nomination of *Nashville* for Best Film of 1970, the 1979 film *Quintet*, perhaps the ------- of his career, earned him only the ------- of the critics.

A. nadir . . disapprobation
B. continuation . . notice
C. denouement . . acclaim
D. climax . . commentary
E. low point . . recommendation

19. Albert's advanced degree in urban planning made him the most qualified person on the committee, but his status as the junior member made his criticism of transportation policy seem ------- even though his remarks were always -------.

A. unwarranted . . superficial
B. opportunistic . . spontaneous
C. presumptuous . . incisive
D. vapid . . insincere
E. practical . . inappropriate

20. The professor's ------- treatment of students in the classroom contrasted with her behavior in the office, where those who sought advice found her to be genuinely ------- to their problems.

A. supercilious . . sympathetic
B. arrogant . . indifferent
C. cavalier . . calloused
D. cautious . . attentive
E. inconsistent . . hardened

21. Legal positivists deny that international law can properly be called law because international organizations can only ------- prohibited conduct but do nothing to ------- it.

A. investigate . . review
B. identify . . encourage
C. provoke . . rectify
D. outline . . satisfy
E. define . . punish

22. Following the ------- emotional pleas for passage of the bill by members known for rambling speeches, the ------- argument for its rejection was a welcome relief for the House.

A. protracted . . trenchant
B. lengthy . . specious
C. flowery . . ornate
D. undisguised . . deceiving
E. blatant . . unfocused

23. In his treatment of science, Ernst Cassirer rejects the traditional ------- of fact and theory, approvingly quoting Goethe as saying "All fact is theory."

A. asymmetry
B. dichotomy
C. frequency
D. conjunction
E. dysfunction

24. Although Jacques Derrida's writings held considerable theoretical promise, deconstructionism in America quickly deteriorated into a ------- as academics of limited intellectual ability mimicked its style without ------- its secrets.

- A. farce . . plumbing
- B. battle . . understanding
- C. burlesque . . concealing
- D. comedy . . purporting
- E. pretense . . sharing

25. Students had become so ------- to the principal's capriciousness that they greeted the announcement of yet another dress code with complete indifference.

- A. receptive
- B. inured
- C. sensitive
- D. attuned
- E. evasive

26. Recent journalistic reports of respected researchers ------- experimental results favorable to their own theories ------- the popular conception of science as a pure search for the truth.

- A. manufacturing . . supports
- B. presenting . . belies
- C. finding . . reinforces
- D. fabricating . . contradicts
- E. concealing . . undermines

27. A recurring theme in science fiction is the contest between good and evil for control over technology that is, in itself, -------.

- A. productive
- B. ill-conceived
- C. independent
- D. amoral
- E. inconsequential

28. In *The Ontology of Political Violence*, Professor Nogarola argues that so-called ------- evidence often dismissed as unreliable would be admissible in a court of law as testimony and has value in the political arena as well.

- A. anecdotal
- B. practical
- C. sensational
- D. collaborative
- E. probative

29. Ironically, the modern Olympic games, which are held up as the ideal of amateur athletics, originated with games in honor of Athena in which winners were rewarded not with laurel wreaths of little ------- worth but oil-filled amphorae with considerable ------- value.

- A. practical . . sentimental
- B. financial . . honorific
- C. market . . aesthetic
- D. capital . . sacrificial
- E. intrinsic . . economic

30. Supply creates its own demand; and advertising, if sufficiently -------, can convince consumers to ------- products for which they have little desire and even less need.

- A. strident . . approve
- B. pervasive . . purchase
- C. unscrupulous . . honor
- D. distasteful . . disregard
- E. vehement . . anticipate

31. In an effort to ------- the strike, the mediators suggested a compromise that they thought would be ------- to both the union and the company.

- A. shorten . . unpalatable
- B. resolve . . satisfactory
- C. end . . unacceptable
- D. extend . . acceptable
- E. accelerate . . puzzling

32. Because of the tremendous magnifying power of the Hubble Telescope, astronomical features that were before ------- are now resolved into fine detail.

A. indistinguishable
B. inapplicable
C. intractable
D. inalienable
E. invaluable

33. Paradoxically, the more the audiences applauded his performances and critics praised his artistic accomplishments, the more ------- Isaac felt about his ability as a musician.

A. decisive
B. insecure
C. confident
D. reluctant
E. assertive

34. An important goal of Black History Month is to ensure that African-Americans who have often received too little credit for their achievements in fields ranging from literature to physics are more widely -------.

A. sustained
B. acknowledged
C. embellished
D. retained
E. envied

35. The directors who favored the plan to diversify overseas operations, though in ------- following their failed experiment on the domestic side, constituted a sufficiently ------- political force on the Board to gain a favorable vote.

A. retreat .. cohesive
B. disarray .. ineffective
C. control .. powerful
D. abeyance .. contentious
E. disfavor .. fragmented

36. Our relegation of the fairy tale to the status of bedtime reading for children has resulted in the ------- of the goriest details from the Grimm tales.

A. ratification
B. reinsertion
C. accentuation
D. expurgation
E. codification

37. For all of his outlandish costumes and immoderate behavior on-stage, rock musician Arlen Quigby was, in his private life, a(n) ------- person who was described by associates as a simple businessman.

A. enigmatic
B. famous
C. conventional
D. unstable
E. flamboyant

38. As vaccines have become increasingly -------, cases of Haemophilus influenza among children under the age of five dropped nearly 99% in the last ten years, and the disease has been nearly -------.

A. routine .. eradicated
B. virile .. annihilated
C. innocuous .. obliterated
D. problematic .. rampant
E. inefficacious .. contained

39. The script writers for the stage version of Kipling's *Just So Stories* wisely decided to make only ------- use of the author's original diction; the occasional flashes of alliteration are charming but overdone; their arcane sound would quickly have become ------- to the modern ear.

A. judicious .. familiar
B. intermittent .. inaudible
C. sporadic .. cloying
D. exacting .. familiar
E. limited .. dissonant

40. Several highly publicized disagreements within the scientific community have become so ------- that many lay people now wonder whether the scientific process is a search for the truth or a contest of -------.

A. repetitive . . platitudes
B. egregious . . wills
C. cacophonous . . theories
D. acrimonious . . egos
E. exuberant . . resources

BUILDING VOCABULARY THROUGH CONTEXT

Unlike other vocabulary books that provide random lists of words and their definitions, this program builds vocabulary by helping you to learn the meaning of words in the context of short stories, essays, and other types of reading selections.

Students often believe that if they don't know what a word means, they won't be able to answer correctly an item that includes that word. This is simply not true. This section will help you to recognize word parts, become more familiar with challenging vocabulary words, and use context clues to determine what difficult words mean. This section will also help you to understand the logical structure of a sentence and how to use that understanding to anticipate appropriate words in vocabulary-related items.

The exercises in this section will enrich and build your vocabulary skills. You will learn vocabulary words in the context of a reading selection (vocabulary-in-context and sentence completion items) so you can actually learn them rather than simply memorize them.

Building Vocabulary Through Context
Exercise 5

DIRECTIONS: The following passage is followed by several items. Read the passage and choose the best answer for each item based on what is stated or implied in the passage. You may refer to the passage as often as necessary to answer the items. Answers are on page 592.

Social Science: The following passage is an excerpt from a history of the political career of Thomas Jefferson, the author of the "Declaration of Independence."

"Heartily tired" from the brutal, almost daily conflicts that erupted over questions of national policy between himself and Alexander Hamilton, Thomas Jefferson resigned his position as Secretary
5 of State in 1793. Although his Federalist opponents were convinced that this was merely a strategic withdrawal to allow him an opportunity to plan and promote his candidacy for the Presidency should Washington step down in 1796, Jefferson insisted
10 that this retirement from public life was to be final.

But even in retirement, the world of politics pursued him. As the election grew nearer and it became apparent that Washington would not seek a third term, rumors of Jefferson's Presidential
15 ambitions grew in intensity. Reacting to these continuous insinuations in a letter to James Madison, Jefferson allowed that while the idea that he coveted the office of chief executive had been originated by his enemies to impugn his political
20 motives, he had been forced to examine his true feelings on the subject for his own peace of mind. In so doing he concluded that his reasons for retirement—the desire for privacy, and the delight of family life—coupled with his now failing health
25 were insuperable barriers to public service. The "little spice of ambition" he had in his younger days had long since evaporated and the question of his Presidency was forever closed.

Jefferson did not actively engage in the
30 campaign on his own behalf. The Republican party, anticipating modern campaign tactics, created grass roots sentiment for their candidate by directing their efforts toward the general populace. In newspapers, Jefferson was presented as the uniform

35 advocate of equal rights among the citizens while Adams was portrayed as the champion of rank, titles, heredity, and distinctions. Jefferson was not certain of the outcome of the election until the end of December. Under the original electoral system
40 established by the Constitution, each Presidential elector cast his ballot for two men without designating between them as to office. The candidate who received the greater number of votes became the President; the second highest, the Vice
45 President. Jefferson foresaw on the basis of his own calculations that the electoral vote would be close. He wrote to Madison that in the event of a tie, he wished for the choice to be in favor of Adams. In public life, the New Englander had always been
50 senior to Jefferson; and so, he explained, the expression of public will being equal, Adams should be preferred for the higher honor. Jefferson, a shrewd politician, realized that the transition of power from the nearly mythical Washington to a
55 lesser luminary in the midst of the deep and bitter political divisions facing the nation could be perilous, and he had no desire to be caught in the storm that had been brewing for four years and was about to break. "This is certainly not a moment to
60 covet the helm," he wrote to Edward Rutledge. When the electoral vote was tallied, Adams emerged the victor. Rejoicing at his "escape," Jefferson was completely satisfied with the decision. Despite their obvious and basic political differences, Jefferson
65 genuinely respected John Adams as a friend and compatriot. Although Jefferson believed that Adams had deviated from the course set in 1776, in Jefferson's eyes he never suffered diminution; and Jefferson was quite confident that Adams would not
70 steer the nation too far from its Republican tack. Within two years, Jefferson's views would be drastically altered as measures such as the Alien and Sedition Acts of 1798 convinced him of the need to wrest control of the government from the
75 Federalists.

1. In line 1, the word *heartily* most nearly means:

   A. sincerely.
   B. vigorously.
   C. zealously.
   D. completely.

2. In line 10, the word *public* most nearly means:

   A. communal.
   B. open.
   C. official.
   D. people.

3. In line 10, the word *final* most nearly means:

   A. last.
   B. closing.
   C. ultimate.
   D. conclusive.

4. In line 17, the word *allowed* most nearly means:

   A. permitted.
   B. admitted.
   C. tolerated.
   D. granted.

5. In line 31, the word *anticipating* most nearly means:

   A. expecting.
   B. presaging.
   C. awaiting.
   D. inviting.

6. In line 34, the word *uniform* most nearly means:

   A. standard.
   B. unchanging.
   C. militant.
   D. popular.

7. In line 36, the word *champion* most nearly means:

   A. victor.
   B. opponent.
   C. colleague.
   D. defender.

8. In line 50, the word *senior* most nearly means:

   A. older in age.
   B. higher in rank.
   C. graduate.
   D. mentor.

9. In line 55, the word *luminary* most nearly means:

   A. bright object.
   B. famous person.
   C. office holder.
   D. candidate.

10. In line 68, the word *diminution* most nearly means:

    A. foreshortening.
    B. shrinkage.
    C. abatement.
    D. degradation.

Vocabulary Builder: Prose Fiction Passages
Exercise 6

DIRECTIONS: Each passage in this exercise is followed by sets of sentence completion and vocabulary-in-context items. In addition to using the passages to infer word meanings, you may use a dictionary.

The first set of items following each passage are sentence completion items based on words from the passage. Each sentence has one blank. Choose the word that best fits the meaning of the sentence in its entirety.

The second set of items following each passage are vocabulary-in-context items based on words from the passage. Choose the best answer for each item based on what is stated or implied in the passage.

Answers are on page 592.

Passage I

Prose Fiction: This passage is adapted from Edgar Allan Poe's "The Oval Portrait."

The portrait was that of a young girl. It was a mere head and shoulders, done in what is technically termed a vignette manner; much in the style of the favorite heads of Sully. The arms, the
5 bosom, and even the ends of the radiant hair, melted imperceptibly into the vague yet deep shadow, which formed the background of the whole. The metallic yellow frame was a valuable oval, richly gilded and filigreed in exquisitely fine detail.
10 As a thing of art nothing could be more admirable than the painting itself. But it could have been neither the execution of the work, nor the immortal beauty of the countenance, which had so suddenly and so vehemently moved me. Least of all could it
15 have been that my fancy, shaken from its half slumber, had mistaken the head for that of a living person. I saw at once that the peculiarities of the design, of the vignetting, and of the frame, must have instantly dispelled such ideas—must have
20 prevented even its momentary entertainment. Thinking earnestly upon these points, I remained, for an hour perhaps, half sitting, half reclining, with my vision riveted upon the portrait. At length, satisfied with the true secret of its effect, I fell back
25 within the bed. I had found the spell of the picture in an absolute *life-likeness* of expression, which at first startling, finally confounded, subdued, and appalled me. With deep and reverent awe, I replaced the candelabrum in its former position. The cause of my
30 deep agitation being thus shut from view, I sought eagerly the volume which discussed the paintings and their histories. Turning to the number which

designated the oval portrait, I there read the vague and quaint words which follow:

35 "She was a maiden of rarest beauty, and not more lovely than full of glee. And evil was the hour when she saw, and loved, and wedded the painter. He, passionate, studious, austere, and having already a bride in his Art; she all light and smiles
40 and frolicsome as the young fawn; loving and cherishing all things: hating only the Art which was her rival; dreading only the palette and brushes and other untoward instruments which deprived her of the countenance of her lover. It was thus a terrible
45 thing for this lady to hear the painter speak of his desire to portray even his young bride. But she was humble and obedient, and sat meekly for many weeks in the dark high turret-chamber where the light dripped upon the pale canvas only from
50 overhead. But he, the painter, took glory in his work, which went on from hour to hour from day to day. And he was a passionate and moody man, who became lost in reveries; so that he *would* not see that the light which fell so ghastly in that lone turret
55 withered the health and the spirits of his bride, who pined visibly to all but him. Yet she smiled on and still on, uncomplainingly, because she saw that the painter (who had great renown) took a fervid and burning pleasure in his task, and wrought day and
60 night to depict her who so loved him, yet who grew daily more dispirited and weak. And in sooth some who beheld the portrait spoke of its resemblance in low words, as of a mighty marvel, and a proof not less of the power of the painter than of his deep love
65 for her, whom he depicted so surpassingly well. But at length, as the labor drew nearer to its conclusion, there were admitted none into the turret; for the painter had grown wild with the ardor of his work, and turned his eyes from the canvas rarely, even to

70 regard the countenance of his wife. And he would
not see that the tints which he spread on the canvas
were drawn from the cheeks of her who sat beside
him. And when many weeks had passed, but little
remained to do, save one brush upon the mouth and
75 one tint upon the eye, the spirit of the lady again
flickered up as the flame within the socket of the
lamp. And then the brush was given, and the tint
was placed; and for one moment, the painter stood
entranced before the work which he had wrought
80 but in the next, while he yet gazed, he grew
tremulous and very pallid, and aghast, and crying
with a loud voice, 'this is indeed *Life* itself!' turned
suddenly to regard his beloved—*She was dead!*"

1. The physical differences between the fraternal
   twins were so ------- that only their family
   members were able to tell them apart.

   A. apparent
   B. invisible
   C. detectable
   D. imperceptible
   E. noticeable

2. Many Republicans are ------- opposed to
   fighting climate change with legislation,
   charging that the Democrat's current bill
   would drastically raise costs for the average
   American family.

   A. impassively
   B. sarcastically
   C. vehemently
   D. ironically
   E. humbly

3. To help control the rapidly increasing national
   debt, the Finance Minister recently announced
   a very ------- set of economic measures that
   drastically cut government services.

   A. mysterious
   B. lackadaisical
   C. lenient
   D. inept
   E. austere

4. The critic wrote in her review of the ballet that
   the ------- and conviction with which the
   dancers performed excused any minor
   imperfections in the overall performance.

   A. doubt
   B. ardor
   C. flawlessness
   D. indifference
   E. deliberation

5. When the animal control officer cornered the
   stray dog in an attempt to catch it, the dog
   bristled and whined in a low ------- tone.

   A. tremulous
   B. confident
   C. unexpected
   D. erratic
   E. passive

6. It can be inferred that the word *vignette*, as it
   is used in line 3, primarily refers to:

   A. a brief incident or scene.
   B. a particular style of brushstroke.
   C. a short musical composition.
   D. a picture with no definite border, shading
      off gradually at its edges.

7. In line 9, *gilded* is best understood to mean:

   A. sponsored.
   B. overlaid with gold.
   C. entangled.
   D. overfilled.

8. In line 9, *filigreed* is best understood to mean:

   A. excessive greed or avarice.
   B. characterized by lack of taste.
   C. adorned with delicate ornamentation.
   D. to be unfounded.

9. As it is used in line 13, the word *countenance*
   most nearly means:

   A. facial features.
   B. approval.
   C. pretense.
   D. motif.

10. In context, *designated* (line 33) most nearly means:

    A. delegated.
    B. indicated.
    C. appointed.
    D. delivered.

11. In line 43, *untoward* most nearly means:

    A. appropriate.
    B. disorderly.
    C. fortunate.
    D. troublesome.

12. It can be inferred that the word *reveries*, as it is used in line 53, primarily refers to:

    A. indifferences.
    B. daydreams.
    C. certainties.
    D. reverences.

13. As it is used in line 56, the word *pined* most nearly means:

    A. longed for.
    B. increased.
    C. wasted away.
    D. imagined.

14. In line 58, *renown* is best understood to mean:

    A. fame.
    B. aptitude.
    C. obscurity.
    D. perseverance.

15. As it is used in line 59, the word *wrought* most nearly means:

    A. hammered.
    B. wreaked havoc.
    C. worked with great care.
    D. operated carelessly.

Passage II

Prose Fiction: This passage is adapted from Arthur Conan Doyle's "The Adventure of the Devil's Foot."

In recording from time to time some of the curious experiences and interesting recollections, which I associate with my long and intimate friendship with Mr. Sherlock Holmes, I have
5 continually been faced with difficulties caused by his own aversion to publicity. To his sombre and cynical spirit all popular applause was always abhorrent, and nothing amused him more at the end of a successful case than to hand over the actual
10 exposure to some orthodox official, and to listen with a mocking smile to the general chorus of misplaced congratulation. It was indeed this attitude upon the part of my friend and certainly not any lack of interesting material which has caused
15 me of late years to lay very few of my records before the public. My participation in some of his adventures was always a privilege, which entailed discretion and reticence upon me.

It was in the spring of the year 1897 that
20 Holmes's iron constitution showed some symptoms of giving way in the face of constant hard work of a most exacting kind, aggravated perhaps by occasional indiscretions of his own. In March of that year Dr. Moore Agar, of Harley Street, whose
25 dramatic introduction to Holmes I may some day recount, gave positive injunctions that the famous private agent lay aside all his cases and surrender himself to complete rest if he wished to avert an absolute breakdown. The state of his health was not
30 a matter in which he himself took the faintest interest, for his mental detachment was absolute, but he was induced at last, on the threat of being permanently disqualified from work, to give himself a complete change of scene and air. Thus, it was that
35 in the early spring of that year we found ourselves together in a small cottage near Poldhu Bay, at the further extremity of the Cornish peninsula.

It was a singular spot, and one peculiarly well suited to the grim humor of my patient. From the
40 windows of our little whitewashed house, which stood high upon a grassy headland, we looked down upon the whole sinister semicircle of Mounts Bay, that old death trap of sailing vessels, with its fringe of black cliffs and surge-swept reefs on which
45 innumerable seamen have met their end. With a northerly breeze it lies placid and sheltered, inviting the storm-tossed craft to tack into it for rest and protection.

Then come the sudden swirl round of the
50 wind, the blustering gale from the south-west, the dragging anchor, the lee shore, and the last battle in the creaming breakers. The wise mariner stands far out from that evil place.

On the land side our surroundings were as
55 sombre as on the sea. It was a country of rolling moors, lonely and dun-colored, with an occasional church tower to mark the site of some old-world village. In every direction upon these moors were traces of some vanished race, which has passed
60 utterly away, and left as its sole record strange monuments of stone, irregular mounds which contained the burned ashes of the dead, and curious earthworks which hinted at prehistoric strife. The glamour and mystery of the place, with its sinister
65 atmosphere of forgotten nations, appealed to the imagination of my friend, and he spent much of his time in long walks and solitary meditations upon the moor. The ancient Cornish language had also arrested his attention, and he had, I remember,
70 conceived the idea that it was akin to Chaldean, and had been largely derived from the Phoenician traders in tin. He had received a consignment of books upon philology and was settling down to develop this thesis when suddenly, to my sorrow,
75 and to his unfeigned delight, we found ourselves, even in that land of dreams, plunged into a problem at our very doors which was more intense, more engrossing, and infinitely more mysterious than any of those which had driven us from London. Our
80 simple life and peaceful, healthy routine were violently interrupted, and we were precipitated into the midst of a series of events which caused the utmost excitement not only in Cornwall but throughout the whole west of England. Many of my
85 readers may retain some recollection of what was called at the time "The Cornish Horror," though a most imperfect account of the matter reached the London press. Now, after some thirteen years, I will give the true details of this inconceivable affair to
90 the public.

16. Due to her strong moral ------- to eating animals or animal by-products, Maggie has been a life-long vegetarian.

  A. adversity
  B. aversion
  C. sympathy
  D. confliction
  E. upbringing

17. Trafficking in human beings and other contemporary forms of slavery constitute a(n) ------- violation of the dignity and rights of human beings.

  A. alluring
  B. laudatory
  C. docile
  D. abhorrent
  E. pedestrian

18. J. D. Salinger was best known for his 1951 novel *The Catcher in the Rye*, as well as his ------- and reclusive nature following his withdrawal from public life in 1965.

  A. arrogance
  B. experience
  C. loquaciousness
  D. nervousness
  E. reticence

19. The governor stepped down from office after his ------- were made public and the state assembly demanded his resignation.

  A. decisions
  B. prudence
  C. indiscretions
  D. responsibilities
  E. virtues

20. In his book, *The Great Crash, 1929*, John Kenneth Galbraith argued that the 1929 stock market crash was ------- by rampant speculation and the belief of participants that they could become rich without work.

  A. considered
  B. precipitated
  C. protracted
  D. belabored
  E. delivered

21. In line 10, *orthodox* is best understood to mean:

  A. conventional.
  B. original.
  C. eccentric.
  D. personal.

22. The word *recount* (line 26) most nearly means to:

  A. conceal facts.
  B. calculate.
  C. reimburse.
  D. tell a story in detail.

23. Based on the use of the word *injunctions* in line 26, it can be inferred that *injunction* primarily refers to a(n):

  A. command.
  B. embargo.
  C. ruling.
  D. reprimand.

24. In line 38, *singular* is closest in meaning to:

  A. simular.
  B. allegorical.
  C. individual.
  D. remarkable.

25. As it is used in line 46, the word *placid* most nearly means:

  A. flabby.
  B. calm.
  C. noisy.
  D. appeasable.

26. It can be inferred that the word *tack*, as it is used in line 47, primarily means to:

    A.   deal fairly.
    B.   fasten.
    C.   change course.
    D.   attack.

27. It can be inferred that the word *lee*, as it is used in line 51, primarily refers to:

    A.   the side sheltered from the wind.
    B.   the rear of a boat.
    C.   a breeze from the west.
    D.   the far side of an object.

28. As it is used in line 72, the word *consignment* most likely refers to:

    A.   a meeting or appointment.
    B.   a homework assignment.
    C.   items in a shipment.
    D.   an error in communication.

29. In line 75, *unfeigned* most nearly means:

    A.   affected.
    B.   legitimate.
    C.   insincere.
    D.   genuine.

30. In line 85, *recollection* refers to a(n):

    A.   collection of items.
    B.   recalled memory.
    C.   religious contemplation.
    D.   act of recoiling.

Passage III

Prose Fiction: This passage is adapted from a letter written by the playwright George Bernard Shaw in response to critics of his plays.

There is a good reason, however, why I should take this haughty attitude towards those representative critics whose complaint is that my plays, though not unentertaining, lack the elevation
5 of sentiment and seriousness of purpose of Shakespeare and Ibsen. They can find, under the surface brilliancy for which they give me credit, no coherent thought or sympathy, and accuse me, in various terms and degrees, of an inhuman and
10 freakish wantonness; of preoccupation with "the seamy side of life"; of paradox, cynicism, and eccentricity, reducible, as some contend, to a trite formula of treating bad as good, and good as bad, important as trivial, and trivial as important, serious
15 as laughable, and laughable as serious and so forth. As to this formula I can only say that if anyone is simple enough to think that even a good comic opera can be produced by it, I invite him to try his hand, and see whether anything remotely
20 resembling one of my plays will result.

I could explain the matter easily enough if I chose, but the result would be that people who misunderstand the plays would misunderstand the explanation ten times more. The particular
25 exceptions taken are seldom more than symptoms of the underlying fundamental disagreement between the romantic morality of the critics and the realistic morality of the plays. For example, I am quite aware the Swiss officer in *Arms and the Man* is
30 not a conventional stage soldier. He suffers from want of food and sleep; his nerves go to pieces after three days under fire, ending in the horrors of a rout and pursuit; he has found by experience it is more important to have a few bits of chocolate to eat than
35 cartridges for his revolver. When many of my critics rejected these circumstances as fantastically improbable and cynically unnatural, it was not necessary to argue them into common sense; all I had to do was to brain them, so to speak, with the
40 first half-dozen military authorities at hand. But when it proved that such unromantic facts implied to them a denial of the existence of courage, patriotism, faith, hope, and charity, I saw it was not really mere matter of fact at issue between us.

45 The real issue between us is whether idealism can survive the general onslaught, which is implicit in *Arms and the Man* and other realistic plays. For my part, I hope not; for idealism, which is only a flattering name for romance in politics and morals,
50 is as obnoxious to me as romance is in ethics or religion. I can no longer be satisfied with fictitious morals and fictitious good conduct, shedding fictitious glory on overcrowding, disease, crime, drink, war cruelty, infant mortality, all the other
55 commonplaces of civilization which drive men to the theater to make foolish pretenses. These things are progress, science, morals, religion, patriotism, imperial supremacy, national greatness, and all the other names the newspapers call them.

60 On the other hand, I see plenty of good in the world working itself out as fast as the idealists will allow it; if they would only leave it alone and learn to respect reality, which would include the beneficial exercise of respecting themselves, and
65 incidentally respecting me, we should all get along much better and faster. At all events, I do not see moral chaos and anarchy as the alternative to romantic convention; furthermore, I am not going to pretend that I do just to please the less clear-sighted
70 people who are convinced the world is only held together by the force of unanimous, strenuous, eloquent, trumpet-tongued lying. To me, the tragedy and comedy of life lie in the consequences, sometimes terrible, sometimes ludicrous, of the
75 persistent attempts to found our institutions on the ideas suggested to our imaginations by our half-satisfied passions, instead of on a genuinely scientific natural history.

31. Dazed by the explosion, nothing Fredrick said was ------; he babbled about the need for lace curtains on the machine shop windows.

A. illogical
B. coherent
C. adequate
D. sensitive
E. informal

32. The suspect drove his car at 60 miles per hour through the school zone, demonstrating a(n) ------- disregard for the safety of the school-children.

A. justifiable
B. moral
C. ambitious
D. lucid
E. wanton

33. The aviation magnate Howard Hughes is remembered for his ------- behavior and reclusive lifestyle in later life, caused in part by a worsening obsessive-compulsive disorder.

A. gregarious
B. customary
C. eccentric
D. habitual
E. extroverted

34. The politician claimed that he would ------- middle-class income taxes by eliminating wasteful government spending and fraud.

A. enhance
B. augment
C. increase
D. reduce
E. maintain

35. Arguably one of the most ------- presidents in American history, John F. Kennedy delivered an inaugural address in 1961 that was an inspirational call to action.

A. inarticulate
B. reticent
C. taciturn
D. belligerent
E. eloquent

36. Based on the use of the word *elevation* in line 4, it can be inferred that *elevate* means to:

A. decrease or drop.
B. raise or lift up.
C. assess or estimate.
D. intensify or accelerate.

37. As it is used in line 11, the word *seamy* most nearly means:

A. wholesome.
B. feeble.
C. unpleasant.
D. vigorous.

38. In line 11, *paradox* is best understood to mean a(n):

A. contradiction.
B. insincerity.
C. intricacy.
D. obscurity.

39. The word *cynicism* (line 11) refers to the belief that:

A. there are not absolute truths about the world.
B. negative perceptions are the cause of negative realities.
C. people and events are inherently good.
D. human nature and motives cannot be trusted.

40. As the word *realistic* is used in line 28, it can be inferred that *realism* refers to the principle of:

A. representation through generalization.
B. representation without idealization.
C. reproduction by individualization.
D. change through moderate action.

41. In line 45, *idealism* refers to behavior or thought based on:

A. a conception of things as one wishes them to be, rather than as they actually are.
B. a conception of how things actually are.
C. a conception of people motivated only by greed or some other selfish motive.
D. delusion of persecution or extreme fear.

42. It can be inferred that the word *onslaught,* as it is used in line 46, primarily refers to a(n):

    A. apology.
    B. justification.
    C. attack.
    D. excuse.

43. Based on the use of the word *pretenses* in line 56, it can be inferred that *pretense* refers to all of the following EXCEPT:

    A. a charade.
    B. pretension.
    C. candor.
    D. a false claim.

44. In line 64, *beneficial* most nearly means:

    A. bountiful.
    B. helpful.
    C. extensive.
    D. refreshing.

45. As it is used in line 67, *anarchy* can be inferred to mean:

    A. lawlessness.
    B. order.
    C. transformation.
    D. reformation.

Vocabulary Builder: Social Science Passages
Exercise 7

DIRECTIONS: Each passage in this exercise is followed by sets of sentence completion and vocabulary-in-context items. In addition to using the passages to infer word meanings, you may use a dictionary.

The first set of items following each passage are sentence completion items based on words from the passage. Each sentence has one blank. Choose the word that best fits the meaning of the sentence in its entirety.

The second set of items following each passage are vocabulary-in-context items based on words from the passage. Choose the best answer for each item based on what is stated or implied in the passage.

Answers are on page 593.

Passage I

Social Science: This passage is adapted from an essay entitled "Animal Images in Human History" in an art history and philosophy anthology.

Among the first images created by man were those of animals, and over the centuries mankind's preoccupation with the nonhuman inhabitants of the earth has never abated. Even when at pains to
5 prove how different he was from the beast, man has depended on the animal world for the imagery by which to explain his interior being as well as his relationship to the cosmos. Endowed with a vitality in common with man, yet following the dictates of
10 an intelligence not readily definable by human reason, the animal, whether wild or domesticated, threatening attacker or docile prey, has remained something of an enigma and often the subject of wonder. To reconstruct the history of religion,
15 philosophy, or art without reference to the animal image would be impossible. Although in our satisfied moment of sophistication, we no longer depend on the literal imagery of hawk-headed gods or rulers with the body of a lion, we still strut like a
20 peacock and search ardently for the dove of peace.

No one knows for sure why the painters in prehistoric times represented bison on the walls of caves, but it is significant that the animals were rendered with more care and completeness than the
25 human creatures. Whatever their utility, the swiftly moving, rhythmic figures show an appreciation for animal beauty that can still be understood with sympathy. "Animal beauty" is a term we tend to use when we wish to describe some particularly adroit
30 and rhythmic coordination of muscles and movement that magnificently fulfills a prescribed

act, an act that seems to be accomplished as answer to an interior impulse untrammeled by rational restraint or an imposed pattern of behavior. There
35 is something magical in an artistic form expressive of such pure vitality, which seems purposive and yet has no rational end. It is as if this summons from far back in the mind a cherished memory of simply being, of existing in a vital continuity not qualified
40 by reason nor limited by concept of time. This particular kind of vital beauty is not the exclusive property of any particular animal; it belongs no less to the hare than to the lion. That remarkable art known as the "animal style," which spread in the
45 early centuries from Central Asia across China and westward through Europe, carried its animal magic through forms that often lose all specific identity. However, the taut, curving forms live with animal exuberance and transform any object they adorn
50 into a living thing. Significantly enough, this intensive vitality was rarely associated with images of human beings. Possibly the human image was not considered to have the same magical power as the animal to bestow perpetual life on the inanimate.

55 Quite probably there are two levels of appeal in this kind of animal beauty in art. One is the promise of an otherwise unattainable sense of muscular triumph, of physical freedom. To run like an antelope or spring like a lion has its reward, even
60 though experienced vicariously. Prudence is not a matter of concern when we identify ourselves with the image of a charging horse or the streamlined form of a plunging hawk. Possibly there is even an element of envy in man's admiration of the animal
65 in which beauty and utility are inseparable, and form and act seem to be one. Blessed with the faculty to cogitate and rationalize conclusions, we

seem also to need moments in which we can live beyond thought.

70   The intuitive basis for action is the other appeal of that beauty we identify as peculiar to the animal and possibly explains in part why animals have so often become cosmic symbols. When in doubt about his own power or the direction of his

75   thinking, man has looked upon the animal as more closely attuned to the universe, living within a natural cycle from which man has been alienated by an excess of his own thought. It is not that most thinking human beings would want to become

80   animals, but the image presented by the animal becomes the foundation upon which a different ordering of the universe can be conceived.

1. Hayley was a very ------- child, naturally inclined to be calm and agreeable.

    A. noisy
    B. feral
    C. orderly
    D. docile
    E. sensitive

2. After thirty years of incarceration, the prisoner was exonerated and released, finally free and -------.

    A. untrammeled
    B. confined
    C. restrained
    D. intractable
    E. unruly

3. In spite of his nervousness, Will finally ------- the courage to telephone Kate and ask her to the prom.

    A. invited
    B. summoned
    C. eliminated
    D. condensed
    E. disparaged

4. The nylon rope was ------- as the rock climber's weight pulled it hard against the cliff.

    A. taunt
    B. slack
    C. pliant
    D. elastic
    E. taut

5. Always late, George ------- misses his bus and is never on time to appointments.

    A. momentarily
    B. perpetually
    C. temporarily
    D. randomly
    E. briefly

6. In context, *abated* (line 4) most nearly means:

    A. increased.
    B. commenced.
    C. continued.
    D. diminished.

7. As it is used in line 6, the word *imagery* most nearly means:

    A. mental images.
    B. paintings.
    C. instruction.
    D. reflections.

8. It can be inferred that the word *endow*, based on the use of *endowed* in line 8, most nearly means to:

    A. be indebted or owing money.
    B. donate goods or services.
    C. have talent or be gifted.
    D. be engaged or betrothed.

9. In line 8, *vitality* is best understood to mean:

    A. lethargy.
    B. life's energy.
    C. humor.
    D. habitat.

10. Based on the word *ardently* as it is used in line 20, *ardent* means to be:

   A. aggressive.
   B. indifferent.
   C. passionate.
   D. persuasive.

11. Based on the word *rendered* as it is used in line 24, *render* means to:

   A. repeat.
   B. tear apart.
   C. raise up.
   D. represent or depict.

12. In line 29, *adroit* is closest in meaning to all of the following EXCEPT:

   A. gauche.
   B. skillful.
   C. dexterous.
   D. clever.

13. In context, *prescribed* (line 31) most nearly means:

   A. spontaneous.
   B. imagined.
   C. donated.
   D. required.

14. As used in line 60, *vicariously* most nearly means:

   A. for a short time.
   B. to behave scandalously.
   C. through imagined participation.
   D. feeling extreme pleasure.

15. In line 70, *intuitive* most nearly means:

   A. intruding.
   B. demanding immediate attention.
   C. conscious reasoning.
   D. possessing insight.

Passage II

Social Science: This passage is adapted from an essay entitled "More on Animal Images in Human History" in an art history and philosophy anthology.

There are aspects of animal beauty other than those of transcendent vitality and natural unity that have a long history of appeal. The gorgeous plumage, intricate patterns, and luxurious fur of the
5   birds and beasts set the standards, and often provided the materials—for man's raiment and domestic decoration from the beginning of history. Although the use of skins might be considered to a degree utilitarian, a more persistent dependence on
10 the animal world was for spectacular adornment, especially for ritualistic occasions. In almost every early culture, most significant decoration has been inseparable from animal inspiration. On the whole, flora played a poor second to fauna in the beginning,
15 although it too had its role to play. It was the animal that taught man to live beyond himself. As theorists have pointed out, only man had to dress himself and felt the need to give decorative meaning to his environment; to meet this peculiarly human need,
20 he depended enthusiastically on the elegant examples provided by his animal associates.

If man has liked to adorn himself in imitation of the animals, he has also found it instructive and useful to depict animals as people, using them as
25 embodiments of human traits or projecting human patterns on their actions. Aesop's fables, the *Panchatantra*, and folk tales from almost every culture put moral judgments in the mouths of animals, as if certain kinds of lessons can best be
30 learned when experienced in a non-human context. Furthermore, we take special pleasure in seeing ourselves—or at least our neighbors—tellingly characterized in the animal world. The cartoon of an irascible duck underscores human traits in a
35 universal way that the likeness of a habitually angry person would not, and a porcine puppet conveys more about some aspects of our life and times than any simple human character could, becoming a kind of popular heroine in the process. The figures of
40 animals have carried much of the social satire in historic times, being immune to the social restrictions that might inhibit our speaking ill of our fellows. Is it our fault a particularly fat man looks like a toad?—or rather, that a picture of a toad is
45 immediately recognized as a likeness of a fat man? Not only has the animal world served to sublimate and personify our aspirations, it also has acted as a mirror to our foibles and a tutor to our ethical behavior.

50 Aside from everything else, man has usually wanted to be liked by animals, as if their affection, or at least recognition, was a mark of special acceptance. Of course, he has also wanted to dominate them, but the compassionate dog, the
55 contented cat, or the wise, devoted parrot make contributions that no amount of dominating can win. In such a relationship, who is the teacher and who is taught?

It is good to know the long traditions of
60 mystery, humor, and wisdom associated with animals have not been entirely lost to modern craftsmen. Even today, we find works that run the full gamut from mysterious symbol to gentle satire. In fact, in recent years, with increasing domination
65 of the man-made and oppressive blunting of sensibility by the preference for generalization over the particular, the threatened animal has assumed an even more poignant role. Perhaps animal imagery can serve to remind us of this important
70 point.

16. Colorado has a very rich -------, with over 3,200 species of seed plants collected, documented, and described by botanists since the first botanical exploration by Edwin James in 1819.

A. culture
B. history
C. flora
D. entourage
E. fauna

17. Carl Linnaeus, Sweden's most famous natural scientist, catalogued the country's animal life, or -------, in 1746.

A. flora
B. society
C. agriculture
D. geography
E. fauna

18. The 1938 Disney cartoon, *Self Control*, features the ------- Donald Duck as he attempts to manage his anger when some pesky insects make it difficult for him to maintain composure.

   A. easygoing
   B. irascible
   C. mysterious
   D. blasé
   E. anxious

19. Although the Russian writer Anton Chekhov sketched his characters with compassionate good-humor, he never abstained from highlighting their ------- and human weaknesses.

   A. talents
   B. accomplishments
   C. traditions
   D. foibles
   E. predilections

20. The novel *Old Yeller*, written by Fred Gipson in 1956, is arguably one of the most disturbing children's stories ever, mainly due to the ------- and emotionally devastating ending.

   A. dispassionate
   B. esoteric
   C. poignant
   D. hackneyed
   E. abstruse

21. In context, *transcendent* (line 2) most nearly means:

   A. extraordinary.
   B. transparent.
   C. conventional.
   D. observable.

22. As it is used in line 6, the word *raiment* most nearly means:

   A. narrative.
   B. evolution.
   C. shelter.
   D. clothing.

23. In line 9, *utilitarian* is best understood to indicate stressing the importance of:

   A. beauty over function.
   B. function over beauty.
   C. free will over fate.
   D. individual freedom.

24. Based on the use of the word *embodiments* in line 25, it can be inferred that *embodiment* refers to the:

   A. deprivation of property or title.
   B. representation of a deity or spirit in earthly form.
   C. concrete expression of some abstract idea or concept.
   D. abstract expression of real objects.

25. Based on the use of the word *projecting* in line 25, it can be inferred that *project* most nearly means to:

   A. imagine.
   B. protect.
   C. build.
   D. predict.

26. It can be inferred that the word *porcine*, as it is used in line 36, primarily refers to something:

   A. related to mushrooms.
   B. made from ceramic.
   C. homemade.
   D. pig-like.

27. In line 46, *sublimate* most nearly means to:

   A. submerge in liquid.
   B. reduce in quality or value.
   C. bring under control or conquer.
   D. make nobler or purer.

28. In context, *gamut* (line 63) most nearly means:

   A. an obstacle course.
   B. the entire range or extent of something.
   C. a division within a classification system.
   D. a collection of many items.

29. In line 65, *oppressive* is closest in meaning to:

    A. uplifting.

    B. tyrannical.

    C. tolerant.

    D. exacting.

30. In line 66, *sensibility* most nearly means the:

    A. inability to feel or perceive emotions.

    B. state of being aware of oneself.

    C. capacity for feeling pain or stimulation.

    D. capacity for being affected emotionally or intellectually.

Passage III

Social Science: This passage is adapted from an article entitled "Early Adolescence and Human Development" in a sociology journal.

Early adolescence is the second most rapid time of growth and change in human development. Only infancy exceeds early adolescence in velocity of growth. Physically, young adolescents are
5 experiencing a growth spurt and the onset of puberty. They have special health, nutritional, and mental health needs in relation to these physical changes. These needs have implications for school curricula. Emotionally and socially, young
10 adolescents are exploring a sense of uniqueness and belonging, of separation and commitment, future goals and their personal pasts. For the first time in their lives, they see themselves as having a personal and a social destiny, and as being part of a
15 generation. Again, these have curricular implications. Intellectually, young adolescents are exploring values and ideas in a new way. Some are beginning to form abstractions, to generalize, to think about thinking. This intellectual development
20 makes it possible for some to become engaged with concepts, imagery, contingencies, logical arguments, and even philosophical speculation. It also enables them to shift from an authoritarian sense of right and wrong to a more open and complex approach to
25 value formation, both personal and social. This cognitive shift makes it possible for young adolescents to struggle for the first time with conflicting concepts like individual rights and "the greater social good"—the underpinnings of
30 democracy. This change in cognitive style has import for curriculum and teaching techniques.

And so, early adolescence is a critical time in human development; critical to the individual, and to the social order. We tend to be fearful of this
35 stage of development. While acknowledging the plasticity of this stage, we anticipate that young adolescents are more receptive to negative than to positive influences. We are apprehensive that the great majority who maneuver their way
40 successfully through a time of life requiring considerable coping skills will "catch" the "diseases" of our "new epidemics"—pregnancy, running away, dropping out of school, alcoholism, drug addiction, violence, and suicide. I do not mean to belittle the
45 personal pain or social risk of such behaviors, but rather to insist that most young adolescents, for many reasons, most of which we do not know,

manage to cope with amazing stability through such a demanding period of life. Partly because of our
50 fears, we label the age group "transitional" and put young adolescents on hold. By doing so, we fail to assign our talents and financial resources to an extremely vulnerable and impressionable age group.

31. To prepare for every ------, the space authorities developed emergency evacuation plans for the International Space Station crew.

    A. criteria
    B. option
    C. inclination
    D. inconsistency
    E. contingency

32. The conference was intended to provide the scientists with a forum to engage in ------- about the origins of the universe and humanity's ultimate destiny.

    A. recklessness
    B. absolution
    C. abolition
    D. speculation
    E. accusation

33. The ------- government maintained its control over the people by severely punishing anyone who even attempted to question its policies.

    A. deposed
    B. authoritarian
    C. antediluvian
    D. bacchanalian
    E. laissez-faire

34. While ------- that he often turned in homework late, the student argued that this did not merit a failing grade in the course.

    A. denying
    B. ignoring
    C. believing
    D. repudiating
    E. acknowledging

35. Since the South African government disbanded the police force's endangered species unit in 2003, black rhinos have become extremely ------- to poaching by organized crime gangs.

    A. impermeable
    B. invincible
    C. amenable
    D. vulnerable
    E. manageable

36. Based on the use of the word *curricula* in line 9, it can be inferred that *curriculum* refers to:

    A. a building code.
    B. a required course of study.
    C. an underground passage.
    D. a standard on which a decision is based.

37. Based on the use of the word *abstractions* in line 18, it can be inferred that *abstraction* most nearly means:

    A. a causal or logical relation or sequence.
    B. the mental act of contemplating the parts of an object as separate from the object itself.
    C. a condition of being clogged or blocked.
    D. an unrestrained expression of feelings.

38. As it is used in line 21, the word *arguments* refers to:

    A. fights or quarrels.
    B. disputed statements.
    C. persuasive reasoning or discussions.
    D. indications or suggestions.

39. The word *underpinnings* (line 29) most nearly means:

    A. growth.
    B. attenuation.
    C. hidden opinions.
    D. foundation.

40. It can be inferred that the word *import*, as it is used in line 31, primarily means to have:

    A. significance.
    B. futility.
    C. foreign origins.
    D. urgency.

41. In line 31, the word *techniques* refers to:

    A. attitudes.
    B. methods.
    C. technologies.
    D. designs.

42. As it is used in line 36, the word *anticipate* most nearly means to:

    A. expect.
    B. disperse.
    C. prevent.
    D. argue.

43. In line 38, *apprehensive* is closest in meaning to:

    A. inexperienced.
    B. assured.
    C. confident.
    D. fearful.

44. In line 42, the word *epidemics* refers to:

    A. characteristics of a particular region.
    B. required courses of study.
    C. outbreaks of sudden rapid growth or development.
    D. cultures or histories.

45. In line 44, *belittle* most nearly means to:

    A. pay tribute.
    B. treat as having little importance.
    C. give emphasis.
    D. express deep regret or remorse.

Passage IV

Social Science: This passage is adapted from a chapter in an agricultural science textbook exploring modern agricultural problems.

Rapid increases in human population have steadily intensified pressures to augment the productivity of existing grazing and agricultural land.

5 Grazing land in the Indian subcontinent and isolated islands in the Philippines have a relatively low carrying capacity and are currently capable of sustaining only marginal levels of subsistence. Over-exploitation has not only decreased their
10 productivity, but is continuously destroying the fertility and stability of affected soils. The problem is particularly injurious in areas of Pakistan and Northeast India, where over-grazing is resulting in desertification. In the Luni blocks of Rajasthan, most
15 pastures now have only 10 to 15 percent of their original carrying capacity and the forage deficit is met by expansion into standing vegetation. Within a twenty-year period, infecund sand cover has increased from 25 to 33 percent of the area.

20 In most Asian countries, rice is the principal food crop. Increased cultivation has barely met the demands of the growing populations. In the Philippines, while food production has increased slightly faster than the size of population, even
25 greater increases in per capita food demand have created new shortfalls. Indonesia, once an important rice exporter, has been dependent on imported rice for several years. Most countries are merely keeping up with their current needs and
30 gross shortages can be anticipated.

The intensified agricultural production required in these countries has potential adverse side effects on other resources. The disruptive effects of the large-scale reservoirs needed for
35 irrigation of more land are self-evident. Some other problems include waterlogging and salinity, soil erosion, increased populations of pests, and agricultural pollution.

Waterlogging and salinity can be a problem
40 wherever surface water is applied to irrigated land with inadequate underground drainage. Water will rise to within a few feet of the surface, vitiating the growth of deep-rooted crops and allowing a concentration of minerals and salt to build up near
45 the surface. This has been seen in China, India, and Pakistan. Control projects involving the construction of new wells and drainage systems have been successful in reversing some of the deleterious effects, but at prodigious costs.

50 The establishment of broad area monoculture, primarily irrigated riceland, can result in difficult pest management problems. Recently, Indonesia has had some destructive and noisome pest outbreaks that have reduced rice yields up to 60
55 percent in the last two years. Double-cropping does not allow dry-season pest population enervation, and their numbers are therefore maintained. An integrated pest management program is needed to realize increased productivity. This program must
60 be done assiduously, not on an intermittent schedule.

Soil erosion is occurring in hilly and mountainous areas, which often constitute the only remaining land available for cultivation. With the
65 monsoon rains, erosion is inevitable unless there is an extensive terracing system. The rivers of Nepal annually carry over 240 million cubic meters of soil to India. This deprivation has been called Nepal's "most dear export."

46. In the nineteenth century, expanding European-American settlement of the United States forced large numbers of Native Americans onto ------- lands.

   A.   valuable
   B.   sustentative
   C.   precarious
   D.   central
   E.   marginal

47. Michael Pollan argues in *The Botany of Desire* that while ------- may offer economic advantages, it invites serious environmental risks because a field of identical plants will always be vulnerable to all the forces of nature.

   A.   agriculture
   B.   monoculture
   C.   nomenclature
   D.   polyculture
   E.   permaculture

48. The neighbors of the confined animal feeding operation complained about the ------- odors and groundwater pollution.

   A. harmless
   B. noisome
   C. helpful
   D. noisy
   E. benign

49. Donna tended her garden -------, taking care to weed every other day and to fertilize with every watering.

   A. inconsistently
   B. strenuously
   C. assiduously
   D. irreverently
   E. respectfully

50. Although a ceasefire had been signed, ------- and sporadic gunfire disturbed the silence of the desert night.

   A. constant
   B. incipient
   C. contented
   D. intermittent
   E. deliberate

51. It can be inferred that the word *augment*, as it is used in line 2, means to:

   A. decrease.
   B. increase.
   C. remain constant.
   D. cease.

52. In context, *subsistence* (line 8) most nearly means:

   A. extinction.
   B. productivity.
   C. wastefulness.
   D. survival.

53. It can be inferred that the word *desertification* (line 14) refers to the process by which:

   A. land becomes wet and humid.
   B. land becomes dry and arid.
   C. air becomes wet and humid.
   D. air becomes dry and arid.

54. As it is used in line 18, the word *infecund* most nearly means:

   A. offensive smelling.
   B. infectious.
   C. unproductive.
   D. fertile.

55. In line 32, *adverse* is best understood to mean:

   A. unfavorable.
   B. constructive.
   C. poisonous.
   D. beneficial.

56. The word *salinity* (line 36) most nearly means:

   A. sourness.
   B. sweetness.
   C. saltiness.
   D. bitterness.

57. As it is used in line 42, the word *vitiating* most nearly means:

   A. assisting or helping.
   B. energizing or strengthening.
   C. depriving of oxygen.
   D. making faulty or defective.

58. It can be inferred that the word *deleterious*, as it is used in line 49, most nearly means:

   A. delicious.
   B. harmless.
   C. involuntary.
   D. destructive.

59. In line 49, *prodigious* most nearly means:

    A. enormous.
    B. marginal.
    C. average.
    D. luxuriant.

60. The word *enervation* (line 56) refers to:

    A. weakening.
    B. strengthening.
    C. extinction.
    D. animation.

Passage V

Social Science: This passage is adapted from an introductory economics course textbook.

The function of payment systems is to provide means for conducting exchanges of values. These values usually involve goods, services, financial obligations, or ownership records on one side,
5 which are exchanged for money from the other party in the transaction. However, in recent years, surrogates for money, such as checks or credit, have received increasing acceptance. Since they facilitate the exchange process, payment systems have
10 become all-persuasive and essential to the operation of modern society. All of us make use of one or more of these systems so easily and casually almost daily, we are seldom aware of the process.

Payment systems have a long history. One of
15 the first steps in organizing any nation is the enactment and promulgation of laws to provide for and regulate the value of some form of money and to enforce, to the greatest extent possible, its universal acceptance. Without widespread use and
20 acceptance of a standardized medium of exchange, the growth of industry and commerce would be stunted.

In early times, coins were the most prevalent form of money and are still widely used for many
25 types of transactions; in fact, during the last two decades, coin transactions have enjoyed a resurgence. The impetus for this increased reliance on coins was the spread of coin-operated vending machines. The development of paper currency
30 provided a more convenient alternative to coins for all except low-value transactions and facilitated the spread of commercial activity. More recently, the large-scale acceptance of checks provided a still better means for making many types of payments,
35 especially those that have to be made over a distance; thus, their growth has been rapid.

A host of other, more specialized instruments have also been developed. Travelers' checks, a widely-accepted and convenient medium of
40 exchange for those away from home, are safer than cash. Letters of credit, which are employed for similar reasons by businesses, usually involve larger amounts than those for which travelers' checks are used. Money orders offer a means for individuals
45 without checking accounts to effect safe and rapid payments at a distance. Telegraph transfers of

money can be relied on where speed is critical. Each system has other distinctive characteristics. Some offer greater safety from loss or theft than do
50 others; some are more susceptible to fraud or misuse. Thus, we can choose among a wide range of options to suit our needs.

The importance of efficient payment mechanisms is amplified by their close relationship
55 to another key social activity—the granting of credit. This relationship derives from the fact that the decision to extend credit is often based to a large extent on the past performance of the recipient in making payments on prior credit
60 offerings. This characteristic makes records of past payments an important component in the credit-granting process.

The most important factor, in social and economic terms, has been the rapid growth in the
65 extension of consumer credit as part of the process of conducting retail sales transactions. Both merchants and financial institutions offering credit—as well as those who receive it—have perceived benefits from the frequent use of short-
70 term credit systems, so a variety of means for providing such credit has arisen in recent years. This has led to a wide-spread and increasing use of credit cards provided by merchants, banks, and independent operators as a substitute for cash or
75 checks when making retail purchases.

Initially, however, credit cards were almost always associated with specific purchases (often from the single company issuing the card), and the grant of credit terminated upon the presentation of
80 a monthly bill. In this forum of use, the dominant features of value to the card-user were the convenience provided when making purchases, the greater safety of carrying smaller amounts of cash, and the possibility of aggregating a number of
85 smaller payments into a single large payment. More recently, and arising primarily from the introduction of bank credit cards, some systems provide extended credit, automatic use of credit when a checking account becomes overdrawn, and
90 opportunities to borrow money unrelated to specific purchases. These features can become more important than the convenience, security, and payments aggregation characteristics. In the process, payments and credit have grown still more
95 tightly related, and the two elements have become increasingly difficult to disentangle.

61. In the United States, the ------- of federal laws occurs upon signing by the President or overriding of a presidential veto.

A. dissimilation
B. promulgation
C. proscription
D. extension
E. destruction

62. To suggest that jazz enjoyed a(n) ------- in the 1980s is to imply that it fell out of favor in the 1970s—a proposition with which many jazz fans would take issue.

A. resurgence
B. acquiescence
C. insurgence
D. disappearance
E. importance

63. After the comptroller was caught embezzling funds from government accounts, her appointment was immediately -------.

A. delegated
B. initiated
C. relegated
D. renegotiated
E. terminated

64. According to Leo Tolstoy, history—that is to say the collective life of the ------- of human beings—turns each moment of a monarch's life to account, and bends kings to its own ends.

A. faction
B. aggregate
C. entourage
D. separation
E. range

65. Because she wrote checks totaling more than the available balance, Jill's bank account became -------.

A. solvent
B. accessible
C. overhauled
D. financed
E. overdrawn

66. In context, *transaction* (line 6) primarily refers to a(n):

A. performance.
B. alteration.
C. transition.
D. business deal.

67. As it is used in line 7, the word *surrogates* refers to:

A. descendants.
B. replications.
C. recipients.
D. substitutes.

68. It can be inferred that the word *facilitate*, as it is used in line 8, most nearly means to:

A. inhibit or slow down.
B. make briefer.
C. make less difficult.
D. complicate.

69. In line 19, *universal* is best understood to mean:

A. used by everyone.
B. the state of being excluded.
C. limited in availability.
D. better than average.

70. According to the passage, the word *prevalent* (line 23) is used to refer to something:

A. exceptional.
B. absent.
C. widespread.
D. current.

71. The word *impetus* (line 27) most nearly means:

A. inertia.
B. stimulus.
C. lethargy.
D. insolence.

72. It can be inferred that the word *currency*, as it is used in line 29, primarily refers to a:

    A. prevalent trend.
    B. technique for making money.
    C. record-keeping device.
    D. medium of trade or exchange.

73. In line 50, *susceptible* most nearly means:

    A. insensitive.
    B. easily affected.
    C. suspicious.
    D. accessible.

74. In line 56, *derives* most nearly means:

    A. comes from a source.
    B. creates from new.
    C. depart from an established course.
    D. expresses contempt.

75. In line 61, *component* refers to a(n):

    A. aggregate.
    B. role or position.
    C. substitute.
    D. part.

Passage VI

Social Science: This passage is adapted from an essay entitled "Customs and Opinions of Ancient Nations" in an introductory sociology textbook.

Nature being everywhere the same, men must necessarily have adopted the same verities, and fallen into the same delusions, in regard to those things which are the immediate objects of sense,
5 and the most striking to the imagination. They simply have ascribed the noise and effects of thunder to some superior being inhabiting the air. The people bordering upon the ocean, seeing great tides inundate their coasts at the time of the full
10 moon, must naturally have imputed to the moon the vicissitudes which attended her cyclical phases.

Among animals, the serpent must have appeared to them to be endowed with superior intelligence; because, seeing it sometimes cast its
15 skin, they had reason to think it became young again. It might, then, by this process of rejuvenation always remain youthful and therefore immortal. In Egypt and Greece, it was the symbol of immortality. The larger serpents found in proximity to fountains
20 deterred the timorous from approaching them, hence they were imagined to be guardians of hidden treasure. Serpents were also found to be mischievous animals, but as they were supposed to possess something divine, nothing less than a deity
25 was imagined capable of destroying them.

Dreams too much have introduced the same superstitions all over the earth. If while awake, I am uneasy for my wife's or son's health, and in my sleep I see them in the agonies of death, should they die a
30 few days later, it cannot be denied the gods sent me this warning. If my dream is not fulfilled? It was a fallacious representation, with which the gods wished to terrify me. Or a woman applies to the oracles to know whether her husband will die
35 within the year. One answers yes, the other no. It is certain that one of them must be correct, and she will proclaim all over the city the wisdom of the one whose prognostication was fulfilled.

The origin of good and evil is a more
40 philosophical question. The first theologians must have put the same question which we all do from the age of fifteen or so: Why is there any evil in the world? It was taught in India, that Adimo, the daughter of Brahma, brought forth from the navel,
45 the just from her right side and the unjust from her left; it was from this left side that evil was originally introduced. We know of Pandora of the Greeks. This is the finest of all the allegories which antiquity has handed down to us.

50 So too all peoples have provided for the expiation of wrongdoing, for where was the man or woman who had not been guilty of some injury against society? Who had not profaned the gods? Who had not debased himself? Where was the
55 person whose natural instinct did not prompt a feeling of remorse? Water cleanses the body and our apparel, and fire purifies metal. It was natural then that water and fire should purge the soul of its guilt, and in every temple were found holy water
60 and sacred fire.

Men plunged themselves into the Ganges, the Indus, and the Euphrates when it was the noon moon. This immersion expiated their sins. If they did not purify themselves in the Nile, it was only for
65 fear that the penitents might have been devoured by crocodiles. However, the priests who purified themselves on the people's behalf immersed themselves in large tubs of water. The Greeks had in all of their temples sacred baths as well as sacred
70 fires, which were universal symbols for all men of the purity of their souls.

76. The authorship of the ancient Sanskrit epic *Mahabharata*, a major text of Hinduism and cornerstone of Hindu mythology, is traditionally ------- to Vyasa.

   A. subscribed
   B. ascribed
   C. delivered
   D. propelled
   E. transmitted

77. The inability of the Congress to pass any legislation was ------- to the Republicans for their perceived refusal to attempt negotiations with the Democrats.

   A. demoted
   B. transferred
   C. promoted
   D. imputed
   E. donated

78. Because Elizabeth was so ------- and lacking in confidence, she was an easy target for every peddler and door-to-door salesperson.

A. brave
B. timorous
C. confrontational
D. outgoing
E. devious

79. The irony of the Nobel Peace Prize bearing the name of the inventor of dynamite has given rise to the myth that Alfred Nobel established the award as a way to ------- his guilty conscience.

A. augment
B. idealize
C. scrutinize
D. justify
E. expiate

80. We hoped that the media would not ------- the memory of our deceased father by reporting the malicious gossip and rumors surrounding his death.

A. profane
B. sustain
C. abolish
D. inflate
E. defend

81. As it is used in line 2, the word *verities* refers to:

A. methods.
B. truths.
C. histories.
D. falsehoods.

82. In context, *inundate* (line 9) most nearly means to:

A. dehydrate.
B. capitulate.
C. overflow.
D. emphasize.

83. In line 11, the word *vicissitudes* refers to:

A. changes in fortune.
B. mental confusion.
C. alteration of plans.
D. fierceness or aggression.

84. It can be inferred that the word *rejuvenation*, as it is used in line 16, primarily refers to the:

A. ending of life.
B. appearance of illusion.
C. personification of characteristics.
D. restoration of youth.

85. The word *proximity* (line 19) is used to indicate:

A. agility.
B. probability.
C. relevance.
D. nearness.

86. Based on the use of the word *oracles* in line 34, it can be inferred that *oracle* primarily refers to a(n):

A. public speech or debate.
B. person believed to foretell the future.
C. organization or coalition.
D. person making a donation.

87. As it is used in line 38, the word *prognostication* refers to a:

A. delay.
B. responsibility.
C. prediction.
D. perception.

88. Based on the use of the word *allegories* in line 48, it can be inferred that *allegory* primarily refers to a(n):

A. unsupported assertion.
B. symbolic story about human existence.
C. musical composition.
D. pledge of allegiance.

89. In line 56, *remorse* is closest in meaning to:

    A. shame.
    B. arrogance.
    C. humility.
    D. compassion.

90. Based on the use of the word *immersion* in line 63, *immerse* most nearly means to:

    A. absorb excess liquid.
    B. confront one's emotions.
    C. rise up from or come into view.
    D. completely cover with liquid.

Vocabulary Builder: Humanities Passages
Exercise 8

DIRECTIONS: Each passage in this exercise is followed by sets of sentence completion and vocabulary-in-context items. In addition to using the passages to infer word meanings, you may use a dictionary.

The first set of items following each passage are sentence completion items based on words from the passage. Each sentence has one blank. Choose the word that best fits the meaning of the sentence in its entirety.

The second set of items following each passage are vocabulary-in-context items based on words from the passage. Choose the best answer for each item based on what is stated or implied in the passage.

Answers are on page 593.

Passage I

Humanities: This passage is adapted from an essay discussing the epic poem *Kalevala*, compiled by Elias Lönnrot from Finnish folklore in the nineteenth century.

Those who enjoyed the *Star Wars* films would probably fall under the spell of the Finnish epic, *Kalevala*. Though first published nearly 150 years ago, many of the adventures in this epic could easily
5 be scripted into scenes for our modern fantasy adventure films. Instead of battling with advanced technological gadgets such as rockets and lasers, however, the heroes of *Kalevala* engage in bouts of wisdom and magic, casting spells of enchantment
10 over their foes. Thus, when wise old Vainamoinen, the greatest singer of the runes, is challenged by a young up-start, Joukahainen, it takes but a few magical charms to cause the young man to sink neck-deep into the seemingly solid ground. The
15 thoroughly intimidated Joukahainen offers his sister, Aino, as ransom for his release, and Vainamoinen accepts. The young girl, dismayed at the prospect of marriage to such an old man, drowns herself and becomes a fish. Vainamoinen
20 later catches the fish, but he fails to recognize her and she escapes, leaving him to grieve.

These fantastic adventures of charm-chanting heroes and sorcerers were known to illiterate Finnish singers for many hundreds of years. The
25 episodes were sung as individual songs by traditional singers who lived in isolated villages along the Finnish-Russian frontier. They became known to the educated, urban Finns only after the texts of some songs were set down on paper.
30 Although a few of the songs had been sporadically

recorded since the eighteenth century, it was primarily the work of one individual—Elias Lönnrot—that clearly demonstrated the richness of these oral traditions. A medical doctor by
35 profession, but an avid folklore collector by avocation, Lönnrot logged many miles on foot in the early 1830s, writing down as many variants as he could find of the songs about Vainamoinen, Lemminkainen, Llmarinen, and others. Instead of
40 publishing the songs as individual pieces, however, he arranged them into a linear story line.

In 1835, he published the *Kalevala* as an epic—the Finnish counterpart to the Nordic *Edda*, the Germanic *Nibelungenlied*, the Scottish Ossian
45 poems, and harkening back to the classics, the Greek *Iliad* and *Odyssey*.

For Finland, the publication of songs sung by the ordinary folk in the hinterlands of their country served as a major stimulus to the building and
50 fostering of a distinct national identity. Until then, the Finnish language and identity were held in rather low esteem; Finland's educated, urban elite had accepted, for the most part, the language, culture, and traditions of the governing Swedes.
55 Through Lönnrot's *Kalevala*, the intelligentsia began to awaken to the richness of the Finnish heritage.

Although it took some time, the *Kalevala* helped to kindle national aspirations that eventually culminated in the establishment of an independent
60 Finland. For the Finnish people, much under the sway of the general Romantic trends of the times, the *Kalevala* presented a past of which they could be proud. Scholars argued about the historicity of the heroes and engaged in discussion about the
65 evolution of the songs through time. It became

required reading in secondary schools, and playwrights, composers, and other artists were soon using its themes and motifs for their own creative ventures.

70   The *Kalevala* was indeed something of which to be proud, for soon after its publication in Finnish, it was translated into Swedish, French, German, and Russian. In America, the work received considerable publicity when Longfellow published his *Song of*
75 *Hiawatha* in 1885, and critics accused him of plagiarizing the Finnish epic. Longfellow admitted that he was acquainted with the work through German translation and that he purposely copied the meter of the *Kalevala* in order to imbue his work
80 with a certain ancient and noble tone and cadence. Prompted by the controversy, the English translation appeared in 1889. Since those times, translations have been printed in 30 languages. The *Kalevala* is probably the best known Finnish literary
85 work throughout the world.

1. Because the dog barked ------- for no apparent reason, we decided he was not a very reliable watchdog.

   A. quietly
   B. callously
   C. temporarily
   D. sporadically
   E. shyly

2. A passionate skateboarder, Jonathan is planning a regional tour of neighborhood community centers to share his ------- love of the sport with underprivileged teens.

   A. apathetic
   B. average
   C. unreasonable
   D. aversive
   E. avid

3. The schedule for the six-week acting workshop indicates it will ------- in the final presentation of a one-act play to the entire student body.

   A. initiate
   B. converge
   C. culminate
   D. founder
   E. corroborate

4. From all around the country, young men with no work and ------- with patriotism rushed to serve in World War I.

   A. subdued
   B. withered
   C. placated
   D. imbued
   E. diminished

5. The high school concert band marched to a swift ------- played by the rhythmic drum section.

   A. dalliance
   B. irreverence
   C. cadence
   D. silence
   E. insurgence

6. In context, *prospect* (line 18) most nearly means:

   A. trust or confidence.
   B. mental consideration.
   C. a declaration.
   D. condition of success.

7. As it is used in line 36, the word *avocation* most nearly means:

   A. hobby.
   B. training.
   C. birth.
   D. job.

8. It can be inferred that the word *hinterlands*, as it is used in line 48, primarily refers to:

   A. areas close to big cities or towns.
   B. areas far from big cities or towns.
   C. capital cities.
   D. elevated or mountainous lands.

9. In line 55, *intelligentsia* is best understood to refer in general to the:

   A. educated class.
   B. uneducated class.
   C. university academic employees.
   D. farmers and peasants.

10. In line 56, *heritage* is best understood as referring to:

    A. innovations.
    B. political systems.
    C. landscape.
    D. customs and traditions.

11. The word *aspirations* (line 58) most nearly means:

    A. failures.
    B. realities.
    C. ambitions.
    D. legends.

12. It can be inferred that the word *establishment*, as it is used in line 59, most nearly means:

    A. destruction.
    B. formation.
    C. interpretation.
    D. purchase.

13. As it is used in line 61, the word *sway* most nearly means:

    A. freedom.
    B. support.
    C. influence.
    D. overindulgence.

14. In line 63, *historicity* most nearly means:

    A. authenticity.
    B. humility.
    C. exaggeration.
    D. origin.

15. In line 68, *motifs* is closest in meaning to:

    A. impulses.
    B. replications.
    C. main elements.
    D. mechanisms.

Passage II

Humanities: This passage is adapted from an essay discussing an anthology of American songs based on the classic, "Tie a Yellow Ribbon."

In 1972, Irwin Levine and L. Russell Brown copyrighted a song with the title of "Tie a Yellow Ribbon Round the Ole Oak Tree," and it was recorded by some 30 different vocalists in the late
5 1970s and sold millions of copies. The hit version was recorded by the popular group Dawn, featuring Tony Orlando. In 1949, Aigosy Pictures released a motion picture starring John Wayne and Joanne Dru, called *She Wore a Yellow Ribbon*. The picture
10 was popular and the theme song, "Round Her Neck She Wore a Yellow Ribbon," became a hit. Not surprisingly, the lyrics make reference to the characters and events in the film. In one form or another, this song antedates both the movie and the
15 hit tune. It has been registered for copyright a number of times, the earliest claim for it being the composition of George Norton in 1917. Norton gave as his title "Round Her Neck She Wears a Yeller Ribbon."

20 It has also been reported as a college song of the 1920s in which environment it displayed considerable variation, both in its symbolism and in its suitability for public expression. A verse typical of the college type:

25 Around her knee, she wore a purple garter;
    She wore it in the Springtime, and in the
        month of May.
    And if you asked her why the Hell she wore it,
    She wore it for her William's man who's far, far
30   away.

Other emblematic appurtenances of the young lady include a baby carriage and a shotgun-wielding father. The color of the ribbon or garter could be varied in order to implicate a student of an
35 appropriate college: crimson for Harvard, orange for Princeton, and so on. It was a slightly refined version of this college tradition, rather than the movie theme song, which became a great favorite on the early 1960s, television show, "Sing Along
40 with Mitch." It appears on pages 22 and 24 of the *Sing Along with Mitch Songbook*, where an accompanying headnote describes it as an "old army marching song (based on a traditional theme)." Although the second verse is essentially

45 the "purple garter" type, the first verse begins, "Around her neck, she wore a yellow ribbon."

It seems likely that Mitch Miller's popular printing, a decade after the motion picture, helped foster the perhaps erroneous idea that wearing a
50 yellow ribbon as a token of remembrance was a custom of the Civil War era, but the song does not appear in any known anthology of Civil War songs. Although it is plausible that the families of Union army troops did adopt such a token, prudent
55 historiography would demand evidence from a diary, photograph, or source contemporary to the war. Without such evidence, it seems likely that distant recollections of the Civil War have subsequently been grafted onto the symbolism of a
60 much later popular motion picture. Occurrences of this sort are often noticed in the study of folk balladry in which the anachronistic combinations are among the more interesting features of the genre.

65 Whether Levine and Brown were consciously or unconsciously influenced by *She Wore a Yellow Ribbon* is not known. If they were, it would be worth noting that the George Norton song that influenced them has a pedigree that stretches far beyond the
70 college environment of the 1920s. A similar song was heard in minstrel shows in this country around 1838: "All Round My Hat," which is unquestionably the ancestor of the later "Round Her Neck She Wore a Yellow Ribbon," with all of its variants and
75 imitations. Likewise, in *Othello*, Shakespeare has Desdemona refer to an earlier version of the song.

In its long descent from Tudor lyric to Cockney ballad to American minstrel ditty to ribald college song to motion picture theme to popular recording,
80 we see garters and ribbons of every hue—and the symbol of constancy in love has been anything but constant itself.

16. Dove releases are traditional following marriage ceremonies because the life-long pairing of doves is ------- of what the state of human marriage should be.

A. antagonistic
B. sympathetic
C. phobic
D. empiric
E. emblematic

17. The Innocence Project is comprised of law professors and their students who re-investigate and challenge the evidence in convictions of murder defendants whose claims of innocence seem -------.

   A. plausible
   B. deniable
   C. expected
   D. unlikely
   E. incredible

18. The mayoral candidate is campaigning on a platform of reigning in government expenditures, stressing that he is fiscally ------- and a friend of the business community.

   A. insensible
   B. furtive
   C. intensive
   D. prudent
   E. supple

19. Mel Brooks' 1974 film *Blazing Saddles*, set in the Wild West in 1874, contains many ------- props from the 1970s, including a stylish Gucci costume for the sheriff and an automobile.

   A. suitable
   B. decorous
   C. mundane
   D. anticlimactic
   E. anachronistic

20. There are a number of criteria by which one may classify musical -------, including the distinction between popular and traditional, regional and national differences, influences, and origins.

   A. instruments
   B. plots
   C. genres
   D. arrangements
   E. conflagrations

21. The word *antedates* (line 14) most nearly means:

   A. anticipates.
   B. precedes.
   C. prevents.
   D. follows.

22. Based on the use of the word *appurtenances* in line 31, it can be inferred that *appurtenance* refers to something:

   A. exaggerated or embellished.
   B. resembling a particular characteristic.
   C. subordinate to another, more important thing.
   D. fundamental in existence.

23. Based on the use of the word *wielding* in line 32, it can be inferred that *wield* means to:

   A. give up.
   B. handle or carry something.
   C. produce or bring forth.
   D. conceal

24. In line 34, *implicate* is best understood to mean to:

   A. make a copy of something.
   B. set about or attempt.
   C. indicate and set apart for a purpose.
   D. involve with or show a connection between things.

25. In line 36, *refined* most nearly means:

   A. defined essential characteristics.
   B. lowered in status or quality.
   C. cultivated or freed from coarseness.
   D. abbreviated or cut short.

26. It can be inferred that the word *anthology*, as it is used in line 52, primarily refers to:

   A. the study of human nature.
   B. an autobiographical account.
   C. an inventory of stock.
   D. a collection of songs.

27. It can be inferred that the word *historiography*, as it is used in line 55, primarily refers to the:

   A.   scholarly study of history.
   B.   process of producing images.
   C.   science of drawing maps.
   D.   deliberate display of emotion for effect.

28. Based on the use of the word *grafted* in line 59, it can be inferred that *graft* most nearly means to:

   A.   work without compensation.
   B.   attach or join together.
   C.   obtain legally.
   D.   duplicate or reproduce.

29. It can be inferred that the word *ditty*, as it is used in line 78, primarily refers to a(n):

   A.   previously mentioned word.
   B.   means of production.
   C.   simple song.
   D.   epic poem.

30. In line 78, *ribald* most nearly means:

   A.   refined.
   B.   popular.
   C.   vulgar.
   D.   mediocre.

Passage III

Humanities: This passage is adapted from an introductory textbook on the history of American music.

Harmonica, mouth organ, French harp, harp—there are dozens of appellations in American English for this simple instrument, evidence of the local and regional level of its widespread appeal.
5 The ubiquitous little music maker may seem homely when compared with more cultivated species, but the hardy perennial has taken root in our musical landscape, and has been owned and played by more Americans than any other instrument. This
10 wildflower has long been mistaken for a weed by stodgy and established musical experts; consequently, there has been little scholarly writing devoted to it.

Like many familiar domestic blooms, the
15 harmonica is an Old World transplant. The ancestral rootstock of the free-reed family, to which the mouth harp belongs, comes from Asia where according to myth, the Chinese female sovereign Nyn-Kwa invented the *sheng* or mouth organ about
20 3000 B.C. Written descriptions of the instrument date from a thousand years later, and examples and representations of *sheng* have been found at grave sites in central China dating from the 5th century B.C. Although its invention has been credited to
25 several people, the first patent for the familiar mouth harmonica was filed in Berlin by Friedrich Buschmann in 1821. Within ten years of its invention, the European mouth organ was being produced commercially in Austria, Switzerland, and
30 the German kingdom of Saxony.

In the second half of the nineteenth century, German manufacturers began the mass production of harmonicas with an eye to the huge export market. Towards the end of the century, German
35 factories were producing up to ten million instruments a year, and more than half were sold in the United States. Popularity of the instrument peaked between the world wars, when it was used for music education in public schools, on the
40 vaudeville stage, and on early blues and "hillbilly" recordings. In the late 1940s, electric "city" blues bands featured amplified harmonicas as lead instruments, and their records, though less popular in black communities since the mid-1960s, continue
45 to be a strong influence on popular music both here and abroad.

With millions of mouth organs imported each year for over a century, the harmonica is the most popular musical instrument in our nation's history.
50 Why, then, the dearth of literature on the harmonica? One explanation is the type of sound produced by the instrument. In reed instruments such as the saxophone or oboe, a flexible sliver of reed is vibrated against something. Once the reed is
55 vibrating, the length of a resonating column of air is varied to produce different pitches. Free-reed instruments, like the harmonica, have reeds that vibrate without touching anything else. As the vibrations of the free reeds are unhindered, the
60 resulting sounds are dense with overtones, producing a timbre alternately described as mellifluous or irritating, according to the tastes of the listener. However, the same may also be said of a "serious" instrument such as the violin. A more
65 likely explanation is the simplicity and cost of the harmonica. Small and cheap, it has been the instrument of choice for children, working people, and vagabonds. Thus, the social status of the most visible harp players has not encouraged the
70 attention of students of "serious" music.

Fortunately, critical neglect has not prevented harmonica players from making good music, much of it endemic to the U.S. Harmonica tune books from the 1920s suggest the instrument's repertory
75 embraced familiar dance tunes, popular songs, and sentimental favorites of the preceding half-century. Prominent among early recordings are entertaining solo pieces in which harmonica virtuosos imitate the sounds of animals, crying babies, electric
80 pumps, and railroads. Train whistles and fox chases pervaded the recorded harmonica repertory.

Other virtuoso pieces make use of "note bending" to make sounds and play pitches which are, in theory, impossible to play on the instrument.
85 The technique, as yet unexplained by acoustic physicists, makes possible the distinctively fluid phrasing and wailing sound of the blues harmonica. By deflecting air with the mouth, the player can "bend" or flatten a note, almost to the tonal value of
90 the next lower-pitched reed. This technique was widely employed by blues players of the 1920s. In some solo recordings, the player sings a line, then uses the mouth harp to play an improvised instrumental response.

95 It is difficult to generalize about an instrument used in making so many different kinds of music, except to say the differences in style between

individuals are stronger than most regional characteristics. There is an intimate relationship be-
100 tween player and harp; the resulting music reflects experience, outlook, and even mood more than with most instruments. While limited in range, the harmonica can speak with a very personal voice. Perhaps its versatile adaptability is the real key to
105 the small instrument's large role in the musical life of America.

31. The ------- presence of the extremely demanding and critical factory owner made the workers fearful for their jobs.

   A. vacuous
   B. ubiquitous
   C. distant
   D. ambiguous
   E. dubious

32. A(n) ------- of certified teachers has forced the school board to hire teachers who are still working on their certification.

   A. abundance
   B. compliment
   C. cooperation
   D. indictment
   E. dearth

33. Although Peter was just over five and half feet tall, when he spoke you had to be impressed by the deep, ------- quality of his voice.

   A. faint
   B. resonant
   C. vulnerable
   D. irreproachable
   E. commendable

34. Articulated in his smooth and ------- prose, the English novelist Colin Thubron's eye for detail and command of scope make for an absorbing, complex read.

   A. callous
   B. terse
   C. temperamental
   D. mellifluous
   E. sarcastic

35. The ------- of the assembly hall were very poor, making it difficult to hear the speaker past the tenth row of seats.

   A. semantics
   B. ballistics
   C. aesthetics
   D. antics
   E. acoustics

36. Based on the use of the word *appellations* in line 2, it can be inferred that *appellation* most nearly means:

   A. name.
   B. appearance.
   C. destination.
   D. manifestation.

37. It can be inferred that the word *perennial*, as it is used in line 7, primarily refers to something that is:

   A. original.
   B. rude in behavior.
   C. continuous.
   D. annoying.

38. As it is used in line 11, the word *stodgy* most nearly means:

   A. substantial.
   B. boring.
   C. unaffected.
   D. lively.

39. In line 18, *sovereign* is best understood to mean:

   A. ruler.
   B. traveler.
   C. explorer.
   D. supplicant.

40. It can be inferred that the word *timbre*, as it is used in line 61, primarily refers to:

   A. a nervous characteristic.
   B. the wood of growing trees.
   C. a short, simple song.
   D. the quality of sound.

41. In line 73, *endemic* most nearly means:

    A. widespread or rapid growth.
    B. characteristic of a particular region.
    C. a long poetic composition.
    D. external to one's country or origin.

42. In line 74, *repertory* most nearly refers to a(n):

    A. musical play or production.
    B. entire collection of works.
    C. place where something is kept safe.
    D. history of development.

43. Based on the use of the word *virtuosos* in line 78, it can be inferred that *virtuoso* primarily refers to a(n):

    A. student.
    B. amateur.
    C. expert.
    D. entertainer.

44. In line 93, *improvised* most nearly means:

    A. skillful or accomplished.
    B. made up or performed spontaneously.
    C. immediately pertinent.
    D. dramatic monologue.

45. Based on its use in line 104, *versatile* can be defined as all of the following EXCEPT:

    A. adaptable.
    B. multipurpose.
    C. resourceful.
    D. inflexible.

Passage IV

Humanities: This passage is adapted from an essay about *La Gioconda*, the painting by Leonardo da Vinci more commonly known as the "Mona Lisa." The actual person in the painting may have been Lisa, the third wife of Francesco del Giocondo.

La Gioconda is, in the truest sense, Leonardo's masterpiece; the revealing paradigm of his mode of thought and work. We all know the face and hands of the figure, set in its marble chair, in that circle of
5 fantastic rocks, as in some faint light under the sea. Perhaps of all ancient pictures, time has chilled it least.

As often happens with works in which genius seems to surpass its limit, there is an element in it
10 transmitted by, but not invented by, the master. In that inestimable folio of drawings, once in the possession of Vasari, were certain designs by Verrocchio, faces of such impressive beauty that Leonardo in his boyhood copied them many times.
15 It is difficult not to see these designs of the elder master as the germinal principle of that unfathomable smile, with its touch of something sinister, which infects all Leonardo's work.

Besides, the picture is a portrait. From
20 childhood, we see this image defining itself on the fabric of his dreams, and were it not for explicit historical testimony, we might fancy this was his ideal lady, embodied and beheld at last.

What was the relationship of a living
25 Florentine to the creature of his thought? By what strange affinities had the dream and the person grown up so apart, and yet so close? Present from the first incorporeal ideas in Leonardo's brain, dimly traced in the designs of Verrocchio, she is
30 found present at last in Il Giocondo's house.

To be sure, it is a portrait, a painting, and legend has it that mimes and musicians were used to protract that smile. Was it in four months or as by a stroke of magic the image was projected?

35 The presence that rises so strangely beside the waters is expressive of what after a thousand years men had come to desire. Hers is the head upon all "the ends of the world are come," and the eyelids are a little weary. It is a beauty brought out from
40 within and deposited upon the flesh, bit by bit, cell by cell—strange thoughts and fantastic reveries and

exquisite passions. Set it for a moment beside one of those Greek statues of beautiful women of antiquity. How they would be troubled by this beauty, into
45 which the soul with all of its maladies had been passed! All the thoughts and experience of the world are etched and molded there: the animalism of Greece, the lust of Rome, the mysticism of the Middle Ages with its spiritual ambition and
50 imaginative loves, the return of the pagan world, the sins of the Borgias.

She is older than the rocks among which she sits. Like the vampire, she has been dead many times, and learned the secrets of the grave; and has
55 submerged herself in deep seas and kept their fallen day about her; and trafficked for some strange webs with Easter merchants and as Leda, the mother of Helen of Troy, and as Saint Anne, the mother of Mary. All of this has been to her but as the sound of
60 lyres and flutes, and lives only in the delicacy with which it has molded the changing lineaments and tinged the eyelids and the hands.

46. The established and successful member-owned cooperative served as a(n) ------- for the small, locally-owned food markets that have recently sprung up in the region.

    A.   benefit
    B.   substitution
    C.   paradigm
    D.   affliction
    E.   anomaly

47. There is such a strong ------- between new cars made by rival automakers today that the casual observer cannot tell them apart.

    A.   dissimilarity
    B.   competition
    C.   deterioration
    D.   affinity
    E.   variation

48. The notion that there is a(n) ------- realm of existence that is distinct from the material universe is fundamental to the belief in a divine being.

A. physical
B. logistical
C. imaginary
D. substitute
E. incorporeal

49. In order to ------- the telephone call long enough to put a trace on it, the detective kept the caller engaged in seemingly pointless conversation.

A. distract
B. mitigate
C. protract
D. contract
E. interrupt

50. Katya's memory of the moment was ------- with sorrow; while her voice was firm, it was obviously touched with grief.

A. confused
B. tipped
C. prolonged
D. tinged
E. arranged

51. In context, *masterpiece* (line 2) most nearly refers to an artist's:

A. most important work.
B. beginning stages of a piece.
C. posthumously published work.
D. rehearsal or practice pieces.

52. As it is used in line 2, the word *mode* most nearly refers to a(n):

A. sound.
B. feeling.
C. asset.
D. method.

53. In line 11, *folio* is best understood to refer to a(n):

A. duplicate.
B. burial.
C. booklet.
D. painting.

54. It can be inferred that the word *germinal*, as it is used in line 16, refers to the:

A. overriding themes.
B. early stages.
C. destructive elements.
D. tutorial process.

55. The word *explicit* (line 21) most nearly means:

A. clearly expressed.
B. involved or entwined.
C. embedded or contained.
D. brought out.

56. In line 42, *exquisite* most nearly means characterized by:

A. an even temperament.
B. expensive taste.
C. mind-numbing detail.
D. intense emotions.

57. It can be inferred that the word *antiquity*, as it is used in line 43, most nearly means belonging to:

A. modern culture.
B. ancient times.
C. the future.
D. prehistory.

58. In line 45, *maladies* is best understood to refer to:

A. dreams.
B. sicknesses.
C. painful emotions.
D. memories.

59. In line 48, *mysticism* refers to:

    A. the historical record.
    B. exciting curiosities.
    C. a belief about spiritual truth.
    D. a political system.

60. It can be inferred that the word *lineaments*, as it is used in line 61, refers to:

    A. skin ointments.
    B. descendants from a common ancestor.
    C. facial features.
    D. ground plans.

Passage V

Humanities: This passage is adapted from an essay about Joseph Turner's 1840 oil painting entitled "Slavers throwing overboard the Dead and Dying—Typhoon coming on," or more commonly, "The Slave Ship."

I think the noblest sea that Turner has ever painted, and so the noblest ever painted by man, is that of "The Slave Ship." It is a sunset on the Atlantic after a prolonged storm, but the storm is partially
5 lulled, and the torn and streaming rain clouds are scudding across the sky in scarlet lines to dissipate into the hollow of the night. The whole surface of the sea comprised within the canvas is divided into two ridges of enormous swell, not high, nor local,
10 but a low, broad heaving of the whole ocean, like the lifting of its bosom by a deep-drawn breath after the torture of the storm. Between these two ridges, the fire of the sunset falls along the trough of the sea, dyeing it with an awful but glorious light, the
15 intense and lurid splendor which burns like gold and bathes like blood.

Along this fiery path and valley, the tossing waves by which the swell of the sea is restlessly divided, lift themselves in the dark, indefinite,
20 fantastic forms, each casting a faint and ghastly shadow behind it along the illumined foam. They do not rise everywhere, but three or four together in wild groups, fitfully and furiously, as the under-strength of the swell compels or permits them;
25 leaving between them treacherous spaces of level and whirling water, now lighted with green lamp-like fire, now flashing back the gold of the declining sun, now fearfully dyed from above with the indistinguishable images of the burning clouds,
30 which fall upon them in flakes of crimson and scarlet and give to the reckless waves the added motion of their own fiery flying.

Purple and blue, the lurid shadows of the hollow breakers are cast upon the mist of night,
35 which gathers cold and low, advancing like the shadow of death upon the guilty ship as it labors amidst the lighting of the sea, its thin masts written upon the sky in lines of blood, girded with condemnation in that fearful hue which signs the
40 sky with horror and mixes its flaming flood with the sunlight, and cast far along the desolate heave of the sepulchral waves, incarnadines the multitudinous sea.

I believe, if I were reduced to rest Turner's
45 immortality upon any single work, I should choose this. Its daring conception—ideal in the highest sense of the word—is based upon the purest truth and wrought out with the concentrated knowledge of a life; its color is absolutely perfect, not one false
50 or morbid hue in any part or line, and so modulated that every square inch of canvas is a perfect composition; its drawing as accurate as it is fearless, the ship buoyant, bending, and full of motion; its tones as true as they are wonderful; and the whole
55 picture dedicated to the most sublime of truths which we have shown to be formed by Turner's works—the power, majesty, and a depth of the open, deep, illimitable sea.

61. The morning fog was quickly ------- by the rays of the sun, allowing us to see the mountains far in the distance.

   A. condensed
   B. extended
   C. accumulated
   D. dissipated
   E. illuminated

62. Known for its sensationalism, the tabloid newspaper reported the horrendous crime in all of its ------- detail.

   A. exquisite
   B. lurid
   C. insipid
   D. ingenuous
   E. modest

63. With a ------- fascination, people flocked to the bombing scene from outer areas to catch a glimpse of the devastation.

   A. intelligent
   B. healthy
   C. cheery
   D. poignant
   E. morbid

64. Towards the end of the song, the Webb sisters' voices began to ------- into pitch-perfect harmony.

    A. vary
    B. intensify
    C. stratify
    D. modulate
    E. displace

65. Although Marie had only known Martin for six months, she felt that her feelings for him were vast and -------.

    A. illimitable
    B. controlled
    C. confidential
    D. definable
    E. inapt

66. As it is used in line 5, the word *lulled* most nearly means to have become:

    A. tense.
    B. calm.
    C. irate.
    D. defeated.

67. Based on the use of the wording *scudding* in line 6, it can be inferred that *scud* most nearly means to:

    A. fall quietly.
    B. pass rapidly.
    C. expand quickly.
    D. slow to a halt.

68. In context, *comprised* (line 8) most nearly means:

    A. pressed together.
    B. prohibited.
    C. exposed to suspicion.
    D. included.

69. As it is used in line 13, *trough* is best understood to refer to:

    A. a receptacle for feeding animals.
    B. low point of a business cycle.
    C. an area of low barometric pressure.
    D. a depression between two waves.

70. The word *ghastly* (line 20) most nearly means:

    A. shockingly frightful.
    B. lacking in substance.
    C. spiritual.
    D. pleasant.

71. As it is used in line 21, the word *illumined* most nearly means:

    A. educated.
    B. extinguished.
    C. lit up.
    D. cast a shadow.

72. It can be inferred that the word *condemnation*, as it is used in line 39, primarily refers to:

    A. praise.
    B. discord.
    C. appeasement.
    D. judgment.

73. It can be inferred that the word *sepulchral*, as it is used in line 42, primarily means:

    A. joyous.
    B. weakening.
    C. overpowering.
    D. dismal.

74. Based on the use of the word *incarnadines* in line 42, it can be inferred that *incarnadine* most nearly means to make:

    A. alive.
    B. red.
    C. dead.
    D. dark.

75. The word *immortality* (line 45) most nearly means:

    A. enduring fame.
    B. immediate demise.
    C. infamous reputation.
    D. collection of works.

Vocabulary Builder: Natural Science Passages
Exercise 9

DIRECTIONS: Each passage in this exercise is followed by sets of sentence completion and vocabulary-in-context items. In addition to using the passages to infer word meanings, you may use a dictionary.

The first set of items following each passage are sentence completion items based on words from the passage. Each sentence has one blank. Choose the word that best fits the meaning of the sentence in its entirety.

The second set of items following each passage are vocabulary-in-context items based on words from the passage. Choose the best answer for each item based on what is stated or implied in the passage.

Answers are on page 594.

Passage I

Natural Science: This passage is adapted from an article entitled "Cosmic Evolution" in a popular cosmology journal.

Through the centuries, man has unceasingly searched the firmament for clues to his destiny. His imagination has been captivated by the stars, his mind challenged by the mystery of their origin and
5 extent, and his spirit imbued with a thirst for some understanding of his role in the cosmos.

Scientific discoveries in fields as diverse as astronomy and molecular biology in the course of the last 15 years have brought us closer to solving
10 three timeless enigmas: How did the universe begin? How did life originate and evolve? What is our place and destiny in the universe?

This burst of interdisciplinary discoveries has given rise to new concepts of the origin of life from
15 inanimate material on primitive Earth, the formation of planets and stars, the synthesis of fundamental particles of matter, and the beginnings of the universe itself. All seem to be founded on the same basic laws of chemistry and physics. The
20 conclusion that the origin and evolution of life is inextricably interwoven with the origin and evolution of the cosmos seems ineluctable. Taken in its totality, this pathway, from fundamental particles to advanced civilizations, constitutes the
25 essence of the concept of cosmic evolution.

To be sure, the sequence from primordial fireball to matter, to stars, to planets, to prebiotic chemistry, to life, and to intelligence, is fragmented and even controversial in some particulars. A broad

30 picture, however, is emerging: a picture that is both imaginative and illuminating.

Man appeared very late in this sequence of events, and with his increased intelligence came civilization, science, and technology. Cultural
35 evolution began and has proceeded very rapidly in the last few millennia. An infinitesimal fraction of the matter of the universe has been converted into the organic matter of the human brain. As a result, one part of the universe can now reflect upon the
40 whole process of cosmic evolution leading to the existence of human cognition. We wonder whether this process is a frequent occurrence in the universe; in doing so, we come to the postulate that life is widespread in the universe and at least in
45 some cases, this life may have evolved to the stage of intelligence and technological civilizations that it did on Earth.

Some of these civilizations may have learned to communicate with each other and achieved
50 major advances in their own evolution as a result. Can we detect them? Although many gaps, puzzles, and uncertainties remain, this unifying concept, in which the expansion of the universe, the birth and death of galaxies and stars, the formation of planets,
55 the origins of life, and the ascent of humans are all explained by the process of cosmic evolution, provides a sound scientific rationale on which to base a program to search for extraterrestrial intelligence.

1. The new Biomedical Research Center, which coordinates many aspects of the university's research, has developed ------- working relationships with the Neuroscience and Medical Physics departments.

   A. adversary
   B. disciplinary
   C. evolutionary
   D. interdisciplinary
   E. reactionary

2. Linus Pauling, winner of the Chemistry Nobel Prize in 1954, was an advocate of high doses of vitamin C, since it is vital to the ------- of collagen, the body's main connective tissue protein.

   A. destruction
   B. analysis
   C. substitution
   D. combination
   E. synthesis

3. An atheist is a person without a belief in, or who does not ------- the existence of, a god or deities.

   A. deny
   B. calculate
   C. postulate
   D. warrant
   E. feign

4. The liberals' ------- for universal health care is that access to high-quality health care is a human right, while the conservatives argue that coverage is a market commodity best left to the free market.

   A. protection
   B. substitution
   C. disagreement
   D. apology
   E. rationale

5. Until Congress canceled its funding, the NASA Deep Space Network used radio dishes to detect non-natural radio emissions from locations outside our solar system in an attempt to discover ------- civilizations.

   A. extraterrestrial
   B. ancient
   C. modern
   D. terrestrial
   E. foreign

6. It can be inferred that the word *firmament*, as it is used in line 2, primarily refers to:

   A. a thin thread or strand.
   B. hell or the underworld.
   C. the heavens.
   D. the earth or material world.

7. It can be inferred that the word *cosmos*, as it is used in line 6, primarily refers to the:

   A. planets.
   B. sky.
   C. universe.
   D. earth.

8. In context, *enigmas* (line 10) most nearly means:

   A. solutions.
   B. puzzles.
   C. doubts.
   D. certainties.

9. Based on the use of the word *inextricably* in line 21, it can be inferred that *inextricable* most nearly means:

   A. indescribable.
   B. incontrollable.
   C. inseparable.
   D. unexplainable.

10. In line 22, *ineluctable* is best understood to mean:

    A. unsolvable.
    B. inescapable.
    C. unappeasable.
    D. avoidable.

11. It can be inferred that the word *primordial*, as it is used in line 26, most nearly means existing:

    A. in the future.
    B. in modern times.
    C. in outer space.
    D. from the beginning of time.

12. It can be inferred that the word *prebiotic*, as it is used in line 27, most nearly means:

    A. existing before the origin of life.
    B. containing beneficial bacteria.
    C. inhibiting bacterial growth.
    D. pertaining to life.

13. The word *millennia* (line 36) refers to:

    A. millions of years.
    B. thousands of years.
    C. hundreds of years.
    D. tens of years.

14. As it is used in line 36, the word *infinitesimal* most nearly means:

    A. extending indefinitely.
    B. immeasurably tiny.
    C. enormous.
    D. calculable.

15. In line 41, *cognition* refers to:

    A. knowledge.
    B. misunderstanding.
    C. unawareness.
    D. existence.

Passage II

Natural Science: This passage is adapted from an essay entitled "Antarctic Exploration" in an introductory earth sciences textbook.

At 3:29 p.m. on November 28, 1929, a heavily laden Ford Trimotor bounced down the rough ice runway of 'Little America' and clawed its way through an Antarctic overcast—embarking on an
5 epic flight that was anything but routine. The little plane, called the Floyd Bennett, weighed only 6,000 pounds. With its four-man crew, extra gasoline, food, and survival gear, it was carrying more than seven tons. The plane's three engines put out 975
10 horsepower; cruising speed was just over 100 miles per hour. For navigating the desolate wastes, there were two drift meters and a sun-compass. The only other scientific instrument aboard was a bulky 100-pound aerial camera. Eighteen hours and 37
15 minutes (and 1,600 miles) later, the Floyd Bennett touched back down on the Little America landing strip, mission completed. Richard E. Byrd and his crew were the first to conquer the South Pole by air, and their historic journey, the consummation of
20 years of work and meticulous planning, had opened a new era of scientific exploration.

Simply establishing the Little America base camp a year earlier was a triumph of logistics. Byrd's men unloaded and hauled several hundred
25 tons of food, fuel, and equipment (including three airplanes) over the crumbling ice barrier on dog sleds. The dismantled all-metal Ford Trimotor was stored that winter in a hangar made of snow blocks. After the long months of darkness set in, Byrd and
30 his companions began final planning for their aerial assault on the South Pole. The 1,600-mile-long flight involved unprecedented features. For hundreds of miles, they would fly over a barren, rolling surface, then climb a mountain rampart 14,000 feet high,
35 with a 10,500-foot pass, and continue the journey across a 10,000-foot plateau. Factors of speed, horsepower, rate of climb, and other engineering problems entailed endless hours of tedious and complicated calculations.

40 Excavated from its snow cave in early November, the Floyd Bennett was reassembled in temperatures that reached 50 degrees below zero. Without photographer Ashley McKinley and his equipment and survival gear, the plane could fly to
45 the South Pole and back with no problem. To Byrd, McKinley's task was the crux of the plan: to

photograph every mile of the flight and to make a permanent record available to science. Since the extra weight would make a nonstop trip impossible,
50 it would be necessary to cache gasoline and food near the base of the mountain range that bordered the high Antarctic plateau. The aircraft would then land and refuel during the return leg of the flight. Even so, weight and fuel consumption calculations
55 were critical. The Floyd Bennett had to be light enough by the time it reached the Queen Maud Mountains to climb 11,000 feet and slip through the pass at the head of the Axel Heiberg glacier.

On November 19, Byrd and his crew flew 400
60 miles to reconnoiter the jagged mountain barrier, then landed to establish their forward camp. On November 28, a geological party radioed that the weather over the mountains was excellent, so that afternoon the Floyd Bennett headed south toward
65 the pole. As the plane neared the Axel Heiberg glacier with its 10,500-foot pass, the men sighted another glacier which seemed low enough and wide enough to cross. The decision had to be made quickly: to tackle the Axel Heiberg, altitude known
70 but air currents unknown—the bordering peaks might be so high that air currents would dash the plane to the ground—or to take the unknown glacier, which looked feasible?

Byrd opted for the unknown glacier. As
75 powerful air currents tossed the plane about, the pilot fought to gain altitude. Suddenly, the wheel turned loosely in his hands. The pass loomed ahead, but the Floyd Bennett would go no higher. If gasoline were jettisoned, it would be impossible to
80 reach the pole and return. If food were thrown overboard, all lives would be endangered in the event of a forced landing. "A bag of food overboard," ordered Byrd. The plane responded immediately and began to climb, but the fast-approaching glacier
85 was higher. Byrd gestured and another 150-pound bag of food careened through the trapdoor of the aircraft. Byrd reported "those were the slowest minutes we ever spent. Finally, we reached the pass. We ambled over—a few hundred yards to spare."

90 The vast Antarctic plateau ranged from 11,000 to 7,000 feet, sloping toward the South Pole. Cruising at only 90 miles per hour against a brisk headwind, Byrd navigated carefully over the jumbled terrain. At 1:14 a.m. on November 29, the
95 big moment had come. The crew dropped an American flag.

Flying at 2,500 feet over the snow, the plane then angled back over the original line of flight to cross again over the pole and make certain the feat
100 was accomplished. Then, the aircraft veered north toward Little America. Byrd's navigation was unerring.

Several hours later, the weary crew spotted the Axel Heiberg glacier in the distance. This time
105 the lightened plane soared through the pass with no difficulty. After landing and refueling, Byrd and his crew resumed the flight. At 10:10 a.m., the Floyd Bennett touched down at Little America. "We were deaf from the roar of the motor," according to Byrd,
110 "tired from the strain of the flight, but we forgot all that in the tumultuous welcome of our companions."

The welcome echoed far beyond the cluster of huts at Little America. Congratulations poured in
115 from all over the world. Byrd was a national hero. His dramatic adventure had captured the imagination of millions of Americans, and Antarctica was etched on the national consciousness.

16. The overly ------- drill sergeant even required the troops to polish the soles of their boots.

    A. solicitous
    B. careless
    C. audacious
    D. meticulous
    E. cautious

17. Though previously the locals remained neutral, recently there has been a(n) ------- surge of support for the fundamentalists that can only be attributed to the U.S. invasion of Afghanistan.

    A. unremarkable
    B. predictable
    C. unprecedented
    D. conventional
    E. predetermined

18. While the negotiators claim there are several issues as stake, the ------- of the matter is really the President's refusal to agree to a reduction in military aid to Latin America.

    A. detail
    B. outcome
    C. adage
    D. crux
    E. mandate

19. In the backyard of the suspect's suburban home, under a doghouse, the police found a ------- of counterfeit bills.

    A. manifesto
    B. cache
    C. exposé
    D. deficit
    E. wealth

20. A roar greeted the appearance of the legendary guitarist on the stage, and the ------- applause did not subside for over twenty minutes.

    A. peaceful
    B. diplomatic
    C. lackadaisical
    D. aggressive
    E. tumultuous

21. As it is used in line 11, the word *desolate* most nearly means:

    A. without human inhabitants.
    B. hopeless.
    C. marked by indulgence.
    D. densely populated.

22. It can be inferred that the word *aerial*, as it is used in line 14, most nearly means:

    A. pertaining to radio.
    B. a small area between things.
    C. of, in, or produced by the air.
    D. a level piece of ground.

23. In context, *consummation* (line 19) most nearly means:

    A. antithesis.
    B. completion.
    C. conservation.
    D. utilization.

24. In line 23, *logistics* refers to:

    A. defense of an encampment.
    B. analysis of data.
    C. planning and coordination of operation details.
    D. the formal principles of knowledge.

25. In line 27, *dismantled* most nearly means:

    A. violently shattered.
    B. deprived of courage.
    C. taken apart and stripped of essential parts.
    D. dismissed or discharged.

26. The word *rampart* is used in line 34 to refer to:

    A. extravagance or absence of restraint.
    B. low place in mountain range.
    C. a way of entrance or exit.
    D. a wall-like ridge or dirt embankment.

27. In line 60, *reconnoiter* most nearly means to:

    A. restore.
    B. explore.
    C. climb.
    D. contemplate.

28. Based on the use of the word *jettisoned* in line 79, it can be inferred that *jettison* most nearly means to:

    A. throw overboard.
    B. burn or extinguish.
    C. overflow.
    D. illuminate.

29. In line 86, *careened* most nearly means:

    A. exploded.
    B. wedged.
    C. lurched.
    D. poked.

30. In line 118, *etched* most nearly means:

    A. misused.
    B. engraved.
    C. irritated.
    D. erased.

Passage III

Natural Science: This passage is adapted from a discussion on the application of science and technology in the field of meteorology.

We can think of science as the attempt to comprehend the workings of nature, and of technology as the practical application of this knowledge. There are three major steps in applying
5 science and technology: experimental observation, analysis, and utilization.

There are two aspects of the experimental observation phase. One is the observation of natural phenomena as they occur. The second is the
10 observation of controlled experiments. The former has necessarily been the way of the past. However, with sounding rockets and satellites, the second became feasible and is being more extensively used.

The observation of natural phenomena as they
15 occur involves the development of sensors to observe important phenomena, and the collection of results into a data inventory that is readily accessible to all. For example, in meteorology, this involves a ground activity of assembling
20 temperature, humidity, wind velocity and direction, and other weather data. This information is observed at myriad locations throughout the world and forwarded regularly to central data collection stations. The development of a wide variety of
25 sensors will be used for continued weather satellite observations to provide an even wider variety of data—daily and on a global scale. A very significant meteorological observation activity now underway is the Global Atmospheric Research Program
30 (GARP). This activity involves a large number of countries throughout the world, cooperating to gather weather data of unprecedented scope on a global scale to help in the understanding of weather systems and phenomena throughout the world and
35 the major factors that control their origin, development, and movement.

The observation of controlled experiments involves the development and use of techniques for conducting both passive and active experiments
40 with natural phenomena and observation of the results. An example of the passive approach is the barium cloud experiment, in which a sounding rocket was used to disperse a quantity of fine barium powder high above the atmosphere in the
45 earth's magnetic field. In this case, the natural phenomena were undisturbed, and the barium cloud was used to chart with considerable definition the earth's magnetic-field lines. An example of an active experiment is the injection of silver iodide
50 pellets in cloud formations to induce rainfall.

In the analysis phase, basic relationships and trends are discerned and a better understanding of the phenomena evolves. From the observed relationships and growing understanding, theories
55 are developed and models of the phenomena are postulated. These theories and models are intended to help understand the complex cause and effect interactions among the many variables involved. Definitive experiments are then sought to test the
60 validity of the theories and models. Such experiments often entail further observations to obtain critical elements of data. It is via progressive iterative steps between experimental observation and analysis that models evolve sufficiently for use
65 on an operational basis. Using meteorology as an example, we currently have general models of weather system behavior. Although these models are limited to very crude weather forecasting, continued satellite observations—together with
70 programs like GARP—can lead to improvements in our global weather models, our understanding, and our ability to predict it.

In the utilization phase, all of the understanding from observations made and models
75 analytically developed is employed to predict what can or will happen under a specified set of conditions. Weather prediction is a typical example of how models are used in conjunction with current observation to develop forecasts for public use. It is
80 the combination of an ability to monitor and forecast events, together with an understanding of the basic mechanisms which cause predicted events—be they natural events or those created by man—that eventually will lead to global systems for
85 management of our resources and control of our environment in ways that best suit the needs of man.

31. Knowledge of the concentration of elements is important in managing a nuclear reactor and requires constant ------- of neutron activation.

A. distention
B. consumption
C. disclosure
D. exploitation
E. analysis

32. The ------- of low-cost recycled material in the production process allowed the manufacturing plant to increase profits by over 35 percent.

A. elimination
B. depreciation
C. utilization
D. accumulation
E. capitulation

33. The plan to build a new highway on the north side of the city is -------, but it will be necessary to raise taxes.

A. feasible
B. imaginary
C. impossible
D. argumentative
E. temporary

34. There are ------- small tasks required to keep an airplane in safe condition, so most pilots keep a detailed log of maintenance and safety checks.

A. moderate
B. generous
C. effusive
D. useful
E. myriad

35. Accustomed to the frequent outbursts of their coach, the team members listened ------- as he shouted at them during half-time.

A. actively
B. passionately
C. favorably
D. passively
E. aggressively

36. In context, *phenomena* (line 9) refers to:

A. unobservable events or facts.
B. observable events or facts.
C. unrecorded events or facts.
D. recorded events or facts.

37. In context, *data* (line 17) refers to:

A. unobservable events or facts.
B. observable events or facts.
C. unrecorded events or facts.
D. recorded events or facts.

38. As used in line 17, the word *inventory* refers to a(n):

A. discovery or finding.
B. secure place of storage.
C. division for classification.
D. organized list of collected information.

39. In line 18, *accessible* most nearly means:

A. easily used.
B. valuable.
C. capable of being estimated.
D. unobtainable.

40. It can be inferred that the word *disperse*, as it is used in line 43, most nearly means to:

A. separate or divide.
B. distribute or scatter.
C. set on fire.
D. replace or drive out.

41. Based on the use of the word *discerned* in line 52, it can be inferred that *discern* most nearly means to:

A. ignore.
B. analyze.
C. identify.
D. eliminate.

42. In line 60, *validity* is best understood to mean:

A. error.
B. illusion.
C. accuracy.
D. strength.

43. As it is used in line 61, the word *entail* most nearly means to:

A. cause to be ineffective.
B. plan or carry out with great care.
C. indicate or set apart.
D. cause or involve by necessity.

44. It can be inferred that the word *iterative*, as it is used in line 63, most nearly means:

A. extreme or outermost.
B. involving repetition.
C. traveling from place to place.
D. obligatory or necessary.

45. In line 78, *conjunction* most nearly means:

A. contradiction.
B. combination.
C. exclusion.
D. estimation.

Passage IV

Natural Science: This passage is adapted from a lecture entitled "Memory and Learning."

Long-term learning—positive and negative—is made possible by the fact that the mind is able to remember virtually all it was ever aware of, including the most trivial details. However, there
5　are several conditions to this process of retention.

One condition is that such memory (learning) is situational: It is determined in part by the nature of the situation in which the learning occurs. Students "pay attention" in school and learn things
10　tied to a concrete, not abstract, teaching/learning situation; they learn something solely for the purpose of earning a grade. Consequently, since most school situations have no counterparts outside of school, a student often develops amnesia and is
15　unable to recall information learned in another context. Memory is like a filing system, in which an item is stored to be retrieved with a code keyed to that specific situation. If the situation eliciting that particular code is not encountered again, the filed
20　item remains untouched and unused. It is important to remember the filed item is not transient; it does not fade or die. It is merely dormant during the time it is not in use.

A second condition of "memory" learning is it
25　appears to be bound to the state of arousal that existed for the original learning. The ability to remember, therefore, depends to some degree on the ability to recreate or re-enter the formative state of arousal: the feeling, tone, or affective quality
30　that characterized the brain at the time of learning. Thus, since there is always some subjective element, some aura of feeling that accompanies all we ever learn, it is simply not enough to consider what so-called objective content or skill is being taught. The
35　student's feelings while or after learning takes place will determine whether learning will be effective.

Since students are often in a classroom for hours, it seems reasonable to assert that teachers must be concerned with the ambience of the
40　classroom. Perhaps teachers should also be more aware of their countenance; even a temporary lapse into boredom or irritation can place the students in a situation which makes learning unnecessarily onerous.

46. The new secretary was so consumed by petty office politics and ------- matters that she failed to take care of the tasks that were vital to the company's daily operations.

   A. vital
   B. voluble
   C. trivial
   D. relevant
   E. complicated

47. The teacher used fun games to aid the students in their ------- of the important concepts, dates, and facts that would be crucial for a passing grade on the exam.

   A. rejection
   B. deletion
   C. miscomprehension
   D. retention
   E. management

48. The general of the American army met with his ------- in the British forces, and they quickly realized that while their uniforms were different, their perspectives were similar.

   A. advisor
   B. prototype
   C. partner
   D. counterpart
   E. superior

49. Because they are ------- during hibernation, ground squirrels prepare for winter by building up a thick insulating layer of body fat during late summer and fall.

   A. active
   B. efficient
   C. dormant
   D. occupied
   E. vigorous

50. The aide had not researched the question completely, but his personal and ------- impression was that the governor should veto the bill.

   A. informed
   B. objective
   C. educated
   D. impartial
   E. subjective

51. In context, *virtually* (line 3) most nearly means:

   A. nearly.
   B. completely.
   C. exclusively.
   D. superficially.

52. As it is used in line 10, the word *concrete* most nearly means:

   A. insubstantial.
   B. significant.
   C. particular or specific.
   D. abstract.

53. In line 12, *consequently* most nearly means:

   A. in addition.
   B. regardless.
   C. for the reason.
   D. as a result.

54. As it is used in line 17, the word *retrieved* most nearly means:

   A. repeated.
   B. recovered.
   C. withdrawn.
   D. deleted.

55. Based on the use of the word *eliciting* in line 18, it can be inferred that *elicit* most nearly means to:

   A. make unlawful.
   B. evoke.
   C. offer.
   D. misplace.

56. It can be inferred that the word *transient*, as it is used in line 21, most nearly means:

   A. easily seen through.
   B. altered.
   C. temporary.
   D. transferrable.

57. In line 29, *affective* most nearly means:

   A. useful.
   B. stern.
   C. aloof.
   D. emotional.

58. It can be inferred that the word *aura*, as it is used in line 32, most nearly means:

   A. of or relating to the ear or sense of hearing.
   B. of, in, or pertaining to air.
   C. distinctive and persuasive quality or atmosphere.
   D. an observable luminous phenomenon.

59. In line 39, *ambience* primarily refers to the:

   A. mood or feeling associated with a place.
   B. decoration and furnishings of a room.
   C. surrounding influences or environment.
   D. structure or foundation of a room.

60. In line 44, *onerous* most nearly means:

   A. effortless.
   B. costly.
   C. burdensome.
   D. mistaken.

Passage V

Natural Science: This passage is adapted from a science news article about the Infrared Astronomical Satellite.

The birth of new stars and the death of old ones will be witnessed by a new Earth-orbiting instrument that will probe through space in quest of celestial phenomena that are invisible to our eyes
5 but glow in the infrared portion of the light spectrum. The instrument's array of infrared detectors will also lift the veil of thick dust clouds that block starlight streaming from the center of our galaxy and sharply limit our study of the densest
10 and most active part of the Milky Way. It will provide a new chart of the universe, mapping perhaps a million infrared sources for future study and will radically transform our concept of the universe. The new instrument is the Infrared
15 Astronomical Satellite (IRAS), and it will be operated by an international team of scientists and engineers.

Infrared astronomy is a recent development in astrophysics because most infrared radiation from
20 space never reaches Earth's surface. Water vapor and other gases in the atmosphere absorb it, hence the importance of situating the telescope above the atmosphere in Earth's orbit. Most infrared observations have been obtained by the use of
25 balloons, sounding rockets, and high-altitude aircraft. The view has been highly circumscribed compared to the broad vista that will be opened to IRAS.

Astronomers have received some tantalizing
30 hints about what may be out there. An exciting example came from a brief survey of infrared objects by the Cambridge Laboratory. It found that some highly evolved stars apparently shed a large percentage of their mass to the interstellar medium.
35 This had not been observed with optical instruments (those that see only visible light). Those highly evolved stars are quite bright at infrared wavelengths, but are only dim specks in conventional star photographs.

40 The theory of star formation accorded general acceptance today says that vast clouds of dust and gas float in space until some mechanism, which is not yet fully understood, triggers gravitational collapse. Over hundreds of thousands of years each
45 mote of dust, each atom of gas, attracts other motes

and atoms until a huge, spinning globe is formed. When gravitational pressure is sufficient and when temperatures at the center of the globe soar high enough—about ten million degrees—
50 thermonuclear reactions commence, and the star begins to glow.

From the time the incipient star is a tenuous dust cloud until soon after the nuclear reactions begin, the heat produced by gravitational collapse is
55 emitted as infrared radiation. That is one of the most exciting prospects of IRAS' mission: the possibility of attending the birth of a star. What appears to be the first nascent star ever observed is buried deep within the nebula or gas cloud in the
60 sword of the constellation Orion, a small dot that while dim by optical measurements, is bright in infrared.

Millions or billions of years after they are born, stars approach their moment of death, when all
65 their nuclear fuel is exhausted. As it begins to die, the star ejects a cloud of dust, and the faint visible light from the moribund star is absorbed by the dust shell and then reemitted as infrared. With IRAS, scientists hope to observe the maternity
70 wards and graveyards of the universe.

61. Though she complained every step of the way, Millie agreed that the panoramic ------- was well worth the four-hour hike to the top of the mountain pass.

A. angle
B. dead end
C. opinion
D. descent
E. vista

62. The ------- descriptions of the products are designed to lure in customers and motivate them to buy what otherwise seems unnecessary.

A. uninspiring
B. disturbing
C. reassuring
D. tantalizing
E. mundane

63. The artist was multitalented and worked in an assortment of -------, including watercolor, oil and acrylic, and sculpture.

A. resources
B. locations
C. incentives
D. processes
E. mediums

64. Because the defendant's hold on reality was so -------, the judge ruled that she was not competent to stand trial.

A. firm
B. discernible
C. tenuous
D. humble
E. convincing

65. The ------- grassroots "tea party" movement is more popular with many conservatives than the long-established Grand Old Party.

A. struggling
B. nascent
C. obsolete
D. mature
E. prosaic

66. It can be inferred that the word *quest*, as it is used in line 3, most nearly means:

A. discovery.
B. deliberation.
C. rotation.
D. search.

67. It can be inferred that the word *celestial*, as it is used in line 4, pertains to the:

A. ancient civilization or world.
B. modern civilization or world.
C. sky or heavens.
D. earth or material world.

68. In context, *radically* (line 13) most nearly means:

A. momentarily.
B. fundamentally.
C. unsubstantially.
D. temporarily.

69. In line 19, *astrophysics* is best understood to refer to the:

A. science of the behavior and physical properties of stars.
B. divination of supposed influences of stars on human affairs.
C. study of objects within the earth's atmosphere.
D. science of the physical properties of the earth's surface.

70. As it is used in line 24, the word *obtained* most nearly means:

A. eliminated.
B. acquired.
C. undermined.
D. negotiated.

71. The word *circumscribed* (line 26) most nearly means:

A. limited.
B. traveled around.
C. surrounded.
D. cut off.

72. In line 45, *mote* is best understood to refer to a:

A. method.
B. feeling.
C. small particle.
D. small creature.

73. It can be inferred that the word *incipient*, as it is used in line 52, most nearly means:

A. lacking taste.
B. in an initial stage.
C. dull or uninteresting.
D. brightly burning.

74. As it is used in line 52, the word *tenuous* most
nearly means:

    A. sturdy.
    B. dense.
    C. unsubstantial.
    D. harmless.

75. It can be inferred that the word *moribund*, as it
is used in line 67, most nearly means:

    A. sinking.
    B. glowing.
    C. thriving.
    D. dying.

Passage VI

Natural Science: This passage is adapted from an essay entitled "The Growth of Intelligence" in an introductory life science textbook.

There is a wide variety of opinions on what evolutionary factors were responsible specifically for hominid intelligence; probably many were important. One theory is that intraspecific warfare
5 plays an important role. War seems to require rapid invention. Strategy discussions that are connected with the planning of warfare tend to involve a kind of verbal competition which requires resourcefulness. Furthermore, intraspecific conflict makes special
10 demands on organisms that their battle with the environment does not: the difference is between intelligence versus intelligence on the one hand, and intelligence versus mere non-intelligence on the other. Finally, warfare involves the young organisms
15 as well, and organisms not suited to it suffer the consequences in that their genes are eliminated from the breeding population. As attractive as the theory is, it is far from having been conclusively proven. Territoriality is a common trait, and some social
20 mammals, such as man and the hyena, exhibit, as a form of territorial behavior, organized violent conflict between social groups. However, territoriality is not a basic biological trait; many species are not afflicted with the desire to make war.

25 More likely, the most important stimuli to the development of intelligence in early hominids were the demands of communication and language. About three million years ago, the rate of evolution in the brain accelerated, and was correlated with the
30 increased use of stone tools. Such artifacts are evidence of complex social structures, which in turn improved communication. At minimum, the techniques for manufacturing the articles had to be transmitted from one generation to the next. Some of
35 the hominids' increased cranial capacity may have been related to a general increase in motor coordination. The notion that man is a puny beast is a spurious one. He is actually fantastically powerful and yet possessing extreme dexterity, possessed as
40 he is with subtle and accurate motor control of the hands and limbs. He also has very complex feedback mechanisms that allow him to determine accurately the course of a thrown projectile with little practice.

There is general agreement that the need to
45 adopt a predatory lifestyle on the savannah stimulated at least the early development of

manipulative ability, motor coordination, and the complex social organization in the hominids. The arboreal environment of the jungle could not have
50 produced these traits. No monkey or ape can control a thrown projectile the way a man can; independent finger control is a uniquely hominid characteristic. Moreover, chimpanzees and other apes, though they use natural objects such as sticks for tools, have
55 never developed a systematic tool-making ability.

Thus, the demands of the savannah environment were probably responsible for the development of intelligence and technological society in man, but it does not follow that this type of
60 environment is a prerequisite to the development of these characteristics. It is possible such characteristics could have developed in entirely different circumstances, nor were the environmental challenges themselves sufficient to produce this
65 result. It was crucial that an animal well-adapted to live in the complex forest environment be pre-adapted to a new ecological niche on the savannah and therefore able to invade it successfully.

76. My dogs are very -------: they bark and act aggressively whenever another dog walks by our yard.

  A. passive
  B. territorial
  C. terrestrial
  D. nonchalant
  E. dormant

77. Advocates of the "war on drugs" argue that strong drug enforcement in the United States is ------- with dramatic reductions in crime, drug use, and drug addiction rates.

  A. disassociated
  B. correlated
  C. motivated
  D. demonstrated
  E. unconnected

78. The new study published in *Genetics and Biotechnology* identifies a mechanism that plays a key role in how mutations are ------- from one generation to the next.

A.   borrowed
B.   disconnected
C.   transmitted
D.   isolated
E.   inflated

79. Recent discoveries in South America and Asia suggest that Tyrannosaurus rex, the largest meat-eating ------- dinosaur, had a range much greater than originally thought.

A.   ambulatory
B.   predatory
C.   satisfactory
D.   reactionary
E.   precursory

80. Very different animals occupy the same ecological ------- in different continents: for example, the bison is the largest land herbivore in America, while in Australia it is the kangaroo.

A.   destination
B.   imperative
C.   prospect
D.   cache
E.   niche

81. It can be inferred that the word *hominid*, as it is used in line 3, refers to all forms, both extinct and living, of:

A.   primate.
B.   animal.
C.   flora.
D.   insect.

82. In context, *intraspecific* (line 4) most nearly means:

A.   eliminating specific characteristics.
B.   mutually joined or related.
C.   occurring between members of the same species.
D.   occurring between members of different species.

83. As it is used in line 24, the word *afflicted* most nearly means:

A.   acted upon.
B.   accomplished by.
C.   inclined toward.
D.   troubled with.

84. In line 30, *artifacts* is best understood to mean:

A.   clever or artful skills.
B.   evidence.
C.   tools used by animals.
D.   human-made objects.

85. It can be inferred that the word *cranial*, as it is used in line 35, pertains to the:

A.   body.
B.   skull.
C.   lungs.
D.   environment.

86. The word *spurious* (line 38) most nearly means:

A.   genuine.
B.   hypocritical.
C.   false.
D.   improbable.

87. It can be inferred that the word *dexterity*, as it is used in line 39, most nearly means:

A.   gentleness.
B.   agility.
C.   clumsiness.
D.   loquaciousness.

88. The word *savannah* (line 45) refers to:

A.   grassland with scattered trees.
B.   tropical rainforest.
C.   an area far from cities or big towns.
D.   temperate hardwood forest.

89. The word *arboreal* (line 49) most nearly means:

A.   native.
B.   flexible.
C.   sheltered.
D.   treelike.

90. In line 60, *prerequisite* most nearly means a(n):

    A. requirement.
    B. option.
    C. development.
    D. opportunity.

Reading Skills Review

Course Concept Outline

I. Honing Your Reading Skills (p. 289)

    A. Understand the Five Elements of Reading Passages (p. 289)

        1. Content (p. 289)
        2. Case (p. 289)
        3. Cause (p. 289)
        4. Context (p. 289)
        5. Character (p. 290)

    B. Use the Six Strategies for Reading Carefully and Comprehensively (p. 290)

    C. Identify the Main Idea (Main Theme) of the Passage (p. 291)

    D. Determine the Outline Employed to Develop the Passage (p. 292)

    E. Locate the Important Specific Details (p. 293)

        1. Prompting Words (p. 294)
        2. Defining Words (p. 294)
        3. Similarity Words (p. 294)
        4. Contrast Words (p. 294)
        5. Example Words (p. 294)

    F. Analyze the Arguments or Persuasive Devices (p. 294)

    G. Consider the Author's Point of View (p. 295)

    H. Probe the Tone of the Passage (p. 296)

    Exercise 1—**Summarize the Main Idea** (Items #1-5, pp. 297-298)

    Exercise 2—**Determine the Main Idea** (Items #1-10, pp. 299-301)

Exercise 3—**Outlining Passages** (pp. 302–303)

Exercise 4—**Locate Verbal Signs** (p. 304)

Exercise 5—**Locate Specific Details** (Items #1–10, pp. 305–306)

Exercise 6—**Analyze the Arguments** (Items #1–10, pp. 307–309)

Exercise 7—**Consider the Author's Point of View** (Items #1–17, pp. 310–313)

Exercise 8—**Probe the Tone of the Passage** (Items #1–2, p. 314)

Exercise 9—**Bonus Passages** (Items #1–16, pp. 315–318)

HONING YOUR READING SKILLS

When you move from reading materials that entertain to reading literature that requires higher levels of critical reading ability and that tests your ability to comprehend complex arguments, you must develop an aptitude for reading carefully and deliberately.

To read a densely written passage carefully for comprehension, there are five major reading elements you should consider when examining the written materials.

Understand the Five Elements of Reading Passages

Content

The content of a passage is made up of the information, data, images, and descriptions found in the text. The author uses words, phrases, and sentences to build the basic facts, figures, illustrations, and examples of a passage. He or she writes to communicate the basic "who," "what," "where," and "when" of the literary piece.

As a reader, you discover the content by asking, "What is the author attempting to tell, show, or explain to me?"

Case

The case (think of a legal case) of the author establishes the reasoning, arguments, or explanations for the content's purpose. The author is attempting to demonstrate that the main point of the content is meaningful, logical, emotionally moving, or important. Even in fictional works, narratives, or poetic literature, authors regularly point directly or indirectly to some reason or explanation for their views.

You discover the case in the passage by asking, "What evidence, arguments, explanations, or reasons does the author use to prove his or her point?"

Cause

The cause (or the "because") is the point of view or perspective from which the author writes. An author may or may not directly tell you his or her point of view. As a critical reader, you may need to "read between the lines" to discover some experience, perspective, background, personal view, opinion, or set of ideas that influence an author to write about specific content or argue in a certain manner.

You discover the cause by asking, "Why is this author exploring this specific content, arguing in this particular style, or writing in this particular manner?"

Context

The context refers to the time and place from which the author writes. All authors write from particular surroundings that influence their understanding of culture, science, history, social structures, etc. For example, an author writing in Spain during the sixteenth century would have a significantly different context than an author writing in New York City during the twenty-first century.

You discover the context by asking, "From when and where did the author write this passage, and how might it influence his or her point of view?"

Character

The character of the passage is the general tone or feeling that an author attempts to communicate. An author may write logically, emotionally, passionately, humorously, whimsically, sarcastically, or in a variety of other styles that project a particular tone.

You discover the character of a passage by asking, "How does the author use his or her style (words, phrases, sentence structure, paragraph patterns, images, illustrations, etc.) to communicate the general tone or feeling of the passage?"

The following strategies will assist you in reading all the previously described reading passage elements. The chart below illustrates how the reading elements correspond to the reading strategies.

READING ELEMENT	QUESTION TO ASK	READING STRATEGY
Content	"What is the author attempting to tell, show, or explain to me?"	• Clearly identify the main idea. • Determine the outline employed to develop the passage. • Locate the important specific details.
Case	"What evidence, arguments, explanations, or reasons does the author use to prove his or her point?"	• Analyze the arguments or persuasive devices.
Cause	"Why is this author exploring this specific content, arguing in this particular style, or writing in this particular manner?"	• Consider the author's point of view.
Context	"From when and where did the author write this passage and how might it influence his or her point of view?"	• Consider the author's point of view.
Character	"How does the author use his or her style (words, phrases, sentence structure, paragraph patterns, images, illustrations, etc.) to communicate the general tone or feeling of the passage?"	• Probe the tone of the passage.

Use the Six Strategies for Reading Carefully and Comprehensively

In the following section, you will learn the six basic strategies of reading passages more seriously, carefully, and comprehensively.

1. Clearly identify the main idea of the written material.
2. Determine the outline employed to develop the passage.
3. Locate the important specific details.
4. Analyze the arguments or persuasive devices.
5. Consider the author's point of view.
6. Probe the tone of the passage.

Identify the Main Idea (Main Theme) of the Passage

In presenting content, an author typically begins writing with a main idea in mind. This may also be called the main theme or the thesis of the passage. All other ideas, examples, facts, or illustrations in the passage are meant to support the main idea.

You discover the main theme by asking the following type of questions:

- What is the primary purpose of this paragraph or passage?

- What is the principal idea or central concept within this particular passage?

- What one statement or sentence best summarizes this reading material?

- What major idea or theme is the author attempting to communicate?

As you read, be careful not to confuse the arguments, examples, or the specific details with the main theme of the passage. The arguments, examples, and details are presented in a passage to support the main theme.

Example:

Though I love planet Earth with her snow-capped mountains, sand-blown deserts, and deep blue oceans, as a scientist and a philosopher, I believe that humanity cannot live here forever.
5 Colonization of other planets, like the red planet Mars, will be necessary. With human population growing so quickly, there will simply not be enough room for all of us on earth by 2050. By that year, food and water will become extremely scarce
10 for all but the most powerful and wealthy, and many will suffer from drought and famine. Because of the growing problems at that time, the governments of nations around the world will need to band together soon to support a long-term
15 plan to colonize other planets by sending humans to live there by 2050. Personally, I am too nervous to be a pioneer on a distant planet, but it will be necessary that some humans undertake this great adventure.

What is the primary purpose of this paragraph?

➢ The main idea of this passage is that colonization of other planets will be necessary by the year 2050. The writer describes why colonization of other planets will be increasingly necessary by 2050. Though the author provides other arguments about why colonization will become necessary and includes thoughts about his or her own nervousness with space travel, the primary purpose is to communicate the coming need to colonize other planets by 2050.

TIP: One practical strategy for determining the main idea is to rephrase the passage into a single, concise sentence that summarizes the entire passage.

Determine the Outline Employed to Develop the Passage

Once you identify the main idea, you need to determine how the author develops that theme using logical arguments, examples, illustrations, facts, or details. A good way to understand the development of a passage is to outline the key ideas, statements, or arguments in that passage. A simple outline provides a way to line up the content in a thoughtful, logical, or sequential manner.

When outlining a passage, find the key statements or thoughts the author uses to support his or her main idea. Ask these questions to help determine the outline:

- What is the main idea of the passage?

- What are the supporting ideas that are used to confirm or strengthen the main idea?

- What primary facts or arguments does the author use to support the main theme?

- What order of ideas or information does the author use to communicate those facts or arguments?

An author may order his or her writing using, among others, one of the following styles:

- *Temporal:* time ordered (e.g., past to present, morning to evening, hours in a day)

- *Sequential:* ordered intervals (e.g., smallest to largest, simplest to most complex, least to most)

- *Categorical:* parts of a system (e.g., classification of animal kingdom, types of stars)

- *Geographical:* locations (e.g., east to west, floor to ceiling, inside to outside)

- *Logical:* rational order (*x* implies *y*, *y* implies *z*, so *x* implies *z*)

- *Emotional:* feeling-related (e.g., least impacting to most impacting, saddest time to happiest time)

Review the following reading passage and outline.

Example:

First-year college students should be required to provide five hours of community service each week. This requirement would greatly benefit the surrounding community. A recent survey shows
5   that communities need more volunteer help. An interview with the mayor demonstrates that her city needs immediate help from more volunteers. This requirement would greatly benefit the student as well. Research demonstrates that students who
10   participate in community service make better grades than those who do not participate in community service. Also, students who participate in community service make more friends than those who do not participate in community service.

Main Idea: First-year college students should be required to provide five hours of community service each week.

1. Fact One: This requirement would greatly benefit the surrounding community.
   a) Argument One: A recent survey shows that communities need more volunteer help.
   b) Argument Two: An interview with the mayor demonstrates that her city needs immediate help from more volunteers.

2. Fact Two: This requirement would greatly benefit the student as well.
   a) Argument One: Research demonstrates that students who participate in community service make better grades than those who do not participate in community service.
   b) Argument Two: Students who participate in community service make more friends than those who do not participate in community service.

Review the following outline that uses a temporal flow (earliest period to latest period).

Example:

Main Idea: A historical overview of book printing

1. Era One: Printing before the invention of movable type
   a) The Egyptian printing methods
   b) The Greco-Roman printing methods
   c) The printing methods of the Middle Ages

2. Era Two: Printing immediately after the invention of movable type
   a) Contemporary practices at the time of Gutenberg's printing press
   b) European printing after Gutenberg's press

3. Era Three: Modern innovations in printing
   a) Innovations before computer technology
   b) Innovations after computer technology

Review the following outline that uses a categorical outline.

Example:

Introduction to Human Anatomy

1. The Digestive System

2. The Reproductive System

3. The Nervous System

4. The Skeletal System

5. The Muscular System

Locate the Important Specific Details

Authors add specific details to a passage to provide necessary information, define terms, add color, or give examples. To skillfully comprehend reading passages, you must locate the most important specific details in a passage.

TIP: One way to identify the most important details is to look for verbal signals. Verbal signals are words or phrases that the author uses to draw attention to significant facts or information.

Prompting Words

Authors use prompting words to clue you that something very important will soon be communicated. Look for words like "significantly," "importantly," "considerably," "vitally," "critically," "notably," or "essentially."

Defining Words

Authors use defining words to introduce a specific meaning of a word, phrase, or idea. A defining word can be as simple as the word "is" (e.g., A totem is a Native American religious symbol carved from wood). Other defining words or phrases include "means," "is defined as," or "that is." Regardless of whether an author uses one of these defining words or phrases, you should take special note whenever he or she provides a definition of a word, phrase, or idea.

Similarity Words

Similarity words make comparisons between a known idea and an unknown idea. "Like" is the most familiar similarity word (e.g., A plant cell is like an animal cell since both have cell walls and genetic material inside those cell walls). Other similarity words or phrases include "comparable," "similar," "equal to," or "related to."

Contrast Words

The word "but" is an extremely important verbal signal. It sets up a contrast between the "prototype" and the "model." Since prototype means the first example, you should expect it to be fairly primitive and the later versions to be more sophisticated (e.g., The Ohio River traffics many shipping barges but not nearly to the extent of the Mississippi River). Other similar verbal clues include "in contrast," "as opposed to," "although," or "unlike."

Example Words

The phrase "for example" serves as a verbal signal that a specific illustration or pattern will follow. The author uses one or more illustrations to support the given argument. Other similar verbal clues include "illustration," "for instance," "model," or "lesson."

Specific details may come in a variety of forms. A detail may be a number, a date, a quote, a definition, a color, a time, a location, etc. Again, a specific detail is not the main idea of the passage, but may play an important supporting role in making the passage more understandable or more readable. Specific details help readers to better understand the meaning of a passage.

Analyze the Arguments or Persuasive Devices

An author may employ a number of persuasive tools or arguments to attempt to prove his or her main ideas. As a critical reader, you will want to note what persuasive tools or arguments are used. In addition, you will want to analyze whether those arguments are valid and truly support the author's ideas.

To discover and analyze the arguments or persuasive devices, ask the following questions:

- How does the author support the main ideas (or supportive ideas) in his or her passage?

- What arguments does the author make for his or her conclusions?

- Is the supporting evidence valid, logical, or reasonable?

- Do the arguments make sense?

The following are various types of evidence or support that an author may use to prove or advance his or her arguments:

- Scientific data or research

- Statistics

- Historical facts

- Quotations from prominent individuals

- Personal experiences

- Logic

- Statements or ideas from other experts

- Emotional statements or stories

TIP: Authors may give direct cues when persuasive tools are used. Look for key words or phrases like "because," "for this reason," "due to," "in order that," "since," "as an example," or "for instance." When not given direct cues, you will need to infer when and how an author argues for his or her propositions.

Consider the Author's Point of View

When considering an author's point of view in a passage, you determine underlying intentions or assumptions of the author. You uncover the reasons why the author wrote on a particular topic using a particular line of reasoning or style of presentation. The author may directly state some of these reasons within the written materials or the author may leave other reasons unstated or hidden. You will need to infer the more implied or hidden reasons from the passage.

An author generally writes from a position of expertise or experience. An author who writes without true expertise in a given area may be writing merely opinion at best or fabrication at worst. This is important to recognize. You should attempt to determine the level of expertise and experience of a writer when reading a passage.

Here are some questions to consider in uncovering an author's point of view:

- What is the author's background (e.g., nationality, economic status, education)?

- What are the author's credentials (e.g., certifications, titles, degrees)?

- What are the author's biases (e.g., strong likes, dislikes, prejudices)?

- What positive/negative experiences have flavored the author's point of view?

- Did the author write simply to inform (e.g., a textbook, factual passages, brochure), or did the author write to persuade?

- What side of the issue does the author take?

- What does the author ultimately want you to believe?

- Why is the author passionate about this issue?

- How did the time or period when the author wrote influence the author?

- How did the place or location of the author influence the writing of the passage?

- To whom was the author writing and how did that influence the passage?

- How did the circumstances of the author's surroundings influence his or her ideas?

Probe the Tone of the Passage

You must take into account the overall tone of a passage. In short, tone could be described as an author's attitude about the subject. Tone can either be stated or implied. The tone of a passage will provide you with cues about the author's intent in writing the passage. An author's tone can be upbeat, sad, humorous, angry, depressed, analytical, entertaining, informational, academic, confused, scholarly, etc.

Here are some questions you may use to increase awareness of the tone of a passage:

- What is the overall feeling of the passage?

- What ideas does the author use to show he or she is passionate or dispassionate about the topic?

- What does the author want the reader to do after reading the passage (e.g., act in a certain way, think more deeply, understand concepts)?

- What emotional words, images, stories, or examples does the author use?

Summarize the Main Idea
Exercise 1

DIRECTIONS: For each of the following passages, choose the statement that best rephrases and summarizes the material. Answers are on page 595.

1. The city of St. Louis has been called the "Gateway to the West" because it was the launching point for many of the trails used during the great westward migration. Many pioneers who ended their migrations as far west as California began their journey in this Missouri river town.

   A. St. Louis is a Missouri river town where many traveling from the west found safety.
   B. Many trails went to California from points east of St. Louis.
   C. St. Louis was the starting location for many migrants who were heading to the western U.S.
   D. Many people from the eastern U.S. traveled to St. Louis to see the "Gateway to the West."

2. Recreational hot air ballooning is restricted to short day trips, so there is little need for navigational instruments. On the other hand, multiple-day hot air ballooning requires a significant number of sophisticated navigational devices.

   F. The length of the flight determines the number of navigational devices on hot air balloons.
   G. Recreational hot air ballooning is restricted to trips that last fewer than four days.
   H. Navigational equipment is necessary for all types of hot air ballooning.
   J. Due to the need for sophisticated navigational devices, rarely do balloons ever attempt longer trips.

3. As new strains of bacteria emerge that have developed immunity to antibiotics, researchers are constantly challenged to discover new treatments that will be effective. It is this constant need for new research that drives up the cost of effective drugs.

   A. Because researchers must constantly find antibiotics for new bacteria, the cost of drugs constantly increases.
   B. Because bacteria are being constantly discovered, researchers need new tools.
   C. Antibiotics are never effective in treating diseases caused by new strains of bacteria.
   D. Bacteria emerge due to effective research.

4. Carbon monoxide, a potentially deadly gas, has no color or odor. Thus, local municipalities now require all new homes to have carbon monoxide detectors that warn homeowners when this gas is leaking from heating units or piping.

   F. Carbon monoxide has the ability to leak from heating units and pipes in newer homes.
   G. Local cities are now requiring new homes to have detectors that identify leaking carbon monoxide, a potentially deadly gas.
   H. As a potentially deadly gas, carbon monoxide has a strong potential for becoming odorless and colorless.
   J. Leaking homes rarely detect carbon monoxide before serious injury occurs to the owner.

5. During the colonial period, the town of New Amsterdam, which was later to become New York City, was founded by the Dutch as a trading post. At the same time, Halifax, which is located in what is now Nova Scotia, Canada, housed a trading post and military fort for the British.

A. New Amsterdam and Halifax are names of cities in New York.

B. Traders often made their base of operations trading posts like New Amsterdam and Nova Scotia.

C. New Amsterdam was once a Dutch trading post for U.S. colonies.

D. The British and the Dutch both established trading posts in North America during the colonial period.

Determine the Main Idea
Exercise 2

DIRECTIONS: For each of the following passages, determine what answer best describes the main idea or main theme of the paragraph. Answers are on page 595.

1. College professors are currently facing a major problem in their classes. While their students are studying as hard as students did ten to fifteen years ago, these same students are failing more classes. After forming a special committee to investigate why students were failing, one college suggested an intriguing theory. They discovered that students are using more text messaging to communicate, and so they have less practice writing in a formal and grammatically acceptable manner.

    A. Colleges should use special committees to investigate failing students.
    B. College professors should teach students proper English grammar.
    C. College students are failing more classes because they no longer practice using formal English grammar.
    D. College students should be persuaded not to use text messaging.

2. Twenty years ago, the African elephant population was declining at an alarming rate due primarily to poaching that supplied a large, illegal trade in ivory. Total elephant numbers declined by as much as 50 percent in the 1970s and 1980s. The Convention on International Trade in Endangered Species (CITES) enacted an international moratorium on the buying and selling of ivory, which was quickly followed by significant declines in ivory trading and in the rate of elephant poaching. Elephant populations in many African countries have since stabilized.

    F. CITES is an organization that helps endangered elephants, especially those who were born prior to 1970.
    G. Though twenty years ago the African elephant population was declining due to illegal hunting, it has now stabilized.
    H. Selling elephant ivory is very profitable.
    J. If trends continue, in twenty years, African elephants will no longer exist.

3. A flood is an overflow of water that covers lands that are normally not covered by water. A flood occurs, for example, when a stream or river overflows its banks. Small streams are subject to flash floods—that is, the very rapid increases in water that may last only a few minutes. In larger streams, floods usually last from several hours to a few days, and a series of storms might keep a river above flood stage for several weeks.

    A. Floods are natural occurrences that result in negative consequences for people.
    B. Rivers sometimes flood.
    C. Small streams are often subject to flash floods that last only a few minutes.
    D. A flood occurs when an overflow of water covers lands not normally covered by water.

4. If I could change one important thing about my country, it would be to have a mandatory service requirement. I mean that everyone who is able would be required to serve his or her country for a one- or two-year period following high school graduation. People would be given a choice about what kind of service they would do. They could choose to enter the military, to work in a poor area in a city, or to serve in a national park.

   F. All high school graduates should be required to spend one or two years fulfilling a mandatory service requirement.
   G. Because my country is not perfect, I would change one thing.
   H. Military service is more important than working in a city or at a national park.
   J. People should be given a choice about what kind of mandatory service they would enjoy, whether working in the military, in an urban area, or in a national park.

5. Like Shakespeare's King Richard, the woman had experienced a winter of discontent when life itself felt cold, wind-blown, and gray. She longed for spring to come to her soul, when she would experience a warming of her moods. But sadness overtook her, like a blizzard covering a street with racing billows of snow. No matter how hard she tried, she could not force spring before the proper time, but simply endured this season of sadness.

   A. Blizzards caused the woman to become sad, much like they did for King Richard.
   B. The woman experienced a sadness that she could not force to go away.
   C. In winter, the woman experienced cold wind and clouds.
   D. The woman desired for her soul to experience the type of winter that Shakespeare experienced.

6. The great Shawnee chief Tecumseh feared that contact between white and Indian civilizations would mean the eventual destruction of the Indian civilization. When the Delawares were pushed out of lands guaranteed to them by treaty, they turned to Tecumseh for leadership. Tecumseh attempted to block the advance of white settlers into the Old Northwest Territory by forming a federation of Indian tribes that reached all the way from Alabama to Minnesota. He met with tribes and explained that he hoped that the white settlers would withdraw peaceably, but if they did not, it was his plan to drive them out by using superior force.

   F. Treaties were often negotiated with a federation of Indian tribes.
   G. Tecumseh believed that white settlers would withdraw peaceably, but if they didn't, he would ask tribes like the Delawares to abandon their lands.
   H. White settlers sought the help of Tecumseh as they entered the Old Northwest Territory.
   J. Tecumseh was a key leader in attempting to block the advance of white settlers into the Old Northwest Territory.

7. According to many current theories of adolescent development, intellectually, young adolescents are exploring values and ideas in a new way. They are beginning to form abstractions, to generalize, and to think about thinking itself. This intellectual development enables them to shift away from an authoritarian and childlike sense of right and wrong to a more open and complex approach to value formation. They begin to struggle with conflicting concepts like individual rights and the overriding social good.

   A. As adolescents develop intellectually, they think with more sophistication about moral values.
   B. Individual rights and the overriding social good cause adolescents to struggle.
   C. A childlike sense of right and wrong is a natural phase in early adolescence.
   D. All adolescents learn to think critically about thinking itself.

8. The history of western medicine can be traced to Hippocrates, a Greek physician who lived on the island of Cos. Few particulars are known about the life of Hippocrates, but the establishment of the school of medicine on Cos is regarded as his most important achievement. The school emphasized reason and observation and regarded disease as having natural, not supernatural, causes. In addition to a systematized body of empirical knowledge free of superstition, the school of Hippocrates evolved into a tradition of the highest standards of conduct.

   F. The life of Hippocrates can be traced to the island of Cos.

   G. The text of the Hippocratic Oath is regularly used by modern doctors.

   H. Hippocrates is the father (founder) of modern medicine.

   J. Superstitions during the time of Hippocrates caused many illnesses to be wrongly treated.

9. Geothermal energy offers enormous potential for many applications. This new renewable source relies on the Earth's own natural energy to heat or cool a house or multi-family dwelling directly. It does not waste energy by needing to convert energy to steam or other high-temperature fluids to create heating and cooling potential. This ultimately brings great cost savings to producers and consumers of heating and cooling energy.

   A. Geothermal energy is better for multi-family dwellings than other forms of energy.

   B. Steam can be used to generate energy for heating and cooling.

   C. Geothermal energy has potentially positive benefits for those who produce and consume it.

   D. Energy always costs producers and consumers a great deal of money.

10. In 1848, gold was discovered in California, and newspapers quickly spread the word. President James K. Polk confirmed the discovery in his 1848 State of the Union message to Congress. The president's words were enough to trigger the greatest national mass migration in U.S. history and a global gold fever. People used their life savings, mortgaged their homes, and sold everything they had to travel to California in hopes of becoming wealthy.

   F. President James K. Polk delivered his State of the Union message in 1948.

   G. Global gold fever is typically started by newspaper announcements.

   H. People will spend their life savings, mortgage their homes, and sell everything in order to become rich.

   J. The California gold discovery of 1848 led to a large migration of people to California.

Outlining Passages
Exercise 3

DIRECTIONS: For each of the following passages, state the main idea and then write an outline that follows the author's development of the content. Examples of outlines are on page 595.

Passage 1

Speaking unscientifically, we say that lightning strikes an object on the ground, but from a scientific point of view, this language is inaccurate. Cloud-to-ground lightning begins when complex
5   meteorological processes cause a tremendous electrostatic charge to build up within a cloud. Typically, the bottom of the cloud is negatively charged. When the charge reaches 50 to 100 million volts, air is no longer an effective insulator, and
10   lightning occurs within the cloud itself. Approximately 10 to 30 minutes after the onset of intra-cloud lightning, negative charges called stepped leaders emerge from the bottom of the cloud, moving toward Earth in 50-meter intervals at
15   speeds of 100 to 200 kilometers per second, creating an ionized channel. As the stepped leaders near Earth, their strong electric field causes streamers of positively charged ions to develop at the tips of pointed objects connected directly or
20   indirectly to the ground. These positively charged streamers flow upward.

When the distance, known as the striking distance, between a stepped leader and one of the streamers reaches 30 to 100 meters, the
25   intervening air breaks down completely and the leader is joined to Earth via the streamer. Now, a pulse of current known as a return stroke ranging from thousands to hundreds of thousands of amperes moves at one-tenth to one third the speed
30   of light from Earth through the object from which the streamer emanated and up the ionized channel to the charge center within the cloud. An ionized channel remains in the air, and additional negative charges called dart leaders will quickly move down
35   this path resulting in further return strokes. It is this multiplicity that causes the flash to flicker. The entire event typically lasts about one second. The return stroke's extremely high temperature creates the visible lightning and produces thunder by
40   instantly turning moisture into steam.

MAIN IDEA

PASSAGE OUTLINE

Passage 2

Twenty years ago, the African elephant population was declining at an alarming rate due primarily to poaching that supplied a large, illegal trade in ivory. Total elephant numbers declined by
5   as much as 50 percent in the 1970s and 1980s. The Convention on International Trade in Endangered Species (CITES) enacted an international moratorium on the buying and selling of ivory, which was quickly followed by significant declines
10 in ivory trading and in the rate of elephant poaching. Elephant populations in many African countries have since stabilized.

U.S. involvement in African elephant conservation, through both its import control
15 provisions and its grant programs, remains important. One of the earliest projects funded was a cooperative effort with the Central African Republic and the World Wildlife Fund. A cooperative effort was underway to establish a reserve in the
20 southeastern portion of that country. While funds for gating the reserve were anticipated, no funds were available for basic equipment and operations of anti-poaching patrols—hired from local communities—until a cooperative project was
25 implemented using funds provided by the United States. When the first patrols were put into place, the only signs of elephants in a local clearing within the park were the carcasses of several poached animals. Today, more than 2,000 individual
30 elephants, young and old, have been identified as using that clearing.

In Senegal, the westernmost population of elephants in Africa is now secure. Through an African elephant conservation fund grant, an
35 anti-poaching program has provided local community employment and protection for the remaining elephant population. For the first time in years, baby elephants are now seen in this small but genetically valuable population. Similar to the
40 projects described above, funds have been provided to augment anti-poaching and management support in Cameroon, Congo, Eritrea, Gabon, Mali, Tanzania, Zambia, and Zimbabwe.

MAIN IDEA

PASSAGE OUTLINE

Locate Verbal Signs
Exercise 4

> **DIRECTIONS:** In the following passage, underline and identify any prompting, defining, similarity, contrast, or example verbal signals. Answers are on page 596.

A flood is an overflow of water that covers lands that are normally not covered by water. A flood occurs, for example, when a stream or river overflows its banks. Small streams are subject to
5 flash floods—that is, the very rapid increases in water that may last only a few minutes. In larger streams, floods usually last from several hours to a few days, and a series of storms might keep a river above flood stage for several weeks.

10 Floods can occur at any time, but weather patterns have a strong influence on when and where floods happen. Cyclones—similar in structure to tornadoes—bring moisture inland from the ocean, causing floods in the spring in the
15 western United States. Thunderstorms are relatively small but intense storms that cause flash floods in smaller streams during the summer in the Southwest. Frontal storms at the edge of large, moist air masses moving across the country cause
20 floods in the northern and eastern parts of the United States during the winter.

The magnitude of a flood is described by a term called the recurrence interval, which is based upon long-term study of flow records for a stream.
25 A five-year flood is one that would occur, on the average, once every five years. Although a 100-year flood is expected to happen only once in a century, it is important to remember that there is a one percent chance that a flood of that size could
30 happen during any given year.

Of course, the frequency and magnitude of floods can be altered if changes are made in the drainage basin of a stream or river. Significantly, harvesting timber or changing land use from
35 farming to housing can cause the runoff to increase, resulting in an increase in the magnitude of flooding. On the other hand, dams can protect against flooding by storing storm runoff. Although the same volume of water must eventually move
40 downstream, the peak flow can be reduced by temporarily storing water and then releasing it when water levels have fallen.

Locate Specific Details
Exercise 5

DIRECTIONS: After reading each of the following passages, select the best answer about the specific details. Answers are on page 596.

Items #1–3 are based on the following passage.

Fraktur is a uniquely American folk art rooted in the Pennsylvania Dutch (Pennsylvania German) culture. In German, *fraktur* refers to a particular typeface used by printers. Derived from the Latin
5   *fractura*, "breaking apart," *fraktur* suggests that the letters are broken apart and reassembled into designs. Fraktur as a genre of folk art refers to a text (usually religious) that is decorated with symbolic designs.

1. Pennsylvania Dutch is the same term as which of the following?

    A. Pennsylvania Irish
    B. Pennsylvania Scottish
    C. Pennsylvania German
    D. Pennsylvania Mennonite

2. The word *"fractura"* in Latin means:

    F. breaking apart.
    G. forging together.
    H. artful lettering.
    J. German lettering.

3. Fraktur would generally appear in what type of text?

    A. Latin
    B. Dutch
    C. Broken
    D. Religious

Items #4–6 are based on the following passage.

Lightning is basically an electrical discharge of immense proportions. Some 80 percent of lightning occurs within clouds; about 20 percent is cloud-to-ground lightning; and an extremely small
5   percentage is cloud-to-sky lightning.

4. According to the passage, lightning is:

    F. an immense proportion.
    G. an electrical discharge.
    H. a natural occurrence for clouds.
    J. always within clouds.

5. What percentage of lightning occurs within clouds?

    A. 10%
    B. 20%
    C. 80%
    D. 100%

6. According to the passage, 20 percent of lightning travels from clouds to:

    F. ground.
    G. sky.
    H. clouds.
    J. electricity.

Items #7–10 are based on the following passage.

We are now in the throes of a third transformation in communications, although when it began exactly is difficult to say. One might choose that evening of 1844 when Samuel Morse
5 telegraphed the message "What has God wrought!" Or possibly one could point to the invention by Charles Babbage of the "Analytic Engine," a mechanical device that prefigured (came before) the modern electronic computer. Or perhaps this
10 third transformation began with the ENIAC computer developed during World War II as the first digital electronic computer. In any case, it is estimated that it took about 150,000 years for human knowledge to first double, then 1,500 years
15 for it to double again, and that it now doubles every 15 years or less.

7. What computer was developed during World War II?

    A. ENIAC
    B. Morse Code
    C. The Analytic Engine
    D. Charles Babbage

8. Who invented the "Analytic Engine"?

    F. Samuel Morse
    G. Charles Babbage
    H. The ENIAC Company
    J. No one can say.

9. How frequently does knowledge currently double?

    A. Every 150,000 years
    B. Every 1,500 years
    C. Every 15 years or less
    D. All of the above

10. According to the passage, the era in communications we are currently experiencing is the:

    F. first transformation.
    G. digital computer age.
    H. doubling of information age.
    J. third transformation.

Analyze the Arguments
Exercise 6

DIRECTIONS: Read the following passages and then answer the corresponding items. Answers are on page 596.

Items #1–2 are based on the following passage.

Alcohol abuse and dependence are serious problems affecting 10 percent of adult Americans, and the toll is high: 3 out of 100 deaths in the United States can be linked directly to alcohol. In addition
5 to traffic crashes, injuries in the home and on the job, and serious long-term medical consequences, alcohol abuse has been implicated in aggression and crime. The cost of alcohol abuse and alcohol dependence is estimated to be as high as $1 trillion
10 annually.

1. In the paragraph above, the author argues that alcohol abuse and dependence are serious problems. Which of the following reasons does he NOT use to support his main idea?

   A. Three out of 100 deaths in the United States can be linked directly to alcohol.
   B. Aggression and crime can be correlated to alcohol abuse.
   C. The cost of alcohol abuse and dependence is as high as $1 trillion annually.
   D. Ten percent of adult Americans experience traffic crashes and injuries in the home and on the job due to alcohol abuse.

2. In the paragraph above, what type of evidence or support does the author use to prove his or her argument?

   F. Historical quotation
   G. Statistics
   H. A personal story
   J. A statement from an expert

Items #3–4 are based on the following passage.

Regardless of where the hopeful migrants originated, the months-long trip to the California gold country was perilous. A journey across the continent meant rough conditions and possibly
5 attacks by Indians or by other emigrants. Those coming by sea from Europe and the eastern United States had to travel around stormy Cape Horn. The sea journey could be shortened by going overland through the jungles of the Isthmus of Panama, but it
10 was a region rife with cholera and other diseases. From San Francisco, getting to the mining areas was difficult. There was little housing, disease was rampant, and food prices were astronomically high.

3. According to the author, the journey to the California gold country was perilous. What dangers does the author suggest that migrants might have experienced?

   A. Attacks by other emigrants
   B. Jungle diseases
   C. Sea storms
   D. All of the above

4. The author claims that when emigrants arrived in California gold country, there was little housing, much disease, and high food prices. What does the author infer?

   F. Even upon arrival at their destination, the emigrants continued to experience great peril.
   G. Many emigrants returned home before arriving in California.
   H. Conditions were less difficult in San Francisco.
   J. Travel by sea was less costly than travel over inland trails.

Items #5–8 are based on the following passage.

During the past decade, the problem of gang-related crime has become a significant policy issue in the United States. According to recent estimates, more than 16,000 gangs are active in this country,
5 with at least half a million members who commit more than 600,000 crimes each year.

Gang membership leads to criminal behavior. A recent study reported that 80 percent of individual gang members said that they had stolen
10 cars, but only 10 percent of at-risk youths who were not gang members said they had stolen cars. Gang members were also more involved with selling drugs.

The study reported similar contrasts for
15 violent crimes. About 40 percent of gang members had participated in a drive-by shooting, compared with two percent of at-risk youths not in gangs. Gang members were far likelier to own guns, and the guns they owned were of a larger caliber.

20 Most gang members join for security and a sense of belonging. As for security, research demonstrates that the benefits of avoiding gang membership far outweigh those of joining. For example, gang members are five times as likely to
25 suffer a violent death as are at-risk youths who are not gang members. As for the sense of belonging, creative prevention that fosters feelings of belonging in the community as a whole might dissuade many of these youths from joining gangs.

5. According to the author, gang membership has become a serious policy issue because:

A. gang members long for a sense of belonging.
B. drive-by shootings are becoming far too frequent.
C. gang members are more likely to be involved in violent crime.
D. gang members are less frequently found to be involved in illegal drug use.

6. The author reasons that gang members are wrong in thinking they will be more secure by joining a gang. Which of the following statements best describes the author's argument?

F. Gang members do not join gangs for security but for a sense of belonging.
G. A gang member is five times as likely to suffer a violent death as those not affiliated with a gang.
H. Research demonstrates that gang members do indeed feel more secure after joining a gang.
J. None of the above

7. The author argues that gang members are more likely to participate in which of the following?

A. Drive-by shootings
B. Selling drugs
C. Gun ownership
D. All of the above

8. The author suggests that potential gang members may be dissuaded from joining a gang if:

F. they owned their own weapons.
G. they felt more of a sense of belonging in their own communities.
H. the government created new policies that punish violent criminals.
J. gang membership did not lead to criminal behavior.

Items #9–10 are based on the following passage.

The Amazon River of South America is the
most environmentally important river in the entire
world. By pure volume of water, it is the largest
river in the world. In fact, by simple calculation of
5   the total flow of water from river to ocean, the
Amazon River disperses more water into the ocean
than the other ten largest rivers flowing into the
ocean combined. By percentage, the Amazon River
expels 20 percent of all the freshwater discharge
10 into the oceans. Though officially the Nile River is
the longest in the world, by volume of water and
percentage of freshwater discharge, the Amazon
River is the queen of the rivers.

9. The author argues that the Amazon River is
the most environmentally important river in
the entire world. What statement does he or
she use to support his or her position?

A. The Amazon River discharges 20 percent
of all freshwater into the oceans.
B. The Nile is the longest river in the world.
C. The Amazon River is in South America.
D. Scientists can calculate the volume of the
Amazon River.

10. What persuasive device does the author use to
support his or her opinion?

F. Famous quotations
G. Life experiences
H. Scientific facts
J. Emotional stories

Consider the Author's Point of View
Exercise 7

DIRECTIONS: Read the following passages and then answer the corresponding questions. Answers are on page 597.

Items #1–6 are based on the following passage.

The history of western medicine can be traced to Hippocrates, a Greek physician who lived on the island of Cos. Few particulars are known about the life of Hippocrates, but the establishment of the
5   school of medicine on Cos is regarded as his most important achievement. The school emphasized reason and observation and regarded disease as having natural, not supernatural, causes. Reason and observation are important elements of modern
10 medicine. In addition to a systematized body of empirical knowledge free of superstition, the school of Hippocrates evolved a tradition of the highest standards of conduct. Today, the Hippocratic Oath, which defines the duties and moral obligations of a
15 physician, is taken by all medical students upon completion of their training.

As a physician myself, I believe all medical students must accept and endorse the methodology of Hippocrates—reason and observation—prior to
20 being admitted to medical school. As one of the older professors in a highly prestigious medical school, I have grown tired of students who desire to be doctors only for fame and fortune and fail to
25 understand the rich scientific foundations of the profession.

1. Who is the author?

   _____

2. Does the author have expertise or experience regarding this particular subject?

   _____

   _____

   _____

3. What are the author's likes or dislikes?

   _____

   _____

   _____

4. Why did the author write this passage?

   _____

   _____

   _____

5. What does this author want you to believe?

   _____

   _____

   _____

6. What is the passage mainly about?

   _____

   _____

   _____

Items #7–11 are based on the following passage.

     After spending 30 years in the American banking industry, I have come to believe strongly that government bailouts of failing banks are harmful because they create incentives that
5 aggravate the underlying economic problems. Indeed, I have seen first-hand how moral hazard incentives are the villains in the recent, unprecedented wave of financial system collapses. Banks willingly and knowingly take on more risks—
10 especially default risks—than they would if they were not protected by government safety nets. In extreme cases, banking collapses lead to the fiscal insolvency of governments that bail out banks and to exchange rate collapse. As one of the first female
15 members of Congress, I wrote legislation that would have kept the government from bailing out failed banks. Unfortunately, few listened to my cogent arguments and instead they foolishly allowed themselves to be deceived by the banks.

7. Who is the author?

_____

_____

_____

8. Does the author have expertise or experience regarding this particular subject?

_____

_____

_____

9. What are the author's likes or dislikes?

_____

_____

_____

10. Why did the author write this passage?

_____

_____

_____

11. What does this author want you to believe?

_____

_____

_____

Items #12–14 are based on the following passage.

The following letter from a citizen was written to the editor of a newspaper in a developing nation in Africa in the 1990s. This nation had recently moved from a military dictatorship to a democratic form of government.

If I could change one important thing about my country, it would be to have a mandatory service requirement. I mean that everyone who is able would be required to serve his or her country for a
5   one- or two-year period. People would be given a choice about what kind of service they would do. You could choose the military, but you would not have to. You could be assigned to work in a poor area in the city or in a rural area. In addition, you
10 could be a carpenter, or a teacher, or whatever. I think that this requirement would be good for three reasons.

First, required service would be good for the people who do it. I have seen many people come
15 back from military service who went in as children but became adults. I think this is because they were treated like adults and asked to do adult things. Also, they learned to work well with other people on a team, and they even learned some valuable
20 skills.

Second, the service would be good for the people who are served. Just think about the different things people could do. One group of people could restore run-down housing in a poor
25 neighborhood and make a place for people to live. Some other people could work in a farm area and help people raise crops. Some other people could be teachers and work in schools. And everyone who was served would benefit.

30 Third, the service would make being a citizen more valuable. We too often take our citizenship for granted. Many people don't even bother to vote. Perhaps that is because if it's free, people don't think that it's worth very much. If people had to
35 "buy" their citizenship with their time, they would think that it was more important.

12. How did the time or period when the author wrote influence the author?

_____

_____

_____

13. How did the place or location of the author influence the writing of the passage?

_____

_____

_____

14. How did the circumstances of the author influence the writing of the passage?

_____

_____

_____

Items #15–17 are based on the following passage.

In this passage, a professor of sociology at a large public university in Los Angeles writes on the criminal behavior of gang members. The article was written in 1978.

During the past decade, the problem of gang-related crime has become a significant policy issue in the United States. According to recent estimates, more than 16,000 gangs are active in this country,
5 with at least half a million members who commit more than 600,000 crimes each year.

Gang membership leads to criminal behavior. The study mentioned in your textbook reported that 80 percent of individual gang members said that
10 they had stolen cars, but only 10 percent of at-risk youths who were not gang members said they had stolen cars. Gang members were also more involved with selling drugs.

The study reports similar contrasts for violent
15 crimes. About 40 percent of gang members had participated in a drive-by shooting, compared with two percent of at-risk youths not in gangs. Gang members were far likelier to own guns, and the guns they owned were of a larger caliber.

20 Most gang members join for security and a sense of belonging. As for security, research demonstrates that the benefits of avoiding gang membership far outweigh those of joining. For example, gang members are five times as likely to
25 suffer a violent death as are at-risk youths who are not gang members. As for the sense of belonging, creative prevention that fosters feelings of belonging in the community as a whole might dissuade many of these youths from joining gangs.

15. How did the time or period when the author wrote influence the author?

_____

_____

16. How did the place or location of the author influence the writing of the passage?

_____

_____

_____

17. How did the circumstances of the author influence the writing of the passage?

_____

_____

_____

Probe the Tone of the Passage
Exercise 8

> **DIRECTIONS:** Read the following passage and then answer the corresponding questions. Answers are on page 598.

The following is a passage from Jonathan Swift's "A Modest Proposal."

It is a melancholy object to those, who walk through this great town, or travel in the country, when they see the streets, the roads and cabin-doors crowded with beggars of the female sex,

5 followed by three, four, or six children, all in rags, and importuning every passenger for an alms. These mothers instead of being able to work for their honest livelihood, are forced to employ all their time in strolling to beg sustenance for their

10 helpless infants who, as they grow up, either turn thieves for want of work, or leave their dear native country, to fight for the Pretender in Spain, or sell themselves to the Barbadoes.

I think it is agreed by all parties, that this

15 prodigious number of children in the arms, or on the backs, or at the heels of their mothers, and frequently of their fathers, is in the present deplorable state of the kingdom, a very great additional grievance; and therefore whoever could

20 find out a fair, cheap and easy method of making these children sound and useful members of the common-wealth, would deserve so well of the public, as to have his statue set up for a preserver of the nation.

25 But my intention is very far from being confined to provide only for the children of professed beggars: it is of a much greater extent, and shall take in the whole number of infants at a certain age, who are born of parents in effect as

30 little able to support them, as those who demand our charity in the streets.

1. What is the tone of the passage?

_____

_____

_____

2. How does the author demonstrate the tone of the passage?

_____

_____

_____

Bonus Passages
Exercise 9

The following bonus passages are provided so that you can practice all of the "Honing Your Reading Skills" strategies comprehensively.

> **DIRECTIONS:** Each passage below is followed by a number of items. Answer each item based upon the content of the passage. Answers are on page 598.

Items #1–10 are based on the following passage.

In 1848, gold was discovered in California, and newspapers quickly spread the word. President James K. Polk confirmed the discovery in his 1848 State of the Union message to Congress. The
5   president's words and the knowledge that taking the precious metal was completely unregulated in California were enough to trigger the greatest national mass migration in U.S. history and a global gold fever. People used their life savings, mortgaged
10 their homes, and sold everything they had to travel to California in hopes of becoming wealthy. At the time gold was discovered, there were approximately 11,000 non-Native Americans living in California. Between the discovery and 1852,
15 some 300,000 people, mostly young and male, traveled to California from all quarters.

Regardless of where the hopeful travelers originated, the months-long trip was perilous. A journey across the continent meant rough
20 conditions and possibly attacks by Indians or by other emigrants. Those coming by sea from Europe and the eastern United States had to travel around stormy Cape Horn. The sea journey could be shortened by going overland through the jungles of
25 the Isthmus of Panama, but it was a region rife with cholera and other diseases. From San Francisco, getting to the mining areas was difficult. There was little housing, disease was rampant, and food prices were astronomically high.

30 There were tales of people finding thousands of dollars of gold in only a few weeks, but most miners just encountered hard times. To survive, some left mining or worked for wages in other men's operations. The problem for many was that
35 they couldn't afford to return home, and any news of other people striking it rich would renew hope. Many people lost, but a few lucky ones won. By 1860, approximately $600 million in gold had been mined—more than $10 billion today.

1. In line 5, the word "precious" most nearly means:

   A. legal.
   B. scarce.
   C. beautiful.
   D. valuable.

2. The author mentions that 300,000 people moved to California in order to:

   F. demonstrate that many people became wealthy.
   G. underscore the size of the migration.
   H. show that they came from all over the world.
   J. explain why so many miners failed to find gold.

3. It can be inferred that some people mortgaged their homes in order to:

   A. get money to travel to California.
   B. ensure a place to return to.
   C. provide insurance against failure.
   D. purchase gold from California.

4. It can be inferred that travelers who crossed the Isthmus of Panama:

   F. generally came from the eastern U.S.
   G. arrived in California after the Gold Rush.
   H. avoided the trip around Cape Horn.
   J. paid less than others for their trip.

5. In line 25, the word "rife" most nearly means:

   A. devoid.
   B. filled.
   C. immune.
   D. suspected.

6. The author mentions all of the following as difficulties facing travelers when they arrived in San Francisco EXCEPT:

   F.   high food prices.
   G.   a housing shortage.
   H.   widespread disease.
   J.   lack of work.

7. In line 18, the word "perilous" most nearly means:

   A.   dangerous.
   B.   lengthy.
   C.   uneventful.
   D.   expensive.

8. In line 35, the phrase "couldn't afford" most nearly means:

   F.   weren't able to sell their gold.
   G.   couldn't find transportation.
   H.   had no money.
   J.   didn't want.

9. According to the selection, why did so many people move to California?

   A.   They hoped to become rich by mining gold.
   B.   President Polk encouraged them to go.
   C.   They wanted to open stores to sell goods to miners.
   D.   They had no homes of their own.

10. What is the main focus of the selection?

   F.   The conditions in San Francisco during the California Gold Rush
   G.   The various modes of transportation available during the mid-1800s
   H.   The demographic characteristics of the people who came to California
   J.   The California migration triggered by the discovery of gold

Items #11–16 are based on the following passage.

Geothermal energy offers enormous potential for direct, low-temperature applications. Unlike indirect applications, this new technology relies on the Earth's natural thermal energy to heat or cool a
5 house or multi-family dwelling directly without the need to convert steam or other high-temperature fluids into electricity using expensive equipment.

A geothermal system consists of a heat pump and exchanger plus a series of pipes, called a loop,
10 installed below the surface of the ground or submerged in a pond or lake. Fluid circulating in the loop is warmed and carries heat to the home. The heat pump and exchanger use an electrically powered vapor compression cycle—the same
15 principle employed in a refrigerator—to concentrate the energy and to transfer it. The concentrated geothermal energy is released inside the home at a higher temperature, and fans then distribute the heat to various rooms through a
20 system of air ducts. In summer, the process is reversed: excess heat is drawn from the home, expelled to the loop, and absorbed by the Earth.

Geothermal systems are more effective than conventional heat pumps that use the outdoor air as
25 their heat source (on cold days) or heat sink (on warm days) because geothermal systems draw heat from a source whose temperature is more constant than that of air. The temperature of the ground or groundwater a few feet beneath the Earth's surface
30 remains relatively stable—between 45°F and 70°F. In winter, it is much easier to capture heat from the soil at a moderate 50°F than from the atmosphere when the air temperature is below zero. Conversely, in summer, the relatively cool ground absorbs a
35 home's waste heat more readily than the warm outdoor air.

The use of geothermal energy through heat pump technology has almost no adverse environmental consequences and offers several
40 advantages over conventional energy sources. Direct geothermal applications are usually no more disruptive of the surrounding environment than are normal water wells. Additionally, while such systems require electricity to concentrate and
45 distribute the energy collected, they actually reduce total energy consumption by one-fourth to two-thirds, depending on the technology used. For every 1,000 homes with geothermal heat pumps, an electric utility can avoid the installation of two to
50 five megawatts of generating capacity. Unfortunately, only a modest part of the potential of this use for geothermal energy has been developed because the service industry is small and the price of competing energy sources is low.

11. The author regards the new technology as:

   A. promising but underutilized.
   B. dependable but costly.
   C. inexpensive but unreliable.
   D. unproven but efficient.

12. The passage implies that a rise in the cost of conventional energy would result in:

   F. a decrease in the cost for installing geothermal heating and cooling equipment.
   G. an economic incentive in favor of the use of conventional energy sources.
   H. an expanded reliance on direct geothermal technology for climate control of smaller structures.
   J. a decrease in the number of new homes constructed using geothermal heating.

13. Which of the following would be the most logical continuation of the passage?

   A. A listing of geological features of the Earth such as geysers and volcanoes that might be potential geothermal energy sources
   B. A review of the history of the use of geothermal energy and associated technologies
   C. A description of experimental techniques for converting geothermal energy into electricity
   D. A discussion of some ways of expanding reliance on geothermal energy for direct, low-temperature applications

14. The author refers to a refrigerator in line 15 in order to:

    F.   demonstrate the feasibility of geothermal technology.

    G.   provide the reader with a familiar example of heat pump technology.

    H.   illustrate the distinction between direct and indirect geothermal technology.

    J.   prove that geothermal energy can cool as well as heat.

15. In line 35, "waste" most nearly means:

    A.   inefficient.

    B.   unused.

    C.   recycled.

    D.   unwanted.

16. Which of the following helps to illustrate why the new technology can be used for air conditioning as well as heating homes?

    F.   A pool of still water freezes faster than a running stream.

    G.   A drink of well water tastes cool on a hot summer day.

    H.   Clothes on a line dry more quickly on a dry day than on a day with high humidity.

    J.   It feels colder on a windy winter day than on a day with the same temperature and no wind.

Reading
Mastery Test

READING MASTERY TEST

42 Items

DIRECTIONS: Each passage below is followed by one or more items based on the passage's content. Answer the items on the basis of what is stated or implied in the corresponding passage. Answers are on page 599.

Passage I

Prose Fiction: This passage is adapted from a short story written by the Russian author Leo Tolstoy.

Near the borders of France and Italy, on the shore of the Mediterranean Sea, lies a tiny little kingdom. There is a King, and he has a palace, courtiers, ministers, and an army. It is not a large
5 army, only 60 men in all, but still it is an army. The King's primary source of revenue is a casino where people play roulette, and whether they win or lose, the King always gets a percentage. The revenue is not great, but it is sufficient for the King and the
10 small country.

Now it happened a few years ago that a murder was committed in the kingdom. No such thing had happened before. The judges assembled with much ceremony and tried the case in the most
15 judicial manner. At last they condemned the criminal to have his head cut off as the law directed. So far, so good. There was only one hitch in the matter. They had neither a guillotine for cutting heads off nor an executioner.

20 At the King's instruction, the Minister of Justice addressed an inquiry to the French government, asking whether the French could not lend them a machine and an expert to cut off the criminal's head; and if so, would the French kindly inform them
25 what the cost would be. A week later the reply came: a machine and an expert could be supplied, and the cost would be 16,000 francs. The King thought it over and said, "Why 16,000 francs is more than two francs apiece from every person in
30 the kingdom. The people won't stand for it. They would riot."

The King told the Minister to send a similar inquiry to the King of Italy. The Italian government wrote that they would supply both a machine and

35 an expert; and the whole cost would be 12,000 francs, including travel expenses. This was cheaper, but still it seemed too much.

The King met with the Minister to consider how the execution could be done with less expense.
40 Could not one of the soldiers perhaps do it, even if in a rough and homely fashion? The General explained to the Minister who told the King that in war, soldiers don't mind killing people. In fact, that is what they are trained to do, but, the General said,
45 they had not been taught the technique of executing a man.

At last the Minister hit upon an idea: the King could commute the death sentence to one of imprisonment for life. In this way, the King would
50 seem to be merciful, plus it would be cheaper. But the small kingdom had no prison. After some searching, the Minister managed to find a house that would serve as a prison, and he put the fellow there and hired a guard. The guard not only had to watch
55 the criminal but also bring him food from the palace kitchen.

The prisoner remained there month after month. When a year had passed, the King, looking over the accounts of his income and expenditures,
60 noticed a new item of expenditure. This was for the upkeep of the criminal, and it wasn't a small sum. There was the prison, the special guard, and the man's food. It came to more than 600 francs for the year. And the worst of it was that the fellow was still
65 young and healthy and might live for 50 years. The King summoned the Minister and told him to fire the guard to save money. "But," the Minister asked, "what if he runs away?" The King replied, "So much the better, for then we save the expense altogether."

70   So, the guard was dismissed, but all that happened was that at dinner time the criminal came out and went to the King's kitchen to get his own dinner. He returned to the prison, shut the door on himself, and stayed inside. Day after day, the same
75 thing occurred. The Minister asked the man, "Why don't you run away? The King won't care." "Maybe the King wouldn't care, but I would," replied the man, "I feel quite at home here."

    Finally, the King decided the only way to get
80 rid of the prisoner was to offer him a pension. "Well," said the prisoner, "I guess I don't mind, so long as you promise to pay it for as long as I live. On that condition, I am willing to go." The amount agreed upon was 600 francs per year. He received
85 one-third of his annuity in advance and left the Kingdom.

    It was only fifteen minutes by rail to the border, and he settled just on the other side, bought a bit of land, and started farming. He still returns
90 every three months to collect his pension and lives quite comfortably on that sum plus the earnings from the farm.

    It is a good thing to know when a kingdom will not pay the expense of cutting off a man's head.

1. Throughout the passage, the narrator is mainly interested in:

    A. why the prisoner committed a crime.
    B. what should be done with the prisoner.
    C. how the General trains soldiers.
    D. where the prisoner should live.

2. Which of the following sentences best describes the prisoner?

    F. The prisoner is clever.
    G. The prisoner is absent-minded.
    H. The prisoner is a coward.
    J. The prisoner is insane.

3. In line 48, the word "commute" means:

    A. murder.
    B. travel.
    C. reduce.
    D. carry out.

4. On the King's instructions, the Minister first contacted:

    F. the General.
    G. the French government.
    H. the King of Italy.
    J. the soldiers.

5. The passage mainly discusses the:

    A. Minister's worries about the prisoner's comfort.
    B. King's concern about the cost of the punishment.
    C. people's reaction to the seriousness of the crime.
    D. importance of protecting the people of the kingdom.

6. Which of the following sentences best describes the Minister's attitude toward the King?

    F. The Minister wants to please the King.
    G. The Minister wants the King to leave the kingdom.
    H. The Minister thinks the King spends too much.
    J. The Minister does not trust the King.

7. The riot that the King feared would occur did not take place because the:

    A. prisoner got his own dinner.
    B. King fired the guard to save money.
    C. King did not pay for an execution.
    D. the criminal was found innocent.

8. The author of the passage describes in the greatest detail the:

    F. life of the criminal after he has left the kingdom.
    G. daily activities of the people who live in the kingdom.
    H. details of the crime that created the need for an execution.
    J. attempts to punish the criminal without spending too much.

9. Which of the following sentences best describes the people in the kingdom?

    A. The people are wasteful.
    B. The people are fearful.
    C. The people are warlike.
    D. The people are law-abiding.

Passage II

Social Studies: The following passage is adapted from a chapter in a history book on the significance of Chicago's Black Metropolis.

At the peak of its prosperity, Chicago's Black Metropolis was recognized as a model of African American achievement. By 1900, a small South Side black community centered at State and 35th Streets
5 began to take on the characteristics of a "city-within-a-city," which paralleled the growth and expansion of the city of Chicago at large. It grew and prospered until the 1930s, when the Great Depression and associated socio-economic
10 conditions virtually halted its further development.

The established white businesses and social communities of Chicago historically had no interest in the black community; consequently, the black community gradually evolved a complete
15 commercial, social, and political base of its own. A great amount of money was generated within the black community, and Joseph Binga established Chicago's first black-owned bank in 1908. With greater access to financial resources, the
20 commercial and business interests of Black Metropolis greatly diversified into a wide range of professional, commercial, and manufacturing interests. The vicinity of State and 35th Streets was rapidly transformed into the Wall Street of the black
25 community.

In marked contrast to the staid banks, insurance companies, and professional offices which conducted business by day on State Street, the area was magically transformed at night by the
30 bright lights and exciting sounds of the numerous nightclubs and all-night restaurants scattered throughout the business district. These were the popular clubs where such notables as King Oliver, Louis Armstrong, and Jelly Roll Morton played and
35 earned Chicago its reputation as a jazz center with a uniquely Chicago style. It was often said that if a horn were held up at the corner of State and 35th Streets, because of all the music in the air, the horn would play itself.

40 Churches played an important role in the development of Black Metropolis, both from a social as well as a spiritual standpoint. Large congregations such as the Olivet Baptist Church and Pilgrim Baptist Church conducted extensive social
45 programs and were instrumental in securing

lodging and employment for the newcomers who arrived from the South during the Great Migration. Similar programs were conducted at the Wabash Avenue YMCA, which opened in 1914 through the
50 impetus of philanthropist Julius Rosenwald, the president of Sears, Roebuck & Company. Programs at the YMCA included extensive job training programs such as auto repair and manual training.

Organized political alliances gave Black
55 Metropolis increased power in Chicago's city government, beginning with the election of Oscar DePriest as the city's first black alderman in 1915. Initially working in alliance with the white Republican bosses who controlled the political
60 destiny of the Black Metropolis wards, DePriest later built a political organization of his own, forming the "People's Movement Club" with headquarters on South Indiana Avenue. The political voting strength of the Black Metropolis
65 wards was such that, by the 1920s, political control was effectively taken from the white political bosses who formerly controlled them and put into the hands of political figures from within the black community. In 1928, Oscar DePriest had the
70 distinction of being the first black from the North to be elected to a seat in the United States House of Representatives, a seat he held for three consecutive terms.

The growth and prosperity of Black Metropolis
75 was directly tied to the rapid growth of the black population, particularly during the Great Migration. The sharp decline in new arrivals during the 1920s weakened the financial base of the community, adversely affecting the businesses that relied on
80 support from within the black community. When white businessmen, who previously had ignored the black community, began to realize the economic potential of the black community, an alternate business area was created along 47th Street by
85 white developers and store owners who controlled the property to such an extent that black-owned businesses were largely excluded from the area. The introduction of established white chain stores and commercial enterprises along 47th Street siphoned
90 off its energy and self-supporting financial base. The final blow to Black Metropolis came from the Great Depression of 1929, which closed down most of its black-owned banks, insurance companies, and other business interests, while many of the businesses of
95 47th Street, with their broader access to credit and

nationwide financial backing, survived. The self-supporting momentum of Black Metropolis, which its backers had hoped would lead to recognition and eventual integration with the downtown business
100 establishment, was thus dealt a serious blow.

10. According to the passage, Joseph Binga was a:

F.   banker.
G.   musician.
H.   politician.
J.   minister.

11. According to the passage, in what year was Oscar DePriest first elected to the United States House of Representatives?

A.   1900
B.   1908
C.   1915
D.   1928

12. According to the passage, the event that led to the closing of most black-owned business in Black Metropolis was:

F.   the Great Migration.
G.   the opening of black-owned banks.
H.   the election of a black alderman.
J.   the Great Depression.

13. The author explains that the black community developed its own businesses because:

A.   white-controlled chain stores dominated 47th Street.
B.   State and 35th Streets were convenient to all Chicago residents.
C.   white businesses were not interested in the black community.
D.   the number of people moving into the area declined sharply.

14. In lines 5–6, the phrase "city-within-a-city" is used by the author to express the idea that Black Metropolis:

F.   had a population larger than that of Chicago.
G.   was largely independent of greater Chicago.
H.   was an important center for jazz music.
J.   had its own city government.

15. Which of the following is NOT mentioned in the passage as a program undertaken by churches with large congregations?

A.   Lending money to black-owned business
B.   Finding housing for recent arrivals
C.   Helping newcomers to find jobs
D.   Conducting extensive social programs

16. All of the following people are mentioned in the passage as being musicians EXCEPT:

F.   Louis Armstrong.
G.   Jelly Roll Morton.
H.   Julius Rosenwald.
J.   King Oliver.

17. The passage states that Oscar DePriest began his political career by first:

A.   building a headquarters on South Indiana Avenue.
B.   working with the powerful white Republican politicians.
C.   forming the People's Movement Club.
D.   being elected to the United States House of Representatives.

Passage III

Humanities: This passage was adapted from a lecture on jazz given to a class by a music professor.

How jazz is defined depends on whom you talk to. There are many types and styles of jazz: jazz-rock, Latin jazz, acid jazz, fusion, and several other "jazzes." The dictionary itself has several
5 definitions. However, most people agree that jazz developed in the early twentieth century, that it was created mainly by Afro-Americans, and that it has elements of European and Afro-American cultures.

As for the origin of the word "jazz," one popular
10 story describes a somewhat inebriated customer in Chicago who, in a moment of excitement, leapt to his feet and shouted to the band, "Jass it up boys, jass it up." The story then goes that through a printer's error "jass" became "jazz," and the name stuck.
15 Perhaps the best response to the question, "What is jazz?" was provided by Louis Armstrong, who, when asked that question, said, "If you don't know, don't mess with it."

Jazz is basically a style of music. It has a lot of
20 the same characteristics as other music but also treats the basic elements of music in a unique way. Any melody can be played in a jazz fashion by putting triplets behind the basic beat. In fact, one of the common practices of jazz players is to quote
25 melodies from various sources, including classical pieces, in their solos. By putting the triplet feeling in their playing, jazz players achieve a "swinging" effect in the playing of the melody. The triplet feeling contrasts with the more common straight
30 eighth note feel that is found in most music. The triplet feel is much "looser" and has a swinging feeling when compared with the eighth note feeling. The ability to play in a swing style is a basic building block for the jazz musician.

35 More important even than interpretation, in fact the most important element of jazz, is improvisation. This is the jazz player's ability to instantaneously compose, edit, revise, and perform. It is also the most difficult element to master, and
40 this is why most players spend their entire lives working and developing this aspect of their playing.

Improvisation is the element by which jazz players are judged and by which they establish their claim to immortality. It is an incredibly complex
45 procedure that encompasses every element of not only jazz but of music itself. It is what makes jazz, jazz. Again, jazz is not the only music to use improvisation, but it uses it to an extent far greater than any other style of music.

50 Rhythm is also important. In this area, jazz distinguishes itself with a tremendous reliance on syncopation. Syncopation is an accent or emphasis where you least expect it. It can happen on a part of a beat or a part of a measure. It gives the music life
55 and provides a tremendous variety in the rhythm of a given piece. Syncopation also occurs when an expected accent is left out by the musician.

Finally, there is tempo. Tempo is just another name for the speed of a piece of music. In jazz, more
60 often than not, the tempo remains steady from the beginning of the piece to the end. This is not the only music where this occurs, but the tempo variations that characterize other types of music are not found in the majority of jazz performances.

65 Although any melody or piece can be played in a jazz style, the blues holds a special place in every jazz performer's heart. It is a very stylized form almost always consisting of twelve measures of music and only three chords. The improviser needs
70 to play only one scale to sound good when he or she solos over the changes (chords). Though blues has a very important influence on jazz, the blues is itself a separate musical entity from jazz.

Is jazz better than classical music? There really
75 is no contest between these two types of music because they have different goals. Jazz is a player's art and classical is a composer's art. In classical music, for the most part, the performers are trying to re-create what the composer had in mind. If you
80 listen to ten recordings of Beethoven's "Ninth Symphony," they would pretty much sound the same. Listen to ten recordings of Duke Ellington's "In a Sentimental Mood" and even the melody would not be treated the same way by the
85 individual players. Individuality is encouraged, sought after, rewarded, and absolutely necessary for the art of jazz to survive.

18. Which of the following sentences about jazz does NOT make a true statement?

F. Jazz originated in the early twentieth century.
G. Jazz has elements of European culture in it.
H. Jazz is a single type of music that is easily defined.
J. Jazz was mainly created by African American musicians.

19. The passage explains that the word "jass" became "jazz" because:

A. the dictionary definition changed.
B. composers preferred jazz to jass.
C. musicians could not define jazz.
D. a printer made a spelling error.

20. According to the passage, jazz musicians create a swinging effect by using:

F. straight eighth notes.
G. triplets.
H. blues scales.
J. tempo variations.

21. In lines 24–25, the phrase "quote melodies from" most nearly means:

A. listen to music from.
B. mention the composers of.
C. play notes from.
D. change the rhythm of.

22. The passage mentions all of the following as typical of jazz music EXCEPT:

F. improvisation.
G. syncopation.
H. interpretation.
J. tempo variations.

23. In line 67, the word "stylized" most nearly means:

A. unusual.
B. predictable.
C. complicated.
D. serious.

24. According to the passage, the blues is characterized by:

F. twelve measures, three chords, and one scale.
G. twelve measures, one chord, and three scales.
H. three measures, one chord, and twelve scales.
J. one measure, twelve chords, and three scales.

25. As used in the passage, improvisation means to:

A. create spontaneously.
B. rehearse carefully.
C. prepare beforehand.
D. follow a plan.

Passage IV

Natural Sciences: This passage was adapted from an article in a science journal.

The Hawaiian Islands, which are entirely of volcanic origin, have formed in the middle of the Pacific Ocean nearly 2,000 miles from the nearest plate boundary. How do the Hawaiian Islands and
5 other volcanoes form in the interior of plates?

J. Tuzo Wilson, a geophysicist, came up with an ingenious idea that became known as the "hotspot" theory. Wilson noted that in certain locations, such as Hawaii, volcanism has been active for very long
10 periods of time. This could only happen if relatively small, long-lasting, and exceptionally hot regions—called hotspots—existed below the plates to provide localized sources of high heat energy, called thermal plumes, to sustain volcanism.

15 Wilson hypothesized that the distinctive linear shape of the Hawaiian Islands resulted from the Pacific Plate moving over a deep, stationary hotspot in the mantle, located beneath the present-day position of the island of Hawaii. Heat from this
20 hotspot produced a persistent source of magma by partly melting the overriding Pacific Plate. The magma, because it is lighter than the surrounding solid rock, then rises through the mantle and crust to erupt onto the seafloor, forming an active
25 seamount. Over time, countless eruptions cause the seamount to grow until it finally emerges above sea level to form an island volcano.

Wilson suggested that continuing plate movement eventually carries the island beyond the
30 hotspot, cutting it off from the magma source, and volcanism ceases. As one island volcano becomes extinct, another develops over the hotspot, and the cycle is repeated. This process of volcano growth and death, over many millions of years, has left a
35 long trail of volcanic islands and seamounts across the Pacific Ocean floor.

According to Wilson's hotspot theory, the volcanoes of the Hawaiian chain should get progressively older and become more eroded the
40 farther they travel beyond the hotspot. The oldest volcanic rocks on Kauai, the most northwestern inhabited Hawaiian island, are about 5.5 million years old and are deeply eroded. By comparison, on the "Big Island" of Hawaii—the most southeastern
45 in the chain and presumably still positioned over the hotspot—the oldest exposed rocks are less than 0.7 million years old and new volcanic rock is continually being formed.

The possibility that the Hawaiian Islands
50 become younger to the southeast was suspected by the ancient Hawaiians, long before any scientific studies were done. Hawaiians noticed the differences in erosion, soil formation, and vegetation and recognized that the islands to the
55 northwest (Niihau and Kauai) were older than those to the southeast (Maui and Hawaii). This idea was handed down from generation to generation in the legends of Pele, the fiery goddess of volcanoes. Pele originally lived on Kauai. When her older sister
60 Namakaokahai, the goddess of the sea, attacked her, Pele fled to the island of Oahu. When she was forced by Namakaokahai to flee again, Pele moved southeast to Maui and finally to Hawaii, where she now lives in the Halemaumau crater at the summit
65 of Kilauea volcano. The mythical flight of Pele from Kauai to Hawaii is consistent with geologic evidence that clearly shows the islands become younger from northwest to southeast.

Although Hawaii is perhaps the best known
70 hotspot, others exist beneath the oceans and continents. More than a hundred hotspots beneath the Earth's crust have been active during the past 10 million years.

A few hotspots are thought to exist below the
75 North American Plate. Perhaps the best known is the hotspot in the region of Yellowstone National Park. Here are found several calderas (large craters formed by the ground collapse accompanying explosive volcanism) that were produced by three
80 gigantic eruptions during the past two million years, the most recent of which occurred about 600,000 years ago. Ash deposits from these powerful eruptions have been mapped as far away as Texas. The thermal energy of the Yellowstone hotspot fuels
85 more than 10,000 hot pools and springs, geysers (like Old Faithful), and pools of boiling mud. A large body of magma, capped by a hydrothermal system (a zone of pressurized steam and hot water), still exists beneath the caldera.

26. Which of the following Hawaiian Islands was formed first?

    F. Kauai
    G. Maui
    H. Oahu
    J. Hawaii

27. According to Wilson's theory, what is the first event that occurs in the formation of a volcanic island like Hawaii?

    A. The plate moves away from the heat plume.
    B. Magma spills onto the ocean floor to make a seamount.
    C. Repeated eruptions increase the height of the seamount.
    D. A seamount emerges to form a volcanic island.

28. According to the passage, all of the following are found in Yellowstone Park EXCEPT:

    F. calderas.
    G. hot springs.
    H. pools of boiling mud.
    J. seamounts.

29. According to Hawaiian legend, after fleeing from Namakaokahai, Pele finally settled on:

    A. Niihau.
    B. Oahu.
    C. Kauai.
    D. Hawaii.

30. According to the passage, the magma produced by a hotspot rises because it is:

    F. lighter than the surrounding rock.
    G. influenced by the plate's movement.
    H. in the middle of the plate.
    J. no longer volcanically active.

31. In line 50, the word "younger" most nearly means:

    A. volcanically inactive.
    B. more thoroughly eroded.
    C. more recently formed.
    D. lacking vegetation.

32. According to the passage, the last major eruption in the Yellowstone Park area occurred:

    F. 10 million years ago.
    G. 2 million years ago.
    H. 600,000 years ago.
    J. 10,000 years ago.

33. The passage explains that the ash from Yellowstone Park found in Texas was deposited there by:

    A. geysers and springs.
    B. volcanic eruptions.
    C. pressurized steam.
    D. collapsing craters.

Passage V

Prose Fiction: This passage is adapted from a short story by George Ade.

"You mean to have somebody get married on Christmas Eve?" asked Mr. Hufty, looking at him coldly.

"That's it exactly," replied Doc with a grin of
5 enthusiasm.

"What's getting married got to do with Christmas?" asked Sam Woodson.

"People get married every day," added Mr. Hufty.

10 "Not the people that I'm thinking about," said Doc, leaning back and looking at them serenely. "Can you imagine what kind of a crowd we'll have in that church if we advertise that old Baz Leonard is going to get married to Miss Wheatley?" said Doc.

15 The other two men gazed at Doc in sheer amazement, stunned by the audacity of his suggestion. Baz Leonard and Miss Wheatley! It took several moments for them to grasp the immensity of the proposition.

20 "Is Baz going to marry her?" asked Sam Woodson.

"He is," replied Doc, "but he don't know it—yet. I'm counting on the fact that he won't miss a chance to get a lot of attention and to show off in public,
25 and that Miss Wheatley is about due to get married to someone—anyone."

"I think you'd be doing her a favor if you picked out somebody besides Baz," suggested the cold and unresponsive Woodson.

30 "Baz is the man," said Doc firmly. "If we've got a character who loves attention in this town it's Baz Leonard. If there's a woman in town that it's time got married, it's poor old Miss Wheatley. After all these years, her getting married to any one would
35 be about the biggest piece of news you could spring on this town. But getting married to Baz Leonard!"

"I don't see how you're going to work it in on a Christmas Eve exhibition," said Woodson, but even as he spoke he chuckled reflectively, and it was

40 evident that the beautiful possibilities of the plan were beginning to occur to him.

"Simplest thing in the world," said Doc. "We announce that we're going to give Miss Wheatley a Christmas present."

45 "You'd better postpone the show till April 1," suggested Mr. Hufty, and then all three men leaned back in their chairs, exchanged glances, and roared with laughter. It was evident that no vote would be necessary.

50 "I've thought it all out," continued Doc. "We can have the regular entertainment, then the distribution of presents. We'll have Santy Claus bring in the marriage license and present it to Baz. Then we'll lead the happy couple to the altar, and
55 after Brother King has done a scientific job of splicing, we'll give them their combination Christmas and wedding presents. The different Sunday-school classes can chip in and buy presents for them. They'll be glad to do it."

60 "It sounds all right, but can we talk 'em into it?" asked Mr. Hufty. "Baz has hung around her a little, but I never thought he wanted to marry her."

"I'll guarantee to have him on hand when the time comes," said Doc. "I want you two fellows to
65 have the women go after Miss Wheatley. Have the women go over and congratulate her, and then convince her that if she has a church wedding she'll get a raft of presents. It's last chance for her."

And so, next day, there began the strangest
70 campaign that ever Cupid waged by proxy. Rumor—strong, persistent, undeniable—had it that Baz Leonard and Miss Beulah Wheatley were to become as "one," or that is the way it was put by the editor of the *Courier*.

34. The story is primarily about how Doc will use his understanding of the personalities of:

    F.   Sam Woodson and Mr. Hufty.
    G.   the church women and Brother King.
    H.   Baz Leonard and Miss Wheatley.
    J.   the editor and townspeople.

35. In line 73, the word "one" most nearly means:

    A.   friend.
    B.   fiancé.
    C.   couple.
    D.   bride.

36. The passage mainly discusses:

    F.   the regular entertainment that the church will present on Christmas Eve.
    G.   the opinions of the editor that are printed in the *Courier*.
    H.   the close friendship between Doc, Sam Woodson, and Mr. Hufty.
    J.   the tricks that Doc thinks will get Baz Leonard and Miss Wheatley married.

37. Throughout the passage, the characters are discussing:

    A.   the plan to have Baz Leonard and Miss Wheatley get married.
    B.   the possibility that Miss Wheatley is already engaged.
    C.   the advantages of getting married in a church on Christmas Eve.
    D.   the best wedding present for Baz Leonard and Miss Wheatley.

38. Which of the following sentences most accurately characterizes Miss Wheatley?

    F.   She is an older woman who is not married.
    G.   She has always wanted to marry Baz Leonard.
    H.   She has only recently moved into the community.
    J.   She is not very involved in church activities.

39. Which of the following sentences best characterizes the relationship of Baz Leonard and Miss Wheatley at the beginning of the story?

    A.   They know each other casually but have no plans to marry.
    B.   They are old friends who spend a lot of time together.
    C.   They were childhood sweethearts who have long planned to marry.
    D.   They have never met before and live in different towns.

40. In the passage, Doc, Mr. Hufty, and Sam Woodson are talking mostly about:

    F.   memories of other weddings held in the town's church.
    G.   plans to get Baz Leonard and Miss Wheatley married.
    H.   advantages of people being married for a long time.
    J.   respect that the townspeople have for Brother King.

41. Which of the following sentences best expresses Doc's attitude about his plan?

    A.   Doc wants Sam and Mr. Hufty to think of a better plan.
    B.   Doc is confident that his plan will be successful.
    C.   Doc is sure that Baz already wants to marry Miss Wheatley.
    D.   Doc knows that his plan will take several years to work.

42. Which of the following sentences best describes Baz Leonard?

    F.   He is extremely shy and rarely goes out in public.
    G.   He is friends with Doc, Sam Woodson, and Mr. Hufty.
    H.   He is handsome and much younger than Miss Wheatley.
    J.   He is vain and likes being the center of attention.

Writing Skills Review

Course Concept Outline

I. Planning an Essay (p. 335)

A. Understand the Assignment (p. 335)

1. Let the Prompt Be Your Topic (p. 335)
2. Develop a Point of View (p. 335)
3. Write Only on the Assigned Topic (p. 335)

B. Organize Your Thoughts (p. 335)

1. Limit the Scope of Your Essay (p. 335)
2. Develop a Thesis (p. 336)
3. Identify Key Points (p. 336)
4. Write an Outline (p. 336)

II. Composition (p. 337)

A. Organize Ideas into Paragraphs (p. 337)

B. Write the Essay (p. 337)

1. The Introduction (p. 338)
2. The Body (p. 338)
3. Transitions (p. 339)
4. The Conclusion (p. 339)

C. Principles of Good Writing (p. 340)

1. Write Grammatically (p. 340)
2. Punctuate and Spell Correctly (p. 341)
3. Write Concisely and Clearly (p. 341)

III. Revision and Scoring (p. 343)

    A. Proofread Your Essay (p. 343)

        1. Proofread for Structural Errors (p. 343)
        2. Proofread for Mechanics/Usage Errors (p. 344)

    B. Scoring Rubric (p. 345)

    Exercise 1—**Sample Essay** (p. 346)

PLANNING AN ESSAY

Understand the Assignment

Let the Prompt Be Your Topic

When presented with a prompt, always read it several times until you are completely familiar with the material. Sometimes it may be helpful to underline key words or phrases that are important.

Usually, the prompt is intended to be your topic and an inspiration for your writing. If you pay careful attention to the language of the prompt, it can actually help you to get started.

Consider this sample essay prompt:

> Human beings are often cruel, but they also have the capacity for kindness and compassion. In my opinion, an example that demonstrates this capacity is ----.

> Complete the statement above with an example from current affairs, history, literature, or your own personal experience. Then write a well-organized essay explaining why you regard that event favorably.

This topic explicitly invites you to choose an example of kindness or compassion from history, current events, literature, or even personal experience. Thus, you could write about the end of a war (history), a mission of humanitarian aid (current events), the self-sacrifice of a fictional character (literature), or even about the day that your family helped a stranded motorist (personal experience). Remember that what you have to say is not as important as how you say it.

Develop a Point of View

Sometimes an essay prompt will invite you to present your opinion on an issue. When you encounter such prompts, you must decide whether you are in agreement or disagreement with the statement given.

Write Only on the Assigned Topic

While the types of prompts may differ among assignments or tests, the directions all agree on this point: you must write on the assigned topic. The assigned topic is often open-ended, so you should have no problem coming up with something to write.

Organize Your Thoughts

Limit the Scope of Your Essay

The requirements of the writing assignment should determine the length and scope of your essay. Always remember to define the scope of an essay before beginning to write. This will improve your focus, and your essay will be more likely to accomplish the assigned task, whether it is to defend a controversial position or to provide a definition. The more limited and specific your topic, the more successful your essay is likely to be since you will be better able to supply the details necessary to give depth and sophistication to your essay. You will also reduce the possibility of either straying onto tangential topics or underdeveloping a specific claim.

Develop a Thesis

A thesis statement provides the scope, purpose, and direction of an essay in one clear and focused statement. A thesis statement usually includes your claims or assertions and the reasoning and evidence you will use to support them. If possible, try to formulate the thesis of your composition in a single sentence during the pre-writing stage. When developing a thesis, keep in mind the following ideas:

IMPORTANT POINTS FOR DEVELOPING A THESIS

1. The thesis must not be too broad or too narrow.

2. The thesis must be clear to both you and the essay reader.

3. Everything in the essay must support your thesis.

4. Use specific details and examples rather than generalizations to support your thesis.

Identify Key Points

Identify the two or three (or perhaps four) important points that you want to make. Then, decide on the order of presentation for those points.

Write an Outline

Once you gain a clear understanding of the assignment and its requirements, it is then important to organize the major points of your essay in a written outline. The purpose of an outline is to develop a logical structure to your arguments and to streamline your essay. An outline should include your thesis statement, the key points of your argument, and the concluding statement of your essay. A sample outline structure is presented below:

SAMPLE OUTLINE

    I. Introduction: Thesis Statement

  II. First Key Point
      A. Sub-Point 1
      B. Sub-Point 2

 III. Second Key Point
      A. Sub-Point 1
      B. Sub-Point 2

 IV. Third Key Point
      A. Sub-Point 1
      B. Sub-Point 2

  V. Conclusion: Restatement of Thesis

COMPOSITION

Organize Ideas into Paragraphs

A good writer uses paragraphs effectively. Paragraphs are important because they provide the structure through which a writer conveys meaning. To illustrate this point with an analogy, imagine a grocery store in which items are not organized into sections. In this store, there is no fresh produce section, no canned goods section, no baked goods section, and no frozen foods section. Consequently, a single bin holds bunches of bananas, cans of beans, loaves of bread, and frozen turkeys. This lack of organization would make shopping very difficult. Likewise, essays without paragraphs (or with poorly organized paragraphs) are very difficult—if not impossible—to understand.

First, you will need to decide how many paragraphs you will write. Your essay should contain two to four important points that develop or illustrate your thesis. Each important point should be treated as its own paragraph.

Do not write simply to fill up space and make it seem like you have many ideas. This approach can result in repetition and wordiness, which are signs of disorganization and unclear thinking. Write enough to demonstrate your writing ability and to prove your thesis. Five paragraphs (an introduction paragraph, three main body paragraphs, and a concluding paragraph) are usually sufficient.

Write the Essay

Many students become frustrated before they even begin to write. They sit and stare at the blank page and complain that they can't think of anything to write. The secret to successfully beginning an essay is simple. After you have completed the pre-writing stage, just start writing. You may need to go back and revise some of your work, but this is the easiest way to avoid writer's block. As you write your essay, follow this simple essay structure:

BASIC ESSAY STRUCTURE

I.   Introduction: State the thesis of your essay.
   A. State your position clearly.
   B. State the elements that you will be using to support your position.

II. Body: Each paragraph in the body of your essay will be devoted to one of the supporting elements that are presented in the introduction. Elaborate on the elements by using examples.

III. Conclusion: Summarize your position and the reasons for your position.

The Introduction

During the pre-writing stage, you analyzed the topic. Now, use the introduction (the first paragraph) to write clear and concise sentences that describe the topic, your point of view on it, and what you plan to say to back up your position. In general, an introduction should let the reader know what direction your essay will take. However, don't spend too much time on an introduction. The remainder of the essay will be where you'll explain your ideas and give your examples in more detail.

When writing your introduction, keep these points in mind:

WRITING AN INTRODUCTION

1. Focus on the essay topic presented in the prompt and clearly state your point of view on this topic.

2. Use a tone that is sincere, straightforward, and clear. DO NOT be cute or funny, ironic or satiric, overly emotional, or too dramatic.

3. DO NOT repeat the writing prompt word-for-word. Instead, paraphrase the prompt in your own words and then clearly state your point of view.

4. After stating your point of view, briefly state the evidence or arguments you will use to support your point of view.

Finally, an effective introduction often accomplishes one of the following tasks as well: it explains why readers should care about the topic at hand, or it grabs the reader's attention by describing briefly an incident in real life that is related to the topic.

The Body

The heart of the essay is the development that takes place in the body paragraphs. Here, the writer must attempt, in paragraph form, to support the main idea of the essay through illustrations, details, and examples. These body, or developmental, paragraphs must serve as a link in the chain of ideas and contribute directly to the essay's main idea or position.

Each paragraph should start with a transitional statement or phrase that describes the relationship of the paragraph to the previous paragraphs. The length of any one of these body paragraphs can vary, but each paragraph should only cover one main idea. You may do this through a style that is descriptive, narrative, or expository. You may take a factual or an anecdotal approach. No matter which approach you choose or style you adopt, your writing must be coherent, logical, unified, and well ordered.

When writing your essay, avoid the following common mistakes:

COMPOSITION ERRORS TO AVOID

1. DO NOT use sentences that include irrelevant material. In each body paragraph, only include sentences that relate specifically to the argument being made in that paragraph.

2. DO NOT use sentences that disrupt logical development. In each body paragraph, make sure each sentence logically follows from the sentence that comes before it.

Transitions

A good writer uses transitional words or phrases to connect thoughts, to provide for a logical sequence of ideas, and to link paragraphs. The following list includes some transitions and the logical relationships they indicate:

TRANSITIONAL WORDS AND PHRASES

Addition
again
also
and
besides
both . . . and
finally
first, second, third
furthermore
in addition
likewise
moreover
not only . . . but (also)
similarly

Alternation
either . . . or
neither . . . nor
nor
or
so that

Cause/Effect/Purpose
accordingly
as
as a consequence
as a result
because
consequently
for
for this purpose
hence
since
therefore
so

Conditions
as if (as though)
if
once . . . then
unless

Contrast
all the same
although
but
even though
however
instead
nevertheless
on the contrary
on the other hand
otherwise
still
though
yet

Space
here
in the middle
nearby
next to
opposite to
there
to the left/right
where
wherever

Support
for example
for instance
in fact
in general
such as

Summary
as shown above
in other words
in brief
in conclusion
in general
in short
in summary
to sum up

Time
after
as soon as
at the present time
before
during
eventually
finally
in (month, year)
later
meanwhile
since
then
until
when
whenever
while

The Conclusion

A successful writer knows when and how to end an essay. To conclude your essay effectively, you should have a strong and clear concluding paragraph. This concluding paragraph should make a reader feel that your essay has made its point, that your thesis has been explained, and that your point of view has been supported by specific examples, ideas, or arguments. A concluding paragraph can be as short as three to six sentences. The following are some guidelines for writing a successful concluding paragraph:

EFFECTIVE METHODS FOR CONCLUDING AN ESSAY

1. Restate your point of view on the essay topic.

2. Summarize the main arguments and evidence you used to support your point of view.

3. If time permits, conclude with a brief statement as to why your point of view is more defensible than a different point of view on the essay topic. What are the positive consequences of holding your point of view? What are the negative consequences of holding the opposite point of view?

The following is a quick overview of ineffective methods for writing a conclusion:

INEFFECTIVE METHODS FOR CONCLUDING AN ESSAY

1. DO NOT apologize for being unable to present all possible arguments in a limited amount of time.

2. DO NOT complain that the topic was uninteresting or too broad.

3. DO NOT introduce new material that you won't have time to develop. DO NOT introduce irrelevant material.

Principles of Good Writing

While writing, keep the three principles of good writing in mind: write grammatically, punctuate and spell correctly, and write concisely and clearly. If you follow these conventions, you will communicate your ideas clearly and effectively.

Write Grammatically

When writing an essay, the following principles of good grammar should be observed:

CORRECT GRAMMAR AND EFFECTIVE ESSAYS

1. Each sentence must have a conjugated (main) verb that agrees with its subject.

2. Each pronoun must have a referent (antecedent) with which it agrees.

3. Similar elements in a sentence must appear in parallel form.

4. Modifiers must agree with what they modify. They must also make sense.

5. Each sentence should use clear and concise language.

Punctuate and Spell Correctly

In addition to writing grammatically, concisely, and formally (without using slang or other informal language), you must punctuate and spell correctly. Since you are in charge of writing the essay, you can choose to avoid many punctuation and spelling errors. If you are unsure about how to punctuate a particular construction or spell a particular word, choose an alternative.

Write Concisely and Clearly

Use simple and direct sentences. Avoid complex and convoluted sentences. In general, the most complicated sentence you should use is one with two independent clauses that are joined by a conjunction such as "and" or "but." Of course, you can also use sentences that include one dependent clause and one independent clause that are joined together by a conjunction such as "while" or "although." Again, though, try to express yourself simply and directly. Avoid using any unnecessary or wordy phrases, such as those illustrated in the following chart:

UNNECESSARY AND WORDY PHRASES TO AVOID	
Instead of:	_Say:_
in my opinion, I believe that	I believe that
in the event of an emergency	in an emergency
on the possibility that it may	since it may
close to the point of	close to
have need for	need
with a view to	to
in view of the fact that	because
give consideration to	consider
mean to imply	imply
disappear from view	disappear
in this day and age	today
the issue in question	the issue

Also, while neatness is not graded, it is almost certainly true that an illegible essay will not receive a good grade.

REVISION AND SCORING

Proofread Your Essay

Proofreading is an essential part of the writing process. The first draft of an essay usually will not be free of errors. This means that you will need to re-read the essay and correct any grammatical errors or logical inconsistencies. There are two categories of errors that generally appear in essays: structural errors and mechanics/usage errors.

Proofread for Structural Errors

When proofreading, first consider the structural elements of an essay. The three most important structural factors in an essay are unity, coherence, and support. Essays are judged by how well they meet these basic requirements. To improve your essay, ask yourself the following questions:

UNITY, COHERENCE, AND SUPPORT

1. Does the essay have a thesis that is clearly stated in the introduction? What is it? What is the essay's point of view on the essay topic?

2. Does the introduction clearly state the arguments and evidence that will support the essay's point of view?

3. Does each body paragraph have a topic sentence? (A topic sentence is the first sentence of a paragraph, and it summarizes what will be argued or presented in that paragraph.)

4. Does each body paragraph make a different argument to support the essay's point of view?

5. Do the other sentences in each body paragraph all support the topic sentence? In other words, do the other sentences all further the argument or present evidence related to the main point made in the topic sentence?

6. Do the body paragraphs include specific details or examples to make the argument more vivid and interesting?

7. Does the essay use transitional words or phrases that allow the reader to move easily from one idea or paragraph to the next?

8. Does the essay have a conclusion that clearly restates the essay's point of view on the essay topic? Does the conclusion explain why this point of view is more defensible than a different point of view on the essay topic?

Proofread for Mechanics/Usage Errors

After reviewing the structure of your essay, look for mechanics/usage errors. Although these are less important, mechanics/usage errors can prevent readers from focusing on the substance of an essay. The following is a list of common mechanics/usage errors:

COMMON MECHANICS/USAGE ERRORS

1. Omission of words—especially "the," "a," and "an"
2. Omission of final letters in words
3. Careless spelling errors
4. Incorrect use of capital letters
5. Faulty punctuation

Scoring Rubric

The following rubric (scoring guide) summarizes how your essay will likely be graded by the essay reader.

ESSAY SCORE QUALIFICATIONS	
Score	*Essay Qualities*
Excellent	• is well organized and fully developed • uses appropriate and innovative examples to support ideas • demonstrates a superior grasp of grammar and style, varies sentence structure, and uses a wide range of vocabulary
Superior	• is generally well organized and adequately developed • uses appropriate examples to support ideas • demonstrates a competent grasp of grammar and style, employs some syntactic variety, and uses appropriate vocabulary
Good	• is organized and somewhat developed • uses examples to support ideas • demonstrates an adequate but inconsistent grasp of grammar and style with minor errors in grammar and diction • displays minimal sentence variety
Average	• may contain one or more of the following weaknesses: inadequate organization or development; inappropriate or insufficient details to support ideas; and an accumulation of errors in grammar, diction, or sentence structure
Below Average	• is flawed by one or more of the following weaknesses: poor organization; thin development; little or inappropriate detail to support ideas; and frequent errors in grammar, diction, and sentence structure
Weak	• is seriously flawed by one or more of the following weaknesses: very poor organization, very thin development, and usage or syntactical errors so severe that meaning is somewhat obscured

N

Sample Essay
Exercise 1

Teachers evaluate the work of students by grading exams, homework, and other assignments, as well as class participation. The end-of-term report card with its letter or numerical grades is a time-honored tradition. Now, some teachers and administrators suggest that students be given the opportunity to grade teachers. They point out that students are in a unique position to assess the effectiveness of their teachers because they spend so much time with the teachers in the classroom. Some of those favoring this idea propose that students complete forms, ranking teachers according to relevant criteria such as "Preparedness" and "Ability to Communicate." Other teachers and administrators oppose this idea and argue that students lack the experience and perspective to determine what makes an effective teacher. They also express concern that the evaluation forms could be used by students to retaliate against teachers for personal reasons. In your opinion, should students be given the opportunity to grade their teachers?

In your essay, take a position on this issue. You can write about either point of view presented here, or you can present a different point of view on this topic. Support your position with relevant reasons and/or examples from your own experience, observations, or reading.

Essay Outline

Math
Skills Review

Math Skills Review

Course Concept Outline

I. Numbers (p. 355)

A. Real Number System (p. 355)

B. Terms and Operations (p. 356)

1. Basic Terms (p. 357)
2. Symbols of Inclusion (p. 357)
3. Order of Operations (p. 357)
4. Factoring and Canceling (p. 358)

C. Properties of the Integers 0 and 1 (p. 358)

D. Factors, Multiples, and Primes (p. 359)

E. Odd and Even Numbers (p. 359)

F. Consecutive Integers (p. 360)

G. Working with Signed Numbers (p. 360)

1. Absolute Value (p. 361)
2. Adding Negative Numbers (p. 361)
3. Subtracting Negative Numbers (p. 362)
4. Multiplying Negative Numbers (p. 363)
5. Dividing Negative Numbers (p. 363)
6. Summary of Signed Numbers (p. 364)

H. Properties of Real Numbers (p. 365)

*Exercise 1—***Numbers** (Items #1–70, pp. 366–370)

II. Fractions (p. 371)

A. Converting Mixed Numbers to Improper Fractions (p. 371)

B. Converting Improper Fractions to Mixed Numbers (p. 372)

C. Reducing Fractions to Lowest Terms (p. 372)

D. Common Denominators (p. 373)

E. Operations of Fractions (p. 374)

1. Adding Fractions (p. 374)
2. Subtracting Fractions (p. 375)
3. "Flying-X" Method (p. 375)
4. Multiplying Fractions (p. 376)
5. Dividing Fractions (p. 376)

F. Comparing Fractions (p. 377)

1. Comparing Decimal Equivalents (p. 377)
2. Upward Cross-Multiplication (p. 377)

*Exercise 2—**Fractions** (Items #1–53, pp. 379–384)*

III. Decimals (p. 385)

A. Converting Fractions to Decimals (p. 385)

B. Converting Mixed Numbers to Decimals (p. 387)

C. Converting Improper Fractions to Decimals (p. 387)

D. Converting Decimals to Fractions and Mixed Numbers (p. 388)

E. Operations of Decimals (p. 389)

1. Adding and Subtracting Decimals (p. 389)
2. Multiplying Decimals (p. 389)
3. Dividing Decimals (p. 390)

*Exercise 3—**Decimals** (Items #1–57, pp. 392–395)*

IV. Percents (p. 397)

A. Converting to and from Percents (p. 397)

B. Operations of Percents (p. 398)

1. Adding and Subtracting Percents (p. 398)
2. Multiplying Percents (p. 398)
3. Dividing Percents (p. 399)

C. Percent Story Problems (p. 399)

1. "What is X Percent of Some Quantity?" (p. 399)
2. "What Percent is This of That?" (p. 400)
3. "This is X Percent of What?" (p. 401)
4. Percent Change (p. 401)

*Exercise 4—**Percents** (Items #1–65, pp. 403–407)*

V. Statistical Measures (p. 409)

A. Mean (p. 409)
1. Calculating a Mean (Average) (p. 409)
2. Determining Missing Elements (p. 409)
3. Calculating Weighted Averages (p. 410)

B. Median (p. 411)

C. Mode (p. 411)

D. Range (p. 411)

E. Frequency Distribution (p. 411)

Exercise 5—**Statistical Measures** (Items #1–52, pp. 413–417)

VI. Ratios and Proportions (p. 419)

A. Working with Ratios (p. 419)
1. Two-Part Ratios (p. 419)
2. Three-Part Ratios (p. 419)
3. Using Ratios to Divide Quantities (p. 420)

B. Working with Proportions (p. 420)
1. Determining the Missing Elements in Proportions (p. 421)
2. Direct Proportions (p. 421)
3. Inverse Proportions (p. 422)

Exercise 6—**Ratios and Proportions** (Items #1–55, pp. 423–428)

VII. Exponents and Radicals (p. 429)

A. Powers and Exponents (p. 429)
1. Powers of Numbers (p. 429)
2. Exponential Notation (p. 430)

B. Operations Involving Exponents (p. 430)
1. Multiplication Involving Exponents (p. 430)
2. Division Involving Exponents (p. 431)
3. Raising a Power to a Power (p. 432)
4. Raising a Product to a Power (p. 432)
5. Raising a Quotient to a Power (p. 432)
6. Negative Exponents (p. 433)
7. Rational (Fractional) Exponents (p. 433)
8. Working with Exponents (p. 434)

C. Roots and Radicals (p. 435)
1. Roots of Numbers (p. 435)
2. Determining Square Roots (p. 436)

D. Operations Involving Radicals (Rational Exponents) (p. 436)

Exercise 7—**Exponents and Radicals** (Items #1–45, pp. 438–441)

VIII. Algebraic Operations (p. 443)

A. Elements of Algebra (p. 443)

1. Algebraic Terms (p. 443)
2. Algebraic Expressions (p. 444)
3. Algebraic Equations (p. 444)

B. Operations of Algebraic Terms (p. 445)

1. Adding and Subtracting Algebraic Terms (p. 445)
2. Multiplying and Dividing Algebraic Terms (p. 446)

C. Operations of Algebraic Fractions (p. 447)

1. Adding and Subtracting Algebraic Fractions (p. 447)
2. Multiplying and Dividing Algebraic Fractions (p. 447)

D. Multiplying Algebraic Expressions (p. 448)

1. Distributive Property (p. 448)
2. FOIL Method (p. 449)

E. Factoring Algebraic Expressions (p. 450)

1. Finding a Common Factor (p. 450)
2. Reversing a Known Polynomial Multiplication Process (p. 451)
3. Reversing an Unknown Polynomial Multiplication Process (p. 451)

F. Absolute Value in Algebraic Expressions (p. 452)

G. Radicals in Algebraic Expressions (p. 452)

Exercise 8—**Algebraic Operations** (Items #1–67, pp. 454–459)

IX. Algebraic Equations and Inequalities (p. 461)

A. Solving Algebraic Formulas (p. 461)

B. Basic Principle of Equations (p. 462)

C. Solving Linear Equations (p. 463)

D. Solving Simultaneous Equations (p. 464)

1. Substitution (p. 464)
2. Linear Combination (Elimination) (p. 465)

E. Solving Quadratic Equations (p. 466)

F. Solving Equations by Factoring (p. 467)

G. Algebraic Inequalities (p. 468)

H. Exponents in Equations and Inequalities (p. 470)

1. Integer and Rational Exponents (p. 470)
2. Algebraic Exponentials (p. 470)
3. Exponential Growth (p. 470)

I. Properties of Functions (p. 471)

J. Rational Equations (p. 472)

K. Radical Equations (p. 473)

L. Absolute Value in Equations and Inequalities (p. 473)

Exercise 9—**Algebraic Equations and Inequalities** (Items #1–67, pp. 474–478)

X. Geometry (p. 479)

A. Geometric Notation (p. 479)

B. Line and Angle Properties (p. 479)

C. Polygon Properties (p. 482)

D. Triangle Properties and Formulas (p. 483)

    1. Properties of Triangles (p. 483)
    2. Pythagorean Theorem (p. 484)
    3. Formulas of Triangles (p. 484)

E. Special Properties of 45°-45°-90° Triangles (p. 485)

F. Special Properties of 30°-60°-90° Triangles (p. 486)

G. Similar Triangles (p. 486)

H. Quadrilateral Properties and Formulas (p. 487)

I. Circle Properties and Formulas (p. 489)

    1. Properties of Circles (p. 489)
    2. Formulas for Circles (p. 492)

J. Surface Area and Volume of Solids (p. 492)

Exercise 10—**Geometry** (Items #1–80, pp. 495–504)

XI. Coordinate Geometry (p. 505)

A. Coordinate Axis System (p. 505)

B. Ordered Pairs (p. 506)

C. Plotting Equations (p. 506)

D. Midpoint of Line Segments (p. 507)

E. Distance Between Two Points (p. 508)

F. Linear Functions (p. 510)

    1. Slope-Intercept Form (p. 510)
    2. Parallel Lines (p. 510)
    3. Perpendicular Lines (p. 510)

G. Quadratic Functions (p. 511)

H. Identifying Graphs of Functions (p. 511)

I. Transformation Effects on Graphs (p. 512)

    1. Vertical Translations (p. 512)
    2. Horizontal Translations (p. 513)

J. Graphing Geometric Figures (p. 513)

Exercise 11—**Coordinate Geometry** (Items #1–42, pp. 516–522)

XII. Story Problems (p. 523)

A. Coin Problems (p. 523)

B. Number and Set Problems (p. 524)

C. Age Problems (p. 525)

D. Interest Problems (p. 526)

1. Simple Interest (p. 526)
2. Compound Interest (p. 526)

E. Mixture Problems (p. 527)

F. Motion Problems (p. 528)

1. Motion in Opposite Directions (p. 528)
2. Motion in the Same Direction (p. 528)
3. Round Trip (p. 528)

G. Rate and Work Problems (p. 529)

1. Rate Problems (p. 529)
2. Work Problems (p. 530)

H. Variation Problems (p. 531)

1. Direct Variation (p. 531)
2. Inverse Variation (p. 531)
3. Joint Variation (p. 532)

I. Percent Problems (p. 533)

1. Percent Increase or Decrease (p. 533)
2. Discounts (p. 533)
3. Profit (p. 533)
4. Commission (p. 534)
5. Taxes (p. 534)

J. Measurement Problems (p. 535)

K. Counting Methods (p. 535)

1. The Multiplication Principle for Counting (p. 535)
2. Permutations (p. 535)
3. Combinations (p. 536)

L. Probability (p. 537)

1. Single-Event Probability (p. 537)
2. Multiple-Event Probability (p. 537)
3. Geometric Probability (p. 539)

M. Data Interpretation: Tables and Graphs (p. 540)

Exercise 12—**Story Problems** (Items #1–53, pp. 541–547)

NUMBERS

Real Number System

All *real numbers* correspond to points on the number line and vice versa. Real numbers include whole numbers, integers, fractions, decimals, and irrational numbers. All real numbers, except zero, are either positive or negative. On the number line, numbers corresponding to points to the left of zero are negative and numbers corresponding to points to the right of zero are positive.

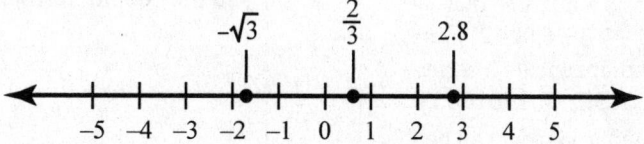

For any two numbers on the number line, the number to the left is *less than* the number to the right. Note that this is the same as saying that for any two numbers on the number line, the number to the right is *greater than* the number to the left. The symbol " < " is used to mean "less than," and the symbol " > " is used to mean "greater than." If a number n is "between 1 and 3" on the number line, then $n > 1$ and $n < 3$; that is, $1 < n < 3$.

Examples:

1. $-5 < -\dfrac{5}{2}$

2. $-0.8 < \dfrac{3}{2} < 2$

3. $2.4 > -\dfrac{1}{4}$

4. $1 > 0.2 > -\sqrt{2}$

The symbol " ≤ " is used to mean "less than or equal to," and the symbol " ≥ " is used to mean "greater than or equal to." Therefore, if a number n is "between 1 and 3, inclusive" on the number line, $1 \le n \le 3$.

The following diagram outlines the subsets of the *real number system*. You should be familiar with the terminology and numbers contained in several of these subsets. Each set is a subset of the one above it; for example, the set of natural numbers is a subset of the set of whole numbers, integers, rational numbers, and real numbers. Natural numbers are whole numbers, integers, rational numbers, and real numbers. Refer back to this diagram as often as necessary.

Real Numbers

Real numbers are all the numbers on the number line including fractions, integers, radicals, negatives, and zero.

Rational Numbers

Rational numbers can be expressed as a ratio of two integers (e.g., $\frac{2}{7}$, $-\frac{8}{2}$, $\frac{9}{10}$). A rational number can be expressed as a number that terminates (e.g., -1, 0, 35, -5.25, 8.0262) or as a non-terminating decimal that repeats a series of digits (e.g., $4.333...$, $3.2525...$, $-0.196196...$). Also, $\sqrt{4}$ is a rational number since it can be expressed as $\frac{2}{1}$, or 2.

Irrational Numbers

Irrational numbers cannot be expressed as a ratio of two integers. No pattern exists when irrational numbers are expressed as decimals and they do not terminate (e.g., $\sqrt{2}$, $-\sqrt{3}$, π).

Integers

Integers are signed (positive and negative) whole numbers and the number zero: $\{...,-2,-1,0,1,...\}$.

Whole Numbers

Whole numbers are the positive integers and the number zero: $\{0,1,2,3,...\}$.

Natural or Counting Numbers

Natural numbers are the numbers used for counting: $\{1,2,3,...\}$.

Terms and Operations

For simplicity, we will introduce the terms and operational concepts associated with all numbers using whole numbers. **Whole numbers** are the positive integers, plus the number zero: $\{0,1,2,3,4,...\}$. Later we will return to the other numbers of the real number system, including fractions, signed numbers, and irrational numbers.

Basic Terms

sum (total): The result of adding numbers together. The *sum*, or total, of 2 and 3 is 5: $2+3=5$.

difference: The result of subtracting one number from another. The *difference* between 5 and 2 is 3: $5-2=3$.

product: The result of multiplying numbers together. The *product* of 2 and 3 is 6: $2 \cdot 3 = 6$.

quotient: The result of dividing one number by another. The *quotient* when 6 is divided by 2 is 3: $6 \div 2 = 3$.

remainder: In division, if the quotient is not itself a whole number, the result can be written as a whole number quotient plus a whole number remainder. For example, $7 \div 3 = 2$, plus a *remainder* of 1.

Symbols of Inclusion

Sets of *parentheses*, *brackets*, and *braces* indicate the order in which operations are to be performed. The innermost symbol of inclusion indicates which operation should be executed first. Generally, operations in parentheses are done first, operations in brackets are done second, and operations in braces are done third. Parentheses, brackets, and braces have the same meaning—three different symbols are used for clarity.

Examples:

1. $(2+3) \cdot 4 = 20$

2. $2+(3 \cdot 4) = 14$

3. $\dfrac{(2 \cdot 3) \cdot (2+1)}{3 \cdot (5-4)} = \dfrac{(6) \cdot (3)}{3 \cdot (1)} = \dfrac{18}{3} = 6$

A particularly complex statement might use parentheses, brackets, and even braces if necessary. With problems such as these, work from the inside out. Start with the operations within parentheses; then do the operations within the brackets; and finally complete the indicated operations.

Example:

$$\{[(2 \cdot 3)-5] \cdot 1\} + [2 \cdot (4-1)] = [(6-5) \cdot 1] + (2 \cdot 3) = (6-5) + 6 = 1 + 6 = 7$$

Order of Operations

Parentheses, brackets, and braces eliminate ambiguity, but they do not always dictate the order in which operations must be done. Use this mnemonic to remember the order of operations for simplifying expressions: *Please Excuse My Dear Aunt Sally.*

Please: **Parentheses, brackets, braces**
Excuse: **Exponents, radicals**
My Dear: **Multiplication** or **Division***
Aunt Sally: **Addition** or **Subtraction***

*Remember: add/subtract and multiply/divide in expressions as the operations occur from left to right.

Examples:

1. $6 + 4 \cdot 3 - 5 = 6 + 12 - 5 = 18 - 5 = 13$

2. $[2(3+4)](3 \cdot 2) = [2(7)](6) = (14)(6) = 84$

3. $\{(2+7) - [(8 \cdot 6) \div 2] + 25\}\{[2 + 3(2-1)] \div 5\} = [(2+7) - (48 \div 2) + 25]\{[2 + 3(1)] \div 5\} = [(2+7) - 24 + 25](5 \div 5) = (9 - 24 + 25)(1) = (-15 + 25) = 10$

Factoring and Canceling

An important point to make is that even when multiplication and addition are combined, you have a choice about order of operations. In the following example, most people would probably do the addition first and then the multiplication. It is also permissible, however, to do the multiplication first.

Example:

$5(2 + 3 + 4) = 5(9) = 45$

$5(2 + 3 + 4) = 5(2) + 5(3) + 5(4) = 10 + 15 + 20 = 45$

Thus, $10 + 15 + 20$ is equal to $5(2) + 5(3) + 5(4)$, which in turn equals $5(2 + 3 + 4)$. This reverse multiplication process is called **factoring**. Factoring can be a tremendous labor-saving device. It is almost always more efficient to first simplify expressions by factoring.

Example:

$(723)(34) - (723)(33) = 24{,}582 - 23{,}859 = 723$

$(723)(34) - (723)(33) = 723(34 - 33) = 723(1) = 723$

Factoring can be combined with division for even greater simplifying power. Division of factors common to both the numerator and the denominator is called **canceling**.

Example:

$\dfrac{24 + 36}{12} = \dfrac{12(2 + 3)}{12} = (1)(2 + 3) = 5$

> In this case, 12 can be factored from both 24 and 36. It is then possible to divide 12 by 12, which is 1.

Properties of the Integers 0 and 1

The integers 0 and 1 have special properties that differ from other integers. First, the integer 0 is neither positive nor negative. If n is any number, then $n \pm 0 = n$ and $n \cdot 0 = 0$. Also, division by 0 is not defined. Therefore, it is never allowable to divide anything by 0. The integer 1 multiplied by any number n is equal to the original number; that is, $1 \cdot n = n$. Also, for any number $n \neq 0$, $n \cdot \dfrac{1}{n} = 1$. Note that the number 1 can be expressed in many ways; for example, $\dfrac{n}{n} = 1$ for any number $n \neq 0$. Finally, multiplying or dividing an expression by 1, in any form, does not change the value of that expression.

Examples:

1. $4 + 0 = 4$

2. $4 - 0 = 4$

3. $3 \cdot 0 = 0$

4. $1 \cdot 5 = 5$

5. $2 \cdot \dfrac{1}{2} = 1$

6. $\dfrac{4}{4} = 1$

Factors, Multiples, and Primes

Numbers that evenly divide another number are called the ***factors*** of that number. If a number is evenly divisible by another number, it is considered a ***multiple*** of that number. 1, 2, 3, 4, 6, and 12 are all factors of 12: 12 is a multiple of 2, a multiple of 3, and so on. Some numbers are not evenly divisible except by 1 and themselves. A number such as this is called a ***prime*** number. For example, 13 is evenly divisible by 1 and 13 but not by 2 through 12. <u>Note:</u> 1 is NOT considered a prime number even though it is not evenly divisible by any other number. The following are examples of prime numbers: 2, 3, 5, 7, 11, 13, 17, 19, and 23.

Example:

Let $D = 120$. How many positive factors, including 1 and 120, does D have?

➢ Express 120 using prime factors: $120 = 2(2)(2)(3)(5) = 2^3(3)(5)$. The exponents of the prime factors 2, 3, and 5, are 3, 1, and 1, respectively. Add 1 to each exponent and multiply the results together: $(3+1)(1+1)(1+1) = (4)(2)(2) = 16$ positive factors.

Odd and Even Numbers

An ***odd number*** is not evenly divisible by 2; an ***even number*** is a number that is divisible by 2. Any number with a last digit that is 0, 2, 4, 6, or 8 is divisible by 2 and is even. Any number with a last digit that is 1, 3, 5, 7, or 9 is not evenly divisible by 2 and is odd. Zero is considered an even number. The following are important principles that govern the behavior of odd and even numbers.

PRINCIPLES OF ODD AND EVEN NUMBERS	
1. EVEN ± EVEN = EVEN	5. EVEN • EVEN = EVEN
2. EVEN ± ODD = ODD	6. EVEN • ODD = EVEN
3. ODD ± EVEN = ODD	7. ODD • EVEN = EVEN
4. ODD ± ODD = EVEN	8. ODD • ODD = ODD

Examples:

1. $2 + 4 = 6$; $2 - 4 = -2$

2. $4 + 3 = 7$; $4 - 3 = 1$

3. $3 + 4 = 7$; $3 - 4 = -1$

4. $3 + 5 = 8$; $3 - 5 = -2$

5. $2 \cdot 4 = 8$

6. $2 \cdot 3 = 6$

7. $3 \cdot 2 = 6$

8. $3 \cdot 5 = 15$

The rules for multiplication DO NOT apply to division. For example, if you divide the even number 4 by the even number 8, the result is $\frac{1}{2}$. Odd and even are characteristics of whole numbers and negative integers, but not fractions. A fraction is neither odd nor even.

Consecutive Integers

Consecutive integers immediately follow one another. For example, 3, 4, 5, and 6 are consecutive integers, but 3, 7, 21, and 45 are not. In a string of consecutive integers, the next number is always one more than the preceding number. Thus, if n is the first number in a string of consecutive integers, the second number is $n+1$, the third number is $n+2$, the fourth number is $n+3$, and so on.

1st	2nd	3rd	4th
n	$n+1$	$n+2$	$n+3$
3	4	5	6

We can also speak of *consecutive even integers* and *consecutive odd integers*. 2, 4, 6, and 8 are consecutive even integers; 3, 5, 7, and 9 are consecutive odd integers. If n is the first number in a string of consecutive even or odd integers, the second number is $n+2$, the third number is $n+4$, the fourth number is $n+6$, and so on.

1st	2nd	3rd	4th
n	$n+2$	$n+4$	$n+6$
3	5	7	9
4	6	8	10

Do not be confused by the fact that the sequence for consecutive odd integers proceeds as n, $n+2$, $n+4$, etc. Even though 2, 4, etc. are even numbers, $n+2$, $n+4$, etc. will be odd numbers when the starting point, n, is odd.

Working with Signed Numbers

Numbers are just positions in a linear system. Each whole number is one greater than the number to its left and one less than the number to its right. The following number line represents the *integer number system*, which consists of the signed (positive and negative) whole numbers and zero:

$$(-) \longleftarrow \underset{-15 \quad -10 \quad -5 \quad 0 \quad 5 \quad 10 \quad 15}{|||||||||||||||||||||||||||||||} \longrightarrow (+)$$

With both positive and negative integers, each position is one more than the position before it and one less than the position after it: −1 is one less than zero and one more than −2; −2 is one less than −1 and one more than −3. The minus sign indicates the direction in which the number system is moving with reference to the origin (zero). If you move to the right, you are going in the positive direction; to the left, in the negative direction.

It is natural to use negative numbers in everyday situations, such as games and banking: An overdrawn checking account results in a negative (minus) balance. You can manipulate negative numbers using the basic operations (addition, subtraction, multiplication, and division). To help explain these operations, we introduce the concept of absolute value.

Absolute Value

A number's ***absolute value*** is its distance on the number line from the origin, without regard to direction: $|x| = |-x|$. The absolute value of a number is its value without any sign and so it is always a positive numerical value: $|x| \geq 0$. Therefore, $|x| = x$ **if** $x \geq 0$ and $|x| = -x$ **if** $x < 0$.

Examples:

1. $|4| = 4$

2. $|-10| = 10$

3. $|5| - |3| = 5 - 3 = 2$

4. $|-2| + |-3| = 2 + 3 = 5$

This idea of value, without regard to direction, helps to clarify negative number operations.

Adding Negative Numbers

To add negative numbers to other numbers, subtract the absolute value of the negative numbers.

Example:

$10 + (-4) = 10 - |-4| = 10 - 4 = 6$

➤ The number line illustrates the logic: Start at 10 and move the counter four units in the negative direction. The result is 6:

Follow this procedure even if you wind up with a negative result, as illustrated in the following example.

Example:

$10 + (-12) = 10 - |-12| = 10 - 12 = -2$

➤ Start at 10 and move the counter 12 units in a negative direction. The result is two units to the left of zero, or −2.

Similarly, the procedure works when you add a negative number to another negative number.

Example:

$-3 + -2 = -3 - |-2| = -3 - 2 = -5$

➤ Begin at –3, and move the counter two units in the negative direction. The result is –5:

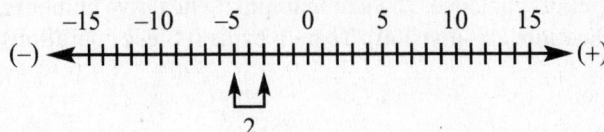

Any addition of a negative number is equivalent to subtraction of a positive number.

Examples:

1. $5+(-2)=5-2=3$

2. $7+(-7)=7-7=0$

Subtracting Negative Numbers

Subtracting negative numbers is a little different. When you subtract a negative number, you are really adding, since the number itself has a negative value. It is like a double negative: "It is not true that Bob's not here" means that Bob is here. To subtract a negative number from another quantity, add the absolute value of the negative number to the other quantity.

Example:

$$10-(-5)=10+\left|-5\right|=10+5=15$$

➤ Start at 10: Since the minus signs cancel each other out, move the counter in the positive direction. The result is 15:

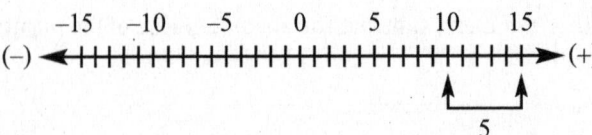

Follow this procedure no matter where you start, even if you are subtracting a negative number from zero or from another negative number.

Example:

$$-5-(-10)=-5+\left|-10\right|=-5+10=5$$

➤ Start at –5: Since the minus signs cancel each other out, move the counter in the positive direction. The result is 5:

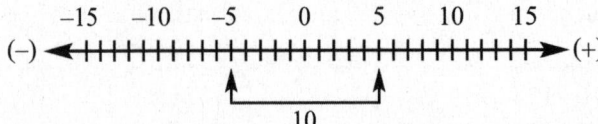

Any subtraction of a negative number is equivalent to addition of a positive number.

Examples:

1. $4-(-4)=4+4=8$

2. $0-(-7)=0+7=7$

3. $-8-(-4)=-8+4=-4$

Multiplying Negative Numbers

We can also explain the rules for multiplying negative numbers through the concept of absolute value. To multiply a positive number by a negative number, simply multiply together the absolute values of the two numbers, and then make the sign of the resultant value negative. The product of two numbers with the same sign is always positive, and the product of two numbers with different signs is always negative.

Examples:

1. $3 \cdot -6 = -(|3| \cdot |-6|) = -(3 \cdot 6) = -18$

2. $-2 \cdot 4 = -(|-2| \cdot |4|) = -(2 \cdot 4) = -8$

A way of remembering this is to think that the minus sign has "tainted" the problem, so the result must be negative.

To multiply a negative number by a negative number, multiply together the absolute values of the two numbers. The product of two negative numbers is always positive.

Example:

$-3 \cdot -6 = |-3| \cdot |-6| = 3 \cdot 6 = 18$

This is like saying that two wrongs DO make a right—a negative times a negative produces a positive.

Any product involving an odd number of negatives will be negative. Any product involving an even number of negatives will be positive.

Examples:

1. $-1 \cdot -2 = 2$

2. $-1 \cdot -2 \cdot -3 = -6$

3. $-1 \cdot -2 \cdot -3 \cdot -4 = 24$

4. $-1 \cdot -2 \cdot -3 \cdot -4 \cdot -5 = -120$

Dividing Negative Numbers

When dividing negative numbers, the same rules apply as with multiplication. If the division involves a positive number and a negative number, divide using the absolute values of the numbers, and then make the sign of the resultant value negative.

Examples:

1. $6 \div -3 = -(|6| \div |-3|) = -(6 \div 3) = -2$

2. $-8 \div 2 = -(|-8| \div |2|) = -(8 \div 2) = -4$

For division involving two negative numbers, divide using the absolute values of the numbers, and then make the sign of this value positive.

Example:

$$-8 \div -4 = |-8| \div |-4| = 8 \div 4 = 2$$

Any quotient involving an odd number of negatives will be negative. Any quotient involving an even number of negatives will be positive.

Examples:

1. $\dfrac{4}{-2} = -2$

2. $\dfrac{(-2)(6)}{-4} = \dfrac{-12}{-4} = 3$

3. $\dfrac{(3)(-2)(-4)}{(-1)(2)} = -(3 \cdot 4) = -12$

Summary of Signed Numbers

PRINCIPLES FOR WORKING WITH NEGATIVE NUMBERS

1. Subtraction of a negative number is equivalent to addition of a positive number.

2. Addition of a negative number is equivalent to subtraction of a positive number.

3. Multiplication or division involving an odd number of negative numbers always results in a negative number.

4. Multiplication or division involving an even number of negative numbers always results in a positive number.

These rules govern operations with all signed numbers. Be careful how you apply the rules to complicated expressions; just take each item step by step.

Example:

$$\dfrac{(2 \cdot -3) - (-2 + -12)}{(-8 \div 2) \cdot (2 + -4)} = \dfrac{(-6) - (-14)}{(-4) \cdot (-2)} = \dfrac{-6 + 14}{4 \cdot 2} = \dfrac{14 - 6}{8} = \dfrac{8}{8} = 1$$

Properties of Real Numbers

The following is a list of the properties of real numbers encountered in this review. Note that these properties apply to all real numbers, not just whole and signed numbers.

PROPERTIES OF REAL NUMBERS (x, y, and z represent real numbers)

1. Commutative Property: $x + y = y + x$ and $xy = yx$.

2. Associative Property: $(x + y) + z = x + (y + z)$ and $(xy)z = x(yz)$

3. Distributive Property: $x(y + z) = xy + xz$

4. If x and y are both positive, then $x + y$ and xy are positive

5. If x and y are both negative, then $x + y$ is negative and xy is positive

6. If x is positive and y is negative, then xy is negative

7. If $xy = 0$, then $x = 0$ or $y = 0$

8. $|x + y| \le |x| + |y|$

Examples:

1. $2 + 4 = 4 + 2 = 6$

2. $(2)(4) = (4)(2) = 8$

3. $(3 + 5) + 6 = 3 + (5 + 6) = 3 + 11 = 14$

4. $\left(2\sqrt{3}\right)(3) = 3\left(2\sqrt{3}\right) = 6\sqrt{3}$

5. $\frac{1}{2}(2 + 4) = \frac{1}{2}(2) + \frac{1}{2}(4) = 1 + 2 = 3$

6. $2x = 0 \Rightarrow x = 0$

7. $|5 + 2| \le |5| + |2| \Rightarrow |7| \le 7 \Rightarrow 7 = 7$

8. $|3 + (-2)| \le |3| + |-2| \Rightarrow |3 - 2| \le 3 + 2 \Rightarrow 1 \le 5$

Numbers
Exercise 1

DIRECTIONS: Choose the correct answer to each of the following items. Answers are on page 605.

1. Subtracting 1 from which digit in the number 12,345 will decrease the value of the number by 1,000?

   A. 1   C. 3   E. 5
   B. 2   D. 4

2. Adding 1 to each digit of the number 222,222 will increase the value of the number by how much?

   A. 333,333   C. 100,000   E. 1
   B. 111,111   D. 10

3. $(1 \cdot 1) + (1 \cdot 10) + (1 \cdot 100) + (1 \cdot 1,000) + (1 \cdot 10,000) = ?$

   A. 5   C. 11,111   E. 1,111,100
   B. 5,000   D. 111,110

4. $(2 \cdot 1,000) + (3 \cdot 100) + (1 \cdot 10,000) + (2 \cdot 10) + 1 = ?$

   A. 11,223   C. 12,321   E. 32,121
   B. 12,132   D. 23,121

5. $(2 \cdot 10,000) + (8 \cdot 1,000) + (4 \cdot 10) = ?$

   A. 284   C. 2,084   E. 28,040
   B. 482   D. 2,840

6. What is the sum of 5, 7, and 8?

   A. 12   C. 20   E. 28
   B. 15   D. 25

7. What is the difference between 8 and 3?

   A. 24   C. 8   E. 3
   B. 11   D. 5

8. What is the product of 2 and 8?

   A. 4   C. 10   E. 24
   B. 6   D. 16

9. What is the product of 12 and 10?

   A. 2   C. 120   E. 300
   B. 22   D. 240

10. What is the difference between $(5 + 2)$ and $(3 \cdot 2)$?

   A. 0   C. 3   E. 14
   B. 1   D. 10

11. What is the sum of the product of 2 and 3 and the product of 3 and 4?

   A. 6   C. 18   E. 72
   B. 12   D. 35

12. What is the remainder when 12 is divided by 7?

   A. 1   C. 3   E. 5
   B. 2   D. 4

13. What is the remainder when 50 is divided by 2?

   A. 0   C. 3   E. 50
   B. 1   D. 25

14. What is the remainder when 15 is divided by 2?

   A. 0   C. 7   E. 14
   B. 1   D. 8

15. When both 33 and 37 are divided by a certain number, the remainder is 1. What is the number?

A. 4   C. 10   E. 18
B. 9   D. 16

16. $(4 \cdot 3) + 2 = ?$

A. 6   C. 12   E. 26
B. 9   D. 14

17. $[2 \cdot (12 \div 4)] + [6 \div (1 + 2)] = ?$

A. 4   C. 8   E. 24
B. 6   D. 18

18. $[(12 \cdot 3) - (3 \cdot 12)] + [(8 \div 2) \div 4] = ?$

A. 0   C. 4   E. 16
B. 1   D. 8

19. Which of the following statements is (are) true?

I. $(4 + 3) - 6 = 4 + (6 - 2)$
II. $3(4 + 5) = (3 \cdot 4) + (3 \cdot 5)$
III. $(3 + 5) \cdot 4 = 4 \cdot (5 + 3)$

A. I only   D. II and III only
B. II only   E. I, II, and III
C. III only

20. $25 + 50 + 100 = ?$

A. $5(1 + 2 + 3)$ D. $25(1 + 2 + 4)$
B. $5(1 + 2 + 4)$ E. $25(1 + 5 + 10)$
C. $25(1 + 2 + 3)$

21. $1,234(96) - 1,234(48) = ?$

A. $1,234 \cdot 48$ D. $(1,234 \cdot 1,234)$
B. $1,234 \cdot 96$ E. $2 \cdot 1,234$
C. $1,234(48 + 96)$

22. How many prime numbers are greater than 50 but less than 60?

A. 0   C. 2   E. 4
B. 1   D. 3

23. Which of the following numbers is (are) prime?

I.   12,345
II. 999,999,999
III. 1,000,000,002

A. I only   D. I, II, and III
B. III only   E. Neither I, II, nor III
C. I and II only

24. What is the largest factor of both 6 and 9?

A. 1   C. 6   E. 12
B. 3   D. 9

25. What is the largest factor of 18, 24, and 36?

A. 6   C. 12   E. 18
B. 9   D. 15

26. What is the smallest multiple of both 5 and 2?

A. 7   C. 20   E. 40
B. 10   D. 30

27. Which of the following is (are) even?

I.   12
II. 36
III. 101

A. I only   D. I and III only
B. II only   E. I, II, and III
C. I and II only

28. Which of the following is (are) even?

I. $333,332 \cdot 333,333$
II. $999,999 + 101,101$
III. $22,221 \cdot 44,441$

A. I only   D. I and III only
B. II only   E. I, II, and III
C. I and II only

29. For any whole number *n*, which of the following MUST be odd?

    I. $3(n+1)$
    II. $3n+2n$
    III. $2n-1$

    A. I only   D. I and II only
    B. II only   E. I, II, and III
    C. III only

30. What is the sum of three consecutive integers the first of which is –5?

    A. –18   C. –5   E. 5
    B. –12   D. 0

31. If the sum of three consecutive odd integers, *x*, *y*, and *z*, is 21, what is the value of *x*?

    A. 5   C. 7   E. 11
    B. 6   D. 9

32. If the sum of three consecutive even integers, *a*, *b*, and *c*, is 24, then what is the value of *c*?

    A. 2   C. 6   E. 10
    B. 4   · D. 8

33. If 15 is the fifth number in a series of five consecutive odd numbers, what is the third number in the series?

    A. 5   C. 9   E. 13
    B. 7   D. 11

34. If $A=2^2(3)(7)=84$, how many positive factors, including 1 and 84, does *A* have?

    A. 12   C. 36   E. 84
    B. 24   D. 42

35. What is the product of 6 and $\frac{1}{6}$?

    A. 0   C. $\frac{1}{6}$ E. 36
    B. 1   D. 6

36. The sum of 7 and 0 is:

    A. –7   C. $\frac{1}{7}$ E. 14
    B. 0   D. 7

37. $\frac{9}{9}$ is equal to which of the following?

    A. 0   C. 9   E. 81
    B. 1   D. 18

38. If $ab(c-d+2e)=-6$, which of the numbers *a*, *b*, *c*, *d*, and *e* CANNOT be 0?

    A. *a* and b only   D. *d* only
    B. *b* only   E. *c* and d only
    C. *c* only

Items #39–46: Each of the following items includes a number line and a counter. Select the letter of the correct position for the counter after the indicated operations. Note that for some items, a letter choice is included for the original position, indicating that the position may or may not have changed following the indicated operations.

Example:

$2+3=?$

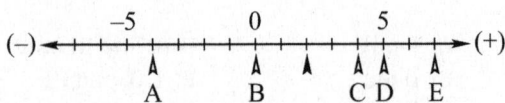

The original position of the counter is 2. If you move it three units in the positive direction, the result is 5, (D).

39. $3+1=?$

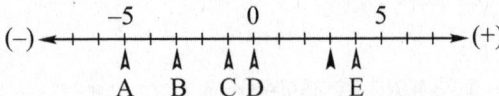

40. $5+(-2)=?$

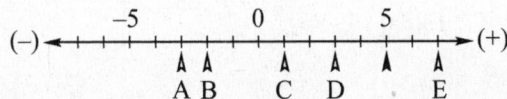

41. $2+(-4)=?$

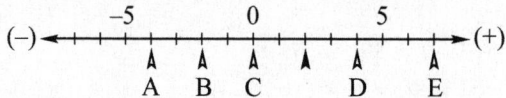

42. $4+(-2)+(-2)=?$

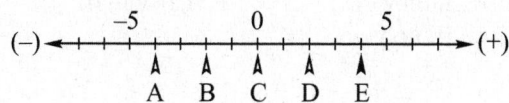

43. $-4+8=?$

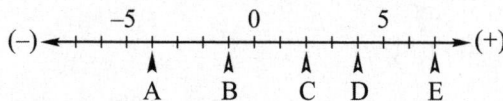

44. $2-(-1)=?$

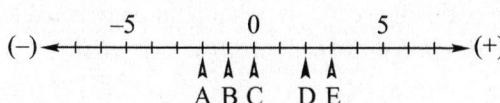

45. $0-(-4)=?$

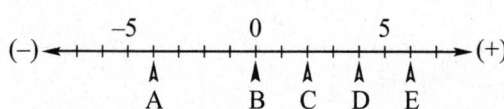

46. $-3-(-1)-(-2)=?$

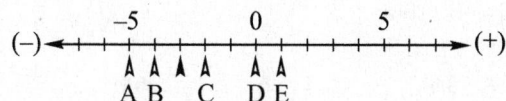

Items #47–66: Determine the correct answer for each of these problems without the aid of a number line.

47. $12-7+6+(-1)=?$

A. 2   C. 10   E. 18
B. 6   D. 14

48. $0+(-12)=?$

A. −12   C. −1   E. 12
B. −6   D. 0

49. $-2+(-6)=?$

A. −8   C. −2   E. 4
B. −4   D. 2

50. $100+(-99)=?$

A. −199   C. −1   E. 99
B. −99   D. 1

51. $2-(-5)=?$

A. 7   C. −2   E. −7
B. 3   D. −3

52. $-2-(-3)=?$

A. −6   C. −1   E. 3
B. −5   D. 1

53. $(5-1)+(1-5)=?$

A. −5   C. 0   E. 5
B. −3   D. 3

54. $1\cdot-2=?$

A. −2   C. $-\dfrac{1}{2}$ E. 2
B. −1   D. 1

55. $-10\cdot-10=?$

A. −100   C. 0   E. 100
B. −20   D. 20

56. $-10\cdot-10\cdot-10=?$

A. −1,000   C. −1   E. 1,000
B. −30   D. 1

57. $-1 \cdot -1 \cdot -1 \cdot -1 \cdot -1 \cdot -1 \cdot -1 \cdot -1 \cdot -1 \cdot -1 = ?$

   A. −10   C. 0   E. 10
   B. −1   D. 1

58. $-12 \div 4 = ?$

   A. −4   C. −2   E. 4
   B. −3   D. 3

59. $[7 - (-6)] + [3 \cdot (2 - 4)] = ?$

   A. −2   C. 7   E. 23
   B. 0   D. 12

60. $(6 \cdot -2) \div (3 \cdot -4) = ?$

   A. −12   C. 1   E. 24
   B. −1   D. 3

61. $[(2 \cdot -1) + (4 \div -2)][(-6 + 6) - (2 - 3)] = ?$

   A. 5   C. −2   E. −23
   B. 2   D. −4

62. $[2(3 - 4)] + [(125 \div -25)(1 \cdot -2)] = ?$

   A. −12   C. 2   E. 125
   B. −8   D. 8

63. $[(2 \cdot 3) \div (-6 \cdot 1)]\left[(21 \div 7) \cdot \frac{1}{3}\right] = ?$

   A. −5   C. 1   E. 36
   B. −1   D. 12

64. $[-3 - (-3)] - [-2 - (-2)] - [-1 - (-1)] = ?$

   A. −12   C. 0   E. 12
   B. −6   D. 6

65. If n is any negative number, which of the following must also be negative?

   I. $n \cdot -n$
   II. $-n \cdot -n$
   III. $-n + n$

   A. I only   D. II and III only
   B. II only   E. I, II, and III
   C. III only

66. If n is any positive number, which of the following must be positive?

   I. $-n - (-n)$
   II. $-n \cdot -n$
   III. $n \div (-n \cdot -n)$

   A. I only   D. I and III only
   B. II only   E. II and III only
   C. III only

67. In the figure below, what point between A and B is two times as far from A as from B?

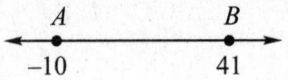

   A. 7   C. 17   E. 31
   B. 10   D. 24

68. $|6| + |6| = ?$

   A. −12   C. 1   E. 36
   B. 0   D. 12

69. $|-8| + |8| = ?$

   A. −16   C. 16   E. 64
   B. 0   D. 24

70. $|1| + |-2| + |3| + |-4| + |5| + |-6| + |7| + |-8| + |9| + |-10| + |11| + |-12| = ?$

   A. −12   C. 6   E. 78
   B. −6   D. 12

FRACTIONS

When one whole number is divided by another whole number and the result is not a third whole number, the result is a ***fraction***. For example, when 2 is divided by 3, the result is not a whole number, but rather it is the fraction $\frac{2}{3}$. Note that any whole number can also be expressed as a fraction; e.g., $\frac{12}{3} = 4$, $7 = \frac{7}{1}$.

The number above the division line in the fraction is called the ***numerator***; the number below the line is called the ***denominator***. In a ***proper fraction***, the numerator is less than the denominator, so the fraction has a value of less than 1, e.g., $\frac{1}{2}$ and $\frac{3}{4}$, which are both less than 1. In an ***improper fraction***, the numerator is greater than the denominator, so the fraction has a value greater than 1, e.g., $\frac{3}{2}$ and $\frac{4}{3}$, which are both greater than 1. A ***mixed number*** consists of both a whole number and a fraction written together. For example, $2\frac{1}{2}$ is equivalent to $2 + \frac{1}{2}$, and $3\frac{4}{5}$ is equivalent to $3 + \frac{4}{5}$.

Converting Mixed Numbers to Improper Fractions

Before you add, subtract, multiply, or divide, convert ***mixed numbers*** to ***improper fractions***. To convert a mixed number to an improper fraction, use the following procedure:

Step 1: Use the denominator of the old fractional part of the mixed number as the new denominator.
Step 2: Multiply the whole number part of the mixed number by the denominator of the old fractional part and add to that product the numerator of the old fractional part. This is the new numerator.

Examples:

1. Rewrite $2\frac{3}{7}$ as an improper fraction.

    ➤ The denominator of the improper fraction is 7. The numerator is determined by multiplying 7 by 2 and adding 3 to the result. To summarize: $2\frac{3}{7} \Rightarrow \frac{(2 \cdot 7) + 3}{7} = \frac{14 + 3}{7} = \frac{17}{7}$.

2. $3\frac{1}{4} = \frac{(3 \cdot 4) + 1}{4} = \frac{13}{4}$

3. $6\frac{2}{5} = \frac{(6 \cdot 5) + 2}{5} = \frac{32}{5}$

4. $2\frac{12}{13} = \frac{(2 \cdot 13) + 12}{13} = \frac{38}{13}$

Converting Improper Fractions to Mixed Numbers

To convert an improper fraction to a mixed number, reverse the process described above.

  Step 1: Divide the denominator into the numerator. The quotient becomes the whole number part of the mixed number.

  Step 2: Use the same denominator for the fraction; the numerator is the remainder of the division process in Step 1.

Examples:

1. Convert $\dfrac{30}{7}$ into a mixed number.

  ➢ Divide 7 into 30; the result is 4 with a remainder of 2. The 4 is the whole number part of the mixed number. Next, the numerator of the fraction is the remainder 2, and the denominator is 7. Therefore, $\dfrac{30}{7} = 4\dfrac{2}{7}$.

2. $\dfrac{29}{5} = 29 \div 5 = 5$ with a remainder of $4 = 5\dfrac{4}{5}$

3. $\dfrac{31}{6} = 31 \div 6 = 5$ with a remainder of $1 = 5\dfrac{1}{6}$

4. $\dfrac{43}{13} = 43 \div 13 = 3$ with a remainder of $4 = 3\dfrac{4}{13}$

Reducing Fractions to Lowest Terms

For reasons of convenience, it is customary to reduce all fractions to their lowest terms. When you reduce a fraction to lowest terms, you really are doing nothing but rewriting it in an equivalent form. This is accomplished by eliminating common factors in both the numerator and the denominator of the fraction.

Example:

$$\frac{8}{16} = \frac{1(8)}{2(8)} = \frac{1}{2}$$

  ➢ There are various ways of describing what goes on when you reduce a fraction. You might think of taking out a common factor, such as 8 in this example, and then dividing 8 into 8 (canceling). It is also possible to think of the process as dividing both the numerator and the denominator by the same number:
  $$\frac{8}{16} = \frac{8 \div 8}{16 \div 8} = \frac{1}{2}.$$

It does not matter how you describe the process, so long as you know how to reduce a fraction to its lowest terms. A fraction is expressed in lowest terms when there is no number (other than 1) that can be evenly divided into both the numerator and the denominator. For example, the fraction $\dfrac{8}{15}$ is in lowest terms, since there is no number (other than 1) that evenly goes into 8 that also evenly goes into 15. On the other hand, the fraction $\dfrac{8}{12}$ is not in lowest terms, since both 8 and 12 can be evenly divided by 4. Reducing $\frac{8}{12}$ by a factor of 4 gives $\frac{2}{3}$, which is in lowest terms since nothing (other than 1) evenly divides into both 2 and 3.

Examples:

1. $\frac{12}{36} = \frac{1 \cdot 12}{3 \cdot 12} = \frac{1}{3}$

2. $\frac{42}{48} = \frac{7 \cdot 6}{8 \cdot 6} = \frac{7}{8}$

3. $\frac{50}{125} = \frac{2 \cdot 25}{5 \cdot 25} = \frac{2}{5}$

If a fraction is particularly large, you may need to reduce it in steps. The process is largely a matter of trial and error, but there are a couple of rules that can guide you. Remember that if both the numerator and the denominator are even numbers, you can reduce the fraction by a factor of 2. Also, if both the numerator and the denominator end in either 0 or 5, they are both divisible by 5.

Examples:

1. $\frac{32}{64} = \frac{16(2)}{32(2)} = \frac{8(2)}{16(2)} = \frac{4(2)}{8(2)} = \frac{2(2)}{4(2)} = \frac{1(2)}{2(2)} = \frac{1}{2}$

2. $\frac{55}{100} = \frac{11(5)}{20(5)} = \frac{11}{20}$

Common Denominators

A ***common denominator*** is a number that is a multiple of the denominators of two or more fractions. For example, 12 is a multiple of both 3 and 4 (both 3 and 4 divide evenly into 12), so it is a suitable common denominator for $\frac{1}{3}$ and $\frac{1}{4}$. Converting a fraction to one with another denominator is the reverse of reducing it to lowest terms. When you multiply both the numerator and the denominator by the same number, you are really just multiplying the fraction by 1, so its value is not changed; e.g., $\frac{3}{3} = 1$.

In grade school, you were taught to find the lowest common denominator for fractions. In truth, any common denominator will work. The easiest way to find a common denominator is to multiply the different denominators together. For example, a common denominator for 2 and 3 is $2 \cdot 3$, or 6; a common denominator for 3 and 4 is $3 \cdot 4$, or 12; a common denominator for 2 and 5 is $2 \cdot 5$, or 10.

What was the big deal about lowest common denominators? It is the same as reducing fractions to lowest terms: It is easier to work with smaller numbers. A common denominator for 2 and 8 is 16, but 8 is also a possibility. It is easier to deal with a fraction of denominator 8 than 16. In the final analysis, you can use any common denominator, because you can always reduce a fraction to its lowest terms.

Operations of Fractions

Adding Fractions

The procedure for adding fractions depends on whether or not the fractions share the same denominator. To add fractions with the same denominator, create a new fraction using that denominator. The new numerator is the sum of the old numerators.

Examples:

1. $\dfrac{3}{7} + \dfrac{2}{7} = \dfrac{5}{7}$

2. $\dfrac{2}{5} + \dfrac{2}{5} = \dfrac{4}{5}$

3. $\dfrac{1}{7} + \dfrac{2}{7} + \dfrac{3}{7} = \dfrac{6}{7}$

To add fractions with different denominators, you must first find a common denominator and convert the fractions in the manner described above. For example, $\dfrac{1}{3}$ and $\dfrac{1}{5}$. Since these fractions have unlike denominators, you must find a common denominator such as 15. Next, you convert each fraction to a fraction with a denominator of 15.

Examples:

1. $\dfrac{1}{3} + \dfrac{1}{5} = \dfrac{1(5)}{3(5)} + \dfrac{1(3)}{5(3)} = \dfrac{5}{15} + \dfrac{3}{15} = \dfrac{8}{15}$

2. $\dfrac{1}{3} + \dfrac{2}{7} = \dfrac{1(7)}{3(7)} + \dfrac{2(3)}{7(3)} = \dfrac{7}{21} + \dfrac{6}{21} = \dfrac{13}{21}$

3. $\dfrac{2}{9} + \dfrac{4}{5} = \dfrac{2(5)}{9(5)} + \dfrac{4(9)}{5(9)} = \dfrac{10}{45} + \dfrac{36}{45} = \dfrac{46}{45}$

To add a fraction and a whole number, you can treat the whole number as a fraction with a denominator of 1.

Example:

$2 + \dfrac{1}{5} + \dfrac{1}{2} = \dfrac{2}{1} + \dfrac{1}{5} + \dfrac{1}{2} = \dfrac{2(10)}{1(10)} + \dfrac{1(2)}{5(2)} + \dfrac{1(5)}{2(5)} = \dfrac{20}{10} + \dfrac{2}{10} + \dfrac{5}{10} = \dfrac{27}{10}$

To add a fraction and a mixed number, add the fractional parts and then add the whole parts.

Example:

$2\dfrac{1}{3} + \dfrac{1}{3} = 2 + \left(\dfrac{1}{3} + \dfrac{1}{3}\right) = 2 + \dfrac{2}{3} = 2\dfrac{2}{3}$

Subtracting Fractions

Follow the same procedures for subtraction of fractions as for addition, except subtract rather than add. When the fractions have the same denominators, simply subtract one numerator from the other.

Examples:

1. $\dfrac{5}{7} - \dfrac{2}{7} = \dfrac{3}{7}$

2. $\dfrac{4}{5} - \dfrac{3}{5} = \dfrac{1}{5}$

When fractions have different denominators, it is first necessary to find a common denominator.

Examples:

1. $\dfrac{7}{8} - \dfrac{3}{5} = \dfrac{7(5)}{8(5)} - \dfrac{3(8)}{5(8)} = \dfrac{35}{40} - \dfrac{24}{40} = \dfrac{11}{40}$

2. $\dfrac{5}{6} - \dfrac{1}{5} = \dfrac{5(5)}{6(5)} - \dfrac{1(6)}{5(6)} = \dfrac{25}{30} - \dfrac{6}{30} = \dfrac{19}{30}$

3. $2 - \dfrac{7}{6} = \dfrac{2}{1} - \dfrac{7}{6} = \dfrac{2(6)}{1(6)} - \dfrac{7(1)}{6(1)} = \dfrac{12}{6} - \dfrac{7}{6} = \dfrac{5}{6}$

"Flying-X" Method

You do not need to worry about finding a lowest common denominator as long as you remember to reduce the result of an operation to lowest terms. This sets up a little trick for adding and subtracting fractions that makes the process a purely mechanical one—one you do not even have to think about. The trick is called the "flying-x."

To add (or subtract) any two fractions with unlike denominators use the following procedure:

Step 1: Multiply the denominators to get a new denominator.
Step 2: Multiply the numerator of the first fraction by the denominator of the second.
Step 3: Multiply the denominator of the first fraction by the numerator of the second.
Step 4: The new numerator is the sum (or difference) of the results of Steps 2 and 3.

Once again, it is more difficult to describe the process than it is to do it. Perhaps the easiest way to learn it is to see it done. To add two fractions: $\dfrac{a}{b} + \dfrac{c}{d} = \dfrac{a}{b} \underset{\longrightarrow}{+} \dfrac{c}{d} = \dfrac{ad + bc}{bd}$.

Example:

$\dfrac{2}{7} + \dfrac{1}{5} = \dfrac{2}{7} + \dfrac{1}{5} = \dfrac{10 + 7}{35} = \dfrac{17}{35}$

As you can see, the connecting arrows make a figure that looks like an "x" floating above the ground, or a "flying x."

The "flying-x" method also works for subtracting fractions.

Examples:

1. $\dfrac{3}{5} - \dfrac{1}{3} = \dfrac{3}{5} \rightleftarrows \dfrac{1}{3} = \dfrac{9-5}{15} = \dfrac{4}{15}$

2. $\dfrac{6}{7} - \dfrac{5}{6} = \dfrac{6}{7} \rightleftarrows \dfrac{5}{6} = \dfrac{36-35}{42} = \dfrac{1}{42}$

Of course, this may not give you the lowest terms of the fractions, so it may be necessary to reduce.

Examples:

1. $\dfrac{3}{4} - \dfrac{1}{8} = \dfrac{3}{4} \rightleftarrows \dfrac{1}{8} = \dfrac{24-4}{32} = \dfrac{20}{32} = \dfrac{5}{8}$

2. $\dfrac{2}{3} - \dfrac{1}{6} = \dfrac{2}{3} \rightleftarrows \dfrac{1}{6} = \dfrac{12-3}{18} = \dfrac{9}{18} = \dfrac{1}{2}$

Multiplying Fractions

Multiplication of fractions does not require a common denominator. To multiply fractions, just multiply numerators to create a new numerator, and multiply denominators to create a new denominator.

Examples:

1. $\dfrac{3}{4} \cdot \dfrac{1}{5} = \dfrac{3 \cdot 1}{4 \cdot 5} = \dfrac{3}{20}$

2. $\dfrac{2}{3} \cdot \dfrac{2}{5} = \dfrac{2 \cdot 2}{3 \cdot 5} = \dfrac{4}{15}$

Dividing Fractions

Division of fractions is the opposite of multiplication. To divide by a fraction, you invert the divisor (the fraction by which you are dividing) and then multiply the two together.

Examples:

1. $2 \div \dfrac{1}{4} = \dfrac{2}{1} \cdot \dfrac{4}{1} = \dfrac{8}{1} = 8$

2. $\dfrac{\frac{2}{3}}{\frac{5}{6}} = \dfrac{2}{3} \cdot \dfrac{6}{5} = \dfrac{12}{15} = \dfrac{4}{5}$

3. $\dfrac{1}{3} \div \dfrac{5}{6} = \dfrac{1}{3} \cdot \dfrac{6}{5} = \dfrac{6}{15} = \dfrac{2}{5}$

4. $\dfrac{2}{7} \div 2 = \dfrac{2}{7} \div \dfrac{2}{1} = \dfrac{2}{7} \cdot \dfrac{1}{2} = \dfrac{2}{14} = \dfrac{1}{7}$

5. $\dfrac{1}{5} \div \dfrac{1}{2} = \dfrac{1}{5} \cdot \dfrac{2}{1} = \dfrac{2}{5}$

6. $3 \div \dfrac{1}{5} = \dfrac{3}{1} \cdot \dfrac{5}{1} = \dfrac{15}{1} = 15$

Comparing Fractions

Comparing Decimal Equivalents

We can compare the values of fractions in several different ways. The first method is the one most commonly used but which often takes up valuable time. Convert the fractions to decimal equivalents and compare these values.

Example:

Find the largest value of the following fractions: $\dfrac{1}{2}, \dfrac{2}{3}, \dfrac{1}{8}$, and $\dfrac{2}{11}$.

➤ Convert the fractions to decimal equivalents: 0.5, $0.6\overline{6}$, 0.125, and $0.18\overline{18}$. Compare the values: $0.6\overline{6}$ is the largest.

Upward Cross-Multiplication

The second method of comparing fractions is often faster. We use ***upward cross-multiplication***—multiply the denominator of the one fraction with the numerator of the other fraction in an upward direction. The fraction with the greatest product above it has the greatest value.

Example:

Find the largest value of the following fractions: $\dfrac{1}{2}, \dfrac{2}{3}, \dfrac{1}{8}$, and $\dfrac{2}{11}$.

➤ Compare $\dfrac{1}{2}$ with $\dfrac{2}{3}$ by multiplying $(3)(1)$ and $(2)(2)$ and place the value above each fraction:

③ ④
$\dfrac{1}{2} \times \dfrac{2}{3} \Rightarrow 4$ is larger than 3, so $\dfrac{2}{3}$ is larger than $\dfrac{1}{2}$. Now, compare $\dfrac{2}{3}$ with the other two remaining

fractions: ⑯ ③ ㉒ ⑥
$\dfrac{2}{3} \times \dfrac{1}{8} \Rightarrow \dfrac{2}{3}$ is larger. $\dfrac{2}{3} \times \dfrac{2}{11} \Rightarrow \dfrac{2}{3}$ is larger. Therefore, $\dfrac{2}{3}$ is the largest value.

Alternatively, you can directly compare fractions by converting all of the fractions to fractions with the same denominator. The fraction with the largest numerator is then the largest value.

Example:

Find the smallest value of the following fractions: $\dfrac{1}{4}, \dfrac{5}{14}, \dfrac{3}{7}$, and $\dfrac{1}{2}$.

➤ Convert the fractions to fractions with the same denominator: $\dfrac{1}{4}\cdot\dfrac{7}{7}=\dfrac{7}{28}$; $\dfrac{5}{14}\cdot\dfrac{2}{2}=\dfrac{10}{28}$; $\dfrac{3}{7}\cdot\dfrac{4}{4}=\dfrac{12}{28}$; $\dfrac{1}{2}\cdot\dfrac{14}{14}=\dfrac{14}{28}$. Since $\dfrac{7}{28}$ is the rewritten fraction with the smallest numerator, the fraction equivalent $\dfrac{1}{4}$ is the smallest value of the given fractions.

Fractions
Exercise 2

DIRECTIONS: Choose the correct answer to each of the following items. Answers are on page 605.

1. $5\frac{3}{8} = ?$

  A. 1 C. $\frac{23}{8}$ E. $\frac{43}{8}$

  B. $\frac{15}{8}$ D. $\frac{35}{8}$

2. $3\frac{1}{12} = ?$

  A. $\frac{13}{2}$ C. $\frac{41}{12}$ E. $\frac{71}{12}$

  B. $\frac{37}{12}$ D. $\frac{53}{12}$

3. $5\frac{2}{7} = ?$

  A. $\frac{5}{14}$ C. $\frac{37}{7}$ E. $\frac{110}{7}$

  B. $\frac{35}{7}$ D. $\frac{70}{7}$

4. $\frac{20}{6} = ?$

  A. $3\frac{1}{3}$ C. $4\frac{1}{6}$ E. 6

  B. $3\frac{2}{3}$ D. $4\frac{1}{3}$

5. $\frac{25}{4} = ?$

  A. $\frac{4}{25}$ C. $1\frac{1}{8}$ E. $6\frac{1}{4}$

  B. $\frac{4}{12}$ D. $1\frac{1}{4}$

6. $\frac{3}{12} = ?$

  A. $\frac{1}{6}$ C. $\frac{1}{3}$ E. $\frac{3}{4}$

  B. $\frac{1}{4}$ D. $\frac{1}{2}$

7. $\frac{125}{625} = ?$

  A. $\frac{1}{10}$ C. $\frac{2}{5}$ E. $\frac{4}{5}$

  B. $\frac{1}{5}$ D. $\frac{7}{10}$

8. $\frac{121}{132} = ?$

  A. $\frac{1}{11}$ C. $\frac{9}{10}$ E. $\frac{11}{12}$

  B. $\frac{1}{10}$ D. $\frac{10}{11}$

9. What is $\frac{4}{28}$ expressed in lowest terms?

  A. $\frac{1}{28}$ C. $\frac{1}{7}$ E. 7

  B. $\frac{2}{14}$ D. 6

10. What is $\frac{8}{30}$ expressed in lowest terms?

A. $\frac{2}{15}$ C. $\frac{4}{15}$ E. $\frac{2}{3}$

B. $\frac{3}{15}$ D. $\frac{1}{5}$

11. What is $\frac{15}{64}$ expressed in lowest terms?

A. $\frac{15}{64}$ C. $\frac{5}{8}$ E. $\frac{64}{15}$

B. $\frac{3}{8}$ D. $\frac{15}{8}$

12. What is $\frac{9}{57}$ expressed in lowest terms?

A. $\frac{1}{57}$ C. $\frac{3}{19}$ E. $\frac{9}{19}$

B. $\frac{1}{9}$ D. $\frac{3}{11}$

13. What is $\frac{0}{1}$ expressed in lowest terms?

A. 0   C. 10   E. 1000
B. 1   D. 100

14. Which of the following is NOT equal to $\frac{3}{8}$?

A. $\frac{6}{16}$ C. $\frac{31}{81}$ E. $\frac{120}{320}$

B. $\frac{15}{40}$ D. $\frac{33}{88}$

15. Which of the following is NOT equal to $\frac{5}{6}$?

A. $\frac{25}{30}$ C. $\frac{50}{60}$ E. $\frac{100}{120}$

B. $\frac{45}{50}$ D. $\frac{55}{66}$

16. $\frac{1}{7}+\frac{2}{7}=?$

A. $\frac{2}{7}$ C. $\frac{6}{7}$ E. $\frac{12}{7}$

B. $\frac{3}{7}$ D. $\frac{8}{7}$

17. $\frac{12}{13}+\frac{12}{13}=?$

A. 0   C. $\frac{12}{26}$ E. $\frac{26}{13}$

B. 1   D. $\frac{24}{13}$

18. $\frac{1}{11}+\frac{2}{11}+\frac{7}{11}=?$

A. $\frac{4}{11}$ C. $\frac{10}{11}$ E. $\frac{11}{7}$

B. $\frac{7}{11}$ D. $\frac{11}{10}$

19. $\frac{1}{8}+\frac{1}{7}=?$

A. $\frac{1}{56}$ C. $\frac{1}{15}$ E. $\frac{15}{56}$

B. $\frac{1}{27}$ D. $\frac{1}{5}$

20. $\frac{3}{5}+\frac{2}{11}=?$

A. $\frac{43}{110}$ C. $\frac{54}{55}$ E. $\frac{100}{43}$

B. $\frac{43}{55}$ D. $\frac{55}{54}$

21. $\frac{2}{3} + \frac{3}{6} + \frac{4}{6} = ?$

    A. $\frac{9}{20}$ C. $\frac{7}{6}$ E. $\frac{16}{3}$

    B. $\frac{6}{7}$ D. $\frac{11}{6}$

22. $\frac{5}{7} - \frac{4}{7} = ?$

    A. $\frac{9}{7}$ C. $\frac{5}{7}$ E. $\frac{1}{49}$

    B. 1 D. $\frac{1}{7}$

23. $\frac{3}{2} - \frac{1}{4} = ?$

    A. $\frac{5}{4}$ C. $\frac{3}{4}$ E. $\frac{1}{3}$

    B. $\frac{4}{5}$ D. $\frac{2}{3}$

24. $2\frac{2}{3} - 1\frac{1}{6} = ?$

    A. $1\frac{1}{6}$ C. $1\frac{1}{2}$ E. 2

    B. $1\frac{1}{3}$ D. $1\frac{2}{3}$

25. $\frac{2}{7} \cdot \frac{1}{4} = ?$

    A. $\frac{1}{63}$ C. $\frac{1}{4}$ E. $\frac{5}{9}$

    B. $\frac{1}{14}$ D. $\frac{3}{8}$

26. $\frac{1}{2} \cdot \frac{1}{2} \cdot \frac{1}{2} = ?$

    A. $\frac{1}{16}$ C. $\frac{3}{16}$ E. $\frac{2}{3}$

    B. $\frac{1}{8}$ D. $\frac{3}{8}$

27. $\frac{1}{4} \cdot \frac{1}{8} \cdot 3 = ?$

    A. $\frac{3}{32}$ C. $\frac{1}{4}$ E. $\frac{3}{4}$

    B. $\frac{1}{8}$ D. $\frac{1}{2}$

28. $\frac{7}{8} \div \frac{3}{4} = ?$

    A. $\frac{7}{6}$ C. $\frac{3}{4}$ E. $\frac{1}{8}$

    B. 1 D. $\frac{1}{3}$

29. $\frac{1}{12} \div \frac{1}{12} = ?$

    A. $\frac{1}{144}$ C. 12 E. 144

    B. 1 D. 18

30. $\frac{8}{9} \div \frac{7}{8} = ?$

    A. $\frac{64}{63}$ C. $\frac{7}{9}$ E. $\frac{1}{3}$

    B. $\frac{9}{7}$ D. $\frac{1}{2}$

31. $\left(\dfrac{1}{4}+\dfrac{2}{3}\right)\cdot\left(\dfrac{3}{2}+\dfrac{1}{4}\right)=?$

   A. $\dfrac{21}{47}$ C. $\dfrac{51}{48}$ E. $\dfrac{105}{51}$

   B. $\dfrac{33}{49}$ D. $\dfrac{77}{48}$

32. $\left(\dfrac{2}{3}\cdot\dfrac{1}{6}\right)\div\left(\dfrac{1}{2}\cdot\dfrac{1}{4}\right)=?$

   A. $\dfrac{1}{18}$ C. $\dfrac{8}{9}$ E. $\dfrac{15}{75}$

   B. $\dfrac{2}{9}$ D. $\dfrac{11}{8}$

33. $\left[\left(\dfrac{1}{3}+\dfrac{1}{2}\right)\cdot\left(\dfrac{2}{3}-\dfrac{1}{3}\right)\right]\cdot 18=?$

   A. 5 C. $\dfrac{5}{6}$ E. $\dfrac{2}{3}$

   B. $\dfrac{7}{8}$ D. $\dfrac{4}{5}$

34. $\left[\left(\dfrac{1}{3}\div\dfrac{1}{6}\right)\cdot\left(\dfrac{2}{3}\div\dfrac{1}{3}\right)\right]\cdot\left(\dfrac{1}{2}+\dfrac{3}{4}\right)=?$

   A. 5 C. 3 E. 1
   B. 4 D. 2

35. $8\left(\dfrac{1}{3}+\dfrac{3}{4}\right)=?$

   A. $\dfrac{1}{3}$ C. $\dfrac{16}{3}$ E. $\dfrac{26}{3}$

   B. $\dfrac{4}{3}$ D. $\dfrac{19}{3}$

36. $\dfrac{1}{4}-\dfrac{1}{5}=?$

   A. $\dfrac{1}{5}$ C. $\dfrac{1}{20}$ E. $\dfrac{4}{5}$

   B. $\dfrac{1}{3}$ D. $\dfrac{3}{4}$

37. $\dfrac{\frac{4}{9}}{\frac{2}{5}}=?$

   A. $\dfrac{1}{2}$ C. $\dfrac{8}{45}$ E. $1\dfrac{1}{9}$

   B. $\dfrac{3}{4}$ D. $\dfrac{11}{9}$

38. Which fraction is the largest?

   A. $\dfrac{9}{16}$ C. $\dfrac{5}{8}$ E. $\dfrac{1}{2}$

   B. $\dfrac{7}{10}$ D. $\dfrac{4}{5}$

39. Which of the following fractions is the largest?

   $\dfrac{4}{7},\dfrac{2}{3},\dfrac{5}{8},\dfrac{9}{20}$

   A. $\dfrac{4}{7}$ C. $\dfrac{5}{8}$ E. all are equal

   B. $\dfrac{2}{3}$ D. $\dfrac{9}{20}$

40. Which of the following fractions is the largest?

   $\dfrac{1}{5},\dfrac{2}{5},\dfrac{3}{8},\dfrac{7}{9}$

   A. $\dfrac{1}{5}$ C. $\dfrac{3}{8}$ E. all are equal

   B. $\dfrac{2}{5}$ D. $\dfrac{7}{9}$

41. Which of the following fractions is the smallest?

$$\frac{2}{7}, \frac{1}{3}, \frac{5}{19}, \frac{3}{7}$$

A. $\frac{2}{7}$ C. $\frac{5}{19}$ E. all are equal

B. $\frac{1}{3}$ D. $\frac{3}{7}$

42. Jughead eats $\frac{2}{5}$ of a pound of cake each day. How many pounds of cake does Jughead eat in 3 weeks?

A. $4\frac{1}{2}$ C. $5\frac{1}{5}$ E. 10

B. $5\frac{3}{4}$ D. $8\frac{2}{5}$

43. Chompa eats $\frac{3}{8}$ of a bag of candy per day. How many weeks will 42 bags of candy last Chompa?

A. 4   C. 9   E. 16
B. 5   D. 12

44. If Bruce can eat $2\frac{1}{2}$ bananas per day, how many bananas can Bruce eat in 4 weeks?

A. 70   C. 80   E. 90
B. 75   D. 85

45. One brass rod measures $3\frac{5}{16}$ inches long and another brass rod measures $2\frac{3}{4}$ inches long. What is the total length, in inches, of the two rods combined?

A. $6\frac{9}{16}$ C. $5\frac{1}{2}$ E. $5\frac{1}{32}$

B. $6\frac{1}{16}$ D. $5\frac{1}{16}$

46. Which of the following equals the number of half-pound packages of tea that can be taken out of a box that holds $10\frac{1}{2}$ pounds of tea?

A. 5   C. 11   E. 21

B. $10\frac{1}{2}$ D. $20\frac{1}{122}$

47. If each bag of tokens weighs $5\frac{3}{4}$ pounds, how many pounds do 3 bags weigh?

A. $7\frac{1}{4}$ C. $16\frac{1}{2}$ E. $17\frac{1}{2}$

B. $15\frac{3}{4}$ D. $17\frac{1}{4}$

48. During one week, a man traveled $3\frac{1}{2}$, $1\frac{1}{4}$, $1\frac{1}{6}$, and $2\frac{3}{8}$ miles. The next week, he traveled $\frac{1}{4}, \frac{3}{8}, \frac{9}{16}, 3\frac{1}{16}, 2\frac{5}{8}$, and $3\frac{3}{16}$ miles. How many more miles did he travel the second week than the first week?

A. $1\frac{37}{48}$ C. $1\frac{3}{4}$ E. $\frac{47}{48}$

B. $1\frac{1}{2}$ D. 1

49. A certain type of board is sold only in lengths of multiples of 2 feet. The shortest board sold is 6 feet and the longest is 24 feet. A builder needs a large quantity of this type of board in $5\frac{1}{2}$-foot lengths. To minimize waste, which of the following board lengths should be ordered?

A. 6-foot   C. 22-foot   E. 26-foot
B. 12-foot   D. 24-foot

50. A man spent $\frac{15}{16}$ of his entire fortune in buying a car for $7,500. How much money did he possess?

A. $6,000   C. $7,000   E. $8,500
B. $6,500   D. $8,000

51. The population of a town was 54,000 in the last census. Since then it has increased by two-thirds. Which of the following equals its present population?

A. 18,000   C. 72,000   E. 108,000
B. 36,000   D. 90,000

52. $\frac{1}{3}$ of the liquid contents of a can evaporates on the first day and $\frac{3}{4}$ of the remainder evaporates on the second day. Which of the following equals the fractional part of the original contents remaining at the close of the second day?

A. $\frac{5}{12}$ C. $\frac{1}{6}$ E. $\frac{4}{7}$

B. $\frac{7}{12}$ D. $\frac{1}{2}$

53. A car is run until the gas tank is $\frac{1}{8}$ full. The tank is then filled to capacity by putting in 14 gallons. What is the gas tank's capacity, in gallons?

A. 14   C. 16   E. 18
B. 15   D. 17

DECIMALS

A ***decimal*** is nothing more than a special way of writing fractions using a denominator of ten, or one hundred, or one thousand, and so on. Decimals are written with a decimal point to the left of the decimal digits in order to distinguish them from whole numbers.

Examples:

1. The fraction $\frac{3}{10}$ written as a decimal is 0.3.

2. The fraction $\frac{72}{100}$ written as a decimal is 0.72.

The positions to the right of the decimal point are called decimal places. Decimal places are analogous to the positions of the digits in whole numbers (units column, tens column, etc.). The number of decimal places indicates the denominator of the fraction. One decimal place indicates a denominator of 10; two places indicate a denominator of 100; three indicate a denominator of 1,000; and so on. 0.335 is read as three hundred thirty-five thousandths and 0.12345 as twelve thousand three hundred forty-five hundred thousandths.

0 . 1 2 3 4 5

TENTHS HUNDREDTHS THOUSANDTHS TEN THOUSANDTHS HUNDRED THOUSANDTHS

When a decimal does not include a positive or negative whole number, a zero is placed to the left of the decimal point. This has no mathematical significance; it is there just to make the decimals more readable. Without the zero, someone might fail to see the decimal point and read .335 as 335. On the exam, all decimals that do not include a positive or negative whole number are written with a zero to the left of the decimal point.

Converting Fractions to Decimals

If the fraction already has a denominator that is ten, one hundred, one thousand, etc., the conversion is very easy. The numerator of the fraction becomes the decimal. The number of zeros in the denominator governs the placement of the decimal point. Starting just to the right of the last digit of the numerator, you count over one digit to the left for each zero in the denominator. For example, to express $\frac{127}{1,000}$ in decimal form, take the numerator, 127, as the decimal. Then, starting just to the right of the 7, count over three places to the left (one for each zero in 1,000). The decimal equivalent is 0.127.

Examples:

1. $\dfrac{3}{10} = 0.3$ (One zero in the denominator indicates one decimal place.)

2. $\dfrac{13}{100} = 0.13$ (Two zeros in the denominator indicate two decimal places.)

3. $\dfrac{522}{1,000} = 0.522$ (Three zeros in the denominator indicate three decimal places.)

If there are fewer digits in the numerator than zeros in the denominator, add zeros to the left of the number until you have enough decimal places. For example, consider $\dfrac{53}{1,000}$: the denominator contains three zeros, but 53 is only a two-digit number. Therefore, add one zero to the left of the 5: $\dfrac{53}{1,000} = 0.053$.

Examples:

1. $\dfrac{3}{100} = 0.03$ (Two zeros mean two decimal places.)

2. $\dfrac{71}{10,000} = 0.0071$ (Four zeros mean four decimal places.)

3. $\dfrac{9}{100,000} = 0.00009$ (Five zeros mean five decimal places.)

To convert a proper fraction with a denominator other than 10, 100, etc., convert the fraction to an equivalent form using a denominator such as ten, one hundred, etc. For example, to convert $\dfrac{3}{4}$ to a decimal, change it into a fraction with a denominator of 100: $\dfrac{3}{4} = \dfrac{3 \cdot 25}{4 \cdot 25} = \dfrac{75}{100}$. Then, $\dfrac{75}{100}$ is written as 0.75, as described in the previous section.

Examples:

1. $\dfrac{2}{5} = \dfrac{2 \cdot 2}{5 \cdot 2} = \dfrac{4}{10} = 0.4$

2. $\dfrac{1}{4} = \dfrac{1 \cdot 25}{4 \cdot 25} = \dfrac{25}{100} = 0.25$

3. $\dfrac{3}{8} = \dfrac{3 \cdot 125}{8 \cdot 125} = \dfrac{375}{1,000} = 0.375$

4. $\dfrac{1}{50} = \dfrac{1 \cdot 2}{50 \cdot 2} = \dfrac{2}{100} = 0.02$

To determine which denominator you should use, divide the denominator of the fraction into 10, then into 100, then into 1,000, until you find the first denominator that is evenly divisible by the denominator of the fraction.

For example, $\frac{3}{8}$ does not have an equivalent form with a denominator of 10, but it does have an equivalent form with a denominator of 1,000. This is the same process used above to find common denominators for fractions. (Note: You can also convert a fraction into a decimal by dividing the numerator of the fraction by its denominator. However, this method obviously presupposes that you know how to divide decimals. We will come back to the topic of converting to decimals when we discuss how to divide decimals.)

Converting Mixed Numbers to Decimals

To change a mixed number to a decimal, convert the fractional part of the mixed number to a decimal as discussed above, and then place the whole number part of the mixed number to the left of the decimal point.

Examples:

1. Convert the mixed number $2\frac{3}{4}$ to a decimal.

   ➤ First, convert $\frac{3}{4}$ to a decimal: $\frac{3}{4} = 0.75$. Then, place the whole-number part to the left of the decimal point: 2.75. Notice that the extra zero is dropped—there is no reason to write 02.75.

2. $6\frac{1}{10} = 6.1$

3. $12\frac{1}{2} = 12.5$

4. $3\frac{7}{8} = 3.875$

Converting Improper Fractions to Decimals

To convert an improper fraction to a decimal, just treat the improper fraction as a mixed number and follow the procedure just outlined.

Examples:

1. $\frac{9}{4} = 2\frac{1}{4} = 2.25$

2. $\frac{7}{2} = 3\frac{1}{2} = 3.5$

3. $\frac{8}{5} = 1\frac{3}{5} = 1.6$

It is also possible, and often easier, to convert improper fractions to decimals by dividing the numerator by the denominator. Again, we will postpone this part of the discussion until we have studied division of decimals.

Converting Decimals to Fractions and Mixed Numbers

To convert a decimal back to a fraction, it is necessary only to create a fraction using the digits of the decimal number as a numerator and a denominator of 1 followed by a number of zeros equal to the number of decimal places.

Examples:

1. Convert 0.125 to a fraction.

   ➤ Use 125 as the numerator and 1,000 as the denominator: $\dfrac{125}{1,000}$. Reduce the fraction to lowest terms:

   $$\dfrac{125}{1,000} = \dfrac{1}{8}.$$

2. $0.04 = \dfrac{4}{100} = \dfrac{1}{25}$

3. $0.25 = \dfrac{25}{100} = \dfrac{1}{4}$

4. $0.005 = \dfrac{5}{1,000} = \dfrac{1}{200}$

Finally, if the decimal consists of both a whole part and a fraction, the conversion will result in a mixed number. The whole part of the mixed number will be the whole part of the decimal. Then, convert the fractional part of the decimal as just shown.

Examples:

1. Convert 2.05 to a mixed number.

   ➤ Write 0.05 as a fraction: $0.05 = \dfrac{5}{100} = \dfrac{1}{20}$. The whole number part is 2, so $2.05 = 2\dfrac{1}{20}$.

2. $1.75 = 1 + \dfrac{75}{100} = 1 + \dfrac{3}{4} = 1\dfrac{3}{4}$

3. $32.6 = 32 + \dfrac{6}{10} = 32 + \dfrac{3}{5} = 32\dfrac{3}{5}$

4. $2.05 = 2 + \dfrac{5}{100} = 2 + \dfrac{1}{20} = 2\dfrac{1}{20}$

5. $357.125 = 357 + \dfrac{125}{1,000} = 357 + \dfrac{1}{8} = 357\dfrac{1}{8}$

Operations of Decimals

Adding and Subtracting Decimals

Decimals can be manipulated in very much the same way as whole numbers. You can add and subtract decimals.

Examples:

1. $0.2+0.3+0.1=0.6$

2. $0.7-0.2=0.5$

Adding zeros to the end of a decimal number does not change the value of that number. If the decimals do not have the same number of decimal places, add zeros to the right of those that do not until every number has the same number of decimal places. Then, line up the decimal points and combine the decimals as indicated. Follow the same process for subtracting decimals.

Examples:

1. $0.75-0.1125 \Rightarrow$
    $$\begin{array}{r} 0.7500 \\ -0.1125 \\ \hline 0.6375 \end{array}$$

2. $0.125+0.6+0.115 \Rightarrow$
    $$\begin{array}{r} 0.125 \\ 0.600 \\ +0.115 \\ \hline 0.840 \end{array}$$

3. $0.999-0.000001 \Rightarrow$
    $$\begin{array}{r} 0.999000 \\ -0.000001 \\ \hline 0.998999 \end{array}$$

4. $2.14+0.125+0.0005 \Rightarrow$
    $$\begin{array}{r} 2.1400 \\ 0.1250 \\ +0.0005 \\ \hline 2.2655 \end{array}$$

5. $0.8-0.1111 \Rightarrow$
    $$\begin{array}{r} 0.8000 \\ -0.1111 \\ \hline 0.6889 \end{array}$$

6. $0.11+0.9+0.033 \Rightarrow$
    $$\begin{array}{r} 0.110 \\ 0.900 \\ +0.033 \\ \hline 1.043 \end{array}$$

Multiplying Decimals

As with fractions, there is no need to find a common denominator or line up the decimal points when multiplying decimals: The multiplication process generates its own common denominator. Simply multiply as with whole numbers and then adjust the decimal point. To find the correct position for the decimal point first, count the total number of decimal places in the numbers that are being multiplied. Then, in the final product, place the decimal point that many places to the left, counting from the right side of the last digit.

Examples:

1. $0.25 \cdot 0.2=?$

    ➤ Ignore the decimals and multiply: $25 \cdot 2=50$. Now, adjust the decimal point. Since 0.25 has two decimal places, and 0.2 has one decimal place, count three places to the left, starting at the right side of the 0 in 50; the final product is $0.050=0.05$.

2. $0.1 \cdot 0.2 \cdot 0.3=0.006$ ($1 \cdot 2 \cdot 3=6$, and there are three decimal places in the multiplication.)

3. $0.02 \cdot 0.008=0.00016$ ($2 \cdot 8=16$, and there are five decimal places in the multiplication.)

4. $2 \cdot 0.5 = 1$ ($2 \cdot 5 = 10$, and there is one decimal place in the multiplication.)

5. $2.5 \cdot 2.5 = 6.25$ ($25 \cdot 25 = 625$, and there are two decimal places in the multiplication.)

6. $0.10 \cdot 0.10 \cdot 0.10 = 0.001$ ($10 \cdot 10 \cdot 10 = 1,000$, and there are six decimal places in the multiplication.)

To simplify the process of multiplying decimals, drop any final zeros before multiplying. Thus, in the case of the last example, $0.10 \cdot 0.10 \cdot 0.10 = 0.1 \cdot 0.1 \cdot 0.1 = 0.001$ since there are three decimal places in the multiplication.

Dividing Decimals

Like multiplication, division generates a common denominator by a suitable adjustment of zeros. However, there are two situations in which division of decimals is a little tricky. Let's review them one at a time.

First, when the divisor (the number doing the dividing) is a whole number, place the decimal point in the quotient (result of division) immediately above the decimal point in the dividend (the number being divided). Then, keep dividing until there is no remainder, adding zeros as needed to the right of the dividend. This is the procedure whenever the divisor is a whole number—even if the dividend is also a whole number.

Examples:

1. $0.25 \div 5 \Rightarrow 5\overline{)0.25}$

    $$\begin{array}{r} 0.05 \\ 5\overline{)0.25} \\ -25 \\ \hline 0 \end{array}$$

2. $2.5 \div 2 \Rightarrow 2\overline{)2.50}$

    $$\begin{array}{r} 1.25 \\ 2\overline{)2.50} \\ -2 \\ \hline 05 \\ -4 \\ \hline 10 \\ -10 \\ \hline 0 \end{array}$$

3. $1.75 \div 25 \Rightarrow 25\overline{)1.75}$

    $$\begin{array}{r} 0.07 \\ 25\overline{)1.75} \\ -175 \\ \hline 0 \end{array}$$

4. $1.44 \div 12 \Rightarrow 12\overline{)1.44}$

    $$\begin{array}{r} 0.12 \\ 12\overline{)1.44} \\ -12 \\ \hline 24 \\ -24 \\ \hline 0 \end{array}$$

5. $0.1 \div 250 \Rightarrow 250\overline{)0.1000}$

    $$\begin{array}{r} 0.0004 \\ 250\overline{)0.1000} \\ -1000 \\ \hline 0 \end{array}$$

6. $9 \div 2 \Rightarrow 2\overline{)9.0}$

    $$\begin{array}{r} 4.5 \\ 2\overline{)9.0} \\ -8 \\ \hline 10 \\ -10 \\ \hline 0 \end{array}$$

The second tricky situation occurs when the divisor is a decimal. In these cases, "clear" the fractional part of the decimal by moving the decimal point to the right. For example, if dividing by 0.1, change 0.1 to 1; if dividing by 2.11, convert that to 211 by moving the decimal point two places to the right. However, you must also move the decimal point of the dividend by the same number of places to ensure that their relative values are not changed. Notice that in the following examples both decimal points are moved the same number of places to the right.

Examples:

1. $5 \div 2.5 \Rightarrow 2.5 \overline{)5.0}$

    $$
    \begin{array}{r}
    2. \\
    2.5\overline{)5.0.} \\
    \underline{-5\ 0} \\
    0
    \end{array}
    $$

2. $10 \div 1.25 \Rightarrow 1.25 \overline{)10.00}$

    $$
    \begin{array}{r}
    8. \\
    1.25\overline{)10.00.} \\
    \underline{-10\ 00} \\
    0
    \end{array}
    $$

3. $50 \div 0.05 \Rightarrow 0.05 \overline{)50.00}$

    $$
    \begin{array}{r}
    1000. \\
    0.05\overline{)50.00.} \\
    \underline{-50\ 00} \\
    0
    \end{array}
    $$

There are two final things to say about dividing decimals. First, as mentioned previously, you can use division of decimals to convert fractions to decimals. For example, to convert $\frac{9}{2}$ to a decimal number, simply divide 9 by 2.

Examples:

1. $\frac{9}{2} = 2\overline{)9} \Rightarrow 2\overline{)9.0}$

    $$
    \begin{array}{r}
    4.5 \\
    2\overline{)9.0} \\
    \underline{-8} \\
    1\ 0 \\
    \underline{-1\ 0} \\
    0
    \end{array}
    $$

2. $\frac{3}{4} = 4\overline{)3} \Rightarrow 4\overline{)3.00}$

    $$
    \begin{array}{r}
    0.75 \\
    4\overline{)3.00} \\
    \underline{-2\ 8} \\
    2\ 0 \\
    \underline{-2\ 0} \\
    0
    \end{array}
    $$

Second, some fractions do not have exact decimal equivalents. Try converting $\frac{1}{3}$ to a decimal using the division route. You will be at it forever, because you get an endless succession of "3"s. Try converting $\frac{1}{9}$ a decimal using the division method. Again, you will get an endless succession, this time of repeating "1"s. By convention, repeating decimals are indicated using an overbar: $0.1\overline{1}$.

Decimals
Exercise 3

DIRECTIONS: Choose the correct answer to each of the following items. Answers are on page 605.

1. What is $\frac{7}{10}$ expressed as a decimal?

A. 70　　C. 0.7　　E. 0.0007
B. 7　　　D. 0.007

2. What is $\frac{21}{1,000}$ expressed as a decimal?

A. 0.21　　C. 0.0021　　E. 0.000021
B. 0.021　　D. 0.00021

3. What is $\frac{34}{10,000}$ expressed as a decimal?

A. 0.00034　　C. 0.034　　E. 3.4
B. 0.0034　　　D. 0.34

4. What is $\frac{30}{100}$ expressed as a decimal?

A. 3　　　C. 0.03　　E. 0.0003
B. 0.3　　D. 0.003

5. Which of the following is (are) equal to $\frac{1}{10}$?

I. 1.0
II. 0.1
III. 0.1000

A. I only　　　　D. II and III only
B. II only　　　　E. I, II, and III
C. III only

6. What is $\frac{257}{100}$ expressed as a decimal?

A. 25.7　　C. 0.257　　E. 0.00257
B. 2.57　　D. 0.0257

7. What is $\frac{5}{8}$ expressed as a decimal?

A. 0.125　　C. 0.850　　E. 5.80
B. 0.625　　D. 1.25

8. What is $\frac{1}{20}$ expressed as a decimal?

A. 0.05　　C. 0.0005　　E. 0.000005
B. 0.005　　D. 0.00005

9. What is $\frac{3}{200}$ expressed as a decimal?

A. 0.15　　C. 0.0015　　E. 0.000015
B. 0.015　　D. 0.00015

10. What is $\frac{17}{500}$ expressed as a decimal?

A. 0.175　　C. 0.0175　　E. 0.00034
B. 0.034　　D. 0.0034

11. What is $7\frac{4}{5}$ expressed as a decimal number?

A. 7.4　　C. 7.8　　E. 39.5
B. 7.45　　D. 8.25

12. What is $9\frac{2}{5}$ expressed as a decimal number?

A. 9.25　　C. 9.8　　E. 45
B. 9.4　　D. 18.5

13. What is $3\frac{5}{8}$ expressed as a decimal number?

A. 3.1　　C. 3.5　　E. 3.625
B. 3.2　　D. 3.6

14. What is $5\frac{3}{4}$ expressed as a decimal number?

   A. 5.3   C. 5.75   E. 5.84
   B. 5.34   D. 5.8

15. What is $2\frac{3}{10}$ expressed as a decimal number?

   A. 2.3   C. 2.7   E. 3.2
   B. 2.6   D. 2.8

16. What is $\frac{16}{5}$ expressed as a decimal number?

   A. 3.1   C. 3.25   E. 3.4
   B. 3.2   D. 3.3

17. What is $\frac{9}{2}$ expressed as a decimal number?

   A. 3.3   C. 4.1   E. 4.6
   B. 4.02   D. 4.5

18. What is $\frac{13}{4}$ expressed as a decimal number?

   A. 2.5   C. 3.1   E. 3.25
   B. 3   D. 3.2

19. What is $\frac{17}{8}$ expressed as a decimal number?

   A. 1.8   C. 2.125   E. 2.5
   B. 2.12   D. 2.2

20. What is $\frac{15}{4}$ expressed as a decimal number?

   A. 3.75   C. 4.1   E. 5
   B. 3.8   D. 4.12

21. What is 2.05 expressed as a fraction?

   A. 2   C. $2\frac{1}{2}$ E. $2\frac{19}{20}$

   B. $2\frac{1}{20}$ D. $2\frac{5}{6}$

22. What is 4.35 expressed as a mixed number?

   A. $4\frac{3}{35}$ C. $4\frac{7}{20}$ E. $4\frac{4}{5}$

   B. $4\frac{6}{20}$ D. $4\frac{3}{5}$

23. What is 7.3 expressed as a mixed number?

   A. $7\frac{3}{100}$ C. $7\frac{3}{5}$ E. $7\frac{3}{10}$

   B. $7\frac{3}{1000}$ D. $7\frac{2}{10}$

24. What is 0.45 expressed as a fraction?

   A. $\frac{8}{20}$ C. $\frac{11}{20}$ E. $\frac{5}{6}$

   B. $\frac{9}{20}$ D. $\frac{3}{5}$

25. What is 9.7 expressed as a mixed number?

   A. $9\frac{7}{10}$ C. $9\frac{9}{10}$ E. $10\frac{7}{10}$

   B. $9\frac{8}{10}$ D. 10

26. $0.1 + 0.1 = ?$

   A. 0.002   C. 0.2   E. 20
   B. 0.02   D. 2

27. $0.528 + 0.116 + 0.227 = ?$

   A. 0.871   C. 0.243   E. 0.0012
   B. 0.583   D. 0.112

28. $1.23 + 0.00001 = ?$

   A. 1.24   C. 1.23001   E. 1.230000001
   B. 1.2301   D. 1.2300001

29. $0.01 + 0.001 + 0.0001 + 0.00001 = ?$

A. 1   C. 0.1111   E. 0.001111
B. 0.10   D. 0.01111

30. $0.27 + 0.36 + 2.1117 + 3.77777 + 1.42 = ?$

A. 5.44   C. 8.11143   E. 14.002785
B. 7.93947   D. 12.223479

31. $0.7 - 0.3 = ?$

A. 0.004   C. 0.04   E. 0.4
B. 0.021   D. 0.21

32. $1.35 - 0.35 = ?$

A. 1   C. 0.1   E. 0.00001
B. 0.35   D. 0.0035

33. $1 - 0.00001 = ?$

A. 0.9   C. 0.999   E. 0.99999
B. 0.99   D. 0.9999

34. $0.1 \cdot 0.1 \cdot 0.1 = ?$

A. 0.3   C. 0.01   E. 0.0001
B. 0.1   D. 0.001

35. $0.11 \cdot 0.33 = ?$

A. 0.363   C. 0.00363   E. 0.0000363
B. 0.0363   D. 0.000363

36. $5 \cdot 0.25 = ?$

A. 1.25   C. 0.0125   E. 0.000125
B. 0.125   D. 0.00125

37. $100 \cdot 0.00052 = ?$

A. 0.0052   C. 5.2   E. 520
B. 0.052   D. 52

38. $1.000 \cdot 1.000 \cdot 1.000 \cdot 1.000 = ?$

A. 1   C. 0.01   E. 0.0001
B. 0.1   D. 0.001

39. $0.2 \div 5 = ?$

A. 0.4   C. 0.004   E. 0.00004
B. 0.04   D. 0.0004

40. $25.1 \div 2.51 = ?$

A. 100   C. 0.1   E. 0.001
B. 10   D. 0.01

41. $0.005 \div 0.005 = ?$

A. 1   C. 0.005   E. 0.00005
B. 0.5   D. 0.0005

42. $2 \div 2.5 = ?$

A. 8   C. 0.8   E. 0.008
B. 5   D. 0.5

43. $111 \div 0.111 = ?$

A. 1   C. 11   E. 1,000
B. 10   D. 110

44. $0.12345 \div 0.012345 = ?$

A. 100   C. 1   E. 0.01
B. 10   D. 0.1

45. $0.002 \div 0.00002 = ?$

A. 100   C. 0.1   E. 0.001
B. 10   D. 0.01

46. Express as a decimal: $\dfrac{3}{5} + \dfrac{5}{8}$.

A. 1.00   C. 1.225   E. 1.75
B. 1.115   D. 1.50

47. Find the average of $\frac{2}{3}$ and 0.75.

A. $\frac{9}{24}$ C. $\frac{17}{24}$ E. $\frac{23}{24}$

B. $\frac{14}{24}$ D. $\frac{21}{24}$

48. Find the average of 0.1, 0.01, and $\frac{1}{4}$.

A. 0.10   C. 0.50   E. 1.0
B. 0.12   D. 0.75

49. $\dfrac{12\frac{1}{3}}{0.2} = ?$

A. $\frac{1}{50}$ C. $\frac{85}{2}$ E. $\frac{225}{4}$

B. $\frac{3}{40}$ D. $\frac{185}{3}$

50. $0.1\left[\frac{1}{3} - 2\left(\frac{1}{2} - \frac{1}{4}\right)\right] = ?$

A. $-\frac{2}{15}$ C. $-\frac{1}{90}$ E. $\frac{3}{4}$

B. $-\frac{1}{60}$ D. $\frac{1}{2}$

51. For three months, Pete saved part of his monthly allowance. He saved $4.56 the first month, $3.82 the second month, and $5.06 the third month. How much did Pete save altogether?

A. $12.04   C. $13.04   E. $14.44
B. $12.44   D. $13.44

52. From an employee's salary of $190.57, an employer deducts $3.05 for social security and $5.68 for pension. What is the final amount of the check?

A. $180.84   C. $181.84   E. $182.84
B. $181.04   D. $182.04

53. If the outer radius of a metal pipe is 2.84 inches and the inner radius is 1.94 inches, what is the thickness, in inches, of the metal?

A. 0.85   C. 1.00   E. 1.25
B. 0.90   D. 1.18

54. Pete earns $20.56 on Monday, $32.90 on Tuesday, and $20.78 on Wednesday. He spends half of all that he earned during the 3 days. How much does he have left?

A. $36.12   C. $37.12   E. $38.12
B. $36.72   D. $37.72

55. What is the total cost of $3\frac{1}{2}$ pounds of meat at $1.70 per pound and 20 lemons at $0.60 per dozen?

A. $5.95   C. $6.95   E. $7.95
B. $6.45   D. $7.45

56. A reel of cable weighs 1,279 pounds. If the empty reel weighs 285 pounds and the cable weighs 7.1 pounds per foot, how many feet of cable are on the reel?

A. 140   C. 160   E. 180
B. 150   D. 170

57. How much will 345 fasteners at $4.20 per hundred cost?

A. $13.29   C. $14.29   E. $14.99
B. $13.99   D. $14.49

PERCENTS

A **percent** is a special type of fraction that always has a denominator equal to 100. The percent sign, "%," is shorthand for "$\dfrac{x}{100}$." For example, $67\% = \dfrac{67}{100}$.

Converting to and from Percents

Since percents are simply a special type of fraction, both fractions and decimals can be converted to percents, and vice versa. The easiest conversion is to change a decimal to a percent: move the decimal point two places to the right and add the percent sign.

Examples:

1. $0.27 = 27\%$

2. $0.50 = 50\%$

3. $0.275 = 27.5\%$

This substitutes "%" for two decimal places—simply a matter of changing things from one form into an equivalent form, which is a process we have already used in several ways. To change a percent back to a decimal, move the decimal point two places to the left and drop the percent sign.

Examples:

1. $27\% = 0.27$

2. $50\% = 0.50$

3. $27.5\% = 0.275$

You already know the rules for converting fractions to decimals, and vice versa. To convert a fraction to a percent, convert the fraction to a decimal and follow the rule above for converting decimals to percents.

Examples:

1. $\dfrac{3}{4} = 0.75 = 75\%$

2. $\dfrac{5}{8} = 0.625 = 62.5\%$

3. $\dfrac{1}{10} = 0.10 = 10\%$

To reverse the process, follow the rule above for converting percents to decimals, and then use the procedure outlined in the previous section for converting decimals to fractions.

Examples:

1. $75\% = 0.75 = \dfrac{75}{100} = \dfrac{3}{4}$

2. $62.5\% = 0.625 = \dfrac{625}{1,000} = \dfrac{5}{8}$

3. $10\% = 0.1 = \dfrac{1}{10}$

There are two tricky types of percents: those greater than 100% and those less than 1%. First, it is possible to have a percent that is larger than 100. This would be the result of converting a mixed number. Second, percents can also be less than 1, in which case they are written with decimals. However, these numbers follow the general rules outlined above. Similarly, fractions smaller than $\dfrac{1}{100}$ will yield a percent less than 1.

Examples:

1. $2\dfrac{3}{4} = 2.75 = 275\%$

2. $0.5\% = 0.005 = \dfrac{5}{1,000} = \dfrac{1}{200}$

3. $\dfrac{1}{2,500} = 0.0004 = 0.04\%$

Operations of Percents

Adding and Subtracting Percents

Percents are fractions, so they can be manipulated like other fractions. All percents have 100 as the denominator. It is easy to add and subtract percents because you already have a common denominator.

Examples:

1. Paul originally owned 25% of the stock of a certain company. He purchased another 15% of the stock privately, and he received a gift of another 10% of the stock. What percent of the stock of the company does Paul now own?

    ➤ $25\% + 15\% + 10\% = 50\%$

2. In a certain election, Peter and Mary received 50% of all the votes that were cast. If Peter received 20% of the votes cast in the election, what percent of the votes did Mary receive?

    ➤ $50\% - 20\% = 30\%$

Multiplying Percents

To multiply percents, first convert them to decimals and then multiply.

Example:

In a certain group, 80% of the people are wearing hats. If 60% of those wearing hats are also wearing gloves, what percent of the entire group is wearing both a hat and gloves?

➢ 60% of 80% = 60% • 80% = 0.60 • 0.80 = 0.48 = 48%

Dividing Percents

To divide percents, first convert them to decimals and then divide.

Example:

Peter is purchasing an item on a lay-away plan. If he pays weekly installments of 12.5% of the purchase price, how many weeks will it take for Peter to pay off the entire purchase price?

➢ $\dfrac{100\%}{12.5\%} = \dfrac{1}{0.125} = 8$ weeks

Percent Story Problems

Four basic variations of percent problems appear on the exam as story problems:

- What is x percent of something?
- This is what percent of that?
- This is a given percent of what?
- What is the percent change from this quantity to that quantity?

Notice that in each of the first three question forms, there is the phrase "of that" and the phrase "is this" ("this is"). When you set up a fraction for the percent, always place the "is this" value over the "of that" value. This allows us to write the "is-over-of" equation for percents: $\dfrac{\text{is}}{\text{of}} = \dfrac{\%}{100}$.

"What Is X Percent of Some Quantity?"

Percents are fractions, so in the question, "What is x percent of some quantity?", the "of" indicates multiplication.

Examples:

1. A certain class is made up of 125 students. If 60% of the students are men, how many men are in the class?

    ➢ 60% of $125 = 60\% • 125 = 0.60 • 125 = 75$.

2. If Sam originally had $25 and gave 25% of that amount to his friend Samantha, how much money did Sam give to Samantha?

    ➢ 25% of $25 = 25\% • 25 = 0.25 • 25 = \$6.25$.

3. If Paula had 50 marbles and gave 20% of them to her friend Paul, how many marbles did Paula give to Paul?

    ➢ 20% of $50 = 20\% • 50 = 0.20 • 50 = 10$.

Noting the slight variation in phrasing, "is this" can be represented by "what number." Therefore, you can use the "is-over-of" equation to solve for the unknown value.

Examples:

1. What number is 20% of 25?

   ➤ Simplify the item stem: "x is 20% of 25." Thus, $\dfrac{is}{of} = \dfrac{\%}{100} \Rightarrow \dfrac{x}{25} = \dfrac{20}{100} \Rightarrow x = \dfrac{20 \cdot 25}{100} = \dfrac{20}{4} = 5$.

2. If Paula had 50 marbles and gave 20% of them to her friend Paul, how many marbles did Paula give to Paul?

   ➤ Simplify the item stem: "x is 20% of 50." Thus, $\dfrac{is}{of} = \dfrac{\%}{100} \Rightarrow \dfrac{x}{50} = \dfrac{20}{100} \Rightarrow x = \dfrac{20 \cdot 50}{100} = \dfrac{20}{2} = 10$.

"What Percent Is This of That?"

A second common item involving percents has the form, "What percent is this of that?"

Example:

What percent is 3 of 12?

➤ Convert $\dfrac{3}{12}$ to a decimal and then change that decimal number to a percent: $\dfrac{3}{12} = \dfrac{1}{4} = 0.25 = 25\%$.

There are other ways of phrasing the same question:

- 3 is what percent of 12?
- Of 12, what percent is 3?

Note that all three versions of the same question are equivalent and represent three general forms:

- What percent is this of that?
- This is what percent of that?
- Of that, what percent is this?

Again, you can set up an "is-over-of" equation and solve for the unknown value.

Example:

5 is what percent of 25? Of 25, what percent is 5? What percent is 5 of 25?

➤ Notice that all three of these questions are equivalent: "5 is x% of 25." Set up the "is-over-of" equation and solve for the unknown: $\dfrac{is}{of} = \dfrac{\%}{100} \Rightarrow \dfrac{5}{25} = \dfrac{x}{100} \Rightarrow x = \dfrac{5 \cdot 100}{25} = \dfrac{100}{5} = 20\%$.

As long as you place the "is this" value in the numerator and the "of that" value in the denominator, you cannot make a mistake.

Examples:

1. What percent is 20 of 50?

   ➤ 20 is x% of 50: $\dfrac{is}{of} = \dfrac{\%}{100} \Rightarrow \dfrac{20}{50} = \dfrac{x}{100} \Rightarrow x = \dfrac{20 \cdot 100}{50} = 20 \cdot 2 = 40\%$.

2. Of 125, what percent is 25?

> 25 is x% of 125: $\dfrac{\text{is}}{\text{of}} = \dfrac{\%}{100} \Rightarrow \dfrac{25}{125} = \dfrac{x}{100} \Rightarrow x = \dfrac{25 \cdot 100}{125} = \dfrac{100}{5} = 20\%$.

3. 12 is what percent of 6?

> 12 is x% of 6: $\dfrac{\text{is}}{\text{of}} = \dfrac{\%}{100} \Rightarrow \dfrac{12}{6} = \dfrac{x}{100} \Rightarrow x = \dfrac{12 \cdot 100}{6} = 2 \cdot 100 = 200\%$.

No matter how wordy or otherwise difficult such items get, you can still use the "is-over-of" method by first simplifying the item stem.

Example:

John received a paycheck for $200. Of that amount, he paid Ed $25. What percent of the paycheck did John give Ed?

> Simplify the item stem: "$25 is x% of $200." Thus, $\dfrac{\text{is}}{\text{of}} = \dfrac{\%}{100} \Rightarrow \dfrac{\$25}{\$200} = \dfrac{x}{100} \Rightarrow x = \dfrac{25 \cdot 100}{200} = \dfrac{25}{2} = 12.5\%$.

"This Is X Percent of What?"

In the third type of percent problem, the task is to manipulate a given value and percent to determine the unknown total value. Again, you can use the "is-over-of" equation for this variation as well—simply solve for the unknown value.

Examples:

1. 5 is 20% of what number?

> 5 is 20% of x: $\dfrac{\text{is}}{\text{of}} = \dfrac{\%}{100} \Rightarrow \dfrac{5}{x} = \dfrac{20}{100} \Rightarrow x = \dfrac{5 \cdot 100}{20} = 5 \cdot 5 = 25$.

2. Seven students attended a field trip. If these seven students were $6\dfrac{1}{4}$% of all the 9th-graders, find the total number of 9th-graders.

> Simplify the item stem: "7 is 6.25% of x." Thus, $\dfrac{\text{is}}{\text{of}} = \dfrac{\%}{100} \Rightarrow \dfrac{7}{x} = \dfrac{6.25}{100} \Rightarrow x = \dfrac{7 \cdot 100}{6.25} = 7 \cdot 16 = 112$.

3. A television set discounted by 18% was sold for $459.20. What was the price of the set before the discount?

> If you take 18% off, then $100\% - 18\% = 82\%$ remains. Simplify the item stem: "$459.20 is 82% of x."
> Thus, $\dfrac{\text{is}}{\text{of}} = \dfrac{\%}{100} \Rightarrow \dfrac{\$459.20}{x} = \dfrac{82}{100} \Rightarrow x = \dfrac{459.20 \cdot 100}{82} = 5.6 \cdot 100 = \$560$.

Percent Change

The fourth type of percent problem involves a quantity change over time. This type of item asks you to express the relationship between the change and the original amount in percent terms. To solve, create a fraction that is then expressed as a percent. Think of this as the "change-over-original" equation, because the fraction places the change over the original amount.

Examples:

1. The price of an item increased from \$20 to \$25. What was the percent increase in the price?

   ➤ $\dfrac{\text{Change}}{\text{Original Amount}} = \dfrac{25 - 20}{20} = \dfrac{5}{20} = \dfrac{1}{4} = 0.25 = 25\%$.

2. Mary was earning \$16 per hour when she received a raise of \$4 per hour. Her hourly wage increased by what percentage?

   ➤ $\dfrac{\text{Change}}{\text{Original Amount}} = \dfrac{4}{16} = 0.25 = 25\%$.

The "change-over-original" trick works for decreases as well.

Examples:

1. A stock's value declined from \$50 per share to \$45 per share. What was the percent decrease in the value of a share?

   ➤ $\dfrac{\text{Change}}{\text{Original Amount}} = \dfrac{45 - 50}{50} = \dfrac{-5}{50} = -0.10 = -10\%$. The negative sign indicates that the percent change was a decrease.

2. Student enrollment at City University dropped from 5,000 students in 2000 to 4,000 students in 2010. What was the percent decrease in the number of students enrolled at City University?

   ➤ $\dfrac{\text{Change}}{\text{Original Amount}} = \dfrac{4{,}000 - 5{,}000}{5{,}000} = \dfrac{-1{,}000}{5{,}000} = -0.20 = -20\%$.

Percents
Exercise 4

DIRECTIONS: Choose the correct answer to each of the following items. Answers are on page 606.

1. What is 0.79 expressed as a percent?

A. 0.0079%   C. 0.79%   E. 79%
B. 0.079%   D. 7.9%

2. What is 0.111 expressed as a percent?

A. 111%   C. 1.11%   E. 0.0111%
B. 11.1%   D. 0.111%

3. What is 0.5555 expressed as a percent?

A. 5,555%   C. 55.55%   E. 0.555%
B. 555.5%   D. 5.555%

4. What is 0.7500 expressed as a percent?

A. 7,500%   C. 75%   E. 0.75%
B. 750%   D. 7.5%

5. What is 1.25 expressed as a percent?

A. 125%   C. 1.25%   E. 0.0125%
B. 12.5%   D. 0.125%

6. What is 0.015 expressed as a percent?

A. 15%   C. 0.15%   E. 0.0015%
B. 1.5%   D. 0.015%

7. What is 0.0333 expressed as a percent?

A. 3.33%   C. 0.0333%   E. 0.000333%
B. 0.333%   D. 0.00333%

8. What is 0.0100 expressed as a percent?

A. 1%   C. 0.001%   E. 0.1%
B. 0.01%   D. 0.0001%

9. What is 56% expressed as a decimal?

A. 5.6   C. 0.056   E. 0.00056
B. 0.56   D. 0.0056

10. What is 100% expressed as a decimal?

A. 100.0   C. 1.0   E. 0.001
B. 10.0   D. 0.1

11. What is 1,000% expressed as a decimal?

A. 1,000.0   C. 10.0   E. 0.01
B. 100.0   D. 1.0

12. What is 0.099% expressed as a decimal?

A. 99   C. 0.099   E. 0.00099
B. 0.99   D. 0.0099

13. What is 0.00100% expressed as a decimal?

A. 0.01   C. 0.0001   E. 0.000001
B. 0.001   D. 0.00001

14. What is $\frac{3}{100}$ expressed as a percent?

A. 300%   C. 3%   E. 0.03%
B. 30%   D. 0.3%

15. What is $\frac{100}{1,000}$ expressed as a percent?

A. 0.1%   C. 10%   E. 1,000%
B. 1.0%   D. 100%

16. What is $\frac{9}{1,000}$ as a percent?

A. 9%   C. 0.09%   E. 0.0009%
B. 0.9%   D. 0.009%

17. What is $\frac{4}{5}$ expressed as a percent?

    A. 4.5%   C. 45%   E. 450%
    B. 8%   D. 80%

18. What is $\frac{3}{75}$ expressed as a percent?

    A. 0.004%   C. 0.4%   E. 40%
    B. 0.04%   D. 4%

19. What is $\frac{111}{555}$ expressed as a percent?

    A. 222%   C. 22%   E. 2%
    B. 200%   D. 20%

20. What is $1\frac{1}{10}$ expressed as a percent?

    A. 110%   C. 1.1%   E. 0.011%
    B. 11%   D. 0.11%

21. What is $3\frac{1}{2}$ expressed as a percent?

    A. 0.35%   C. 35%   E. 3,500%
    B. 3.5%   D. 350%

22. What is $10\frac{1}{5}$ expressed as a percent?

    A. 10.02%   C. 100.2%   E. 1,020%
    B. 10.2%   D. 102%

23. What is $\frac{111}{100}$ expressed as a percent?

    A. 1,110%   C. 11.1%   E. 0.0111%
    B. 111%   D. 1.11%

24. What is $\frac{13}{5}$ expressed as a percent?

    A. 260%   C. 2.6%   E. 0.026%
    B. 26%   D. 0.26%

25. What is $\frac{22}{5}$ expressed as a percent?

    A. 440%   C. 4.4%   E. 0.044
    B. 44%   D. 0.44%

26. Which of the following is equal to 18%?

    A. $\frac{18}{1}$ C. $\frac{18}{100}$ E. $\frac{18}{10,000}$
    B. $\frac{18}{10}$ D. $\frac{18}{1,000}$

27. Which of the following is equal to 45%?

    A. $\frac{1}{9}$ C. $\frac{11}{19}$ E. $\frac{9}{10}$
    B. $\frac{9}{20}$ D. $\frac{3}{4}$

28. Which of the following is equal to 13.2%?

    A. 0.0132   C. 1.32   E. 132
    B. 0.132   D. 13.2

29. Which of the following is equal to 10.101%?

    A. 0.0010101   C. 0.10101   E. 10.101
    B. 0.010101   D. 1.0101

30. Which of the following is equal to 80.1%?

    A. $80\frac{1}{10}$ C. $\frac{801}{1,000}$ E. 0.00801
    B. 8.01   D. 0.0801

31. Which of the following is equal to 250%?

    A. $\frac{25}{1,000}$ C. $\frac{1}{4}$ E. 25
    B. $\frac{25}{100}$ D. 2.5

32. 37% + 42% = ?

    A. 6%   C. 106%   E. 154%
    B. 79%   D. 110%

33. 8% + 9% + 10% + 110% = ?

    A. 17%   C. 180%   E. 18,000%
    B. 137%   D. 1,800%

34. 0.02% + 0.005% = ?

    A. 7%   C. 1%   E. 0.025%
    B. 2.5%   D. 0.07%

35. 100% − 0.99% = ?

    A. 1%   C. 11%   E. 99.99%
    B. 9.9%   D. 99.01%

36. If John read 15% of the pages in a book on Monday and another 25% on Tuesday, what percent of the book did he read on Monday and Tuesday combined?

    A. 7.5%   C. 55%   E. 80%
    B. 40%   D. 75%

Items #37–38 refer to the following table:

SCHEDULE FOR COMPLETING PROJECT X					
	Mon.	Tues.	Wed.	Thurs.	Fri.
% of work to be completed each day	8%	17%	25%	33%	17%

37. By the end of which day is one-half of the work scheduled to be completed?

    A. Monday   C. Wednesday E. Friday
    B. Tuesday   D. Thursday

38. If production is on schedule, during which day will $\frac{2}{3}$ of the project have been completed?

    A. Monday   C. Wednesday E. Friday
    B. Tuesday   D. Thursday

39. If Edward spends 15% of his allowance on a book and another 25% on food, what percent of his allowance remains?

    A. 10%   C. 45%   E. 80%
    B. 40%   D. 60%

40. 1% of 100% = ?

    A. 0.01%   C. 1%   E. 100%
    B. 0.1%   D. 10%

41. If 75% of 240 cars in a certain parking lot are sedans, how many of the cars in the parking lot are sedans?

    A. 18   C. 60   E. 210
    B. 24   D. 180

42. What percent of 10 is 1?

    A. 0.1%   C. 10%   E. 1,000%
    B. 1%   D. 100%

43. 50 is what percent of 40?

    A. 125%   C. 80%   E. 8%
    B. 90%   D. 12.5%

44. What number is 250% of 12?

    A. 3   C. 24   E. 36
    B. 15   D. 30

45. If 25 of the employees at a bank are women and 15 are men, then what percent of the bank's employees are women?

    A. 37.5%   C. 60%   E. 90%
    B. 40%   D. 62.5%

46. If the price of an item increases from $5.00 to $8.00, the old price is what percent of the new price?

A. 20%   C. 62.5%   E. 160%
B. 60%   D. 92.5%

47. If the price of a share of stock drops from $200 to $160, the old price is what percent of the new price?

A. 20%   C. 50%   E. 125%
B. 25%   D. 80%

Items #48–50 refer to the following table:

ENROLLMENTS FOR A ONE-WEEK SEMINAR	
Week Number	**Number of Enrollees**
1	10
2	25
3	20
4	15
5	30

48. The number of people who enrolled for the seminar in Week 1 was what percent of the number of people who enrolled in Week 2?

A. 5%   C. 50%   E. 250%
B. 40%   D. 80%

49. The number of people who enrolled for the seminar in Week 5 was what percent of the number of people who enrolled in Week 4?

A. 15%   C. 50%   E. 200%
B. 25%   D. 100%

50. What was the percent decrease in the number of people enrolled for the seminar from Week 3 to Week 4?

A. 25%   C. 75%   E. $133\frac{1}{3}$%

B. $33\frac{1}{3}$%   D. 125%

51. If a textbook costs $30 plus 8.5% sales tax, what is the total cost of one textbook?

A. $3.55   C. $23.55   E. $33.55
B. $12.55   D. $32.55

52. How much is 2.3% of 90?

A. 1.07   C. 2.17   E. 2.3
B. 2.07   D. 2.7

53. The number of the question you are now reading is what percent of 1,000?

A. 0.053%   C. 5.3%   E. 530%
B. 0.53%   D. 53%

54. 80 is what percent of 20?

A. 4%   C. 40%   E. 400%
B. 8%   D. 200%

55. Mary's factory produces pencils at a cost to her company of $0.02 per pencil. If she sells them to a wholesaler at $0.05 each, what is her percent of profit based on her cost of $0.02 per pencil?

A. 25%   C. 75%   E. 150%
B. 50%   D. 100%

56. If the Wildcats won 10 out of 12 games, to the nearest whole percent, what percentage of their games did the Wildcats win?

A. 3   C. 38   E. 94
B. 8   D. 83

57. A stereo was discounted by 20% and sold at the discount price of $256. Which of the following equals the price of the stereo before the discount?

A. less than $300
B. between $300 and $308
C. between $308 and $316
D. between $316 and $324
E. more than $324

58. The regular price of a TV set is $118.80. Which of the following equals the price of the TV set after a sale reduction of 20%?

A. $158.60   C. $138.84   E. $29.70
B. $148.50   D. $95.04

59. Two dozen shuttlecocks and four badminton rackets are to be purchased for a playground. The shuttlecocks are priced at $0.35 each and the rackets at $2.75 each. The playground receives a discount of 30% from these prices. Which of the following equals the total cost of this equipment?

A. $7.29   C. $13.58   E. $19.40
B. $11.43   D. $18.60

60. A bag contains 800 coins. Of these, 10% are dimes, 30% are nickels, and the rest are quarters. Which of the following equals the amount of money in the bag?

A. less than $150
B. between $150 and $300
C. between $301 and $450
D. between $450 and $800
E. more than $800

61. A man insures 80% of his property and pays a $2\frac{1}{2}$% premium amounting to $348. What is the total value of his property?

A. $19,000   C. $18,000   E. $13,920
B. $18,400   D. $17,400

62. In a school in which 40% of the enrolled students are boys, 80% of the boys are present on a certain day. If 1,152 boys are present, which of the following equals the total school enrollment?

A. 1,440   C. 3,600   E. 5,760
B. 2,880   D. 5,400

63. The population of Stormville has increased from 80,000 to 100,000 in the last 20 years. Find the percent increase.

A. 20%   C. 80%   E. 10%
B. 25%   D. 60%

64. The Rubins bought their home for $120,000 and sold it for $240,000. Find the percent increase.

A. 100%   C. 200%   E. 150%
B. 50%   D. 300%

65. If enrollment at City University grew from 3,000 to 12,000 in the last 10 years, what was the percent increase in enrollment?

A. 25%   C. 300%   E. 400%
B. 125%   D. 330%

STATISTICAL MEASURES

Mean (or average), ***median***, ***mode***, ***range***, ***standard deviation***, and ***frequency distribution*** are types of statistics that can be determined for a given set of numbers. These statistics provide particular information about a particular set of data.

Mean

Calculating a Mean (Average)

To calculate an ***average (arithmetic mean)***, add the quantities contributing to the average and then divide that sum by the number of quantities involved. For example, the average of 3, 7, and 8 is $\frac{3+7+8}{3} = \frac{18}{3} = 6$. Typically, on the exam, the term "average" is used instead of "mean" or "arithmetic mean." The generalized formula for an average is given by the following equation.

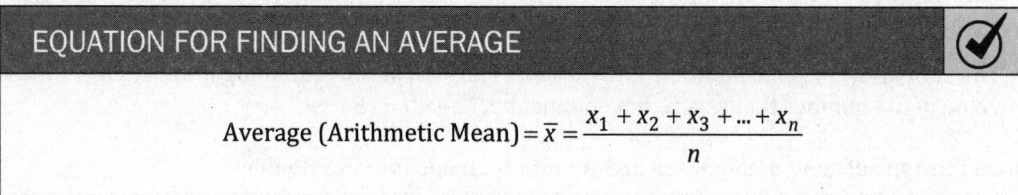

EQUATION FOR FINDING AN AVERAGE

$$\text{Average (Arithmetic Mean)} = \overline{x} = \frac{x_1 + x_2 + x_3 + \dots + x_n}{n}$$

Example:

A student's final grade is the average of her scores on five exams. If she receives scores of 78, 83, 82, 88, and 94, what is her final grade?

➢ To find the average, add the five grades and divide that sum by 5: $\frac{78 + 83 + 82 + 88 + 94}{5} = \frac{425}{5} = 85$.

It is possible that an easy item might ask that you find the average of a few numbers, as in the example above; however, items about averages can take several other forms.

Determining Missing Elements

Some items provide the average of a group of numbers and some—but not all—of the quantities involved. You are then asked to find the ***missing element(s)***. For example, if the average of 3, 8, and x is 6, what is the value of x? Since the average of the three numbers is 6, the sum or total of the three numbers is $3 \cdot 6 = 18$. The two given numbers are equal to $3 + 8 = 11$, so the third number must be $18 - 11 = 7$. Check the solution by averaging 3, 8, and 7: $\frac{3+8+7}{3} = \frac{18}{3} = 6$.

Examples:

1. For a certain five-day period, the average high temperature (in degrees Fahrenheit) for Chicago was 30°. If the high temperatures recorded for the first four of those days were 26°, 32°, 24°, and 35°, what was the high temperature recorded on the fifth day?

   ➢ The sum of the five numbers is $5 \cdot 30 = 150$. The sum for the four days we know about is: $26 + 32 + 24 + 35 = 117$. Thus, the fifth day must have had a high temperature of $150 - 117 = 33$. Note that this is the same as setting up an equation for the average and solving for the missing element:
   $$\frac{26 + 32 + 24 + 35 + x}{5} = 30 \Rightarrow x = (30 \cdot 5) - (26 + 32 + 24 + 35) = 150 - 117 = 33.$$

2. The average of Jose's scores on four tests is 90. If three of those scores are 89, 92, and 94, what is his fourth score?

   ➢ The sum of all four scores must be $4 \cdot 90 = 360$. The sum of the three known scores is $89 + 92 + 94 = 275$. Thus, the remaining score must be $360 - 275 = 85$. Note that this is the same as setting up an equation for the average and solving for the missing element:
   $$\frac{89 + 92 + 94 + x}{4} = 90 \Rightarrow x = (90 \cdot 4) - (89 + 92 + 94) = 360 - 275 = 85.$$

3. The average of a group of eight numbers is 9. If one of these numbers is removed from the group, the average of the remaining numbers is 7. What is the value of the number removed?

   ➢ The sum of the original numbers is $8 \cdot 9 = 72$. The sum of the remaining numbers is $7 \cdot 7 = 49$, so the value of the number that was removed must be $72 - 49 = 23$.

A variation on this type of an item might ask about more than one missing element.

Example:

In a group of children, three of the children are ages 7, 8, and 10, and the other two are the same age. If the average of the ages of all five children is 7, what is the age of the other two children?

➢ The total sum of the five ages must be $5 \cdot 7 = 35$. The known ages total only $7 + 8 + 10 = 25$, so the ages of the two other children must total 10. Since there are two of them, each one must be 5 years old.

Calculating Weighted Averages

In the average problems discussed thus far, each element in the average has been given equal weight. Sometimes, averages are created that give greater weight to one element than to another.

Example:

Cody bought 4 books that cost $6.00 each and 2 books that cost $3.00 each. What is the average cost of the 6 books?

➢ The average cost of the 6 books is not just the average of $6.00 and $3.00, which is $4.50. He bought more of the higher priced books, so the average must reflect that fact. One method is to treat each book as a separate expense: $\frac{6 + 6 + 6 + 6 + 3 + 3}{6} = \frac{30}{6} = 5$. Another method is to "weigh" the two different costs: $\frac{6(4) + 3(2)}{6} = \frac{30}{6} = 5$.

Median

The *median* of an odd number of data values is the middle value of the data set when it is arranged in ascending or descending order. The median of an even number of data values is the average of the two middle values of the data set when it is arranged in ascending or descending order.

Examples:

1. What is the median of $\{1, 1, 2, 3, 4, 5, 6, 7, 7, 7, 8, 8, 9\}$?

    ➤ The set contains an odd number of data values, so the median is the middle value: 6.

2. What is the median of $\{7, 9, 10, 16\}$?

    ➤ The set contains an even number of data values, so the median is the average of the two middle values: $\dfrac{9+10}{2} = 9.5$.

Mode

The *mode* is the value that appears most frequently in a set of data. Depending on the values in a particular set, some data sets have multiple modes, while others have no modes.

Examples:

1. The mode of $\{2, 4, 5, 5, 5, 6, 6, 19, 2\}$ is 5.

2. The group of numbers $\{-3, 5, 6, -3, -2, 7, 5, -3, 6, 5, 5, -3\}$ is bimodal: -3 and 5 each occur four times.

Range

There are several ways to measure the degree to which numerical data are spread out or dispersed. The *range* of a set of numbers is the simplest measure of the spread of the data. The range is the difference between the highest and lowest numbers in the set. Note that the range depends on only these two values in the data: the greater the spread in the data, the greater the range.

Example:

The range of $\{5, 10, 3, 24, 11, 4\}$ is $24 - 3 = 21$.

Frequency Distribution

Finally, a frequency distribution is a simple way of displaying how numerical data are distributed. This method arranges the data according to the varying frequencies with which the data occurs.

Example:

Display the following 15 numbers using a frequency distribution:
$\{-2, 0, 2, 0, 1, -1, 2, -1, 4, 0, -2, 2, -1, -1, 1\}$.

➢ Create a table that lists the different numerical values, x, in the data set and the frequencies, f, with which they occur:

x	f
−2	2
−1	4
0	3
1	2
2	3
4	1
Total	15

Statistical Measures
Exercise 5

DIRECTIONS: Choose the correct answer to each of the following items. Answers are on page 606.

1. What is the average of 8, 6, and 16?

    A. 10   C. 13   E. 18
    B. 12   D. 15

2. What is the average of 0 and 50?

    A. 0   C. 10   E. 50
    B. 5   D. 25

3. What is the average of 5, 11, 12, and 8?

    A. 6   C. 9   E. 12
    B. 8   D. 10

4. What is the average of 25, 28, 21, 30, and 36?

    A. 25   C. 29   E. 44
    B. 28   D. 34

5. What is the average of $\frac{1}{4}$, $\frac{3}{4}$, $\frac{5}{8}$, $\frac{1}{2}$, and $\frac{3}{8}$?

    A. $\frac{3}{32}$ C. $\frac{1}{2}$ E. $\frac{27}{32}$

    B. $\frac{5}{16}$ D. $\frac{5}{8}$

6. What is the average of $0.78, $0.45, $0.36, $0.98, $0.55, and $0.54?

    A. $0.49   C. $0.56   E. $0.61
    B. $0.54   D. $0.60

7. What is the average of 0.03, 0.11, 0.08, and 0.5?

    A. 0.18   C. 0.28   E. 1.0
    B. 0.25   D. 0.50

8. What is the average of 1,001, 1,002, 1,003, 1,004, and 1,005?

    A. 250   C. 1,003   E. 5,000
    B. 1,000   D. 2,500

9. What is the average of -8, -6, and -13?

    A. -15 C. -12 E. -8
    B. -13 D. -9

10. Jordan receives test scores of 79, 85, 90, 76, and 80. What is the average of these test scores?

    A. 82   C. 84   E. 86
    B. 83   D. 85

11. Mr. Whipple bought five different items costing $4.51, $6.25, $3.32, $4.48, and $2.19. What is the average cost of the five items?

    A. $3.40   C. $3.90   E. $4.15
    B. $3.80   D. $4.00

12. Nadia received scores of 8.5, 9.3, 8.2, and 9.0 in four different gymnastics events. What is the average of her scores?

    A. 8.5   C. 8.9   E. 9.1
    B. 8.75   D. 9

13. Five people have ages of 44, 33, 45, 44, and 29 years. What is the average of their ages in years?

    A. 36   C. 40   E. 43
    B. 39   D. 41

14. In a certain government office, if 360 staff hours are needed to process 120 building permit applications, on the average how long (in hours) does it take to process one application?

A. 3   C. 12   E. 36
B. 6   D. 24

15. In a chemical test for Substance X, a sample is divided into five equal parts. If the purity of the five parts is 84%, 89%, 87%, 90%, and 80%, then what is the overall purity of the sample (expressed as a percent of Substance X)?

A. 83   C. 86   E. 88
B. 84   D. 87

16. The average of three numbers is 24. If two of the numbers are 21 and 23, what is the third number?

A. 20   C. 26   E. 30
B. 24   D. 28

17. The average of three numbers is 5. If two of the numbers are zero, what is the third number?

A. 1   C. 5   E. 15
B. 3   D. 10

18. The average of the weight of four people is 166 pounds. If three of the people weigh 150 pounds, 200 pounds, and 180 pounds, what is the weight of the fourth person?

A. 134   C. 155   E. 165
B. 140   D. 161

19. For a certain student, the average of five test scores is 83. If four of the scores are 81, 79, 85, and 90, what is the fifth test score?

A. 83   C. 81   E. 79
B. 82   D. 80

20. Sue bought 10 items at an average price of $3.60. The cost of eight of the items totaled $30. If the other two items were the same price, what was the price she paid for each?

A. $15.00   C. $6.00   E. $1.50
B. $7.50   D. $3.00

21. In a certain shipment, the weights of 12 books average 2.75 pounds. If one of the books is removed, the weights of the remaining books average 2.70 pounds. What was the weight, in pounds, of the book that was removed?

A. 1.7   C. 3.0   E. 4.5
B. 2.3   D. 3.3

22. The average of a group of seven test scores is 80. If the lowest and the highest scores are thrown out, the average of the remaining scores is 78. What is the average of the lowest and highest scores?

A. 100   C. 90   E. 85
B. 95   D. 88

23. In a certain group, twelve of the children are age 10, and eight are age 15. What is the average of the ages of all the children in the group?

A. 9.5   C. 11   E. 12
B. 10.5   D. 11.5

24. Robert made the following deposits in a savings account:

Amount	Frequency
$15	4 times
$20	2 times
$25	4 times

What was the average of all the deposits Robert made?

A. $18.50   C. $21.50   E. $22.50
B. $20.00   D. $22.00

25. The average of the weights of six people sitting in a boat is 145 pounds. After a seventh person gets into the boat, the average of the weights of all seven people in the boat is 147 pounds. What is the weight, in pounds, of the seventh person?

A. 160   C. 155   E. 147
B. 159   D. 149

26. Find the mean of the following 5 numbers: 2, 3, 13, 15, and 1.

A. 4.6   C. 6.8   E. 16.8
B. 6.2   D. 8.6

27. Find the mean of the following 6 numbers: -3, 2, 6, 5, 2, and 0.

A. 1   C. 5   E. 8
B. 2   D. 6

28. If the mean of 6 numbers is 10, what is the sixth number if the five given numbers are -3, 5, 6, 13, and 17?

A. 12   C. 18   E. 22
B. 16   D. 20

29. The average of 5 numbers is 56. If two new numbers are added to the list, the average of the 7 numbers is 58. Which of the following equals the average of the two new numbers?

A. 64   C. 62   E. 60
B. 63   D. 61

30. Arranged in some order, $3x+1$, $2x+4$, and $x+10$ represent 3 consecutive whole numbers. If x represents a whole number and the average of the 3 numbers is 13, then solve for x.

A. 2   C. 6   E. 10
B. 4   D. 8

31. The ages of 100 female corporate officers is described in the frequency table below. What is the average of the women's ages?

Ages	Frequency
25	12
35	26
45	28
55	34

A. 16   C. 43.4   E. 45
B. 43   D. 44.3

Items #32–34 refer to the following information:

During the last 14 games, a basketball player scored the following points per game: 42, 35, 29, 42, 33, 37, 26, 38, 42, 47, 51, 33, 30, and 40.

32. What is the median score?

A. 35.4   C. 36   E. 38
B. 35.7   D. 37.5

33. What is the mode?

A. 35.4   C. 38   E. 44
B. 37.5   D. 42

34. If after one more game, the player's average for points per game is exactly 37, how many points did the player score in the fifteenth game?

A. 30   C. 37.5   E. 44
B. 37   D. 42

35. Find the median of the following 5 numbers: 1, 3, 7, 2, and 8.

A. 1   C. 3   E. 7
B. 2   D. 4.2

36. Find the median for the following data set: {2, −3, 8, 4, 9, −16, 12, 0, 4, 2, 1}.

    A. 4   C. 2   E. 0
    B. 2.1   D. 1

37. Find the median for the following data set: {2, −3, 8, 4, 9, −16, 12, 8, 4, 2}.

    A. 2   C. 3.5   E. 4.2
    B. 3   D. 4

38. Find the mode of the following five numbers: 4, 8, 10, 8, and 15.

    A. 4   C. 9   E. 15
    B. 8   D. 10

39. Find the mode of the following data set: {6, 8, 10, 2, −2, 2, 8, 4, 2}.

    A. 6   C. 4   E. 1
    B. 4.4   D. 2

40. A set of seven numbers contains the numbers 1, 4, 5, and 6. The other three numbers are represented by $2x+8$, $x-4$, and $7x-4$. If the mode of these seven numbers is a negative even integer, then what is a possible value for x?

    A. 0   C. 2   E. 5
    B. 1   D. 4

41. The grades received on a test by twenty students were 100, 55, 75, 80, 65, 65, 95, 90, 80, 45, 40, 50, 85, 85, 85, 80, 80, 70, 65, and 60. What is the average of these grades?

    A. 70.5   C. 77   E. 100
    B. 72.5   D. 80.3

42. Mr. Rodriquez had to purchase rulers for the students working on a schoolwide project. The frequency table below indicates the type, cost, and number of rulers purchased. What was the average price per ruler?

Type	Cost	Frequency
Six-inch	15¢	75
One-foot	30¢	100
One-yard	72¢	50

    A. $26\frac{1}{8}$ ¢   C. 39¢   E. $77\frac{1}{4}$ ¢

    B. $34\frac{1}{3}$ ¢   D. 42¢

43. What is the average grade for a student who received 90 in English, 84 in algebra, 75 in French, and 76 in music, if the subjects have the following weights: English 4, algebra 3, French 3, and music 1?

    A. 81   C. 82   E. 83

    B. $81\frac{1}{2}$ D. $82\frac{1}{2}$

Items #44–46 refer to the following information:

A census shows that on a certain neighborhood block the number of children in each family is 3, 4, 4, 0, 1, 2, 0, 2, and 2.

44. Find the average number of children per family.

    A. 4   C. $3\frac{1}{2}$ E. $1\frac{1}{2}$

    B. 3   D. 2

45. Find the median number of children.

    A. 1   C. 3   E. 5
    B. 2   D. 4

46. Find the mode of the number of children.

A. 0   C. 2   E. 4
B. 1   D. 3

47. What is the range for the set:
{2, 6, 35, 4, 42, 7, 16}?

A. 2   C. 16   E. 40
B. 7   D. 20

48. What is the range for the set:
{12, 3, 8, 23, 17, 45, 9}?

A. 7   C. 42   E. no range
B. 23   D. 45

49. Lucy went to the store and purchased five different bags of candy priced at $3.19, $2.99, $2.29, $3.09, and $2.49. What is the range of prices for the bags of candy purchased?

A. $0.59   C. $0.90   E. $1.29
B. $0.80   D. $1.00

50. The diameter of a rod is required to be 1.51 ± 0.015 inches. Which of the following represents the possible range of measurements for the rod's diameter?

A. 1.490 inches to 1.520 inches
B. 1.495 inches to 1.520 inches
C. 1.495 inches to 1.525 inches
D. 1.495 inches to 1.530 inches
E. 1.500 inches to 1.530 inches

51. A is a set containing five different numbers. B is a set containing four different numbers, all of which are members of A. Which of the following statements CANNOT be true?

A. The mean of A is equal to the mean of B.
B. The median of A is equal to the median of B.
C. The range of A is equal to the range of B.
D. The mean of A is greater than the mean of B.
E. The range of A is less than the range of B.

52. If the variables A, B, and C take on only the values 1, 2, 3, 4, or 5 with frequencies indicated by the shaded regions below, for which of the frequency distributions is the mean equal to the median?

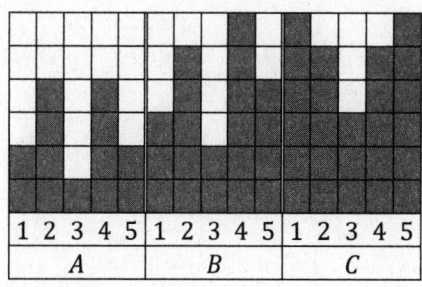

A. A only
B. B only
C. C only
D. A and C only
E. A, B, and C

RATIOS AND PROPORTIONS

Working with Ratios

Two-Part Ratios

A **ratio** is a statement about the relationship between any two quantities, or we might say a ratio is a statement that compares any two quantities. Suppose that in an English class there are five girls and eight boys. We can compare those quantities by saying that the ratio of girls to boys is 5 to 8. Conversely, the ratio of boys to girls is 8 to 5. Notice that order is very important in stating a ratio. The order of the numbers in the ratio must reflect the order of the categories being compared. In our example, it would be incorrect to say that the ratio of girls to boys is 8 to 5.

A phrase such as "5 to 8" is one way of stating a ratio, but there are several other ways. A ratio can also be described using a colon: "the ratio of girls to boys is $5:8$" and "the ratio of boys to girls is $8:5$." Alternatively, the ratio can be written in fraction form: "the ratio $\frac{girls}{boys}$ is $\frac{5}{8}$" and "the ratio $\frac{boys}{girls}$ is $\frac{8}{5}$."

Ratios of the form $a:b$ or $\frac{a}{b}$ can also refer to numbers instead of a number of objects. We can speak abstractly of the ratio $5:8$, which is the ratio of any set of five things to any set of eight things. Consequently, ratios can be manipulated in the same way as fractions. Just as you could rewrite a fraction to get a form with a different denominator, you can convert a ratio to an equivalent form by multiplying both terms of the ratio by the same number. For example, $\frac{5}{8} = \frac{5 \cdot 2}{8 \cdot 2} = \frac{10}{16}$ and $\frac{8}{5} = \frac{8 \cdot 3}{5 \cdot 3} = \frac{24}{15}$.

It is customary to reduce a ratio to its lowest terms just as you would reduce fractions to their lowest terms. For example, in a certain classroom, there are ten girls and sixteen boys; the ratio of girls to boys is $\frac{10}{16}$, which is $\frac{5}{8}$.

Although you may not be aware of it, you probably also use ratios informally in ordinary conversation. A common phrase that signifies a ratio is "for every (number)...there are (number)...." For example, in the classroom just described, for every 10 girls there are 16 boys, or in lowest terms, for every 5 girls there are 8 boys, and for every 8 boys there are 5 girls.

Finally, a ratio can also be stated as a rate using the word "per." If a car travels 200 miles and uses 10 gallons of fuel, the car gets 200 miles per 10 gallons, or 20 miles per gallon. Cost, too, is often described as a ratio. If it is possible to purchase a dozen greeting cards for $2.40, the cost of the cards is $2.40 per dozen, or 20 cents per card.

Three-Part Ratios

When three quantities are to be compared, they can be stated using ordinary ratios. For example, if a bowl of fruit contains two apples, three pears, and five oranges, the ratio of apples to pears is $2:3$; the ratio of apples to oranges is $2:5$; and the ratio of pears to oranges is $3:5$. This same information can also be conveyed in a single statement: the ratio of apples to pears to oranges is $2:3:5$.

A ***three-part ratio*** depends on the middle term to join the two outside terms. In our example, the ratio of apples to pears is $2:3$, and the ratio of pears to oranges is $3:5$. Since 3 is common to both ratios, it can be the middle term. Sometimes it will be necessary to find a common middle term.

Example:

On a certain day, a bank has the following rates of exchange: $\dfrac{\text{dollar}}{\text{mark}} = \dfrac{1}{3}$ and $\dfrac{\text{mark}}{\text{pound}} = \dfrac{6}{1}$. What is the ratio of dollars to pounds?

➤ To find the ratio dollars : pounds, we will use marks as the middle term. However, the ratio of dollars to marks is $1:3$, and the ratio of marks to pounds is $6:1$. We must change the first ratio to express it in terms of six marks rather than three marks. This is like finding a common denominator before adding fractions: $\dfrac{1}{3} = \dfrac{1 \cdot 2}{3 \cdot 2} = \dfrac{2}{6}$, so the ratio of dollars to marks is $2:6$, and the ratio of dollars to marks to pounds is $2:6:1$. Thus, the ratio of dollars to pounds is $2:1$.

Using Ratios to Divide Quantities

An item may require that you divide a quantity according to a certain ratio.

Examples:

1. A $100 prize is divided between two contestants according to the ratio $2:3$. How much does each contestant receive?

   ➤ Add the terms of the ratio to determine by how many parts the prize is to be divided. Divide the prize by that many parts, and multiply the result by the number of parts to be given to each contestant. The ratio $2:3$ has $2+3=5$ parts, so each part is $\$100 \div 5 = \$20$. One contestant receives $2 \cdot \$20 = \$40$, and the other contestant receives $3 \cdot \$20 = \$60$.

2. Bronze is 16 parts tin and 9 parts copper. If a bronze ingot weighs 100 pounds, how much does the tin weigh (in pounds)?

   ➤ First, the number of parts in the ratio $16:9$ is $16+9=25$. Second, $100 \div 25 = 4$, so each part is worth 4 pounds. Since there are 16 parts of tin, the tin must weigh $16 \cdot 4 = 64$ pounds.

Working with Proportions

A ***proportion*** is the mathematical equivalent of a verbal analogy. For example, $2:3::8:12$ is equivalent to "two is to three as eight is to twelve." The main difference between an analogy and a proportion is the precision. A verbal analogy depends upon words that do not have unique and precise meanings, while mathematical proportions are made up of numbers, which are exact.

In a mathematical proportion, the first and last terms are called the "extremes" of the proportion because they are on the extreme outside, and the two middle terms are called the "means" ("mean" can mean "middle"). In a mathematical proportion, the product of the extremes is always equal to the product of the means. For example, in the proportion $2:3::8:12$, $2 \cdot 12 = 3 \cdot 8$.

Determining the Missing Elements in Proportions

Since any ratio can be written as a fraction, a proportion, which states that two ratios are equivalent, can also be written in fractional form as an equation. This is the foundation for the process called cross-multiplication—a process that is useful in solving for an unknown element in a proportion.

Examples:

1. $\dfrac{2}{3} = \dfrac{8}{12} \Rightarrow \dfrac{2}{3} \diagup\!\!\!\!\diagdown \dfrac{8}{12} \Rightarrow 2 \cdot 12 = 3 \cdot 8$

2. $\dfrac{6}{9} = \dfrac{12}{x} \Rightarrow \dfrac{6}{9} \diagup\!\!\!\!\diagdown \dfrac{12}{x} \Rightarrow 6x = 108 \Rightarrow x = \dfrac{108}{6} = 18$

   ➤ Check the solution by substitution: $\dfrac{6}{9} \overset{?}{=} \dfrac{12}{18} \Rightarrow \dfrac{6}{9} \overset{?}{\diagup\!\!\!\!\diagdown} \dfrac{12}{18} \Rightarrow 6 \cdot 18 \overset{?}{=} 9 \cdot 12 \Rightarrow 108 = 108$.

3. $\dfrac{3}{15} = \dfrac{x}{45} \Rightarrow \dfrac{3}{15} \diagup\!\!\!\!\diagdown \dfrac{x}{45} \Rightarrow 3 \cdot 45 = 15x \Rightarrow x = \dfrac{135}{15} = 9$

   ➤ Check the solution by substitution: $\dfrac{3}{15} \overset{?}{=} \dfrac{9}{45} \Rightarrow \dfrac{3}{15} \overset{?}{\diagup\!\!\!\!\diagdown} \dfrac{9}{45} \Rightarrow 3 \cdot 45 \overset{?}{=} 15 \cdot 9 \Rightarrow 135 = 135$.

Direct Proportions

The use of proportions can be a powerful problem-solving tool. **Direct proportions** equate ratios of two quantities having a direct relationship. The more there is of one quantity, the more there is of the other quantity, and vice versa.

Example:

If the cost of a dozen donuts is \$3.60, what is the cost of 4 donuts? Assume there is no discount for buying in bulk.

➤ One method for solving this item is to calculate the cost of one donut $(\$3.60 \div 12 = \$0.30)$, and then multiply that cost by four $(\$0.30 \cdot 4 = \$1.20)$. While this approach is not incorrect, the same result can be reached in a conceptually simpler way. The more donuts being purchased, the greater the total cost, and vice versa. Relate the quantities using a direct proportion: $\dfrac{\text{Total Cost } X}{\text{Total Cost } Y} = \dfrac{\text{Number } X}{\text{Number } Y} \Rightarrow$

$$\dfrac{\$3.60}{x} = \dfrac{12 \text{ donuts}}{4 \text{ donuts}} \Rightarrow x = \dfrac{4 \cancel{\text{ donuts}} \cdot \$3.60}{12 \cancel{\text{ donuts}}} = \dfrac{\$3.60}{3} = \$1.20.$$

Note that in the previous example, we set up the proportion by grouping "like terms": the "cost of the donuts" is on one side of the proportion and the number of donuts is on the other side. It is equally correct to set up the proportion as $\dfrac{\text{Total Cost } X}{\text{Number } X} = \dfrac{\text{Total Cost } Y}{\text{Number } Y}$ or $\dfrac{\text{Number } X}{\text{Total Cost } X} = \dfrac{\text{Number } Y}{\text{Total Cost } Y}$. However, setting up direct proportions by grouping like terms is the first step in solving inverse proportions, as we'll see in the next subsection, so it is generally a good idea to group like terms to avoid confusion. The following examples illustrate additional typical situations involving direct proportions.

- The LONGER the travel time, the GREATER the distance traveled (and vice versa), assuming a CONSTANT speed.

  Example:

  If a plane moving at a constant speed flies 300 miles in 6 hours, how far will the plane fly in 8 hours?

  Use a direct proportion: $\dfrac{300 \text{ miles}}{x} = \dfrac{6 \text{ hours}}{8 \text{ hours}} \Rightarrow x = \dfrac{8 \text{ hours} \cdot 300 \text{ miles}}{6 \text{ hours}} = 400 \text{ miles}$.

- The LONGER the time of operation, the GREATER the output (and vice versa).

  Example:

  If an uninterrupted stamping machine operating at a constant rate postmarks 320 envelopes in 5 minutes, how long will it take the machine to postmark 480 envelopes?

  Use a direct proportion: $\dfrac{320 \text{ envelopes}}{480 \text{ envelopes}} = \dfrac{5 \text{ minutes}}{x} \Rightarrow x = \dfrac{480 \text{ envelopes} \cdot 5 \text{ minutes}}{320 \text{ envelopes}} = 7.5 \text{ minutes}$.

- The GREATER the number of items, the GREATER the weight (and vice versa).

  Example:

  If 20 jars of preserves weigh 25 pounds, how much do 15 jars of preserves weigh?

  Use a direct proportion: $\dfrac{20 \text{ jars}}{15 \text{ jars}} = \dfrac{25 \text{ pounds}}{x} \Rightarrow x = \dfrac{15 \text{ jars} \cdot 25 \text{ pounds}}{20 \text{ jars}} = 18.75 \text{ pounds}$.

Inverse Proportions

In some situations, quantities are related inversely; that is, an increase in one results in a decrease in the other, and vice versa. For example, the more workers doing a job, the less time it takes to finish the job. In this case, quantities are related inversely to each other. To solve problems involving inverse relationships, use the following procedure to set up an inverse proportion.

Step 1: Set up an ordinary proportion—make sure to group like terms.
Step 2: Invert one side of the proportion.
Step 3: Solve for the unknown quantity.

Example:

Traveling at a constant rate of 150 miles per hour, a plane makes the trip from Phoenix to Grand Junction in 4 hours. How long will the trip take if the plane flies at a constant rate of 200 miles per hour?

➤ The greater the rate of travel, the shorter the duration of the trip, so use an inverse proportion. First, set up a direct proportion, grouping like terms: $\dfrac{150 \text{ mph}}{200 \text{ mph}} = \dfrac{4 \text{ hours}}{x}$. Now, invert one side of the equation

and solve for the unknown quantity: $\dfrac{150 \text{ mph}}{200 \text{ mph}} = \dfrac{x}{4 \text{ hours}} \Rightarrow x = \dfrac{4 \text{ hours} \cdot 150 \text{ mph}}{200 \text{ mph}} = 3 \text{ hours}$.

While it is possible, though not advised, to set up a direct proportion without grouping like terms, for inverse proportions it is essential to group like terms. This is sufficient reasoning to always begin by grouping like terms, whether solving direct or inverse proportions.

Ratios and Proportions
Exercise 6

DIRECTIONS: Choose the correct answer to each of the following items. Answers are on page 606.

1. If a jar contains 3 blue marbles and 8 red marbles, what is the ratio of blue marbles to red marbles?

   A. 3:11   C. 8:3   E. 4:1
   B. 3:8   D. 11:3

2. If a school has 24 teachers and 480 students, what is the ratio of teachers to students?

   A. $\frac{1}{20}$ C. $\frac{1}{48}$ E. $\frac{1}{200}$

   B. $\frac{1}{24}$ D. $\frac{1}{56}$

3. If a library contains 12,000 works of fiction and 3,000 works of nonfiction, what is the ratio of works of fiction to works of nonfiction?

   A. $\frac{1}{9}$ C. $\frac{1}{4}$ E. $\frac{5}{1}$

   B. $\frac{1}{5}$ D. $\frac{4}{1}$

4. Which of the following is (are) equivalent to $\frac{1}{3}$?

   I. $\frac{40}{120}$

   II. $\frac{75}{100}$

   III. $\frac{120}{360}$

   A. I only   D. II and III only
   B. III only   E. I, II, and III
   C. I and III only

Items #5–6 refer to the following table:

STUDENTS AT TYLER JUNIOR HIGH SCHOOL		
	7th Grade	8th Grade
Girls	90	80
Boys	85	75

5. What is the ratio of the number of seventh-grade girls to the total number of girls at Tyler Junior High School?

   A. $\frac{9}{17}$ C. $\frac{18}{17}$ E. $\frac{17}{9}$

   B. $\frac{8}{9}$ D. $\frac{9}{8}$

6. What is the ratio of the number of eighth-grade girls to the total number of students at Tyler Junior High School?

   A. $\frac{8}{33}$ C. $\frac{8}{15}$ E. $\frac{17}{30}$

   B. $\frac{9}{33}$ D. $\frac{8}{17}$

7. If an airplane flies 275 miles on 25 gallons of fuel, then what is the average fuel consumption for the entire trip expressed in miles per gallon?

   A. 25   C. 15   E. 7
   B. 18   D. 11

8. An assortment of candy includes 12 chocolates, 6 caramels, and 9 mints. What is the ratio of chocolates : caramels : mints ?

   A. 4:3:2   C. 3:4:2   E. 2:4:3
   B. 4:2:3   D. 3:2:4

9. If Lucy has twice the amount of money that Ricky has, and Ricky has three times the amount of money that Ethel has, then what is the ratio of the amount of money Ethel has to the amount of money Lucy has?

A. $\dfrac{1}{8}$ C. $\dfrac{1}{4}$ E. $\dfrac{2}{1}$

B. $\dfrac{1}{6}$ D. $\dfrac{1}{2}$

10. If three farkels buy two kirns, and three kirns buy five pucks, then nine farkels buy how many pucks?

A. 2   C. 8   E. 17
B. 5   D. 10

11. If Machine X operates at twice the rate of Machine Y, and Machine Y operates at $\dfrac{2}{3}$ the rate of Machine Z, then what is the ratio of the rate of operation of Machine X to the rate of operation of Machine Z?

A. $\dfrac{4}{1}$ C. $\dfrac{4}{3}$ E. $\dfrac{1}{3}$

B. $\dfrac{3}{1}$ D. $\dfrac{3}{4}$

12. If 48 marbles are to be divided between Bill and Carl in the ratio of $3:5$, how many marbles should Bill get?

A. 6   C. 18   E. 30
B. 8   D. 24

13. If $10 is to be divided between Janeway and Nelix so that Nelix receives $\dfrac{1}{4}$ of what Janeway receives, then how much should Janeway receive?

A. $10.00   C. $7.50   E. $2.00
B. $8.00   D. $6.00

14. If a $1,000 reward is to be divided among three people in the ratio of $2:3:5$, what is the largest amount that will be given to any one of the three recipients?

A. $200   C. $500   E. $900
B. $300   D. $750

15. If $\dfrac{6}{8}=\dfrac{x}{4}$, then $x=?$

A. 12   C. 4   E. 2
B. 6   D. 3

16. If $\dfrac{14}{x}=\dfrac{2}{7}$, then $x=?$

A. 7   C. 28   E. 343
B. 14   D. 49

17. If $\dfrac{3}{4}=\dfrac{4}{x}$, then $x=?$

A. $\dfrac{3}{16}$ C. $\dfrac{4}{3}$ E. $\dfrac{16}{3}$

B. $\dfrac{3}{4}$ D. $\dfrac{7}{3}$

18. If 240 widgets cost $36, what is the cost of 180 widgets?

A. $8   C. $24   E. $32
B. $16   D. $27

19. If a kilogram of a certain cheese costs $9.60, what is the cost of 450 grams of the cheese? $\left(1 \text{ kilogram}=1,000 \text{ grams}\right)$

A. $2.78   C. $3.88   E. $5.12
B. $3.14   D. $4.32

20. If 50 feet of electrical wire cost $4.80, then $10.80 will buy how many feet of the wire?

A. 60   C. 67.25   E. 112.5
B. 62.5   D. 75

21. In a certain group of people, 100 people have red hair. If only 25% of the people have red hair, then how many people do not have red hair?

A. 75   C. 300   E. 500
B. 125   D. 400

22. If a certain fundraising project has raised $12,000, which is 20% of its goal, how much money will have been raised when 50% of the goal has been reached?

A. $60,000   C. $18,000   E. $4,800
B. $30,000   D. $15,000

23. If 48 liters of a certain liquid weigh 50 kilograms, then how much, in kilograms, will 72 liters of the liquid weigh?

A. 25   C. 75   E. 120
B. 60   D. 90

24. If the trip from Soldier Field to Wrigley Field takes two hours walking at a constant rate of four miles per hour, how long (in hours) will the same trip take walking at a constant rate of five miles per hour?

A. 2.5   C. 1.6   E. 1.25
B. 1.75   D. 1.5

25. A swimming pool is filled by either of two pipes. Pipe A supplies water at the rate of 200 gallons per hour and takes eight hours to fill the pool. If Pipe B can fill the pool in five hours, what is the rate (in gallons per hour) at which Pipe B supplies water?

A. 125   C. 360   E. 575
B. 320   D. 480

26. What is the ratio of 3 to 8 expressed as a decimal?

A. 0.125   C. 0.375   E. 1
B. 0.25   D. 0.50

27. If the ratio of 3 to 4 is the same as the ratio of 15 to x, find x.

A. 5   C. 15   E. 25
B. 10   D. 20

28. Annika can solve 10 math problems in 30 minutes. At this rate, how many math problems can she solve in 48 minutes?

A. 8   C. 32   E. 56
B. 16   D. 46

29. Seung can walk up 6 flights of stairs in 4 minutes. At this rate, how many flights of stairs could he walk up in 18 minutes?

A. 4   C. 14   E. 27
B. 10   D. 20

30. If 4 candy bars cost $1.04, how much should 6 candy bars cost?

A. $0.96   C. $1.56   E. $2.06
B. $1.25   D. $1.85

31. If Baby Andrew takes 8 steps to walk 2 yards, how many steps will he take to walk 5 yards?

A. 5   C. 15   E. 25
B. 10   D. 20

32. If a 40-inch stick is divided in a 3:5 ratio, how long, in inches, is the shorter piece?

A. 5   C. 15   E. 25
B. 10   D. 20

33. If Maria bicycles at an average speed of 15 miles per hour, her trip from the park to her house takes 3 hours. How long will the trip take, in hours, if she bicycles at an average rate of 20 miles per hour?

A. 2   C. 2.5   E. 2.8
B. 2.25   D. 2.75

34. If El kayaks at an average speed of 6 miles per hour, the trip across the lake takes 2 hours. How long will the trip take, in hours, if El's average speed is 5 miles per hour?

A. 1   C. 1.6   E. 2.4
B. 1.5   D. 2

35. If 6 printing presses all operating at the same rate take 10 hours to produce a run of books, how long will it take, in hours, for 8 such printing presses operating at the same rate to produce the same run of books?

A. 8.25   C. 7.5   E. 6
B. 8   D. 6.75

36. If a water hose flowing at a constant rate of 65 gallons per hour fills up a child's swimming pool in 1.4 hours, how long will it take, in hours, to fill the pool if the rate flowing through the hose is decreased to a constant rate of 25 gallons per hour?

A. 2.60   C. 3.50   E. 3.86
B. 3.28   D. 3.64

37. Carla has a small collection of 5 parrots which eat 3 pounds of sunflower seeds in 30 days. At this rate, if Carla decides to buy 3 more parrots, how long will it take, in days, for the parrots to eat the three-pound bag of sunflower seeds?

A. 18.75   C. 22.45   E. 25.2
B. 20.25   D. 25

38. Orville claims that 3 bags of his popcorn will yield 28 ounces when popped. If this is the case, how many ounces will 5 bags of his popcorn yield when popped?

A. 23   C. $54\frac{1}{2}$ E. $64\frac{2}{3}$

B. $46\frac{2}{3}$ D. 64

39. In a poll of 1,000 people, 420 said they would vote for Mason. Based on this poll, how many people would be expected to vote for Mason if 60,000,000 people actually vote?

A. 25,200,000 C. 26,000,000 E. 26,500,000
B. 25,500,000 D. 26,200,000

40. In 4 days, a worm grew from 5 centimeters to 12 centimeters. At this rate, how long, in centimeters, will the worm be in another 6 days?

A. 10.5   C. 22.25   E. 23
B. 22   D. 22.5

41. Elan can mow 3 lawns in 85 minutes. At this rate, how long would he need to mow 5 lawns?

A. 140 minutes, 20 seconds
B. 141 minutes
C. 141 minutes, 40 seconds
D. 142 minutes
E. 142 minutes, 50 seconds

42. Sarah does $\frac{1}{5}$ of a job in 6 minutes. At this rate, what fraction of the job will she do in 10 minutes?

A. $\frac{1}{4}$ C. $\frac{1}{2}$ E. $\frac{3}{2}$

B. $\frac{1}{3}$ D. $\frac{3}{4}$

43. A snapshot measures $2\frac{1}{2}$ inches by $1\frac{7}{8}$ inches. If it is enlarged so that the longer dimension is 4 inches, what is the length, in inches, of the enlarged shorter dimension?

A. $2\frac{1}{2}$ C. $3\frac{3}{8}$ E. 5

B. 3   D. 4

44. Three of the men's white handkerchiefs cost $2.29. How much will a dozen of those handkerchiefs cost?

A. $27.48 C. $9.16 E. $4.58
B. $13.74 D. $6.87

45. A certain pole casts a 24-foot-long shadow. At the same time another pole that is 3 feet high casts a 4-foot-long shadow. How high, in feet, is the first pole, given that the heights and shadows are in proportion?

A. 18 C. 20 E. 24
B. 19 D. 21

46. If a drawing is scaled $\frac{1}{8}$ inch to the foot, what is the actual length, in feet, represented by $3\frac{1}{2}$ inches on the drawing?

A. 3.5 C. 21 E. 120
B. 7 D. 28

47. Aluminum bronze consists of copper and aluminum, usually in the ratio of 10:1 by weight. If an object made of this alloy weighs 77 pounds, how many pounds of aluminum does it contain?

A. 0.7 C. 7.7 E. 77.0
B. 7.0 D. 70.7

48. It costs 31 cents per square foot to lay vinyl flooring. How much will it cost to lay 180 square feet of flooring?

A. $16.20 C. $55.80 E. $180.00
B. $18.60 D. $62.00

49. If Tuvak earns $352 in 16 days, how much will he earn in 117 days?

A. $3,050 C. $2,285 E. $1,170
B. $2,574 D. $2,080

50. Assuming that on a blueprint $\frac{1}{8}$ inch equals 12 inches of actual length, what is the actual length, in inches, of a steel bar represented on the blueprint by a line $3\frac{3}{4}$ inches long?

A. $3\frac{3}{4}$ C. 36 E. 450
B. 30 D. 360

51. Blake, James, and Staunton invested $9,000, $7,000, and $6,000, respectively. Their profits were to be divided according to the ratio of their investments. If James uses his share of the firm's profit of $825 to pay a personal debt of $230, how much will he have left?

A. $30.50 C. $34.50 E. $37.50
B. $32.50 D. $36.50

52. If on a road map $1\frac{5}{8}$ inches represents 10 miles, how many miles does 2.25 inches represent?

A. $\frac{180}{13}$ miles C. $\frac{57}{4}$ miles E. 3 miles
B. $\frac{53}{4}$ miles D. $\frac{27}{2}$ miles

53. Jake and Jessie are standing next to each other in the sun. If Jake's shadow is 48 inches long, and he is 72 inches tall, how long is Jessie's shadow, in inches, if she is 66 inches tall?

A. 42 C. 44 E. 46
B. 43 D. 45

54. A blueprint allows 1 inch for every 12 feet. At that rate, 7 inches represents how many yards?

A. $\frac{28}{3}$ C. 84 E. 336
B. 28 D. 252

55. A bug crawls clockwise around the outside rim of a clock from the 12 to the 4 and travels 7 inches. If a second bug crawls around the outside rim from the 6 to the 11, in the same direction, how many inches did the bug travel?

A. 7.75   C. 8.25   E. 8.75

B. 8   D. 8.5

EXPONENTS AND RADICALS

Powers and Exponents

Powers of Numbers

A ***power*** of a number indicates repeated multiplication. For example, "3 to the fifth power" means $3 \cdot 3 \cdot 3 \cdot 3 \cdot 3$, which equals 243. Therefore, 3 raised to the fifth power is 243.

Examples:

1. 2 to the second power $= 2 \cdot 2 = 4$.

2. 2 to the third power $= 2 \cdot 2 \cdot 2 = 8$.

3. 2 to the fourth power $= 2 \cdot 2 \cdot 2 \cdot 2 = 16$.

4. 3 to the second power $= 3 \cdot 3 = 9$.

5. 3 to the third power $= 3 \cdot 3 \cdot 3 = 27$.

The second power of a number is also called the square of the number. This refers to a square with sides equal in length to the number; the square of the number is equal to the area of the aforementioned square.

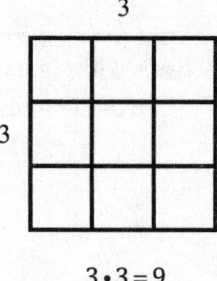

$$3 \cdot 3 = 9$$

The third power of a number is also called the cube of the number, which refers to a cube with sides equal in length to the number; the cube of the number is equal to the volume of the cube with sides equal in length to that number.

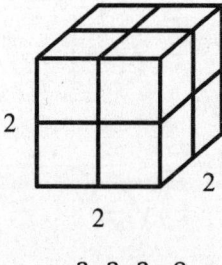

$$2 \cdot 2 \cdot 2 = 8$$

Beyond the square and the cube, powers are referred to by their numerical names, e.g., fourth, fifth, sixth, and so on.

Exponential Notation

The notation system for designating the power of a number is a superscript following the number. The number being multiplied is the **base**, and the superscript is the **exponent**. The exponent indicates the operation of repeated multiplication.

Examples:

1. The third power of 2 is written as 2^3 : base $\rightarrow 2^3 \leftarrow$ exponent $= 2 \cdot 2 \cdot 2$.

2. The fifth power of 3 is written as 3^5 : base $\rightarrow 3^5 \leftarrow$ exponent $= 3 \cdot 3 \cdot 3 \cdot 3 \cdot 3$.

A base without an exponent is unchanged and represents the **first power** of the number. Since $x^1 = x$, the exponent 1 is not explicitly noted.

Examples:

1. $2^1 = 2$

2. $1{,}000^1 = 1{,}000$

Operations Involving Exponents

There are special rules that apply to operations involving exponents. When you begin working with radicals (fractional exponents) and algebraic expressions, these same rules will apply.

Multiplication Involving Exponents

The **product rule** is used to multiply two identical bases with similar or different exponents. To multiply powers of the same base, add the exponents: $x^m \cdot x^n = x^{m+n}$. To better understand this rule, explicitly write out the multiplication indicated by the exponents.

Example:

$$2^2 \cdot 2^3 = 2^{2+3} = 2^5 = (2 \cdot 2)(2 \cdot 2 \cdot 2)$$

➤ Writing out the expression and using the product rule give you the same result, but it is much faster to apply the latter.

Therefore, the product rule provides an easy shortcut for multiplying identical bases with exponents.

Examples:

1. $3^2 \cdot 3^5 = 3^{(2+5)} = 3^7$

2. $5^2 \cdot 5^3 \cdot 5^5 = 5^{(2+3+5)} = 5^{10}$

3. $x^3 \cdot x^4 = x^{(3+4)} = x^7$

4. $y^7 \cdot y^2 \cdot y^4 = y^{(7+2+4)} = y^{13}$

Notice that each of these examples has only one base. The product rule does NOT apply to terms with different bases.

Example:

$2^4 \cdot 3^4 = ?$

➢ The product rule cannot be used since 2 and 3 are not equal bases. You must explicitly multiply all of the numbers: $2^4 \cdot 3^4 = (2 \cdot 2 \cdot 2 \cdot 2)(3 \cdot 3 \cdot 3 \cdot 3 \cdot) = 16 \cdot 81 = 1,296$.

Finally, the product rule does NOT apply to addition or subtraction of bases with exponents, even if the bases are identical.

Example:

$2^2 + 2^3 \neq 2^5$, since $2^2 + 2^3 = (2 \cdot 2) + (2 \cdot 2 \cdot 2) = 4 + 8 = 12$ and $2^5 = 2 \cdot 2 \cdot 2 \cdot 2 \cdot 2 = 32$.

Division Involving Exponents

The **quotient rule** is used for division involving identical bases with exponents. When dividing similar bases, subtract the exponent in the denominator from the exponent in the numerator: $\dfrac{x^m}{x^n} = x^{m-n}$. As with the product rule, the quotient rule can be verified by explicitly carrying out the indicated operations, as illustrated in the first of the following examples.

Examples:

1. $\dfrac{2^5}{2^3} = 2^{(5-3)} = 2^2$

   ➢ Writing out the expression and using the quotient rule give you the same result:
   $$\frac{2^5}{2^3} = \frac{2 \cdot 2 \cdot 2 \cdot 2 \cdot 2}{2 \cdot 2 \cdot 2} = \frac{32}{8} = 4 = 2^2.$$

2. $\dfrac{5^{10}}{5^9} = 5^{(10-9)} = 5^1 = 5$

3. $\dfrac{x^8}{x^6} = x^{(8-6)} = x^2$

4. $\dfrac{y^3}{y^2} = y^{(3-2)} = y^1 = y$

An **exponent of zero** results whenever a quantity is divided into itself. Since a quantity divided into itself is equal to 1, any base (except zero) with an exponent of zero is also equal to 1: $x^0 = 1$ **if** $x \neq 0$. 0^0 is an undefined operation in math.

Examples:

1. $\dfrac{5^3}{5^3} = 5^{(3-3)} = 5^0 = 1$

2. $\dfrac{x^{12}}{x^{12}} = x^{(12-12)} = x^0 = 1$

Raising a Power to a Power

The **power rule** is used when a power of a number is raised to another power. This is done by multiplying the exponents together: $\left(x^m\right)^n = x^{mn}$. Again, we can prove the validity of this shortcut by explicitly carrying out the indicated multiplications.

Examples:

1. $\left(2^2\right)^3 = 2^{(2 \cdot 3)} = 2^6$

   ➤ Writing out the expression and using the power rule give you the same result: $\left(2^2\right)^3 = (2 \cdot 2)^3 = 4^3 = 4 \cdot 4 \cdot 4 = 64 = 2^6$.

2. $\left(x^3\right)^4 = x^{(3 \cdot 4)} = x^{12}$

Raising a Product to a Power

The **product power rule** is used when a product with exponents is raised to a power. The exponent outside the parentheses governs all the factors inside the parentheses. When raising a product to a power, first multiply the exponent on the outside by each exponent on the inside: $\left(x^m y^p\right)^n = x^{mn} \cdot y^{pn}$.

Examples:

1. $(2 \cdot 3)^2 = 2^2 \cdot 3^2 = 4 \cdot 9 = 36$

   ➤ Writing out the expression and using the product power rule give you the same result:
   $(2 \cdot 3)^2 = (6)^2 = 36$.

2. $\left(2^2 \cdot 3^3\right)^2 = 2^{(2 \cdot 2)} \cdot 3^{(3 \cdot 2)} = \left(2^4\right)\left(3^6\right) = (16)(729) = 11{,}664$

3. $\left(x^2 \cdot y^3\right)^4 = x^{(2 \cdot 4)} \cdot y^{(3 \cdot 4)} = x^8 y^{12}$

Raising a Quotient to a Power

The **quotient power rule** is used when a quotient with exponents is raised to a power. It is essentially the same as the previous rule for determining the power of a product. The exponent outside the parentheses governs all the factors inside the parentheses. Determine the power of a quotient by multiplying the exponent on the outside by each exponent on the inside: $\left(\dfrac{x^m}{y^p}\right)^n = \dfrac{x^{mn}}{y^{pn}}$.

Examples:

1. $\left(\dfrac{2}{3}\right)^3 = \dfrac{2^3}{3^3} = \dfrac{8}{27}$

   ➤ Writing out the expression and using the quotient power rule give you the same result:

   $\left(\dfrac{2}{3}\right)^3 = \dfrac{2}{3} \cdot \dfrac{2}{3} \cdot \dfrac{2}{3} = \dfrac{2 \cdot 2 \cdot 2}{3 \cdot 3 \cdot 3} = \dfrac{8}{27}$.

2. $\left(\dfrac{1^2}{3^3}\right)^2 = \dfrac{1^{(2 \cdot 2)}}{3^{(3 \cdot 2)}} = \dfrac{1^4}{3^6} = \dfrac{1}{729}$

3. $\left(\dfrac{x^2}{y^3}\right)^2 = \dfrac{x^{(2 \cdot 2)}}{y^{(3 \cdot 2)}} = \dfrac{x^4}{y^6}$

Negative Exponents

Negative exponents do not signify negative numbers. Instead, they signify fractions. Specifically, a negative exponent indicates the power of the ***reciprocal*** of the base: $x^{-n} = \dfrac{1}{x^n}$.

Examples:

1. $\dfrac{2^2}{2^3} = 2^{(2-3)} = 2^{-1} = \dfrac{1}{2^1} = \dfrac{1}{2}$

2. $\dfrac{2^2}{2^3} = \dfrac{2 \cdot 2}{2 \cdot 2 \cdot 2} = \dfrac{4}{8} = \dfrac{1}{2}$

3. $3^{-2} = \left(\dfrac{1}{3}\right)^2 = \dfrac{1}{9}$

4. $x^{-3} = \left(\dfrac{1}{x}\right)^3 = \dfrac{1}{x^3}$

Rational (Fractional) Exponents

Exponents are not restricted to integer values. ***Rational (fractional) exponents*** are also possible. Later in this chapter, we will use rational exponents when working with radicals. Rational exponents also appear in algebraic expressions, functions, and equations. The rules for working with rational exponents are the same as those for integer exponents.

Examples:

1. $2^{\frac{1}{2}} \cdot 2^{\frac{1}{2}} = 2^{\frac{1}{2} + \frac{1}{2}} = 2^1 = 2$

2. $\left(x^2 y^4\right)^{\frac{1}{4}} = x^{2 \cdot \frac{1}{4}} y^{4 \cdot \frac{1}{4}} = x^{\frac{1}{2}} y$

Working with Exponents

Complex expressions may require the application of two or more operations involving exponents. No matter how complex an item gets, it can be solved by a series of simple steps following the five rules that are explained above for working with exponents. Remember to follow the rules for order of operations. Also, be careful when negative signs are involved.

Examples:

1. $\left(2^3 \cdot 3^2\right)^2 = 2^{3 \cdot 2} \cdot 3^{2 \cdot 2} = 2^6 \cdot 3^4$

2. $\left(\dfrac{3^3 \cdot 5^5}{3^2 \cdot 5^2}\right)^2 = \left(3^{3-2} \cdot 5^{5-2}\right)^2 = \left(3^1 \cdot 5^3\right)^2 = 3^2 \cdot 5^6$

3. $\left(\dfrac{x^2 \cdot y^3}{x \cdot y^2}\right)^2 = \left(x^{2-1} \cdot y^{3-2}\right)^2 = (x \cdot y)^2 = x^2 y^2$

4. $(-3)^3 (-2)^6 = (-27)(64) = -1{,}728$

5. $-2^4 (-3)^2 = -(2^4)(-3)^2 = -(16)(9) = -144$

These rules for working with exponents provide simple shortcuts, as verified by explicitly executing all indicated operations. When you begin to manipulate algebraic expressions, not only will these same shortcuts apply, but they will become indispensable.

SUMMARY OF OPERATIONS INVOLVING EXPONENTS

1. $x^1 = x$

2. $x^0 = 1$, if $x \neq 0$

3. Product Rule: $x^m \cdot x^n = x^{m+n}$

4. Quotient Rule: $\dfrac{x^m}{x^n} = x^{m-n}$

5. Power Rule: $\left(x^m\right)^n = x^{m \cdot n}$

6. Product Power Rule: $\left(x^m \cdot y^p\right)^n = x^{mn} \cdot y^{pn}$

7. Quotient Power Rule: $\left(\dfrac{x^m}{y^p}\right)^n = \dfrac{x^{mn}}{y^{pn}}$

8. Negative Exponents: $x^{-n} = \left(\dfrac{1}{x}\right)^n = \dfrac{1}{x^n}$

Roots and Radicals

Roots of Numbers

A ***square root*** of a number x is a solution to the equation $\sqrt{x} = b$, in which $x = b^2$. When you perform the multiplication indicated by an exponent, you are in effect answering the question, "What do I get when I multiply this number by itself so many times?" Now ask the opposite question, "What number, when multiplied by itself so many times, will give me a certain value?" For example, when you raise 2 to the third power, you find out that $2^3 = 8$. Now, ask the question in the other direction. What number, when raised to the third power, is equal to 8?

This reverse process is called "finding the root of a number." Why roots? Look at the following diagram; since $2^6 = 64$, the sixth root of 64 is 2. The picture resembles plant roots.

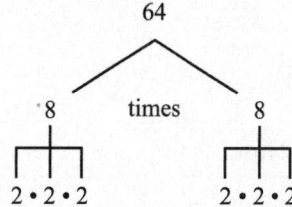

Of course, we rarely deal with sixth roots. Mostly, we deal with two roots: $2 \cdot 2 = 4$, so the second or ***square root*** of 4 is 2; and occasionally with numbers having three roots: $2 \cdot 2 \cdot 2 = 8$, so the third or ***cube root*** of 8 is 2.

The operation of taking a square root of a number is signaled by the ***radical*** sign, $\sqrt{\ }$. ***Radical*** comes from the Latin word "rad," which means "root."

Examples:

1. $\sqrt{1} = 1$	4. $\sqrt{16} = 4$	7. $\sqrt{49} = 7$	10. $\sqrt{100} = 10$
2. $\sqrt{4} = 2$	5. $\sqrt{25} = 5$	8. $\sqrt{64} = 8$	11. $\sqrt{121} = 11$
3. $\sqrt{9} = 3$	6. $\sqrt{36} = 6$	9. $\sqrt{81} = 9$	12. $\sqrt{144} = 12$

The symbol $\sqrt{\ }$ always denotes a positive number. Later, when we get to the topic of quadratic equations in algebra, we will run across a "$\pm$" sign preceding the radical; this signifies both the positive and negative values of the root.

If a radical sign is preceded by a superscript number, then the number, or ***index***, indicates a root other than the square root. In the notation $\sqrt[n]{a}$, n is the root or index, $\sqrt{\ }$ is the radical, and a is the radicand.

Examples:

1. $\sqrt[3]{8} = 2 \Rightarrow$ The cube root of 8 is 2.

2. $\sqrt[4]{81} = 3 \Rightarrow$ The fourth root of 81 is 3.

3. $\sqrt[6]{64} = 2 \Rightarrow$ The sixth root of 64 is 2.

Determining Square Roots

If a number is a perfect square (e.g., 4, 9, 16, etc.), then extracting its square root is easy. Simply use the values given in the examples of square roots above. Not every number, however, has an exact square root. In such cases, you can do one of two things. First, you may be able to find in the number a factor that does have an exact square root and extract that factor from under the radical sign.

Examples:

1. $\sqrt{125} = ?$

   ➤ 125 does not have a perfect square root. However, 25 has a perfect square and is a factor of 125, so factor 125 into 25 and 5: $\sqrt{125} = \sqrt{25 \cdot 5}$. Then, take the square root of 25, which is 5; $\sqrt{25} \cdot \sqrt{5} = 5 \cdot \sqrt{5}$. The final expression is $5\sqrt{5}$, which means 5 multiplied by the square root of 5: $\sqrt{125} = 5\sqrt{5}$.

2. $\sqrt{27} = \sqrt{9 \cdot 3} = \sqrt{9} \cdot \sqrt{3} = 3 \cdot \sqrt{3} = 3\sqrt{3}$

3. $\sqrt{32} = \sqrt{16 \cdot 2} = \sqrt{16} \cdot \sqrt{2} = 4 \cdot \sqrt{2} = 4\sqrt{2}$

4. $\sqrt{52} = \sqrt{4 \cdot 13} = \sqrt{4} \cdot \sqrt{13} = 2 \cdot \sqrt{13} = 2\sqrt{13}$

For the purposes of the exam, knowledge of the approximate values for common square roots may save valuable test time. For example, it is useful to know that $\sqrt{2}$ is approximately 1.4 and that $\sqrt{3}$ is approximately 1.7. Other values can be approximated by using ranges; e.g., $\sqrt{7}$ must be between 2 and 3 ($\sqrt{4} < \sqrt{7} < \sqrt{9}$). Since 7 is closer to 9 than to 4, a good approximation of $\sqrt{7}$ is 2.6 to 2.7.

Operations Involving Radicals (Rational Exponents)

Radicals can be rewritten using *rational (fractional) exponents*. This simplifies the process of working with radicals, since all of the rules for exponents apply to fractional exponents and thus to radicals. The relationship between a rational exponent and the radical representing a given root is: $\sqrt[n]{x^m} = x^{\frac{m}{n}}$, where m and n are integers, and $n \neq 0$.

Examples:

1. $\sqrt{4} = 4^{\frac{1}{2}} = 2$

2. $\sqrt[3]{8} = 8^{\frac{1}{3}} = 2$

When you multiply a square root by itself, the result is the radicand: $\left(\sqrt{x}\right)\left(\sqrt{x}\right) = x$. This can be explained using the product rule for exponents as illustrated in the following example.

Example:

$$\left(\sqrt{2}\right)\left(\sqrt{2}\right) = 2^{\frac{1}{2}} \cdot 2^{\frac{1}{2}} = 2^1 = 2$$

The power rules for working with exponents are the ones you are most likely to use when working with radicals. The following example illustrates how the product power rule applies to radicals.

Example:

$$\sqrt{125} = 125^{\frac{1}{2}} = (25 \cdot 5)^{\frac{1}{2}} = 25^{\frac{1}{2}} \cdot 5^{\frac{1}{2}} = \left(\sqrt{25}\right)\left(\sqrt{5}\right) = 5\sqrt{5}$$

Notice that this is just the process of extracting a square root by finding a factor, but what makes this process work is the product power rule of exponents. The quotient power rule is used in the following example.

Example:

$$\sqrt{\frac{4}{9}} = \left(\frac{4}{9}\right)^{\frac{1}{2}} = \frac{4^{\frac{1}{2}}}{9^{\frac{1}{2}}} = \frac{\sqrt{4}}{\sqrt{9}} = \frac{2}{3}$$

Importantly, since radicals are fractional exponents and obey the rules for exponents, you cannot simply add radicals. $\sqrt{4} + \sqrt{9}$ is not equal to $\sqrt{13}$, and you can prove this by taking the square root of 4, which is 2, and the square root of 9, which is 3. $2 + 3$ is 5, which does not equal $\sqrt{13}$.

OPERATIONS INVOLVING RADICALS (RATIONAL EXPONENTS)

1. **Product Rule:** $\sqrt{x} \cdot \sqrt{x} = x^{\frac{1}{2}} x^{\frac{1}{2}} = x^1 = x$

2. **Quotient Rule:** $\dfrac{\sqrt[m]{x}}{\sqrt[n]{x}} = \dfrac{x^{\frac{1}{m}}}{x^{\frac{1}{n}}} = x^{\left(\frac{1}{m} - \frac{1}{n}\right)}$

3. **Power Rule:** $\left(\sqrt[m]{x}\right)^n = \left(x^{\frac{1}{m}}\right)^n = x^{\frac{n}{m}}$

4. **Product Power Rule:** $\sqrt[m]{x^n y^p} = \left(x^n y^p\right)^{\frac{1}{m}} = x^{\frac{n}{m}} y^{\frac{p}{m}} = \sqrt[m]{x^n} \cdot \sqrt[m]{y^p}$

5. **Quotient Power Rule:** $\sqrt[m]{\dfrac{x^n}{y^p}} = \left(\dfrac{x^n}{y^p}\right)^{\frac{1}{m}} = \dfrac{x^{\frac{n}{m}}}{y^{\frac{p}{m}}} = \dfrac{\sqrt[m]{x^n}}{\sqrt[m]{y^p}}$

Exponents and Radicals
Exercise 7

DIRECTIONS: Choose the correct answer to each of the following items. Answers are on page 607.

1. What is the third power of 3?

A. 1   C. 9   E. 27
B. 3   D. 15

2. What is the fourth power of 2?

A. 2   C. 8   E. 32
B. 4   D. 16

3. What is the first power of 1,000,000?

A. 0   C. 1   E. 1,000,000

B. $\dfrac{1}{1,000,000}$ D. 10

4. $100^0 = ?$

A. 0   C. 10   E. 100,000
B. 1   D. 100

5. $2^3 \cdot 2^2 = ?$

A. 6   C. 2^5 E. 4^6
B. 8   D. 2^6

6. $3^{10} \cdot 10^3 = ?$

   I. 30^{30}
  II. $300 \cdot 1,000$
 III. $30 + 30$

A. I only   D. II and III only
B. II only   E. Neither I, II, nor III
C. I and III only

7. $5^4 \cdot 5^9 = ?$

A. 25^{36} C. 5^{13} E. 5
B. 5^{36} D. 5^5

8. $2^3 \cdot 2^4 \cdot 2^5 = ?$

A. 2^{12} C. 8^{12} E. 8^{60}
B. 2^{60} D. 4^{60}

9. $(2+3)^{20} = ?$

A. 5^{20} C. 6^{20} E. 20^6
B. $2^{20} + 3^{20}$ D. 20^5

10. $\dfrac{2^5}{2^3} = ?$

A. 2^2 C. 2^8 E. 2^{15}
B. 4^4 D. 4^8

11. $\dfrac{3^{10}}{3^8} = ?$

A. 3   C. 9^2 E. 3^{80}
B. 3^2 D. 3^{18}

12. $\dfrac{5^2}{5^2} = ?$

   I. 0
  II. 1
 III. 5^0

A. I and II only   D. III only
B. I and III only   E. Neither I, II, nor III
C. II and III only

13. $\dfrac{3^2}{3^3} = ?$

    I. 3^{-1}

    II. $\dfrac{1}{3}$

    III. -1

A. I only   D. I and III only
B. II only   E. I, II, and III
C. I and II only

14. $\left(2^2\right)^3 = ?$

A. 2^5 C. 4^5 E. 6^5
B. 2^6 D. 4^6

15. $\left(5^2\right)^6 = ?$

A. 5^8 C. 10^4 E. 10^{12}
B. 5^{12} D. 10^8

16. $\left(7^7\right)^7 = ?$

A. 21 C. 7^{49} E. 49^{49}
B. 7^{14} D. 21^7

17. $(3 \cdot 2)^2 = ?$

    I. 36
    II. $3 \cdot 3 \cdot 2 \cdot 2$
    III. $3^2 \cdot 2^2$

A. I only   D. I and III only
B. II only   E. I, II, and III
C. III only

18. $(5 \cdot 3)^2 = ?$

    I. 15^2
    II. $5^2 \cdot 3^2$
    III. 8^2

A. I only   D. I and II only
B. II only   E. I, II, and III
C. III only

19. $\left(\dfrac{8}{3}\right)^2 = ?$

    I. $\dfrac{64}{9}$

    II. $\dfrac{8^2}{3^2}$

    III. 11^2

A. I only   D. I and III only
B. II only   E. I, II, and III
C. I and II only

20. $\left(\dfrac{4}{9}\right)^2 = ?$

A. $\dfrac{2}{3}$ C. $\dfrac{16}{81}$ E. $\dfrac{4}{9^2}$

B. $\dfrac{4}{9}$ D. $\dfrac{4^2}{9}$

21. $\left(2 \cdot 2^2 \cdot 2^3\right)^2 = ?$

A. 2^8 C. 2^{12} E. 2^{18}
B. 2^{10} D. 2^{16}

22. $\left(\dfrac{2^4 \cdot 5^4}{2^2 \cdot 5^2}\right)^2 = ?$

A. $2^4 \cdot 5^4$ C. 4^6 E. 24
B. $2^6 \cdot 2^6$ D. 4^8

23. $\dfrac{3^6 \cdot 5^3 \cdot 7^9}{3^4 \cdot 5^3 \cdot 7^8} = ?$

   A. $3^2 \cdot 5 \cdot 7$ C. $3 \cdot 5 \cdot 7$ E. $3^2 \cdot 7$

   B. $3^2 \cdot 5 \cdot 7^2$ D. $3^2 \cdot 5$

24. $\left(\dfrac{5^{12} \cdot 7^5}{5^{11} \cdot 7^5} \right)^2 = ?$

   A. 25   C. 5^7 E. 7^5

   B. 49   D. 5^{11}

25. $\left(\dfrac{12^{12} \cdot 11^{11} \cdot 10^{10}}{12^{12} \cdot 11^{11} \cdot 10^9} \right)^2 = ?$

   A. 0   C. 10   E. 1,000

   B. 1   D. 100

26. $\sqrt{36} = ?$

   I. 6
   II. −6
   III. $3\sqrt{3}$

   A. I only   D. II and III only
   B. I and II only   E. I, II, and III
   C. I and III only

27. $\sqrt{27} = ?$

   A. 3   C. $3\sqrt{9}$ E. 81

   B. $3\sqrt{3}$ D. 27

28. $\sqrt{52} = ?$

   A. $\sqrt{5} + \sqrt{2}$ C. $2\sqrt{13}$ E. 13^2

   B. 7   D. $13\sqrt{4}$

29. $\sqrt{\dfrac{9}{4}} = ?$

   A. $\dfrac{\sqrt{3}}{2}$ C. $\dfrac{3}{2}$ E. $\sqrt{5}$

   B. $\dfrac{3}{\sqrt{2}}$ D. 5

30. $\dfrac{\sqrt{81}}{\sqrt{27}} = ?$

   A. $\sqrt{3}$ C. $3\sqrt{3}$ E. $9\sqrt{3}$

   B. 3   D. 9

31. $2\sqrt{2}$ is approximately equal to which of the following?

   A. 2.8   C. 4   E. 12

   B. 3.4   D. 7

32. $\sqrt{27}$ is approximately equal to which of the following?

   A. 3   C. 4.5   E. 9

   B. 4   D. 5.1

33. $\sqrt{12}$ is approximately equal to which of the following?

   A. 2   C. 4   E. 8

   B. 3.4   D. 6

34. $\sqrt{23}$ is approximately equal to which of the following?

   A. 4   C. 6   E. 8

   B. 4.8   D. 7

35. $\sqrt{45}$ is approximately equal to which of the following?

   A. 5   C. 6.6   E. 7.5

   B. 5.5   D. 7

36. $\sqrt{2} \cdot 2\sqrt{3} = ?$

    A. $-2\sqrt{6}$ C. 2   E. $2\sqrt{6}$
    B. $-\sqrt{6}$ D. $\sqrt{6}$

37. $\sqrt{3^2 + 5^2} = ?$

    A. 6   C. 7   E. 8
    B. $\sqrt{34}$ D. $\sqrt{51}$

38. $\sqrt{\left(2\sqrt{3}\right)^2 + 2^2} = ?$

    A. 1   C. 3   E. 5
    B. 2   D. 4

39. $\dfrac{15\sqrt{96}}{5\sqrt{2}} = ?$

    A. $7\sqrt{3}$ C. $11\sqrt{3}$ E. $40\sqrt{3}$
    B. $7\sqrt{12}$ D. $12\sqrt{3}$

40. Which of the following radicals is a perfect square?

    A. $\sqrt{0.4}$ C. $\sqrt{0.09}$ E. $\sqrt{0.025}$
    B. $\sqrt{0.9}$ D. $\sqrt{0.02}$

41. $\left(-\dfrac{1}{3}\right)^4 = ?$

    A. $-\dfrac{1}{81}$ C. $-\dfrac{1}{12}$ E. $-\dfrac{1}{64}$

    B. $\dfrac{1}{81}$ D. $\dfrac{1}{12}$

42. $-4^4 = ?$

    A. -256 C. -16 E. -8
    B. 256   D. 16

43. $\sqrt[12]{x^6} = ?$

    A. x^6 C. x^2 E. x^{-2}
    B. x^{-6} D. $x^{\frac{1}{2}}$

44. $\sqrt[k]{6^{2km}}$ MUST be a positive integer if:

    A. k is a positive integer.
    B. k is a multiple of 3.
    C. $k < 0$.
    D. m is a non-negative common fraction.
    E. m is a non-negative integer.

45. If n is an integer and 0.012345×10^n is greater than 10,000, what is the least possible value of n?

    A. 2   C. 4   E. 6
    B. 3   D. 5

ALGEBRAIC OPERATIONS

Algebra is the branch of mathematics that uses letter symbols to represent numbers. The letter symbols are, in essence, placeholders. They function somewhat like "someone" or "somewhere" in that they do not represent a definite value. For example, in the sentence "Someone took the book and put it somewhere," neither the identity of the person in question nor the new location of the book is known. We can rewrite this sentence in algebraic terms: "x put the book in y place." The identity of x is unknown, and the new location of the book is unknown. It is for this reason that letter symbols in algebra are often referred to as "unknowns."

Algebra, like English, is a language, and for making certain statements, algebra is much better than English. For example, the English statement "There is a number such that, when you add 3 to it, the result is 8" can be rendered more easily in algebraic notation: $x + 3 = 8$. In fact, learning the rules of algebra is really very much like learning the grammar of any language. Keeping this analogy between algebra and English in mind, let's begin by studying the components of the algebraic language.

Elements of Algebra

Algebraic Terms

The basic unit of the English language is the word. The basic unit of algebra is the **term**. In English, a word consists of one or more letters. In algebra, a term consists of one or more letters or numbers. For example, x, $2z$, xy, N, 2, $\sqrt{7}$, and π are all algebraic terms. A term can be a product, quotient, or single symbol.

In English, a word may have a root, a prefix, a suffix, an ending, and so on. In algebra, a term may have a coefficient, an exponent, and a sign, etc. Of course, algebraic terms also include a variable, also referred to as the base.

$$\underset{\text{coefficient}}{\nearrow} 3\underset{\text{variable}}{x}^{\overset{\text{exponent}}{\nwarrow}2} \qquad \underset{\text{coefficient}}{\nearrow}-2\underset{\text{variable}}{b}^{\overset{\text{exponent}}{\nwarrow}3} \qquad \underset{\text{variable}}{x}^{\overset{\text{exponent}}{\nwarrow}4}$$

Just as with numbers, when the sign of an algebraic term is positive, the " + " is not written; e.g., $3x$ is equivalent to $+3x$. Additionally, when the coefficient is 1, it is understood to be included and is not written out; e.g., x rather than $1x$.

The elements in an algebraic term are all joined by the operation of multiplication. The coefficient and its sign are multiplied by the variable. For example: $-3x = (-3)(x)$; $5a = (+5)(a)$; and $\frac{1}{2}N = (+\frac{1}{2})(N)$.

The exponent, as you have already learned, also indicates multiplication. Thus, x^2 means x times x; a^3 means a times a times a; and N^5 means N times N times N times N times N. Be careful not to confuse the coefficient with the exponent. $3x$ means "+3 times x," while x^3 means "x times x times x." Of course, many terms have both a coefficient and an exponent. Thus, $3x^2$ means "+3 times x times x," and $-5a^3$ means "−5 times a times a times a."

Algebraic Expressions

In English, words are organized into phrases. In algebra, terms are grouped together in ***expressions***. An expression is a collection of algebraic terms that are joined by addition, subtraction, or both.

Examples:

1. $x + y$

2. $-2x + 3y + z$

3. $3x^2 - 2y^2$

4. $x^2 + y^{20}$

A ***rational expression*** is a fraction containing algebraic terms. In other words, rational expressions are algebraic fractions.

Examples:

1. $\dfrac{1}{x}$

2. $\dfrac{x^2}{xy - y^2}$

3. $\dfrac{3 + \dfrac{1}{x}}{9 - \dfrac{1}{x^2}}$

Algebraic expressions are classified according to the number of terms the expression contains. A ***monomial*** is an algebraic expression with exactly one term. A ***polynomial*** is an algebraic expression with more than one term. A ***binomial*** is a polynomial with exactly two terms. A ***trinomial*** is a polynomial with exactly three terms.

The highest power of the variable term in any polynomial expression determines the degree of the polynomial. A ***first degree*** (or ***linear***) ***polynomial*** has 1 as the highest power of its variable. For example, $y + 3$ is a linear polynomial because the highest power of y is 1. A ***second degree*** (or ***quadratic***) ***polynomial*** has 2 as the highest power of its variable. For example, $3x^2 - 8x - 3$ is a quadratic polynomial because the highest power of x is 2.

Algebraic Equations

In algebra, a complete sentence is called an equation. An equation asserts that two algebraic expressions are equal. Equations involving rational expressions are called ***rational equations.***

Examples:

1. $2x + 4 = 3x - 2$

2. $\dfrac{y^2 - 5y}{y^2 - 4y - 5} = \dfrac{y}{y + 1}$

Operations of Algebraic Terms

Adding and Subtracting Algebraic Terms

Addition and subtraction are indicated in algebra, as they are in arithmetic, with the signs " + " and " − ." In arithmetic, these operations combine the numbers into one number. For example, the addition of 2 and 3 is equivalent to combining 2 and 3 to form the number 5: $2+3=5$.

In algebra, however, only **similar (like) terms** may be combined. Similar terms are terms with the same variables having the same exponent values. Coefficients do not factor into whether or not terms are similar.

Examples:

1. $3x^2$, $40x^2$, $-2x^2$, and $\sqrt{2}x^2$ are similar terms.

2. xy, $5xy$, $-23xy$, and πxy are similar terms.

3. $10xyz$, $-xyz$, and xyz are similar terms.

4. $3x$ and $3x^2$ are NOT similar terms.

5. xy and $x^2 y$ are NOT similar terms.

6. xy, yz, and xz are NOT similar terms.

To simplify an algebraic expression, group similar terms and add/subtract the numerical coefficients of each group. Variables and exponents of combined similar terms remain unchanged.

Examples:

1. $x^2 + 2x^2 + 3x^2 = ?$

   ➤ All three terms are similar since each includes x^2. Combine the terms by adding the coefficients: $1+2+3=6$. Thus, the result is $6x^2$.

2. $y + 2x + 3y - x = ?$

   ➤ With two different types of terms, group the similar terms together: $(2x - x) + (y + 3y)$. Add the coefficients for each type of term. For the x terms, the combined coefficient is $2-1=1$; for the y terms, $1+3=4$. The result is $x + 4y$.

3. $x - 3x + 5x - 2x = (1 - 3 + 5 - 2)x = x$

4. $2x - y - 3x + 4y + 5x = (2x - 3x + 5x) + (4y - y) = 4x + 3y$

5. $5x^2 + 3x^3 - 2x^2 + 4x^3 = \left(5x^2 - 2x^2\right) + \left(3x^3 + 4x^3\right) = 3x^2 + 7x^3$

Notice that when you have combined all similar terms, it is not possible to carry the addition or subtraction any further.

Multiplying and Dividing Algebraic Terms

Use the arithmetic **rules of exponents** to multiply or divide algebraic terms. Remember that $x^0 = 1$ **when** $x \neq 0$, and $x^1 = x$.

> ### OPERATIONS OF ALGEBRAIC TERMS
>
> 1. Product Rule: $x^m \cdot x^n = x^{m+n}$ and $ax^m \cdot bx^n = abx^{m+n}$
>
> 2. Quotient Rule: $\dfrac{x^m}{x^n} = x^{m-n}$
>
> 3. Power Rule: $\left(x^m\right)^n = x^{mn}$
>
> 4. Product Power Rule: $\left(x^m \cdot y^p\right)^n = x^{mn} \cdot y^{pn}$
>
> 5. Quotient Power Rule: $\left(\dfrac{x^m}{y^p}\right)^n = \dfrac{x^{mn}}{y^{pn}}$
>
> 6. Negative Exponents: $x^{-n} = \dfrac{1}{x^n}$

Examples:

1. *Product Rule:*

   a) $\left(x^2\right)\left(x^3\right) = x^{(2+3)} = x^5$

   b) $\left(3x^2\right)(xy) = (3 \cdot 1)\left(x^2 \cdot xy\right) = 3 \cdot x^{(2+1)} \cdot y = 3x^3 y$

   c) $(2xyz)(3xy)(4yz) = (2 \cdot 3 \cdot 4)(xyz \cdot xy \cdot yz) = 24 \cdot x^{(1+1)} \cdot y^{(1+1+1)} \cdot z^{(1+1)} = 24x^2 y^3 z^2$

2. *Quotient Rule:*

   a) $\dfrac{x^3}{x^2} = x^{(3-2)} = x^1 = x$

   b) $\dfrac{2x^4 y^3}{x^2 z} = \dfrac{2}{1} \cdot \dfrac{x^4 y^3}{x^2 z} = 2 \cdot \dfrac{x^{(4-2)} y^3}{z} = \dfrac{2x^2 y^3}{z}$

3. *Power Rule:* $\left(x^2\right)^3 = x^{(2)(3)} = x^6$

4. *Product Power Rule:* $\left(x^2 y^3\right)^2 = x^{(2)(2)} y^{(3)(2)} = x^4 y^6$

5. *Quotient Power Rule:* $\left(\dfrac{x^2}{y^3}\right)^2 = \dfrac{x^{(2)(2)}}{y^{(3)(2)}} = \dfrac{x^4}{y^6}$

Operations of Algebraic Fractions

Adding and Subtracting Algebraic Fractions

Adding and subtracting algebraic fractions, like adding and subtracting numerical fractions, require common denominators. If the denominators are the same, simply add/subtract the numerators: $\dfrac{a}{x} \pm \dfrac{b}{x} = \dfrac{a \pm b}{x}$.

Examples:

1. $\dfrac{5}{x} + \dfrac{3}{x} = \dfrac{5+3}{x} = \dfrac{8}{x}$

2. $\dfrac{2x}{y} - \dfrac{x}{y} = \dfrac{2x-x}{y} = \dfrac{x}{y}$

3. $\dfrac{a}{cd} + \dfrac{x}{cd} = \dfrac{a+x}{cd}$

To add or subtract algebraic fractions with unlike denominators, you must first find a common denominator. Usually, this can be accomplished by using the same method as with numerical fractions: $\dfrac{a}{x} \pm \dfrac{b}{y} = \dfrac{ay}{xy} \pm \dfrac{bx}{xy} = \dfrac{ay \pm bx}{xy}$.

Example:

$$\dfrac{2x}{y} + \dfrac{3y}{x} = \dfrac{2x}{y} \searrow + \nearrow \dfrac{3y}{x} = \dfrac{2x^2 + 3y^2}{xy}$$

Multiplying and Dividing Algebraic Fractions

To multiply algebraic fractions, follow the rule for multiplying numeric fractions. Multiply terms in the numerators to create a new numerator, and multiply terms in the denominator to create a new denominator: $\dfrac{a}{c} \cdot \dfrac{b}{d} = \dfrac{ab}{cd}$.

Examples:

1. $\dfrac{2}{x} \cdot \dfrac{3}{y} = \dfrac{6}{xy}$

2. $\dfrac{x^2 y^3}{z} \cdot \dfrac{x^3 y^2}{wz} = \dfrac{x^5 y^5}{wz^2}$

To divide algebraic fractions, follow the rule for dividing numeric fractions. Invert the divisor, or second fraction, and multiply: $\dfrac{a}{c} \div \dfrac{b}{d} = \dfrac{a}{c} \cdot \dfrac{d}{b} = \dfrac{ad}{cb}$.

Examples:

1. $\dfrac{2}{y} \div \dfrac{3}{x} = \dfrac{2}{y} \cdot \dfrac{x}{3} = \dfrac{2x}{3y}$

2. $\dfrac{2x^2}{y} \div \dfrac{y}{x} = \dfrac{2x^2}{y} \cdot \dfrac{x}{y} = \dfrac{2x^3}{y^2}$

Multiplying Algebraic Expressions

A *polynomial* is an algebraic expression with one or more terms involving only the operations of addition, subtraction, and multiplication of variables. Polynomial means "many terms," although it is possible to get a monomial by adding two polynomials. A multiplication item such as $(x+y)(x+y)$ requires a special procedure. The fundamental rule for multiplying is that every term of one expression must be multiplied by every term of the other expression.

Distributive Property

First, let's look at the case in which a polynomial is to be multiplied by a single term. One way of solving the item is to first add and then multiply. Alternatively, we can use the **distributive property** to multiply every term inside the parentheses by the term outside the parentheses, and then we can add the terms: $x(y+z) = xy + xz$. The result is the same regardless of the method used. The following example illustrates these two methods using real numbers.

Example:

$2(3+4+5) = 2(12) = 24$

➤ The distributive property returns the same result: $2(3+4+5) = (2 \cdot 3) + (2 \cdot 4) + (2 \cdot 5) = 6 + 8 + 10 = 24$.

When working with algebraic expressions, use the distributive property, since you cannot add unlike terms. The following examples apply the distributive property to algebraic expressions.

Examples:

1. $x(y+z) = xy + xz$

2. $a(b+c+d) = ab + ac + ad$

To multiply two polynomials, either add the polynomials before multiplying them, or reverse the order of operations using the distributive property.

Example:

$(2+3)(1+3+4) = (5)(8) = 40$

➤ The distributive property returns the same result:

$(2+3)(1+3+4) = (2 \cdot 1) + (2 \cdot 3) + (2 \cdot 4) + (3 \cdot 1) + (3 \cdot 3) + (3 \cdot 4) = 2 + 6 + 8 + 3 + 9 + 12 = 40$.

FOIL Method

To multiply two binomials using the **FOIL method**, follow these steps for combining the binomial terms: (1) multiply the first terms, (2) multiply the outer terms, (3) multiply the inner terms, (4) multiply the last terms, and (5) combine like terms. The FOIL method is simply a mnemonic shortcut derived from the distributive property. The following diagram illustrates application of the FOIL method.

MULTIPLYING TWO BINOMIALS ✓

(FOIL: First, Outer, Inner, Last)

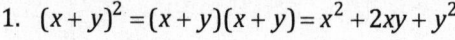

$$(x + y)(x + y) = x^2 + xy + xy + y^2 = x^2 + 2xy + y^2$$

Examples:

1. $(x + y)(x - y) = ?$

   ➢ First: $(x)(x) = x^2$.
   Outer: $(x)(-y) = -xy$.
   Inner: $(y)(x) = xy$.
   Last: $(y)(-y) = y^2$.
   Add: $x^2 - xy + xy + y^2 = x^2 + y^2$.

2. $(x - y)(x - y) = ?$

   ➢ First: $(x)(x) = x^2$.
   Outer: $(x)(-y) = -xy$.
   Inner: $(-y)(x) = -xy$.
   Last: $(-y)(-y) = y^2$.
   Add: $x^2 - xy - xy + y^2 = x^2 - 2xy + y^2$.

Three situations, one in addition to the two illustrated in the previous examples, arise with such frequency that you should memorize the results to simplify the calculation.

THREE COMMON MULTIPLICATIONS INVOLVING POLYNOMIALS ♞

1. $(x + y)^2 = (x + y)(x + y) = x^2 + 2xy + y^2$

2. $(x - y)^2 = (x - y)(x - y) = x^2 - 2xy + y^2$

3. $(x + y)(x - y) = x^2 - y^2$

You might be asked to multiply something more complex than two binomials. The process is tedious and time-consuming, but ultimately it is executed the same way.

Example:

$(x+y)^3 = ?$

➢ Apply the FOIL method to the first two binomials, then multiply the last binomial to the resultant trinomial of the first two binomials:

$$(x+y)^3 = (x+y)(x+y)(x+y)$$
$$= \left(x^2 + 2xy + y^2\right)(x+y)$$
$$= x\left(x^2\right) + x(2xy) + x\left(y^2\right) + y\left(x^2\right) + y(2xy) + y\left(y^2\right)$$
$$= x^3 + 2x^2 y + xy^2 + x^2 y + 2xy^2 + y^3$$
$$= x^3 + 3x^2 y + 3xy^2 + y^3$$

Factoring Algebraic Expressions

Although the term ***factoring*** intimidates many students, factoring is really nothing more than reverse multiplication. For example, if $(x+y)(x+y) = x^2 + 2xy + y^2$, then $x^2 + 2xy + y^2$ can be factored into $(x+y)(x+y)$. Fortunately, for the purposes of taking the test, any factoring you might need to do will fall into one of three categories.

Finding a Common Factor

If all the terms of an algebraic expression contain a common factor, then that term can be factored out of the expression.

Examples:

1. $ab + ac + ad = a(b+c+d)$

2. $abx + aby + abz = ab(x+y+z)$

3. $x^2 + x^3 + x^4 = x^2\left(1 + x + x^2\right)$

4. $3a + 6a^2 + 9a^3 = 3a\left(1 + 2a + 3a^2\right)$

Reversing a Known Polynomial Multiplication Process

Three patterns recur with such frequency on the exam that you should memorize them. These patterns are the same as the ones you were encouraged to memorize in the discussion of the FOIL method.

THREE COMMON POLYNOMIAL MULTIPLICATION REVERSALS

1. Perfect square trinomial: $x^2 + 2xy + y^2 = (x+y)(x+y)$

2. Perfect square trinomial: $x^2 - 2xy + y^2 = (x-y)(x-y)$

3. Difference of two squares: $x^2 - y^2 = (x+y)(x-y)$

Reversing an Unknown Polynomial Multiplication Process

Occasionally, you may find it necessary to factor an expression that does not fall into one of the three categories presented above. The expression will most likely have the form $ax^2 + bx + c$; e.g., $x^2 + 2x + 1$. To factor such expressions, set up a blank diagram: $(\quad)(\quad)$. Then, fill in the diagram by answering the following series of questions.

Step 1: What factors will produce the first term, ax^2?
Step 2: What possible factors will produce the last term, c?
Step 3: Which of the possible factors from step 2, when added together, will produce the middle term, bx?

Examples:

1. Factor $x^2 + 3x + 2$.

   ➤ What factors will produce the first term, ax^2, where $a = 1$? x times x yields x^2, so the factors, in part, are $(x\quad)(x\quad)$. What possible factors will produce the last term? The possibilities are $\{2, 1\}$ and $\{-2, -1\}$. Which of the two sets of factors just mentioned, when added together, will produce a result of $+3x$? The answer is $\{2, 1\}$: $2 + 1 = 3$, as the FOIL method confirms: $(x+2)(x+1) =$ $x^2 + x + 2x + 2 = x^2 + 3x + 2$.

2. Factor $x^2 + 4x - 12$.

   ➤ What factors will generate x^2? $(x\quad)(x\quad)$. What factors will generate -12? $\{1, -12\}$, $\{12, -1\}$, $\{2, -6\}$, $\{6, -2\}$, $\{3, -4\}$, and $\{4, -3\}$. Which factors, when added together, will produce the middle term of $+4x$? The answer is $\{6, -2\}$: $6 + (-2) = 4$. Thus, the factors are $(x+6)$ and $(x-2)$, as the FOIL method confirms: $(x+6)(x-2) = (x+6)(x-2) = x^2 - 2x + 6x - 12 = x^2 + 4x - 12$.

Absolute Value in Algebraic Expressions

Algebraic terms involving absolute values are treated the same way as numeric absolute values. Remember that the absolute value of any term is always a positive numerical value.

Examples:

1. If $w = -3, |w| = ?$

   ➤ Since the value of w is less than zero, $|w| = -w = -(-3) = 3$.

2. Let x be a member of the following set: $\{-11, -10, -9, -8, -7, -6, -5, -4, -3, -2, -1, 0, 1, 2, 3, 4\}$. $\dfrac{|2x - |x||}{3}$ is a positive integer for how many different numbers in the set?

   ➤ If $x < 0$, then $|x| = -x$: $\dfrac{|2x - |x||}{3} = \dfrac{|2x - (-x)|}{3} = \dfrac{|2x + x|}{3} = \dfrac{|3x|}{3} = |x|$, which is always a positive. Therefore, $\dfrac{|2x - |x||}{3}$ is a positive integer for all numbers in the set less than zero. If $x \geq 0$, then $|x| = x$: $\dfrac{|2x - |x||}{3} = \dfrac{|2x - x|}{3} = \dfrac{|x|}{3} = \dfrac{x}{3}$. Thus, the only other number in the set that returns a positive integer is 3. The total number of values in the set that satisfy the condition is: $11 + 1 = 12$.

Radicals in Algebraic Expressions

Radicals in algebraic expressions are manipulated in the same way as numeric radicals using the rules of exponents.

Example:

Does $\dfrac{3\sqrt{x} + \sqrt{x^3}}{x} = \dfrac{3}{\sqrt{x}} + \sqrt{x}$?

➤ $\dfrac{3\sqrt{x} + \sqrt{x^3}}{x} = \dfrac{3\sqrt{x}}{x} + \dfrac{\sqrt{x^3}}{x} = \dfrac{3x^{\frac{1}{2}}}{x} + \dfrac{x^{\frac{3}{2}}}{x} = 3x^{\left(\frac{1}{2} - 1\right)} + x^{\left(\frac{3}{2} - 1\right)} = 3x^{-\frac{1}{2}} + x^{\frac{1}{2}} = \dfrac{3}{\sqrt{x}} + \sqrt{x}$.

When simplifying expressions containing roots and radicals that are inverse operations of one another, it is important to note that the sign of the variable impacts the sign of the result. Consider $\sqrt{x^2}$. If $x \geq 0$, then $\sqrt{x^2} = x$; if $x < 0$, then $\sqrt{x^2} = -x$.

Examples:

1. $\sqrt{2^2} = 2$.

2. $\sqrt{(-2)^2} = -(-2)^2 = 2$.

Algebraic Operations
Exercise 8

DIRECTIONS: Choose the correct answer to each of the following items. Answers are on page 607.

1. Which of the following is (are) like terms?

 I. $34x$ and $-18x$
 II. $2x$ and $2xy$
 III. x^3 and $3x$

A. I only
B. II only
C. I and III only
D. II and III only
E. I, II, and III

2. Which of the following is a binomial?

A. x
B. $2x$
C. x^2
D. $x+1$
E. $1x^2+2x+2$

3. What is the coefficient in the algebraic expression $\frac{3}{4}y^2$?

A. 2
B. 3
C. 4
D. $\frac{3}{4}$
E. y

4. What is the exponent in the algebraic expression x ?

A. 0
B. 1
C. x
D. -1
E. There is no exponent

5. $x+2x+3x=?$

A. $6x^6$
B. x^6
C. $6x$
D. $x+6$
E. $x-6$

6. $a^3+a^2+a=?$

A. $3a^3$
B. a^3
C. $2a^2$
D. a^2
E. a^3+a^2+a

7. $a^3-12a^3+15a^3+2a^3=?$

A. $6a^3$
B. $2a^2$
C. $6a$
D. $3a$
E. a

8. $-7nx+2nx+2n+7x=?$

A. 0
B. $-5nx+2n+7x$
C. $18nx$
D. $9nx+9xn$
E. $4nx$

9. $2x^2+2x^2+2x^2=?$

A. $6x^6$
B. $2x^6$
C. $6x^2$
D. $6x$
E. 6

10. $x^2+2xy-3x+4xy-6y+2y^2+3x-2xy+6y=?$

A. $x^2-2xy+y^2$
B. $x^2+y^2+3x+2y$
C. $x^2+2y^2+4xy+6x+6y$
D. $x^2+2y+4xy+6x$
E. x^2+2y^2+4xy

11. $pqr+qrs+rst+stu=?$

A. $pqrst$
B. $pq+qr+rs+st+tu$
C. $pqr+rst$
D. $4pqrst$
E. $pqr+qrs+rst+stu$

12. $(a)\left(a^2\right)\left(a^3\right)\left(a^4\right)=?$

A. $10a$
B. $24a$
C. a^5
D. a^{10}
E. a^{24}

13. $\left(x^2y\right)\left(xy^2\right) = ?$

   A. $4xy$ C. xy^4 E. xy^{16}

   B. x^3y^3 D. x^4y^4

14. $\left(xy^2\right)\left(x^2z\right)\left(y^2z\right) = ?$

   A. $8xyz$ C. $x^3y^4z^2$ E. $x^3y^3z^3$

   B. x^2y^4z D. $x^3y^3z^2$

15. $\dfrac{a^3b^4c^5}{abc} = ?$

   A. $a^2b^3c^4$ C. $(abc)^3$ E. $(abc)^{60}$

   B. $a^3b^4c^5$ D. $(abc)^{12}$

16. $\left(\dfrac{a^2}{b^3}\right)^3 = ?$

   A. $\dfrac{a^5}{b}$ C. a^5b E. a^6b^9

   B. $\dfrac{a^6}{b^9}$ D. a^6b

17. $\left(\dfrac{c^4d^2}{c^2d}\right)^3 = ?$

   A. c^5d^3 C. c^6d^3 E. c^6d^6

   B. c^5d^5 D. c^6d^4

18. $\left(\dfrac{abc^2}{abc^3}\right)\left(\dfrac{a^2b^2c}{ab}\right) = ?$

   A. $\dfrac{ab}{c}$ C. ab E. 1

   B. $\dfrac{bc}{a}$ D. c

19. $\dfrac{a}{c} + \dfrac{b}{c} = ?$

   A. $\dfrac{ab}{c}$ C. $\dfrac{a+b}{2c}$ E. $\dfrac{a+b}{abc}$

   B. $\dfrac{a+b}{c}$ D. $\dfrac{a+b}{c^2}$

20. $\dfrac{ab}{x} + \dfrac{bc}{x} + \dfrac{cd}{x} = ?$

   A. $\dfrac{abcd}{x}$ D. $\dfrac{ab+bc+cd}{3x}$

   B. $\dfrac{a+b+c+d}{x}$ E. $\dfrac{ab+bc+cd}{x^3}$

   C. $\dfrac{ab+bc+cd}{x}$

21. $\dfrac{2x}{z} - \dfrac{y}{z} = ?$

   A. $\dfrac{2x-y}{z}$ C. $\dfrac{2x-y}{x^2}$ E. $\dfrac{2xy}{2z}$

   B. $\dfrac{2x-y}{2z}$ D. $\dfrac{2xy}{z}$

22. $\dfrac{a}{b} - \dfrac{b}{a} = ?$

   A. $\dfrac{ab}{a-b}$ C. $\dfrac{a-b}{ab}$ E. $\dfrac{a^2-b^2}{ab}$

   B. $\dfrac{a-b}{b-a}$ D. $\dfrac{ab-ba}{ab}$

23. $\dfrac{x}{a} + \dfrac{y}{b} + \dfrac{z}{c} = ?$

   A. $\dfrac{xyz}{abc}$ D. $\dfrac{xbc+yac+zab}{a+b+c}$

   B. $\dfrac{x+y+z}{a+b+c}$ E. $\dfrac{xa+yb+zc}{abc}$

   C. $\dfrac{xbc+yac+zab}{abc}$

24. $2(x+y)=?$

  A. $2xy$ C. $2+x+2y$ E. $2x^2+2y^2$

  B. $2x+2y$ D. $4x$

25. $3(a+b+c+d)=?$

  A. $3abcd$

  B. $3a+b+c+d$

  C. $3a+3b+3c+3d$

  D. $3ab+3bc+3cd$

  E. $12a+12b+12c+12d$

26. $3a^2(ab+ac+bc)=?$

  A. $3a^3b^2c$ D. $3a^3b+3a^3c+3a^2bc$

  B. $3a^3+3b^3+3c$ E. $3a^5b+3a^5c$

  C. $3a^2b+3a^2c+3a^2bc$

27. $(a+b)^2=?$

  A. a^2+b^2 D. $a^2-2ab+b^2$

  B. a^2-b^2 E. $a^2+2ab+b^2$

  C. $a^2+2ab-b^2$

28. $(a+b)(a-b)=?$

  A. a^2-b^2 D. $a^2-2ab+b^2$

  B. a^2+b^2 E. $a^2+2ab-b^2$

  C. $a^2+2ab+b^2$

29. $(2-x)^2=?$

  A. $4-x^2$ C. x^2+4x+4 E. x^2-4x-4

  B. x^2+4 D. x^2-4x+4

30. $(x-y)(x+2)=?$

  A. $x^2+2xy+2y$ D. $x^2-xy+2x-2y$

  B. $x^2+2xy+x+y$ E. $x^2+2x+2y-2$

  C. $x^2+2xy+x-2y$

31. $(w+x)(y-z)=?$

  A. $wxy-z$ D. $wy+wz+xy-xz$

  B. $wy+xy-yz$ E. $wy-wz+xy-xz$

  C. $wy-wz+xy+xz$

32. $(2+x)(3+x+y)=?$

  A. $x^2+6xy+6$

  B. $x^2+6xy+3x+2y+6$

  C. $x^2+2xy+6x+6y+6$

  D. $x^2+xy+5x+2y+6$

  E. $x^2+3xy+2x+y+6$

33. $(x-y)^3=?$

  A. $x^3-3x^2y+3xy^2-y^3$

  B. $x^3+3x^3y+3xy^3+y^3$

  C. $x^3+3x^2y-3xy^2-y^3$

  D. $x^3+6x^2y^2+y^3$

  E. $x^2+6x^2y^2-y^3$

34. $2a+2b+2c=?$

  A. $2(a+b+c)$ D. $6(a+b+c)$

  B. $2(abc)$ E. $8(a+b+c)$

  C. $2(ab+bc+ca)$

35. $2x^2+4x^3+8x^4=?$

  A. $2x^2\left(1+2x+4x^2\right)$ D. $2x^2\left(x+2x^2+4x^3\right)$

  B. $2x^2\left(1+2x+4x^3\right)$ E. $2x^2\left(x^2+2x^3+4x^4\right)$

  C. $2x^2\left(x+2x+4x^2\right)$

36. $x^2y^2 + x^2y + xy^2 = ?$

    A. $(x+y)^2$ D. $xy(xy+x+y)$

    B. x^2+y^2 E. $xy(x+y+1)$

    C. $x^2y^2(x+y)$

37. $144^2 - 121^2 = ?$

    A. 23

    B. $(144+121)(144-121)$

    C. $(144+121)(144+121)$

    D. 23^2

    E. $(144+121)^2$

38. $x^2 + 2x + 1 = ?$

    A. $(x+1)(x-1)$ D. x^2-1

    B. $(x+1)(x+1)$ E. x^2+1

    C. $(x-1)(x-1)$

39. $x^2 + 3x + 2 = ?$

    A. $(x+1)(x-2)$ D. $(x-2)(x-1)$

    B. $(x+2)(x+1)$ E. $(x+3)(x-1)$

    C. $(x+2)(x-1)$

40. $p^2 + 4p + 3 = ?$

    A. $(p+3)(p+1)$ D. $(p+3)(p+4)$

    B. $(p+3)(p-1)$ E. $(p+3)(p-4)$

    C. $(p-3)(p-1)$

41. $x^2 + x - 20$

    A. $(x+5)(x-4)$ D. $(x+10)(x-2)$

    B. $(x+4)(x-5)$ E. $(x+20)(x-1)$

    C. $(x+2)(x-10)$

42. $x^2 + 8x + 16 = ?$

    A. $(x+2)(x+8)$ D. $(x+4)(x-4)$

    B. $(x+2)(x-8)$ E. $(x+4)(x+4)$

    C. $(x-4)(x-4)$

43. $a^2 - 3a + 2 = ?$

    A. $(a-2)(a-1)$ D. $(a-3)(a+1)$

    B. $(a-2)(a+1)$ E. $(a+3)(a+1)$

    C. $(a+1)(a-2)$

44. $x^2 - 8x + 16 = ?$

    A. $x+2$ C. $(x+2)^2$ E. $(x+4)^3$

    B. $x+4$ D. $(x-4)^2$

45. What number must be added to $4x^2 - 12x$ to make the resulting trinomial expression a perfect square?

    A. 2   C. 9   E. 16

    B. 4   D. 12

46. $2x^2 + 5x - 3 = ?$

    A. $(x-1)(x+3)$ D. $(3x+1)(x+3)$

    B. $(2x-1)(x+3)$ E. $(3x-1)(2x+3)$

    C. $(2x+1)(x-3)$

47. $ax^2 + 3ax = ?$

    A. $3ax$ C. $ax(x+3)$ E. $ax^2(x+3)$

    B. $ax(x-3)$ D. $ax^2(-3)$

48. If $15x^2 + ax - 28 = (5x-4)(3x+7)$, then $a = ?$

    A. 7   C. 23   E. 33

    B. 14   D. 28

49. $x^2 - 9y^4 = ?$

   A. $\left(x + 3y^2\right)\left(x - 3y^2\right)$

   B. $\left(x - 3y^2\right)\left(x - 3y^2\right)$

   C. $\left(x + 3y^2\right)\left(x + 3y^2\right)$

   D. $\left(2x + 3y^2\right)\left(2x + 3y^2\right)$

   E. $\left(2x - 3y^2\right)\left(2x - 3y^2\right)$

50. If $x = -2$, then $\left| x - 2 \right| =$

   A. –4   C. 0   E. 4
   B. –2   D. 2

51. If $x = -1$ and $y = 3$, then $\left| 2x - y \right| =$

   A. –5   C. –1   E. 5
   B. –3   D. 1

52. If $x = -2$ and $y = 4$, then $\left| x \right| + \left| y \right| =$

   A. –8   C. –2   E. 6
   B. –6   D. 2

53. $\dfrac{8x^{-4}}{2x} = ?$

   A. $\dfrac{2}{x^5}$ C. $\dfrac{3}{x^5}$ E. $\dfrac{8}{x^5}$

   B. $\dfrac{4}{x^4}$ D. $\dfrac{4}{x^5}$

54. $\dfrac{6x^{-5}y^2}{3^{-1}x^{-4}y} = ?$

   A. $\dfrac{12y^4}{x^4}$ C. $\dfrac{16y^5}{x^4}$ E. $\dfrac{18y^5}{x^6}$

   B. $\dfrac{16y^4}{x^5}$ D. $\dfrac{18y}{x}$

55. If $x = -2$, $x^2 = ?$

   A. –4   C. 6   E. 10
   B. 4   D. 8

56. If $x = -2$ and $y = -3$, then $x^2 - 4xy - x = ?$

   A. –24   C. –18   E. –14
   B. –20   D. –16

57. $\left(2x + \sqrt{3}\right)^2 = ?$

   A. $3x^2 + 3x\sqrt{3} + 3$ D. $-4x^2 + 4x\sqrt{3} + 3$

   B. $4x^2 - 4x\sqrt{3} + 3$ E. $4x^2 + 4x\sqrt{3} + 3$

   C. $4x^2 - 4x\sqrt{3} - 3$

58. $\left(\dfrac{x^2 y^3 x^5}{2^{-1}}\right)^2 = ?$

   A. $4x^{12}y^4$ C. $4x^{14}y^4$ E. $4x^{14}y^6$

   B. $4x^{12}y^{66}$ D. $4x^{12}y^6$

59. $\sqrt{(x + y)^2} = ?$

   A. $\sqrt{x^2 + y^2}$

   B. $\sqrt{x^2 + xy + y^2}$

   C. $x^2 + y^2$

   D. $x^2 + 2xy + y^2$

   E. None of the above.

60. $\dfrac{6}{\sqrt{2a-3c}} = ?$

A. $\dfrac{6\sqrt{2a-3c}}{2a-3c}$

B. $\dfrac{6\sqrt{2a+3c}}{2a+3c}$

C. $\dfrac{6\sqrt{2a+3c}}{2a-3c}$

D. $\dfrac{6\sqrt{2a-3c}}{2a+3c}$

E. None of the above.

61. $1 - \dfrac{x}{y} = ?$

A. $\dfrac{1-x}{y}$ C. $\dfrac{x-y}{y}$ E. $\dfrac{y-x}{xy}$

B. $\dfrac{y-x}{y}$ D. $\dfrac{1-x}{1-y}$

62. $\dfrac{1 + \dfrac{1}{x}}{\dfrac{y}{x}} = ?$

A. $\dfrac{x+1}{y}$ C. $\dfrac{x+1}{xy}$ E. $\dfrac{y+1}{y}$

B. $\dfrac{x+1}{x}$ D. $\dfrac{x^2+1}{xy}$

63. $\dfrac{\dfrac{1}{x} + \dfrac{1}{y}}{3} = ?$

A. $\dfrac{3x+3y}{xy}$ C. $\dfrac{xy}{3}$ E. $\dfrac{y+x}{3}$

B. $\dfrac{3xy}{x+7}$ D. $\dfrac{y+x}{3xy}$

64. If $x \geq 0$, then $\sqrt{\dfrac{x^2}{9} + \dfrac{x^2}{16}} = ?$

A. $\dfrac{25x^2}{144}$ C. $\dfrac{5x^2}{12}$ E. $\dfrac{7x}{12}$

B. $\dfrac{5x}{12}$ D. $\dfrac{x}{7}$

65. If $x \geq 0$, then $\sqrt{\dfrac{x^2}{64} - \dfrac{x^2}{100}} = ?$

A. $\dfrac{x}{40}$ C. $\dfrac{x}{2}$ E. $\dfrac{3x}{80}$

B. $-\dfrac{x}{2}$ D. $\dfrac{3x}{40}$

66. $\sqrt{a^2 + b^2} = ?$

A. $a+b$ D. $(a+b)(a-b)$

B. $a-b$ E. None of these

C. $\sqrt{a^2} + \sqrt{b^2}$

67. When factored as completely as possible with respect to the integers, $16x^4 - 81y^{16} = ?$

A. $\left(4x^2 + 9y^4\right)\left(4x^2 - 9y^4\right)$

B. $\left(4x^2 + 9y^8\right)\left(4x^2 - 9y^8\right)$

C. $\left(4x^2 + 9y^4\right)(2x + 3y)(2x - 3y)$

D. $\left(4x^2 + 9y^8\right)\left(2x + 3y^4\right)\left(2x - 3y^4\right)$

E. $16x^4 - 81y^{16}$

ALGEBRAIC EQUATIONS AND INEQUALITIES

Pursuing the analogy between English and algebra as a language, the algebraic analogue of a complete sentence in English (with subject and verb) is an equation. An **algebraic equation** is a statement that two algebraic expressions are equivalent.

Examples:

English	*Algebra*
Ed is three years older than Paul	$E = P + 3$
Paul is twice as old as Mary	$P = 2M$
Ned has \$2 more than Ed	$N = E + \$2$
Bill has three times as much money as does Ted	$B = 3T$

Solving Algebraic Formulas

An **algebraic formula** is an equation that typically involves a relationship between literal quantities. Problems that involve formulas often ask you to solve for a particular unknown (variable) using substitution. Algebraic formulas can take many different forms, including functions, scientific equations, geometric formulas, and story problems. Regardless of the format, the concept is the same: replace the variables with the values that are given and solve for the unknown variable.

Examples:

1. For all real numbers x and y, $x \oplus y = 2x + y^2$. What is the value of $3 \oplus 7$?

   ➤ Substitute 3 for x and 7 for y in the given expression: $x \oplus y = 2x + y^2 \Rightarrow 3 \oplus 7 = 2(3) + (7)^2 = 6 + 49 = 55$.

2. The formula that relates Fahrenheit temperature to Celsius temperature is: $F = 1.8C + 32$, where F is Fahrenheit degrees (°F) and C is Celsius degrees (°C). What is the temperature, in Fahrenheit degrees, if the temperature is 25°C?

   ➤ Substitute 25 for C in the given equation and solve for F: $F = 1.8C + 32 = 1.8(25) + 32 = 45 + 32 = 77$°F.

3. The volume of a sphere is: $V = \dfrac{4\pi r^3}{3}$, where r is the radius of the sphere. Find the volume of a sphere with a radius of 6.

   ➤ Substitute 6 for r in the given formula and solve for V: $V = \dfrac{4\pi r^3}{3} = \dfrac{4\pi(6)^3}{3} = 4\pi \cdot 72 = 288\pi$.

4. If a person must pick one object from a group of x objects and then one object from a group of y objects, the number of possible combinations is xy. Jan must select 1 candy bar from 7 different candy bars and 1

pack of gum from 3 different packs of gum. What is the maximum number of combinations available to Jan?

➤ Substitute 7 for x and 3 for y in the given expression: number of combinations $= xy = (7)(3) = 21$.

Formulas that represent real life situations often involve variables with units of measure, such as inches or gallons. You must ensure that all variables have similar units on both sides of the equation in order for the equality to remain true. To maintain consistency, it may be necessary to convert units using equivalent expressions (e.g., 12 inches/foot, 1 foot/12 inches, 60 minutes/hour, 1 hour/60 minutes). Thus, when dealing with quantities given in units of any type, it helps to explicitly write out the units in the expressions.

Example:

If string costs k cents per foot at the hardware store, how much will w feet and j inches of the string cost, in dollars?

➤ Explicitly write out the units in the expression and cancel like units in the numerator and denominator:

$$\text{Cost of string (dollars)} = \frac{k \text{ cents}}{1 \text{ ft. of string}} \cdot \text{length of string (ft.)} \cdot \frac{1 \text{ dollar}}{100 \text{ cents}}$$

$$= \frac{k \text{ cents}}{1 \text{ ft.}} \cdot \left[w \text{ ft.} + \left(j \text{ in.} \cdot \frac{1 \text{ ft.}}{12 \text{ in.}} \right) \right] \cdot \frac{1 \text{ dollar}}{100 \text{ cents}}$$

$$= \frac{k \text{ cents}}{1 \text{ ft.}} \cdot \left[w \text{ ft.} + \left(j \text{ in.} \cdot \frac{1 \text{ ft.}}{12 \text{ in.}} \right) \right] \cdot \frac{1 \text{ dollar}}{100 \text{ cents}}$$

$$= \frac{k \text{ cents}}{1 \text{ ft.}} \cdot \left(w + \frac{j}{12} \right)(\text{ft.}) \cdot \frac{1 \text{ dollar}}{100 \text{ cents}}$$

$$= k \text{ cents} \cdot \left(w + \frac{j}{12} \right) \cdot \frac{1 \text{ dollar}}{100 \text{ cents}}$$

$$= \frac{k}{100} \left(w + \frac{j}{12} \right)$$

Therefore, the cost of the string, in dollars, is: $\frac{k}{100} \left(w + \frac{j}{12} \right)$.

Basic Principle of Equations

The fundamental rule for working with any equation is: Whatever you do to one side of an equation, you must do exactly the same thing to the other side of the equation. This rule implies that you can add, subtract, multiply, and divide both sides of the equality by any value without changing the statement of equality. The only exception is that you cannot divide by zero. The following example illustrates the validity of this principle using an equation containing only real numbers.

Example:

$5 = 5$

➤ This is obviously a true statement. You can add any value to both sides of the equation, say 10, and the statement will remain true. Add 10: $5 + 10 = 5 + 10 \Rightarrow 15 = 15$. You can also subtract the same value from both sides, e.g., 7: $15 - 7 = 15 - 7 \Rightarrow 8 = 8$. You can multiply both sides by the same value, e.g., -2: $8 \cdot -2 = 8 \cdot -2 \Rightarrow -16 = -16$. Finally, you can divide both sides by the same value (except zero); e.g., -4: $-16 \div -4 = -16 \div -4 \Rightarrow 4 = 4$.

This principle for manipulating equations applies to algebraic equations with variables, as the following example illustrates.

Example:

$5 + x = 5 + x$

➤ Add x: $5 + x + x = 5 + x + x \Rightarrow 5 + 2x = 5 + 2x$. Whatever x is, since it appears on both sides of the equation, both sides of the equation must still be equal. Now, subtract a value, e.g., y: $5 + 2x - y = 5 + 2x - y$. Again, since y appears on both sides of the equation, the statement that the two expressions are equal remains true.

DO NOT multiply both sides of an equation by zero if the equation contains a variable. You may lose special characteristics of the variable. For example, the equation $2x = 8$ is true only if $x = 4$. However, the equation $0(2x) = 0(8)$ is true for any value of x.

Solving Linear Equations

Equations that have only variables of the first power are called equations of the first degree or **linear equations**. While a linear equation can have any number of different variables, equations with one or two variables are most common on the exam.

The fundamental rule of equations is the key to solving linear equations. To solve for an unknown variable, identically manipulate both sides of the equation to isolate the variable on one side. Be sure to reduce the other side of the equation by combining similar terms.

Examples:

1. If $2x + 3 = x + 1$, then what is the value of x?

   ➤ To solve for x, manipulate the equation to isolate x. Subtract x from both sides: $2x + 3 - x = x + 1 - x \Rightarrow x + 3 = 1$. Next, subtract 3 from both sides: $x + 3 - 3 = 1 - 3 \Rightarrow x = -2$.

2. If $4x + 2 = 2x + 10$, then what is the value of x?

   ➤ Subtract $2x$ from both sides of the equation: $4x + 2 - 2x = 2x + 10 - 2x \Rightarrow 2x + 2 = 10$. Then, subtract 2 from both sides: $2x + 2 - 2 = 10 - 2 \Rightarrow 2x = 8$. Divide both sides by 2: $2x \div 2 = 8 \div 2 \Rightarrow x = 4$.

3. If $3y - 2x = 12$, then what is the value of y in terms of x?

   ➤ Add $2x$ to both sides of the equation: $3y - 2x + 2x = 12 + 2x \Rightarrow 3y = 12 + 2x$. Divide both sides by 3:
   $$y = \frac{2x}{3} + 4.$$

So far, we have been very formal in following the fundamental rule for working with equations. The process is simplified using a shortcut called **transposition**. Transposing is the process of moving a term or a factor from one side of the equation to the other by changing it into its mirror image. Perform these "inverse operations" until the variable is isolated. Note that this shortcut does not change the fundamental rule or its outcome: it simply bypasses the formal steps.

To transpose a term that is added or subtracted, move it to the other side of the equation and change its sign. Thus, a term with a positive sign on one side is moved to the other side and becomes negative, and vice versa. It is imperative when using transposition that you do not forget to change signs when terms change sides.

Examples:

1. $x + 5 = 10$

    ➤ Rather than going through the formal steps of subtracting 5 from both sides of the equality, simply transpose the 5: move it from the left side to the right side and change its sign from " $+$ " to " $-$ ": $x = 10 - 5 \Rightarrow x = 5$.

2. $x - 5 = 10 \Rightarrow x = 10 + 5 \Rightarrow x = 15$

3. $3x = 5 + 2x \Rightarrow 3x - 2x = 5 \Rightarrow x = 5$

To transpose a multiplicative factor, move the factor to the opposite side of the equation and invert it; that is, replace it with its reciprocal.

Example:

$$\frac{2x + 5}{3} = 9$$

➤ $2x$ and 5 are both divided by 3; in other words, they are both multiplied by $\frac{1}{3}$. Therefore, the $\frac{1}{3}$ must be transposed first. Move it to the opposite side of the equation and invert it: $2x + 5 = 9(3) = 27$. Now the 5 can be transposed: $2x = 27 - 5 = 22$. Finally, solve for x by transposing the 2: $x = 22 \cdot \frac{1}{2} = 11$.

Solving Simultaneous Equations

Ordinarily, if an equation has more than one variable, it is not possible to determine the unique numeric solution for any individual variable. For example, the equation $x + y = 10$ does not have one unique solution set for x and y: x and y could be 1 and 9, 5 and 5, −2 and 12, and so on. However, if there are as many equations as there are variables, the equations can be manipulated as a system to determine the value of each variable. This technique is called **solving simultaneous equations** because the equations are taken to be true at the same time, or simultaneously, in order to determine the variable value. On the exam, simultaneous equations are typically limited to two equations and two unknowns.

Example:

Given $x + y = 10$ and $x - y = 6$, solve for x and y.

➤ If we treat both of the equations as making true statements at the same time, then there is only one solution set for x and y, for there is only one pair of numbers that will satisfy both equations, $x = 8$ and $y = 2$.

It is easy to see the answer to the previous example, but solutions will not always be this obvious. How do you find the specific solution for a given set of equations? There are two methods for solving simultaneous equations: substitution and linear combination (elimination).

Substitution

The steps for **substitution** are as follows:

Step 1: Pick one of the two given equations and define one variable in terms of the other.
Step 2: Substitute the defined variable into the other equation and solve.
Step 3: Substitute the solution back into either equation and solve for the remaining variable.

Examples:

1. If $2x + y = 13$ and $x - y = 2$, what are the values of x and y?

    ➤ Redefine one variable in terms of the other. Since y is already a single variable in both equations, define y in terms of x: $y = 13 - 2x$. Substitute $13 - 2x$ for y in the second equation and solve for x: $x - (13 - 2x) = 2 \Rightarrow x - 13 + 2x = 2 \Rightarrow 3x = 15 \Rightarrow x = 5$. Finally, solve for y by substituting 5 for x in either equation: $2x + y = 13 \Rightarrow 2(5) + y = 13 \Rightarrow y = 3$.

2. If $3x + 2y = 16$ and $2x - y = 6$, what are the values of x and y?

    ➤ Since y is a simple term in the second equation, define y in terms of x: $2x - y = 6 \Rightarrow y = 2x - 6$. Substitute this expression for y in the first equation and solve for x: $3x + 2(2x - 6) = 16 \Rightarrow 3x + 4x - 12 = 16 \Rightarrow 7x = 28 \Rightarrow x = 4$. Finally, solve for y by substituting 4 for x in either equation: $2x - y = 6 \Rightarrow 2(4) - y = 6 \Rightarrow y = 2$.

3. If $y = 7 + x$ and $3x + 2y = 4$, what are the values of x and y?

    ➤ Substitute $7 + x$ for y in the second equation and solve for x: $3x + 2y = 4 \Rightarrow 3x + 2(7 + x) = 4 \Rightarrow 3x + 14 + 2x = 4 \Rightarrow 5x = -10 \Rightarrow x = -2$. Substitute -2 for x in the first equation and solve for y: $y = 7 + x = 7 - 2 = 5$.

Linear Combination (Elimination)

The second method for solving simultaneous equations is **linear combination** or **elimination**. Eliminate one of the two variables by adding or subtracting the two equations. If necessary, division of one equation by another may eliminate one of two variables.

Examples:

1. If $2x + y = 8$ and $x - y = 1$, what are the values of x and y?

    ➤ In this pair of simultaneous equations, there is a "$+y$" term in one equation and a "$-y$" term in the other. Since $+y$ and $-y$ added together yields zero, eliminate the y term by adding the two equations together. (Actually, you will be adding the left side of the second equation to the left side of the first equation and the right side of the second to the right side of the first, but it is easier to speak of the process as "adding equations.") $[2x + y = 8] + [(x - y = 1)] = [3x = 9] \Rightarrow x = 3$. Find the value of y by substituting 3 for x in either equation: $2x + y = 8 \Rightarrow 2(3) + y = 8 \Rightarrow y = 8 - 6 = 2$.

2. If $4x + 3y = 17$ and $2x + 3y = 13$, what are the values of x and y?

    ➤ In this pair, each equation has a $+3y$ term, which you can eliminate by subtracting the second equation from the first. $[4x + 3y = 17] - [2x + 3y = 13] = [2x = 4] \Rightarrow x = 2$. Solve for y by substituting 2 for x in either equation: $4x + 3y = 17 \Rightarrow 4(2) + 3y = 17 \Rightarrow 8 + 3y = 17 \Rightarrow 3y = 9 \Rightarrow y = 3$.

3. $x^5 = 6y$ and $x^4 = 2y$; x is a real number such that $x \neq 0$ and y is a real number. Solve for x.

    ➤ The system of equations is reduced to one equation and one variable by dividing the first equation by the second equation: $\dfrac{x^5}{x^4} = \dfrac{6y}{2y} \Rightarrow x = 3$.

If a system of equations has more variables than equations, then not every variable value can be determined. Instead, you will be asked to solve for one or more variables in terms of another variable.

Examples:

1. If $y = 2a$ and $3x + 8y = 28a$, find x in terms of a.

   ➤ Substitute $2a$ for y and solve for x: $3x + 8(2a) = 28a \Rightarrow 3x = 28a - 16a \Rightarrow 3x = 12a \Rightarrow x = \dfrac{12a}{3} = 4a$.

2. In terms of a, solve the following pair of equations for x and y: $3x - 4y = 10a$ and $5x + 2y = 8a$.

   ➤ First, solve for either x or y in terms of a alone. To solve for x, multiply the second equation by 2 and add the result to the first equation.
   $[2(5x + 2y = 8a)] + [3x - 4y = 10a] = [10x + 4y = 16a] + [3x - 4y = 10a] = 13x = 26a \Rightarrow x = 2a$. To find y

   in terms of a, substitute $2a$ for x in either equation: $5x + 2y = 8a \Rightarrow y = \dfrac{8a - 5(2a)}{2} \Rightarrow y = \dfrac{-2a}{2} = -a$.

Solving Quadratic Equations

Equations that involve variables of the second power (e.g., x^2) are called ***quadratic equations***. Unlike a linear equation with a single variable, which has a single solution, a quadratic may have two solutions. By convention, quadratic equations are written so that the right side of the equation is equal to zero. The general form is: $ax^2 + bx + c = 0$.

Example:

Solve for x: $x^2 + x - 2 = 0$.

➤ To solve the quadratic equation, factor the left side of the equation: $x^2 + x - 2 = 0 \Rightarrow (x + 2)(x - 1) = 0$. For the equality to hold true, $x + 2$ or $x - 1$ must equal zero. Therefore, $x = -2$ or 1, so this quadratic equation has two solutions.

This last example illustrates the ***zero product property***: if $xy = 0$, then $x = 0$ or $y = 0$.

Example:

$x^2 - 3x - 4 = 0$

➤ Factor the left side of the equation: $(x + 1)(x - 4) = 0$. Either $x + 1 = 0$, in which case $x = -1$, or $x - 4 = 0$, in which case $x = 4$. Therefore, the solution set for this quadratic equation is $\{-1, 4\}$.

However, not every quadratic equation has two different solutions.

Example:

$x^2 + 2x + 1 = 0$

➤ Factor the left side of the equation: $(x + 1)(x + 1) = 0$. Since the two factors are the same, the equation has one solution: -1.

For quadratic equations not in standard form, you must first group like terms and rearrange the equation into standard form.

Examples:

1. Solve for x: $2x^2 + 12 - 3x = x^2 + 2x + 18$.

> Rewrite the equation by grouping like terms and simplifying:

$$2x^2 + 12 - 3x = x^2 + 2x + 18$$
$$\left(2x^2 - x^2\right) + (-3x - 2x) + (12 - 18) = 0$$
$$x^2 - 5x - 6 = 0$$
$$(x - 6)(x + 1) = 0$$

Either $x - 6 = 0$ or $x + 1 = 0$. Therefore the set of all possible values for x is $\{-1, 6\}$.

2. Solve for x: $x(8 + x) = 2x + 36 + 6x$.

> Rewrite the equation by grouping like terms and simplifying:

$$x(8 + x) = 2x + 36 + 6x$$
$$8x + x^2 = 8x + 36$$
$$x^2 = 36$$

Since squaring a negative number yields a positive and squaring a positive number yields a positive, $x = \pm 6$.

Some higher degree equations can also be solved if they can be written in quadratic form.

Example:

Solve for x: $x^4 - 13x^2 + 36 = 0$.

> Factor: $\left(x^2 - 9\right)\left(x^2 - 4\right) = 0$. Factor again: $(x + 3)(x - 3)(x + 2)(x - 2) = 0$. To find the four possible values of x, set each factor equal to zero and solve each for x: $x + 3 = 0 \Rightarrow x = -3$; $x - 3 = 0 \Rightarrow x = 3$; $x + 2 = 0 \Rightarrow x = -2$; and $x - 2 = 0 \Rightarrow x = 2$. Therefore, the solution set is: $\{-3, 3, -2, 2\}$.

Alternatively, you can use the quadratic formula, $x = \dfrac{-b \pm \sqrt{b^2 - 4ac}}{2a}$, to solve quadratic equations.

Example:

Solve for x: $3 - x = 2x^2$.

> $3 - x = 2x^2 \Rightarrow 2x^2 + x - 3 = 0$. $a = 2, b = 1, c = -3$. Substitute these values into the quadratic formula and solve for x: $x = \dfrac{-b \pm \sqrt{b^2 - 4ac}}{2a} = \dfrac{-1 \pm \sqrt{1^2 - 4(2)(-3)}}{2(2)} = \dfrac{-1 \pm \sqrt{1 + 24}}{4} = \dfrac{-1 \pm 5}{4}$. So, the solution set for x is $\left\{1, -\dfrac{3}{2}\right\}$.

Solving Equations by Factoring

Factoring is an alternative shortcut method for solving some equations. Before factoring, rewrite the equation with all of the terms on one side of the equation and 0 on the other side. If the nonzero side of the equation can be factored into a product of expressions, then use the following property to yield simpler equations that can be solved: if $xy = 0$, then $x = 0$ or $y = 0$. The solutions of the simpler equations will be solutions of the factored equation. The solutions of an equation are also called the **roots** of the equation.

Examples:

1. $\dfrac{\left(4x^2 - 1\right)(x + 2)}{x + 4} = 0$

   ➤ Either $4x^2 - 1 = 0$ or $x + 2 = 0$. In each instance, solve for x:

   $$4x^2 - 1 = 0$$

   $$x^2 = \frac{1}{4}$$

   $$x = \pm\frac{1}{2}$$

   $$x + 2 = 0$$

   $$x = -2$$

   Therefore, the set of all possible values for x is $\left\{-2, -\dfrac{1}{2}, \dfrac{1}{2}\right\}$.

2. Solve for x: $x^3 + 2x^2 + x = 3(x + 1)^2$.

   ➤ Move all the terms to one side of the equality and simplify by factoring like terms:

   $$x^3 + 2x^2 + x - 3(x + 1)^2 = 0$$

   $$x\left(x^2 + 2x + 1\right) - 3(x + 1)^2 = 0$$

   $$x(x + 1)^2 - 3(x + 1)^2 = 0$$

   $$(x - 3)(x + 1)^2 = 0$$

   $$x - 3 = 0 \text{ or } x + 1 = 0$$

   The solution set is $\{-1, 3\}$.

Algebraic Inequalities

An **inequality** is very much like an equation except, as the name implies, it is a statement that two quantities are not equal. Four different symbols are used to make statements of inequality:

- $>$ greater than
- $<$ less than
- $\geq$ greater than or equal to
- $\leq$ less than or equal to

Examples:

$5 > 1$ ....5 is greater than 1.
$2 > -2$ ....2 is greater than −2.
$x > 0$ ....x is greater than zero.
$x > y$ ....x is greater than y.
$8 < 9$ ....8 is less than 9.
$-4 < -1$ ....−4 is less than −1.
$x < 0$ ....x is less than zero.
$y < x$ ....y is less than x.

$x \geq 0$ ....x is greater than or equal to zero. (x could be zero or any number larger than zero.)
$x \geq y$ ....x is greater than or equal to y. (Either x is greater than y, or x and y are equal.)
$x \leq 0$ ....x is less than or equal to zero. (x could be zero or any number less than zero.)
$x \leq y$ ....x is less than or equal to y. (Either x is less than y, or x and y are equal.)

The fundamental rule for working with inequalities is similar to that for working with equalities: Treat each side of the inequality exactly the same. You can add or subtract the same value to each side of an inequality without changing the inequality, and you can multiply or divide each side of an inequality by any *positive* value without changing the inequality.

Example:

$$5 > 2$$
$$\text{Add 25 to both sides. } 5 + 25 > 2 + 25$$
$$30 > 27$$
$$\text{Subtract 6 from both sides. } 30 - 6 > 27 - 6$$
$$24 > 21$$
$$\text{Multiply both sides by 2. } 24 \cdot 2 > 21 \cdot 2$$
$$48 > 42$$
$$\text{Divide both sides by 6. } 48 \div 6 > 42 \div 6$$
$$8 > 7$$

However, if you multiply or divide an inequality by a *negative* number, the direction of the inequality is reversed. Therefore, remember to change the direction of the inequality when multiplying or dividing by a negative number.

Example:

$$4 > 3$$
$$\text{Multiply both sides by } -2. \ 4(-2) < 3(-2)$$
$$-8 < -6$$

These properties hold true for inequalities containing variables, as the following two examples illustrate.

Examples:

1. For what values of x is $3(2-x) + 7x > 30$?

   ➤ Solve for x: $3(2-x) + 7x > 30$
   $$6 - 3x + 7x > 30$$
   $$6 + 4x > 30$$
   $$4x > 24$$
   $$x > 6$$

2. For what values of x is $3(2-x) + x > 30$?

   ➤ Solve for x: $3(2-x) + x > 30$
   $$6 - 3x + x > 30$$
   $$6 - 2x > 30$$
   $$-2x > 24$$
   $$x < -12$$

Exponents in Equations and Inequalities

Integer and Rational Exponents

Algebraic equations and inequalities can include terms with integer and rational exponents. The rules of exponents apply when manipulating these terms.

> **Examples:**
>
> 1. If $x = 2$, then what is the value of x^{2x}?
>
>   ➤ Substitute $x = 2$ into the given expression: $x^{2x} = (2)^{2(2)} = (2)^4 = 16$.
>
> 2. Find the value of $x^{-\frac{2}{3}}$ when $x = 27$.
>
>   ➤ Substitute $x = 27$: $x^{-\frac{2}{3}} = (27)^{-\frac{2}{3}} = \dfrac{1}{27^{\frac{2}{3}}} = \dfrac{1}{\left(\sqrt[3]{27}\right)^2} = \dfrac{1}{3^2} = \dfrac{1}{9}$.

Algebraic Exponentials

When solving equations that involve algebraic exponential terms, try to find a common base to use throughout the problem.

> **Example:**
>
> Solve for x: $4^{x+2} = 8^{3x-6}$
>
> ➤ Since $4 = 2^2$ and $8 = 2^3$, the common base in this item is 2. Thus:
>
> $$4^{x+2} = 8^{3x-6}$$
> $$\left(2^2\right)^{x+2} = \left(2^3\right)^{3x-6}$$
> $$2^{2x+4} = 2^{9x-18}$$
>
> Now, drop the common base and solve for x:
>
> $$2x + 4 = 9x - 18$$
> $$22 = 7x$$
> $$x = \frac{22}{7}$$

Exponential Growth

Items that involve exponential growth test knowledge of exponential growth sequences, also called geometric sequences. In a geometric sequence, the ***ratio***, r, of any term to its preceding term is constant. If the terms of a geometric sequence are designated by a_1, a_2, a_3, ..., a_n, then $a_n = a_1 r^{n-1}$. Sequences that involve exponential growth have real-life applications, such as determining population growth over a specific period.

Examples:

1. Find the 5th term of the geometric sequence {4, 12, 36, ...}.

   ➤ In this geometric sequence, the ratio between the terms is $\dfrac{12}{4} = 3$. The 5th term is:

   $$a_n = a_1 r^{n-1} \Rightarrow a_5 = 4(3)^{5-1} = 4(3)^4 = 4 \cdot 81 = 324.$$

2. On June 1, 1990, the population of Grouenphast was 50,250. If the population is increasing at an annual rate of 8.4%, what is the approximate population of Grouenphast on June 1, 2010?

   ➤ An annual increase of 8.4% means that each year the population will be 108.4% of the previous year's population. Thus, the ratio between terms, r, is 1.084. The population on June 1, 1990 is the starting term: $a_1 = 50,250$. Since June 1, 2010 is 20 years later, the population at that time is the 21st term in the sequence: $n = 21$. So the population on June 1, 2010 is: $a_n = a_1 r^{n-1} \Rightarrow$

   $$a_{21} = 50,250(1.084)^{20} \approx 252,186.$$

The previous example involving growth over time suggests an alternate form of the geometric sequence equation called the ***exponential growth equation***: $a_t = a_0 r^{\frac{t}{T}}$. In this equation, a_t is the amount after time t; a_0 is the initial amount ($t = 0$), r is the proportionality constant, t is the total period of growth, and T is the time per cycle of growth. Note that this equation also applies to exponential decay, where the initial amount is larger than the amount after time t.

Example:

The number of rabbits in a certain population doubles every 3 months. Currently, there are 5 rabbits in the population. How many rabbits will there be 3 years from now?

➤ In this case, the total time of growth is 3 years. Since the population doubles every 3 months, the time per cycle of growth is one-fourth of a year. Using the formula for exponential growth: $a_t = a_0 r^{\frac{t}{T}} \Rightarrow$

$a_3 = (5)(2)^{\frac{3}{0.25}} = (5)(2)^{12} = 20,480$. We can verify this solution by working out the values, allowing the population to double every 3 months.

Period (months)	0	3	6	9	12	15	18	21	24	27	30	33	36
Population Size	5	10	20	40	80	160	320	640	1,280	2,560	5,120	10,240	20,480

Properties of Functions

A function is a set of ordered pairs (x, y) such that for each value of x, there is exactly one value of y. By convention, we say that "y is a function of x," which is written as: $y = f(x)$ or $y = g(x)$, etc. The set of x-values for which the set is defined is called the ***domain*** of the function. The set of corresponding values of y is called the ***range*** of the function.

Example:

What are the domain and range of the function $y = |x|$?

➤ The function is defined for all real values of x. Hence the domain is the set of all real numbers. Since $y = |x|$ can only be a positive number or zero, the range of the function is given by the set of all real numbers equal to or greater than zero.

When we speak of $f(a)$, we mean the value of $y = f(x)$ when $x = a$ is substituted in the expression for $f(x)$. If $z = f(y)$ and $y = g(x)$, we say that $z = f[g(x)]$. Thus, z is in turn a function of x.

This function notation is a short way of writing the result of substituting a value for a variable. Once a function $f(x)$ is defined, think of the variable x as an input and $f(x)$ as the corresponding output. In any function, there can be no more than one output for a given input. Note, however, that there may be more than one input that returns the same output.

Examples:

1. If $f(x) = 2x^x - 3x$, find the value of $f(3)$.

   ➤ Substitute 3 for x in the given expression:
   $$f(x) = 2x^x - 3x \Rightarrow f(3) = 2(3)^3 - 3(3) = 2(27) - 9 = 54 - 9 = 45.$$

2. If $f(x) = 2x - 9^{\frac{1}{x}}$, what is $f(-2)$?

   ➤ $f(-2) = 2(-2) - 9^{-\frac{1}{2}} = -4 - \frac{1}{\sqrt{9}} = -4 - \frac{1}{3} = -\frac{13}{3}.$

3. If $z = f(y) = 3y + 2$ and $y = g(x) = x + 2$, then $z = ?$

   ➤ $z = f[g(x)] = 3[g(x)] + 2 = 3(x + 2) + 2 = 3x + 6 + 2 = 3x + 8.$

In the previous chapter we introduced geometric sequences as an example of working with exponents. Note that a geometric sequence ($a_n = a_1 r^{n-1}$) is actually a function. In general, a **sequence**, a_n, is any function $a(n)$ with a domain consisting of only the positive integers and possibly zero; that is, $n = 0, 1, 2, 3, \ldots$, or $n = 1, 2, 3, \ldots$. Note that a sequence is often written by listing its values in the order $a_1, a_2, a_3, \ldots, a_n, \ldots$. For example, $a_n = (-1)^n (n!)$ for $n = 1, 2, 3, \ldots$, is written as $-1, 2, -6, \ldots, (-1)^n (n!), \ldots$.

Example:

1. What is the fifth term of the sequence defined by $a_n = 3n^2 + 2$ for $n = 1, 2, 3, \ldots$?

   ➤ The fifth term of the sequence is for $n = 5$. Substitute 5 for n in the function $3n^2 + 2$: $3(5)^2 + 2 = 77$.

2. Find the fourth term of the sequence with values $-1, 2, -6, \ldots, (-1)^n (n!), \ldots$.

   ➤ The values of n for any sequence are consecutive integers, so determine the value of n for the fourth term of the sequence by finding the first n value. Test $n = 1$: $(-1)^1 (1) = -1$. Therefore, the fourth value of n must be 4: $(-1)^4 (4!) = 4 \cdot 3 \cdot 2 \cdot 1 = 24$.

Rational Equations

Algebraic equations may include rational (fractional) expressions. When manipulating rational expressions, follow the same rules as discussed with equations, inequalities, and algebraic fractions.

Example:

If $\dfrac{x}{x+6} = \dfrac{y^3-1}{(y+1)(y^2-y+1)+4}$, then $x = ?$

➤ $\dfrac{x}{x+6} = \dfrac{y^3-1}{y^3-y^2+y+y^2-y+1+4} = \dfrac{y^3-1}{y^3+5} = \dfrac{y^3-1}{y^3-1+6} = \dfrac{y^3-1}{(y^3-1)+6}$. Therefore, $x = y^3-1$.

Radical Equations

Expressions in algebraic equations may include radicals. The same principles for working with equations and inequalities apply when manipulating radicals.

Example:

$5\sqrt{x-4} - 28 = 12$ for what value of x?

➤ Solve for x:

$$5\sqrt{x-4} - 28 = 12$$
$$5\sqrt{x-4} = 40$$
$$\sqrt{x-4} = 8$$
$$\left(\sqrt{x-4}\right)^2 = 8^2$$
$$x-4 = 64$$
$$x = 68$$

Absolute Value in Equations and Inequalities

Expressions in algebraic equations and inequalities may include absolute values. The same principles for working with equations and inequalities apply when manipulating absolute values.

Examples:

1. What is the sum of all different integers that can be substituted for x such that $|x| + |x-3| = 3$?

   ➤ The absolute value of any real number, including integers, is always zero or more. Therefore, try only $-3, -2, -1, 0, 1, 2, 3$. The last four work in the equality: $|0| + |0-3| = 0+3 = 3$; $|1| + |1-3| = 1+2 = 3$; $|2| + |2-3| = 2+1 = 3$; $|3| + |3-3| = 3+0 = 3$. Thus, $0+1+2+3 = 6$.

2. If x represents an integer, $|x-3| + |x+2| < 7$ for how many different values of x?

   ➤ Absolute values are always equal to or greater than zero. Thus, if $x = -4$, $|x-3| = |-4-3| = 7$; there is no need to try any integers less than -3. Similarly, if $x = 5$, $|x+2| = |5+2| = 7$, there is no need to try any integers greater than 4. Therefore, test only the integers between -3 and 4. Six integers satisfy the inequality: $\{-2, -1, 0, 1, 2, 3\}$.

Algebraic Equations and Inequalities
Exercise 9

DIRECTIONS: Choose the correct answer to each of the following items. Answers are on page 607.

1. If $3x = 12$, then $x = ?$

   A. 2   C. 4   E. 10
   B. 3   D. 6

2. If $7x - 5x = 12 - 8$, then $x = ?$

   A. 0   C. 2   E. 4
   B. 1   D. 3

3. If $a - 8 = 10 - 2a$, then $a = ?$

   A. −2   C. 2   E. 6
   B. 0   D. 4

4. If $12x + 3 - 4x - 3 = 8$, then $x = ?$

   A. −5   C. 0   E. 5
   B. −1   D. 1

5. If $a + 2b - 3 + 3a = 2a + b + 3 + b$, then $a = ?$

   A. −1   C. 2   E. 6
   B. 0   D. 3

6. If $-4 - x = 12 + x$, then $x = ?$

   A. −8   C. 1   E. 4
   B. −2   D. 2

7. If $\dfrac{2x}{3} + \dfrac{x}{4} + 4 = \dfrac{x}{6} + 10$, then $x = ?$

   A. $\dfrac{11}{12}$ C. 5   E. 20

   B. $\dfrac{3}{2}$ D. 8

8. If $\dfrac{1}{p} + \dfrac{2}{p} + \dfrac{3}{p} = 1$, then $p = ?$

   A. $\dfrac{2}{3}$ C. 1   E. 6

   B. $\dfrac{3}{4}$ D. 2

9. If $\dfrac{5 - x}{5} = 1$, then $x = ?$

   A. −5   C. 0   E. 5
   B. −1   D. 1

10. If $\dfrac{5}{x + 1} + 2 = 5$, then $x = ?$

   A. $-\dfrac{2}{7}$ C. $\dfrac{7}{2}$ E. 10

   B. $\dfrac{2}{3}$ D. 7

11. If $3x + y = 10$ and $x + y = 6$, then $x = ?$

   A. 1   C. 3   E. 5
   B. 2   D. 4

12. If $x + 3y = 5$ and $2x - y = 3$, then $x = ?$

   A. 2   C. 5   E. 9
   B. 4   D. 6

13. If $a + b = 5$ and $2a + 3b = 12$, then $b = ?$

   A. 1   C. 3   E. 6
   B. 2   D. 4

14. If $k - n = 5$, and $2k + n = 16$, then $k = ?$

   A. −3   C. 1   E. 7
   B. 0   D. 5

15. If $a + 5b = 9$ and $a - b = 3$, then $a = ?$

   A. 1   C. 5   E. 11
   B. 4   D. 7

16. If $\frac{x+y}{2}=4$ and $x-y=4$, then $x=?$

A. 1   C. 4   E. 8
B. 2   D. 6

17. If $x+y+z=10$ and $x-y-z=4$, then $x=?$

A. 2   C. 6   E. 12
B. 3   D. 7

18. If $x+y+z=6$, $x+y-z=4$, and $x-y=3$, then $x=?$

A. −2   C. 4   E. 8
B. 0   D. 6

19. If $x^2-3x-4=0$, then $x=?$

A. −4 or 1   C. −1 or 2   E. 6 or −1
B. −2 or 2   D. 4 or −1

20. If $x^2-3x+2=0$, then $x=?$

A. −2 or −1   C. 1 or 2   E. 3 or 5
B. −1 or 2   D. 2 or 3

21. If $x^2+5x=-4$, then $x=?$

A. −1 or −4   C. 1 or 2   E. 2 or 6
B. −1 or −2   D. 1 or 4

22. If $k^2-10=-3k$, then $k=?$

A. −10 and −1   C. −5 and 3   E. 2 and −5
B. −10 and 1   D. −3 and 5

23. If $3x^2=12x$, then $x=?$

A. 0 or 3   C. −2 or 2   E. 3 or 12
B. 0 or 4   D. 2 or 4

24. For what values of x is $3+4x<28$?

A. $x<4$ C. $x<6.25$ E. $x\ge0$
B. $x>4$ D. $x>6.25$

25. For what values of x is $8-3x>35$?

A. $x>0$ C. $x\ge0$ E. $x\ge9$
B. $x>-3$ D. $x<-9$

26. If $(x-8)(x+2)=0$, then $x=?$

A. −8 or −2   C. 4 or −2   E. 10 or −5
B. −4 or −2   D. 8 or −2

27. If $\frac{x+5}{4}=17$, then $x=?$

A. 13 or 25   C. 63   E. 124
B. 54   D. 75 or −24

28. If $0.02x+1.44=x-16.2$, then $x=?$

A. 18   C. 14   E. 10
B. 16   D. 12

29. If $x^2-9x=22$, then $x=?$

A. −11 or 2   C. 2 or 3   E. 11
B. 3   D. 11 or −2

30. If $2x+3y=12$ and $x=-6$, then $y=?$

A. 2   C. 8   E. 12
B. 4   D. 10

31. If $3x+5y=10$, then $y=?$

A. $-0.6x-2$ C. $0.5x-4$ E. $-0.6x+2$
B. $-0.4x+2$ D. $0.6x-2$

32. If $8x+16=(x+2)(x+5)$, then $x=?$

A. 3 or −2   C. −2   E. 3
B. −3   D. 2 or 3

33. If $\frac{0.2+x}{3}=\frac{\frac{5}{6}}{4}$, then $x=?$

A. $-\frac{40}{17}$ C. 0   E. $\frac{40}{17}$
B. $-\frac{17}{40}$ D. $\frac{17}{40}$

34. If x is an integer and $5 \le x \le 7$, then which of the following values is (are) possible for x?

   I. 5
   II. 6
   III. 7

   A. II only
   B. I and II only
   C. I and III only
   D. II and III only
   E. I, II, and III

35. If x and y are integers, $5 > x \ge 2$, and $6 < y \le 9$, then which of the following is the *minimum* value of xy?

   A. 14
   B. 18
   C. 20
   D. 45
   E. 54

36. If $3^{8x+4} = 27^{2x+12}$, then $x = ?$

   A. $\dfrac{1}{4}$
   B. $\dfrac{1}{9}$
   C. 4
   D. 9
   E. 16

37. For what value of x is $\sqrt{x} + 3 = 5$?

   A. 2
   B. 4
   C. 8
   D. 9
   E. 16

38. The formula for determining the volume of a cone is: $V = \dfrac{\pi r^2 h}{3}$ where V is volume, h is height, and r is the radius of the base. Which of the following equations can be used to determine the height, h, of a cone with volume V and a base with radius r?

   A. $h = \dfrac{\pi r^2}{3V}$
   B. $h = \dfrac{3\pi r^2}{V}$
   C. $h = \dfrac{\pi r^2 V}{3}$
   D. $h = \dfrac{3V}{\pi r^2}$
   E. $h = \dfrac{\pi r^2}{3V}$

39. If $2(x+3) = 18a + 10$, then $x = ?$

   A. $9a + 2$
   B. $9a + 5$
   C. $16a + 4$
   D. $9a + 3.5$
   E. 11

40. If x is a real number such that $x \ne 0$, y is a real number, $x^5 = 8y$, and $x^4 = y$, then which of the following is true?

   A. $x = 7y$
   B. $x = 8y$
   C. $x = 8y^2$
   D. $x = 7y^2$
   E. $x = 8$

41. What is the tenth term of the sequence $\{1, 4, 9, 16, ...\}$?

   A. 25
   B. 36
   C. 49
   D. 81
   E. 100

42. For what value of x is $6 - 2\sqrt{x} = 0$?

   A. –3
   B. 0
   C. 3
   D. 9
   E. 12

43. Which of the following values for c returns two distinct real solutions to the equation $x^2 - 8x + c = 0$?

   A. –20
   B. 17
   C. 18
   D. 19
   E. 20

44. If $4y + 2x = 2y + 8 - 6x$, then which of the following equations correctly expresses y in terms of x?

   A. $y = 4 - 4x$
   B. $y = 2 + 4x$
   C. $y = -2 + x$
   D. $y = 4 - x$
   E. $y = 2 - 2x$

45. For what value of x is $2\sqrt{x+3} + 5 = 21$?

   A. 16
   B. 34
   C. 61
   D. 64
   E. 163

46. If $\dfrac{3x}{4} = 1$, then $\dfrac{2x}{3} = ?$

   A. $\dfrac{1}{3}$
   B. $\dfrac{1}{2}$
   C. $\dfrac{2}{3}$
   D. $\dfrac{8}{9}$
   E. 2

47. If $|x|+3=10$, then $x=?$

A. 7   C. 13, –13   E. 6
B. 7, –7   D. 13

48. What are the roots of the equation $(2x+5)(x-4)=0$?

A. 2.5 and –4   C. 2.5 and 4   E. 2 and –5
B. –2.5 and 4   D. –2.5 and –4

49. If $2|x-4|-3=-1$, then $x=?$

A. 3, 5   C. –2, 2   E. 5
B. 3, –5   D. 3

50. If $|x-1|<5$, then which of the following correctly describes all possible values of x?

A. $x<4$ C. $-4<x<6$ E. $-4<x<4$
B. $x<6$ D. $-6<x<6$

51. What are the roots of the equation $x^2-4x-12=0$?

A. 4 and –3   C. –6 and 2   E. 6 and –2
B. –4 and 3   D. 6 and 2

52. If x represents a real number, how many different values of x satisfy the equation $x^{128}=16^{32}$?

A. 0
B. 1
C. 2
D. more than 2, but not infinite
E. infinite

53. If $y=3^x$, then $3^{x+2}=?$

A. y^2 C. $y+3$ E. $y+9$
B. 2^y D. $9y$

54. If $3x^2-9x=0$, then $x=?$

A. 3 and –9   C. 0 and 3   E. 2 and –3
B. 3 and 9   D. –3 and –9

55. Let $f(x)=\dfrac{x-2}{2x-13}$. If x represents a whole number, what is the largest value of x such that $f(x)<0$?

A. –1   C. 1   E. 8
B. 0   D. 6

56. If $-5<x<-1$, and $f(x)=|14-|1+2x||$, then $f(x)=?$

A. $13-2x$ C. $13+2x$ E. $13+3x$
B. $15+2x$ D. $2x-13$

57. If $|2x-3|\geq7$, then which of the following describes all possible values of x?

A. $x\geq5$ D. $-2\leq x\leq5$
B. $x\geq2$ E. $x\leq1$ or $x\geq10$
C. $x\leq-2$ or $x\geq5$

58. If $y=2x+1$ and the domain for x is the set of all non-negative integers, then the range for y is the set of which of the following?

A. Non-negative integers
B. Non-negative even integers
C. Odd integers
D. Positive odd integers
E. Real numbers equal to or greater than 1

59. How many whole numbers are not in the domain of values for x if $y=\dfrac{(x-1)(x-2)(x-3)}{x^2-11x+30}$?

A. 1   C. 3   E. 5
B. 2   D. 4

60. $f(x)$ and $g(x)$ represent linear functions. If $f(x)=5$ for $x=1$, $g(x)=3x+8$, and $f(x)=g(x)$ for $x=2$, then what is the value of $f(4)$?

A. 12   C. 20   E. 32
B. 16   D. 24

61. If $10x^2 = 30$ and $(6+y)y = 6y + 52$, then
$2x^2 + 2y^2 = ?$

    A. 110   C. 82   E. 55
    B. 96   D. 72

62. A geometric sequence is a sequence of numbers formed by continually multiplying by the same number; e.g., {81, 27, 9, 3, ...} is a geometric sequence formed by continually multiplying by $\frac{1}{3}$. What is the next term in the geometric sequence of {2, 8, 32, 128, ...}?

    A. 132   C. 384   E. 1,024
    B. 256   D. 512

63. An arithmetic sequence is a sequence of numbers formed by continually adding the same number; e.g., {1, 3, 5, 7, 9, 11, ...} is an arithmetic sequence formed by continually adding 2. What is the ninth term in the arithmetic sequence of {1, 4, 7, 10, 13, ...}?

    A. 16   C. 19   E. 25
    B. 17   D. 21

64. If $x = k + \frac{1}{2} = \frac{k+3}{2}$, then $x = ?$

    A. $\frac{1}{3}$ C. 1   E. $\frac{5}{2}$

    B. $\frac{1}{2}$ D. 2

65. Let $y = 2^x$ and $w = 8^x$. For what value of x does $w = 2y$?

    A. A rational number between 0 and 2
    B. A whole number between 2 and 8
    C. A irrational number between 2 and 8
    D. No such value of x exists.
    E. More than one such value of x exists.

66. Let n be a member of the set {5, 6, 7, 8, 9, 10, 11, 12, 13, 14, 15, 16}. For how many different values of n is the following equation true?

$$\frac{1 + 2 + \ldots + n}{2 + 4 + \ldots + 2n} = \frac{1}{2}$$

    A. 0   C. 6   E. 12
    B. 1   D. 11

67. If $f(x) = \frac{kx}{3x+5}$, $x \neq -\frac{5}{3}$, k is a constant, and $f(x)$ satisfies the equation $f(f(x)) = x$ for all real values of x except for $x = -\frac{5}{3}$, what is the value of k?

    A. k cannot be uniquely determined.
    B. k does not equal any real value.
    C. $k = -\frac{5}{3}$

    D. $k = -\frac{3}{5}$

    E. $k = -5$

GEOMETRY

If you have ever taken a basic course in geometry, you probably remember having to memorize theorems and do formal proofs. Fortunately, you will not be asked to do any formal proofs on the exam, and the formulas you need to know are few and relatively simple. Most often, test items ask you to find the measure of an angle, the length of a line, or the area of a figure.

Geometric Notation

The ACT test includes items that test standard geometric notation for length, segments, lines, rays, and congruence. For example, $\overline{PQ}$ represents a line segment with points P and Q as endpoints, and PQ represents the length of $\overline{PQ}$. A line passing through points P and Q is represented by $\overleftrightarrow{PQ}$, while $\overrightarrow{PQ}$ represents the ray beginning at point P and passing through point Q. Finally, the symbol "$\cong$" represents the term "congruent."

> **Example:**
>
> If $\overleftrightarrow{AB}$ does not contain point C, but it does contain point D, what is the maximum number of points in the intersection of $\overleftrightarrow{AB}$ and $\overleftrightarrow{CD}$?
>
> ➤ $\overleftrightarrow{AB}$ and $\overleftrightarrow{CD}$ are different lines, so the maximum number of points at which they can intersect is one point, point D.

Line and Angle Properties

For the purposes of this review and the test, the word **line** means a straight line:

$$P \qquad Q$$
$$\bullet\!\!-\!\!-\!\!-\!\!-\!\!-\!\!\bullet\!\!-\!\!-\!\!-\ l$$

The line above is designated line l. The portion of line l from point P to point Q is called "line segment PQ," or "$\overline{PQ}$."

When two lines intersect, they form an **angle**, and their point of intersection is called the **vertex** of that angle.

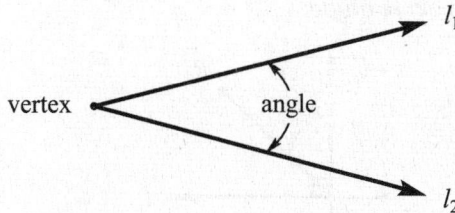

The size of an angle is measured in *degrees*. Degrees are defined in reference to a circle. By convention, a circle is divided into 360 equal parts, or degrees.

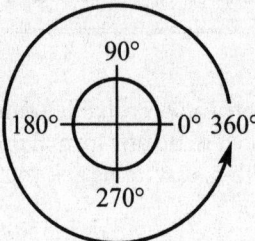

A 90° angle is also called a ***right angle***. A right angle is often indicated in the following way:

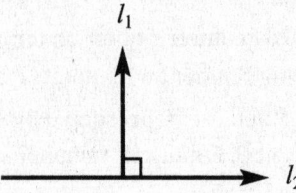

Two right angles form a straight line:

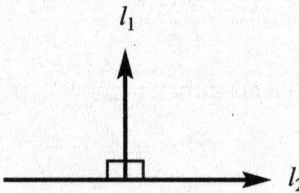

Since two right angles form a straight line, the degree measure of the angle of a straight line is $90° + 90° = 180°$:

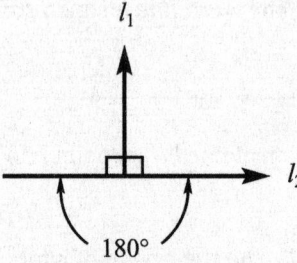

An angle that is less than 90° is called an ***acute angle***:

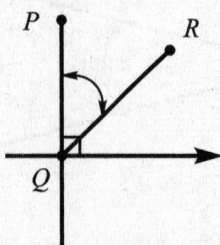

In the figure above, $\angle PQR$ is an acute angle.

An angle that is greater than 90° but less than 180° is called an **obtuse angle**:

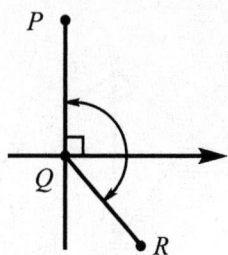

In the figure above, $\angle PQR$ is an obtuse angle.

When two lines intersect, the opposite (or vertical) angles created by their intersection are congruent, or equal:

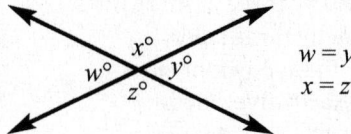

Two lines that do not intersect regardless of how far they are extended are **parallel** to each other. In the following figure, the symbol ∥ indicates that l_1 and l_2 are parallel.

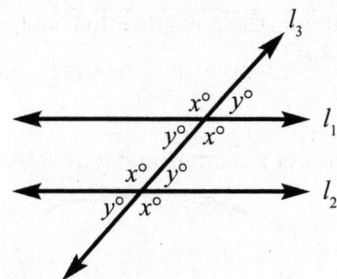

When parallel lines are intersected by a third line, a **transversal**, the following angle relationships are created:

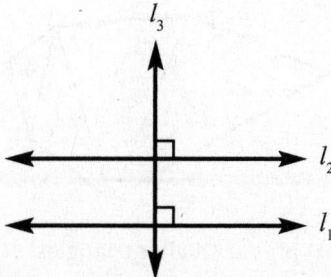

All angles labeled x are equal.
All angles labeled y are equal.
Any x plus any y totals 180.

Two lines that are **perpendicular** to the same line are parallel to each other:

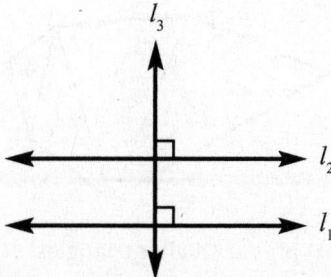

Since l_1 and l_2 are both perpendicular to l_3, we can conclude that l_1 and l_2 are parallel to each other.

A line segment that **bisects** another line, segment, or angle divides that line, segment, or angle into two congruent halves.

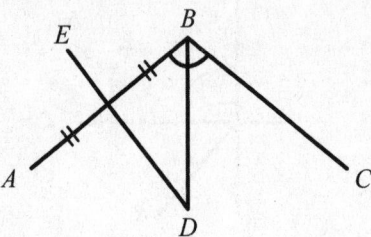

Polygon Properties

- A **polygon** is a closed figure created by three or more lines.
- A **triangle** is any polygon with exactly three sides.
- A **quadrilateral** is any polygon with exactly four sides.
- A **pentagon** is any polygon with exactly five sides.
- A **hexagon** is any polygon with exactly six sides.

A polygon with more than six sides is usually referred to as a polygon with a certain number of sides; for example, a polygon with ten sides is called a ten-sided polygon. A **regular polygon** is a polygon with equal sides and equal angles (e.g., a square). The sum of the degree measures of the **exterior angles** of a polygon is 360. The sum of the degree measures of the **interior angles** of a polygon can be expressed as $180(n-2)$, where n is the number of sides in the polygon.

Furthermore, note that any polygon is made up of a number of smaller triangles: a quadrilateral consists of two triangles, a pentagon consists of three triangles, an octagon consists of six triangles, etc. Therefore, the sum of the angles of a polygon can be found by partitioning the polygon into triangles and summing the angle measures of those triangles, each of which is equal to 180°.

Example:

What is the sum of the degree measures of the interior angles of the following six-sided polygon?

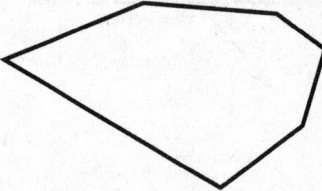

➤ If you remember the formula, use it: $180(n-2) = 180(6-2) = 180 \cdot 4 = 720°$. Otherwise, partition the polygon into smaller triangles:

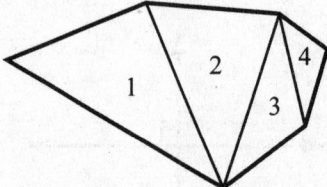

Since the six-sided polygon consists of four smaller triangles, each of which has an interior degree measure of 180°, the polygon's interior degree measure must be $4 \cdot 180 = 720°$.

Triangle Properties and Formulas

Properties of Triangles

A *triangle* is a three-sided figure. Within a given triangle, the larger an angle is, the longer the opposite side of the angle is; conversely, the longer a side is, the larger the opposite angle is.

Examples:

1. In the following figure, since $\overline{PR} > \overline{QR} > \overline{PQ}$, $\angle Q > \angle P > \angle R$.

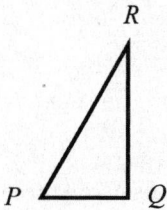

2. In the following figure, since $\angle P > \angle Q > \angle R$, $\overline{QR} > \overline{PR} > \overline{PQ}$.

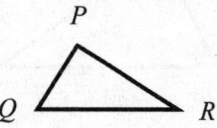

Within a given triangle, if two sides are equal, then the angles opposite the two sides are equal, and vice versa:

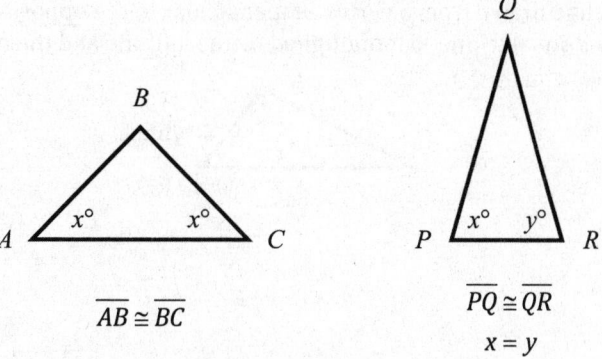

$\overline{AB} \cong \overline{BC}$

$\overline{PQ} \cong \overline{QR}$

$x = y$

A triangle with exactly two equal sides is called an *isosceles triangle*. A triangle with exactly three equal sides is called an *equilateral triangle*.

Example:

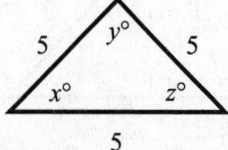

➢ An equilateral triangle has three equal sides and therefore three equal angles: $x = y = z$. Thus, each angle must be $60°$.

A triangle with a right angle is called a *right triangle*. The longest side of the right triangle, which is opposite the $90°$ angle, is called the *hypotenuse*.

Pythagorean Theorem

The sides of every right triangle fit a special relationship called the ***Pythagorean theorem***: the square of the hypotenuse is equal to the sum of the squares of the other two sides. This is easier to understand when it is summarized in a formula.

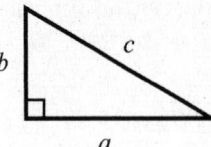

Pythagorean Theorem: $c^2 = a^2 + b^2$

Formulas of Triangles

The ***perimeter*** of a triangle is the sum of the lengths of the three sides:

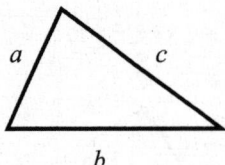

Triangle Perimeter: $P_{triangle} = a + b + c$

The ***altitude*** of a triangle is a line drawn from a vertex perpendicular to the opposite side. The formula for finding the ***area*** of a triangle is equal to one-half multiplied by the altitude and the base.

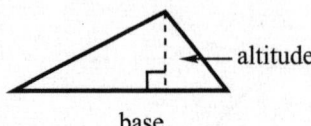

Triangle Area: $A_{triangle} = \dfrac{ab}{2}$

Example:

In the following figure, what is the area of the triangle?

➤ $A_{triangle} = \dfrac{ab}{2} = \dfrac{4 \cdot 5}{2} = 10$

Special Properties of 45°-45°-90° Triangles

The sides of **45°-45°-90° triangles** share special relationships. In a triangle with angles of 45°-45°-90°, the length of the hypotenuse is equal to the length of either side multiplied by the square root of two. Conversely, the length of each of the two sides is equal to one-half the length of the hypotenuse multiplied by the square root of two.

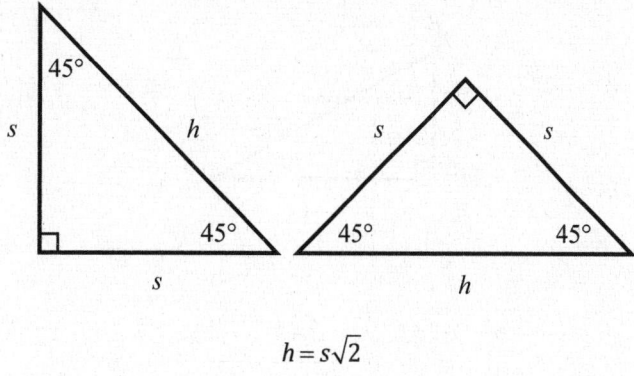

$$h = s\sqrt{2}$$

Examples:

1. In $\triangle ABC$, both $\angle A$ and $\angle C$ are $45°$. If the length of $\overline{AB}$ is 3, what is the length of $\overline{AC}$?

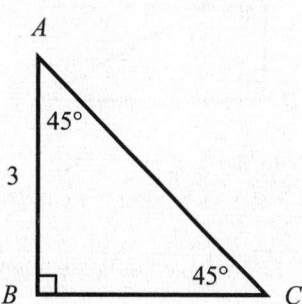

> $h = s\sqrt{2} \Rightarrow AC = AB\left(\sqrt{2}\right) = 3\sqrt{2}$

2. In $\triangle LMN$, both $\angle L$ and $\angle N$ are $45°$. If the length of $\overline{LN}$ is 4, what is the length of $\overline{MN}$?

> $h = s\sqrt{2} \Rightarrow 4 = s\sqrt{2} \Rightarrow s = \dfrac{4}{\sqrt{2}} = \dfrac{4}{\sqrt{2}} \cdot \dfrac{\sqrt{2}}{\sqrt{2}} = \dfrac{4\sqrt{2}}{2} = 2\sqrt{2}$

Special Properties of 30°-60°-90° Triangles

Similarly, the sides of **30°-60°-90° triangles** also share special relationships. In triangles with angles of 30°-60°-90°, the length of the side opposite the 30° angle is equal to one-half the length of the hypotenuse, and the length of the side opposite the 60° angle is equal to one-half the length of the hypotenuse multiplied by $\sqrt{3}$.

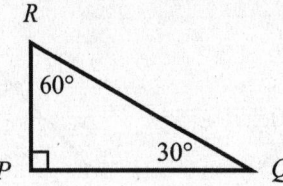

$$PR = \frac{QR}{2}; \ PQ = \frac{QR\sqrt{3}}{2}$$

Examples:

1. In $\triangle ABC$, $\angle A = 60°$ and $\angle C = 30°$. If the length of $\overline{AC}$ is 6, what are the lengths of $\overline{AB}$ and $\overline{BC}$?

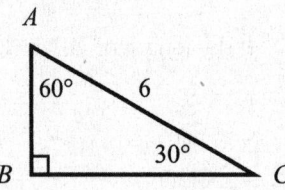

> $AB = \dfrac{AC}{2} = \dfrac{6}{2} = 3 \Rightarrow BC = \dfrac{AC\sqrt{3}}{2} = \dfrac{6\sqrt{3}}{2} = 3\sqrt{3}$

2. In $\triangle FGH$, $\angle F = 60°$. If the length of $\overline{FH}$ is 14, what is the length of $\overline{FG}$?

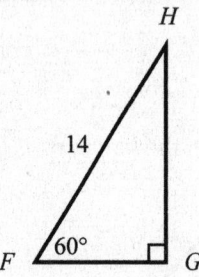

> The length of the side opposite the 30° angle, $\overline{FG}$, is equal to one-half the length of the side opposite the 90° angle, $\overline{FH}$: $FG = \dfrac{FH}{2} = \dfrac{14}{2} = 7$.

Similar Triangles

"Real world" items such as blueprints, scale drawings, microscopes, and photo enlargements involve similar figures. **Similar triangles** are frequently encountered on the exams. The symbol for similarity is "∼." If two triangles are similar, the corresponding sides have the same ratio, and their matching angles are **congruent**; that is, they have the same number of degrees. Again, the symbol for congruency is "≅ ."

Examples:

1. In the following figure, $\triangle ABC \sim \triangle DEF$. Find the length of $\overline{AC}$.

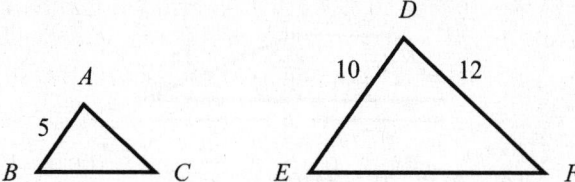

> The triangles are similar, so create a proportion relating the similar sides:
>
> $\dfrac{AC}{5} = \dfrac{12}{10} \Rightarrow 10(AC) = 5(12) \Rightarrow 10AC = 60 \Rightarrow AC = 6$.

2. Right triangle *PQR* is similar to right triangle *STV*. The hypotenuse of $\triangle PQR$ is 12 units long and one of the legs is 6 units long. Find the smallest angle of $\triangle STV$.

> Any right triangle in which one leg is equal to one-half the hypotenuse must be a 30°-60°-90° triangle. Since the two triangles are similar, the matching angles are congruent. Therefore, the smallest angle of $\triangle STV$ is 30°.

Quadrilateral Properties and Formulas

A *quadrilateral* is a closed, four-sided figure in two dimensions. Common quadrilaterals are the parallelogram, rectangle, and square. The sum of the four angles of a quadrilateral is 360°. A *parallelogram* is a quadrilateral in which both pairs of opposite sides are parallel. Opposite sides of a parallelogram are equal, or congruent. Similarly, opposite angles of a parallelogram are also equal, or congruent. Again, the symbol for congruency is "$\cong$."

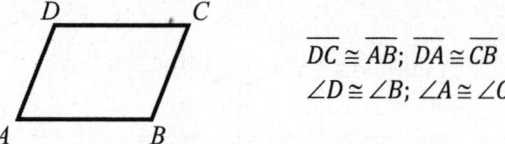

$$\overline{DC} \cong \overline{AB};\ \overline{DA} \cong \overline{CB}$$
$$\angle D \cong \angle B;\ \angle A \cong \angle C$$

The area of a parallelogram is found by multiplying the base times its height. The height must be measured at a right angle to the base.

Example:

In the following figure, find the area of the parallelogram.

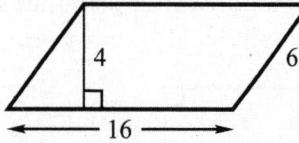

> The base of the parallelogram is 16 and the height is 4 (not 6). Remember, the height must be measured at a right angle to the base. Therefore, the area is: $16 \cdot 4 = 64$.

A *trapezoid* is a quadrilateral with only two parallel sides. The area of a trapezoid is equal to one-half of the height times the sum of the two bases, which are the two parallel sides. Alternatively, a trapezoid can be broken down into triangles and rectangles, and the sum of these areas equals the trapezoid's area. The following example illustrates both methods.

Example:

In the following figure, find the area of the trapezoid.

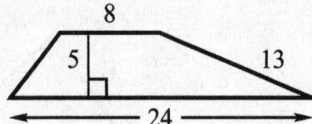

➢ The area of a trapezoid is: $\dfrac{(b_1 + b_2)h}{2} = \dfrac{(8+24)(5)}{2} = 80$. However, if you do not remember the formula, simply break down the trapezoid into two triangles and a rectangle:

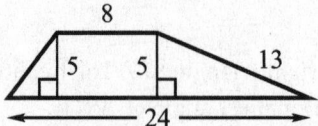

Use the Pythagorean theorem to find the base of the right-hand triangle: $x^2 + 5^2 = 13^2 \Rightarrow x = \sqrt{169 - 25} = \sqrt{144} = 12$. This implies that the base of the left-hand triangle is: $24 - 12 - 8 = 4$. Thus, the left-hand triangle's area is: $\dfrac{4 \cdot 5}{2} = 10$; the right-hand triangle's area is: $\dfrac{12 \cdot 5}{2} = 30$; and the rectangle's area $= 8 \cdot 5 = 40$. The trapezoid area is: $10 + 30 + 40 = 80$.

FORMULAS FOR PARALLELOGRAMS AND TRAPEZOIDS ✓

Parallelogram Area: $A_{\text{parallelogram}} = b \cdot h$

Trapezoid Area: $A_{\text{trapezoid}} = \dfrac{(b_1 + b_2)h}{2}$

A ***rectangle*** is any four-sided figure that has four right angles. Since the opposite sides of a rectangle are congruent, it is customary to speak of the two dimensions of a rectangle: width and length. A ***square*** is a rectangle with four congruent sides.

To find the ***perimeter*** of either a rectangle or a square, simply add the lengths of the four sides. To find the ***area*** of a rectangle, multiply the width times the length. In a square, the sides are all congruent, so there is no difference between length and width. To find the area of a square, just square the length of one side.

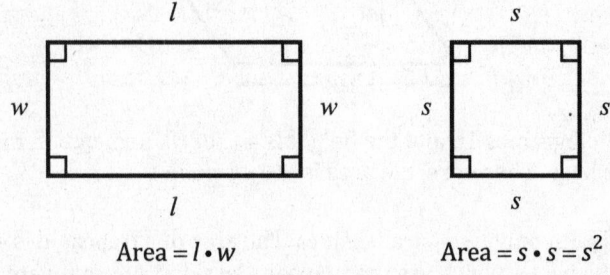

FORMULAS FOR RECTANGLES AND SQUARES

Rectangular Perimeter: $P_{rectangle} = 2(width) + 2(length) = 2w + 2l = 2(w + l)$

Rectangular Area: $A_{rectangle} = w \cdot l$

Square Perimeter: $P_{square} = 4(side) = 4s$

Square Area: $A_{square} = s \cdot s = s^2$

Circle Properties and Formulas

Properties of Circles

A *circle* is a closed plane curve, all points of which are equidistant from the center. A complete circle contains 360°, and a semicircle contains 180°. The distance from the center of the circle to any point on the circle is called the *radius*.

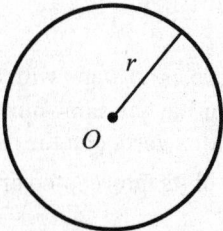

A line segment that passes through the center of the circle and that has endpoints on the circle is called the *diameter*. The diameter of a circle is twice the radius.

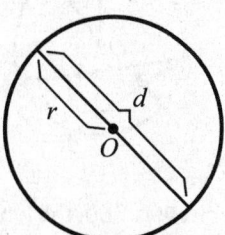

A *chord* is a line segment that connects any two points on a circle. A *secant* is a chord that extends in either one or both directions. A *tangent* is a line that touches a circle at one and only one point. A line that is tangent to a circle is perpendicular to a radius drawn to the point of tangency. The *circumference*, or perimeter, is the curved line that bounds the circle. An *arc* of a circle is any part of the circumference. The symbol for arc is " $\frown$."

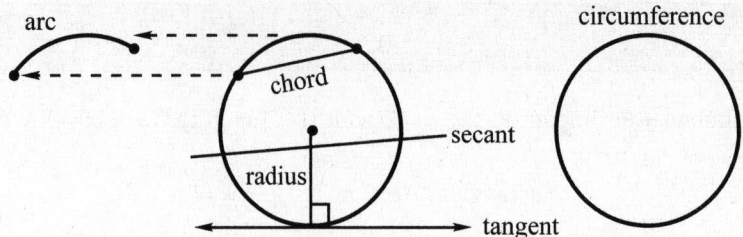

Example:

Two different circles lie in a flat plane. The circles may or may not intersect, but neither circle lies entirely within the other. What is the difference between the minimum and maximum number of lines that could be common tangents to both circles?

➤ Three cases are possible for the orientation of the two circles:

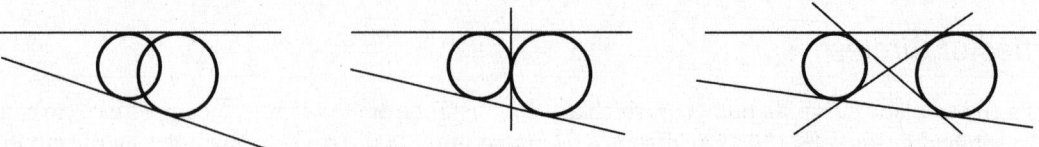

The difference between the minimum and maximum number of tangents that could be common to both circles is: $4-2=2$.

A **central angle**, such as $\angle AOB$ in the next figure, is an angle with a vertex at the center of the circle and with sides that are radii. A central angle is equal to, or has the same number of degrees as, its intercepted arc. An **inscribed angle**, such as $\angle MNP$, is an angle with a vertex on the circle and with sides that are chords. An inscribed angle has half the number of degrees of its intercepted arc. $\angle MNP$ intercepts $\overset{\frown}{MP}$ and has half the degrees of $\overset{\frown}{MP}$.

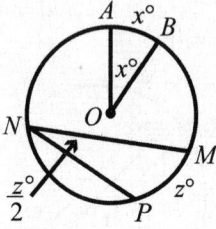

Since the number of degrees of arc in an entire circle is 360, the length of the intercepted arc of a central angle is $\dfrac{x}{360}$ of the circumference of the circle, where x is the degree measure of the central angle.

Example:

In the following circle with center O, if $x = 60$ and the diameter of the circle is 12, what is the length of $\overset{\frown}{MN}$?

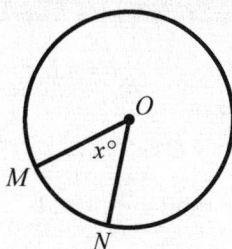

➤ Since the $\angle MON$ is a central angle, it has the same number of degrees as the intercepted $\overset{\frown}{MN}$. Thus, the length of $\overset{\frown}{MN}$ is: $\dfrac{x}{360} = \dfrac{60}{360} = \dfrac{1}{6}$ of the circumference of the circle. The circumference of the circle is:

$C = 2\pi r = 2\pi \cdot \dfrac{d}{2} = \pi d = 12\pi$. Therefore, the length of $\overset{\frown}{MN}$ is: $\dfrac{12\pi}{6} = 2\pi$.

If each side of a polygon is tangent to a circle, the polygon is *circumscribed* about the circle and the circle is *inscribed* in the polygon. Conversely, if each vertex of a polygon lies on a circle, then the polygon is *inscribed* in the circle and the circle is *circumscribed* about the polygon.

Example:

In the following figure, $\triangle ABC$ is circumscribed about a circle and square $DEFG$ is inscribed in a circle.

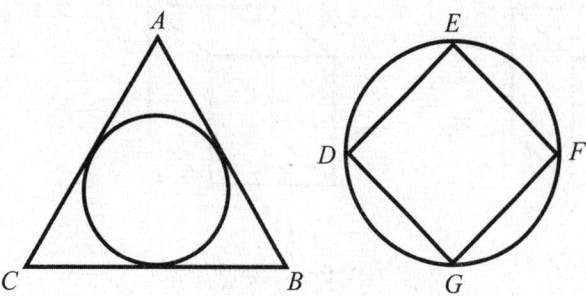

An angle inscribed in a semicircle is a right angle because the semicircle has a measure of 180°.

Example:

In the following figure, $\overset{\frown}{NP}$ has a degree measure of 180°; therefore, the degree measure of $\angle NMP$ must be 90°.

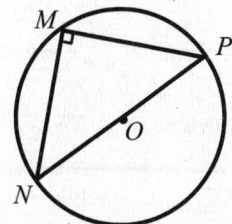

Formulas for Circles

FORMULAS FOR CIRCLES

Circle Circumference: $C_{circle} = 2\pi r = \pi d$; $r = $ radius, $d = $ diameter

Circle Area: $A_{circle} = \pi r^2$

$$\pi(\text{pi}) \approx \frac{22}{7} \approx 3.14$$

Surface Area and Volume of Solids

In a three-dimensional figure, the total space contained within the figure is called the ***volume***; it is expressed in ***cubic denominations*** (e.g., cm^3). The total outside surface is called the ***surface area***; it is expressed in ***square denominations*** (e.g., cm^2). In computing volume and surface area, express all dimensions in the same denomination.

A ***rectangular solid*** is a figure of three dimensions having six rectangular faces that meet each other at right angles. The three dimensions are length, width, and height. A ***cube*** is a rectangular solid whose edges are equal. A ***cylinder*** is a solid composed of two circular, parallel planes joined at the edges by a curved surface. The centers of the circular planes both lie in a line perpendicular to both planes.

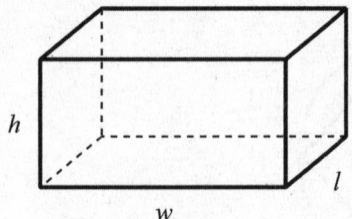

Volume $= w \cdot l \cdot h$

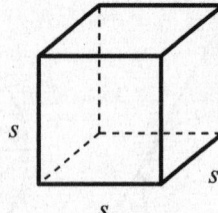

Cube Volume $= s^3$

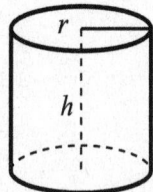

Cylinder Volume $= h\pi r^2$

FORMULAS FOR RECTANGULAR SOLIDS, CUBES, AND CYLINDERS

Rectangular Solid Volume: $V_{rectangular\ solid} = \text{width} \cdot \text{length} \cdot \text{height} = w \cdot l \cdot h$

Rectangular Solid Surface Area: $A_{rectangular\ solid} = 2(w \cdot l) + 2(l \cdot h) + 2(h \cdot w)$

Cube Volume: $V_{cube} = \text{side}^3 = s^3$

Cube Surface Area: $SA_{cube} = 6s^2$

Cylinder Volume: $V_{cylinder} = \text{height} \cdot \text{end area} = h\left(\pi r^2\right)$

Cylinder Surface Area: $SA_{cylinder} = (2\pi r \cdot h) + 2\left(\pi r^2\right)$

Examples:

1. What is the volume and surface area of the following rectangular solid?

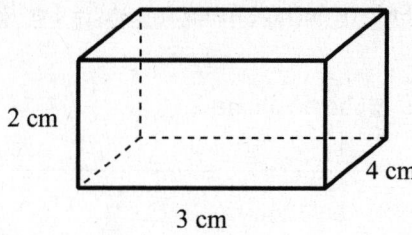

$$\text{Volume} = w \cdot l \cdot h = 3 \cdot 4 \cdot 2 = 24 \text{ cm}^3$$

$$\text{Surface Area} = 2(w \cdot l) + 2(l \cdot h) + 2(h \cdot w) = 2(3 \cdot 4) + 2(4 \cdot 2) + 2(2 \cdot 3) = 24 + 16 + 12 = 52 \text{ cm}^2$$

2. What is the volume and surface area of the following cube?

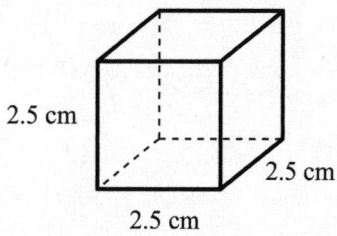

$$\text{Volume} = s^3 = (2.5)^3 = 15.625 \text{ cm}^3$$

$$\text{Surface Area} = 6s^2 = 6(2.5)^2 = 37.5 \text{ cm}^2$$

3. What is the volume and surface area of the following cylindrical solid?

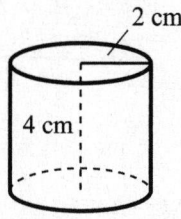

$$\text{Volume} = h\left(\pi r^2\right) = 4\left(\pi \cdot 2^2\right) = 16\pi \text{ cm}^3$$

$$\text{Surface Area} = (2\pi r \cdot h) + 2\left(\pi r^2\right) = (2\pi \cdot 2 \cdot 4) + 2\left(\pi \cdot 2^2\right) = 16\pi + 8\pi = 24\pi \text{ cm}^2$$

The ***surface area of a sphere*** is 4π multiplied by the radius squared. The ***volume of a sphere*** is $\dfrac{4\pi}{3}$ multiplied by the radius cubed.

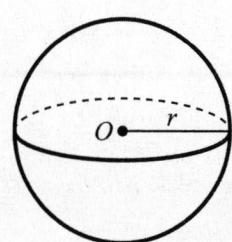

FORMULAS FOR SPHERES

Sphere Surface Area: $SA_{sphere} = 4\pi r^2$

Sphere Volume: $V_{sphere} = \dfrac{4\pi r^3}{3}$

Geometry
Exercise 10

DIRECTIONS: Choose the correct answer to each of the following items. Answers are on page 608.

1. In the figure below, $x = ?$

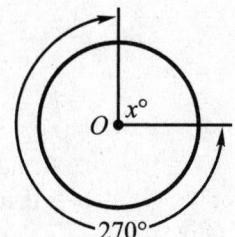

O is the center of the circle.

A. 30   C. 90   E. 270
B. 60   D. 120

2. In the figure below, $x = ?$

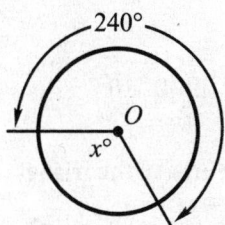

A. 60   C. 120   E. 180
B. 90   D. 150

3. In the figure below, $x = ?$

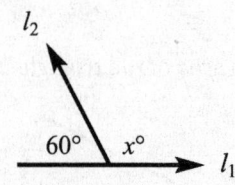

A. 15°   C. 45   E. 120
B. 30   D. 90

4. In the figure below, $x = ?$

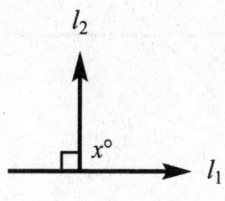

A. 15   C. 45   E. 90
B. 30   D. 60

5. In the figure below, $x = ?$

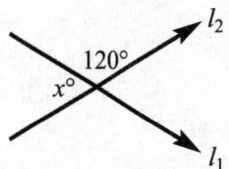

A. 45   C. 75   E. 120
B. 60   D. 90

6. Which of the following is (are) true of the figure below?

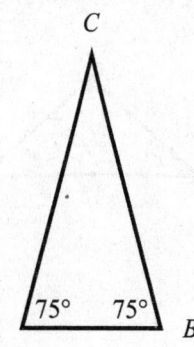

I. $\overline{AB} \cong \overline{BC}$
II. $\overline{BC} \cong \overline{AC}$
III. $\overline{AC} \cong \overline{AB}$

A. I only   D. I and III only
B. II only   E. I, II, and III
C. I and II only

Items #7–8 are based on the following figure:

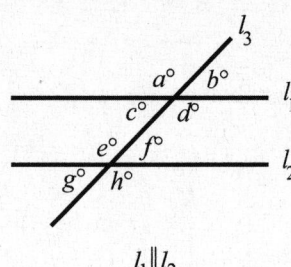

$l_1 \| l_2$

7. Which of the following is (are) necessarily true?

    I. $b = c$
   II. $d = c$
  III. $g = e$

A. I only
B. III only
C. I and III only
D. II and III only
E. I, II, and III

8. If $e = 120$, then $g = ?$

A. 60
B. 90
C. 120
D. 150
E. 180

9. Which of the following is (are) true of the figure below?

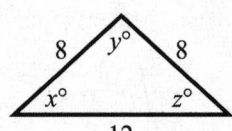

    I. $x = y$
   II. $y = z$
  III. $z = x$

A. I only
B. II only
C. III only
D. I and II only
E. I, II, and III

10. Which of the following is (are) true of the figure below?

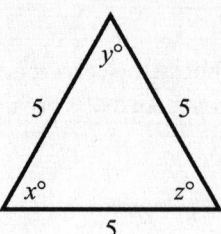

    I. $x = y$
   II. $y = z$
  III. $z = x$

A. I only
B. I and II only
C. I and III only
D. II and III only
E. I, II, and III

11. What is the perimeter of the triangle below?

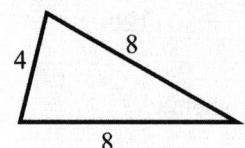

A. 20
B. 18
C. 12
D. 10
E. 8

12. What is the area of the triangle below?

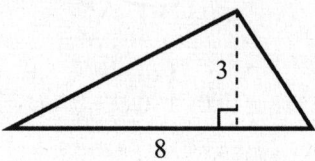

A. 3
B. 6
C. 12
D. 18
E. 24

13. What is the area of the triangle below?

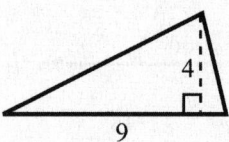

A. 6
B. 12
C. 15
D. 18
E. 24

14. In the figure below, what is the length of $\overline{AB}$?

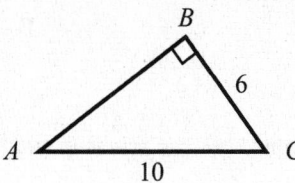

A. 4   C. 12   E. 24
B. 8   D. 16

15. In the figure below, what is the length of $\overline{AC}$?

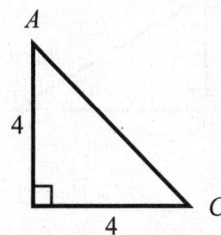

A. 2   C. 4   E. 8
B. $2\sqrt{2}$ D. $4\sqrt{2}$

16. What is the area of the parallelogram below?

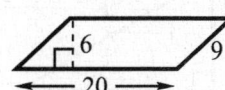

A. 180   C. 58   E. 15
B. 120   D. 29

17. What is the area of the parallelogram below?

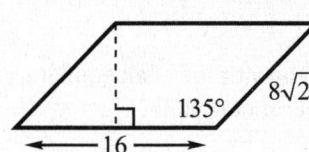

A. $128\sqrt{3}$ C. 128   E. 64
B. $128\sqrt{2}$ D. $64\sqrt{2}$

18. In $\triangle ABC$, the measure of $\angle A$ is 23° and the measure of $\angle B$ is 84°. What is the longest side of $\triangle ABC$?

A. $\overline{AC}$
B. $\overline{AB}$
C. $\overline{BC}$
D. $\overline{AC} \cong \overline{AB}$ (there is no longest side)
E. $\overline{AC} \cong \overline{BC}$ (there is no longest side)

19. In $\triangle ABC$, the measure of $\angle A$ is 40° and the measure of $\angle B$ is 70°. What is the longest side of $\triangle ABC$?

A. $\overline{AC}$
B. $\overline{AB}$
C. $\overline{BC}$
D. $\overline{AC} \cong \overline{AB}$ (there is no longest side)
E. $\overline{AC} \cong \overline{BC}$ (there is no longest side)

20. Each side of a cube is a square with an area of 49 square centimeters. What is the volume of the cube, in cubic centimeters?

A. 49   C. 7^4 E. 7^{49}
B. 7^3 D. 49^7

21. What is the area of the trapezoid below?

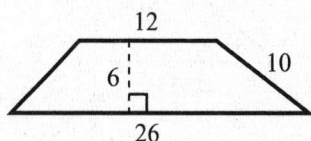

A. 260   C. 120   E. 58
B. 130   D. 114

22. The volume of a sphere is: $V_{sphere} = \dfrac{4}{3}\pi r^3$,

where r is the radius of the sphere. If the surface area of the sphere is 324π, what is the sphere's volume?

A. 243π C. 729π E. $1{,}296\pi$
B. 324π D. 972π

23. What is the perimeter of the figure below?

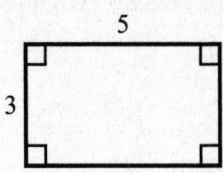

A. 8 C. 14 E. 16
B. 12 D. 15

24. What is the area of the figure below?

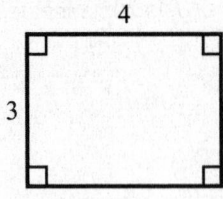

A. 6 C. 12 E. 24
B. 8 D. 16

25. In the figure below, $\overline{AB} = 5$. What is the area of square $ABCD$?

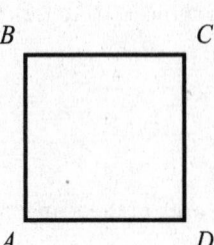

A. 5 C. 20 E. 40
B. 10 D. 25

26. If the diameter of a circle is 10, what is the radius?

A. 2 C. 8 E. 20
B. 5 D. 15

27. If the radius of a circle is 5, what is the circumference?

A. 5π C. 15π E. 24π
B. 10π D. 20π

28. If the radius of a circle is 3, what is the area?

A. π C. 6π E. 12π
B. 3π D. 9π

29. If the diameter of a circle is 8, what is the area?

A. 16π C. 10π E. 4π
B. 12π D. 8π

30. In the figure below, what are a and b?

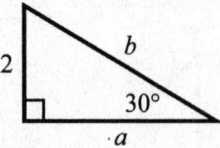

A. $a = \sqrt{3}$, $b = 2$ D. $a = 4$, $b = 2\sqrt{3}$
B. $a = 2\sqrt{3}$, $b = 4$ E. $a = 4$, $b = 4\sqrt{3}$
C. $a = 2$, $b = 2$

31. In the figure below, what are e and f?

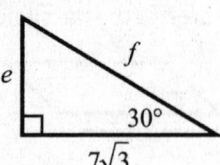

A. $e = 2$, $f = 6$ D. $e = 7$, $f = 10$
B. $e = \sqrt{2}$, $f = 8$ E. $e = 7$, $f = 14$
C. $e = 4$, $f = 3\sqrt{5}$

32. What is the altitude of an equilateral triangle with a perimeter of 24?

A. $2\sqrt{3}$ C. 6 E. 8
B. $4\sqrt{3}$ D. $4\sqrt{5}$

33. In the figure below, what are k and m?

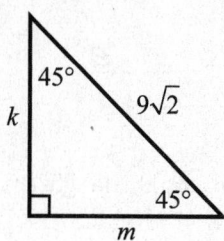

A. $k=3$, $m=3$ D. $k=9$, $m=9$
B. $k=2\sqrt{3}$, $m=3$ E. $k=3$, $m=9$
C. $k=4$, $m=6$

34. If the perimeter of a square is equal to 40, what is the length of the diagonal?

A. $10\sqrt{2}$ C. 10 E. 14
B. $5\sqrt{3}$ D. $3\sqrt{5}$

35. In the circle below, $\overline{RS}$ is parallel to diameter $\overline{PQ}$, and $\overline{PQ}$ has a length of 12. What is the length of minor arc $\overset{\frown}{RS}$?

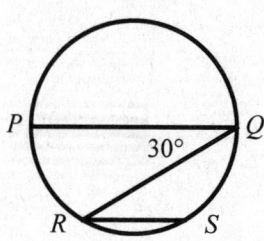

A. $\dfrac{\pi}{2}$ C. 2π E. $\dfrac{7\pi}{2}$

B. π D. $\dfrac{3\pi}{2}$

36. What is the radius of a circle with an area of 49?

A. 7 C. $\dfrac{7}{\sqrt{\pi}}$ E. π^2

B. 7π D. $\dfrac{7}{\pi}$

37. A circle has an area of $36\pi^3$. What is the radius of the circle?

A. 6 C. $6\pi^2$ E. $6\pi^4$
B. 6π D. $6\pi^3$

38. In the figure below, what is the value of the shaded area?

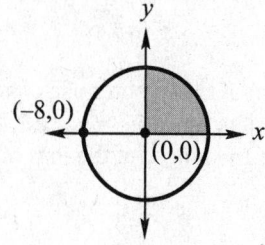

A. 16π C. 64π E. $16\pi^2$
B. 32π D. 66π

39. Two congruent legs of a triangle with angles of degree measures of 45, 45, and 90 are 5. What is the length of the hypotenuse?

A. 5 B. $5\sqrt{2}$ C. $5\sqrt{3}$
D. $6\sqrt{2}$ E. $6\sqrt{3}$

40. The area of a square is $64x^2y^{16}$. What is the length of a side of the square?

A. $8xy^8$ C. $8x^2y^{16}$ E. $20x^2y^4$
B. $8xy^4$ D. $16x^2y^{16}$

41. What is the area of a right triangle with legs of lengths 4 and 5?

A. 6 C. 12 E. 24
B. 10 D. 20

42. In the figure below, rectangle *ABCD* has an area of 15. What is the length of the diagonal $\overline{AC}$?

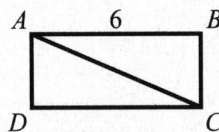

A. 4   C. 6.5   E. 7.5
B. 5   D. 7

43. The length of the hypotenuse of a triangle with angles of degree measures of 45, 45, and 90 is 6. What is the length of the legs of the triangle?

A. 3   C. $3\sqrt{3}$ E. $4\sqrt{2}$
B. $3\sqrt{2}$ D. 4

44. If the diagonal of a square is $5\sqrt{2}$, what is the area of the square?

A. 10   C. 25   E. 35
B. 20   D. 30

45. In the figure below, what is *x* equal to?

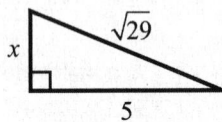

A. $\sqrt{29}-5$ C. 24   E. $\sqrt{2}$
B. $\sqrt{24}$ D. 2

46. In the figures below, what is the ratio of the perimeter of $\triangle ABC$ to the perimeter of $\triangle DEF$?

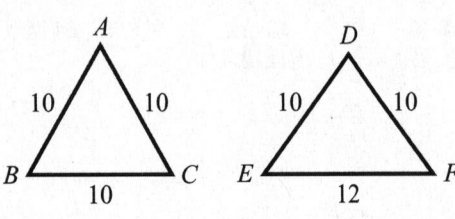

A. 1:1   C. 15:16   E. 7:3
B. 5:6   D. 6:5

47. What is the radius of a circle whose area is 12π?

A. 40π C. $2\sqrt{3}$ E. 3
B. 1   D. 2

48. If the legs of a right triangle are 2 and 5, what is the hypotenuse?

A. $\sqrt{22}$ C. $5\sqrt{2}$ E. 6
B. $\sqrt{29}$ D. $\sqrt{35}$

49. If $2\sqrt{12}$, $3\sqrt{6}$, and $4\sqrt{3}$ are the dimensions of a rectangular solid, what is the volume of the solid?

A. $216\sqrt{24}$ C. $144\sqrt{6}$ E. $\sqrt{24}$
B. $\sqrt{5,184}$ D. 5,184

50. In the figure below, what is *x* equal to?

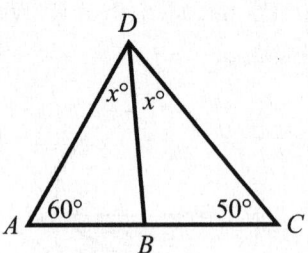

A. 30   C. 35   E. 70
B. 32   D. 40

51. In the figure below, what is the length of $\overline{JK}$?

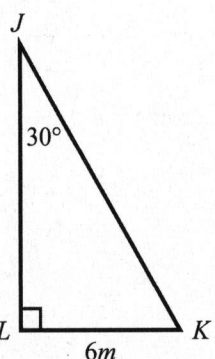

A. $6m\sqrt{3}$ C. $12m$ E. $14m$
B. $9m$ D. $12m\sqrt{3}$

52. If the longest side of a 30°-60°-90° triangle is $2\sqrt{3}$, what is the area of the triangle?

    A. 8   C. $1.5\sqrt{3}$ E. 1
    B. 4   D. 2

53. The length of the hypotenuse of a triangle of degree measures 45, 45, and 90 is 7. What is the length of the legs of the triangle?

    A. $\dfrac{7\sqrt{3}}{3}$ C. $7\sqrt{2}$ E. 8

    B. $\dfrac{7\sqrt{2}}{2}$ D. $7\sqrt{3}$

54. In the figure below, a equals all of the following EXCEPT

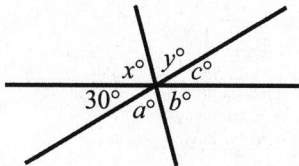

    A. y C. $180-b-c$ E. $180-x-y$
    B. $150-x$ D. $150-b$

55. In the figure below, if $\overline{AE}\parallel\overline{BD}$ and $\overline{BD}\cong\overline{DC}$, then what is $\angle BDC$ equal to?

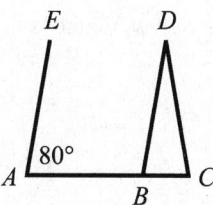

    A. 10°   C. 18°   E. 24°
    B. 15°   D. 20°

56. In the figure below, what is the value of x?

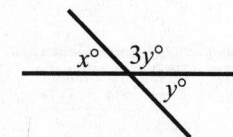

    A. 30   C. 60   E. 80
    B. 45   D. 65

57. In the figure below, $\overline{OM}\parallel\overline{PJ}$, and $\overline{FG}$ and $\overline{EG}$ divide $\angle CGO$ into 3 congruent angles. What is the degree measure of $\angle EGC$?

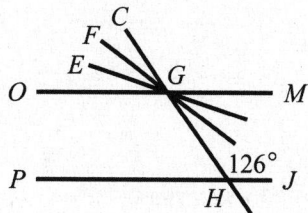

    A. 18°   C. 42°   E. 63°
    B. 36°   D. 54°

58. A triangle with sides of 12, 14, and 20 is similar to a second triangle that has one side with a length of 40. What is the smallest possible perimeter of the second triangle?

    A. 48   C. 120   E. 180
    B. 92   D. 160

59. If the perimeter of a rectangle is 68 yards and the width is 48 feet, what is the length?

    A. 10 yards   C. 20 feet   E. 54 feet
    B. 18 feet   D. 46 feet

60. An umbrella 50" long can lie diagonally on the bottom of a trunk with a length and width that are which of the following, respectively?

    A. 26", 30"   C. 31", 31"   E. 40", 30"
    B. 30", 36"   D. 40", 21"

61. $\triangle ABC$ is similar to $\triangle XYZ$. $\overline{AB}=4$, $\overline{XY}=12$, and $\overline{AC}=6$. What is the length of $\overline{XZ}$?

    A. 8   C. 12   E. 18
    B. 10   D. 16

62. A rectangular bin 4 feet long, 3 feet wide, and 2 feet high is solidly packed with bricks whose dimensions are 8 inches by 4 inches by 2 inches. What is the number of bricks in the bin?

A. 54
B. 320
C. 648
D. 848
E. Cannot be determined from the given information

63. A piece of wire is shaped to enclose a square, whose area is 121 square inches. It is then reshaped to enclose a rectangle whose length is 13 inches. What is the area of the rectangle, in square inches?

A. 64   C. 117   E. 234
B. 96   D. 144

64. The area of a circle is 49π. What is its circumference, in terms of π?

A. 14π C. 49π E. 147π
B. 28π D. 98π

65. A box is 12 inches in width, 16 inches in length, and 6 inches in height. How many square inches of paper would be required to cover it on all sides?

A. 192   C. 720   E. 1,440
B. 360   D. 900

66. In the figure below, $x = ?$

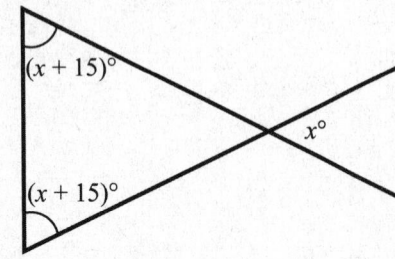

A. 20   C. 50   E. 90
B. 35   D. 65

67. A triangle with sides of 4, 6, and 8 has the same perimeter as an equilateral triangle with sides of length equal to which of the following?

A. 2   C. 3   E. 8
B. $\frac{3}{2}$ D. 6

68. If the area of the rectangle shown below is equal to 1, then $l = ?$

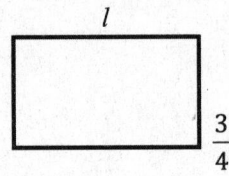

A. $\frac{4}{9}$ C. $\frac{4}{3}$ E. 2
B. 1   D. $\frac{9}{4}$

69. In the figure below, $x = ?$

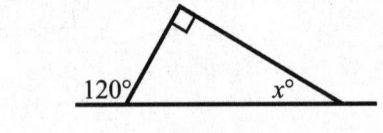

A. 15   C. 45   E. 90
B. 30   D. 60

70. In the figure below, which is not necessarily drawn to scale, $\angle A \cong \angle C$ and $\angle B \cong \angle D$.

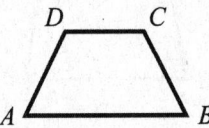

How many of the following four statements of congruence must be true?

$\angle A \cong \angle B$
$\overline{AB} \cong \overline{DC}$
$\overline{AD} \cong \overline{BC}$
$\overline{AB} \cong \overline{BC} \cong \overline{CD} \cong \overline{AD}$

A. 0   C. 2   E. 4
B. 1   D. 3

71. In the diagram below, $\overline{AD} \cong \overline{AE}$ and $\overline{AB} \cong \overline{BF} \cong \overline{CE} \cong \overline{CF} \cong \overline{DE}$.

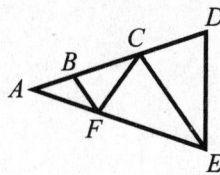

What is the degree measure of $\angle DAE$?

A. 20°   C. 25°   E. 35°
B. 24°   D. 30°

72. At 3:00 in the afternoon, Linda, who is 68 inches tall, casts a shadow 3.2 feet long while her daughter casts a shadow 1.8 feet long. How tall, in inches, is Linda's daughter?

A. 21.25   C. 36.50   E. 42.75
B. 28.36   D. 38.25

73. The figure below shows a circle of area 144π square inches with a radius drawn to the point of tangency of the circle on the *x*-axis.

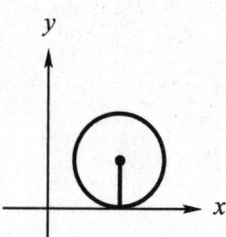

If this point of tangency is 16 inches from the origin, then the number of inches from the origin to the center of the circle is:

A. 12   C. 16   E. 20
B. $12\sqrt{2}$ D. $16\sqrt{2}$

74. In the figure below, which is not necessarily drawn to scale, $\angle ABC = 90°$, $\overline{AB} = 10$, and $\dfrac{\overline{AB}}{\overline{BC}} = 1$. What is the length of $\overline{AC}$?

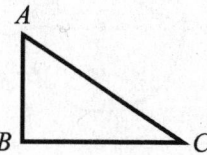

A. 10   C. $10\sqrt{2}$ E. $20\sqrt{3}$
B. 20   D. $10\sqrt{3}$

75. The volume of a cone is $\dfrac{\pi r^2 h}{3}$, where *r* is the radius of the cone base and *h* is the cone height. What is the volume, in cubic inches, of a cone of height 12 inches that has a base of radius 3 inches?

A. 144π C. 72π E. 36π
B. 108π D. 54π

76. In the figure below, a circle with an area of 144π is inscribed in a square. What is the area of the shaded region?

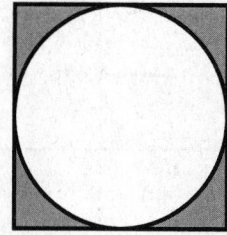

A. $576 - 144\pi$ D. $1,728 - 144\pi$
B. $216 - 72\pi$ E. $256 - 24\pi$
C. $144 - 24\pi$

77. At 12 cents per square foot, how much will it cost to paint the rectangular slab in the figure below?

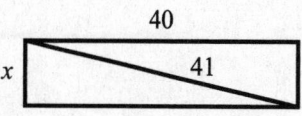

A. $43.20   C. $98.40   E. $201.50
B. $46.40   D. $196.80

78. In the figure below, if $\overset{\frown}{BC}$ equals 60°, then what is the area of $\triangle ABC$?

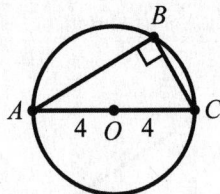

A. 16　　 C. $8\sqrt{3}$　　 E. $10\sqrt{2}$
B. $4\sqrt{3}$　　 D. 12

79. A certain triangle has side lengths of 6, 8, and 10. A rectangle equal in area to that of the triangle has a width of 3. What is the perimeter of the rectangle?

A. 11　　 C. 22　　 E. 30
B. 16　　 D. 24

80. The figure below shows a circle with center O, two radii $\overline{OA}$ and $\overline{OB}$, and two tangents $\overline{AC}$ and $\overline{BC}$. What is the area of the shaded region?

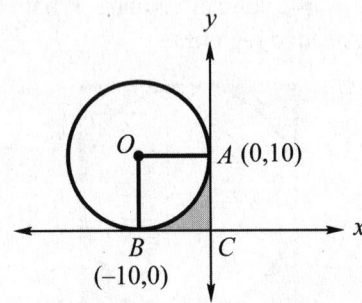

A. $100 - 100\pi$　 C. $50 - 50\pi$　 E. $100 - 25\pi$
B. $50 - 100\pi$　 D. $50 - 25\pi$

COORDINATE GEOMETRY

Coordinate Axis System

The easiest way to understand the coordinate axis system is as an analog to the points of the compass. If we take a plot of land, we can divide it into quadrants:

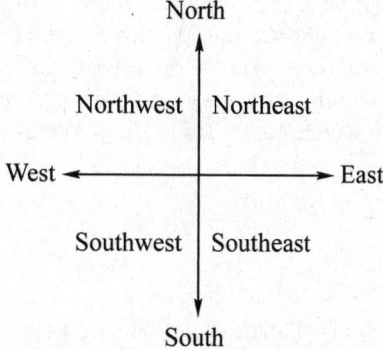

Now, if we add measuring units along each of the directional axes, we can actually describe any location on this piece of land by two numbers.

Example:

Point *P* is located at 4 units East and 5 units North. Point *Q* is located at 4 units West and 5 units North. Point *R* is located at 4 units West and 2 units South. Point *T* is located at 3 units East and 4 units South.

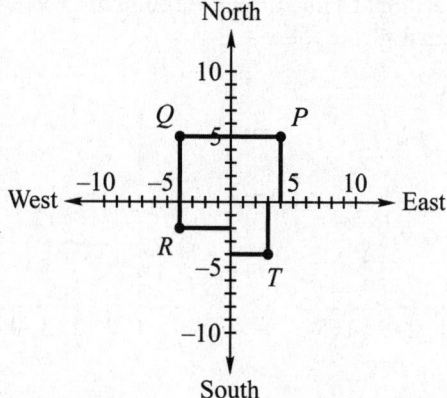

The coordinate system used in coordinate geometry differs from our map of a plot of land in that it uses *x*- and *y*-axes divided into negative and positive regions.

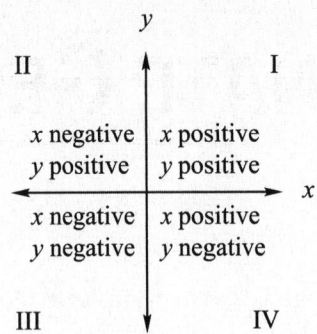

It is easy to see that **Quadrant I** corresponds to our Northeast quarter, in which the measurements on both the x- and y-axes are positive. **Quadrant II** corresponds to our Northwest quarter, in which the measurements on the x-axis are negative and the measurements on the y-axis are positive. **Quadrant III** corresponds to our Southwest quarter, in which both the x-axis measurements and the y-axis measurements are negative. Finally, **Quadrant IV** corresponds to our Southeast quarter, in which the x-values are positive while the y-values are negative.

Ordered Pairs

An **ordered pair** of coordinates has the general form (x, y). The first element refers to the **x-coordinate**: the distance left or right of the **origin**, or intersection of the axes. The second element gives the **y-coordinate**: the distance up or down from the origin.

Example:

Plot $(3,2)$.

➤ Move to the positive 3 value on the x-axis. Then, from there move up two units on the y-axis, as illustrated by the graph on the left. The graph on the right demonstrates an alternative method: the point $(3,2)$ is located at the intersection of a line drawn through the x-value 3 parallel to the y-axis and a line drawn through the y-value 2 parallel to the x-axis.

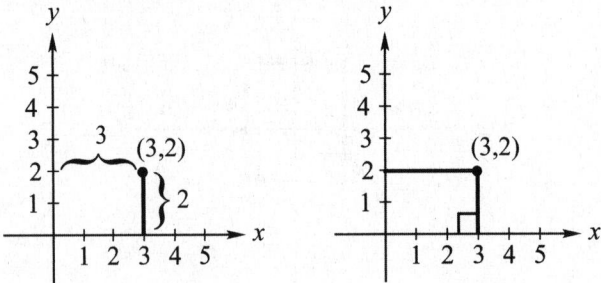

Plotting Equations

The coordinate axis system provides a framework for plotting equations. Simply plot several pairs of points for the given equation.

Examples:

1. Plot the equation $x = y$.

➤ This equation has an infinite number of solutions:

x	1	2	3	5	0	-3	-5	...
y	1	2	3	5	0	-3	-5	...

Plot these pairs of x and y on the axis system. Draw a line through them to produce a plot of the original equation. The complete picture of the equation $x = y$ is a straight line including all the real numbers such that x is equal to y.

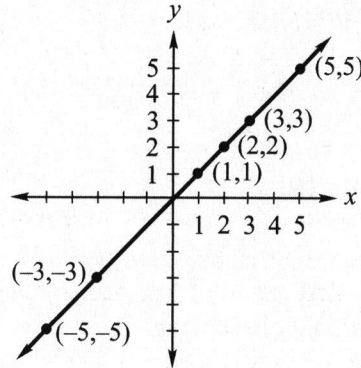

2. Plot the equation $y = 2x$.

   ➢ This equation has an infinite number of solutions:

x	-4	-2	-1	0	1	2	4	...
y	-8	-4	-2	0	2	4	8	...

After entering the points on the graph, complete the picture. It is a straight line, but it rises more rapidly than does $x = y$.

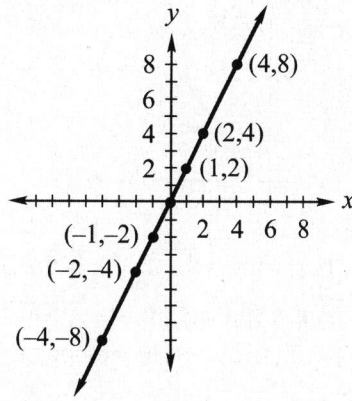

Midpoint of Line Segments

For a line segment between two points, (x_1, y_1) and (x_2, y_2), the ***midpoint*** $= \left(\dfrac{x_1 + x_2}{2}, \dfrac{y_1 + y_2}{2} \right)$. The x-coordinate of the midpoint is the average of the two x-axis endpoints and the x-coordinate of the midpoint is the average of the two y-axis endpoints.

Examples:

1. Find the midpoint between (−5,8) and (11,34).

➤ The midpoint is $\left(\dfrac{x_1+x_2}{2},\dfrac{y_1+y_2}{2}\right)=\left(\dfrac{-5+11}{2},\dfrac{8+34}{2}\right)=\left(\dfrac{6}{2},\dfrac{42}{2}\right)=(3,21)$.

2. One endpoint of a circle diameter is located at $(13,1)$. If the center of the circle is $(15,10)$, find the other endpoint.

➤ The midpoint of the diameter is $(15,10)$, so $15=\dfrac{x_1+x_2}{2}=\dfrac{13+x_2}{2}$ and $10=\dfrac{y_1+y_2}{2}=\dfrac{1+y_2}{2}$.

$x_2=(15\cdot 2)-13=17$ and $y_2=(10\cdot 2)-1=19$. Thus, $(x_2,y_2)=(17,19)$.

Distance Between Two Points

To determine the distance between two points on a coordinate graph, consider points P and Q. For simplicity's sake, we will confine the discussion to the first quadrant, but the method generally works in all quadrants and even with lines covering two or more quadrants. Assign the value (x_1,y_1) to point P and (x_2,y_2) to point Q:

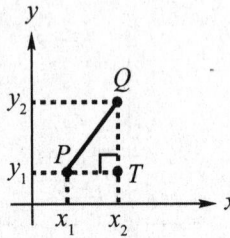

To find distance between points P and Q, construct a triangle:

Point T now has the coordinates (x_2,y_1). To calculate the length of $\overline{PT}$, find the distance moved on the x-axis: x_2-x_1 units. The y-coordinate does not change. Similarly, the length of $\overline{QT}$ will be y_2-y_1 since the distance is purely vertical, moving up from y_1 to y_2, with no change in the x-value. Apply the Pythagorean theorem:

$$(PQ)^2=(PT)^2+(QT)^2=\left(x_2-x_1\right)^2+\left(y_2-y_1\right)^2 \Rightarrow PQ=\sqrt{\left(x_2-x_1\right)^2+\left(y_2-y_1\right)^2}$$

Example:

In the following figure, what is the length of $\overline{PQ}$?

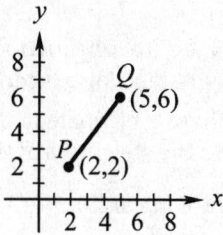

➤ Find the length of $\overline{PQ}$ by constructing a triangle:

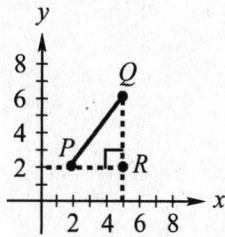

$\overline{QR}$ runs from $(5,6)$ to $(5,2)$, so it must be 4 units long. $\overline{PR}$ runs from $(2,2)$ to $(5,2)$, so it is 3 units long. Use the Pythagorean theorem: $\left(\overline{PQ}\right)^2 = \left(\overline{QR}\right)^2 + \left(\overline{PR}\right)^2 = 4^2 + 3^2 = 16 + 9 = 25$. Therefore, $\overline{PQ} = \sqrt{25} = 5$.

Therefore, you can find the length of any line segment drawn in a coordinate axis system between points (x_1, y_1) and (x_2, y_2) using this ***distance formula***: $d = \sqrt{(x_2 - x_1)^2 + (y_2 - y_1)^2}$. Notice that it does not actually matter which point is considered the start of the line and the end of the line, since the change in each coordinate is squared in the distance formula.

Example:

In the following figure, what is the distance between P and Q?

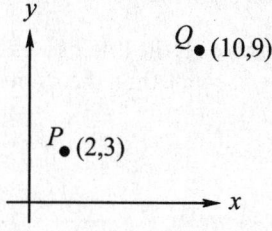

➤ The distance between P and Q is: $\sqrt{(x_2 - x_1)^2 + (y_2 - y_1)^2} = \sqrt{(10-2)^2 + (9-3)^2} = \sqrt{64 + 36} = \sqrt{100} = 10$.

Linear Functions

Slope-Intercept Form

If x and y are related by a linear equation, then y is a **linear function**. Except for a vertical line, every linear equation is a linear function that can be represented in **slope-intercept form**: $y = mx + b$. m is the slope of the line and b is the y-intercept. The y-intercept is the y-coordinate of the point where the line intersects the y-axis, or where $x = 0$. The **slope**, m, of a line describes the steepness of the line. It is defined as the change in y-values divided by the change in x-values, or rise over run: $slope = m = \dfrac{y_2 - y_1}{x_2 - x_1} = \dfrac{rise}{run}$.

Examples:

1. Find the slope of the line containing $(3,2)$ and $(8,22)$.

   ➤ $m = \dfrac{y_2 - y_1}{x_2 - x_1} = \dfrac{22 - 2}{8 - 3} = \dfrac{20}{5} = 4$.

2. Find the slope of the line given by the equation $6x + 12y = 13$.

   ➤ $6x + 12y = 13 \Rightarrow 12y = -6x + 13 \Rightarrow y = \dfrac{-6x + 13}{12} \Rightarrow y = -\dfrac{x}{2} + \dfrac{13}{12}$. Therefore, the slope is $-\dfrac{1}{2}$.

3. The points $(-5,12)$, $(0,7)$ and $(10,-3)$ lie on a line. What is the y-intercept of this line?

   ➤ The x-coordinate of the second point is 0. Therefore, this point's y-coordinate, 7, is the y-intercept of the line.

Parallel Lines

The equation of a line that is parallel to the x-axis is $y = k$, where is a constant. The equation of a line that is parallel to the y-axis is $x = c$, where c is a constant. If two lines are parallel, their slopes are equal.

Example:

Find the equation for a line that passes through the point $(0,12)$ and is parallel to the line $y = 7x - 15$.

   ➤ A line has slope-intercept form $y = mx + b$. If the line passes through the y-axis at $(0,12)$, then the y-intercept $b = +12$. If the two lines are parallel, then the slopes are equal and $m = +7$. Therefore, the line equation is $y = mx + b \Rightarrow y = 7x + 12$.

Perpendicular Lines

If two perpendicular lines have slopes m_1 and m_2, then $m_1 = -\dfrac{1}{m_2}$ and vice versa.

Example:

The equation of a line is $y = \dfrac{x}{4} + 10$. If a second line is perpendicular to the line, what is the slope of this line?

➤ If two lines are perpendicular to one another, their slopes are opposite reciprocals of one another. The first line has a slope of $\dfrac{1}{4}$; thus, the line perpendicular to it has a slope of -4.

Quadratic Functions

If y is expressed in the form $y = ax^2 + bx + c$, where $a \neq 0$ and b is any real number, y is a ***quadratic function***. Graphs of quadratic functions are called parabolas.

Example:

A quadratic function of the form $y = ax^2 + bx + c$ includes the following ordered pairs of (x, y): $(1, 17)$, $(5, 61)$, and $(7, 95)$. What is the value of c for this quadratic function?

➤ Set up the system of three simultaneous equations that are generated by the three ordered pairs:

$$17 = a(1)^2 + b(1) + c \Rightarrow 17 = a + b + c$$
$$61 = a(5)^2 + b(5) + c \Rightarrow 61 = 25a + 5b + c$$
$$95 = a(7)^2 + b(7) + c \Rightarrow 95 = 49a + 7b + c$$

Use the method of solving simultaneous equations (system of equations) to determine the values of a, b, and c. Multiply the first equation by -1, and add it to the other two equations to eliminate c:

$$\begin{array}{ll} -1(17 = a + b + c) & -1(17 = a + b + c) \\ +\;\; 61 = 25a + 5b + c & +\;\; 95 = 49a + 7b + c \\ \hline \quad\; 44 = 24a + 4b & \quad\;\; 78 = 48a + 6b \end{array}$$

Now, combine these new equations to eliminate a. Multiply the first equation by -2, and add it to the second equation to eliminate a:

$$\begin{array}{l} -2(44 = 24a + 4b) \\ +\;\; 78 = 48a + 6b \\ \hline \;\; -10 = -2b \Rightarrow b = 5 \end{array}$$

Substitute 5 for b in either of the new equations and solve for a: $44 = 24a + 4(5) \Rightarrow 24a = 24 \Rightarrow a = 1$. Finally, substitute the values for a and b into any of the three original equations to solve for c. Since the first equation is simplest, we'll use that one: $17 = a + b + c \Rightarrow 17 = 1 + 5 + c \Rightarrow c = 11$.

Identifying Graphs of Functions

You may be asked simply to identify graphs of linear and quadratic functions. The graph of a linear function is a straight line, while the graph of a quadratic function is called a parabola. The basic quadratic graph that you need to know is $f(x) = x^2$, as illustrated in the second of the following examples.

Examples:

1. The line of best fit for $y = f(x)$ for the ordered pairs $(-4,-18)$, $(1,3)$, $(2,6)$, $(3,8)$, and $(4,14)$ is best represented by which of the following graphs?

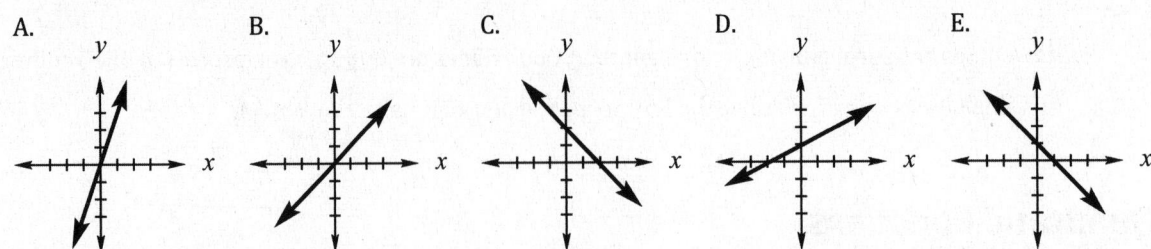

A.   B.   C.   D.   E.

> The correct answer is (A). Both x and y increase in value for each ordered pair, so eliminate (C) and (E). You can eliminate (B) since the values of x and y in the given ordered pairs clearly indicate that $x \neq y$. Finally, eliminate (D) because when $x = 1$, $y = 3$, whereas in the graph of (D), $y < 3$ when $x = 1$.

2. Which of the following graphs depicts a quadratic function?

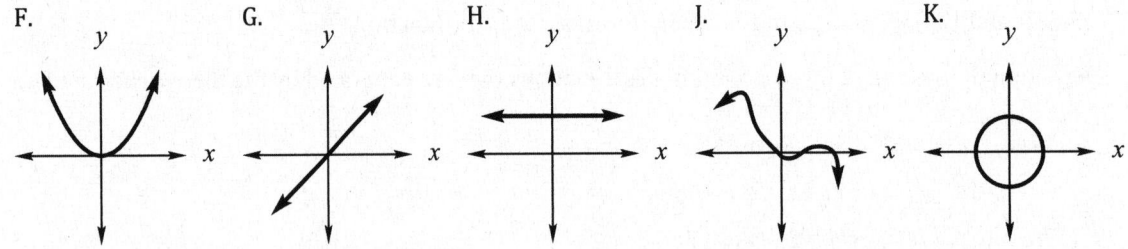

F.   G.   H.   J.   K.

> All quadratic equations can be written in the form $y = ax^2 + bx + c$. (G) is a linear plot with the y-intercept equal to 0: $y = ax$. (H) is a constant value for y: $y = k$. (K) is a plot of a circle: $x^2 + y^2 = k$, where k is a constant. (J) is a complicated function without a standard form of equation. Only (F) is a quadratic equation: $y = ax^2$.

Functions can be also mathematical models of real-life situations. For example, an item might present information about the projected sales of a product at various prices and ask for a mathematical model in the form of a graph or equation that represents projected sales as a function of price.

Transformation Effects on Graphs

When you alter a graph, you transform it. If you transform a graph without changing its shape, you translate it. Vertical and horizontal transformations are translations. Items on the exam may test knowledge of the effects of simple translations of graphs of functions. For example, the graph of a function $f(x)$ could be given and you might be asked questions about the graph of the function $f(x+2)$.

Vertical Translations

To move a function up or down, you add or subtract outside the function. That is, $f(x)+b$ is $f(x)$ moved up b units, and $f(x)-b$ is $f(x)$ moved down b units.

Example:

In order to obtain the graph of $y = (x+2)^2 + 6$ from the graph of $y = x^2 + 4x + 11$, how should the graph of $y = x^2 + 4x + 11$ be moved?

➤ Rewrite the original in the form $f(x) + b$: $y = x^2 + 4x + 11 \Rightarrow y = x^2 + 4x + 4 + 7 = (x+2)^2 + 7$. Thus, to obtain the graph of $y = (x+2)^2 + 6$ from the graph of $y = (x+2)^2 + 7$, the graph must be moved one unit down.

Horizontal Translations

To shift a function to the left or to the right, add or subtract inside the function. That is, $f(x+b)$ is $f(x)$ shifted b units to the left, and $f(x-b)$ is $f(x)$ shifted b units to the right.

Example:

The following graph is of the function $y = |x|$.

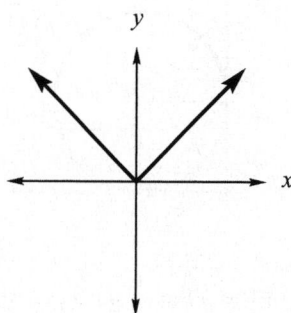

Which of the following is a graph of the function $y = |x+3|$?

A.   B.   C.   D.   E.

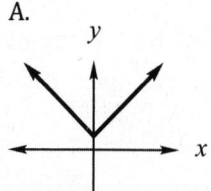 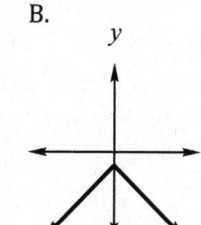 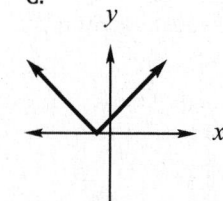 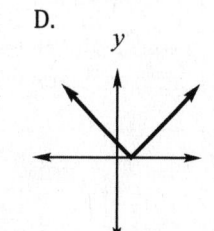 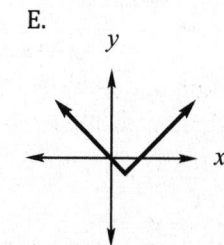

➤ By translation of the original graph from $y = |x|$ to $y = |x+3|$, the original graph is moved three units to the left, (C). Alternatively, substitute values for x and y: $y = 0$ for $x = -3$. (C) is the only graph that contains the point $(-3, 0)$.

Graphing Geometric Figures

You can also use the coordinate system for graphing geometric figures. The following figure is a graph of a square whose vertices are at coordinates $(0,0)$, $(4,0)$, $(4,4)$, and $(0,4)$.

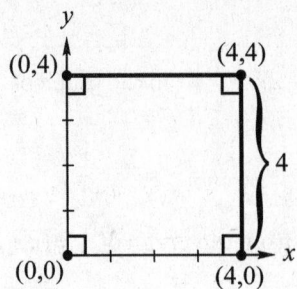

Each side of the square is equal to 4 since each side is 4 units long and parallel to either the x- or y-axis. Since every coordinate point is the perpendicular intersection of two lines, it is possible to measure distances in the coordinate system.

Examples:

1. In the following figure, what is the area of the circle?

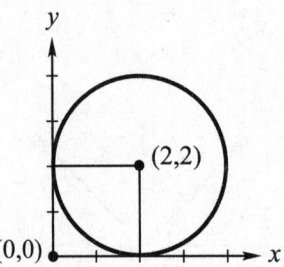

> ➤ To solve this problem, find the radius of the circle. The center of the circle is located at the intersection of $x = 2$ and $y = 2$, or the point $(2,2)$. Thus, the radius is 2 units long and the area is 4π.

2. $\triangle ABC$ has coordinates A, B, and C equal to $(5,3)$, $(19,7)$ and $(17,25)$, respectively. By how much does the largest slope for any median of $\triangle ABC$ exceed the largest slope for any altitude of $\triangle ABC$?

> ➤ The largest slope occurs for the steepest ascent for increasing values of x. Draw a figure of the given information in the coordinate plane:

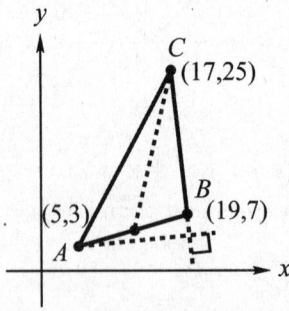

A median is drawn from one angle of a triangle to the midpoint of the opposite side. Of the three possible medians, the median that connects C to the midpoint of $\overline{AB}$ has the largest slope. The midpoint of $\overline{AB}$ is $\left(\dfrac{5+19}{2}, \dfrac{7+3}{2} \right) = (12,5)$. Therefore, the slope of the median is $\dfrac{25-5}{17-12} = 4$. An altitude is drawn from one angle of a triangle to the opposite side at a right angle. Of the three possible altitudes, the altitude that connects A to $\overline{BC}$ has the largest slope. Since this altitude is perpendicular to $\overline{BC}$, its slope is the opposite reciprocal of the slope of $\overline{BC}$. The slope of $\overline{BC}$ is

$\dfrac{25-7}{17-19} = \dfrac{18}{-2} = -9$, so the slope of the altitude $\dfrac{1}{9}$. Therefore, the amount by which the slope of the

median is larger than the slope of the altitude is: $4 - \dfrac{1}{9} = \dfrac{36}{9} - \dfrac{1}{9} = \dfrac{35}{9}$.

Coordinate Geometry
Exercise 11

1. Which of the following graphs represents a relation of which the domain is the set of all real numbers and the range is the set of all non-negative real numbers?

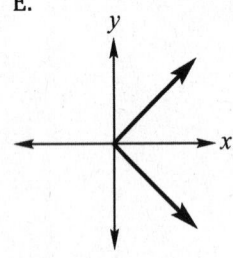

A.

B.

C.

D.

E.

2. Which of the lettered points on the number line below could represent the result when the coordinate of point F is divided by the coordinate of point X?

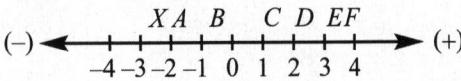

$$X \, A \quad B \quad C \, D \, EF$$
$$(-) \longleftarrow \underset{-4\;-3\;-2\;-1\;\;0\;\;1\;\;2\;\;3\;\;4}{|\;\;|\;\;|\;\;|\;\;|\;\;|\;\;|\;\;|\;\;|} \longrightarrow (+)$$

A. A   C. C   E. E
B. B   D. D

3. $\overline{AB}$ is the diameter of a circle whose center is point O. If the coordinates of point A are $(2,6)$ and the coordinates of point B are $(6,2)$, find the coordinates of point O.

A. $(4,4)$ C. $(2,-2)$ E. $(2,2)$
B. $(4,-4)$ D. $(0,0)$

4. $\overline{AB}$ is the diameter of a circle whose center is point O. If the coordinates of point O are $(2,1)$ and the coordinates of point B are $(4,6)$, find the coordinates of point A.

A. $\left(3, 3\tfrac{1}{2}\right)$ C. $(0,-4)$ E. $\left(-1, -2\tfrac{1}{2}\right)$
B. $\left(1, 2\tfrac{1}{2}\right)$ D. $\left(2\tfrac{1}{2}, 1\right)$

5. Find the distance from the point whose coordinates are $(4,3)$ to the point whose coordinates are $(8,6)$.

A. 5   C. $\sqrt{7}$ E. 15
B. 25   D. $\sqrt{67}$

6. The vertices of a triangle are $(2,1)$, $(2,5)$, and $(5,1)$. What is the area of the triangle?

A. 12   C. 8   E. 5
B. 10   D. 6

7. The area of a circle whose center is at $(0,0)$ is 16π. The circle does NOT pass through which of the following points?

A. $(4,4)$ C. $(4,0)$ E. $(0,-4)$
B. $(0,4)$ D. $(-4,0)$

8. What is the slope of a line that passes through $(0,-5)$ and $(8,27)$?

   A. 4   C. $\dfrac{8}{32}$ E. −4

   B. 2   D. $-\dfrac{8}{32}$

9. The slope of a line that passes through points $(3,7)$ and $(12,y)$ is $\dfrac{1}{3}$. What is the value of y?

   A. 2   C. $6\dfrac{2}{3}$ E. 10

   B. 4   D. $7\dfrac{1}{3}$

10. What is the slope of the line $y = 5x + 7$?

    A. 7   C. 2   E. $\dfrac{1}{5}$

    B. 5   D. $\dfrac{7}{5}$

11. A line passes through points $(3,8)$ and $(w,2k)$. If $w \neq 3$, what is the slope of the line?

    A. $\dfrac{8-2k}{3+w}$ C. $\dfrac{2k-8}{w-3}$ E. $\dfrac{3}{8}$

    B. $\dfrac{2k+8}{w+3}$ D. $\dfrac{w-3}{2k-8}$

12. What is the equation of the line that passes through the point $(0,13)$ and is parallel to the line $4x + 2y = 17$?

    A. $4x + 2y = 13$
    B. $4x + 2y = -13$
    C. $y = -2x + 13$
    D. $y = 2x + 13$
    E. Cannot be determined from the given information

13. A line passes through the point $(0,-5)$ and is perpendicular to the line $y = -\dfrac{x}{2} + 5$. What is the equation of the line?

    A. $y = -\dfrac{x}{2} - 5$
    B. $y = 2x - 5$
    C. $y = -2x - 5$
    D. $y = -\dfrac{x}{2} + 13$
    E. Cannot be determined from the given information

14. If point P has coordinates $(-2,2)$ and point Q has coordinates $(2,0)$, what is the distance from point P to point Q?

    A. −4   C. $4\sqrt{5}$ E. 6
    B. $2\sqrt{5}$ D. 4

15. If point R has coordinates (x,y) and point S has coordinates $(x+1, y+1)$, what is the distance between point R and point S?

    A. $\sqrt{2}$ D. $\sqrt{x^2 + y^2 + 2}$
    B. 2   E. $x + y + 1$
    C. $\sqrt{x^2 + y^2}$

16. Will is standing 40 yards due north of point P. Grace is standing 60 yards due west of point P. What is the shortest distance between Will and Grace?

    A. 20 yards   D. 80 yards
    B. $4\sqrt{13}$ yards   E. $80\sqrt{13}$ yards
    C. $20\sqrt{13}$ yards

17. On a coordinate graph, what is the distance between points $(5,6)$ and $(6,7)$?

    A. $\sqrt{2}$ C. 2   E. $6\sqrt{2}$
    B. 1   D. 4

18. On a coordinate plane, point B is located 7 units to the left of point A. The x-coordinate of point A is x, and the y-coordinate of point A is y. What is the x-coordinate of point B?

A. $x-7$

B. $x+7$

C. $y+7$

D. $y-7$

E. Cannot be determined from the given information

19. Point R is represented on the coordinate plane by (x,y). The vertical coordinate of point S is three times the vertical coordinate of point R and the two points have the same horizontal coordinate. The ordered pair that represents point S is:

A. $(3x,y)$ C. $(x,y-3)$ E. $(x,3y)$

B. $(x,y+3)$ D. $(3x,3y)$

20. A square is drawn in a coordinate plane. Which of the following transformations of the square will shift the square 7 units to the right and 5 units downward?

A. Add 7 to each x-coordinate and add 5 to each y-coordinate.

B. Multiply each x-coordinate by 7 and divide each y-coordinate by 5.

C. Add 7 to each x-coordinate and subtract 5 from each y-coordinate.

D. Subtract 7 from each x-coordinate and subtract 5 from each y-coordinate.

E. Subtract 7 from each x-coordinate and add 5 to each y-coordinate.

21. In the rectangular coordinate system below, if $x = 4.2$, then y equals which of the following?

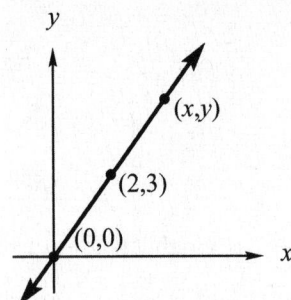

A. 2.8   C. 4.8   E. 6.3

B. 3.4   D. 6.2

22. Points $(x,-4)$ and $(-1,y)$ (not shown in the figure below) are in Quadrants III and II, respectively. If x and $y \neq 0$, in which quadrant is point (x,y)?

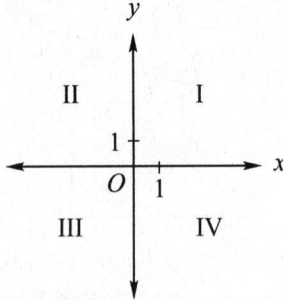

A. I

B. II

C. III

D. IV

E. Cannot be determined from the given information

23. If Sam lives 8 miles west of Jeni, and Molly lives 10 miles north of Jeni, approximately how many miles less would Molly walk if she walks directly to Sam's house, rather than first to Jeni's house and then to Sam's house?

A. 1   C. 3   E. 5

B. 2   D. 4

24. If point B (not shown in the figure below) lies below the x-axis at point $(4,-4)$, what is the area of $\triangle ABC$?

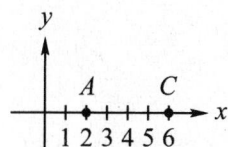

A. 2   C. 6   E. 16
B. 4   D. 8

25. On a coordinate graph, what is the distance between points $(-1,4)$ and $(2,8)$?

A. 3   C. 5   E. 8
B. 4   D. 6

26. In the figure below, $\overline{AB}$ is the base of a water ski ramp and is 18 feet long. The slope (rise divided by run) of the ramp is m. If the ramp is y feet high, then what is the value of y?

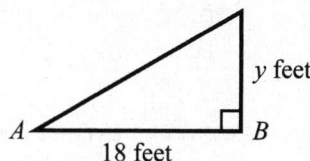

A. $\dfrac{m}{18}$ C. $18-m$ E. $m+18$
B. $18m$ D. $m-18$

27. What is the midpoint between $(-2,15)$ and $(8,17)$?

A. $(6,16)$ C. $(5,16)$ E. $(6,32)$
B. $(3,16)$ D. $(5,32)$

28. In the figure below, $\overline{AB}$ is the diameter of a circle whose center is at point P. What are the coordinates for point B?

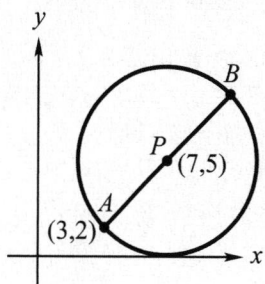

A. $(10,7)$ C. $(12,7)$ E. $(11,7)$
B. $(5,2.5)$ D. $(11,8)$

29. How many of the following graphs are graphs of linear functions?

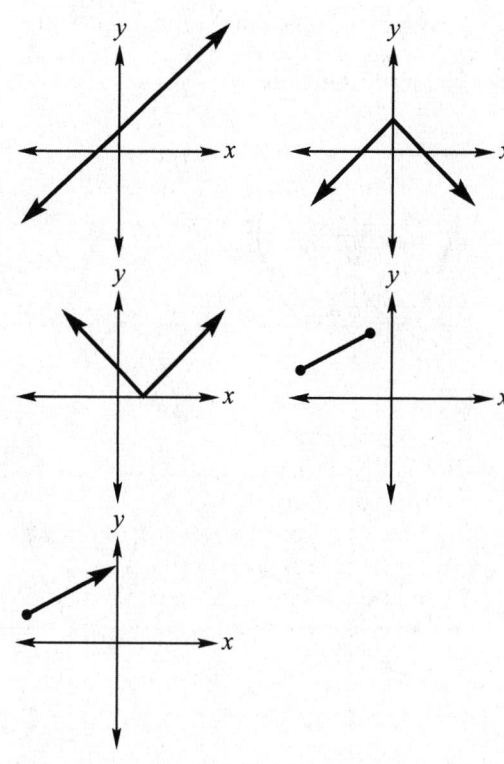

A. 1   C. 3   E. 5
B. 2   D. 4

30. In each of the following four sets, the three ordered pairs belong to a linear function. In how many of the four sets is the value of the variable x less than zero?

$\{(0,1), (-4,7), (x,0)\}$
$\{(0,2), (-5,52), (x,12)\}$
$\{(2,-5), (-2,-17), (x,13)\}$
$\{(6,17), (8,25), (x,4)\}$

A. 0   C. 2   E. 4
B. 1   D. 3

31. If $y = mx + b$, $x = 5$ for $y = 20$, and $x = 9$ for $y = 32$, then $m + b$ is:

A. 76   C. 14   E. 3
B. 52   D. 8

32. Which of the following graphs depicts the quadratic functions $y = \dfrac{x^2}{2}$ and $y = -\dfrac{x^2}{2}$?

A.
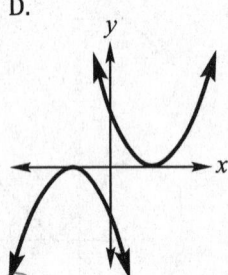

D.

B.
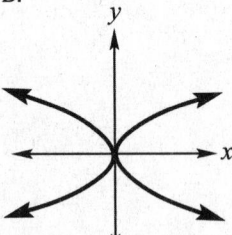

E.
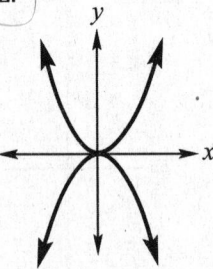

C.
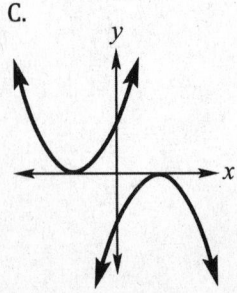

33. If $y = -2x^2 + 16x - 1$, what is the largest possible value for y?

A. −1
B. 13
C. 31
D. 32
E. Cannot be determined from the given information

34. The graph of $y = 4x^2$ intersects the graph of $y = x^2 + 3x$ at how many points?

A. 0   C. 2   E. 4
B. 1   D. 3

35. The graph of the following ordered pairs for (x,y) is approximately a straight line of the form $y = mx + b$: $(1,18), (2,23), (3,27),$ $(4,32), (5,38)$. Which of the following best approximates the value of b?

A. 13   C. 20   E. 25
B. 18   D. 23

36. The figure below shows two parallel lines with coordinates of points as shown. What is the slope of the line passing through point $(0,6)$?

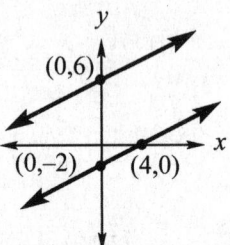

A. $\dfrac{1}{2}$ C. $\dfrac{1}{4}$ E. $\dfrac{1}{6}$

B. $\dfrac{1}{3}$ D. $\dfrac{1}{5}$

37. The center of a circle is located at $(19,7)$. If one of the endpoints of the circle's diameter is located at $(4,6)$, then the second end of the diameter is located at:

A. $(11.5, 6.5)$ C. $(34,8)$ E. $(38,8)$
B. $(11.5, 13)$ D. $(38,14)$

38. In the figure below, which is not necessarily drawn to scale, $ABCD$ is a square and $\angle FGH \cong \angle A$.

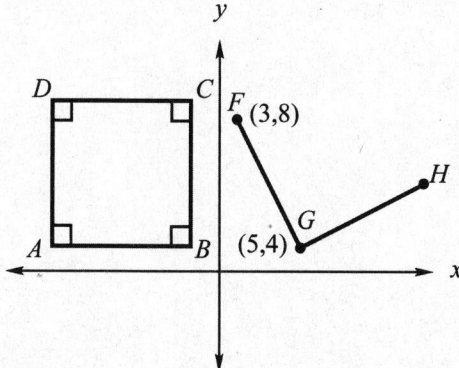

If points F and G have the coordinates as indicated in the figure, how many of the following four ordered pairs could possibly represent point H?

$(8,6), (9,6), (11,7), (13,8)$

A. 0   C. 2   E. 4
B. 1   D. 3

39. The line that passes through $(1,5)$ and $(-2,17)$ is parallel to the line that passes through $(17,6)$ and $(13,y)$. What is the value of y?

A. 10   C. 16   E. 22
B. 14   D. 18

40. What is the distance from the point $(-2,5)$ to the point $(7,-7)$?

A. 9   C. 15   E. 24
B. 12   D. 18

41. The figure below shows a circle with an area of 9π.

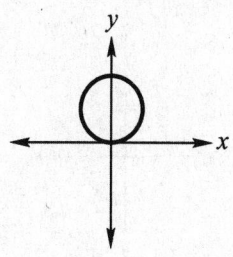

The circle is tangent to the x-axis at $(0,0)$ and the center of the circle lies on the y-axis. The constant function $y = k$ intersects the circle at exactly one point. If $k > 0$, what is the value of k?

A. 1   C. 3   E. 9
B. 2   D. 6

42. The graph below shows a circle whose equation is $x^2 + y^2 = 16$.

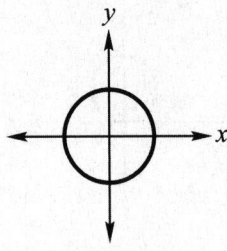

The graph is moved by the following transformations: four units to the right and two units up. Which of the following is the correctly transformed graph?

A.

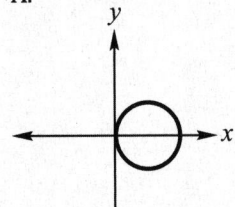

D.

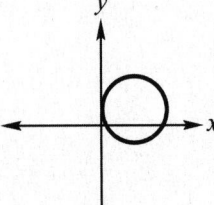

B.

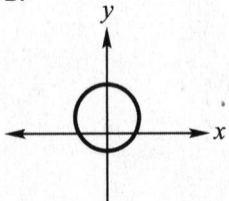

E.

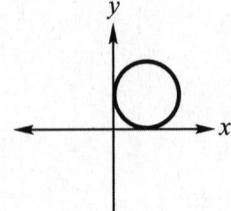

C.

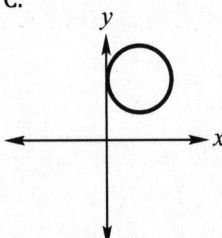

STORY PROBLEMS

Story problems may test arithmetic, algebra, or geometry in the context of a "story." You should have everything you need to solve these problems. However, remember that if a math story item stumps you, you have the answer at hand. Simply work backwards from the answer choices—the right answer has to be one of the choices. Since quantitative (i.e., numerical value) choices are arranged in size order, starting with the middle answer choice will result in the fewest calculations.

In solving story problems, the most important technique is to read accurately. Be sure you clearly understand what you are asked to find. Then, evaluate the item in common sense terms to eliminate answer choices. For example, if two people are working together, their combined speed is greater than either individual speed, but not more than twice as fast as the fastest speed. Finally, be alert for the "hidden equation"—some necessary information so obvious that the item assumes that you know it.

Examples:

1. boys + girls = total class

2. imported wine + domestic wine = all wine

3. wall + floor = right angle (Pythagorean theorem)

Some of the frequently encountered types of problem-solving problems are described in this section, although not every item you may encounter will fall into one of these categories. However, thoroughly familiarizing yourself with the types of problems that follow will help you to develop the skills to translate and solve all kinds of verbal problems.

Coin Problems

For *coin problems*, change the value of all monies involved to cents before writing an equation. The number of nickels must be multiplied by 5 to give their value in cents; dimes must be multiplied by 10; quarters by 25; half-dollars by 50; and dollars by 100.

Example:

Richard has $3.50 consisting of nickels and dimes. If he has 5 more dimes than nickels, how many dimes does he have?

➤ Let x equal the number of nickels, $x + 5$ equal the number of dimes, $5x$ equal the value of the nickels in cents, $10(x + 5) = 10x + 50$ equal the value of the dimes in cents, and 350 equal the value of the money he has in cents. Thus, $5x + 10x + 50 = 350 \Rightarrow 15x = 300 \Rightarrow x = 20$. Therefore, Richard has 20 nickels and 25 dimes.

In an item such as this, you can be sure that 20 would be among the multiple-choice answers. You must be sure to read carefully what you are asked to find and then continue until you have found the quantity sought.

Number and Set Problems

Number problems can be story problems that require knowledge of the properties of numbers in order to solve the item. Typically, number problems involve ***consecutive integers*** or ***consecutive odd/even numbers***. Consecutive integers are one number apart and can be represented by x, $x+1$, $x+2$, etc. Consecutive even or odd integers are two numbers apart and can be represented by x, $x+2$, $x+4$, etc.

Example:

Three consecutive odd integers have a sum of 33. Find the average of these integers.

➤ Represent the integers as x, $x+2$, and $x+4$. Write an equation indicating the sum is 33: $x+x+2+x+4 = 3x+6 = 33 \Rightarrow 3x = 27 \Rightarrow x = 9$. Thus, the integers are 9, 11, and 13. In the case of evenly spaced numbers such as these, the average is the middle number, 11. Since the sum of the three numbers was given originally, all we really had to do was to divide this sum by 3 to find the average, without ever knowing what the numbers were.

Set problems test understanding of relationships between different sets of numbers or ***elements***. A ***set*** is a collection of things; e.g., the set of positive integers.

DEFINITIONS FOR WORKING WITH SETS

1. The ***number of elements*** in set P is: $n(P)$.

2. The ***union*** of two sets P and Q is the set of all elements in *either* P or Q, or both: $P \cup Q$.

3. The ***intersection*** of two sets P and Q is the set of all elements in *both* P and Q: $P \cap Q$.

4. The ***cardinal number theorem*** is used to find the number of elements in a union of two sets: $n(P \cup Q) = n(P) + n(Q) - n(P \cap Q)$

Examples:

1. Let $S = \{3, 5, x\}$. If exactly one subset of S contains two different elements whose sum is 12, what value(s) can x be?

   ➤ Since either $3 + x = 12$ or $5 + x = 12$, then $x = 9$ or $x = 7$.

2. In a class of 30 students, 15 students are learning French, 11 students are learning Spanish, and 7 students are learning neither French nor Spanish. How many students in the class are learning both French and Spanish?

   ➤ Use the cardinal number theorem:

   $$n(F \cup S) = n(F) + n(S) - n(F \cap S)$$
   $$30 - 7 = 15 + 11 - n(F \cap S)$$
   $$n(F \cap S) = 3$$

The cardinal number theorem is also known as the ***addition principle for counting*** and is the first of several useful methods for counting objects and sets of objects without actually listing the elements to be counted. According to the theorem, if set A contains m objects, set B contains n objects, and there are no objects common to the two sets, then the total number of objects in the two sets combined is $m+n$. However, if there are k objects common to the two sets, then the total in the combined set is $m+n-k$. In other words, you must take into account the double-counting of objects common to both sets.

Example:

Of a group of students at a campus cafe, 9 ate pizza and 5 had salad. If 3 had both pizza and salad, how many had either pizza or salad?

➤ The question describes two sets: one consisting of students that ate pizza (set P: $m=9$), and one consisting of students that had salad (set S: $n=5$). Since the question states that 3 students had both pizza and salad, the number of students common to the two sets is 3 ($k=3$). Therefore, the total in the combined set (number of students who had either pizza or salad) is: $m+n-k=9+5-3=11$.

This kind of situation involving sets that overlap is most easily handled by displaying the given information in a **Venn diagram**.

Example:

Two circles are drawn on a floor. 20 people are standing in circle A. 15 people are standing in circle B. 9 people are standing in both circles. Find the total number of people standing in the two circles.

➤ The item can be symbolized with a Venn diagram:

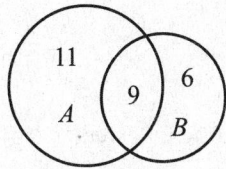

From the diagram, it can be seen that there are a total of $11+9+6$ or 26 people.

Age Problems

Age problems involve a comparison of ages at the present time, several years from now, or several years ago. A person's age x years from now is found by adding x to his present age. A person's age x years ago is found by subtracting x from his present age.

Examples:

1. Michelle was 12 years old y years ago. What is her age b years from now?

   ➤ Michelle's present age is $12+y$. In b years, her age will be $12+y+b$.

2. Logan is 5 years older than Florencia. Three years ago, Logan was twice as old as Florencia. How old is Logan?

   ➤ If you have trouble setting up the equations, use numbers. Suppose that Florencia is 11. If Logan is 5 years older than Florencia, then Logan must be $11+5=16$. Thus, if L is Logan's age and F is Florencia's age, $L=F+5$. Three years ago, Logan was $L-3$ and Florencia was $F-3$. So, since 3 years ago, Logan was twice as old as Florencia, $L-3=2(F-3) \Rightarrow L-3=2F-6 \Rightarrow L=2F-3$. Substitute $L=F+5 \Rightarrow F=L-5$ for F in the equation $L=2F-3$ to find Logan's current age: $L=2F-3=2(L-5)-3=2L-13 \Rightarrow L=13$.

Interest Problems

Simple Interest

Simple interest is computed on the principal (amount of initial investment) only. To calculate the amount of simple interest paid on an investment, multiply the principal invested by the rate (percent) of interest paid and the time of the investment: **Simple interest income = principal • rate • time.**

Examples:

1. If $4,000 is invested at 3% simple annual interest, how much interest is earned in 4 months?

   ➤ Since the annual interest is 3%, the interest for 1 year is: $4,000(0.03) = $120. Thus, the interest earned in 4 months, or $\frac{1}{3}$ of a year is: $\frac{$120}{3} = 40.

2. Mr. Krecker invests $4,000, part at 6% and part at 7%; the first year return is $250. Find the amount invested at 7%.

   ➤ Let x equal the amount invested at 7%. Thus, $4,000 - x$ equals the amount invested at 6%; $0.07x$ equals the income from the 7% investment; and $0.06(4,000 - x)$ equals the income from the 6% investment. Therefore:

   $$0.07x + 0.06(4,000 - x) = 250$$
   $$7x + 6(4,000 - x) = 25,000$$
   $$7x + 24,000 - 6x = 25,000$$
   $$x = 1,000 \ (\$1,000 \text{ invested at } 7\%)$$

Compound Interest

Compound interest is computed on the principal as well as on any interest already earned. The interest already earned is determined as simple interest for each period that the interest is compounded with the principal increasing to include the previously earned interest. If annual interest is compounded for a given period, the interest rate for that period is only a fraction of the interest rate, as determined by the number of periods for which the interest is compounded.

Example:

If $2,000 is invested at 4% annual interest, compounded quarterly, what is the balance after 9 months?

   ➤ Since the interest is compounded quarterly, figure the interest for the four periods, with each successive interest computed for the principal plus all prior interest income. Since the interest rate is 4% annually, compounded four times a year, the interest rate for each period is 1%. The balance after the first 3 months (one-quarter of a year) would be: $2,000 + ($2,000)(0.01) = $2,000 + $20 = $2,020. The balance after the second 3 months would be: $2,020 + ($2,020)(0.01) = $2,020 + $20.20 = $2,040.20. The total balance after the final 3 months would be: $2,040.20 + ($2,040.20)(0.01) = $2,040.20 + $20.40 = $2060.60.

The previous example illustrates how if interest is compounded, the interest is computed on the principal as well as on any interest earned. The general formula for compounded interest follows:

$$\textbf{Final Balance} = \textbf{Principal} \cdot \left(1 + \frac{\textbf{interest rate}}{C}\right)^{(\textbf{time})(C)}$$

where C is the number of times the interest is compounded annually.

Example:

If \$12,000 is invested at 8% annual interest, compounded semiannually, what is the balance after one year?

➢ The interest is compounded twice a year, so $C = 2$. Therefore, the final balance is $12,000\left(1 + \dfrac{0.08}{2}\right)^{(1)(2)} =$

$12,000(1.04)^2 = \$12,979.20$.

Mixture Problems

You should be familiar with two kinds of *mixture problems*. The first type is sometimes referred to as dry mixture, in which dry ingredients of different values, such as nuts or coffee, are mixed. For this type of problem, it is best to organize the data in a chart of three rows and three columns labeled as illustrated in the following problem.

Example:

A dealer wishes to mix 20 pounds of nuts selling for 45 cents per pound with some more expensive nuts selling for 60 cents per pound to make a mixture that will sell for 50 cents per pound. How many pounds of the more expensive nuts should he use?

➢ Create a table summarizing the provided information:

	No. of lbs. ×	Price/lb. =	Total Value
Original	20	0.45	0.45(20)
Added	x	0.60	0.60(x)
Mixture	$20 + x$	0.50	0.50(20 + x)

The value of the original nuts plus the value of the added nuts must equal the value of the mixture:

$$0.45(20) + 0.60(x) = 0.50(20 + x)$$
$$45(20) + 60(x) = 50(20 + x)$$
$$900 + 60x = 1,000 + 50x$$
$$10x = 100$$
$$x = 10$$

Therefore, he should use 10 lbs. of 60-cent nuts.

The second type of mixture item deals with percents and amounts rather than prices and value.

Example:

How much water must be added to 20 gallons of solution that is 30% alcohol to dilute it to a solution that is only 25% alcohol?

➢ Create a table summarizing the provided information:

	No. of gals. ×	% alcohol =	Amt. alcohol
Original	20	0.30	0.30(20)
Added	x	0	0
Mixture	$20 + x$	0.25	0.25(20 + x)

Note that the percentage of alcohol in water is zero. Had pure alcohol been added to strengthen the solution, the percentage would have been 100%. Thus, the amount of alcohol added (none) plus the original amount must equal the amount of alcohol in the new solution:

$$0.30(20) = 0.25(20 + x)$$
$$30(20) = 25(20 + x)$$
$$600 = 500 + 25x$$
$$100 = 25x$$
$$x = 4 \, \text{gallons}$$

Motion Problems

The fundamental relationship in all **motion problems** is **distance = rate • time**. The problems at the level of this examination usually derive their equation from a relationship concerning distance. Most problems fall into one of three types.

Motion in Opposite Directions

When two objects moving at the same speed start at the same time and move in opposite directions, or when two objects start at points at a given distance apart and move toward each other with the same speed until they meet, then the distance the second travels will equal one-half the total distance covered. Either way, the total distance $= d_1 + d_2$:

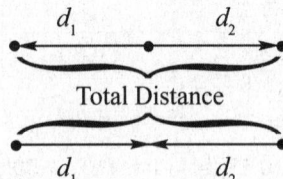

Motion in the Same Direction

This type of item is sometimes called the "catch-up" problem. Two objects leave the same place in the same direction at different times and at different rates, but one "catches up" to the other. In such a case, the two distances must be equal.

Round Trip

In this type of problem, the rate going is usually different from the rate returning. The times are also different. But if we go somewhere and then return to the starting point, the distances must be the same.

To solve any motion problem, it is helpful to organize the data in a box with columns for rate, time, and distance. A separate line should be used for each moving object. Remember that if the rate is given in *miles per hour*, the time must be in *hours* and the distance in *miles*.

Examples:

1. Two cars leave a restaurant at 1 p.m., with one car traveling east at 60 miles per hour and the other west at 40 miles per hour along a straight highway. At what time will they be 350 miles apart?

   ➤ Create a table summarizing the provided information:

	Rate	×	Time	=	Distance
Eastbound	60		x		$60x$
Westbound	40		x		$40x$

Notice that the time is unknown, since we must determine the number of hours traveled. However, since the cars start at the same time and stop when they are 350 miles apart, their times are the same: $60x + 40x = 350 \Rightarrow 100x = 350 \Rightarrow x = 3.5$. Therefore, in 3.5 hours, it will be 4:30 p.m.

2. Gloria leaves home for school, riding her bicycle at a rate of 12 miles per hour. Twenty minutes after she leaves, her mother sees Gloria's English paper on her bed and leaves to bring it to her. If her mother drives at 36 miles per hour, how far must she drive before she reaches Gloria?

   ➢ Create a table summarizing the provided information:

	Rate	×	Time	=	Distance
Gloria	12		x		$12x$
Mother	36		$x - \dfrac{1}{3}$		$36\left(x - \dfrac{1}{3}\right)$

The 20 minutes has been converted to $\dfrac{1}{3}$ of an hour. In this problem, the times are not equal, but the distances are: $12x = 36\left(x - \dfrac{1}{3}\right) = 36x - 12 \Rightarrow 12 = 24x \Rightarrow x = \dfrac{1}{2}$. Thus, if Gloria rode for $\dfrac{1}{2}$ hour at 12 miles per hour, the distance covered was 6 miles. So, Gloria's mother must drive 6 miles before she reaches Gloria.

3. Nisha leaves home at 11 a.m. and rides to Andrea's house to return her bicycle. She travels at 12 miles per hour and arrives at 11:30 a.m. She turns right around and walks home. How fast does she walk if she returns home at 1 p.m.?

   ➢ Create a table summarizing the provided information:

	Rate	×	Time	=	Distance
Going	12		$\dfrac{1}{2}$		6
Return	x		$1\dfrac{1}{2}$		$\dfrac{3x}{2}$

The distances are equal: $6 = \dfrac{3x}{2} \Rightarrow 12 = 3x \Rightarrow x = 4$ miles per hour.

Rate and Work Problems

Rate Problems

We introduced rate problems in the section above on motion problems, since distance traveled per unit time is a rate. Anytime you compare two quantities with different units, you are finding a **rate**. To find a rate, look for the different units and their corresponding numbers. Rate problems can be solved by using ratios.

Examples:

1. If Save-A-Lot Grocery advertises 2 pounds of cherries for $2.20, how much would 3 pounds of cherries costs?

    ➤ Create two ratios corresponding to the different units and their corresponding numbers. Set the ratios equal to one another and solve for the unknown quantity. The rate in the question is quantity of cherries per price (or price per quantity of cherries), and the unknown is the cost of 3 pounds of cherries: $\dfrac{2 \text{ pounds}}{\$2.20} = \dfrac{3 \text{ pounds}}{x} \Rightarrow x = \dfrac{3}{2}(\$2.20) = \$3.30$.

2. During a 4-hour party, 5 adults consumed drinks costing $120. For the same drink costs per person per hour, what would be the cost of drinks consumed by 4 adults during a 3-hour party?

    ➤ The ratio in question is drink costs per person per hour, so equate two ratios and solve for the missing value: $\dfrac{\$120}{5 \text{ adults}/4 \text{ hours}} = \dfrac{x}{4 \text{ adults}/3 \text{hours}} \Rightarrow \dfrac{120 \cdot 4}{5} = \dfrac{x \cdot 3}{4} \Rightarrow x = \dfrac{120 \cdot 16}{15} = 8 \cdot 16 = \$128$.

Note that the following words are frequently used in rate problems: *for, in, per, to, each*. For example: $100 *for* 5 hours of work, 3 widgets produced *in* 5 minutes, 55 miles *per* hour, 13 floors *to* a building, 7 cards *to each* person.

Work Problems

Combined rate, or **work**, problems concern the speed with which work can be accomplished and the time necessary to perform a task, if the size of the workforce is changed. Thus, work problems involve combining individual rates into a combined rate.

Example:

If Tess alone can weed a garden in 3 days and Rio can weed the same garden in 5 days, how long will it take them to weed the garden if they work together?

➤ Let x equal number of days required if Tess and Rio work together to weed the garden and create a table summarizing the given information:

	Tess	Rio	Together
Days to weed garden	3	5	x
Part weeded in 1 day	$\dfrac{1}{3}$	$\dfrac{1}{5}$	$\dfrac{1}{x}$

Since the part done by Tess in one day plus the part done by Rio in one day equals the part done by both in one day, we have: $\dfrac{1}{3} + \dfrac{1}{5} = \dfrac{1}{x}$. Multiply each part of the equation by $15x$ to clear the fractions:

$$\dfrac{1}{3}(15x) + \dfrac{1}{5}(15x) = \dfrac{1}{x}(15x) \Rightarrow 5x + 3x = 15 \Rightarrow 8x = 15 \Rightarrow x = 1\dfrac{7}{8} \text{ days.}$$

From the previous example, we can see that the basic formula for solving work problems is: $\dfrac{1}{a} + \dfrac{1}{b} = \dfrac{1}{c}$, where a and b are the number of minutes, days, hours, etc. that it takes the two individuals, respectively, to complete a job when working alone, and c is the number of minutes, days, hours, etc. that it takes the two individuals to do the job when working together.

Example:

When working alone, Machine X can fill a production order in 4 hours, and Machine Y can fill the same order in y hours. When the two machines operate simultaneously to fill the production order, it takes them 2.5 hours to complete the job. What is the value of y?

> $\frac{1}{4} + \frac{1}{y} = \frac{1}{2.5} \Rightarrow \frac{1}{4}(10y) + \frac{1}{Y}(10y) = \frac{1}{2.5}(10y) \Rightarrow 2.5y + 10 = 4y \Rightarrow \frac{3}{2}(y) = 10 \Rightarrow y = \frac{20}{3} = 6\frac{2}{3}$. Thus, working alone, Machine Y can fill the production order in $6\frac{2}{3}$ hours.

Variation Problems

Variation in mathematics refers to the interrelationship of variables in such a manner that a change of value for one variable produces a corresponding change in another. There are three basic types of variation: ***direct***, ***inverse***, and ***joint***.

Direct Variation

The expression "x varies directly with y" can be described by either of the following equations:

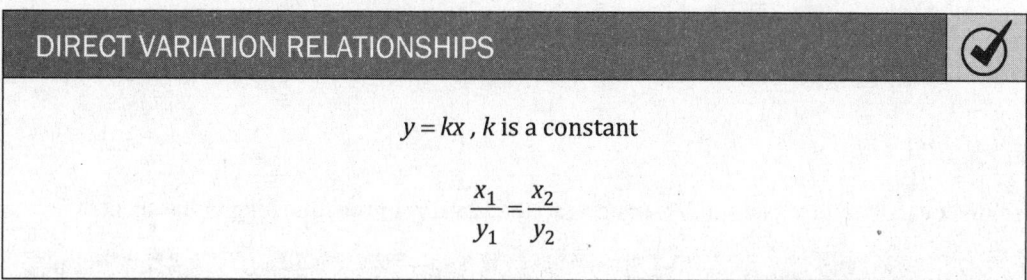

DIRECT VARIATION RELATIONSHIPS

$y = kx$, k is a constant

$$\frac{x_1}{y_1} = \frac{x_2}{y_2}$$

Two quantities are said to vary directly if they change in the same direction. As one increases, the other increases and their ratio is equal to the positive constant.

For example, the amount you must pay for milk varies directly with the number of quarts of milk you buy. The amount of sugar needed in a recipe varies directly with the amount of butter used. The number of inches between two cities on a map varies directly with the number of miles between these cities.

Example:

If x varies directly as y^2, and $x = 12$ when $y = 2$, what is the value of x when $y = 3$?

> Notice that the variation involves the square of y. Therefore, $\frac{x_1}{y_1^2} = \frac{x_2}{y_2^2} \Rightarrow \frac{12}{2^2} = \frac{x}{3^2} \Rightarrow \frac{12}{4} = \frac{x}{9} \Rightarrow x = 27$.

Inverse Variation

The expression "x varies inversely as y" can be described by either of the following equations:

INVERSE VARIATION RELATIONSHIPS

$$xy = k \text{ , } k \text{ is a constant}$$

$$\frac{x_1}{y_2} = \frac{x_2}{y_1}$$

Two quantities vary inversely if they change in opposite directions. As one quantity increases, the other quantity decreases.

For example, the number of people hired to paint a house varies inversely with the number of days the job will take. A doctor's stock of flu vaccine varies inversely with the number of patients she injects. The number of days a given supply of cat food lasts varies inversely with the number of cats being fed.

Example:

The time t to empty a container varies inversely with the square root of the number of men m working on the job. If it takes 3 hours for 16 men to do the job, how long will it take 4 men working at the same rate to empty the container?

➤ $\dfrac{t_1}{\sqrt{m_2}} = \dfrac{t_2}{\sqrt{m_1}} \Rightarrow t_1\sqrt{m_1} = t_2\sqrt{m_2} \Rightarrow 3\sqrt{16} = t\sqrt{4} \Rightarrow t = 3 \cdot \dfrac{\sqrt{16}}{\sqrt{4}} = 3\left(\sqrt{4}\right) = 3 \cdot 2 = 6$.

Joint Variation

The expression "x varies jointly as y and z" can be described by any of the following equations:

JOINT VARIATION RELATIONSHIPS

$$\frac{x}{yz} = k \text{ , } k \text{ is a constant}$$

$$\frac{x_1}{y_1 z_1} = \frac{x_2}{y_2 z_2} \Leftrightarrow \frac{x_1}{x_2} = \left(\frac{y_1}{y_2}\right)\left(\frac{z_1}{z_2}\right)$$

Example:

The area, A, of a triangle varies jointly as the base b and the height h. If $A = 20$ when $b = 10$ and $h = 4$, what is the value of A when $b = 6$ and $h = 7$?

➤ $\dfrac{A_1}{b_1 h_1} = \dfrac{A_2}{b_2 h_2} \Rightarrow \dfrac{20}{(10)(4)} = \dfrac{A_2}{(6)(7)} \Rightarrow A_2 = 21$.

Percent Problems

Many problem-solving items involve percents as they apply to certain types of business situations.

Percent Increase or Decrease

Percent increase or decrease is found by putting the amount of increase or decrease over the original amount and changing this fraction to a percent.

Example:

A company normally employs 100 people. During a slow spell, it fired 20% of its employees. By what percentage must it now increase its staff to return to full capacity?

➤ $20\% = \frac{1}{5} \cdot 100 = 20$. The company now has $100 - 20 = 80$ employees. If it then increases by 20 employees, the percentage increase is $\frac{20}{80} = \frac{1}{4}$, or 25%.

Discounts

A discount is expressed as a percent of the original price that will be deducted from that price to determine the sale price.

Examples:

1. Bill's Hardware offers a 20% discount on all appliances during a sale week. How much must Mrs. Russell pay for a washing machine marked at $280?

   ➤ $20\% = \frac{1}{5} \Rightarrow \frac{1}{5} \cdot \$280 = \$56$ discount $\Rightarrow \$280 - \$56 = \$224$ sale price. Alternatively, the following shortcut simplifies the solution: if there is a 20% discount, Mrs. Russell will pay 80% of the marked price: $80\% = \frac{4}{5} \Rightarrow \frac{4}{5} \cdot \$280 = \$224$ sale price.

2. A store offers a television set marked at $340 less consecutive discounts of 10% and 5%. Another store offers the same set marked at $340 less a single discount of 15%. How much does the buyer save buying at the better price?

   ➤ In the first store, the initial 10% discount means the buyer will pay 90%, or $\frac{9}{10}$ of $340, which is $306. Now, the second discount must be figured on the first sale price. The additional 5% discount means the buyer will pay 95% of $306, or $290.70. In the second store, the single discount of 15% means the buyer will pay 85% of $340, or $289. Thus, the second store will have a lower sale price, and the buyer saves $290.70 - \$289 = \$1.70$ buying at that better price.

Profit

Gross profit is equal to revenues minus expenses, that is, the selling price minus cost.

Example:

A used car lot paid $5,000 for a trade-in car. At what price should the salesman sell the used car in order to make a gross profit of 60% of the cost of the car?

> The cost of the car is $5,000, so the gross profit is 60% of $5,000, or $0.6(5,000) = \$3,000$. Since the gross profit is equal to the selling price minus cost, the selling price of the car must be gross profit plus cost, or $\$3,000 + \$5,000 = \$8,000$.

Commission

Many salespeople earn money on a commission basis. In order to inspire sales, they are paid a percentage of the value of goods that they personally sell. This amount is called a commission.

Examples:

1. Mr. Saunders works at Brown's Department Store, where he is paid $80 per week in salary plus a 4% commission on all his sales. How much does he earn in a week in which he sells $4,032 worth of merchandise?

   > Find 4% of $4,032 and add this amount to $80: $\$4,032 \cdot 0.04 = \$161.28 \Rightarrow \$161.28 + \$80 = \$241.28$.

2. Bill Olson delivers newspapers for a dealer and keeps 8% of all money collected. In one month, he was able to keep $16. How much did he forward to the dealer?

   > First, find how much he collected by asking $16 is 8% of what number: $\$16 = 0.08x \Rightarrow \$1,600 = 8x \Rightarrow x = \$200$. Then, subtract the amount Bill kept ($16) from the total collected ($200). Therefore, Bill forwarded $184 to the dealer.

Taxes

Taxes are a percent of money spent or money earned.

Examples:

1. Dane County collects a 7% sales tax on automobiles. If the price of a used Ford is $5,832 before taxes, what will it cost when the sales tax is added in?

   > Find 7% of $5,832 to determine the amount of tax and then add that amount to $5,832. This can be done in one step by finding 107% of $5,832: $\$5,832 \cdot 1.07 = \$6,240.24$.

2. If income is taxed at the rate of 10% for the first $10,000 of earned income, 15% for the next $10,000, 20% for the next $10,000, and 25% for all earnings over $30,000, how much income tax must be paid on a yearly income of $36,500?

   > Find the income tax collected at each percentage rate and add them:

   $$10\% \text{ of first } \$10,000 = \$1,000$$
   $$15\% \text{ of next } \$10,000 = \$1,500$$
   $$20\% \text{ of next } \$10,000 = \$2,000$$
   $$+\ 25\% \text{ of next } \$6,500 = \$1,625$$
   $$\text{Total Tax} = \$6,125$$

Measurement Problems

Some questions may involve different units of measure. For any problem requiring conversion from one unit of measure to another, other than for units of time, the relationship between those units will be given.

Example:

A car travels at a constant rate of 37 miles per hour. If 1 kilometer is equal to 0.62 miles, approximately how many kilometers does the car travel in 20 minutes?

> 1 kilometer equals 0.62 miles, so multiply the given speed by $\dfrac{1 \text{ kilometer}}{0.62 \text{ miles}}$ to convert it to kilometers per
>
> hour: $\dfrac{37 \text{ miles}}{\text{hour}} \cdot \dfrac{1 \text{ kilometer}}{0.62 \text{ miles}} \approx 60$ kilometers per hour. Thus, in 20 minutes, or one-third of an hour, the
>
> car travels $\dfrac{60}{3} = 20$ kilometers.

Counting Methods

The Multiplication Principle for Counting

The **multiplication principle for counting** states that if an object is to be chosen from a set of m objects and a second object is to be chosen from a different set of n objects, the total number of ways of choosing both object simultaneously is mn. In other words, if an operation takes two steps and the first step can be performed in m ways, and if, for each of those ways, the second step can be performed in n ways, the total number of ways of performing the operation is mn.

Examples:

1. A litter of boxer puppies contains 4 with brindle coloring and 5 with fawn coloring. In how many ways can one choose a pair of one brindle puppy and one fawn puppy from this litter of puppies?

> You have 4 choices for a brindle puppy and 5 choices for a fawn puppy. By the multiplication principle, the total number of possible pairs is: $4 \cdot 5 = 20$.

2. From a garden with 6 flower varieties, a bouquet of 3 different types of flowers is to be picked. How many different possible bouquets are there?

> Extend the multiplication principle to a three-step process: there are 6 choices of flower for the first pick of the bouquet, for each of which there are 5 choices for the second flower (because one flower type has been eliminated, having been picked as the first flower in the bouquet). Furthermore, for each of these pairs, there are 4 remaining flower choices for the third pick (because two flower types have been eliminated, having been picked as the first and second flowers in the bouquet). Therefore, the total number of possible bouquets is: $6 \cdot 5 \cdot 4 = 120$.

Permutations

A natural extension of the multiplication principle is the concept of **permutations**, or orderings in distinct arrangements of n distinguishable objects in a row. If a set of n objects is to be ordered from 1st to n^{th}, then there are n choices for the first object, $n-1$ choices for the second object, $n-2$ choices for the third object, and so on, until there is only one choice for the nth object. Therefore, the number of ways of ordering the n objects, also called **n factorial**, is as follows:

$$n! = n(n-1)(n-2)\ldots(3)(2)(1)$$

Examples:

1. If five spices (rosemary, oregano, basil, sage, and pepper) are arranged randomly on a shelf, what is the chance that they will be in alphabetical order from left to right?

    ➤ There are five distinguishable objects that can be arranged in $5! = 5 \cdot 4 \cdot 3 \cdot 2 \cdot 1 = 120$ ways. In only one of these ways will they be in alphabetical order. Therefore, the chance is $\frac{1}{120}$ that the spices will be arranged in alphabetical order from left to right.

2. In how many ways can five spices (rosemary, oregano, basil, sage, and pepper) be arranged on the shelf if the oregano and the basil must be next to each other?

    ➤ Since the oregano and the basil must be next to each other, treat the two together as one spice, thereby reducing the total number of spices to be arranged from five to four. These four spices— rosemary, oregano/basil, sage, and pepper—can be arranged in $4! = 4 \cdot 3 \cdot 2 \cdot 1 = 24$ ways. However, for each of these ways, we could have set up the "glued" spices in two sequences: oregano/basil or basil/oregano. Therefore, there is a total of $2 \cdot 24 = 48$ ways in which the spices can be arranged with the oregano and basil next to each other.

If you are asked to find the number of ways to arrange a smaller group that is being drawn from a larger group, you can use the following *permutation formula*:

$$P = \frac{n!}{(n-k)!}$$

where n is the number of elements in the larger set and k is the number of elements being arranged.

Example:

Five candidates are running for office. The candidates who come in first, second, and third place will be elected president, vice-president, and treasurer, respectively. How many outcomes for president, vice-president, and treasurer are there?

➤ Using the permutation formula: $P = \frac{n!}{(n-k)!} = \frac{5!}{(5-3)!} = \frac{5!}{2!} = \frac{5 \cdot 4 \cdot 3 \cdot 2 \cdot 1}{2 \cdot 1} = 5 \cdot 4 \cdot 3 = 60$. Notice that the formula is the same as applying the following logic: Any of the five candidates could come in first place, leaving four candidates who could come in second place, leaving three candidates who could come in third place, for a total of $5 \cdot 4 \cdot 3 = 60$ possible outcomes for president, vice-president, and treasurer.

Combinations

A *combination* problem is one in which the order or arrangement of the smaller group that is being drawn from the larger group does NOT matter. Rather than the permutation formula, use the following *combination formula*:

$$C = \frac{n!}{k!(n-k)!}$$

where n is the number of elements in the larger set and k is the number of elements being arranged.

Example:

How many different ways are there to choose four socks from a drawer containing nine socks?

➤ Since the order or arrangement of the four socks being drawn from the drawer containing nine socks does not matter, use the combination formula: $C = \dfrac{9!}{4!(9-4)!} = \dfrac{9!}{4! \cdot 5!} = \dfrac{9 \cdot 8 \cdot 7 \cdot \cancel{6} \cdot \cancel{5}!}{4 \cdot \cancel{3} \cdot \cancel{2} \cdot 1 \cdot \cancel{5}!} = \dfrac{9 \cdot 8 \cdot 7}{4} = 126$.

Probability

Single-Event Probability

Probability is concerned with experiments that have a finite number of outcomes. Probabilities occur in games, sports, weather reports, etc. The probability that some particular outcome or set of outcomes (called an ***event***) will occur is expressed as a ratio. The numerator of a probability ratio is the number of ways that the event of interest can occur. The denominator is the total number of outcomes that are possible. This ***probability ratio*** is true for experiments in which all of the individual outcomes are equally likely:

$$\text{Probability of event} = \frac{\textbf{number of ways that event can happen}}{\textbf{total number of outcomes possible}}$$

Example:

If a six-sided die is tossed, what is the probability that you will get a number greater than 4?

➤ There are a total of six ways a die can land: 1, 2, 3, 4, 5, or 6. Each of these six events is equally likely. There are two possible outcomes that are greater than 4: 5 or 6. Therefore, the probability of the die landing with a number greater than 4 is $\dfrac{2}{6} = \dfrac{1}{3}$.

Note that the probability that an event occurs is a number between 0 and 1, inclusive. If the event has no outcomes, then it is impossible and its probability is 0. If the event is the set of all possible outcomes, then it is certain to occur and its probability is 1.

Multiple-Event Probability

Another type of probability involves finding the probability of a certain outcome after multiple events. One type of ***multiple-event probability*** involves individual events that must occur a certain way. For these experiments, figure out the probability for each individual event and multiply the individual probabilities together.

Example:

If two marbles are randomly chosen from a jar with three red marbles and seven black marbles, what is the probability that both marbles will be red?

➤ Since three out of the ten marbles are red, the probability that the first marble chosen is red is $\dfrac{3}{10}$. After choosing one red marble, this leaves two red marbles in the jar out of nine. Therefore, the probability that the second marble chosen will also be red is $\dfrac{2}{9}$. The probability that both marbles chosen will be red is: $\dfrac{3}{10} \cdot \dfrac{2}{9} = \dfrac{6}{90} = \dfrac{1}{15}$.

A second type of multiple-event probability involves individual events that can have different outcomes. For these experiments, create a probability ratio by dividing the number of desired outcomes by the total number of possible outcomes. The total number of possible outcomes is found by multiplying together the number of possible outcomes for each individual event. The number of desired outcomes can be determined by counting the possibilities.

Example:

If a dime is tossed three times, what is the probability that at least two of the three tosses will be heads up?

➤ There are two possible outcomes for each toss (heads or tails), so after three tosses there are a total of $2^3 = 2 \cdot 2 \cdot 2 = 8$ possible outcomes. Next, list all the possibilities where at least two of the three tosses are heads up: H, H, H; H, H, T; H, T, H; T, H, H. Thus, the total number of desired outcomes is four.

Therefore, the probability that at least two of the three tosses will be heads up is: $\dfrac{4}{8} = \dfrac{1}{2}$.

Probabilities can also be determined for an experiment with two different events, A and B. The probability of A occurring is denoted by $P(A)$, and the probability of B occurring is denoted by $P(B)$. Given these two events, there are three additional events that can be defined. "Not A" is the set of outcomes that are not outcomes in A; "A or B" is the set of outcomes in A or B or both ($A \cup B$); "A and B" is the set of outcomes in both A and B ($A \cap B$). If the event "A and B" is impossible, because A and B cannot happen at the same time, then A and B are said to be **mutually exclusive**. If the occurrence of either event A or B does not alter the probability that the other event occurs, then A and B are said to be **independent**.

PROBABILITIES FOR MULTIPLE EVENT EXPERIMENTS

(An experiment with events A and B)

1. "Not A": $P(\text{not } A) = 1 - P(A)$

2. "A or B": $P(A \text{ or } B) = P(A) + P(B) - P(A \text{ and } B)$

3. "A and B" (A and B are mutually exclusive): $P(A \text{ and } B) = 0$

4. "A and B" (A and B are independent): $P(A \text{ and } B) = P(A)P(B)$

Example:

If a six-sided die is tossed, what is the probability that you will roll a prime number or an even number?

➤ Let A be the event that the outcome is a prime number, $\{2, 3, 5\}$, and let B be the event that the outcome is an even number, $\{2, 4, 6\}$. Since 3 outcomes are prime, $P(A) = \dfrac{3}{6} = \dfrac{1}{2}$. Similarly, $P(B) = \dfrac{1}{2}$. $P(A \text{ and } B)$, or the probability that the outcome is both even and prime, is $\dfrac{1}{6}$ since only 2 is both even and prime.

Therefore, $P(A \text{ or } B) = \dfrac{1}{2} + \dfrac{1}{2} - \dfrac{1}{6} = \dfrac{5}{6}$. Note that this is the same as reasoning that the set of prime and even numbers on the die is $\{2, 3, 4, 5, 6\}$, so the probability of getting one of these numbers is $\dfrac{5}{6}$.

Geometric Probability

Some items on the exam may involve geometric probability. For example, if a point is to be chosen at random from the interior of a region, part of which is shaded, you might be asked to find the probability that the point chosen will be from the shaded portion of the region. Such an item might be presented in a specific context, such as throwing darts at a target.

Examples:

1. The figure below shows a circle inscribed in a square. The area of the square is 324. If a point is selected at random in the interior of the square, what is the approximate probability that the point also lies in the interior of the circle?

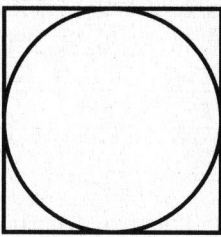

➤ Since the area of the square is 324, $A_{square} = s^2 \Rightarrow s = 18$. The side of the square is equal to the diameter of the circle, so the radius of the circle is $18 \div 2 = 9$. The area of the circle is: $A_{circle} = \pi r^2 = \pi(9)^2 = 81\pi$. Therefore, the probability that a point chosen at random in the interior of the square will also be in the interior of the circle is: $\dfrac{A_{circle}}{A_{square}} = \dfrac{81\pi}{324} = \dfrac{\pi}{4} \approx 0.785$.

2. The figure below shows a rectangle that is bounded by the two axes and two lines whose respective equations are $y = 8$ and $x = 6$. The shaded trapezoidal region is bounded on three sides by portions of three sides of the rectangle. The fourth unbounded side of the shaded trapezoidal region is a line segment that is a portion of the line whose equation is $2y = x + 4$. If a point is selected at random in the interior of the rectangle, what is the probability that the point also lies in the shaded region?

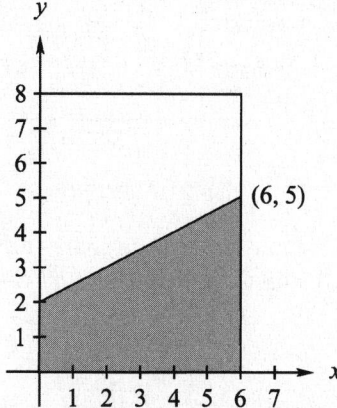

➤ For the line $2y = x + 4$, substitute values for x and solve for y. If $x = 0$, $2y = 0 + 4 \Rightarrow y = 2$. If $x = 6$, $2y = 6 + 4 \Rightarrow y = 5$. The parallel sides of the trapezoid have lengths of 2 and 5; the altitude of the trapezoid is 6. Therefore, the probability that the point will be in both the interior of the rectangle and the interior of the shaded region is: $\dfrac{A_{shaded}}{A_{rectangle}} = \dfrac{\frac{6(2+5)}{2}}{6 \cdot 8} = \dfrac{3 \cdot 7}{48} = \dfrac{21}{48} = \dfrac{7}{16}$.

Data Interpretation: Tables and Graphs

You are expected to be able to interpret data displayed in tables, charts, and graphs.

Example:

The tables below show the number, type, and cost of candy bars bought during one week at two local drugstores.

NUMBER OF CANDY BARS BOUGHT						
	Type A		Type B		Type C	
	Large	Giant	Large	Giant	Large	Giant
Drugstore P	60	20	69	21	43	17
Drugstore Q	44	18	59	25	38	13

COST PER CANDY BAR		
	Large	Giant
Type A	$0.45	$0.69
Type B	$0.45	$0.79
Type C	$0.55	$0.99

What is the total cost of all Type B candy bars bought at these two drugstores during the week?

➤ Total the cost of all Type B bars bought at the two drugstores: $69(0.45) + 21(0.79) + 59(0.45) + 25(0.79) =$ $93.94.

The test may also ask about the line of best fit for a scatterplot. A scatterplot is really just a plot of various data points for which a line of best fit can be drawn. For example, an item may require you to identify that a line of best fit for a scatterplot has a slope that is positive but less than 1. You are not expected to use formal methods for finding the equation of a line of best fit.

Example:

The points in the scatterplot below show the relationship between 14 students' test scores on a mid-term test and a final test. What is the approximate average (arithmetic mean) of the scores on the final test for all students who scored above 90 on the midterm test?

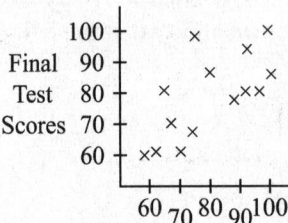

Mid-Term Test Scores

➤ Five students scored above 90 on the mid-term. Their marks are the five to the right on the scatterplot. The five corresponding scores on the final are approximately 80, 80, 85, 95, and 100. The average of these scores is approximately 88.

Story Problems
Exercise 12

DIRECTIONS: Choose the correct answer to each of the following items. Answers are on page 608.

1. A suit is sold for $68 while marked at $80. What is the rate of discount?

    A. 15%   C. $17\frac{11}{17}$%   E. 24%

    B. 17%   D. 20%

2. Ten dollars is placed into an account that earns 3.5% interest compounded monthly. Using the formula for compound interest,

    $A = P\left(1 + \dfrac{r}{n}\right)^{nt}$,where A is the final amount of

    the investment, P is the amount of the initial investment, r is the annual percentage interest rate, t is the time period in years, and n is the number of times per year the interest is compounded, determine the amount in the account after 5 years.

    A. $11.91   C. $13.23   E. $35.95
    B. $12.60   D. $14.74

3. Colin and Shaina wish to buy a gift for a friend. They combine their money and find they have $4.00, consisting of quarters, dimes, and nickels. If they have 35 coins and the number of quarters is half the number of nickels, how many quarters do they have?

    A. 5   C. 20   E. 36
    B. 10   D. 23

4. Three times the smallest of three consecutive odd integers is 3 more than twice the largest. Find the largest integer.

    A. 9   C. 13   E. 17
    B. 11   D. 15

5. If 60 feet of uniform wire weigh 80 pounds, what is the weight, in pounds, of 2 yards of the same wire?

    A. $2\frac{2}{3}$ C. 80   E. 2,400

    B. 8   D. 120

6. Robert is 15 years older than Stan. However, y years ago Robert was twice as old as Stan. If Stan is now b years old and $b > y$, find the value of $b - y$.

    A. 13   C. 15   E. 17
    B. 14   D. 16

7. A gear 50 inches in diameter turns a smaller gear 30 inches in diameter. If the larger gear makes 15 revolutions, how many revolutions does the smaller gear make in that time?

    A. 9   C. 20   E. 30
    B. 12   D. 25

8. How many ounces of pure acid must be added to 20 ounces of a solution that is 5% acid to strengthen it to a solution that is 24% acid?

    A. $2\frac{1}{2}$ C. 6   E. 10

    B. 5   D. $7\frac{1}{2}$

9. A certain radio costs a merchant $72. At what price must he sell it if he is to make a profit of 20% of the selling price?

    A. $86.40   C. $90   E. $148
    B. $88   D. $144

10. In Juanita's purse, she has 24 coins made up of nickels and dimes. She also knows that she has three times as many dimes as nickels. What is the total value of coins in her purse?

 A. $1.50 C. $2.20 E. $2.40
 B. $2.10 D. $2.35

11. If a furnace uses 40 gallons of oil in a week, how many gallons, to the nearest gallon, does it use in 10 days?

 A. 57 C. 28 E. 4
 B. 44 D. 20

12. The sum in years of Sam's and Suzie's ages is 18. If Sam is half as old as Suzie, how old is Suzie?

 A. 4 C. 8 E. 12
 B. 6 D. 10

13. A baseball team has won 40 games out of 60 played. It has 32 more games to play. How many of these must the team win to make its record 75% for the season?

 A. 28 C. 30 E. 34
 B. 29 D. 32

14. Peter invested some money at 6% interest compounded quarterly. Peter made no other deposits or any withdrawals, and at the end of ten years, the value of his investment was $907. Using the formula for compound interest, $A = P\left(1 + \dfrac{r}{n}\right)^{nt}$, where A is the final amount, P is the initial investment, r is the annual percentage interest rate, t is the time period in years, and n is the number of times per year the interest is compounded, approximately how much was his initial investment?

 A. $475 C. $595 E. $650
 B. $500 D. $635

15. Ivan left Austin to drive to Boxville at 6:15 p.m. and arrived at 11:45 p.m. If he averaged 30 miles per hour and stopped one hour for dinner, how many miles is Boxville from Austin?

 A. 120 C. 180 E. 190
 B. 135 D. 185

16. How much water must be added to 30 gallons of a 50% alcohol solution to obtain a 40% alcohol solution?

 A. 7.5 C. 10.25 E. 14.5
 B. 9 D. 12

17. If a car can drive 25 miles on two gallons of gasoline, how many gallons will be needed for a trip of 150 miles?

 A. 12 C. 16 E. 20
 B. 13 D. 17

18. How many different ways can you arrange all the letters in the word "STUDY" such that the arrangement begins with the letter D?

 A. 5 C. 12 E. 24
 B. 6 D. 16

19. A salesperson earns a commission of 5% on all sales between $200 and $600, and 8% on all sales over $600. What is the commission earned in a week in which sales total $800?

 A. $20 C. $48 E. $88
 B. $36 D. $78

20. Two boats leave the dock at the same time. One boat is traveling north at 30 miles per hour and the other boat is traveling south at 50 miles per hour. After how many hours will they be 200 miles apart?

 A. 1 hour C. 2 hours E. 3 hours
 B. 1.5 hours D. 2.5 hours

21. Mr. Bridges can wash his car in 15 minutes, while his son Dave takes twice as long to do the same job. If they work together, how many minutes will the job take them?

A. 5　　　　C. 10　　　　E. 30

B. $7\frac{1}{2}$　　D. $22\frac{1}{2}$

22. Leah has been saving quarters and dimes in her treasure chest. If the total value of the 26 coins in her treasure chest is $4.40, how many dimes has she saved?

A. 8　　　　C. 14　　　　E. 18
B. 12　　　D. 17

23. At c cents per pound, what is the cost of a ounces of salami?

A. $\frac{c}{a}$　　　C. ac　　　E. $\frac{16c}{a}$

B. $\frac{a}{c}$　　　D. $\frac{ac}{16}$

24. Jack is 5 years older than his sister, Kate. Six years ago, Jack was twice as old as Kate. How old is Jack now?

A. 11　　　C. 15　　　E. 19
B. 13　　　D. 16

25. If 4 workers take an hour to pave a road, how long should it take 12 workers to pave the same road?

A. $\frac{1}{4}$ hour　　C. $\frac{1}{2}$ hour　　E. 1 hour

B. $\frac{1}{3}$ hour　　D. $\frac{3}{4}$ hour

26. A baker mixes 10 pounds of dark chocolate selling for $2.00 per pound with some white chocolate selling for $1.50 per pound to make a mixture that sells for $1.80 per pound. Approximately how many pounds of the white chocolate should she use?

A. 4 lbs.　　C. 6.67 lbs　　E. 8.33 lbs
B. 5.33 lbs.　D. 7.67 lbs.

27. If p pencils cost d dollars, how many pencils can be bought for c cents?

A. $\frac{100pc}{d}$　　C. $\frac{pd}{c}$　　E. $\frac{cd}{p}$

B. $\frac{pc}{100d}$　　D. $\frac{pc}{d}$

28. Blake runs to the bike shop at a rate of 4 miles per hour to pick up his bike. He gets to the bike shop in 20 minutes. He rides his bike back home in 10 minutes. How fast does he ride his bike home?

A. 6 mph　　C. 8 mph　　E. 10 mph
B. 7 mph　　D. 9 mph

29. There are two drains, Drain 1 and Drain 2, in a pool. If both drains are opened, the pool is emptied in 20 minutes. If Drain 1 is closed and Drain 2 is open, the pool will be emptied in 30 minutes. If Drain 2 is closed and Drain 1 is open, how many minutes will it take to empty the pool?

A. 20　　　C. 50　　　E. 120
B. 30　　　D. 60

30. If the number n of newspapers sold per week varies with the price p in dollars according to the equation $n = 40 - 3p$, what would be the total weekly revenue from the sale of $1 newspapers?

A. $30　　C. $35　　E. $40
B. $33　　D. $37

31. A candy manufacturer produces 400 bars of a certain chocolate each month at a cost to the manufacturer of 25 cents per bar and all the produced chocolate bars are sold each month. What is the minimum selling price per bar that will ensure that the monthly profit on the sales of these chocolate bars will be at least $420?

A. $1.00   C. $1.20   E. $1.30
B. $1.10   D. $1.25

32. The variable m varies directly as the square of t. If m is 7 when $t = 1$, what is the value of m when $t = 2$?

A. 28   C. 7   E. 2
B. 14   D. $3\frac{1}{2}$

33. If the value of a piece of property decreases by 10% while the tax rate on the property increases by 10%, what is the effect on taxes?

A. Taxes increase by 10%.
B. Taxes increase by 1%.
C. There is no change in taxes.
D. Taxes decrease by 1%.
E. Taxes decrease by 10%.

34. Of the Coral Estates residents, 95% live in private homes. Of those, 40% live in air-conditioned homes. What percent of the residents of Coral Estates live in air-conditioned homes?

A. 3%   C. 30%   E. 38%
B. 3.8%   D. 34%

35. Mr. Carlson receives a salary of $500 a month and a commission of 5% on all sales. What must be the amount of his sales in July so that his total monthly income is $2,400?

A. $48,000   C. $7,600   E. $2,000
B. $38,000   D. $3,800

36. In a run/walk marathon, Weber runs x miles in h hours, then walks the remainder of the marathon route, y miles, in the same number of hours. Which of the following represents Weber's average speed, in miles per hour, for the entire marathon?

A. $\dfrac{x-y}{h}$ C. $\dfrac{2(x+y)}{h}$ E. $\dfrac{x+y}{2h}$

B. $\dfrac{x-y}{2h}$ D. $\dfrac{2(x+y)}{2h}$

37. Let $R = \{3, 5, 6, 7, 9\}$. How many different subsets of R with 1, 2, 3, or 4 elements contain one or more odd numbers?

A. 31   C. 29   E. 27
B. 30   D. 28

38. Sixty students are enrolled in French, Spanish, or German. Forty-five students are in French, 35 are in Spanish, and 20 are in German. Fifteen students are enrolled in all three of the courses. How many of the students are enrolled in exactly two of the courses?

A. 5   C. 12   E. 20
B. 10   D. 15

39. Set X is the set of all positive integral multiples of 8: $X = \{8, 16, 24, 32, ...\}$. Set Y is the set of all positive integral multiples of 6: $Y = \{6, 12, 18, 24, ...\}$. The intersection of these two sets is the set of all positive integral multiples of:

A. 2   C. 14   E. 48
B. 4   D. 24

40. Of the 50 children in a school sports program, 40% will be assigned to softball, and the remaining 60% to baseball. However, 70% of the children prefer softball and 30% prefer baseball. What is the least possible number of children who will NOT be assigned to the sport they prefer?

A. 10   C. 20   E. 35
B. 15   D. 30

41. If y varies directly with x and the constant of variation is 3, then $y = 12.3$ when $x = 4.1$. If y varies directly with x and $y = 6.72$ when $x = 4.2$, then what is the constant of variation?

A. 3.1   C. 2.52   E. 2.50
B. 4.2   D. 1.6

42. At a constant temperature, the resistance of a wire varies directly with length and inversely with the square of the wire diameter. A piece of wire that is 0.1 inch in diameter and 50 feet long has a resistance of 0.1 ohm. What is the resistance, in ohms, of a wire of the same material that is 9,000 feet long and 0.3 inches in diameter?

A. 0.3   C. 2   E. 9
B. 0.9   D. 3

43. The perimeter of a square varies directly as the length of one side of the square with a constant of variation of 4. The circumference of a circle varies directly as the circle's radius and a constant of variation equal to:

A. π C. 1   E. $\dfrac{1}{n}$
B. 2π D. 2

44. The formula for compound interest is $A = P\left(1 + \dfrac{r}{n}\right)^{nt}$, where A is the final amount, P is the initial investment, r is the annual percentage interest rate, t is the time period, and n is the number of times per year that the interest is compounded. If an initial investment of \$10,000 accrues compound interest at a percentage rate of 4.16% and is worth \$10,424.02, \$10,866.03, \$11,326.77, and \$11,807.06 after 1, 2, 3, and 4 years, respectively, then n is approximately equal to:

A. 1   C. 4   E. 12
B. 2   D. 6

45. The probability that an event will happen can be shown by the fraction $\dfrac{\text{winning events}}{\text{total events}}$ or $\dfrac{\text{favorable events}}{\text{total events}}$. From the 8-digit number 12,344,362, Helen selects a digit at random. What is the probability that she selected 4?

A. $\dfrac{1}{8}$ C. $\dfrac{1}{4}$ E. $\dfrac{4}{1}$
B. $\dfrac{1}{5}$ D. $\dfrac{1}{2}$

46. George must select 1 pencil from 6 different pencils and 1 pen from 5 different pens. How many different combinations can George make?

A. 5   C. 30   E. 65
B. 11   D. 56

47. One of the letters in the alphabet is selected at random. What is the probability that the letter selected is a letter found in the word "MATHEMATICS"?

A. $\dfrac{1}{26}$ C. $\dfrac{5}{13}$ E. $\dfrac{6}{13}$
B. $\dfrac{4}{13}$ D. $\dfrac{11}{26}$

48. If 5 books are lined up in random order on a shelf, what is the probability that the oldest book will be on the left end and the newest book will be on the right end?

A. $\dfrac{1}{20}$ C. $\dfrac{1}{6}$ E. $\dfrac{1}{4}$
B. $\dfrac{1}{8}$ D. $\dfrac{1}{5}$

49. In the figure below, two sides of the rectangle *ABGF* lie on two sides of the square *ACDE*. $\overline{AF} = 9$, $\overline{BC} = 8$, and $\overline{FE} = 1$.

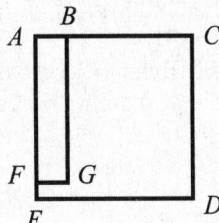

If a point is chosen at random in the interior of the square, what is the probability that the point also lies in the interior of the rectangle?

A. $\dfrac{1}{50}$ C. $\dfrac{7}{50}$ E. $\dfrac{11}{50}$

B. $\dfrac{3}{50}$ D. $\dfrac{9}{50}$

50. The table below shows the daily change in the weather temperatures for a certain city last week. What was the net change (total change), in degrees Celsius, in the weather temperature for the week?

Day	Daily Change in Temperature (°C)
Sunday	+5.5
Monday	+1.7
Tuesday	−3.9
Wednesday	−3.3
Thursday	−0.5
Friday	+0.8
Saturday	−0.2

A. −5.7   C. 0.1   E. 5.7
B. −0.1   D. 5.3

51. The table below shows the number of students in three sports at East High School. 8 students are in both basketball and tennis, 5 students are in both basketball and volleyball, and 3 students are in both volleyball and tennis. No student is in all three sports. What is the total number of students that participate only in basketball or tennis?

Sport	Number of Students
Basketball	35
Volleyball	15
Tennis	40

A. 22   C. 50   E. 75
B. 29   D. 51

52. The stronger the relationship between two variables, the more closely the points on a scatter plot will approach some linear or curvilinear pattern. Which of the scatter plots below represents the strongest relationship between the two variables?

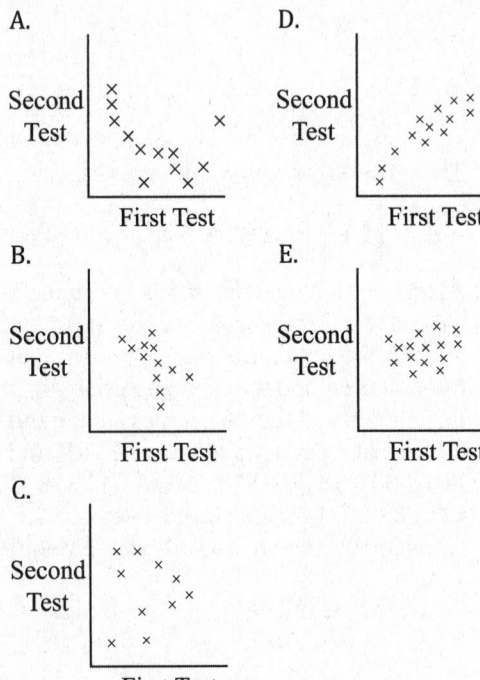

53. The table below represents the number of voters in five counties that voted in a general election and the percent change in the number of voters from the previously held primary election. Which county had the greatest net increase in voters between the primary and the general elections?

County	Number of Voters in General Election (in Millions)	Percent Change from Primary Election
M	5.67	−23%
N	2.34	+14%
O	1.25	−2%
P	4.56	+4%
Q	6.23	+8%

A. County M
B. County N
C. County O
D. County P
E. County Q

Math
Mastery Test

MATH MASTERY TEST

45 Items

DIRECTIONS: Solve each problem and choose the correct answer from the choices given. Then, fill in the corresponding oval on the bubble sheet. Calculator use is permitted, though some items are best solved without a calculator. Answers are on page 611.

NOTE: Unless otherwise stated, illustrative figures are NOT necessarily drawn to scale. The word *average* indicates arithmetic mean. The word *line* indicates a straight line. Assume geometric figures lie in a plane.

1. What is the correct order of the following numbers from least to greatest?

  I.   0.00692
  II. 0.007
  III. 0.0069
  IV. 0.0071

A. I, II, III, IV
B. I, III, II, IV
C. III, I, II, IV
D. III, I, IV, II
E. III, II, I, IV

2. Beth cut 11 pieces of electrical wire from a spool, each 14 feet long, leaving a piece 9 feet long on the spool. How many feet long was the wire on the spool before Beth started?

F. 99
G. 113
H. 145
J. 154
K. 163

3. On a number line, M has coordinate -6 and N has coordinate 6. If $\overline{MN}$ is divided into three equal parts, what is the length of each part?

A. 0
B. 3
C. 4
D. 6
E. 12

4. Which of the following numbers is the <u>LEAST</u>?

F. 0.0011
G. 0.00111
H. 0.00101
J. 0.00011
K. 0.0001

5. On the real number line shown below, which point has a coordinate that is less than -0.6 but greater than -0.7?

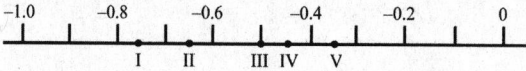

A. I
B. II
C. III
D. IV
E. V

6. During an assembly program, 379 students, all of them in the 9th, 10th, or 11th grade, are seated in an auditorium. If 121 of the students are 9th graders and 135 of them are 10th graders, how many of the students seated in the auditorium are 11th graders?

F. 14
G. 123
H. 244
J. 256
K. 258

7. Jon bought a motorcycle for $6,000. He initially paid 20% of the purchase price and agreed to pay the balance in six equal monthly payments without interest. How much will each monthly payment be?

    A. $48
    B. $200
    C. $800
    D. $1,000
    E. $1,200

8. Admission to the Drama Club's annual production costs $7 for tickets purchased in advance and $9 for tickets at the door. On the night of the performance, 187 tickets had already been sold for $7 each. How many tickets had to be sold at the door to ensure that the $2,100 cost of the production was covered by ticket sales?

    F.   87
    G.   88
    H.   278
    J.   801
    K. 1,309

9. $(\sqrt{2})^2 + (\sqrt{3})^2 = ?$

    A. $\sqrt{5}$
    B. $\sqrt{6}$
    C. 5
    D. 6
    E. 7

10. A group of five students wants to buy their coach a gift that costs $30. If the students agree to share the cost of the gift equally, how much should each student contribute to the cost of the gift? (Ignore any tax.)

    F. $5
    G. $6
    H. $11
    J. $25
    K. $150

11. $(3\sqrt{2} + 2\sqrt{3})^2 = ?$

    A. 10
    B. 12
    C. $30 + 6\sqrt{6}$
    D. $30 + 12\sqrt{6}$
    E. $55\sqrt{6}$

12. What is the smallest integer, x, such that $x - \sqrt{7}$ is positive?

    F. 1
    G. 2
    H. 3
    J. 4
    K. 5

13. Shayna ran 1.8 miles in 20 minutes. What was her average running speed in miles per hour?

    A. 0.6
    B. 1.2
    C. 2.0
    D. 4.8
    E. 5.4

14. Which of the following points on the real number line shown below is closest to $-\frac{1}{2}$?

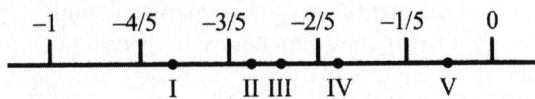

    F. I
    G. II
    H. III
    J. IV
    K. V

15. $(1.2 \cdot 10^4)(2.5 \cdot 10^5) = ?$

    A. $3.0 \cdot 10^{\frac{4}{5}}$

    B. $3.0 \cdot 10^{\frac{5}{4}}$

    C. $3.0 \cdot 10^9$

    D. $3.0 \cdot 10^{10}$

    E. $3.0 \cdot 10^{20}$

16. One day at 6:00 a.m., the temperature in Northern City was −18 °F. At 12:00 noon, the temperature was 12°F. By how many degrees did the temperature change?

    F.   1.5
    G.   3
    H.   6
    J.   15
    K.   30

17. Which of the following pairs of numbers should be placed in the blanks below, in the order shown, so that the difference between consecutive numbers is the same?

$$7\frac{1}{3}, \underline{\quad}, \underline{\quad}, 7\frac{3}{5}$$

    A. $7\frac{1}{5}, 7\frac{2}{5}$

    B. $7\frac{2}{5}, 7\frac{2}{3}$

    C. $7\frac{2}{5}, 7\frac{8}{15}$

    D. $7\frac{5}{15}, 7\frac{9}{15}$

    E. $7\frac{19}{45}, 7\frac{23}{45}$

18. On the number line shown below, if P has coordinate −2 and R has coordinate 12, then what is the coordinate of Q?

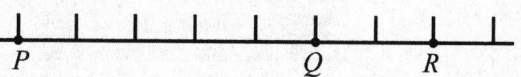

    F.   3
    G.   4
    H.   5
    J.   8
    K.   10

19. A book on etiquette recommends that diners tip an amount that it is in constant proportion to the total bill. If the recommended tip for a dinner check totaling $20.00 is $3.60, what is the recommended tip for a dinner check totaling $15.00?

    A. $1.40
    B. $2.70
    C. $4.17
    D. $4.80
    E. $7.50

20. If $a = 2$, $b = -5$, and $c = -3$, what is the value of $\dfrac{(a+b)c}{(a+c)b}$?

    F.   −9

    G. $\dfrac{9}{5}$

    H. $\dfrac{7}{3}$

    J.   5

    K. $\dfrac{35}{3}$

21. Eight people spent a total of S dollars at a bookstore. Which of the following expressions can be used to determine the average amount spent per person?

    A. $8S$

    B. $S + 8$

    C. $8S + 8$

    D. $\dfrac{S}{8}$

    E. $\dfrac{(8S + 8)}{8}$

22. Ramon took part in a fishing contest and caught three fish of different weights as shown in the table below.

Weights
2 pounds, 3 ounces
3 pounds, 12 ounces
3 pounds, 6 ounces

What was the total weight, in <u>ounces</u>, of the fish that Ramon caught? (1 pound is equal to 16 ounces.)

F.   21 ounces
G.   29 ounces
H.   101 ounces
J.   149 ounces
K.   1,681 ounces

23. Which of the following correctly orders the mixed numbers shown below from least to greatest?

$$\text{I.} \quad -2\frac{11}{16}$$

$$\text{II.} \quad -3\frac{1}{12}$$

$$\text{III.} \quad -2\frac{3}{8}$$

$$\text{IV.} \quad -2\frac{4}{9}$$

A.   I, IV, II, III
B.   II, I, IV, III
C.   II, I, III, IV
D.   II, IV, I, III
E.   III, IV, I, II

24. Traveling at approximately 186,000 miles per second, approximately how many miles will a beam of light travel in 10 hours?

F. $1.86 \cdot 10^6$

G. $1.11 \cdot 10^7$

H. $6.11 \cdot 10^8$

J. $1.11 \cdot 10^9$

K. $6.69 \cdot 10^9$

25. If $x \lozenge y$ is defined as $3x - 2y$, then what is the value of $2 \lozenge 3$?

A.   0
B.   1
C.   5
D.   12
E.   30

26. The instructions on the packaging of a fresh turkey advise cooking the turkey in a 325°F oven 1 hour for every 4 pounds it weighs. Approximately how long should a 21-pound turkey cook?

F.   1 hour and 21 minutes
G.   1 hour and 55 minutes
H.   3 hours and 30 minutes
J.   5 hours and 15 minutes
K.   5 hours and 25 minutes

27. What is the perimeter of the square shown below?

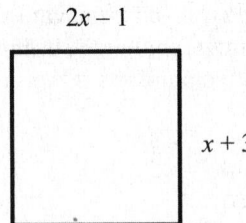

A.   4
B.   7
C.   16
D.   28
E.   49

28. The expression $-2x^2 + 3x - 4 + 6x^2 + 3 - 2x = $?

F. $-12x^2 + 5x + 7$

G. $4x^2 + x - 1$

H. $4x^2 + 5x - 1$

J. $4x^2 + 5x + 7$

K. $12x^2 + 5x + 7$

29. The expression $(3x-2)^2$ is equivalent to

    A. $6x^2+4$

    B. $6x^2-4$

    C. $9x^2-6x+4$

    D. $9x^2-6x-4$

    E. $9x^2-12x+4$

30. According to a company's product description, a certain photocopy machine makes 72 copies every 15 seconds. How many copies does the machine make per <u>minute</u>?

    F. 18

    G. 36

    H. 57

    J. 72

    K. 288

31. The toll for a car to cross the Narrows Bridge is $12.00, but a motorist can buy a roll of ten tokens for $110.00. If a token is good for one trip across the bridge, how much will a motorist save <u>per trip</u> by buying the roll of tokens?

    A. $0.98

    B. $1.00

    C. $1.40

    D. $10.00

    E. $11.00

32. In response to a newspaper ad, 30 students applied for summer jobs with the Parks Department. If 6 students will be hired, what percentage of the total number of students will be hired?

    F. 5%

    G. 18%

    H. 20%

    J. 24%

    K. 36%

33. In his job as a fundraiser, Jess is paid $50 a day plus a bonus for each telephone call that he completes. On Wednesday, Jess completed 22 calls and earned total of $72. On Thursday, he completed 8 more telephone calls than he did on Wednesday. Jess's total earnings on Thursday were how much more than his total earnings on Wednesday?

    A. $8

    B. $14

    C. $22

    D. $30

    E. $80

34. What is the perimeter of the equilateral triangle shown below?

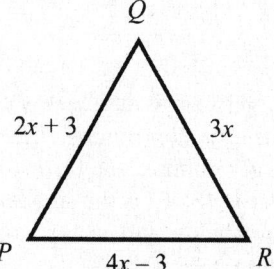

    F. 3

    G. 6

    H. 9

    J. 27

    K. 30

35. During a certain sale, tires are advertised as "Get four tires but pay only for three." The cost of four tires on sale is what fraction of the cost of four tires at the regular price?

    A. $\dfrac{1}{4}$

    B. $\dfrac{1}{3}$

    C. $\dfrac{3}{4}$

    D. $\dfrac{4}{3}$

    E. $\dfrac{3}{2}$

36. $-x - 2x + 3x + x = ?$

    F. x^4
    G. $8x$
    H. $5x$
    J. x
    K. 1

37. The expression $(2x - 3y)(3x + y)$ is equivalent to:

    A. $6x^2 - 11xy + 3y^2$
    B. $6x^2 - 7xy - 3y^2$
    C. $6x^2 - 7xy + 3y^2$
    D. $6x^2 - 3xy + 3y^2$
    E. $6x^2 + 11xy - 3y^2$

38. The larger of two numbers is 3 greater than twice the smaller number. The sum of twice the larger number and three times the smaller number is 45. If x is the smaller number, which equation below can be used to determine the value of x?

    F. $2(2x + 3) + 3x = 45$
    G. $2(3x - 3) + 3x = 45$
    H. $3(2x + 3) + 2x = 45$
    J. $3(2x - 3) + 2x = 45$
    K. $2(2x + 3) - 3x = 45$

39. A certain city estimates that 120 people move into the city every 5 days and 96 leave the city every 7 days. At these rates, which of the following is the best estimate of the change in the total population of the city for one year?

    A.   An increase of 3,800 people
    B.   An increase of 8,440 people
    C.   An increase of 13,200 people
    D.   A decrease of 4,800 people
    E.   A decrease of 8,440 people

40. The current standard for drinking water in a certain country establishes a maximum safe arsenic level of 0.005 milligrams of arsenic per liter. The country's health authority proposes to reduce that amount to $\dfrac{1}{100}$ of the current standard. What would be the maximum allowable concentration, in milligrams per liter, of arsenic in drinking water under the new standard?

    F. $5.0 \cdot 10^{-5}$
    G. $5.0 \cdot 10^{-3}$
    H. $2.0 \cdot 10^{-2}$
    J. $5.0 \cdot 10^{3}$
    K. $5.0 \cdot 10^{5}$

41. $2a + 6a - 4a - 5a + a = ?$

    A. 0
    B. 1
    C. a
    D. $-a$
    E. $-2a$

42. The expression $(a - b) - (b + a) + b$ is equivalent to which of the following?

    F. $a - b$
    G. $b - a$
    H. $3b$
    J. $2b$
    K. $-b$

43. The expression $(3a - 2b)(a + 3b)$ is equivalent to:

    A. $3a^2 - 11ab + 6b^2$
    B. $3a^2 - 9ab - 6b^2$
    C. $3a^2 - 8ab + 6b^2$
    D. $3a^2 + 7ab - 6b^2$
    E. $6a^2 + 7ab - 6b^2$

44. If the lengths of the adjacent sides of a rectangular parking lot are represented by $5x - 3$ and $3x + 2$, then which of the following expressions represents the perimeter of the parking lot?

F. $7x$
G. $8x + 5$
H. $8x - 1$
J. $16x - 2$
K. $32x - 4$

45. An integer, n, is added to 5. That sum is then multiplied by 4. The result is 12 less than 3 times the original integer. Which of the following equations represents this relationship?

A. $4n + 5 = 3n - 12$
B. $4n + 5 = 3(n - 12)$
C. $4(n + 5) = 3n - 12$
D. $4(n + 5) = 12 + 3n$
E. $4n + 5 = 12 - 3n$

Appendix A:
Answers and Explanations

GRAMMAR AND MECHANICS SKILLS REVIEW

Parts of Speech (p. 9)
Exercise 1

1. taxi = noun
   traffic = noun
   it = pronoun
   hurried = verb
   airport = noun

2. movers = noun
   unloaded = verb
   and = conjunction
   it = pronoun
   in = preposition

3. dark = modifier
   clouds = noun
   blocked = verb
   our = pronoun
   and = conjunction

4. dinner = noun
   cleared = verb
   table = noun
   and = conjunction
   sat = verb

5. room = noun
   was filled = verb
   with = preposition
   authors = noun
   Polish = modifier

6. first = modifier
   shows = noun
   were = verb
   earlier = modifier
   programs = noun

7. waiter = noun
   arrived = verb
   Victor = noun
   ordered = verb
   and = conjunction

8. inspector = noun
   finally = modifier
   approved = verb
   and = conjunction
   allowed = verb

9. notified = verb
   in = preposition
   water = noun
   would be = verb
   hours = noun

10. band = noun
    finished = verb
    crowd = noun
    burst = verb
    loud = modifier

11. called = verb
    her = pronoun
    would be = verb
    their = pronoun
    date = noun

12. cat = noun
    slept = verb
    warmth = noun
    of = preposition
    sun = noun

13. train = noun
    pulled = verb
    called = verb
    name = noun
    and = conjunction

14. we = pronoun
    children = noun
    were = verb
    in = preposition
    rear = noun

15. they = pronoun
    leave = verb
    teach = verb
    hikers = noun
    and = conjunction

16. covered = verb
    steaming = modifier
    melted = modifier
    sticky = modifier
    syrup = noun

17. weekend = noun
    made = verb
    special = modifier
    brilliant = modifier
    beautiful = modifier

18. eventful = modifier
    wrote = verb
    but = conjunction
    his = pronoun
    unopened = modifier

19. barely = modifier
    make out = verb
    bus = noun
    as = conjunction
    it = pronoun

20. offered = verb
    us = pronoun
    or = conjunction
    were = verb
    delicious = modifier

Common Grammatical Errors (p. 25)
Exercise 2

1. A	5. C	9. A	13. B	17. A	21. D	25. A
2. J	6. J	10. H	14. G	18. J	22. J	
3. D	7. B	11. C	15. B	19. B	23. D	
4. H	8. G	12. J	16. J	20. G	24. H	

26. The adverb "slowly" is the correct answer choice.

27. The adverb phrase "really well" is the correct answer choice.

28. The adjective "polite" is the correct answer choice.

29. The adverb "well" is the correct answer choice.

30. The adjective "good" is the correct answer choice.

31. The adjective "terrible" is the correct answer choice.

32. The adjective "awful" is the correct answer choice.

33. The adverb "terribly" is the correct answer choice.

34. The adverb "well" is the correct answer choice.

35. The adverb "well" is the correct answer choice.

36. The adverb "hard" is the correct answer choice.

37. The adverb "fast" is the correct answer choice.

38. The adjective "near" is the correct answer choice.

39. The adverb "slowly" is the correct answer choice.

40. The adjective "healthy" is the correct answer choice.

41. The adjective "heavy" is the correct answer choice.

42. The plural subject "many people" requires the plural form "receive."

43. The plural subject "books" requires the plural form "were."

44. The plural subject "stores" requires the plural form "offer."

45. The plural subject "bottles" requires the plural form "remain."

46. The singular subject "tourist" requires the singular form "is."

47. The plural subject "several different species" requires the plural form "were."

48. The plural subject "young boys" requires the plural form "were."

49. The plural subject "several barrels" requires the plural form "have."

50. The plural subject "sponsors" requires the plural form "hope."

51. The plural subject "Dawn, Harriet, and Gloria" requires the plural form "are."

52. The singular subject "the mayor" requires the singular form "worries."

53. The plural subject "acts" requires the plural form "have been."

54. The plural subject "rock musicians" requires the plural form "lose."

55. The plural subject "the leaves" requires the plural form "fall."

56. The plural subject "the computer and the printer" requires the plural form "have."

57. The singular subject "Theresa" requires the singular form "was."

58. The singular subject "the film critic" requires the singular form "writes."

59. The plural subject "ingredients" requires the plural form "have."

60. The singular subject "the computer" requires the singular form "was."

61. The singular subject "support" requires the singular form "has."

62. The plural subject "Bill and Jean" requires the plural form "are."

63. The plural subject "several students" requires the plural form "were."

64. The singular pronoun "his or her" is the correct answer choice.

65. The singular pronoun "her" is the correct answer choice.

66. The singular subject "music" requires the singular form "is."

Analyzing Sentence Structure (p. 37)
Exercise 3

1. D	10. J	19. A	28. H	37. A	46. J	55. E
2. G	11. C	20. H	29. C	38. H	47. B	56. J
3. E	12. K	21. A	30. G	39. B	48. H	57. D
4. G	13. A	22. K	31. A	40. H	49. C	
5. A	14. K	23. C	32. J	41. C	50. G	
6. H	15. B	24. G	33. C	42. H	51. C	
7. D	16. K	25. D	34. J	43. D	52. J	
8. K	17. B	26. H	35. B	44. H	53. C	
9. C	18. K	27. E	36. F	45. B	54. J	

Problems of Logical Expression (p. 47)
Exercise 4

1. C	5. A	9. C	13. B	17. A	21. D	25. D
2. G	6. F	10. K	14. G	18. F	22. G	26. J
3. C	7. B	11. A	15. C	19. D	23. A	27. A
4. K	8. K	12. F	16. F	20. K	24. J	

Idioms and Clarity of Expression (p. 56)
Exercise 5

1. The adjective "principal" is the correct answer choice.

2. The verb "accept" is the correct answer choice.

3. The noun "weather" is the correct answer choice.

4. The preposition "into" is the correct answer choice.

5. The verb "advise" is the correct answer choice.

6. The conjunction "than" is the correct answer choice.

7. The phrase "all ready" is the correct answer choice.

8. The noun "stationery" is the correct answer choice.

9. The noun "effect" is the correct answer choice.

10. The verb "sit" is the correct answer choice.

11. The verb "lie" is the correct answer choice.

12. The adverb "altogether" is the correct answer choice.

13. The past tense verb "passed" is the correct answer choice.

14. The noun "dessert" is the correct answer choice.

15. The verb "lose" is the correct answer choice.

16. The verb "affect" is the correct answer choice.

17. The contraction "you're" is the correct answer choice.

18. "Used" is the correct answer choice.

19. The verb "rise" is the correct answer choice.

20. "Supposed" is the correct answer choice.

21. The possessive pronoun "its" is the correct answer choice.

22. The adjective "conscious" is the correct answer choice.

23. The verb "seem" is the correct answer choice.

24. The plural noun "allusions" is the correct answer choice.

25. The noun "complement" is the correct answer choice.

26. The adjective "later" is the correct answer choice.

27. The noun "build" is the correct answer choice.

28. The past tense verb "knew" is the correct answer choice.

29. The adjective "personal" is the correct answer choice.

30. The noun "course" is the correct answer choice.

31. The adjective "cloth" is the correct answer choice.

32. The verb "elude" is the correct answer choice.

33. The adverb "no" is the correct answer choice.

34. The prefix "ante" is the correct answer choice.

35. The noun "morale" is the correct answer choice.

36. The adjective "capital" is the correct answer choice.

37. The verb "faze" is the correct answer choice.

38. "Excess" is the correct answer choice.

39. The verb "proceed" is the correct answer choice.

40. The noun "forte" is the correct answer choice.

41. The verb "disperse" is the correct answer choice.

42. The adverb "formally" is the correct answer choice.

43. The adjective "averse" is the correct answer choice.

44. The noun "incidence" is the correct answer choice.

45. The adjective "dual" is the correct answer choice.

46. The verb "expend" is the correct answer choice.

47. The noun "discomfort" is the correct answer choice.

48. The noun "idol" is the correct answer choice.

49. The verb "emigrate" is the correct answer choice.

50. The noun "clique" is the correct answer choice.

51. The noun "prophecy" is the correct answer choice.

52. The noun "lightning" is the correct answer choice.

53. The adjective "whatever" is the correct answer choice.

54. The adjective "imminent" is the correct answer choice.

55. The verb "adapt" is the correct answer choice.

56. The noun "epitaphs" is the correct answer choice.

57. The preposition "among" is the correct answer choice.

58. The noun "benefit" is the correct answer choice.

59. The adverb "a lot" is the correct answer choice.

60. The noun "number" is the correct answer choice.

61. The adverb "almost" is the correct answer choice.

62. The adjective "all right" is the correct answer choice.

63. The verb "annoy" is the correct answer choice.

64. The singular noun "alumnus" is the correct answer choice.

65. The adverb "alongside" is the correct answer choice.

66. The conjunction "since" is the correct answer choice.

67. The adjective "eager" is the correct answer choice.

68. The verb "meet" is the correct answer choice.

69. The adverb "awhile" is the correct answer choice.

70. The adverb "about" is the correct answer choice.

71. "Couple of" is the correct answer choice.

72. "You and me" is the correct answer choice.

73. The adjective "continuous" is the correct answer choice.

74. "Seems unable" is the correct answer choice.

75. The verb "assume" is the correct answer choice.

76. The adjective "uninterested" is the correct answer choice.

77. "Just as" is the correct answer choice.

78. The conjunction "that" is the correct answer choice.

79. The pronoun "one another" is the correct answer choice.

80. The conjunction "whether" is the correct answer choice.

81. The plural noun "human beings" is the correct answer choice.

82. The verb "finalize" is the correct answer choice.

83. The past tense verb "flouted" is the correct answer choice.

84. The adjective "healthful" is the correct answer choice.

85. The noun "slander" is the correct answer choice.

86. "Regard" is the correct answer choice.

87. The adverb "regardless" is the correct answer choice.

88. The verb "lend" is the correct answer choice.

89. The singular verb "is" is the correct answer choice.

90. The preposition "off" is the correct answer choice.

91. The verb "stop" is the correct answer choice.

92. The conjunction "that" is the correct answer choice.

93. The verb "manage" is the correct answer choice.

94. The singular pronoun "his or her" is the correct answer choice.

95. "Any other" is the correct answer choice.

96. The conjunction "but" is the correct answer choice.

97. "Try to" is the correct answer choice.

98. "Whoever" is the correct answer choice.

99. The preposition "for" is the correct answer choice.

100. C	107. C	114. A	121. D	128. H	135. B	142. H
101. A	108. C	115. B	122. J	129. C	136. G	143. C
102. B	109. A	116. J	123. C	130. J	137. B	
103. B	110. B	117. B	124. J	131. B	138. G	
104. B	111. A	118. G	125. D	132. F	139. C	
105. C	112. B	119. A	126. J	133. A	140. G	
106. A	113. C	120. H	127. C	134. G	141. C	

Punctuation (p. 77)
Exercise 6

1. He was not aware that you had lost your passport.

2. Did you report the loss to the proper authorities?

3. I suppose you had to fill out many forms.

4. What a nuisance!

5. I hate doing so much paperwork!

6. Did you ever discover where the wallet was?

7. I imagine you wondered how it was misplaced.

8. Good for you!

9. At least you now have your passport.

10. What will you do if it happens again?

11. I don't know if they are coming, though I sent them an invitation weeks ago.

12. Neurology is the science that deals with the anatomy, physiology, and pathology of the nervous system.

13. Nursery lore, like everything human, has been subject to many changes over long periods of time.

    Nursery lore—like everything human—has been subject to many changes over long periods of time.

14. Bob read Joyce's *Ulysses* to the class; everyone seemed to enjoy the reading.

15. In order to provide more living space, we converted an attached garage into a den.

16. Because he is such an industrious student, he has many friends.

17. I don't recall who wrote *A Midsummer Night's Dream*.

18. In the writing class, students learned about coordinating conjunctions—and, but, so, or, yet, for, and nor.

    In the writing class, students learned about coordinating conjunctions: and, but, so, or yet, for, and nor.

19. "Those who do not complain are never pitied" is a familiar quotation by Jane Austen.

20. Howard and his ex-wife are on amicable terms.

21. Her last words were, "Call me on Sunday," and she jumped on the train.

22. He is an out-of-work carpenter.

23. This is what is called a "pregnant chad."

24. "Come early on Monday," the teacher said, "to take the exit exam."

25. The dog, man's best friend, is a companion to many.

    The dog—man's best friend—is a companion to many.

26. The winner of the horse race is, to the best of my knowledge, Silver.

    The winner of the horse race is—to the best of my knowledge—Silver.

27. Every time I see him, the dentist asks me how often I floss.

28. The off-duty officer witnessed the crime.

29. *Anna Karenina* is my favorite movie.

30. Red, white, and blue are the colors of the American flag.

31. Stop using "stuff" in your essays; it's too informal.

32. She was a self-made millionaire.

33. The Smiths, who are the best neighbors anyone could ask for, have moved out.

    The Smiths—who are the best neighbors anyone could ask for—have moved out.

34. My eighteen-year-old daughter will graduate this spring.

35. Dracula lived in Transylvania.

36. The students were told to put away their books.

37. Begun while Dickens was still at work on *Pickwick Papers*, *Oliver Twist* was published in 1837 and is now one of the author's most widely read works.

38. Given the great difficulties of making soundings in very deep water, it is not surprising that few such soundings were made until the middle of this century.

39. Did you finish writing your thesis prospectus on time?

40. The root of modern Dutch was once supposed to be Old Frisian, but the general view now is that the characteristic forms of Dutch are at least as old as those of Old Frisian.

41. Moose, once scarce because of indiscriminate hunting, are protected by law, and the number of moose is once again increasing.

    Moose—once scarce because of indiscriminate hunting—are protected by law, and the number of moose is once again increasing.

42. He ordered a set of books, several records, and a film almost a month ago.

43. Perhaps the most interesting section of New Orleans is the French Quarter, which extends from North Rampart Street to the Mississippi River.

44. Writing for a skeptical and rationalizing age, Shaftesbury was primarily concerned with showing that goodness and beauty are not determined by revelation, authority, opinion, or fashion.

45. We tried our best to purchase the books, but we were completely unsuccessful even though we went to every bookstore in town.

46. A great deal of information regarding the nutritional requirements of farm animals has been accumulated over countless generations by trial and error; however, most recent advances have come as the result of systematic studies at schools of animal husbandry.

47. *Omoo*, Melville's sequel to *Typee*, appeared in 1847 and went through five printings in that year alone.

    Omoo—Melville's sequel to *Typee*—appeared in 1847 and went through five printings in that year alone.

48. "Go to Florence for the best gelato in all of Italy," said the old man to the young tourist.

49. Although the first school for African Americans was a public school established in Virginia in 1620, most educational opportunities for African Americans before the Civil War were provided by private agencies.

50. As the climate of Europe changed, the population became too dense for the supply of food obtained by hunting, and other means of securing food, such as the domestication of animals, were necessary.

    As the climate of Europe changed, the population became too dense for the supply of food obtained by hunting, and other means of securing food—such as the domestication of animals—were necessary.

51. In Faulkner's poetic realism, the grotesque is somber, violent, and often inexplicable; in Caldwell's writing, it is lightened by a ballad-like, humorous, sophisticated detachment.

52. The valley of the Loire, a northern tributary of the Loire at Angers, abounds in rock villages; they occur in many other places in France, Spain, and northern Italy.

    The valley of the Loire—a northern tributary of the Loire at Angers—abounds in rock villages; they occur in many other places in France, Spain, and northern Italy.

53. The telephone rang several times; as a result, his sleep was interrupted.

54. He has forty-three thousand dollars to spend; however, once that is gone, he will be penniless.

55. Before an examination, do the following: review your work, get a good night's sleep, eat a balanced breakfast, and arrive on time to take the test.

DIAGRAMMING SENTENCES SKILLS REVIEW

Subjects and Verbs (p. 90)
Exercise 1

1. Ducks quack.

Ducks	quack

   The subject of the sentence is "ducks." The verb "quack" is in the present tense.

2. Mosquitoes are buzzing.

Mosquitoes	are buzzing

   The subject of the sentence is "mosquitoes." The verb "are buzzing" is a progressive form of the present tense.

3. People have been talking.

People	have been talking

   The subject of the sentence is "people." The verb "have been talking" is present-perfect progressive.

4. They will be captured.

They	will be captured

   The subject of the sentence is "they," a personal pronoun. The verb "will be captured" is in the future tense, passive voice.

5. Money had been collected.

Money	had been collected

   The subject of the sentence is "money." "Had been collected" is in the past-perfect tense, passive voice.

Modal Auxiliary Verbs (p. 95)
Exercise 2

1. You may stay.

You	may stay

   The verb consists of the present modal auxiliary verb "may" and the basic present tense form of "stay."

2. They should be scolded.

They	should be scolded

   The verb consists of the present modal auxiliary verb "should" and the basic present passive form of "scold."

3. She must have been delayed.

She	must have been delayed

   The verb consists of the present modal auxiliary verb "must" and the basic present-perfect passive form of "delay."

4. That could have been done.

That	could have been done

   The verb consists of the present subjunctive of the modal auxiliary verb "can" and the basic present-perfect passive form of "do."

5. They might be coming.

They	might be coming

   The verb consists of the present subjunctive form of the modal auxiliary verb "may" and the basic present progressive form of "come."

Conjunctions (p. 100)
Exercise 3

1. Buses come and go.

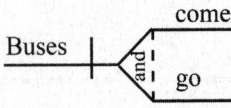

   "Come and go" is a compound verb. Since it constitutes the entire predicate, it is also a compound predicate.

2. Deer were running and jumping.

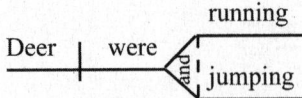

   Together with the helping verb "were," the compound present participle "running and jumping" forms the past progressive.

3. Children run, jump, and play.

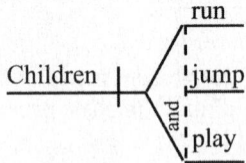

   This compound predicate consists of three verbs.

4. Doctors and nurses are scurrying.

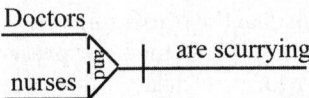

   "Doctors and nurses" is a compound subject. The coordinating conjunction "and" joins the two nouns. The verb "are scurrying" is a progressive form of the present tense.

5. Bombs fell and people died.

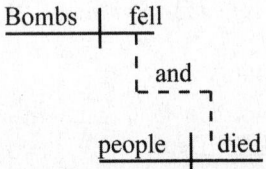

   This is a compound sentence. In other words, it consists of two independent clauses joined by a coordinating conjunction.

Articles, Attributive Adjectives, and Direct Objects (p. 106)
Exercise 4

1. We must consider a different plan.

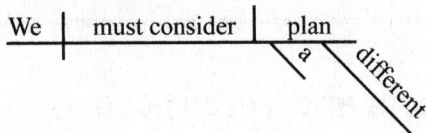

   "Plan" is a direct object. "Different" is an attributive adjective.

2. Either the county or the city must assume primary responsibility.

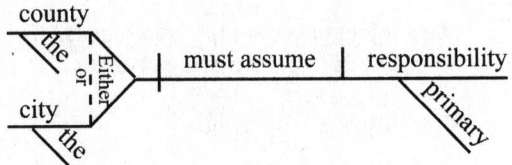

   "Responsibility" is a direct object. "Either . . . or" is called a correlative conjunction.

3. The new store sells athletic clothing and equipment.

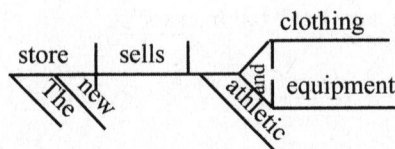

   Since athletic modifies both "clothing" and "equipment," its line is attached to the part of the direct-object line that belongs to both objects.

4. Employers appreciate honest and diligent employees.

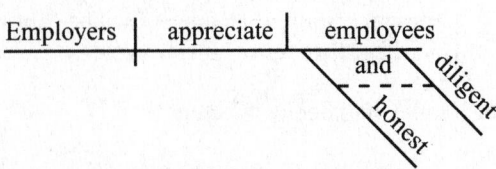

   "Honest and diligent" is a compound attributive adjective.

5. She buys and restores old furniture.

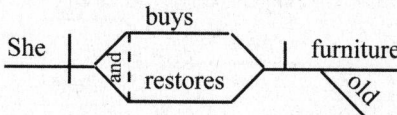

The verbs "buys" and "restores" have the same direct object: "furniture."

Adverbs (p. 111)
Exercise 5

1. Angrily and inexorably the storm devastated the coastal regions.

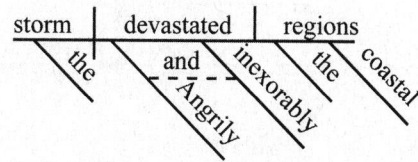

"Angrily and inexorably" is a compound adverb.

2. Not all Americans favor bigger and more expensive cars.

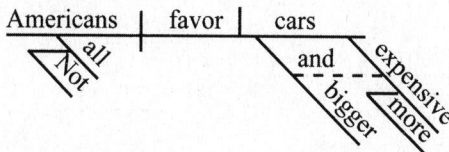

The adverbs "not" and "more" modify the attributive adjectives "all" and "expensive," respectively. "Bigger and more expensive" is a compound attributive adjective.

3. I did the assignment fast and inattentively.

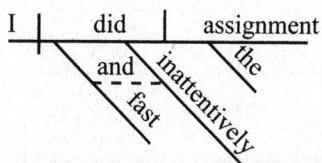

"Fast and inattentively" is a compound adverb.

4. She wrote an exceedingly but unexpectedly beautiful poem.

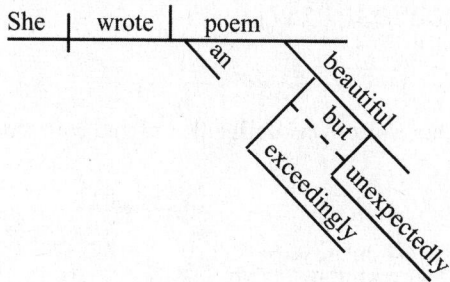

The compound adverb "exceedingly but unexpectedly" modifies the attributive adjective "beautiful."

5. This subdivision has about fifty residences.

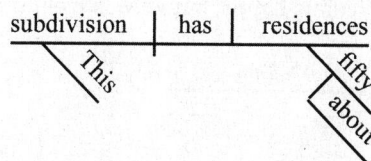

"This" is called a demonstrative adjective. "About" is an adverb modifying the adjective "fifty."

Subjective Complements: Predicate Nominatives and Predicate Adjectives (p. 117)

Exercise 6

1. Our waiter was both efficient and courteous.

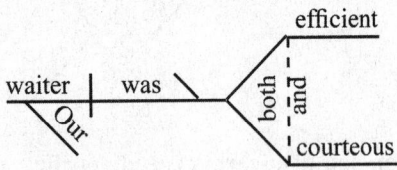

"Our" is a possessive pronoun. "Both" and "and" are correlative coordinating conjunctions.

2. She was feeling happy, but he was feeling sad.

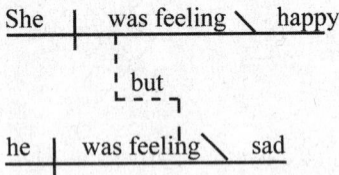

This is a compound sentence whose two main clauses are joined by the coordinating conjunction "but." "Was feeling" is a linking verb. "Happy" and "sad" are predicate adjectives.

3. He is a truly remarkable scholar but a lousy poet.

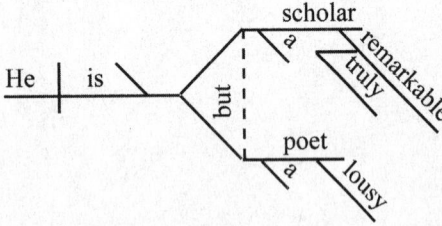

This sentence features a compound predicate nominative.

4. He became angry and silent and left the room.

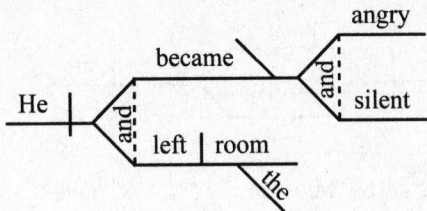

The first branch of the compound predicate contains a compound predicate adjective ("angry and silent"), the second a direct object ("room").

5. She has been, is, and will be a very effective mayor.

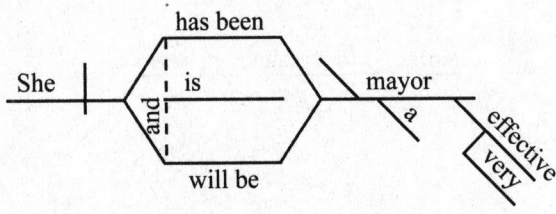

The compound, tripartite verb "has been, is, and will be" has "mayor" as its predicate nominative.

Appositives (p. 122)

Exercise 7

1. Her cousins Jack and Jill climbed a hill.

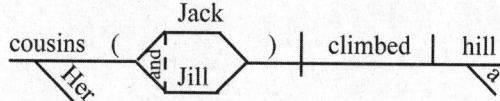

"Jack and Jill" is a compound restrictive appositive. It is in apposition with the subject "cousins."

2. J. J., a four-year band member, was chosen as the most outstanding musician.

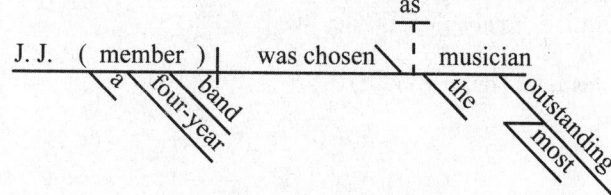

"Member," a nonrestrictive appositive, is in apposition with the subject "J. J." The passive verb "was chosen" functions as a linking verb. "Musician" is a predicate nominative, and "as" is an expletive.

3. The renters altered, that is, nearly destroyed, the apartment.

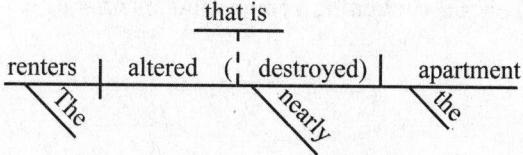

The verb phrase "nearly destroyed" is in apposition with the main verb "altered." "That is" is an expletive. Other such function words and phrases, which are sometimes called appositive conjunctions because they are not entirely devoid of meaning, are "especially," "for example," "in other words," and "or."

4. They have strength, speed, and mental toughness—the right qualities.

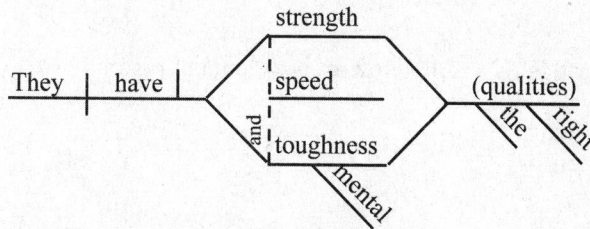

"Qualities" is in apposition with the compound direct object "strength, speed, and mental toughness."

5. Have you met my friend Marcy?

you | Have met | friend (Marcy)
                      my

"Marcy" is a restrictive appositive. It is in apposition with the direct object "friend."

Prepositional Phrases (p. 127)
Exercise 8

1. Early in the week, friends of ours are coming for dinner.

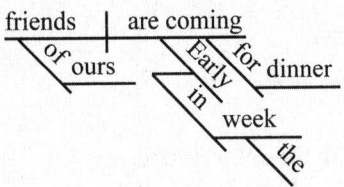

"In the week" and "for dinner" are adverbial prepositional phrases. The former modifies the adverb "early," and the latter modifies the verb "are coming." "Ours" is an absolute possessive.

2. They approach every new challenge with enthusiasm and determination.

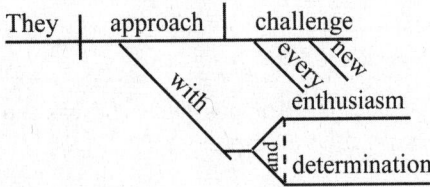

"With enthusiasm and determination" is a prepositional phrase containing a compound object.

3. We can go through the narrow tunnel or over the narrow bridge.

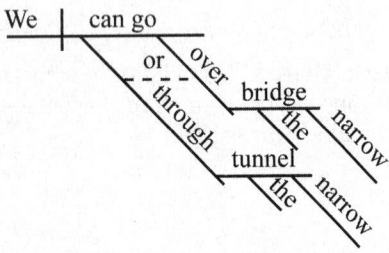

"Through the narrow tunnel or over the narrow bridge" is a compound prepositional phrase.

4. The principal is taking a group of teachers out for lunch.

"Out for" is not a phrasal preposition. "Out" is an adverb in this sentence.

5. She acted in accordance with the express wishes of her clients.

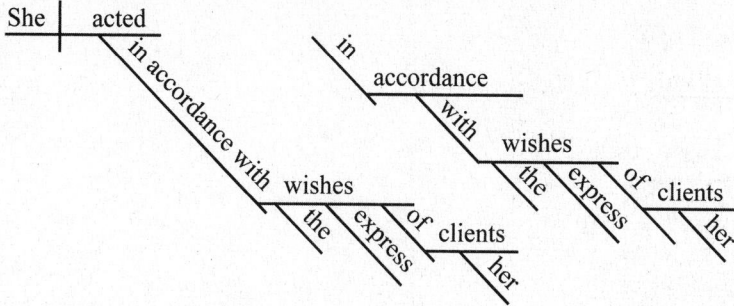

"In accordance with" can be considered a phrasal preposition; however, it can also be diagrammed as a prepositional phrase.

Indirect Objects and Objective Complements (p. 133)
Exercise 9

1. John gave Judy an engagement ring.

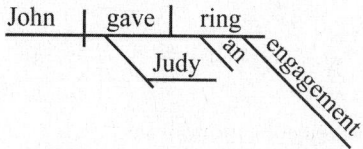

"Judy" (the person to whom something was given) is an indirect object. "Engagement" is a noun used as an adjective.

2. The governor gave each distinguished student and his or her mentor a monetary award.

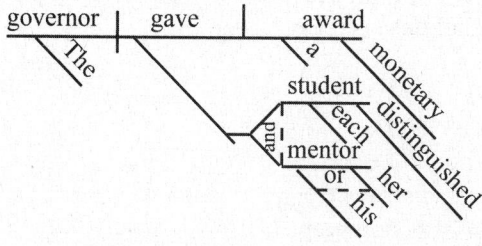

"Student" and "mentor" constitute a compound indirect object.

3. The rescue team found the campers alive and declared them extremely fortunate.

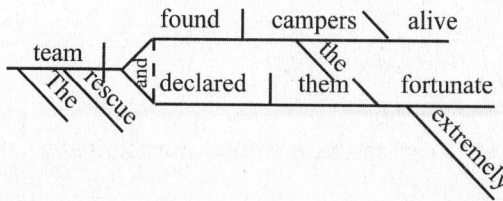

"Alive" cannot be recognized as an objective complement by asking "what?" Like all objective complements, it completes the action of the verb with respect to the direct object.

4. Jamie told Shanika, her next-door neighbor, the news about their friend Pam.

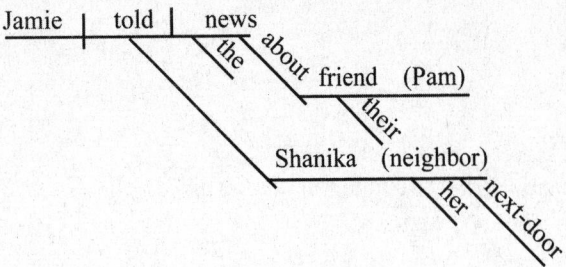

"Neighbor" is in apposition with "Shanika," an indirect object, while "Pam" is in apposition with "friend," the object of the preposition "about."

5. Humpty-Dumpty was found in pieces, and neither the king's horses nor the king's men could make him whole again.

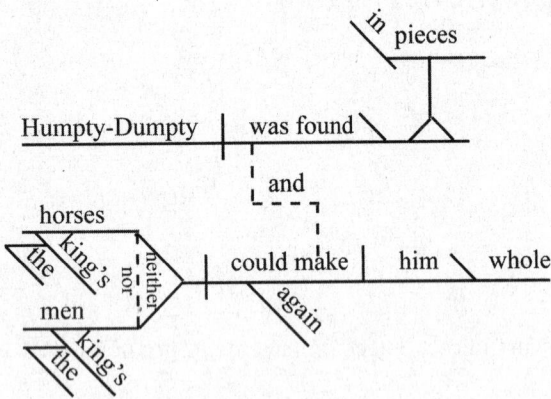

The passive verb "was found" functions here as a linking verb, and the prepositional phrase "in pieces" serves as a predicate adjective. If the first main clause were active ("they found him in pieces"), "in pieces" would be an objective complement, like "alive" in sentence 3 of this exercise.

Infinitives (p. 142)
Exercise 10

1. Their plan was to fly to Seattle and rent a car.

The compound infinitive phrase "to fly to Seattle and rent a car" serves as a predicate nominative.

2. That is easy to promise but hard to do.

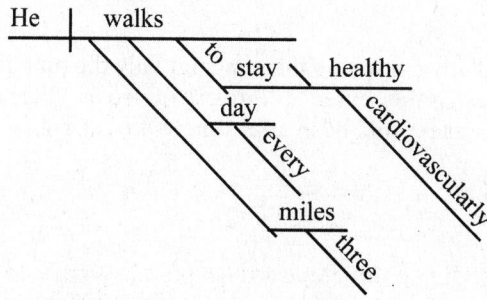

The infinitives "to promise" and "to do" function here as adverbial modifiers. They modify the predicate adjectives "easy" and "hard," respectively.

3. She spoke too softly to be understood.

The present passive infinitive "to be understood" modifies the adverb "softly."

4. He walks three miles every day to stay cardiovascularly healthy.

The infinitive phrase "to stay cardiovascularly healthy" functions as a modifier of the verb "walks"; it tells why he walks. "Miles" and "day" are adverbial objectives.

5. Domestic responsibilities compelled them to stay at home.

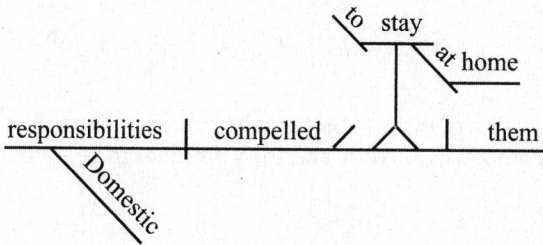

The infinitive phrase "to stay at home" functions here as an objective complement.

6. The students are to go immediately to their desks.

"To go" is a complementary infinitive. A verb and its complementary infinitive are, taken together, often equivalent to a verb phrase using a modal auxiliary verb or to a future-tense verb form. In this case, "are to go" can be expressed as "must go."

7. For them to become angry is not helpful to our cause.

The word "for" as used in this sentence can be called an expletive. It has no meaning but only the function of introducing an infinitive phrase and its objective-case subject. If the sentence were expressed as "It is not helpful to our cause for them to become angry," the "for" phrase would be in apposition with the subject "it."

8. To have to be told three times to behave is a sign of immaturity.

The infinitive phrase "to have to be told three times to behave" is the subject of the sentence, the infinitive phrase "to be told three times to behave" has a complementary function, and the infinitive "to behave" is a direct object.

9. She said for the children to be ready to leave in ten minutes.

The infinitive phrase introduced by the expletive "for" is the direct object of "said." "Children" is the subject of the infinitive "to be."

10. They are thought to have been kidnapped by insurgents.

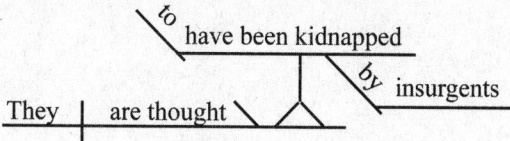

The present-perfect passive infinitive "to have been kidnapped," along with its modifying prepositional phrase, functions here as a predicate adjective. The passive verb "are thought" acts as a linking verb.

Gerunds (p. 149)
Exercise 11

1. Ms. Shelby, a teacher at our school, calls her friendship with Mr. Moss, a teacher at a rival school, "fraternizing with the enemy."

The gerund phrase "fraternizing with the enemy" is an objective complement, which is diagrammed here in the traditional manner.

2. Something worth quoting is worth quoting accurately.

Each "quoting" is an adverbial objective. The first modifies an attributive adjective, the second a predicate adjective.

3. The landlord increased his profit by raising the rent and reducing the amenities.

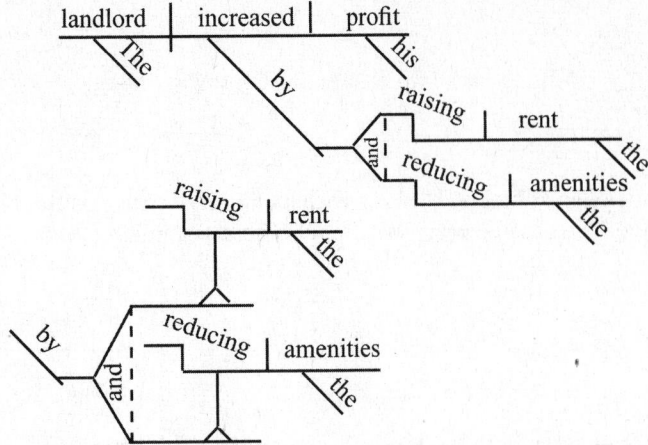

The compound gerund phrase "raising the rent and reducing the amenities" is the object of the preposition "by." The second diagram above is another way of diagramming the compound gerund phrase.

4. The men are playing golf and the women are going shopping.

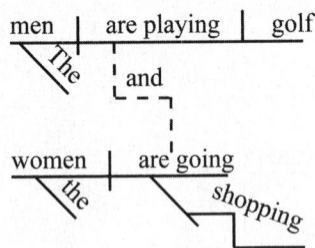

"Shopping" is a gerund used as an adverbial objective. It tells where the women are going. "Playing" and "going" are participial components of progressive verb forms.

5. The joylessness in Mudville is the result of Casey's not having hit a home run.

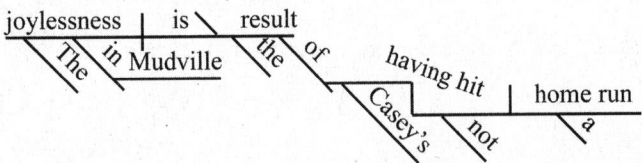

The gerund phrase "Casey's not having hit a home run" contains the adjectival modifier "Casey's" and the adverbial modifier "not." "Having hit" is a present-perfect active gerund.

Participles (p. 156)
Exercise 12

1. Still running smoothly after twenty-five miles, she left the park and headed for the finish line.

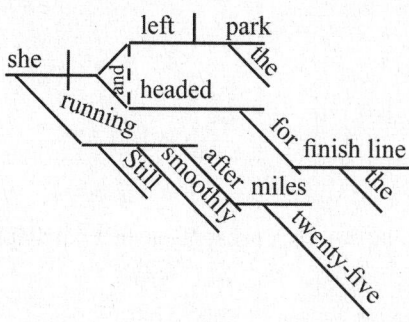

"Running" is a present participle. It introduces a participial phrase that modifies the subject of the sentence, "she." The sentence has a compound predicate.

2. Chewing, spitting, and occasionally talking, the three old-timers watched the people and the trains go by.

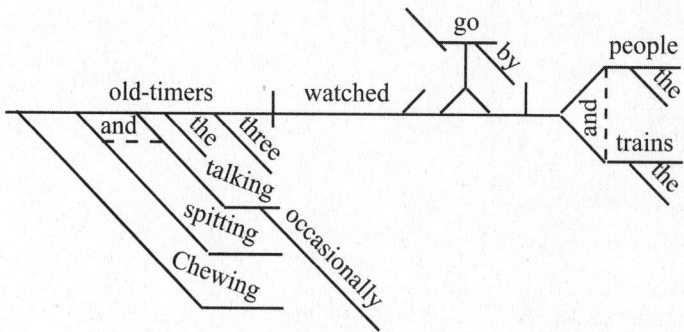

A compound participial phrase featuring three present participles modifies the subject of the sentence, "old-timers." "Go by" is a "*to*-less" infinitive phrase used as an objective complement. It is diagrammed here in the traditional way.

3. Having reached the end of her twelve-hour shift, the exhausted nurse heaved a sigh of relief.

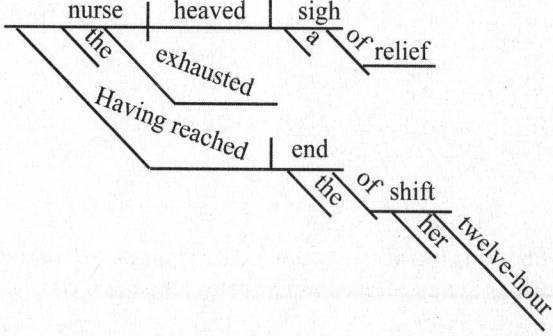

The present-perfect active participle "having reached" introduces a participial phrase that modifies the subject of the sentence, "nurse." "Exhausted" is a past participle.

4. The bridge having collapsed, some interstate commuters were forced to drive much farther each day.

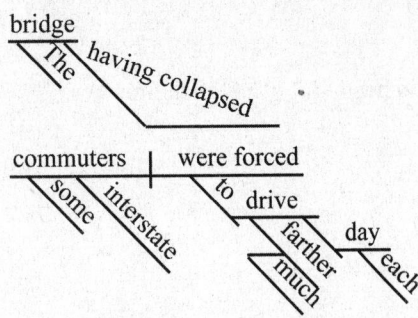

"The bridge having collapsed" is a nominative absolute. "Having collapsed" is a present-perfect participle.

5. Speaking of rascals, Oscar just knocked at the door.

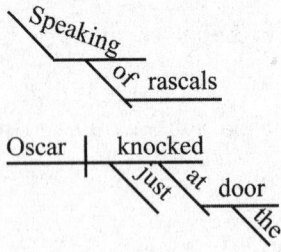

"Speaking of rascals" is a dangling participle.

Adverb Clauses (p. 164)
Exercise 13

1. Although snow was expected later in the day, most schools were open.

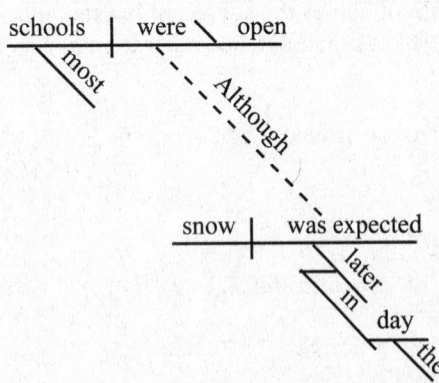

"Although" is a subordinating conjunction; such conjunctions introduce subordinate clauses. No matter where it may appear in a sentence, a subordinate clause is always diagrammed below the main clause.

2. She knows a lot about the world because she travels a lot.

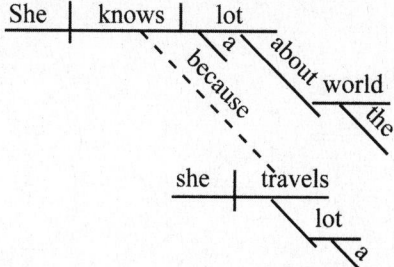

The subordinate clause "because she travels a lot" is introduced by the subordinating conjunction "because." The second "lot" is an adverbial objective.

3. When they entered the theater, they went to their seats immediately.

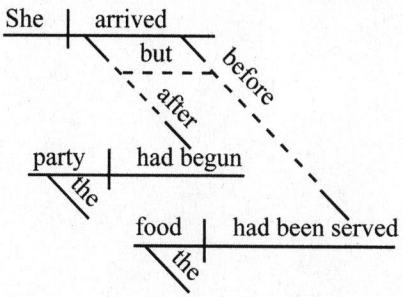

"When" is equivalent to two prepositional phrases: "at the time" and "at which," the second of which includes a relative pronoun. That "when" modifies both "went" and "entered" is shown in the diagram by the solid ends of the line upon which "when" rests.

4. She arrived after the party had begun but before the food had been served.

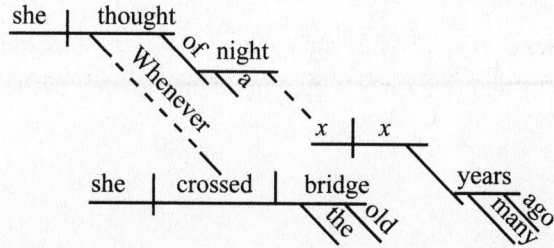

The coordinating conjunction "but" connects two adverb clauses, each introduced by a relative adverb.

5. Whenever she crossed the old bridge, she thought of a night many years ago.

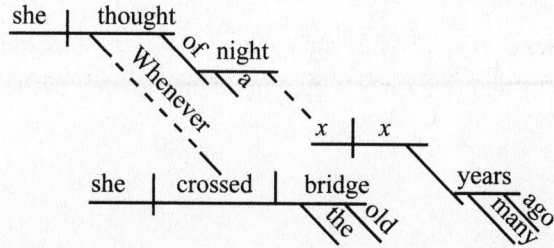

"Whenever" ("at any time at which") is an indefinite relative adverb. The left-hand x represents the unexpressed relative pronoun "that," and the right-hand *x* represents the unexpressed verb "was." "Years" is an adverbial objective.

6. The more it rains, the faster the grass grows.

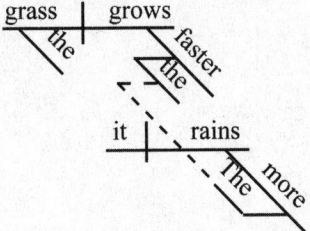

This sentence features the correlatives "the . . . the." Think: "the grass grows faster according to the extent to which it rains more." "The" modifying "faster" is an ordinary adverb; "the" modifying "more" is a relative adverb.

7. It was so late that no more trick-or-treaters were expected.

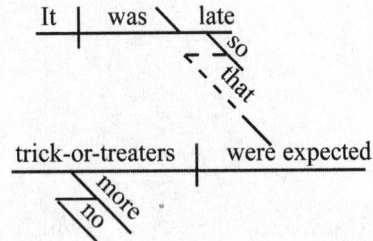

Think: "it was late to a degree in which no more trick-or-treaters were expected."

8. After the guests arrive, but before the food is brought out, let's remind them of the reason for the party.

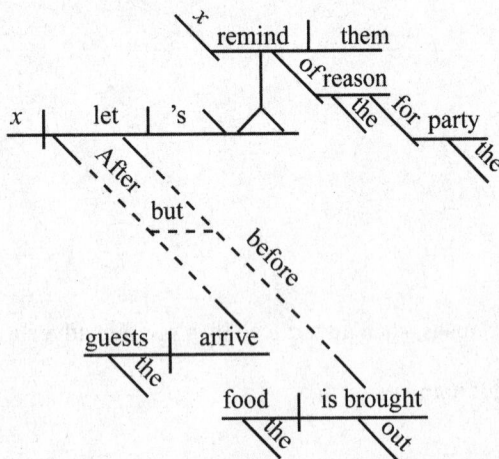

This complex sentence features two adverb clauses. The main clause is "let's remind them of the reason for the party."

9. He is kinder and more generous than his sister.

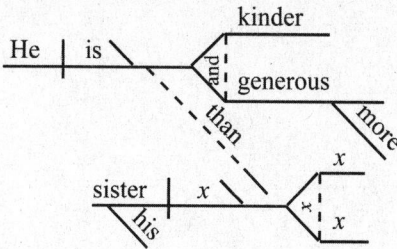

This comparative sentence contains a compound comparative adjective. The relative adverb is "than."

10. When our family does a jigsaw puzzle, the children always put in more pieces than the parents.

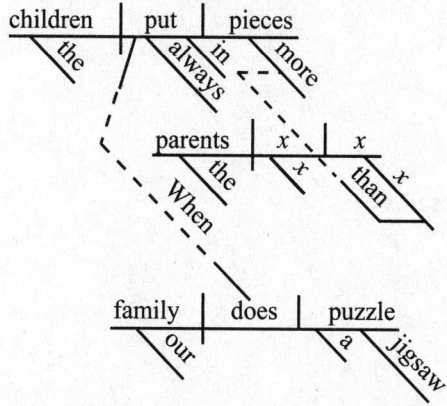

This sentence has two subordinate clauses: the first is introduced by "when," a relative adverb of time; the second is introduced by "than," a relative adverb of comparison. As for the four instances of *x*, they stand for "put in many pieces."

Adjective Clauses (p. 171)
Exercise 14

1. Choose carefully the person in whom you place your full trust.

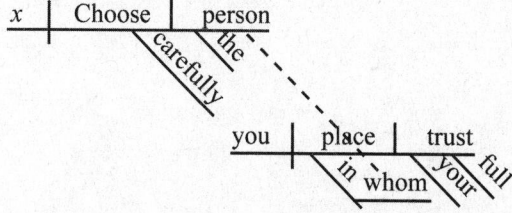

The relative pronoun "whom" is the object of the preposition "in." Its antecedent is "person."

2. The guy whose car is parked illegally may soon be looking for a ride.

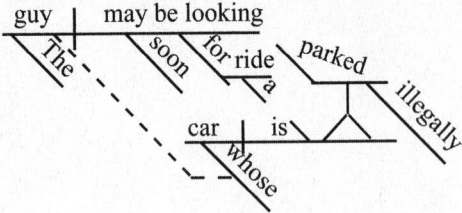

The relative pronoun "whose," a possessive modifier of the noun "car," has "guy" as its antecedent.

3. The accident happened on the day they arrived in Miami.

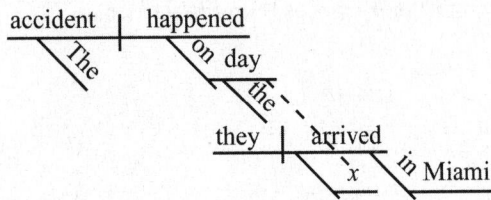

The relative pronoun "that," an adverbial objective, is unexpressed.

4. The other prizes will be given to whoever answers correctly.

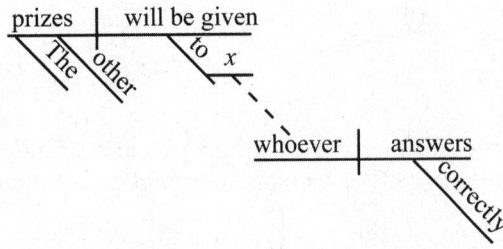

"Whoever" is the subject of the relative clause "whoever answers correctly." Its antecedent is the unexpressed object of the preposition "to."

5. I have already told you the reason I can't be there.

The noun "reason" is modified by "[why] I can't be there," an adjective clause introduced by the unexpressed relative adverb "why."

Noun Clauses (p. 177)
Exercise 15

1. An unintended result of the experiment was that many birds died.

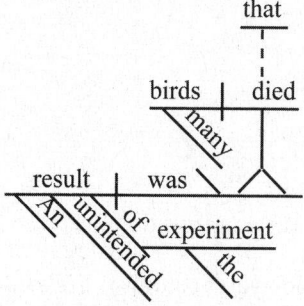

The expletive "that" introduces a noun clause ("that many birds died"); the noun clause functions as a predicate nominative.

2. It is a widespread belief that poinsettias are poisonous.

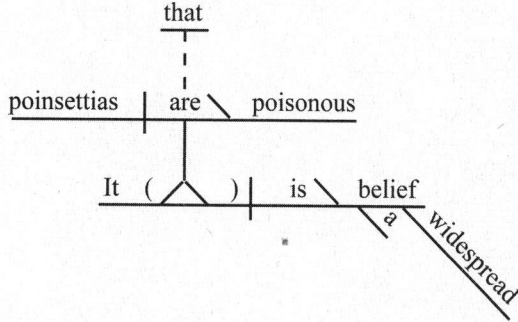

The noun clause "that poinsettias are poisonous" functions as an appositive. It is in apposition with the subject of the sentence, "it." "That" is an expletive.

3. The professor attempted to find out who damaged his car.

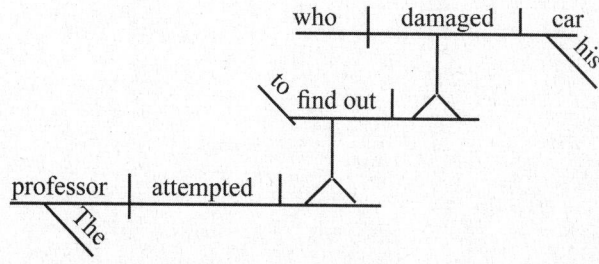

The interrogative pronoun "who" introduces a noun clause that functions as the direct object of the phrasal verb "find out."

4. The station manager claimed to be uncertain as to why the station had lost so many listeners.

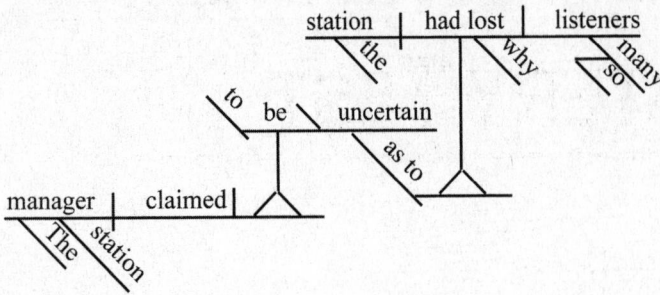

The noun clause introduced by the adverb "why" acts as the object of the phrasal preposition "as to."

5. How many angels could fit on the head of a pin was a question that some medieval theologians are said to have found intriguing.

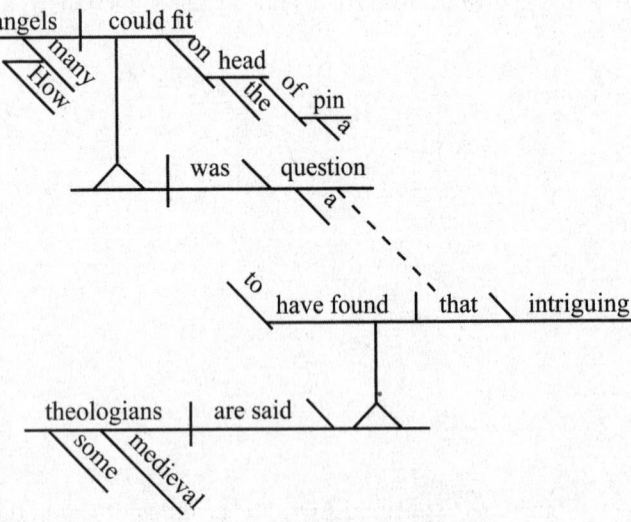

The noun clause introduced by the interrogative adverb "how" is the subject of the sentence. "That" is a relative pronoun. The passive verb "are said" functions as a linking verb, the infinitive phrase as a predicate adjective.

ENGLISH/WRITING MASTERY TEST

Answer Key (p. 193)

1. D	9. C	17. A	25. C	33. D	41. D	49. D
2. G	10. F	18. J	26. J	34. F	42. H	50. J
3. B	11. D	19. D	27. A	35. C	43. B	51. B
4. J	12. F	20. J	28. J	36. J	44. J	52. J
5. B	13. C	21. A	29. A	37. B	45. A	53. A
6. F	14. H	22. G	30. F	38. H	46. H	54. G
7. B	15. C	23. C	31. B	39. D	47. D	
8. H	16. J	24. F	32. J	40. J	48. F	

VOCABULARY SKILLS REVIEW

Anticipating Sentence Completions (p. 213)
Exercise 1

1. exceed, surpass

2. climax, high point, zenith

3. boring, dull, uninspiring

4. serious, severe, large-scale

5. complete, comprehensive

6. complete, total, authoritarian

7. hides, camouflages, conceals

8. wanted, infamous, notorious

9. dazed, confused, disoriented

10. generate, spark, increase

11. E	**13.** B	**15.** C	**17.** B	**19.** B
12. A	**14.** D	**16.** A	**18.** E	**20.** A

Analyzing Sentence Completions (p. 216)
Exercise 2

1. dead, spirits, ghosts

2. reform, improvement

3. flammable

4. start, beginning

5. tolerant, understanding

6. weaknesses, shortcomings

7. the elderly, senior citizens

8. disrupted, interrupted

9. cooperation, accord

10. annihilation, death

11. B	**13.** A	**15.** A	**17.** C	**19.** A
12. E	**14.** E	**16.** A	**18.** B	**20.** E

Substituting Sentence Completions (p. 219)
Exercise 3

1. C	**4.** D	**7.** C	**10.** C	**13.** A	**16.** B
2. B	**5.** A	**8.** E	**11.** A	**14.** B	**17.** E
3. E	**6.** B	**9.** D	**12.** B	**15.** E	

Building Vocabulary with Sentence Completions (p. 221)
Exercise 4

1. A	**7.** D	**13.** B	**19.** C	**25.** B	**31.** B	**37.** C
2. B	**8.** E	**14.** A	**20.** A	**26.** D	**32.** A	**38.** A
3. D	**9.** C	**15.** D	**21.** E	**27.** D	**33.** B	**39.** C
4. E	**10.** B	**16.** E	**22.** A	**28.** A	**34.** B	**40.** D
5. A	**11.** B	**17.** E	**23.** B	**29.** E	**35.** A	
6. C	**12.** B	**18.** A	**24.** A	**30.** B	**36.** D	

Building Vocabulary Through Context (p. 228)
Exercise 5

1. D	**3.** D	**5.** B	**7.** D	**9.** B
2. C	**4.** B	**6.** B	**8.** B	**10.** D

Vocabulary Builder: Prose Fiction Passages (p. 230)
Exercise 6

1. D	**8.** C	**15.** C	**22.** D	**29.** D	**36.** B	**43.** C
2. C	**9.** A	**16.** B	**23.** A	**30.** B	**37.** C	**44.** B
3. E	**10.** B	**17.** D	**24.** D	**31.** B	**38.** A	**45.** A
4. B	**11.** D	**18.** E	**25.** B	**32.** E	**39.** D	
5. A	**12.** B	**19.** C	**26.** C	**33.** C	**40.** B	
6. D	**13.** C	**20.** B	**27.** A	**34.** D	**41.** A	
7. B	**14.** A	**21.** A	**28.** C	**35.** E	**42.** C	

Vocabulary Builder: Social Science Passages (p. 239)
Exercise 7

1. D	15. D	29. B	43. D	57. D	71. B	85. D
2. A	16. C	30. D	44. C	58. D	72. D	86. B
3. B	17. E	31. E	45. B	59. A	73. B	87. C
4. E	18. B	32. D	46. E	60. A	74. A	88. B
5. B	19. D	33. B	47. B	61. B	75. D	89. A
6. D	20. C	34. E	48. B	62. A	76. B	90. D
7. A	21. A	35. D	49. C	63. E	77. D	
8. C	22. D	36. B	50. D	64. B	78. B	
9. B	23. B	37. B	51. B	65. E	79. E	
10. C	24. C	38. C	52. D	66. D	80. A	
11. D	25. A	39. D	53. B	67. D	81. B	
12. A	26. D	40. A	54. C	68. C	82. C	
13. D	27. D	41. B	55. A	69. A	83. A	
14. C	28. B	42. A	56. C	70. C	84. D	

Vocabulary Builder: Humanities Passages (p. 256)
Exercise 8

1. D	12. B	23. B	34. D	45. D	56. D	67. B
2. E	13. C	24. D	35. E	46. C	57. B	68. D
3. C	14. A	25. C	36. A	47. D	58. B	69. D
4. D	15. C	26. D	37. C	48. E	59. C	70. A
5. C	16. E	27. A	38. B	49. C	60. C	71. C
6. B	17. A	28. B	39. A	50. D	61. D	72. D
7. A	18. D	29. C	40. D	51. A	62. B	73. D
8. B	19. E	30. C	41. B	52. D	63. E	74. B
9. A	20. C	31. B	42. B	53. C	64. D	75. A
10. D	21. B	32. E	43. C	54. B	65. A	
11. C	22. C	33. B	44. B	55. A	66. B	

Vocabulary Builder: Natural Science Passages (p. 270)

Exercise 9

1. D	14. B	27. B	40. B	53. D	66. D	79. B
2. E	15. A	28. A	41. C	54. B	67. C	80. E
3. C	16. D	29. C	42. C	55. B	68. B	81. A
4. E	17. C	30. B	43. D	56. C	69. A	82. C
5. A	18. D	31. E	44. B	57. D	70. B	83. D
6. C	19. B	32. C	45. B	58. C	71. A	84. D
7. C	20. E	33. A	46. C	59. A	72. C	85. B
8. B	21. A	34. E	47. D	60. C	73. B	86. C
9. C	22. C	35. D	48. D	61. E	74. C	87. B
10. B	23. B	36. B	49. C	62. D	75. D	88. A
11. D	24. C	37. D	50. E	63. E	76. B	89. D
12. A	25. C	38. D	51. A	64. C	77. B	90. A
13. B	26. D	39. A	52. C	65. B	78. C	

READING SKILLS REVIEW

Summarize the Main Idea (p. 297)
Exercise 1

1. C	2. F	3. A	4. G	5. D

Determine the Main Idea (p. 299)
Exercise 2

1. C	3. D	5. B	7. A	9. C
2. G	4. F	6. J	8. H	10. J

Outlining Passages (p. 302)
Exercise 3

Passage 1

Main Idea
Lightning is a complex meteorological process in which an electric current moves through an ionized channel between a cloud and the ground.

Passage Outline
  I. A tremendous electrostatic charge builds up within a cloud.
  II. Lightning occurs within the cloud itself.
  III. Negative charges called stepped leaders emerge from the bottom of the cloud, moving toward Earth and creating an ionized channel.
  IV. A strong electric field causes streamers of positively charged ions to develop and flow upward.
  V. A return stroke moves through the object from which the streamer emanated and up the ionized channel to the charge center within the cloud.
  VI. An ionized channel remains in the air, and dart leaders will quickly move down this path, resulting in further return strokes.

Passage 2

Main Idea
Due to anti-poaching and conservation programs, endangered African elephant populations have begun to stabilize.

Passage Outline
  I. The efforts of the Convention on International Trade in Endangered Species
    a. An international moratorium was enacted on the buying and selling of ivory.
    b. The moratorium prompted significant declines in ivory trading and in the rate of elephant poaching.
  II. The cooperative effort of the U.S. with the Central African Republic and the World Wildlife Fund
    a. A reserve has been established in the southeastern portion of that country.

b. Anti-poaching patrols were established using funds provided by the U.S.
III. The efforts of Senegal's anti-poaching program
    a. An African elephant conservation fund grant has provided protection for the elephant population.
    b. Similar protection projects have begun in Cameroon, Congo, Eritrea, Gabon, Mali, Senegal, Tanzania, Zambia, and Zimbabwe.

Locate Verbal Signs (p. 304)
Exercise 4

A <u>flood is an overflow of water that covers lands that are normally not covered by water</u> (*defining*). A <u>flood occurs, for example, when a stream or river overflows its banks</u> (*example*). Small streams are subject to <u>flash floods—that is, the very rapid increases in water that may last only a few minutes</u> (*defining*). In larger streams, floods usually last from several hours to a few days, and a series of storms might keep a river above flood stage for several weeks.

Floods can occur at any time, but weather patterns have a strong influence on when and where floods happen. Cyclones—<u>similar in structure to tornadoes</u> (*similarity*)—bring moisture inland from the ocean, causing floods in the spring in the western United States. Thunderstorms are relatively small but intense storms that cause flash floods in smaller streams during the summer in the Southwest. Frontal storms at the edge of large, moist air masses moving across the country cause floods in the northern and eastern parts of the United States during the winter.

The <u>magnitude of a flood is described by a term called the recurrence interval</u> (*defining*) which is based upon long-term study of flow records for a stream. A <u>five-year flood is one that would occur, on the average, once every five years</u> (*defining*). Although <u>a 100-year flood is expected to happen only once in a century</u> (*defining*), it is <u>important to remember</u> (*prompting*) that there is a one percent chance that a flood of that size could happen during any given year.

Of course, the frequency and magnitude of floods can be altered if changes are made in the drainage basin of a stream or river. <u>Significantly, harvesting timber or changing land use from farms to housing can cause the runoff to increase</u> (*prompting*), resulting in an increase in the magnitude of flooding. <u>On the other hand, dams can protect against flooding</u> (*contrast*) by storing storm runoff. Although the same volume of water must eventually move downstream, the peak flow can be reduced by temporarily storing water and then releasing it when water levels have fallen.

Locate Specific Details (p. 305)
Exercise 5

1. C	**3.** D	**5.** C	**7.** A	**9.** C
2. F	**4.** G	**6.** F	**8.** G	**10.** J

Analyze the Arguments (p. 307)
Exercise 6

1. D	**3.** D	**5.** C	**7.** D	**9.** A
2. G	**4.** F	**6.** G	**8.** G	**10.** H

Consider the Author's Point of View (p. 310)
Exercise 7

1. The author claims to be both a physician and a professor at a prestigious medical school.

2. One could assume that the author, as a physician, has a working knowledge of the field of medicine. One could also assume that the author, as a professor at a prestigious medical school, is well-versed in the needs of the medical community and the status of students entering medical school.

3. The author most certainly has the highest respect for the application of the Hippocratic method of reason and observation within the medical practice. The author also dislikes, or holds in contempt, medical students who pursue medical careers for the reasons of fame and fortune.

4. The author is attempting to change what he or she perceives as problems in the attitudes and perceptions of medical students.

5. The author wants you to believe that the Hippocratic method of observation and reason is essential for medical students. He or she also wants you to believe that this perspective must be acquired prior to being admitted into medical school.

6. The passage discusses the origins of modern medicine; specifically, the passage is about Hippocrates in the role of father (or founder) of modern medicine.

7. The author has spent 30 years in the American banking industry, was one of the first female members of Congress, and wrote legislation regarding banking.

8. The author has 30 years of banking experience and knowledge regarding banking laws.

9. The author strongly dislikes or disagrees with the idea that government bailouts of failing banks are helpful to the economy.

10. The author writes to go on record as having denounced government bailouts of banks.

11. The author wants you to believe that government bailouts of banks have detrimental results to the economy as a whole.

12. Writing in the 1990s, the author is certainly influenced by the democratic ideals of citizenship that have influenced many nations in the twentieth century.

13. Writing in Africa, the author writes with the knowledge of a poorer, agrarian culture.

14. Moving from being a citizen under a military dictatorship to being a citizen within a democratic government has influenced the author to desire others to be more actively involved in the growth and development of his or her nation.

15. The author wrote this piece at a time when gang influence was having a detrimental effect on urban cultures and urban economies.

16. Since the location was Los Angeles, the author writes about gang issues in an urban center that was greatly affected by gang activity.

17. The author certainly writes with a negative point of view regarding gangs and gang members. He also appears to write from an outsider's view of gang involvement. As a sociologist, he is interested in the social aspects of gangs, but mostly from an academic viewpoint.

Probe the Tone of the Passage (p. 314)
Exercise 8

1. The mood of the passage is quite depressing and bleak. The passage might be described as somber or dark.

2. The author uses the terms "melancholy," "deplorable," and "helpless infants." He verbally paints a picture of begging mothers and children in need of charity.

Bonus Passages (p. 315)
Exercise 9

1. D	4. H	7. A	10. J	13. D	16. G
2. G	5. B	8. H	11. A	14. G	
3. A	6. J	9. A	12. H	15. D	

READING MASTERY TEST

Answer Key (p. 321)

1. B	10. F	19. D	28. J	37. A
2. F	11. D	20. G	29. D	38. F
3. C	12. J	21. C	30. F	39. A
4. G	13. C	22. J	31. C	40. G
5. B	14. G	23. B	32. H	41. B
6. F	15. A	24. F	33. B	42. J
7. C	16. H	25. A	34. H	
8. J	17. B	26. F	35. C	
9. D	18. H	27. B	36. J	

Sample Essay (p. 346)
Exercise 1

Above Average Response

Parents, educators, and government leaders are increasingly concerned about the quality of education in our schools. Recently, the government instituted a policy of comprehensive testing to ensure that all students are getting a quality education and that no child is left behind. The theory is that these tests show what students have learned. If the students in a particular school don't score high enough, then that school is deemed to be failing its students. At that point, special programs are made available to provide additional instruction and tutoring to the school's students. The additional opportunities are supposed to help students learn and then perform better on the tests.

If you think about the structure of education, you'll see that it involves teachers and students in a school setting. Teachers have always evaluated students. Periodically, teachers give us tests, and we get report cards to tell our parents how we are doing in school. The new government testing is designed to find out whether schools are doing a good job. But in all of this, no one is testing the teachers. I think that if everyone is serious about improving the quality of education, then it would be a good idea to have students give their teachers report cards.

From a school improvement standpoint, teacher evaluations would help administrators learn which teachers are doing a good job and which teachers are not. When a student performs poorly in math, everyone assumes that it is the student who is at fault. And with the new testing program, if the average math score is low, then it must be the school that is failing. But it might also be the case that a single bad teacher is the real cause. A teacher who can't make math concepts clear to students could easily have an entire class with students getting poor grades on their report cards. Parents will lecture their children but never realize that the whole class has the same problem. The school may get blamed for not providing a quality education, but maybe there are other classes in the school that don't have this problem. In other words, student evaluations could be a valuable tool for identifying the real problem.

Another advantage of student evaluations would be improving the quality of teaching. Let's say, for example, that a particular teacher speaks softly and is hard to hear. Students might not want to say anything about the teacher. If only one or two students complain, they may be considered trouble-makers. But if the entire class fills out an evaluation form and under "Ability to Communicate" says "The teacher is hard to hear," then the problem can be addressed. Administrators could meet with the teacher and go over the evaluations. They could suggest to the teacher to speak up more clearly.

The objection that students might retaliate personally is really just a red herring. Students are already permitted to vote for the "Outstanding Teacher" award (or similar awards) given by most schools. Additionally, it would be obvious from the tone of the evaluations if the teacher had been unfairly criticized. Statements like "A rotten teacher" or "Can't really help us" wouldn't carry much weight. Statements like "Speaks too softly" or "Doesn't answer questions about difficult topics" are useful. Finally, a structured evaluation would make it less likely that students would comment on irrelevant factors like a teacher's personal habits.

If you listen to the debate about education, you can't help but notice that the issues are complicated. A quality education is not a simple matter. You need the right setting, the proper tools, motivated students, effective teachers, and good administration. It's like a complex recipe that calls for good ingredients mixed up in the right proportions and cooked at the right temperature for the correct length of time. Student evaluations of teachers is not going to solve all of the education world's problems. But student evaluations could be an important part of a successful recipe.

Position on issue: The writer clearly states the position at the end of the second paragraph.

Topic development and essay organization: Although the structure of the essay isn't articulated in outline form (such as "Point 1," "Point 2," etc.), the structure is evident. The writer uses paragraphing and transitional phrases, such as "another advantage," to help the reader follow the train of thought. The writer develops the points within each paragraph. In the next-to-the-last paragraph, for example, the writer offers three reasons for believing that the danger of personal retaliation is not very significant.

Language usage, sentence structure, and punctuation: The essay might be subjected to two related criticisms. One, sometimes the examples seem to be a little abstract. The example of math scores never really gets very specific, though it is difficult to say exactly how the writer could improve on what is written.

Additionally, the prose, while effective, seems a little dry. It lacks zip. Even the recipe analogy in the last paragraph seems flat. Maybe the writer could have mentioned a specific dish, say gumbo, in which several ingredients have to be mixed together to get the desired result. Even that little flair would have lightened up the writing style.

Summary and conclusions: This is a very strong response. Most readers would say it fits the qualifications of a "Superior" or "Excellent" essay (see the "Essay Score Qualifications" table on p. 345).

Below Average Response

In my opinion, students should not get to evaluate teachers because it wouldn't mean anything, and it would just be a chance for some students to dump on teachers they don't like.

Teachers give students grades for a reason. Teachers know more than the students do because they've been to college. So when a teacher gives a test, that teacher knows the right answer and can mark the papers accordingly. This system makes sense. Students have not been to college. They don't have experience teaching classes. Most, if not all, students couldn't make up an exam to test a teacher's ability to teach. They wouldn't know which questions to ask on the exam and wouldn't know what the right answers are. So students really don't know how to grade a teacher on ability to teach.

Also, some, maybe even many, students would use the evaluation to take pot shots at teachers they don't like or have a grudge about. This would be especially dangerous if students got together to say the same thing. If only one student says a teacher is rude, then no one might care. If half the class says a teacher is rude, the principal would figure where there's smoke there's fire.

The evaluations could also be unfair to hard teachers. No students like to have a lot of homework, but homework is important. It's a given fact that some teachers give more homework than others. So would students give low marks to the teachers who gave the most homework? That seems like it might happen.

Even if there were an evaluation form with categories, this would still be a problem. Everyone could agree to mark low on "Preparedness" and "Ability to Communicate." That way, there wouldn't be any question asked about retribution. The students would be using the form.

Student evaluations of teachers is not a good idea. The whole thing won't help and it could really hurt some good teachers.

Position on issue: The writer conveys the position in the first sentence. Although the position is clearly stated, the prose used is not an effective manner in which to start the essay.

Topic development and essay organization: This essay is pretty rough, but it does contain some relevant ideas. The writer explains that the evaluations would have limited utility and, further, that the system could be abused. The second point is developed in greater detail than the first. The writer argues that students might conspire against an unpopular teacher and that the evaluations might be used to retaliate against taskmasters. The final point in this development—that the evaluation form itself might mask this phenomenon—is particularly interesting.

The essay lacks coherent structure. The writer fails to outline her ideas in the introductory paragraphs and does not use helpful transitional phrases.

Language usage, sentence structure, and punctuation: The essay suffers from informal language and glaring grammatical errors.

Summary and conclusions: The prose is not polished. Nonetheless, it is an honest effort and addresses the topic. This essay would likely fit the qualifications of an "Average" essay (see the "Essay Score Qualifications" table on p. 345). Some readers might not score it quite that high, and it would be surprising if it were categorized as "Good."

MATH SKILLS REVIEW

Numbers (p. 366)
Exercise 1

1. B	12. E	23. E	34. A	45. D	56. A	67. D
2. B	13. A	24. B	35. B	46. D	57. D	68. D
3. C	14. B	25. A	36. D	47. C	58. B	69. C
4. C	15. A	26. B	37. B	48. A	59. C	70. E
5. E	16. D	27. C	38. A	49. A	60. C	
6. C	17. C	28. C	39. E	50. D	61. D	
7. D	18. B	29. C	40. D	51. A	62. D	
8. D	19. D	30. B	41. B	52. D	63. B	
9. C	20. D	31. A	42. C	53. C	64. C	
10. B	21. A	32. E	43. D	54. A	65. A	
11. C	22. C	33. D	44. E	55. E	66. E	

Fractions (p. 379)
Exercise 2

1. E	9. C	17. D	25. B	33. A	41. C	49. C
2. B	10. C	18. C	26. B	34. A	42. D	50. D
3. C	11. A	19. E	27. A	35. E	43. E	51. D
4. A	12. C	20. B	28. A	36. C	44. A	52. C
5. E	13. A	21. D	29. B	37. E	45. B	53. C
6. B	14. C	22. D	30. A	38. D	46. E	
7. B	15. B	23. A	31. D	39. B	47. D	
8. E	16. B	24. C	32. C	40. D	48. A	

Decimals (p. 392)
Exercise 3

1. C	5. D	9. B	13. E	17. D	21. B	25. A
2. B	6. B	10. B	14. C	18. E	22. C	26. C
3. B	7. B	11. C	15. A	19. C	23. E	27. A
4. B	8. A	12. B	16. B	20. A	24. B	28. C

29. D	34. D	39. B	44. B	49. D	54. C
30. B	35. B	40. B	45. A	50. B	55. C
31. E	36. A	41. A	46. C	51. D	56. A
32. A	37. B	42. C	47. C	52. C	57. D
33. E	38. A	43. E	48. B	53. B	

Percents (p. 403)
Exercise 4

1. E	11. C	21. D	31. D	41. D	51. D	61. D
2. B	12. E	22. E	32. B	42. C	52. B	62. C
3. C	13. D	23. B	33. B	43. A	53. C	63. B
4. C	14. C	24. A	34. E	44. D	54. E	64. A
5. A	15. C	25. A	35. D	45. D	55. E	65. C
6. B	16. B	26. C	36. B	46. C	56. D	
7. A	17. D	27. B	37. C	47. E	57. D	
8. A	18. D	28. B	38. D	48. B	58. D	
9. B	19. D	29. C	39. D	49. E	59. C	
10. C	20. A	30. C	40. C	50. A	60. A	

Statistical Measures (p. 413)
Exercise 5

1. A	10. A	19. D	28. E	37. D	46. C
2. D	11. E	20. D	29. B	38. B	47. E
3. C	12. B	21. D	30. B	39. D	48. C
4. B	13. B	22. E	31. C	40. A	49. C
5. C	14. A	23. E	32. D	41. B	50. C
6. E	15. C	24. B	33. D	42. B	51. E
7. A	16. D	25. B	34. A	43. E	52. D
8. C	17. E	26. C	35. C	44. D	
9. D	18. A	27. B	36. C	45. B	

Ratios and Proportions (p. 423)
Exercise 6

1. B	4. C	7. D	10. D	13. B	16. D	19. D
2. A	5. A	8. B	11. D	14. C	17. E	20. E
3. D	6. A	9. B	12. C	15. D	18. D	21. C

22. B	28. B	34. C	40. D	46. D	52. A
23. C	29. E	35. C	41. C	47. B	53. C
24. C	30. C	36. D	42. B	48. C	54. B
25. B	31. D	37. A	43. B	49. B	55. E
26. C	32. C	38. B	44. C	50. D	
27. D	33. B	39. A	45. A	51. B	

Exponents and Radicals (p. 438)
Exercise 7

1. E	8. A	15. B	22. A	29. C	36. E	43. D
2. D	9. A	16. C	23. E	30. A	37. B	44. E
3. E	10. A	17. E	24. A	31. A	38. D	45. E
4. B	11. B	18. D	25. D	32. D	39. D	
5. C	12. C	19. C	26. A	33. B	40. C	
6. E	13. C	20. C	27. B	34. B	41. B	
7. C	14. B	21. C	28. C	35. C	42. A	

Algebraic Operations (p. 454)
Exercise 8

1. A	11. E	21. A	31. E	41. A	51. E	61. B
2. D	12. D	22. E	32. D	42. E	52. E	62. A
3. D	13. B	23. C	33. A	43. A	53. D	63. D
4. B	14. C	24. B	34. A	44. D	54. D	64. B
5. C	15. A	25. C	35. A	45. C	55. B	65. D
6. E	16. B	26. D	36. D	46. B	56. C	66. E
7. A	17. C	27. E	37. B	47. C	57. E	67. D
8. B	18. C	28. A	38. B	48. C	58. E	
9. C	19. B	29. D	39. B	49. A	59. E	
10. E	20. C	30. D	40. A	50. E	60. A	

Algebraic Equations and Inequalities (p. 474)
Exercise 9

1. C	5. D	9. C	13. B	17. D	21. A	25. D
2. C	6. A	10. B	14. E	18. C	22. E	26. D
3. E	7. D	11. B	15. B	19. D	23. B	27. C
4. D	8. E	12. A	16. D	20. C	24. C	28. A

29. D	35. A	41. E	47. B	53. D	59. B	65. A
30. C	36. E	42. D	48. B	54. C	60. E	66. E
31. E	37. B	43. A	49. A	55. D	61. A	67. E
32. A	38. D	44. A	50. C	56. B	62. D	
33. D	39. A	45. C	51. E	57. C	63. E	
34. E	40. E	46. D	52. C	58. D	64. E	

Geometry (p. 495)
Exercise 10

1. C	13. D	25. D	37. B	49. C	61. E	73. E
2. C	14. B	26. B	38. A	50. C	62. C	74. C
3. E	15. D	27. B	39. B	51. C	63. C	75. E
4. E	16. B	28. D	40. A	52. C	64. A	76. A
5. B	17. C	29. A	41. B	53. B	65. C	77. A
6. B	18. B	30. B	42. C	54. E	66. C	78. C
7. A	19. D	31. E	43. B	55. D	67. D	79. C
8. A	20. B	32. B	44. C	56. B	68. C	80. E
9. C	21. D	33. D	45. D	57. B	69. B	
10. E	22. D	34. A	46. C	58. B	70. C	
11. A	23. E	35. C	47. C	59. E	71. A	
12. C	24. C	36. C	48. B	60. E	72. D	

Coordinate Geometry (p. 516)
Exercise 11

1. B	7. A	13. B	19. E	25. C	31. D	37. C
2. A	8. A	14. B	20. C	26. B	32. E	38. D
3. A	9. E	15. A	21. E	27. B	33. C	39. E
4. C	10. B	16. C	22. B	28. D	34. C	40. C
5. A	11. C	17. A	23. E	29. C	35. A	41. D
6. D	12. C	18. A	24. D	30. B	36. A	42. D

Story Problems (p. 541)
Exercise 12

1. A	4. D	7. D	10. B	13. B	16. A	19. B
2. A	5. B	8. B	11. A	14. B	17. A	20. D
3. B	6. C	9. C	12. E	15. B	18. E	21. C

22. C	27. B	32. A	37. C	42. C	47. B	52. D
23. D	28. C	33. D	38. B	43. B	48. A	53. E
24. D	29. D	34. E	39. D	44. E	49. D	
25. B	30. D	35. B	40. B	45. C	50. C	
26. C	31. E	36. E	41. D	46. C	51. D	

MATH MASTERY TEST

Answer Key (p. 551)

1. C	10. G	19. B	28. G	37. B
2. K	11. D	20. G	29. E	38. F
3. C	12. H	21. D	30. K	39. A
4. K	13. E	22. J	31. B	40. F
5. B	14. H	23. B	32. H	41. A
6. G	15. C	24. K	33. A	42. K
7. C	16. K	25. A	34. J	43. D
8. G	17. E	26. J	35. C	44. J
9. C	18. J	27. D	36. J	45. C

Appendix B:
Progress Reports

PROGRESS REPORTS

The progress reports on the following pages are designed to help you monitor your progress throughout the skills reviews in this book. Complete the assigned items by the due date given by your instructor. Correct your answers using the answers and explanations in Appendix A of this book*, and record both the number and percentage of items answered correctly on the *student copies* of the progress reports. Identify the date on which you completed each exercise. List the numbers of any items that you would like your instructor to review in class. Then, transfer this information to the corresponding *instructor copies* of the reports and give them to your instructor. Be sure to leave the last three columns of the *instructor copies* blank; these are for your instructor's use in evaluating your progress. (**NOTE:** In the first column of each report, the numbering refers to the exercises and the page numbers refer to the locations of those exercises in this book.)

*Consult with your instructor to determine whether you will use Appendix A to complete the Progress Reports.

Grammar and Mechanics Skills Review
(Student Copy)

Exercise	Total # of Items			% of Items Correct	Date Completed	Item #s to Review
	Possible	Assigned	Correct			
1. Parts of Speech (p. 9)	20					
2. Common Grammatical Errors (p. 25)	66					
3. Analyzing Sentence Structure (p. 37)	57					
4. Problems of Logical Expression (p. 47)	27					
5. Idioms and Clarity of Expression (p. 56)	143					
6. Punctuation (p. 77)	55					

Diagramming Sentences Skills Review

(Student Copy)

Exercise	Total # of Items			% of Items Correct	Date Completed	Item #s to Review
	Possible	Assigned	Correct			
1. Subjects and Verbs (p. 90)	5					
2. Modal Auxiliary Verbs (p. 95)	5					
3. Conjunctions (p. 100)	5					
4. Articles, Attributive Adjectives, and Direct Objects (p. 106)	5					
5. Adverbs (p. 111)	5					
6. Subjective Complements: Predicate Nominatives and Predicate Adjectives (p. 117)	5					
7. Appositives (p. 122)	5					
8. Prepositional Phrases (p. 127)	5					
9. Indirect Objects and Objective Complements (p. 133)	5					
10. Infinitives (p. 142)	10					
11. Gerunds (p. 149)	5					
12. Participles (p. 156)	5					
13. Adverb Clauses (p. 164)	10					
14. Adjective Clauses (p. 171)	5					
15. Noun Clauses (p. 177)	5					

Vocabulary Skills Review
(Student Copy)

Exercise	Total # of Items			% of Items Correct	Date Completed	Item #s to Review
	Possible	Assigned	Correct			
1. Anticipating Sentence Completions (p. 213)	20					
2. Analyzing Sentence Completions (p. 216)	20					
3. Substituting Sentence Completions (p. 219)	17					
4. Building Vocabulary with Sentence Completions (p. 221)	40					
5. Building Vocabulary Through Context (p. 228)	10					
6. Vocabulary Builder: Prose Fiction Passages (p. 230)	45					
7. Vocabulary Builder: Social Science Passages (p. 239)	90					
8. Vocabulary Builder: Humanities Passages (p. 256)	75					
9. Vocabulary Builder: Natural Science Passages (p. 270)	90					

Reading Skills Review
(Student Copy)

Exercise	Total # of Items			% of Items Correct	Date Completed	Item #s to Review
	Possible	Assigned	Correct			
1. Summarize the Main Idea (p. 297)	5					
2. Determine the Main Idea (p. 299)	10					
3. Outlining Passages (p. 302)	2		N/A	N/A		N/A
4. Locate Verbal Signs (p. 304)	1		N/A	N/A		N/A
5. Locate Specific Details (p. 305)	10					
6. Analyze the Arguments (p. 307)	10					
7. Consider the Author's Point of View (p. 310)	17					
8. Probe the Tone of the Passage (p. 314)	2					
9. Bonus Passages (p. 315)	16					

Writing Skills Review
(Student Copy)

Exercise	Total # of Items			% of Items Correct	Date Completed	Item #s to Review
	Possible	Assigned	Correct			
1. Sample Essay (p. 346)	1		N/A	N/A		N/A

Math Skills Review
(Student Copy)

Exercise	Total # of Items			% of Items Correct	Date Completed	Item #s to Review
	Possible	Assigned	Correct			
1. Numbers (p. 366)	70					
2. Fractions (p. 379)	53					
3. Decimals (p. 392)	57					
4. Percents (p. 403)	65					
5. Statistical Measures (p. 413)	52					
6. Ratios and Proportions (p. 423)	55					
7. Exponents and Radicals (p. 438)	45					
8. Algebraic Operations (p. 454)	67					
9. Algebraic Equations and Inequalities (p. 474)	67					
10. Geometry (p. 495)	80					
11. Coordinate Geometry (p. 516)	42					
12. Story Problems (p. 541)	53					

Mastery Tests
(Student Copy)

Exercise	Total # of Items			% of Items Correct	Date Completed	Item #s to Review
	Possible	Assigned	Correct			
1. English/Writing (p. 193)	54					
2. Reading (p. 321)	42					
3. Math (p. 551)	45					

Grammar and Mechanics Skills Review
(Instructor Copy)

Name _____ Student ID Number _____

Date _____ Instructor _____ Course/Session Number _____

Exercise	Total # of Items			% of Items Correct	Date Completed	Item #s to Review	Instructor Skill Evaluation (Check One Per Section)		
	Possible	Assigned	Correct				Mastered	Partially Mastered	Not Mastered
1. Parts of Speech (p. 9)	20								
2. Common Grammatical Errors (p. 25)	66								
3. Analyzing Sentence Structure (p. 37)	57								
4. Problems of Logical Expression (p. 47)	27								
5. Idioms and Clarity of Expression (p. 56)	143								
6. Punctuation (p. 77)	55								

Diagramming Sentences Skills Review
(Instructor Copy)

Name _____   Student ID Number _____

Date _____   Instructor _____   Course/Session Number _____

Exercise	Total # of Items			% of Items Correct	Date Completed	Item #s to Review	Instructor Skill Evaluation (Check One Per Section)		
	Possible	Assigned	Correct				Mastered	Partially Mastered	Not Mastered
1. Subjects and Verbs (p. 90)	5								
2. Modal Auxiliary Verbs (p. 95)	5								
3. Conjunctions (p. 100)	5								
4. Articles, Attributive Adjectives, and Direct Objects (p. 106)	5								
5. Adverbs (p. 111)	5								
6. Subjective Complements: Predicate Nominatives and Predicate Adjectives (p. 117)	5								
7. Appositives (p. 122)	5								

8. Prepositional Phrases (p. 127)	5								
9. Indirect Objects and Objective Complements (p. 133)	5								
10. Infinitives (p. 142)	10								
11. Gerunds (p. 149)	5								
12. Participles (p. 156)	5								
13. Adverb Clauses (p. 164)	10								
14. Adjective Clauses (p. 171)	5								
15. Noun Clauses (p. 177)	5								

Vocabulary Skills Review
(Instructor Copy)

Name _____   Student ID Number _____

Date _____   Instructor _____   Course/Session Number _____

Exercise	Total # of Items			% of Items Correct	Date Completed	Item #s to Review	Instructor Skill Evaluation (Check One Per Section)		
	Possible	Assigned	Correct				Mastered	Partially Mastered	Not Mastered
1. Anticipating Sentence Completions (p. 213)	20								
2. Analyzing Sentence Completions (p. 216)	20								
3. Substituting Sentence Completions (p. 219)	17								
4. Building Vocabulary with Sentence Completions (p. 221)	40								
5. Building Vocabulary Through Context (p. 228)	10								
6. Vocabulary Builder: Prose Fiction Passages (p. 230)	45								
7. Vocabulary Builder: Social Science Passages (p. 239)	90								
8. Vocabulary Builder: Humanities Passages (p. 256)	75								
9. Vocabulary Builder: Natural Science Passages (p. 270)	90								

Reading Skills Review
(Instructor Copy)

Name _____   Student ID Number _____

Date _____   Instructor _____   Course/Session Number _____

Exercise	Total # of Items			% of Items Correct	Date Completed	Item #s to Review	Instructor Skill Evaluation (Check One Per Section)		
	Possible	Assigned	Correct				Mastered	Partially Mastered	Not Mastered
1. Summarize the Main Idea (p. 297)	5								
2. Determine the Main Idea (p. 299)	10								
3. Outlining Passages (p. 302)	2		N/A	N/A		N/A			
4. Locate Verbal Signs (p. 304)	1		N/A	N/A		N/A			
5. Locate Specific Details (p. 305)	10								
6. Analyze the Arguments (p. 307)	10								
7. Consider the Author's Point of View (p. 310)	17								
8. Probe the Tone of the Passage (p. 314)	2								
9. Bonus Passages (p. 315)	16								

Writing Skills Review
(Instructor Copy)

Name _____   Student ID Number _____

Date _____   Instructor _____   Course/Session Number _____

Exercise	Total # of Items			% of Items Correct	Date Completed	Item #s to Review	Instructor Skill Evaluation (Check One Per Section)		
	Possible	Assigned	Correct				Mastered	Partially Mastered	Not Mastered
1. Sample Essay (p. 346)	1		N/A	N/A		N/A			

Math Skills Review
(Instructor Copy)

Name

Student ID Number

Date

Instructor

Course/Session Number

Exercise	Total # of Items			% of Items Correct	Date Completed	Item #s to Review	Instructor Skill Evaluation (Check One Per Section)		
	Possible	Assigned	Correct				Mastered	Partially Mastered	Not Mastered
1. Numbers (p. 366)	70								
2. Fractions (p. 379)	53								
3. Decimals (p. 392)	57								
4. Percents (p. 403)	65								
5. Statistical Measures (p. 413)	52								
6. Ratios and Proportions (p. 423)	55								
7. Exponents and Radicals (p. 438)	45								
8. Algebraic Operations (p. 454)	67								
9. Algebraic Equations and Inequalities (p. 474)	67								
10. Geometry (p. 495)	80								
11. Coordinate Geometry (p. 516)	42								
12. Story Problems (p. 541)	53								

Mastery Tests
(Instructor Copy)

Exercise	Total # of Items			% of Items Correct	Date Completed	Item #s to Review
	Possible	Assigned	Correct			
1. English/Writing (p. 193)	54					
2. Reading (p. 321)	42					
3. Math (p. 551)	45					

The Big Book of Skills, 11th Edition
Error Correction and Suggestion Form

Name/Location: _____ Day Phone: _____ E-mail Address: _____

Part of Materials: ☐ Student Text, Specify Subject: _____ Page: _____ Item: _____

☐ Teacher's Guide, Specify Subject: _____ Page: _____ Item: _____

Error/Suggestion: _____

_____

_____

Part of Materials: ☐ Student Text, Specify Subject: _____ Page: _____ Item: _____

☐ Teacher's Guide, Specify Subject: _____ Page: _____ Item: _____

Error/Suggestion: _____

_____

_____

Part of Materials: ☐ Student Text, Specify Subject: _____ Page: _____ Item: _____

☐ Teacher's Guide, Specify Subject: _____ Page: _____ Item: _____

Error/Suggestion: _____

_____

_____

Part of Materials: ☐ Student Text, Specify Subject: _____ Page: _____ Item: _____

☐ Teacher's Guide, Specify Subject: _____ Page: _____ Item: _____

Error/Suggestion: _____

_____

_____

Part of Materials: ☐ Student Text, Specify Subject: _____ Page: _____ Item: _____

☐ Teacher's Guide, Specify Subject: _____ Page: _____ Item: _____

Error/Suggestion: _____

_____

_____

Part of Materials: ☐ Student Text, Specify Subject: _____ Page: _____ Item: _____

☐ Teacher's Guide, Specify Subject: _____ Page: _____ Item: _____

Error/Suggestion: _____

_____

_____

Mail form to Cambridge Educational Services, Inc. or fax form to 1-847-299-2933. For teacher's assistance, call 1-800-444-4373 or e-mail solutions@CambridgeEd.com. Visit our Web site at www.CambridgeEd.com.